# MODERN DRAMA FOR ANALYSIS

PAUL M. CUBETA
WILLIAMS COLLEGE

# Modern Drama
# *for* Analysis

WILLIAM SLOANE
ASSOCIATES, INC.
*Publishers ... New York*

6266-304

# CONTENTS

# ACKNOWLEDGMENTS

The editor makes grateful acknowledgment to the following publishers for permission to reprint the plays included in *Modern Drama for Analysis:*

Harper and Brothers for *The Skin of Our Teeth* by Thornton Wilder, copyright 1942 by Thornton Wilder.

The Macmillan Company for *Juno and the Paycock* by Sean O'Casey, copyright 1925 by The Macmillan Company and used with their permission.

Random House, Inc., for *Watch on the Rhine* by Lillian Hellman, copyright 1941 by Lillian Hellman; for *The Glass Menagerie*, copyright 1945 by Tennessee Williams and Edwina D. Williams; for *The Emperor Jones* by Eugene O'Neill, copyright 1921 and 1948 by Eugene O'Neill; and for *The Playboy of the Western World* by John M. Synge, copyright 1935 by Modern Library, Inc., and reprinted by permission of Random House, Inc.

# NOTE TO THE INSTRUCTOR

The basic problem in introducing drama to the student is to make him realize that a play is primarily a theater piece to be seen and heard, not to be read as one would read a novel. Yet without rigorous textual analysis and without a keen awareness of the functions of various stage techniques, the student will most often read merely for plot and "message." Once he is shown the relationship of such basic stage devices as sets, costumes, and sound effects to the literary qualities of the entire play, he will approach his reading with an active imagination and will learn to visualize the actual performance.

I believe that the student should become acquainted first with the stage of his own times, so that when he does attend the theater, he will better understand the significance and value of the complex workings of the spectacle before him. Consequently, I have limited my collection to plays of the relatively modern period. Greek or Elizabethan drama, for example, would necessitate an understanding of the quite different theatrical conventions, styles of acting, and physical characteristics of their respective theaters.

Most modern drama collections of this size are based on different principles from those I have followed. One basis of selection is dramatic types; another is representative geographical distribution; still another attempts to exemplify major modern theatrical developments; while a more recent trend demands plays that mirror cultural changes. Excellent as these approaches may be for specialized study, I have found that collections based on them teach the student little about the play-going experience.

Although I have given consideration both to variety of nationality and to dramatic types by including plays which illustrate most of the important trends of the last sixty years, my primary concern has been to select teachable plays of intrinsic merit which at the same time admirably demonstrate the techniques of the playwright and the resources of the modern theater. I have avoided theatrical novelty for its own sake, for I believe that only the best plays make the most successful use of the assets of the stage.

In this book the plays are arranged in such an order that the study of the dramatic techniques they employ can be exploited to fullest advantage. Hence the first play, *The Emperor Jones*, not only is a relatively simple one to analyze, but also introduces the student to a wide range of techniques which he may not have been aware of previously. Subsequent plays deal in more detail and on an increasingly difficult level with one or more theatrical effects. Each play is accompanied by the date and place of its first production, a brief biographical note on the dramatist, a list of his important works, and a short bibliography.

I decided against including an introduction on the history of drama, because by means of close reading methods I hope to focus the attention of the student on the play itself. Nor is critical analysis of the individual plays included in the anthology, because I believe that such an analysis may color the student's understanding of the play and incline him to lean on this material rather than to think for himself. All too often immature students are found doggedly maintaining an editor's opinions which, because they are in print, seem to them to have greater validity than the oral arguments of their instructor.

The detailed analyses omitted from the book are found in a Teaching Guide for the instructor, published separately. The Guide suggests a classroom approach and includes an explication of each play based on the techniques of close reading. The first of these explore fully the importance of sheer theatrical effects. Subsequent ones focus attention primarily upon the specific new problems arising: the dramatization of a theme, the dramatic use of symbols, the means of establishing the tonal complexities of a play, and so forth. Although I have found the teaching method outlined in the Guide the most successful in my experience, it is by no means the only way in which this anthology can be used. The plays themselves are durable and varied enough for many approaches, each as valid as mine. My chief intention has been to provide a collection of teachable plays suitable for an introductory course in the methods of dramatic analysis.

It would be impossible for me to acknowledge individually my debt to all those who have so willingly helped me with suggestions and advice. Special thanks, however, must go to the members of the Department of English at Williams College and in particular to Robert W. Watson, whose very generous assistance made the editing of this text possible, as well as to Elizabeth B. Cubeta, who devoted many hours helping to prepare the manuscripts of the text and the teaching manual.

P. M. C.

EUGENE O'NEILL

# The Emperor Jones

*The Emperor Jones* was first produced by the Province-town Players at the Playwrights' Theater, New York City, on November 3, 1920.

# CHARACTERS

BRUTUS JONES ................................................................................ *Emperor*

HENRY SMITHERS .......................................................... *A Cockney Trader*

AN OLD NATIVE WOMAN

LEM ............................................................................................ *A Native Chief*

SOLDIERS ...................................................................... *Adherents of Lem*

*The Little Formless Fears; Jeff; The Negro Convicts; The Prison Guard; The Planters; The Auctioneer; The Slaves; The Congo Witch-Doctor; The Crocodile God.*

*The action of the play takes place on an island in the West Indies as yet not self-determined by white Marines. The form of native government is, for the time being, an empire.*

# Scene One

SCENE: *The audience chamber in the palace of the Emperor—a spacious, high-ceilinged room with bare, white-washed walls. The floor is of white tiles. In the rear, to the left of center, a wide archway giving out on a portico with white pillars. The palace is evidently situated on high ground for beyond the portico nothing can be seen but a vista of distant hills, their summits crowned with thick groves of palm trees. In the right wall, center, a smaller arched doorway leading to the living quarters of the palace. The room is bare of furniture with the exception of one huge chair made of uncut wood which stands at center, its back to rear. This is very apparently the Emperor's throne. It is painted a dazzling, eye-smiting scarlet. There is a brilliant orange cushion on the seat and another smaller one is placed on the floor to serve as a footstool. Strips of matting, dyed scarlet, lead from the foot of the throne to the two entrances.*

*It is late afternoon but the sunlight still blazes yellowly beyond the portico and there is an oppressive burden of exhausting heat in the air.*

*As the curtain rises, a native Negro woman sneaks in cautiously from the entrance on the right. She is very old, dressed in cheap calico, bare-footed, a red bandana handkerchief covering all but a few stray wisps of white hair. A bundle bound in colored cloth is carried over her shoulder on the end of a stick. She hesitates beside the doorway, peering back as if in extreme dread of being discovered. Then she begins to glide noiselessly, a step at a time, toward the doorway in the rear. At this moment,* SMITHERS *appears beneath the portico.*

SMITHERS *is a tall, stoop-shouldered man about forty. His bald head, perched on a long neck with an enormous Adam's apple, looks like an egg. The tropics have tanned his naturally pasty face with its small, sharp features to a sickly yellow, and native rum has painted his pointed nose to a startling red. His little, washy-blue eyes are red-rimmed and dart about him like a ferret's. His expression is one of unscrupulous meanness, cowardly and dangerous. He is dressed in a worn riding suit of dirty white drill, puttees, spurs, and wears a*

3

*white cork helmet. A cartridge belt with an automatic revolver is around his waist. He carries a riding whip in his hand. He sees the woman and stops to watch her suspiciously. Then, making up his mind, he steps quickly on tiptoe into the room. The woman, looking back over her shoulder continually, does not see him until it is too late. When she does* SMITHERS *springs forward and grabs her firmly by the shoulder. She struggles to get away, fiercely but silently.*

SMITHERS (*tightening his grasp—roughly*): Easy! None o' that, me birdie. You can't wriggle out now. I got me 'ooks on yer.

WOMAN (*seeing the uselessness of struggling, gives way to frantic terror, and sinks to the ground, embracing his knees supplicatingly*): No tell him! No tell him, Mister!

SMITHERS (*with great curiosity*): Tell 'im? (*Then scornfully*) Oh, you mean 'is bloomin' Majesty. What's the gaime, any 'ow? What are you sneakin' away for? Been stealin' a bit, I s'pose. (*He taps her bundle with his riding whip significantly.*)

WOMAN (*shaking her head vehemently*): No, me no steal.

SMITHERS: Bloody liar! But tell me what's up. There's somethin' funny goin' on. I smelled it in the air first thing I got up this mornin'. You blacks are up to some devilment. This palace of 'is is like a bleedin' tomb. Where's all the 'ands? (*The woman keeps sullenly silent.* SMITHERS *raises his whip threateningly.*) Ow, yer won't, won't yer? I'll show yer what's what.

WOMAN (*coweringly*): I tell, Mister. You no hit. They go—all go. (*She makes a sweeping gesture toward the hills in the distance.*)

SMITHERS: Run away—to the 'ills?

WOMAN: Yes, Mister. Him Emperor—Great Father. (*She touches her forehead to the floor with a quick mechanical jerk.*) Him sleep after eat. Then they go—all go. Me old woman. Me left only. Now me go too.

SMITHERS (*his astonishment giving way to an immense, mean satisfaction*): Ow! So that's the ticket! Well, I know bloody well wot's in the air—when they runs orf to the 'ills. The tom-tom 'll be thumping out there bloomin' soon. (*With extreme vindictiveness*) And I'm bloody glad of it, for one! Serve 'im right! Puttin' on airs, the stinkin' nigger! 'Is Majesty! Gawd blimey! I only 'opes I'm there when they takes 'im out to shoot 'im. (*Suddenly*) 'E's still 'ere all right, ain't 'e?

WOMAN: Yes. Him sleep.

SMITHERS: 'E's bound to find out soon as 'e wakes up. 'E's cunnin' enough to know when 'is time's come. (*He goes to the doorway on right and whistles shrilly with his fingers in his mouth. The old woman springs to her feet and runs out of the doorway, rear.* SMITHERS *goes after her, reaching for his revolver.*) Stop or I'll shoot! (*Then stopping—indifferently*) Pop orf then, if yer like, yer black cow. (*He stands in the doorway, looking after her.*)

(JONES *enters from the right. He is a tall, powerfully-built, full-blooded Negro of middle age. His features are typically negroid, yet there is something decidedly distinctive about his face—an underlying strength of will, a hardy, self-reliant confidence in himself that inspires respect. His eyes are alive with a keen, cunning intelligence. In manner he is shrewd, suspicious, evasive. He wears a light blue uniform coat, sprayed with brass buttons, heavy gold chevrons on his shoulders, gold braid on the collar, cuffs, etc. His pants are bright red with a light blue stripe down the side. Patent-leather laced boots with brass spurs, and a belt with a long-barreled, pearl-handled revolver in a holster complete his make up. Yet there is something not altogether ridiculous about his grandeur. He has a way of carrying it off.*)

JONES (*not seeing anyone—greatly irritated and blinking sleepily—shouts*): Who dare whistle dat way in my palace? Who dare wake up de Emperor? I'll git de hide fravled off some o' you niggers sho'!

SMITHERS (*showing himself—in a manner half-afraid and half-defiant*): It was me whistled to yer. (*As* JONES *frowns angrily*) I got news for yer.

JONES (*putting on his suavest manner, which fails to cover up his contempt for the white man*): Oh, it's you, Mister Smithers. (*He sits down on his throne with easy dignity.*) What news you got to tell me?

SMITHERS (*coming close to enjoy his discomfiture*): Don't yer notice nothin' funny today?

JONES (*coldly*): Funny? No. I ain't perceived nothin' of de kind!

SMITHERS: Then yer ain't so foxy as I thought yer was. Where's all your court? (*Sarcastically*) The Generals and the Cabinet Ministers and all?

JONES (*imperturbably*): Where dey mostly runs de minute I closes my eyes—drinkin' rum and talkin' big down in de town. (*Sarcastically*) How come you don't know dat? Ain't you sousin' with 'em most every day?

SMITHERS (*stung but pretending indifference—with a wink*): That's part of the day's work. I got ter—ain't I—in my business?

JONES (*contemptuously*): Yo' business!

SMITHERS (*imprudently enraged*): Gawd blimey, you was glad enough for me ter take yer in on it when you landed here first. You didn' 'ave no 'igh and mighty airs in them days!

JONES (*his hand going to his revolver like a flash—menacingly*): Talk polite, white man! Talk polite, you heah me! I'm boss heah now, is you fergettin'? (*The Cockney seems about to challenge this last statement with the facts but something in the other's eyes holds and cows him.*)

SMITHERS (*in a cowardly whine*): No 'arm meant, old top.

JONES (*condescendingly*): I acccpts yo' apology. (*Lets his hand fall from his revolver*) No use'n rakin' up ole times. What I was den is one thing. What I is now 's another. You didn't let me in on yo' crooked work out o' no kind feelin's dat time. I done de dirty work fo' you—and most o' de brain work, too, fo' dat matter—and I was wu'th money to you, dat's de reason.

SMITHERS: Well, blimey, I give yer a start, didn't I—when no one else would. I wasn't afraid to 'ire yer like the rest was—'count of the story about your breakin' jail back in the States.

JONES: No, you didn't have no s'cuse to look down on me fo' dat. You been in jail you'self more'n once.

SMITHERS (*furiously*): It's a lie! (*Then trying to pass it off by an attempt at scorn*) Garn! Who told yer that fairy tale?

JONES: Dey's some tings I ain't got to be tole. I kin see 'em in folk's eyes. (*Then after a pause—meditatively*) Yes, you sho' give me a start. And it didn't take long from dat time to git dese fool, woods' niggers right where I wanted dem. (*With pride*) From stowaway to Emperor in two years! Dat's goin' some!

SMITHERS (*with curiosity*): And I bet you got yer pile o' money 'id safe some place.

JONES (*with satisfaction*): I sho' has! And it's in a foreign bank where no pusson don't ever git it out but me no matter what come. You didn't s'pose I was holdin' down dis Emperor job for de glory in it, did you? Sho'! De fuss and glory part of it, dat's only to turn de heads o' de low-flung, bush niggers dat's here. Dey wants de big circus show for deir money. I gives it to 'em an' I gits de money. (*With a grin*) De long green, dat's me every time! (*Then rebukingly*) But you ain't got no kick agin me, Smithers. I'se paid you back all you done for me many times. Ain't I pertected you and winked at all de crooked tradin' you been doin' right out in de broad day? Sho' I has—and me makin' laws to stop it at de same time! (*He chuckles.*)

SMITHERS (*grinning*): But, meanin' no 'arm, you been grabbin' right and left yourself, ain't yer? Look at the taxes you've put on 'em! Blimey! You've squeezed 'em dry!

JONES (*chuckling*): No, dey ain't *all* dry yet. I'se still heah, ain't I?

SMITHERS (*smiling at his secret thought*): They're dry right now, you'll find out. (*Changing the subject abruptly*) And as for me breakin' laws, you've broke 'em all yerself just as fast as yer made 'em.

JONES: Ain't I de Emperor? De laws don't go for him. (*Judicially*) You heah what I tells you, Smithers. Dere's little stealin' like you does, and dere's big stealin' like I does. For de little stealin' dey gits you in jail soon or late. For de big stealin' dey makes you Emperor and puts you in de Hall o' Fame when you croaks. (*Reminiscently*) If dey's one thing I learns in ten years on the Pullman ca's listenin' to de white quality talk, it's dat same fact. And when I gits a chance to use it I winds up Emperor in two years.

SMITHERS (*unable to repress the genuine admiration of the small fry for the large*): Yes, yer turned the bleedin' trick, all right. Blimey, I never seen a bloke 'as 'ad the bloomin' luck you 'as.

JONES (*severely*): Luck? What you mean—luck?

SMITHERS: I suppose you'll say as that swank about the silver bullet ain't luck—and that was what first got the fool blacks on yer side the time of the revolution, wasn't it?

JONES (*with a laugh*): Oh, dat silver bullet! Sho' was luck! But I makes dat luck, you heah? I loads de dice! Yessuh! When dat murderin' nigger ole Lem hired to kill me takes aim ten feet away and his gun misses fire and I shoots him dead, what you heah me say?

SMITHERS: You said yer'd got a charm so's no lead bullet'd kill yer. You was so strong only a silver bullet could kill yer, you told 'em. Blimey, wasn't that swank for yer—and plain, fat-'eaded luck?

JONES (*proudly*): I got brains and I uses 'em quick. Dat ain't luck.

SMITHERS: Yer know they wasn't 'ardly liable to get no silver bullets. And it was luck 'e didn't 'it you that time.

JONES (*laughing*): And dere all dem fool, bush niggers was kneelin' down and bumpin' deir heads on de ground like I was a miracle out o' de Bible. Oh Lawd, from dat time on I has dem all eatin' out of my hand. I cracks de whip and dey jumps through.

SMITHERS (*with a sniff*): Yankee bluff done it.

JONES: Ain't a man's talkin' big what makes him big—long as he makes folks believe it? Sho', I talks large when I ain't got nothin' to back it up, but I ain't talkin' wild just de same. I knows I kin fool 'em—I *knows* it—and dat's backin' enough fo' my game. And ain't I got to learn deir lingo and teach some of dem English befo' I kin talk to 'em? Ain't dat wuk? You ain't never learned ary word er it, Smithers, in de ten years you been heah, dough yo' knows it's money in yo' pocket tradin' wid 'em if you does. But you'se too shiftless to take de trouble.

SMITHERS (*flushing*): Never mind about me. What's this I've 'eard about yer really 'avin' a silver bullet moulded for yourself?

JONES: It's playin' out my bluff. I has de silver bullet moulded and I tells 'em when de time comes I kills myself wid it. I tells 'em dat's 'cause I'm de on'y man in de world big enuff to git me. No use'n deir tryin'. And dey falls down and bumps deir heads. (*He laughs*) I does dat so's I kin take a walk in peace widout no jealous nigger gunnin' at me from behind de trees.

SMITHERS (*astonished*): Then you 'ad it made—'onest?

JONES: Sho' did. Heah she be. (*He takes out his revolver, breaks it, and takes the silver bullet out of one chamber.*) Five lead an' dis silver baby at de last. Don't she shine pretty? (*He holds it in his hand, looking at it admiringly, as if strangely fascinated.*)

SMITHERS: Let me see. (*Reaches out his hand for it.*)

JONES (*harshly*): Keep yo' hands whar dey b'long, white man. (*He replaces it in the chamber and puts the revolver back on his hip.*)

SMITHERS (*snarling*): Gawd blimey! Think I'm a bleedin' thief, you would.

JONES: No, 'tain't dat. I knows you'se scared to steal from me. On'y I ain't 'lowin' nary body to touch dis baby. She's my rabbit's foot.

SMITHERS (*sneering*): A bloomin' charm, wot? (*Venomously*) Well, you'll need all the bloody charms you 'as before long, s' 'elp me!

JONES (*judicially*): Oh, I'se good for six months yit 'fore dey gits sick o' my game. Den, when I sees trouble comin', I makes my get-away.

SMITHERS: Ho! You got it all planned, ain't yer?

JONES: I aint no fool. I knows dis Emperor's time is sho't. Dat why I make hay when de sun shine. Was you thinkin' I'se aimin' to hold down dis job for life? No, suh! What good is gittin' money if you stays back in dis raggedy country? I wants action when I spends. And when I sees dese niggers gittin' up deir nerve to tu'n me out, and I'se got all de money in sight, I resigns on de spot and beats it quick.

SMITHERS: Where to?

JONES: None o' yo' business.

SMITHERS: Not back to the bloody States, I'll lay my oath.

JONES (*suspiciously*): Why don't I? (*Then with an easy laugh*) You mean 'count of dat story 'bout me breakin' from jail back dere? Dat's all talk.

SMITHERS (*skeptically*): Ho, yes!

JONES (*sharply*): You ain't 'sinuatin' I'se a liar, is you?

SMITHERS (*hastily*): No. Gawd strike me! I was only thinkin' o' the bloody lies you told the blacks 'ere about killin' white men in the States.

JONES (*angered*): How come dey're lies?

SMITHERS: You'd 'ave been in jail if you 'ad, wouldn't yer then? (*With venom*) And from what I've 'eard, it ain't 'ealthy for a black to kill a white man in the States. They burns 'em in oil, don't they?

JONES (*with cool deadliness*): You mean lynchin' 'd scare me? Well, I tells you, Smithers, maybe I does kill one white man back dere. Maybe I does. And maybe I kills another right heah 'fore long if he don't look out.

SMITHERS (*trying to force a laugh*): I was on'y spoofin' yer. Can't yer take a joke? And you was just sayin' you'd never been in jail.

JONES (*in the same tone—slightly boastful*): Maybe I goes to jail dere for gettin' in an argument wid razors ovah a crap game. Maybe I gits twenty years when dat colored man die. Maybe I gits in 'nother argument wid de prison guard was overseer ovah us when we're wukin' de roads. Maybe he hits me wid a whip and I splits his head wid a shovel and runs away and files de chain off my leg and gits away safe. Maybe I does all dat an' maybe I don't. It's a story I tells you so's you knows I'se de kind of man dat if you evah repeats one word of it, I ends yo' stealin' on dis yearth mighty damn quick!

SMITHERS (*terrified*): Think I'd peach on yer? Not me! Ain't I always been yer friend?

JONES (*suddenly relaxing*): Sho' you has—and you better be.

SMITHERS (*recovering his composure—and with it his malice*): And just to show yer I'm yer friend, I'll tell yer that bit o' news I was goin' to.

JONES: Go ahead! Shoot de piece. Must be bad news from de happy way you look.

SMITHERS (*warningly*): Maybe it's gettin' time for you to resign—with that bloomin' silver bullet, wot? (*He finishes with a mocking grin.*)

JONES (*puzzled*): What's dat you say? Talk plain.

SMITHERS: Ain't noticed any of the guards or servants about the place today, I 'aven't.

JONES (*carelessly*): Dey're all out in de garden sleepin' under de trees. When I sleeps, dey sneaks a sleep, too, and I pretends I never suspicions it. All I got to do is to ring de bell and dey come flyin', makin' a bluff dey was wukin' all de time.

SMITHERS (*in the same mocking tone*): Ring the bell now an' you'll bloody well see what I means.

JONES (*startled to alertness, but preserving the same careless tone*): Sho' I rings. (*He reaches below the throne and pulls out a big, common dinner bell which is painted the same vivid scarlet as the throne. He rings this vigorously—then stops to listen. Then he goes to both doors, rings again, and looks out.*)

SMITHERS (*watching him with malicious satisfaction, after a pause—mockingly*): The bloody ship is sinkin' an' the bleedin' rats 'as slung their 'ooks.

JONES (*in a sudden fit of anger flings the bell clattering into a corner*): Low-flung, woods' niggers! (*Then catching Smithers' eye on him, he controls himself and suddenly bursts into a low chuckling laugh.*) Reckon I overplays my hand dis once! A man can't take de pot on a bob-tailed flush all de time. Was I sayin' I'd sit in six months mo'? Well, I'se changed my mind den. I cashes in and resigns de job of Emperor right dis minute.

SMITHERS (*with real admiration*): Blimey, but you're a cool bird, and no mistake.

JONES: No use'n fussin'. When I knows de game's up I kisses it good-bye widout no long waits. Dey've all run off to de hills, ain't dey?

SMITHERS: Yes—every bleedin' man jack of 'em.

JONES: Den de revolution is at de post. And de Emperor better git his feet smokin' up de trail. (*He starts for the door in rear.*)

SMITHERS: Goin' out to look for your 'orse? Yer won't find any. They steals the 'orses first thing. Mine was gone when I went for 'im this mornin'. That's wot first give me a suspicion of wot was up.

JONES (*alarmed for a second, scratches his head, then philosophically*): Well, den I hoofs it. Feet do yo' duty! (*He pulls out a gold watch and looks at it.*) Three-thuty. Sundown's at six-thuty or dereabouts. (*Puts his watch back—with cool confidence*) I got plenty o' time to make it easy.

SMITHERS: Don't be so bloomin' sure of it. They'll be after you 'ot and 'eavy. Ole Lem is at the bottom o' this business an' 'e 'ates you like 'ell. 'E'd rather do for you than eat 'is dinner, 'e would!

JONES (scornfully): Dat fool no-count nigger! Does you think I'se scared o' him? I stands him on his thick head more'n once befo' dis, and I does it again if he come in my way . . . (Fiercely) And dis time I leave him a dead nigger fo' sho'!

SMITHERS: You'll 'ave to cut through the big forest—an' these blacks 'ere can sniff and follow a trail in the dark like 'ounds. You'd 'ave to 'ustle to get through that forest in twelve hours even if you knew all the bloomin' trails like a native.

JONES (with indignant scorn): Look-a-heah, white man! Does you think I'se a natural bo'n fool? Give me credit fo' havin' some sense, fo' Lawd's sake! Don't you s'pose I'se looked ahead and made sho' of all de chances? I'se gone out in dat big forest, pretendin' to hunt, so many times dat I knows it high an' low like a book. I could go through on dem trails wid my eyes shut. (With great contempt) Think dese ign'rent bush niggers dat ain't got brains enuff to know deir own names even can catch Brutus Jones? Huh, I s'pects not! Not on yo' life! Why, man, de white men went after me wid bloodhounds where I come from an' I jes' laughs at 'em. It's a shame to fool dese black trash around heah, dey're so easy. You watch me, man! I'll make dem look sick, I will. I'll be 'cross de plain to de edge of de forest by time dark comes. Once in de woods in de night, dey got a swell chance o' findin' dis baby! Dawn tomorrow I'll be out at de oder side and on de coast whar dat French gunboat is stayin'. She picks me up, take me to Martinique when she go dar, and dere I is safe wid a mighty big bankroll in my jeans. It's easy as rollin' off a log.

SMITHERS (maliciously): But s'posin' somethin' 'appens wrong an' they do nab yer?

JONES (decisively): Dey don't—dat's de answer.

SMITHERS: But, just for argyment's sake—what'd you do?

JONES (frowning): I'se got five lead bullets in dis gun good enuff fo' common bush niggers—and after dat I got de silver bullet left to cheat 'em out o' gittin' me.

SMITHERS (jeeringly): Ho, I was fergettin' that silver bullet. You'll bump yourself orf in style, won't yer? Blimey!

JONES (*gloomily*): You kin bet yo whole roll on one thing, white man. Dis baby plays out his string to de end and when he quits, he quits wid a bang de way he ought. Silver bullet ain't none too good for him when he go, dat's a fac'! (*Then shaking off his nervousness—with a confident laugh*) Sho'! What is I talkin' about? Ain't come to dat yit and I never will—not wid trash niggers like dese yere. (*Boastfully*) Silver bullet bring me luck anyway. I kin outguess, outrun, outfight, an' outplay de whole lot o' dem all ovah de board any time o' de day er night! You watch me! (*From the distant hills comes the faint, steady thump of a tom-tom, low and vibrating. It starts at a rate exactly corresponding to normal pulse beat—72 to the minute—and continues at a gradually accelerating rate from this point uninterruptedly to the very end of the play.*)

(JONES *starts at the sound. A strange look of apprehension creeps into his face for a moment as he listens. Then he asks, with an attempt to regain his most casual manner.*) What's dat drum beatin' fo'?

SMITHERS (*with a mean grin*): For you. That means the bleedin' ceremony 'as started. I've 'eard it before and I knows.

JONES: Cer'mony? What cer'mony?

SMITHERS: The blacks is 'oldin' a bloody meetin', 'avin' a war dance, gettin' their courage worked up b'fore they starts after you.

JONES: Let dem! Dey'll sho' need it!

SMITHERS: And they're there 'oldin' their 'eathen religious service—makin' no end of devil spells and charms to 'elp 'em against your silver bullet. (*He guffaws loudly.*) Blimey, but they're balmy as 'ell!

JONES (*a tiny bit awed and shaken in spite of himself*): Huh! Takes more'n dat to scare dis chicken!

SMITHERS (*scenting the other's feeling—maliciously*): Ternight when it's pitch black in the forest, they'll 'ave their pet devils and ghosts 'oundin' after you. You'll find yer bloody 'air 'll be standin' on end before termorrow mornin'. (*Seriously*) It's a bleedin' queer place, that stinkin' forest, even in daylight. Yer don't know what might 'appen in there, it's that rotten still. Always sends the cold shivers down my back minute I gets in it.

JONES (*with a contemptuous sniff*): I ain't no chicken-liver like you is. Trees an' me, we'se friends, and dar's a full moon comin' bring me light. And let dem po' niggers make all de fool spells dey'se a min' to. Does yo' s'pect I'se silly enuff to b'lieve in ghosts an' ha'nts an' all dat ole woman's talk? G'long, white man! You ain't talkin' to me. (*With a chuckle*) Doesn't you know dey's got to do wid a man was member in good standin' o' de Baptist Church? Sho' I was dat when I was porter on de Pullmans, befo' I gits into my little trouble. Let dem try deir heathen tricks. De Baptist Church done pertect me and land dem all in hell. (*Then with more confident satisfaction*) And I'se got little silver bullet o' my own, don't forgit.

SMITHERS: Ho! You 'aven't give much 'eed to your Baptist Church since you been down 'ere. I've 'eard myself you 'ad turned yer coat an' was takin' up with their blarsted witch-doctors, or whatever the 'ell yer calls the swine.

JONES (*vehemently*): I pretends to! Sho' I pretends! Dat's part o' my game from de fust. If I finds out dem niggers believes dat black is white, den I yells it out louder 'n deir loudest. It don't git me nothin' to do missionary work for de Baptist Church. I'se after de coin, an' I lays my Jesus on de shelf for de time bein'. (*Stops abruptly to look at his watch—alertly*) But I ain't got de time to waste no more fool talk wid you. I'se gwine away from heah dis secon'. (*He reaches in under the throne and pulls out an expensive Panama hat with a bright multi-colored band and sets it jauntily on his head.*) So long, white man! (*With a grin*) See you in jail sometime, maybe!

SMITHERS: Not me, you won't. Well, I wouldn't be in yer bloody boots for no bloomin' money, but 'ere's wishin' yer luck just the same.

JONES (*contemptuously*): You're de frightenedest man evah I see! I tells you I'se safe's 'f I was in New York City. It takes dem niggers from now to dark to git up de nerve to start somethin'. By dat time, I'se got a head start dey never kotch up wid.

SMITHERS (*maliciously*): Give my regards to any ghosts yer meets up with.

JONES (*grinning*): If dat ghost got money, I'll tell him never ha'nt you less'n he wants to lose it.

SMITHERS (*flattered*): Garn! (*Then curiously*) Ain't yer takin' no luggage with yer?

JONES: I travels light when I wants to move fast. And I got tinned grub buried on de edge o' de forest. (*Boastfully*) Now say dat I don't look ahead an' use my brains! (*With a wide, liberal gesture*) I will all dat's left in de palace to you—and you better grab all you kin sneak away wid befo' dey gits here.

SMITHERS (*gratefully*): Righto—and thanks ter yer. (*As* JONES *walks toward the door in rear—cautioningly*) Say! Look 'ere, you ain't goin' out that way, are yer?

JONES: Does you think I'd slink out de back door like a common nigger? I'se Emperor yit, ain't I? And de Emperor Jones leaves de way he comes, and dat black trash don't dare stop him—not yit, leastways. (*He stops for a moment in the doorway, listening to the far-off but insistent beat of the tom-tom.*) Listen to dat roll-call, will you? Must be mighty big drum carry dat far. (*Then with a laugh*) Well, if dey ain't no whole brass band to see me off, I sho' got de drum part of it. So long, white man. (*He puts his hands in his pockets and with studied carelessness whistling a tune, he saunters out of the doorway and off to the left.*)

SMITHERS (*looks after him with a puzzled admiration*): 'E's got 'is bloomin' nerve with 'im, s'elp me! (*Then angrily*) Ho—the bleedin' nigger—puttin' on 'is bloody airs! I 'opes they nabs 'im an' gives 'im what's what! (*Then putting business before the pleasure of this thought, looking around him with cupidity*) A bloke ought to find a 'ole lot in this palace that'd go for a bit of cash. Let's take a look, 'Arry, me lad. (*He starts for the doorway on right as*

*The Curtain Falls.*)

# Scene Two

SCENE: *Nightfall. The end of the plain where the Great Forest begins. The foreground is sandy, level ground dotted by a few stones and clumps of stunted bushes cowering close against the earth to escape the buffeting of the trade wind. In the rear the forest is a wall of darkness dividing the world. Only when the eye becomes accustomed to the gloom can the outlines of separate trunks of the nearest trees be made out, enormous pillars of deeper blackness. A somber monotone of wind lost in the leaves moans in the air. Yet this sound serves but to intensify the impression of the forest's relentless immobility, to form a background throwing into relief its brooding, implacable silence.*

(JONES *enters from the left, walking rapidly. He stops as he nears the edge of the forest, looks around him quickly, peering into the dark as if searching for some familiar landmark. Then, apparently satisfied that he is where he ought to be, he throws himself on the ground, dog-tired.*)

Well, heah I is. In de nick o' time, too! Little mo' an' it'd be blacker'n de ace of spades heahabouts. (*He pulls a bandana handkerchief from his hip pocket and mops off his perspiring face.*) Sho'! Gimme air! I'se tuckered out sho' 'nuff. Dat soft Emperor job ain't no trainin' fo' a long hike ovah dat plain in de brilin' sun. (*Then with a chuckle*) Cheah up, nigger, de worst is yet to come. (*He lifts his head and stares at the forest. His chuckle peters out abruptly. In a tone of awe.*) My goodness, look at dem woods, will you? Dat nocount Smithers said dey'd be black an' he sho' called de turn. (*Turning away from them quickly and looking down at his feet, he snatches at a chance to change the subject—solicitously.*) Feet, you is holdin' up yo' end fine an' I sutinly hopes you ain't blisterin' none. It's time you git a rest. (*He takes off his shoes, his eyes studiously avoiding the forest. He feels of the soles of his feet gingerly.*) You is still in de pink—on'y a little mite feverish. Cool yo'selfs. Remember you done got a long journey yit befo' you. (*He sits in a weary attitude, listening to the rhythmic beating of the tom-tom. He grumbles in a loud*

16

*tone to cover up a growing uneasiness*.) Bush niggers! Wonder dey wouldn' git sick o' beatin' dat drum. Sound louder, seem like. I wonder if dey's startin' after me? (*He scrambles to his feet, looking back across the plain*.) Couldn't see dem now, nohow, if dey was hundred feet away. (*Then shaking himself like a wet dog to get rid of these depressing thoughts*) Sho', dey's miles an' miles behind. What you gittin' fidgety about? (*But he sits down and begins to lace up his shoes in great haste, all the time muttering reassuringly*.) You know what? Yo' belly is empty, dat's what's de matter wid you. Come time to eat! Wid nothin' but wind on yo' stumach, o' course you feels jiggedy. Well, we eats right heah an' now soon's I gits dese pesky shoes laced up! (*He finishes lacing up his shoes*.) Dere! Now le's see. (*Gets on his hands and knees and searches the ground around him with his eyes*) White stone, white stone, where is you? (*He sees the first white stone and crawls to it—with satisfaction*.) Heah you is! I knowed dis was de right place. Box of grub, come to me. (*He turns over the stone and feels in under it—in a tone of dismay*.) Ain't heah! Gorry, is I in de right place or isn't I? Dere's 'nother stone. Guess dat's it. (*He scrambles to the next stone and turns it over*.) Ain't heah, neither! Grub, whar is you? Ain't heah. Gorry, has I got to go hungry into dem woods—all de night? (*While he is talking he scrambles from one stone to another, turning them over in frantic haste. Finally, he jumps to his feet excitedly*.) Is I lost de place? Must have! But how dat happen when I was followin' de trail across de plain in broad daylight? (*Almost plaintively*) I'se hungry, I is! I gotta git my feed. Whar's my strength gonna come from if I doesn't? Gorry, I gotta find dat grub high an' low somehow! Why it come dark so quick like dat? Can't see nothin'. (*He scratches a match on his trousers and peers about him. The rate of the beat of the far-off tom-tom increases perceptibly as he does so. He mutters in a bewildered voice*.) How come all dese white stones come heah when I only remembers one? (*Suddenly, with a frightened gasp, he flings the match on the ground and stamps on it*.) Nigger, is you gone crazy mad? Is you lightin' matches to show dem whar you is? Fo' Lawd's sake, use yo' haid. Gorry, I'se got to be careful! (*He stares at the plain behind him apprehensively, his hand on his revolver*.) But how come all dese white stones? And whar's dat tin box o' grub I had all wrapped up in oil cloth?

(*While his back is turned, the* LITTLE FORMLESS FEARS *creep out from the deeper blackness of the forest. They are black, shapeless, only their glittering little eyes can be seen. If they have any describable form at all it is that of a grubworm about the size of a creeping child. They move noiselessly, but with deliberate, painful effort, striving to raise themselves on end, failing and sinking prone again.* JONES *turns about to face the forest. He stares up at the tops of the trees, seeking vainly to discover his whereabouts by their conformation.*)

Can't tell nothin' from dem trees! Gorry, nothin' 'round heah look like I evah seed it befo'. I'se done lost de place sho' 'nuff! (*With mournful foreboding*) It's mighty queer! It's mighty queer! (*With sudden forced defiance—in an angry tone*) Woods, is you tryin' to put somethin' ovah on me?

(*From the formless creatures on the ground in front of him comes a tiny gale of low mocking laughter like a rustling of leaves. They squirm upward toward him in twisted attitudes.* JONES *looks down, leaps backward with a yell of terror, yanking out his revolver as he does so—in a quavering voice.*) What's dat? Who's dar? What is you? Git away from me befo' I shoots you up! You don't? . . .

(*He fires. There is a flash, a loud report, then silence broken only by the far-off, quickened throb of the tom-tom. The formless creatures have scurried back into the forest.* JONES *remains fixed in his position, listening intently. The sound of the shot, the reassuring feel of the revolver in his hand, have somewhat restored his shaken nerve. He addresses himself with renewed confidence.*)

Dey're gone. Dat shot fix 'em. Dey was only little animals—little wild pigs, I reckon. Dey've maybe rooted out yo' grub an' eat it. Sho', you fool nigger, what you think dey is—ha'nts? (*Excitedly*) Gorry, you give de game away when you fire dat shot. Dem niggers heah dat fo' su'tin! Time you beat it in de woods widout no long waits. (*He starts for the forest—hesitates before the plunge—then urging himself in with manful resolution.*) Git in, nigger! What you skeered at? Ain't nothin' dere but de trees! Git in! (*He plunges boldly into the forest.*)

# Scene Three

---

SCENE: *Nine o'clock. In the forest. The moon has just risen. Its beams, drifting through the canopy of leaves, make a barely perceptible, suffused, eerie glow. A dense low wall of underbrush and creepers is in the nearer foreground, fencing in a small triangular clearing. Beyond this is the massed blackness of the forest like an encompassing barrier. A path is dimly discerned leading down to the clearing from left, rear, and winding away from it again toward the right. As the scene opens nothing can be distinctly made out. Except for the beating of the tom-tom, which is a trifle louder and quicker than in the previous scene, there is silence, broken every few seconds by a queer, clicking sound. Then gradually the figure of the negro,* JEFF, *can be discerned crouching on his haunches at the rear of the triangle. He is middle-aged, thin, brown in color, is dressed in a Pullman porter's uniform, cap, etc. He is throwing a pair of dice on the ground before him, picking them up, shaking them, casting them out with the regular, rigid, mechanical movements of an automaton. The heavy, plodding footsteps of someone approaching along the trail from the left are heard and* JONES' *voice, pitched in a slightly higher key and strained in a cheering effort to overcome its own tremors.*

De moon's rizen. Does you heah dat, nigger? You gits more light from dis out. No mo' buttin' yo' fool head agin' de trunks an' scratchin' de hide off yo' legs in de bushes. Now you sees whar yo'se gwine. So cheer up! From now on you has a snap. (*He steps just to the rear of the triangular clearing and mops off his face on his sleeve. He has lost his Panama hat. His face is scratched, his brilliant uniform shows several large rents.*) What time's it gittin' to be, I wonder? I dassent light no match to find out. Phoo'. It's wa'm an' dat's a fac'! (*Wearily*) How long I been makin' tracks in dese woods? Must be hours an' hours. Seems like fo'evah! Yit can't be, when de moon's jes' riz. Dis am a long night fo' yo', yo' Majesty! (*With a mournful chuckle*) Majesty! Der ain't much majesty 'bout dis baby now. (*With attempted cheerfulness*) Never min'. It's all part o' de game.

Dis night come to an end like everything else. And when you gits dar safe and has dat bankroll in yo' hands you laughs at all dis. (*He starts to whistle but checks himself abruptly.*) What yo' whistlin' for, you po' dope! Want all de worl' to heah you? (*He stops talking to listen.*) Heah dat ole drum! Sho' gits nearer from de sound. Dey're packin' it along wid 'em. Time fo' me to move. (*He takes a step forward, then stops—worriedly.*) What's dat odder queer clickety sound I heah? Dere it is! Sound close! Sound like—sound like— Fo' God sake, sound like some nigger was shootin' crap! (*Frightenedly*) I better beat it quick when I gits dem notions. (*He walks quickly into the clear space—then stands transfixed as he sees* JEFF—*in a terrified gasp.*) Who dar? Who dat? Is dat you, Jeff? (*Starting toward the other, forgetful for a moment of his surroundings and really believing it is a living man that he sees—in a tone of happy relief*) Jeff! I'se sho' mighty glad to see you! Dey tol' me you done died from dat razor cut I gives you. (*Stopping suddenly, bewilderedly*) But how you come to be heah, nigger? (*He stares fascinatedly at the other who continues his mechanical play with the dice.* JONES' *eyes begin to roll wildly. He stutters.*) Ain't you gwine—look up—can't you speak to me? Is you—is you—a ha'nt? (*He jerks out his revolver in a frenzy of terrified rage.*) Nigger, I kills you dead once. Has I got to kill you again? You take it den. (*He fires. When the smoke clears away* JEFF *has disappeared.* JONES *stands trembling—then with a certain reassurance.*) He's gone, anyway. Ha'nt or no ha'nt, dat shot fix him. (*The beat of the far-off tom-tom is perceptibly louder and more rapid.* JONES *becomes conscious of it—with a start, looking back over his shoulder.*) Dey's gittin' near! Dey's comin' fast! And heah I is shootin' shots to let 'em know jes' whar I is. Oh, Gorry, I'se got to run. (*Forgetting the path he plunges wildly into the underbrush in the rear and disappears in the shadow.*)

# Scene Four

SCENE: *Eleven o'clock. In the forest. A wide dirt road runs diagonally from right, front, to left, rear. Rising sheer on both sides the forest walls it in. The moon is now up. Under its light the road glimmers ghastly and unreal. It is as if the forest had stood aside momentarily to let the road pass through and accomplish its veiled purpose. This done, the forest will fold in upon itself again and the road will be no more.* JONES *stumbles in from the forest on the right. His uniform is ragged and torn. He looks about him with numbed surprise when he sees the road, his eyes blinking in the bright moonlight. He flops down exhaustedly and pants heavily for a while. Then with sudden anger.*

I'm meltin' wid heat! Runnin' an' runnin' an' runnin'! Damn dis heah coat! Like a strait-jacket! (*He tears off his coat and flings it away from him, revealing himself stripped to the waist.*) Dere! Dat's better! Now I kin breathe! (*Looking down at his feet, the spurs catch his eye.*) And to hell wid dese high-fangled spurs. Dey're what's been a-trippin' me up an' breakin' my neck. (*He unstraps them and flings them away disgustedly.*) Dere! I gits rid o' dem frippety Emperor trappin's an' I travels lighter. Lawd! I'se tired! (*After a pause, listening to the insistent beat of the tom-tom in the distance*) I must 'a put some distance between myself an' dem—runnin' like dat—and yit—dat damn drum sound jes' de same—nearer, even. Well, I guess I a'most holds my lead anyhow. Dey won't never catch up. (*With a sigh*) If on'y my fool legs stands up. Oh, I'se sorry I evah went in for dis. Dat Emperor job is sho' hard to shake. (*He looks around him suspiciously.*) How'd dis road evah git heah? Good level road, too. I never remembers seein' it befo'. (*Shaking his head apprehensively*) Dese woods is sho' full o' de queerest things at night. (*With a sudden terror*) Lawd God, don't let me see no more o' dem ha'nts! Dey gits my goat! (*Then trying to talk himself into confidence*) Ha'nts! You fool nigger, dey ain't no such things! Don't de Baptist parson tell you dat many time? Is you civilized, or is you like dese ign'rent black niggers heah? Sho'! Dat was all in yo'

21

own head. Wasn't nothin' dere. Wasn't no Jeff! Know what? You jus' get seein' dem things 'cause yo' belly's empty and you's sick wid hunger inside. Hunger 'fects yo' head and yo' eyes. Any fool know dat. (*Then pleading fervently*) But bless God, I don't come across no more o' dem, whatever dey is! (*Then cautiously*) Rest! Don't talk! Rest! You needs it. Den you gits on yo' way again. (*Looking at the moon*) Night's half gone a'most. You hits de coast in de mawning! Den you'se all safe.

(*From the right forward a small gang of Negoes enter. They are dressed in striped convict suits, their heads are shaven, one leg drags limpingly, shackled to a heavy ball and chain. Some carry picks, the others shovels. They are followed by a white man dressed in the uniform of a prison guard. A Winchester rifle is slung across his shoulders and he carries a heavy whip. At a signal from the* GUARD *they stop on the road opposite where* JONES *is sitting.* JONES, *who has been staring up at the sky, unmindful of their noiseless approach, suddenly looks down and sees them. His eyes pop out, he tries to get to his feet and fly, but sinks back, too numbed by fright to move. His voice catches in a choking prayer.*)

Lawd Jesus!

(*The* PRISON GUARD *cracks his whip—noiselessly—and at that signal all the convicts start to work on the road. They swing their picks, they shovel, but not a sound comes from their labor. Their movements, like those of* JEFF *in the preceding scene, are those of automatons,— rigid, slow, and mechanical. The* PRISON GUARD *points sternly at* JONES *with his whip, motions him to take his place among the other shovelers.* JONES *gets to his feet in a hypnotized stupor. He mumbles subserviently.*)

Yes, suh! Yes, suh! I'se comin'.

(*As he shuffles, dragging one foot, over to his place, he curses under his breath with rage and hatred.*)

God damn yo' soul, I gits even wid you yit, sometime.

(*As if there were a shovel in his hands he goes through weary, mechanical gestures of digging up dirt, and throwing it to the roadside. Suddenly the* GUARD *approaches him angrily, threateningly. He raises his whip and lashes* JONES *viciously across the shoulders with it.* JONES *winces with pain and cowers abjectly. The* GUARD *turns his back on him and walks away contemptuously. Instantly* JONES *straightens up. With arms upraised as if his shovel were a club in his hands he springs murderously at the unsuspecting* GUARD. *In the act of crashing down his shovel on the white man's skull,* JONES *suddenly becomes aware that his hands are empty. He cries despairingly.*)

Whar's my shovel? Gimme my shovel till I splits his damn head! (*Appealing to his fellow convicts*) Gimme a shovel, one o' you, fo' God's sake!

(*They stand fixed in motionless attitudes, their eyes on the ground. The* GUARD *seems to wait expectantly, his back turned to the attacker.* JONES *bellows with baffled, terrified rage, tugging frantically at his revolver.*)

I kills you, you white debil, if it's de last thing I evah does! Ghost or debil, I kill you again!

(*He frees the revolver and fires point blank at the* GUARD'S *back. Instantly the walls of the forest close in from both sides, the road and the figures of the convict gang are blotted out in an enshrouding darkness. The only sounds are a crashing in the underbrush as* JONES *leaps away in mad flight and the throbbing of the tom-tom, still far distant, but increased in volume of sound and rapidity of beat.*)

# Scene Five

SCENE: *One o'clock. A large circular clearing, enclosed by the serried ranks of gigantic trunks of tall trees whose tops are lost to view. In the center is a big dead stump worn by time into a curious resemblance to an auction block. The moon floods the clearing with a clear light.* JONES *forces his way in through the forest on the left. He looks wildly about the clearing with hunted, fearful glances. His pants are in tatters, his shoes cut and misshapen, flapping about his feet. He slinks cautiously to the stump in the center and sits down in a tense position, ready for instant flight. Then he holds his head in his hands and rocks back and forth, moaning to himself miserably.*

Oh Lawd, Lawd! Oh Lawd, Lawd! (*Suddenly he throws himself on his knees and raises his clasped hands to the sky—in a voice of agonized pleading.*) Lawd Jesus, heah my prayer! I'se a po' sinner, a po' sinner! I knows I done wrong, I knows it! When I cotches Jeff cheatin' wid loaded dice my anger overcomes me and I kills him dead! Lawd, I done wrong! When dat guard hits me wid de whip, my anger overcomes me, and I kills him dead. Lawd, I done wrong! And down heah whar dese fool bush niggers raises me up to the seat o' de mighty, I steals all I could grab. Lawd, I done wrong! I knows it! I'se sorry! Forgive me, Lawd! Forgive dis po' sinner! (*Then beseeching terrifiedly.*] And keep dem away, Lawd! Keep dem away from me! And stop dat drum soundin' in my ears! Dat begin to sound ha'nted, too. (*He gets to his feet, evidently slightly reassured by his prayer—with attempted confidence.*) De Lawd'll preserve me from dem ha'nts after dis. (*Sits down on the stump again*) I ain't skeered o' real men. Let dem come. But dem odders . . . (*He shudders—then looks down at his feet, working his toes inside the shoes—with a groan.*) Oh, my po' feet! Dem shoes ain't no use no more 'ceptin' to hurt. I'se better off widout dem. (*He unlaces them and pulls them off—holds the wrecks of the shoes in his hands and regards them mournfully.*) You was real, A-one patin' leather, too. Look at you now. Emperor, you'se gittin' mighty low!

(*He sits dejectedly and remains with bowed shoulders, staring*

24

*him to the purchaser*) And *you* sells me? And *you* buys me? I shows you I'se a free nigger, damn yo' souls! (*He fires at the* AUCTIONEER *and at the* PLANTER *with such rapidity that the two shots are almost simultaneous. As if this were a signal the walls of the forest fold in. Only blackness remains and silence broken by* JONES *as he rushes off, crying with fear—and by the quickened, ever louder beat of the tom-tom.*)

*down at the shoes in his hands as if reluctant to throw them away. While his attention is thus occupied, a crowd of figures silently enter the clearing from all sides. All are dressed in Southern costumes of the period of the fifties of the last century. There are middle-aged men who are evidently well-to-do planters. There is one spruce, authoritative individual—the* AUCTIONEER. *There is a crowd of curious spectators, chiefly young belles and dandies who have come to the slave-market for diversion. All exchange courtly greetings in dumb show and chat silently together. There is something stiff, rigid, unreal, marionettish about their movements. They group themselves about the stump. Finally a batch of slaves are led in from the left by an attendant—three men of different ages, two women, one with a baby in her arms, nursing. They are placed to the left of the stump, beside* JONES.

*The white planters look them over appraisingly as if they were cattle, and exchange judgments on each. The dandies point with their fingers and make witty remarks. The belles titter bewitchingly. All this in silence save for the ominous throb of the tom-tom. The* AUCTIONEER *holds up his hand, taking his place at the stump. The group strain forward attentively. He touches* JONES *on the shoulder peremptorily, motioning for him to stand on the stump—the auction block.*

JONES *looks up, sees the figures on all sides, looks wildly for some opening to escape, sees none, screams and leaps madly to the top of the stump to get as far away from them as possible. He stands there, cowering, paralyzed with horror. The* AUCTIONEER *begins his silent spiel. He points to* JONES, *appeals to the planters to see for themselves. Here is a good field hand, sound in wind and limb as they can see. Very strong still in spite of his being middle-aged. Look at that back. Look at those shoulders. Look at the muscles in his arms and his sturdy legs. Capable of any amount of hard labor. Moreover, of a good disposition, intelligent and tractable. Will any gentleman start the bidding? The* PLANTERS *raise their fingers, make their bids. They are apparently all eager to possess* JONES. *The bidding is lively, the crowd interested. While this has been going on,* JONES *has been seized by the courage of desperation. He dares to look down and around him. Over his face abject terror gives way to mystification, to gradual realization—stutteringly.*)

What you all doin', white folks? What's all dis? What you all looking at me fo'? What you doin' wid me, anyhow? (*Suddenly convulsed with raging hatred and fear*) Is dis a auction? Is you sellin' me like dey uster befo' de war? (*Jerking out his revolver just as the* AUCTIONEER *knocks him down to one of the planters—glaring from*

# Scene Six

SCENE: *Three o'clock. A cleared space in the forest. The limbs of the trees meet over it forming a low ceiling about five feet from the ground. The interlocked ropes of creepers reaching upward to entwine the tree trunks give an arched appearance to the sides. The space thus enclosed is like the dark, noisome hold of some ancient vessel. The moonlight is almost completely shut out and only a vague, wan light filters through. There is the noise of someone approaching from the left, stumbling and crawling through the undergrowth.* JONES' *voice is heard between chattering moans.*

Oh, Lawd, what I gwine do now? Ain't got no bullet left on'y de silver one. If mo' o' dem ha'nts come after me, how I gwine skeer dem away? Oh, Lawd, on'y de silver one left—an' I gotta save dat fo' luck. If I shoots dat one I'm a goner sho'! Lawd, it's black heah! Whar's de moon? Oh, Lawd, don't dis night evah come to an end? (*By the sounds, he is feeling his way cautiously forward.*) Dere! Dis feels like a clear space. I gotta lie down an' rest. I don't care if dem niggers does cotch me. I gotta rest.

(*He is well forward now where his figure can be dimly made out. His pants have been so torn away that what is left of them is no better than a breech cloth. He flings himself full length, face downward on the ground, panting with exhaustion. Gradually it seems to grow lighter in the enclosed space and two rows of seated figures can be seen behind* JONES. *They are sitting in crumpled, despairing attitudes, hunched, facing one another with their backs touching the forest walls as if they were shackled to them. All are Negroes, naked save for loin cloths. At first they are silent and motionless. Then they begin to sway slowly forward toward each other and back again in unison, as if they were laxly letting themselves follow the long roll of a ship at sea. At the same time, a low, melancholy murmur rises among them, increasing gradually by rhythmic degrees which seem to be directed and controlled by the throb of the tom-tom in the distance, to a long, tremulous wail of despair that reaches a certain pitch, unbearably acute, then falls by slow gradations of tone into*)

27

*silence and is taken up again.* JONES *starts, looks up, sees the figures, and throws himself down again to shut out the sight. A shudder of terror shakes his whole body as the wail rises up about him again. But the next time, his voice, as if under some uncanny compulsion, starts with the others. As their chorus lifts he rises to a sitting posture similar to the others, swaying back and forth. His voice reaches the highest pitch of sorrow, of desolation. The light fades out, the other voices cease, and only darkness is left.* JONES *can be heard scrambling to his feet and running off, his voice sinking down the scale and receding as he moves farther and farther away in the forest. The tom-tom beats louder, quicker, with a more insistent, triumphant pulsation.*)

# Scene Seven

SCENE: *Five o'clock. The foot of a gigantic tree by the edge of a great river. A rough structure of boulders, like an altar, is by the tree. The raised river bank is in the nearer background. Beyond this the surface of the river spreads out, brilliant and unruffled in the moonlight, blotted out and merged into a veil of bluish mist in the distance.* JONES' *voice is heard from the left rising and falling in the long, despairing wail of the chained slaves, to the rhythmic beat of the tom-tom. As his voice sinks into silence, he enters the open space. The expression of his face is fixed and stony, his eyes have an obsessed glare, he moves with a strange deliberation like a sleepwalker or one in a trance. He looks around at the tree, the rough stone altar, the moonlit surface of the river beyond, and passes his hand over his head with a vague gesture of puzzled bewilderment. Then, as if in obedience to some obscure impulse, he sinks into a kneeling, devotional posture before the altar. Then he seems to come to himself partly, to have an uncertain realization of what he is doing, for he straightens up and stares about him horrifiedly—in an incoherent mumble.*

What—what is I doin'? What is—dis place? Seems like—seems like I know dat tree—an' dem stones—an' de river. I remember—seems like I been heah befo'. (*Tremblingly*) Oh, Gorry, I'se skeered in dis place! I'se skeered! Oh, Lawd, pertect dis sinner!

(*Crawling away from the altar, he cowers close to the ground, his face hidden, his shoulders heaving with sobs of hysterical fright. From behind the trunk of the tree, as if he had sprung out of it, the figure of the* CONGO WITCH DOCTOR *appears. He is wizened and old, naked except for the fur of some small animal tied about his waist, its bushy tail hanging down in front. His body is stained all over a bright red. Antelope horns are on each side of his head, branching upward. In one hand he carries a bone rattle, in the other a charm stick with a bunch of white cockatoo feathers tied to the end. A great number of glass beads and bone ornaments are about his neck, ears, wrists, and ankles. He struts noiselessly with a queer prancing*

29

*step to a position in the clear ground between* JONES *and the altar. Then with a preliminary, summoning stamp of his foot on the earth, he begins to dance and to chant. As if in response to his summons the beating of the tom-tom grows to a fierce, exultant boom whose throbs seem to fill the air with vibrating rhythm.* JONES *looks up, starts to spring to his feet, reaches a half-kneeling, half-squatting position and remains rigidly fixed there, paralyzed with awed fascination by this new apparition. The* WITCH DOCTOR *sways, stamping with his foot, his bone rattle clicking the time. His voice rises and falls in a weird, monotonous croon, without articulate word divisions. Gradually his dance becomes clearly one of a narrative in pantomime, his croon is an incantation, a charm to allay the fierceness of some implacable deity demanding sacrifice. He flees, he is pursued by devils, he hides, he flees again. Ever wilder and wilder becomes his flight, nearer and nearer draws the pursuing evil, more and more the spirit of terror gains possession of him. His croon, rising to intensity, is punctuated by shrill cries.* JONES *has become completely hypnotized. His voice joins in the incantation, in the cries, he beats time with his hands and sways his body to and fro from the waist. The whole spirit and meaning of the dance has entered into him, has become his spirit. Finally the theme of the pantomime halts on a howl of despair, and is taken up again in a note of savage hope. There is a salvation. The forces of evil demand sacrifice. They must be appeased. The* WITCH-DOCTOR *points with his wand to the sacred tree, to the river beyond, to the altar, and finally to* JONES *with a ferocious command.* JONES *seems to sense the meaning of this. It is he who must offer himself for sacrifice. He beats his forehead abjectly to the ground, moaning hysterically.*)

Mercy, Oh Lawd! Mercy! Mercy on dis po' sinner.

(*The* WITCH-DOCTOR *springs to the river bank. He stretches out his arms and calls to some god within its depths. Then he starts backward slowly, his arms remaining out. A huge head of a crocodile appears over the bank and its eyes, glittering greenly, fasten upon* JONES. *He stares into them fascinatedly. The* WITCH-DOCTOR *prances up to him, touches him with his wand, motions with hideous command toward the waiting monster.* JONES *squirms on his belly nearer and nearer, moaning continually.*)

Mercy, Lawd! Mercy!

(*The crocodile heaves more of his enormous bulk onto the land.* JONES *squirms toward him. The* WITCH-DOCTOR'S *voice shrills out in furious exultation, the tom-tom beats madly.* JONES *cries out in a fierce, exhausted spasm of anguished pleading.*)

Lawd, save me! Lawd Jesus, heah my prayer!

*(Immediately, in answer to his prayer, comes the thought of the one bullet left him. He snatches at his hip, shouting defiantly.)*

De silver bullet! You don't git me yit!

*(He fires at the green eyes in front of him. The head of the crocodile sinks back behind the river bank, the* WITCH-DOCTOR *springs behind the sacred tree and disappears.* JONES *lies with his face to the ground, his arms outstretched, whimpering with fear as the throb of the tom-tom fills the silence about him with a somber pulsation, a baffled but revengeful power.)*

# Scene Eight

SCENE: *Dawn. Same as Scene Two, the dividing line of forest and plain. The nearest tree trunks are dimly revealed but the forest behind them is still a mass of glooming shadows. The tom-tom seems on the very spot, so loud and continuously vibrating are its beats.* LEM *enters from the left, followed by a small squad of his soldiers, and by the Cockney trader,* SMITHERS. LEM *is a heavy-set, ape-faced old savage of the extreme African type, dressed only in a loin cloth. A revolver and cartridge belt are about his waist. His soldiers are in different degrees of rag-concealed nakedness. All wear broad palm-leaf hats. Each one carries a rifle.* SMITHERS *is the same as in Scene One. One of the soldiers, evidently a tracker, is peering about keenly on the ground. He grunts and points to the spot where* JONES *entered the forest.* LEM *and* SMITHERS *come to look.*

SMITHERS (*after a glance, turns away in disgust*): That's where 'e went in right enough. Much good it'll do yer. 'E's miles orf by this an' safe to the Coast, damn 'is 'ide! I tole yer yer'd lose 'im, didn't I? —wastin' the 'ole bloomin' night beatin' yer bloody drum and castin' yer silly spells! Gawd blimey, wot a pack!

LEM (*gutturally*): We cotch him. You see. (*He makes a motion to his soldiers who squat down on their haunches in a semicircle.*)

SMITHERS (*exasperatedly*): Well, ain't yer goin' in an' 'unt 'im in the woods? What the 'ell's the good of waitin'?

LEM (*imperturbably—squatting down himself*): We cotch him.

SMITHERS (*turning away from him contemptuously*): Aw! Garn! 'E's a better man than the lot o' you put together. I 'ates the sight o' 'im but I'll say that for 'im. (*A sound of snapping twigs comes from the forest. The soldiers jump to their feet, cocking their rifles alertly.* LEM *remains sitting with an imperturbable expression, but listening intently. The sound from the woods is repeated.* LEM *makes a quick signal with his hand. His followers creep quickly but noiselessly into the forest, scattering so that each enters at a different spot.*)

32

SMITHERS (*in the silence that follows—in a contemptuous whisper*): You ain't thinkin' that would be 'im, I 'ope?

LEM (*calmly*): We cotch him.

SMITHERS: Blarsted fat 'eads! (*Then after a second's thought—wonderingly*) Still an' all, it might 'appen. If 'e lost 'is bloody way in these stinkin' woods 'e'd likely turn in a circle without 'is knowin' it. They all does.

LEM (*peremptorily*): Sssh! (*The reports of several rifles sound from the forest, followed a second later by savage, exultant yells. The beating of the tom-tom abruptly ceases.* LEM *looks up at the white man with a grin of satisfaction.*) We cotch him. Him dead.

SMITHERS (*with a snarl*): 'Ow d'yer know it's 'im an' 'ow d'yer know 'e's dead?

LEM: My mens dey got 'um silver bullets. Dey kill him shore.

SMITHERS (*astonished*): They got silver bullets?

LEM: Lead bullet no kill him. He got um strong charm. I cook um money, make um silver bullet, make um strong charm, too.

SMITHERS (*light breaking upon him*): So that's wot you was up to all night, wot? You was scared to put after 'im till you'd moulded silver bullets, eh?

LEM (*simply stating a fact*): Yes. Him got strong charm. Lead no good.

SMITHERS (*slapping his thigh and guffawing*): Haw-haw! If yer don't beat all 'ell! (*Then recovering himself—scornfully*) I'll bet yer it ain't 'im they shot at all, yer bleedin' looney!

LEM (*calmly*): Dey come bring him now. (*The soldiers come out of the forest, carrying* JONES' *limp body. There is a little reddish-purple hole under his left breast. He is dead. They carry him to* LEM, *who examines his body with great satisfaction.* SMITHERS *leans over his shoulder—in a tone of frightened awe.*) Well, they did for yer right enough, Jonsey, me lad! Dead as a 'erring! (*Mockingly*) Where's yer 'igh an' mighty airs now, yer bloomin' Majesty? (*Then with a grin*) Silver bullets! Gawd blimey, but yer died in the 'eighth o' style, any'ow! (LEM *makes a motion to the soldiers to carry the body out left.* SMITHERS *speaks to him sneeringly.*)

SMITHERS: And I s'pose you think it's yer bleedin' charms and yer silly beatin' the drum that made 'im run in a circle when 'e'd lost 'imself, don't yer? (*But* LEM *makes no reply, does not seem to hear the question, walks out left after his men.* SMITHERS *looks after him with contemptuous scorn.*) Stupid as 'ogs, the lot of 'em! Blarsted niggers!

(*The Curtain Falls.*)

LILLIAN HELLMAN

# Watch
# on the Rhine

*Watch on the Rhine* was first produced at the Martin Beck Theater, New York City, on April 1, 1941.

# CHARACTERS

ANISE

JOSEPH

FANNY FARRELLY

DAVID FARRELLY

MARTHE DE BRANCOVIS

TECK DE BRANCOVIS

SARA MÜLLER

JOSHUA MÜLLER

BODO MÜLLER

BABETTE MÜLLER

KURT MÜLLER

The time of the play is late spring, 1940.

# Act One

---

SCENE: *The living room of the Farrelly house, about twenty miles from Washington, D. C., on a warm spring morning.*

*Center stage are large French doors leading to an elevated open terrace. On the terrace are chairs, tables, a large table for dining. Some of this furniture we can see; most of it is on the left side of the terrace, beyond our sight. Left stage in an arched entrance, leading to the oval reception hall. We can see the main staircase as it goes off to the back of the hall. Right stage is a door leading to a library. The Farrelly house was built in the early nineteenth century. It has space, simplicity, style. The living room is large. Up stage right is a piano; down stage left, a couch; down stage right, a couch and chairs; up stage a few smaller chairs. Four or five generations have furnished this room and they have all been people of taste. There are no styles, no periods; the room has never been refurnished. Each careless aristocrat has thrown into the room what he or she liked as a child, what he or she brought home when grown up. Therefore the furniture is of many periods: the desk is English, the couch is Victorian, some of the pictures are modern, some of the ornaments French. The room has too many things in it: vases, clocks, miniatures, boxes, china animals. On the right wall is a large portrait of a big kind-faced man in an evening suit of 1900. On another wall is a large, very ugly landscape. The room is crowded. But it is cool and clean and its fabrics and woods are in soft colors.*

AT RISE: ANISE, *a thin Frenchwoman of about sixty, in a dark housekeeper's dress, is standing at a table sorting mail. She takes the mail from a small basket, holds each letter to the light, reads each postal card, then places them in piles. On the terrace,* JOSEPH, *a tall, middle-aged Negro butler, wheels a breakfast wagon. As he appears,* FANNY FARRELLY *comes in from the hall. She is a handsome woman of about sixty-three. She has on a fancy, good-looking dressing-gown.*

*Left and right are the audience's left and right.*

FANNY (*stops to watch* ANISE. *Sees* JOSEPH *moving about on terrace. Calls*): Joseph! (*To* ANISE) Morning.

ANISE (*continues examining mail*): Good morning, Madame.

JOSEPH (*comes to terrace door*): Yes'm?

FANNY: Everybody down?

JOSEPH: No'm. Nobody. I'll get your tea. (*He returns to breakfast wagon on terrace.*)

FANNY: Mr. David isn't down yet? But he knows he is to meet the train.

JOSEPH (*comes in from the terrace with the cup of tea*): He's got plenty of time, Miss Fanny. The train ain't in till noon.

FANNY: Breakfast is at nine o'clock in this house and will be until the day after I die. Ring the bell.

JOSEPH: It ain't nine yet, Miss Fanny. It's eight-thirty.

FANNY: Well, put the clocks up to nine and ring the bell.

JOSEPH: Mr. David told me not to ring it any more. He says it's got too mean a ring, that bell. It disturbs folks.

FANNY: That's what it was put there for. I like to disturb folks.

JOSEPH: Yes'm.

FANNY: You slept well, Anise. You were asleep before I could dismantle myself.

ANISE: I woke several times during the night.

FANNY: Did you? Then you were careful not to stop snoring. We must finally get around to rearranging your room. (ANISE *hands her three or four letters*) Even when you don't snore, it irritates me. (FANNY *opens a letter, begins to read it. After a minute*) What time is it?

ANISE: It is about eight-thirty. Joseph just told you.

FANNY: I didn't hear him. I'm nervous. Naturally. My mail looks dull. (*Reading the letter*) Jenny always tells you a piece of gossip three times, as if it grew fresher with the telling. Did you put flowers in their room?

ANISE: Certainly.

FANNY: David ought to get to the station by eleven-thirty.

ANISE (*patiently*): The train does not draw in until ten minutes past noon.

FANNY: But it might come in early. It's been known.

ANISE: Never. Not in the Union Station in Washington, the District of Columbia.

FANNY (*irritably*): But it might. It might. Don't argue with me about everything. What time is it?

ANISE: It's now twenty-seven minutes before nine. It will be impossible to continue telling you the time every three minutes from now until Miss Sara arrives. I think you are having a nervous breakdown. Compose yourself.

FANNY: It's been twenty years. Any mother would be nervous. If your daughter were coming home and you hadn't seen her, and a husband, *and* grandchildren—

ANISE: I do not say that it is wrong to be nervous. I, too, am nervous. I say only that you are.

FANNY: Very well. I heard you. *I* say that I am. (*She goes back to reading her letter. Looks up*) Jenny's still in California. She's lost her lavallière again. Birdie Chase's daughter is still faire l'amouring with that actor. Tawdry, Jenny says it is. An actor. Fashions in sin change. In my day, it was Englishmen. I don't understand infidelity. If you love a man, then why? If you don't love him, then why stay with him? (*Without turning, she points over her head to Joshua Farrelly's portrait*) Thank God, I was in love. I thought about Joshua last night. Three grandchildren. He would have liked that. I hope I will. (*Points to other letters*) Anything in anybody else's mail?

ANISE: Advertisements for Mr. David and legal things. For our Count and Countess, there is nothing but what seems an invitation to a lower-class embassy tea and letters asking for bills to get paid.

FANNY: That's every morning. (*Thoughtfully*) In the six weeks the Balkan nobility have been with us, they seem to have run up a great many bills.

ANISE: Yes, *I* told you that. Then there was a night-letter for Mr. David.

(*A very loud, very unpleasant bell begins to ring.*)

FANNY (*through the noise*): Really? From whom?

ANISE: From her. I took it on the telephone, and—

(*Bell drowns out her voice.*)

FANNY: Who is "her"? (*Bell becomes very loud*) Go tell him to stop that noise—

ANISE (*goes toward terrace, calling*): Joseph! Stop that bell. Miss Fanny says to stop it.

JOSEPH (*calls*): Miss Fanny said to start it.

FANNY (*shouts out to him*): I didn't tell you to hang yourself with it.

JOSEPH (*appears on terrace*): I ain't hung. Your breakfast is ready. (*Disappears.*)

FANNY (*to* ANISE): Who is "her"?

ANISE: That Carter woman from Lansing, Michigan.

FANNY: Oh, my. Is she back in Washington again? What did the telegram say?

ANISE: It said the long sickness of her dear Papa had terminated in full recovery.

FANNY: That's too bad.

ANISE: She was returning, and would Mr. David come for dinner a week from Thursday? "Love," it said, "to you and your charming mother." (*To* FANNY) That's you. I think Miss Carter from Lansing, Michigan, was unwise in attending the illness of her Papa.

FANNY: I hope so. Why?

ANISE (*shrugs*): There is much winking of the eyes going on between our Countess and Mr. David.

FANNY (*eagerly*): I know that. Anything new happen?

ANISE (*too innocently*): Happen? I don't know what you mean?

FANNY: You know damn well what I mean.

ANISE: *That?* Oh, no, I don't think that.

JOSEPH (*appears in the door*): The sausage cakes is shrinking.

FANNY (*rises. To* ANISE): I want everybody down here immediately. Is the car ready? (ANISE *nods*) Did you order a good dinner? (*Shrieks*) David! Oh.

(DAVID FARRELLY, *a pleasant-looking man of thirty-nine, comes in from the entrance hall, almost bumps into* FANNY.)

DAVID: Good morning, everybody.

ANISE (*to* FANNY): Everything is excellent. You have been asking the same questions for a week. You have made the kitchen very nervous.

DAVID (*to* JOSEPH): Why did you ring that air-raid alarm again?

JOSEPH: Ain't me, Mr. David. I don't like no noise. Miss Fanny told me.

FANNY: Good morning, David.

DAVID (*to* JOSEPH): Tell Fred to leave the car. I'll drive to the station.

JOSEPH (*nods*): Yes, sir. (*Exits.*)

DAVID (*to* FANNY, *half amused, half annoyed, as he begins to read his mail*): Mama, I think we'll fix up the chicken-house for you as a playroom. We'll hang the room with bells and you can go into your second childhood in the proper privacy.

FANNY: I find it very interesting. You sleep soundly, you rise at your usual hour—although your sister, whom you haven't seen in years, is waiting at the station—

DAVID: She is not waiting at the station. (*Laughs*) The train does not come in until ten minutes past twelve.

FANNY (*airily*): It's almost that now.

ANISE (*turns to look at her*): Really, Miss Fanny, contain yourself. It is twenty minutes before nine.

DAVID: And I have *not* slept soundly. And I've been up since six o'clock.

FANNY: The Balkans aren't down yet. Where are they?

DAVID: I don't know.

ANISE: There's nothing in your mail, Mr. David. Only the usual advertisements.

DAVID: And for me, that is all that is ever likely to come—here.

ANISE (*haughtily, as she starts toward hall*): I cannot, of course, speak for Miss Fanny. *I* have never opened a letter in my life.

DAVID: I know. You don't have to. For you they fly open.

FANNY (*giggles*): It's true. You're a snooper, Anise. (ANISE *exits.* FANNY *talks as* ANISE *moves out*) I rather admire it. It shows an interest in life. (*She looks up at Joshua's portrait*) You know, I've been lying awake most of the night wondering what Papa would have thought about Sara. He'd have been very pleased, wouldn't he? I always find myself wondering what Joshua would have felt.

DAVID: Yes. But maybe it would be just as well if you didn't expect me to be wondering about it, too. I wasn't married to him, Mama. He was just my father.

FANNY: My. You got up on the wrong side of the bed. (*She moves past him. Points to the mail which he is still opening*) The bills are for our noble guests. Interesting, how many there are every morning. How much longer are they going to be with us?

DAVID (*without looking at her*): I don't know.

FANNY: It's been six weeks. Now that Sara and her family are coming, even this house might be a little crowded—(*He looks up at her. Quickly*) Yes. I know I invited them. I felt sorry for Marthe, and Teck rather amused me. He plays good cribbage, and he tells good jokes. But that's not enough for a lifetime guest. If you've been urging her to stay, I wish you'd stop it. They haven't any money; all right, lend them some—

DAVID: I have been urging them to stay?

FANNY: I'm not so old I don't recognize flirting when I see it.

DAVID: But you're old enough not to be silly.

FANNY: I'm not silly. I'm charming.

(MARTHE DE BRANCOVIS, *an attractive woman of thirty-one or thirty-two, enters.*)

MARTHE: Good morning, Fanny. Morning, David.

FANNY: Good morning, Marthe.

DAVID (*warmly*): Good morning.

MARTHE: Fanny, darling, couldn't you persuade yourself to let me have a tray in bed and some cotton for my ears?

DAVID: Certainly not. My father ate breakfast at nine; and whatever my father did . . .

FANNY (*carefully, to* DAVID): There was a night-letter for you from that Carter woman in Lansing, Michigan. She is returning and you are to come to dinner next Thursday. (*As she exits on terrace*) C-A-R-T-E-R. (*Pronounces it carefully*) Lansing, Michigan.

DAVID (*laughs*): I know how to spell Carter, but thank you. (FANNY *exits.* DAVID *looks up at* MARTHE) Do you understand my mother?

MARTHE: Sometimes.

DAVID: Miss Carter was done for your benefit.

MARTHE (*smiles*): That means she has guessed that I would be jealous. And she has guessed right.

DAVID (*looks at her*): Jealous?

MARTHE: I know I've no right to be, but I am. And Fanny knows it.

DAVID (*carelessly*): Don't pay any attention to Mama. She has a sure instinct for the women I like, and she begins to hammer away early. Marthe— (*Goes to decanter on side-table*) I'm going to have a drink. I haven't had a drink before breakfast since the day I took my bar examination. (*Pours himself a drink, gulps it down*) What's it going to be like to stand on a station platform and see your sister after all these years? I'm afraid, I guess.

MARTHE: Why?

DAVID: I don't know. Afraid she won't like me— (*Shrugs*) We were very fond of each other, but it's been a long time.

MARTHE: I remember Sara. Mama brought me one day when your father was stationed in Paris. I was about six and Sara about fifteen and you were—

DAVID: You were a pretty little girl.

MARTHE: Do you really remember me? You never told me before.

FANNY (*yelling from the terrace*): David! Come to breakfast.

DAVID (*as if he had not been listening*): You know, I've never met Sara's husband. Mama did. I think the first day Sara met him, in Munich. Mama didn't like the marriage much in those days—and Sara didn't care, and Mama didn't like Sara not caring. Mama cut up about it, bad.

MARTHE: Why?

DAVID: Probably because they didn't let her arrange it. Why does Mama ever act badly? She doesn't remember ten minutes later.

MARTHE: Wasn't Mr. Müller poor?

DAVID: Oh, Mama wouldn't have minded that. If they'd only come home and let her fix their lives for them—(*Smiles*) But Sara didn't want it that way.

MARTHE: You'll have a house full of refugees—us and—

DAVID: Are you and Teck refugees? I'm not sure I know what you're refugees from.

MARTHE: From Europe.

DAVID: From what Europe?

MARTHE (*smiles, shrugs*): I don't know. I don't know myself, really. Just Europe. (*Quickly, comes to him*) Sara will like you. I like you. (*Laughs*) That doesn't make sense, does it?

(*On her speech*, TECK DE BRANCOVIS *appears in the hall. He is a good-looking man of about forty-five. She stops quickly.*)

TECK (*to* MARTHE *and* DAVID): Good morning.

(*The bell gives an enormous ring.*)

DAVID (*goes to terrace*): Good morning, Teck. For years I've been thinking they were coming for Mama with a net. I'm giving up hope. I may try catching her myself. (*Disappears, calling*) Mama! Stop that noise.

TECK: I wonder if science has a name for women who enjoy noise? (*Goes to table, picks up his mail*) Many mistaken people, Marthe, seem to have given you many charge accounts.

MARTHE: The Countess de Brancovis. That still does it. It would be nice to be able to pay bills again—

TECK: Do not act as if I refused to pay them. I did not sleep well last night. I was worried. We have eighty-seven dollars in American Express checks. (*Pleasantly, looking at her*) That's all we have, Marthe.

MARTHE (*shrugs*): Maybe something will turn up. It's due.

TECK (*carefully*): David? (*Then, as she turns to look at him*) The other relatives will arrive this morning?

MARTHE: Yes.

TECK (*points to porch*): I think Madame Fanny and Mr. David may grow weary of accents and charity guests. Or is the husband of the sister a rich one?

MARTHE: No. He's poor. He had to leave Germany in '33.

TECK: A Jew?

MARTHE: No. I don't think so.

TECK: Why did he have to leave Germany?

MARTHE (*still reading*): Oh, I don't know, Teck. He's an anti-Nazi.

TECK: A political?

MARTHE: No, I don't think so. He was an engineer. I don't know. I don't know much about him.

TECK: Did you sleep well?

MARTHE: Yes. Why not?

TECK: Money does not worry you?

MARTHE: It worries me very much. But I just lie still now and hope. I'm glad to be here. (*Shrugs*) Maybe something good will happen. We've come to the end of a road. That's been true for a long time. Things will have to go one way or the other. Maybe they'll go well, for a change.

TECK: I have not come to the end of any road.

MARTHE (*looks at him*): No? I admire you.

TECK: I'm going into Washington tonight. Phili has a poker game every Wednesday evening. He has arranged for me to join it.

MARTHE (*after a pause*): Have you been seeing Phili?

TECK: Once or twice. Why not? Phili and I are old friends. He may be useful. I do not want to stay in this country forever.

MARTHE: You can't leave them alone. Your favorite dream, isn't it, Teck? That they will let you play with them again? I don't think they will, and I don't think you should be seeing Phili, or that you should be seen at the Embassy.

TECK (*smiles*): You have political convictions now?

MARTHE: I don't know what I have. I've never liked Nazis, as you know, and you should have had enough of them. They seem to have had enough of you, God knows. It would be just as well to admit they are smarter than you are and let them alone.

TECK (*looking at her carefully, after a minute*): That is interesting.

MARTHE: What is interesting?

TECK: I think you are trying to say something to me. What is it?

MARTHE: That you ought not to be at the Embassy, and that it's insane to play cards in a game with Von Seitz with eighty-seven dollars in your pocket. I don't think he'd like your not being able to pay up. Suppose you lose?

TECK: I shall try not to lose.

MARTHE: But if you do lose and can't pay, it will be all over Washington in an hour. (*Points to terrace*) They'll find out about it, and we'll be out of here when they do.

TECK: I think I want to be out of here. I find that I do not like the picture of you and our host.

MARTHE (*carefully*): There is no picture, as you put it, to like or dislike.

TECK: Not yet? I am glad to hear that. (*Comes toward her slowly*) Marthe, you understand that I am not really a fool? You understand that it is unwise to calculate me that way?

MARTHE (*slowly, as if it were an effort*): Yes, I understand that. And I understand that I am getting tired. Just plain tired. The whole thing's too much for me. I've always meant to ask you, since you played on so many sides, why we didn't come out any better. I've always wanted to ask you what happened. (*Sharply*) I'm tired, see? And I just want to sit down. Just to sit down in a chair and stay.

TECK (*carefully*): Here?

MARTHE: I don't know. Any place—

TECK: You have thus arranged it with David?

MARTHE: I've arranged nothing.

TECK: But you are trying, eh? (*He comes close to her*) I think not. I would not like that. Do not make any arrangements, Marthe. I may not allow you to carry them through. (*Smiles*) Come to breakfast now. (*He passes her, disappears on the terrace. She stands still and thoughtful. Then she, too, moves to the terrace, disappears.* JOSEPH *appears on the terrace, carrying a tray toward the unseen breakfast table. The stage is empty. After a minute, there are sounds of footsteps in the hall.* SARA MÜLLER *appears in the doorway, comes toward the middle of the room as if expecting to find somebody, stops, looks around, begins to smile. Behind her in the doorway, are three children; behind them,* KURT MÜLLER. *They stand waiting, watching* SARA. SARA *is forty-one or forty-two, a good-looking woman, with a well-bred, serious face. She is very badly dressed. Her dress is too long, her shoes were bought a long time ago and have no relation to the dress, and the belt of her dress has become untied and is hanging down. She looks clean and dowdy. As she looks around the room, her face is gay and surprised. Smiling, without turning, absently, she motions to the children and* KURT. *Slowly, the children come in.* BODO MÜLLER, *a boy of nine, comes first. He is carrying coats. Behind him, carrying two cheap valises, is* JOSHUA MÜLLER, *a boy of four-*

*teen. Behind him is* BABETTE MÜLLER, *a pretty little girl of twelve. They are dressed for a much colder climate. They come forward, look at their mother, then move to a couch. Behind them is* KURT MÜLLER, *a large, powerful, German-looking man of about forty-seven. He is carrying a shabby valise and a brief-case. He stands watching* SARA. JOSHUA *puts down the valises, goes to his father, takes the valise from* KURT, *puts it neatly near his, and puts the brief-case near* KURT. BABETTE *goes to* SARA, *takes a package from her, places it near the valise. Then she turns to* BODO, *takes the coats he is carrying, puts them neatly on top of the valises. After a second,* KURT *sits down. As he does so, we see that his movements are slow and careful, as if they are made with effort.*)

BABETTE (*points to a couch near which they are standing. She has a slight accent*): Is it allowed?

KURT (*smiles. He has an accent*): Yes. It is allowed. (BABETTE *and* BODO *sit stiffly on the couch.*)

JOSHUA (*nervously. He has a slight accent*): But we did not sound the bell—

SARA (*idly, as she wanders around the room, her face excited*): The door isn't locked. It never was. Never since I can remember.

BODO (*softly, puzzled*): The entrance of the home is never locked. So.

KURT (*looks at him*): You find it curious to believe there are people who live and do not need to watch, eh, Bodo?

BODO: Yes, Papa.

KURT (*smiles*): You and I.

JOSHUA (*smiles*): It is strange. But it must be good, I think.

KURT: Yes.

SARA: Sit back. Be comfortable. I—I wonder where Mama and David— (*Delighted, sees portrait of Joshua Farrelly, points to it*) And that was my Papa. That was the famous Joshua Farrelly. (*They all look up at it. She wanders around the room*) My goodness, isn't it a fine room? I'd almost forgotten— (*Picks up a picture from the table*) And this was my grandmother. (*Very nervously*) Shall I go and say we're here? They'd be having breakfast, I think. Always on the side terrace in nice weather. I don't know. Maybe— (*Picks up another picture*) "To Joshua and Fanny Farrelly. With admiration. Alfonso, May 7, 1910." I had an ermine boa and a pink coat. I was angry because it was too warm in Madrid to wear it.

BODO: Alfons von Spanien? Der hat immer Bilder von sich verschenkt. Ein schlectes Zeichen für einen Mann.

JOSHUA: Mama told you it is good manners to speak the language of the country you visit. Therefore, speak in English.

BODO: I said he seemed always to give his photograph. I said that is a bad flag on a man. Grow fat on the poor people and give pictures of the face. (JOSHUA *sits down.*)

SARA: I remember a big party and cakes and a glass of champagne for me. I was ten, I guess— (*Suddenly laughs*) That was when Mama said the first time a king got shot at, he was a romantic, but the fifth time he was a comedian. And when my father gave his lecture in Madrid, he repeated it—right in Madrid. It was a great scandal. You know, Alfonso was always getting shot at or bombed.

BODO (*shrugs*): Certainement.

JOSHUA: Certainement? As-tu perdu la tête?

BABETTE: Speak in English, please.

KURT (*without turning*): You are a terrorist, Bodo?

BODO (*slowly*): No.

JOSHUA: Then since when has it become *natural* to shoot upon people?

BODO: Do not give me lessons. It is neither right nor natural to shoot upon people. I know that.

SARA (*looks at* BABETTE, *thoughtfully*): An ermine boa. A boa is a scarf. I should like to have one for you, Babbie. Once, in Prague, I saw a pretty one. I wanted to buy it for you. But we had to pay our rent. (*Laughs*) But I almost bought it.

BABETTE: Yes, Mama. Thank you. Tie your sash, Mama.

SARA (*thoughtfully*): Almost twenty years.

BODO: You were born here, Mama?

SARA: Upstairs. And I lived here until I went to live with your father. (*Looks out beyond terrace*) Your Uncle David and I used to have a garden, behind the terrace. I wonder if it's still there. I like a garden. I've always hoped we'd have a house some day and settle down— (*Stops, nervously, turns to stare at* KURT, *who is looking at her*) I am talking so foolish. Sentimental. At my age. Gardens and ermine boas. I haven't wanted anything—

KURT (*comes toward her, takes her hand*): Sara. Stop it. This is a fine room. A fine place to be. Everything is so pleasant and full of comfort. This will be a good piano on which to play again. And it is all so clean. I like that. Now, you shall not be a baby. You must enjoy your house, and not be afraid that you hurt me with it. Yes?

BABETTE: Papa, tie Mama's sash, please.

SARA (*shyly smiles at him as he leans down to tie the belt*): Yes, of course. It's strange, that's all. We've never been in a place like this together—

KURT: That does not mean, and should not mean, that we do not remember how to enjoy what comes our way. We are on a holiday.

JOSHUA: A holiday? But for how long? And what plans afterward?

KURT (*quietly*): We will have plans when the hour arrives to make them. (ANISE *appears from the hall. She starts into the room, stops, bewildered. The* MÜLLERS *have not seen her. Then, as* SARA *turns,* ANISE *speaks. As she speaks, the children rise.*)

ANISE: What? What?

SARA (*softly*): Anise. It's me. It's Sara.

ANISE (*coming forward slowly*): What? (*Then as she approaches* SARA, *she begins to run toward her*) Miss Sara! Miss Sara! (*They reach each other, both laugh happily.* SARA *kisses* ANISE) I would have known you. Yes, I would. I would have known— (*Excited, bewildered, nervous, she looks toward* KURT) How do you do, sir? How do you do? (*Turns toward the children*) How do you do?

JOSHUA: Thank you, Miss Anise. We are in good health.

SARA (*very happily*): You look the same. I think you look the same. Just the way I've always remembered. (*To the others*) This is the Anise I have told you about. She was here before I was born.

ANISE: But how— Did you just come in? What a way to come home! And after all the plans we've made! But you were to come on the twelve o'clock train, and Mr. David was to meet you—

BABETTE: The twelve o'clock train was most expensive. We could not have come with that train. We liked the train we came on. It was most luxurious.

ANISE (*very nervously, very rattled*): But Madame Fanny will have a fit. I will call her— She will not be able to contain herself. She—

SARA (*softly*): I wanted a few minutes. I'm nervous about coming home, I guess.

BODO (*conversationally*): You are French, Madame Anise?

ANISE: Yes, I am from the Bas Rhin. (*She looks past* SARA, *and bobs her head idiotically at* KURT) Sara's husband. That is nice. That is nice.

BODO: Yes. Your accent is from the North. That is fine country. We were in hiding there once. (BABETTE *quickly pokes him.*)

ANISE: Hiding? You— (*Turns nervously to* KURT) But here we stand and talk. You have not had your breakfast, sir!

BABETTE (*simply, eagerly*): It would be nice to have breakfast.

ANISE: Yes, of course— I will go and order it.

SARA (*to the children*): What would you like for breakfast?

BABETTE (*surprised*): What would we like? Why, Mama, we will have anything that can be spared. If eggs are not too rare or too expensive—

ANISE (*amazed*): Rare? Why— Oh, I—I must call Miss Fanny now. It is of a necessity. (*Excited, rushing toward terrace, calling*) Miss Fanny. Miss Fanny. (*Back to* SARA) Have you forgotten your Mama's nature? She cannot bear not knowing things. Miss Fanny! What a way to come home! After twenty years and nobody at the station—

FANNY'S VOICE: Don't yell at me. What is the matter with you?

ANISE (*excitedly, as* FANNY *draws near*): She's here. They're here. Miss Sara. She's here, I tell you. (FANNY *comes up to her, stares at her, then looks slowly around until she sees* SARA.)

SARA (*softly*): Hello, Mama.

FANNY (*after a long pause, softly, coming toward her*): Sara. Sara, darling. You're here. You're really here. (*She reaches her, takes her arms, stares at her, smiles*) Welcome. Welcome. Welcome to your house. (*Slowly*) You're not young, Sara.

SARA (*smiles*): No, Mama. I'm forty-one.

FANNY (*softly*): Forty-one. Of course. (*Presses her arms again*) Oh, Sara, I'm— (*Then quickly*) You look more like Papa now. That's good. The years have helped you. (*Turns to look at* KURT) Welcome to this house, sir.

KURT (*warmly*): Thank you, Madame.

FANNY (*turns to look at* SARA *again, nervously pats her arm. Nods, turns again to stare at* KURT. *She is nervous and chatty*): You are a good-looking man, for a German. I didn't remember you that way. I like a good-looking man. I always have.

KURT (*smiles*): I like a good-looking woman. I always have.

FANNY: Good. That's the way it should be.

BODO (*to* SARA): Ist das Grossmama?

FANNY (*looks down*): Yes. I am your grandmother. Also, I speak German, so do not talk about me. I speak languages very well. But there is no longer anybody to speak with. Anise has half forgotten her French, which was always bad; and I have nobody with whom to speak my Italian or German or—Sara, it's very good to have you home. I'm chattering away, I—

JOSHUA: Now you have us, Madame. We speak ignorantly, but fluently, in German, French, Italian, Spanish—

KURT: And boastfully in English.

BODO: There is never a need for boasting. If we are to fight for the good of all men, it is to be accepted that we must be among the most advanced.

ANISE: My God.

FANNY (*to* SARA): Are these your *children?* Or are they dressed up midgets?

SARA (*laughs*): These are my children, Mama. This, Babette. (BABETTE *bows*) This, Joshua. (JOSHUA *bows*) This is Bodo. (BODO *bows*.)

FANNY: Joshua was named for Papa. You wrote me. (*Indicates picture of Joshua Farrelly*) You bear a great name, young man.

JOSHUA (*smiles, indicates his father*): My name is Müller.

FANNY (*looks at him, laughs*): Yes. You look a little like your grandfather. (*To* BABETTE) And so do you. You are a nice-looking girl. (*To* BODO) You look like nobody.

BODO (*proudly*): I am not beautiful.

FANNY (*laughs*): Well, Sara, well. Three children. You have done well. (*To* KURT) You, too, sir, of course. Are you quite recovered? Sara wrote that you were in Spain and—

BODO: Did Mama write that Papa was a great hero? He was brave, he was calm, he was expert, he was resourceful, he was—

KURT (*laughs*): My biographer. And as unprejudiced as most of them.

SARA: Where is David? I am so anxious— Has he changed much? Does he . . .

FANNY (*to* ANISE): Don't stand there. Go and get him right away. Go get David. (*As* ANISE *exits*) He's out having breakfast with the titled folk. Do you remember Marthe Randolph? I mean, do you remember Hortie Randolph, her mother, who was my friend? Can you follow what I'm saying? I'm not speaking well today.

SARA (*laughs*): Of course I remember Marthe and Hortie. You and she used to scream at each other.

FANNY: Well, Marthe, her daughter, married Teck de Brancovis. *Count* de Brancovis. He was fancy when she married him. Not so fancy now, I suspect. Although still chic and tired. You know what I mean, the way they are in Europe. Well, they're here.

SARA: What's David like now? I—

FANNY: Like? Like? I don't know. He's a lawyer. You know that. Papa's firm. He's never married. You know that, too—

SARA: Why hasn't he married?

FANNY: Really, I don't know. I don't think he likes his own taste. Which is very discriminating of him. He's had a lot of girls, of course, one more ignorant and silly than the other— (*Goes toward terrace, begins to scream*) And where is he? David! David!

ANISE'S VOICE: He's coming, Miss Fanny. He's coming. Contain yourself. He was down at the garage getting ready to leave—

FANNY: I don't care where he is. Tell him to come.— David! (*Suddenly points to picture of Joshua*) That's my Joshua. Handsome, eh? We were very much in love. Hard to believe of people nowadays, isn't it?

SARA: Kurt and I love each other.

FANNY: Oh. You do? I daresay. But there are ways and ways of loving.

SARA: How dare you, Mama—

KURT (*laughs*): Ladies, ladies.

SARA (*giggles*): Why, I almost got mad then. You know, I don't think I've been mad since I last saw you.

BODO: My! You and Mama must not get angry. Anger is protest. And so you must direction it to the proper channels and then harness it for the good of other men. That is correct, Papa?

FANNY (*peers down at him*): If you grow up to talk like that, and stay as ugly as you are, you are going to have one of those successful careers on the lecture platform. (JOSHUA *and* BABETTE *laugh*.)

JOSHUA (*to* BODO): Ah. It is a great pleasure to hear Grandma talk with you.

BODO (*to* FANNY, *tenderly*): We will not like each other. (KURT *has wandered to the piano. Standing, he touches the keys in the first bars of a Mozart Rondo.*)

FANNY: You are wrong. I think we are rather alike; if that is so, let us at least remember to admire each other. (DAVID *comes running in from the entrance hall. At the door he stops, stares at* SARA.)

DAVID (*to* SARA): Sara. Darling—

SARA (*wheels, goes running toward him. She moves into his arms. He leans down, kisses her with great affection*): David. David.

DAVID (*softly*): It's been a long, long time. I got to thinking it would never happen. (*He leans down, kisses her hair. After a minute, he smiles, presses her arm.*)

SARA (*excited*): David, I'm excited. Isn't it strange? To be here, to see each other— But I am forgetting. This is my husband. These are my children. Babette, Joshua, Bodo. (*They all three advance, stand in line to shake hands.*)

BODO (*shaking hands*): How do you do, Uncle David?

DAVID: How do you do, Bodo? (DAVID *shakes hands with* JOSHUA) Boys can shake hands. But so pretty a girl must be kissed. (*He kisses* BABETTE. *She smiles, very pleased, and crosses to the side of* SARA.)

BABETTE: Thank you. Fix your hairpin, Mama. (SARA *shoves back a falling hairpin.*)

DAVID (*crossing to* KURT): I'm happy to meet you, sir, and to have you here.

KURT: Thank you. Sara has told me so much from you. You have a devoted sister.

DAVID (*very pleased*): Have I? Still? That's mighty good to hear. (ANISE *comes in from the library.*)

ANISE: Your breakfast is coming. Shall I wash the children, Miss Sara?

JOSHUA (*amazed*): Wash us? Do people wash each other?

SARA: No, but the washing is a good idea. Go along now, and hurry. (*All three start for the hall*) And then we'll all have a fine, big breakfast again. (*The children exit.*)

FANNY: Again? Don't you usually have a good breakfast?

KURT (*smiles*): No, Madame. Only sometimes.

SARA (*laughs*): Oh, we do all right, usually. (*Very happily, very gaily*) Ah, it's good to be here. (*Puts her arm in* DAVID's) We were kids. Now we're all grown up! I've got children, you're a lawyer, and a fine one, I bet—

FANNY: The name of Farrelly on the door didn't, of course, hurt David's career.

DAVID (*smiles*): Sara, you might as well know Mama thinks of me only as a monument to Papa and a not very well-made monument at that. I am not the man Papa was.

SARA (*to* FANNY, *smiles*): How do you know he's not?

FANNY (*carefully*): I beg your pardon. That is the second time you have spoken disrespectfully of your father. (SARA *and* DAVID *laugh.* FANNY *turns to* KURT) I hope you will like me.

KURT: I hope so.

SARA (*pulls him to the couch, sits down with him*): Now I want to hear about you— (*Looks at him, laughs*) I'm awfully nervous about seeing you. Are you, about me?

DAVID: Yes. I certainly am.

SARA (*looks around*): I'm like an idiot. I want to see everything right away. The lake, and my old room—and I want to talk and ask questions . . .

KURT (*laughs*): More slow, Sara. It is most difficult to have twenty years in a few minutes.

SARA: Yes, I know, but— Oh, well. Kurt's right. We'll say it all slowly. It's just nice being back. Haven't I fine children?

DAVID: Very fine. You're lucky. I wish I had them.

FANNY: How could you have them? All the women you like are too draughty, if you know what I mean. I'm sure that girl from Lansing, Michigan, would be sterile. Which is as God in his wisdom would have it.

SARA: Oh. So you have a girl?

DAVID: I have no girl. This amuses Mama.

FANNY: He's very attractive to some women. (*To* KURT) Both my children are attractive, whatever else they're not. Don't you think so? (*Points to* DAVID) He's flirting with our Countess now, Sara. You will see for yourself.

DAVID (*sharply*): You are making nervous jokes this morning, Mama. And they are not very good ones.

FANNY (*gaily*): I tell the truth. If it turns out to be a joke, all the better.

SARA (*affectionately*): Ah, Mama hasn't changed. And that's good, too.

FANNY: Don't mind me, Sara. I, too, am nervous about seeing you. (*To* KURT) You'll like it here. You are an engineer?

KURT: Yes.

FANNY: Do you remember the day we met in München? The day Sara brought you to lunch? I thought you were rather a clod and that Sara would have a miserable life. I think I was wrong. (*To* DAVID) You see? I always admit when I'm wrong.

DAVID: You are a woman who is noble in all things, at all times.

FANNY: Oh, you're mad at me. (*To* KURT) As I say, you'll like it here. I've already made some plans. The new wing will be for you and Sara. The old turkey-house we'll fix up for the children. A nice, new bathroom, and we'll put in their own kitchen, and Anise will move in with them—

SARA: That's kind of you, Mama. But—but—we won't make any plans for a while— (*Very quietly*) A good, long vacation; God knows Kurt needs it—

FANNY: A vacation? You'll be staying here, of course. You don't have to worry about work—engineers can always get jobs, David says, and he's already begun to inquire—

KURT: I have not worked as an engineer since many years, Madame.

DAVID: Haven't you? I thought— Didn't you work for Dornier?

KURT: Yes. Before '33.

FANNY: But you have worked in other places. A great many other places, I should say. Every letter of Sara's seemed to have a new postmark.

KURT (*smiles*): We move most often.

DAVID: You gave up engineering?

KURT: I gave it up? (*Shrugs*) One could say it that way.

FANNY: What do you do?

SARA: Mama, we—

KURT: It is difficult to explain.

DAVID (*after a slight pause*): If you'd rather not.

FANNY: No, I—I'm trying to find out something. (*To* KURT) May I ask it, sir?

KURT: Let me help you, Madame. You wish to know whether not being an engineer buys adequate breakfasts for my family. It does not. I have no wish to make a mystery of what I have been doing; it is only that it is awkward to place neatly. (*Smiles, motions with his hand*) It sounds so big: it is so small. I am an Anti-Fascist. And that does not pay well.

FANNY: Do you mind questions?

SARA: Yes.

KURT (*sharply*): Sara. (*To* FANNY) Perhaps I shall not answer them. But I shall try.

FANNY: Are you a radical?

KURT: You would have to tell me what that word means to you, Madame.

FANNY (*after a slight pause*): That is just. Perhaps we all have private definitions. We all are Anti-Fascists, for example—

SARA: Yes. But Kurt works at it.

FANNY: What kind of work?

KURT: Any kind. Anywhere.

FANNY (*sharply*): I will stop asking questions.

SARA (*very sharply*): That would be sensible, Mama.

DAVID: Darling, don't be angry. We've been worried about you, naturally. We knew so little, except that you were having a bad time.

SARA: I didn't have a bad time. We never—

KURT: Do not lie for me, Sara.

SARA: I'm not lying. I didn't have a bad time, the way they mean. I—

FANNY (*slowly*): You had a bad time just trying to live, didn't you? That's obvious, Sara, and foolish to pretend it isn't. Why wouldn't you take money from us? What kind of nonsense—

SARA (*slowly*): We've lived the way we wanted to live. I don't know the language of rooms like this any more. And I don't want to learn it again.

KURT: Do not bristle about it.

SARA: I'm not bristling. (*To* FANNY) I married because I fell in love. You can understand that.

FANNY (*slowly*): Yes.

SARA: For almost twelve years, Kurt went to work every morning and came home every night, and we lived modestly, and happily— (*Sharply*) As happily as people could in a starved Germany that was going to pieces—

KURT: Sara, please. You are angry. I do not like it that way. I will try to find a way to tell you with quickness. Yes. (SARA *turns, looks at him, starts to speak, stops*) I was born in a town called Fürth. (*Pauses. Looks up, smiles*) There is a holiday in my town. We call it Kirchweih. It was a gay holiday with games and music and a hot white sausage to eat with the wine. I grow up, I move away—to school, to work—but always I come back for Kirchweih. It is for me, the great day of the year. (*Slowly*) But after the war, that day begins to change. The sausage is made from bad stuff, the peasants come in without shoes, the children are too sick— (*Carefully*) It is bad for my people, those years, but always I have hope. In the festival of August, 1931, more than a year before the storm, I give up that hope. On that day, I see twenty-seven men murdered in a Nazi street fight. I cannot stay by now and watch. My time has come to move. I say with Luther, "Here I stand. I can do nothing else. God help me. Amen."

SARA: It doesn't pay well to fight for what we believe in. But I wanted it the way Kurt wanted it. (*Shrugs*) They don't like us in Europe; I guess they never did. So Kurt brought us home. You've always said you wanted us. If you don't, I will understand.

DAVID: Darling, of course we want you—

FANNY (*rises*): I am old. And made of dry cork. And bad-mannered. Please forgive me.

SARA (*goes quickly to* FANNY): Shut up, Mama. We're all acting like fools. I'm glad to be home. That's all I know. So damned glad.

DAVID: And we're damned glad to have you. Come on. Let's walk to the lake. We've made it bigger and planted the island with black-berries— (*She smiles and goes to him. Together they move out the hall entrance.*)

FANNY (*after a silence*): They've always liked each other. We're going to have Zwetschgen-Knoedel for dinner. You like them?

KURT: Indeed.

FANNY: I hope you like decent food.

KURT: I do.

FANNY: That's a good sign in a man.

MARTHE (*coming in from the terrace. Stops in the doorway*): Oh, I'm sorry, Fanny. We were waiting. I didn't want to interrupt the family reunion. I—

FANNY: This is my son-in-law, Herr Müller. The Countess de Brancovis.

KURT AND MARTHE (*together*): How do you do?

MARTHE: And how is Sara, Herr Müller? I haven't seen her since I was a little girl. She probably doesn't remember me at all (TECK *comes in from the hall. She turns*) This is my husband, Herr Müller.

KURT: How do you do?

TECK: How do you do, sir? (KURT *bows. They shake hands*) Would it be impertinent for one European to make welcome another?

KURT (*smiles*): I do not think so. It would be friendly.

BODO (*appears at the hall door*): Papa— (*Sees* TECK *and* MARTHE, *bows*) Oh, good morning. Miss Anise says you are the Count and Countess. Once before we met a Count and Countess. They had a small room bordering on ours in Copenhagen. They were more older than you, and more poor. We shared with them our newspaper.

MARTHE (*laughs*): It wasn't us, but it might have been. What's your name?

TECK (*laughs*): We hope you will be as kind to us.

BODO: My name is Bodo. It's a strange name. No? (*To* KURT) Papa, this is the house of great wonders. Each has his bed, each has his bathroom. The arrangement of it, that is splendorous.

FANNY (*laughs*): You are a fancy talker, Bodo.

KURT: Oh, yes. In many languages.

BODO (*to* FANNY): Please to correct me when I am wrong. Papa, the plumbing is such as you have never seen. Each implement is placed on the floor, and all are simultaneous in the same room. You will therefore see that being placed most solidly on the floor allows of no rats, rodents or crawlers, and is most sanitary. (*To the others*) Papa will be most interested. He like to know how each thing of everything is put together. And he is so fond of being clean—

KURT (*laughs. To* FANNY): I am a hero to my children. It bores everybody but me.

TECK: It is most interesting, Herr Müller. I thought I had a good ear for the accents of your country. But yours is most difficult to place. It is Bayrisch? Or is it—

BODO: That's because Papa has worked in so many—

KURT (*quickly*): German accents are the most difficult to identify. I, myself, when I try, am usually incorrect. It would be particularly difficult with me because I speak other languages. Yours would be Roumanian?

MARTHE (*laughs*): My God, is it that bad?

KURT (*smiles*): I am showing off. I know the Count de Brancovis is Roumanian.

TECK (*heartily*): So? We have met before? I thought so, but I cannot remember—

KURT: No, sir. We have not met before. I read your name in the newspapers.

TECK (*to* KURT): Strange. I was sure I had met you. I was in the Paris Legation for many years, and I thought perhaps—

KURT: Oh no. If it is possible to believe, I am the exile who is not famous. (*To* FANNY) I have been thinking with pleasure, Madame Fanny, of breakfast on your porch. (*He points to the picture of Joshua Farrelly*) Your husband once wrote: "I am getting older now and Europe seems far away. Fanny and I will have an early breakfast on the porch and then I shall drive the bays into Washington." (*Remembering*) And then he goes on: "Henry Adams tells me he has been reading Karl Marx. I shall have to tell him my father made me read Marx many years ago and that, since he proposes to exhibit himself to impress me, will spoil Henry's Sunday."

FANNY (*laughs, delighted. Takes* KURT'S *arm*): And so it did. I had forgotten that. I am pleased with you. I shall come and serve your food myself. I had forgotten Joshua ever wrote it. (*They start out of the terrace doors together, followed by* BODO.)

KURT (*as they disappear*): I try to impress you. I learned it last night. (FANNY *laughs. They disappear.*)

TECK (*smiles*): He is a clever man. A quotation from Joshua Farrelly is a sure road to Fanny's heart. Where did you say Herr Müller was from?

MARTHE: Germany.

TECK: I know that. (*Goes to a valise. He leans over, stares at it, looks at the labels, pushes the lock. The lock opens; he closes it. Then he turns and, as he speaks, picks up the brief-case*) What part of Germany?

MARTHE: I don't know. And I never knew you were an expert on accents.

TECK: I never knew it either. Are you driving into Washington with David this morning?

MARTHE: I was going to. But he may not be going to the office, now that Sara's here. I was to have lunch with Sally Tyne. (TECK *puts down the brief-case*) What are you doing?

TECK: Wondering why luggage is unlocked and a shabby brief-case is so carefully locked.

MARTHE: You're very curious about Mr. Müller.

TECK: Yes. And I do not know why. Something far away . . . I am curious about a daughter of the Farrellys' who marries a German who has bullet scars on his face and broken bones in his hands.

MARTHE (*sharply*): Has he? There are many of them now, I guess.

TECK: So there are. But this one is in this house. (*He goes to the bell cord, pulls it. She watches him nervously.*)

MARTHE: Is it—is he any business of yours?

TECK: What is my business? Anything might be my business now.

MARTHE: Yes—unfortunately. You might inquire from your friend Von Seitz. They always know their nationals.

TECK (*pleasantly, ignoring the sharpness with which she has spoken*): Oh, yes, I will do that, of course. But I do not like to ask questions without knowing the value of the answers.

MARTHE: Teck. This man is a little German Sara married years ago. I remember Mama talking about it. He was nothing then and he isn't now. They've had a tough enough time already without—

TECK: Have you— Have you been sleeping with David?

MARTHE (*stops, stares at him, then simply*): No. I have not been. And that hasn't been your business for a good many years now.

TECK: You like him?

MARTHE (*nervously*): What's this for, Teck?

TECK: Answer me, please.

MARTHE: I— (*She stops.*)

TECK: Yes? Answer me.

MARTHE: I do like him.

TECK: What does he feel about you?

MARTHE: I don't know.

TECK: But you are trying to find out. You have made plans with him?

MARTHE: Of course not. I—

TECK: But you will try to make him have plans. I have recognized it. Well, we have been together a long— (JOSEPH *enters.* TECK *stops*) Joseph, Miss Fanny wishes you to take the baggage upstairs.

JOSEPH: Yes, sir. I was going to. (*He begins to pick up the baggage.* MARTHE *has turned sharply and is staring at* TECK. *Then she rises, watches* JOSEPH *pick up the baggage, turns again to look at* TECK.)

TECK: As I was saying. It is perhaps best that we had this talk.

MARTHE (*she stops, waits for* JOSEPH *to move off. He exits, carrying the valises*): Why did you do that? Why did you tell Joseph that Fanny wanted him to take the baggage upstairs?

TECK: Obviously it is more comfortable to look at baggage behind closed doors.

MARTHE (*very sharply*): What kind of silliness is this now? Leave these people alone— (*As he starts to exit*) I won't let you—

TECK: What? (*As he moves again, she comes after him.*)

MARTHE: I said I won't let you. You are not—

TECK: How many times have you seen me angry? (MARTHE *looks up, startled*) You will not wish to see another. Run along now and have lunch with something you call Sally Tyne. But do not make plans with David. You will not be able to carry them out. You will go with me, when I am ready to go. You understand. (*He exits during his speech. The last words come as he goes through the door, and as the curtain falls.*)

# Act Two

SCENE: *The same as Act One, about ten days later. During the act it will begin to grow dark; but the evening is warm and the terrace doors are open.*

AT RISE: SARA *is sitting on the couch, crocheting.* FANNY *and* TECK *are sitting at a small table playing cribbage.* BODO *is sitting near them, at a large table, working on a heating pad. The cord is torn from the bag, the bag is ripped open.* ANISE *sits next to him, anxiously watching him. Outside on the terrace,* JOSHUA *is going through baseball motions, coached by* JOSEPH. *From time to time they move out of sight, reappear, move off again.*

FANNY (*playing a card*): One.

BODO (*after a minute, to* TECK): The arrangement of this heating pad grows more complex.

TECK (*smiles, moves on the cribbage board*): And the more wires you remove, the more complex it will grow.

BODO (*points to the bag*): Man has learned to make man comfortable. Yet all cannot have the comforts. (*To* ANISE) How much did this cost you?

ANISE: It cost me ten dollars. And you have made a ruin of it.

BODO: That is not yet completely true. (*To* FANNY) Did I not install for you a twenty-five-cent button-push for your radio?

TECK (*playing a card*): Two and two. (*Moves pegs on the cribbage board.*)

FANNY: Yes, you're quite an installer.

BODO (*to* TECK): As I was wishing to tell you, Count de Brancovis, comfort and plenty exist. Yet all cannot have them it. Why?

TECK: I do not know. It has worried many men. Why?

65

ANISE (*to* BODO): Yes, why?

BODO (*takes a deep breath, raises his finger as if about to lecture*): Why? (*Considers a moment, then deflates himself*) I am not as yet sure.

ANISE: I thought not.

FANNY (*turns to look at* JOSHUA *and* JOSEPH *on the terrace*): Would you mind doing that dancing some place else?

JOSEPH (*looking in*): Yes'm. That ain't dancing. I'm teaching Josh baseball.

FANNY: Then maybe he'd teach you how to clean the silver.

JOSEPH: I'm a good silver-cleaner, Miss Fanny.

FANNY: But you're getting out of practice.

JOSEPH (*after a moment's thought*): Yes'm. I see what you mean. (*He exits.*)

FANNY (*playing a card*): Three.

JOSHUA: It is my fault. I'm crazy about baseball.

BODO: Baseball players are among the most exploited people in this country. I read about it.

FANNY: You never should have learned to read.

BODO: Their exploited condition is foundationed on the fact that—

JOSHUA (*bored*): All right, all right. I still like baseball.

SARA: Founded, Bodo, not foundationed.

JOSHUA: He does it always. He likes long words. In all languages.

TECK: How many languages do you children speak?

BODO: Oh, we do not really know any very well, except German and English. We speak bad French and—

SARA: And bad Danish and bad Czech.

TECK: You seem to have stayed close to the borders of Germany. Did Herr Müller have hopes, as so many did, that National Socialism would be overthrown on every tomorrow?

SARA: We have not given up that hope. Have you, Count de Brancovis?

TECK: I never had it.

JOSHUA (*pleasantly*): Then it must be most difficult for you to sleep.

TECK: I beg your pardon?

SARA: Schweig doch, Joshua!

FANNY (*to* TECK): Sara told Joshua to shut up. (*Playing a card*) Twelve.

TECK: I have offended you, Mrs. Müller. I am most sorry.

SARA (*pleasantly*): No, sir, you haven't offended me. I just don't like polite political conversations any more.

TECK (*nods*): All of us, in Europe, had too many of them.

SARA: Yes. Too much talk. By this time all of us must know where we are and what we have to do. It's an indulgence to sit in a room and discuss your beliefs as if they were a juicy piece of gossip.

FANNY: You know, Sara, I find it very pleasant that Kurt, considering his history, doesn't make platform speeches. He hasn't tried to convince anybody of anything.

SARA (*smiles*): Why should he, Mama? You are quite old enough to have your own convictions—or Papa's.

FANNY (*turns to look at her*): I am proud to have Papa's convictions.

SARA: Of course. But it might be well to have a few new ones, now and then.

FANNY (*peers over at her*): Are you criticizing me?

SARA (*smiles*): Certainly not.

BABETTE (*comes running in from the right entrance door. She has on an apron and she is carrying a plate. She goes to* FANNY): Eat it while it's hot, Grandma.

(FANNY *peers down, takes the fork, begins to eat.* ANISE *and* BODO *both rise, move to* FANNY, *inspect the plate.*)

FANNY (*to them*): Go away.

ANISE: It is a potato pancake.

FANNY: And the first good one I've eaten in many, many years. I love a good potato pancake.

BODO: I likewise.

BABETTE: I am making a great number for dinner. Move away, Bodo.

TECK (*playing a card*): Fifteen and two.

ANISE (*who has followed* BODO *back to the table, leans over to look at the heating pad*): You've ruined it! I shall sue you.

JOSHUA: I told you not to let him touch it.

SARA (*laughs*): I remember you were always saying that, Anise—that you were going to sue. That's very French. I was sick once in Paris, and Babbie stayed up for a whole night and day and finished a dress I was making for a woman in the Rue Jacob. I told her to tell the woman she'd done it—I thought perhaps the woman would give her a candy or something—and anyway, I was very proud of her work. But no. The woman admitted the dress was well done, but said she was going to sue because I hadn't done it myself. Fancy that.

FANNY (*slowly*): You sewed for a living?

SARA: Not a very good one. But Babbie and I made a little something now and then. Didn't we, darling?

FANNY (*sharply*): Really, Sara, were these—these things necessary? Why couldn't you have written?

SARA (*laughs*): You've asked me that a hundred times in the last week.

JOSHUA (*gently*): I think it is only that Grandma feels sorry for us. Grandma has not seen much of the world.

FANNY: Don't you start giving me lectures, Joshua. I'm fond of you. And of you, Babbie. (*To* ANISE) Are there two desserts for dinner? And are they sweet?

ANISE: Yes.

FANNY (*turns to* BODO): I wish I were fond of you.

BODO: You are. (*Happily*) You are very fond of me.

FANNY (*playing a card*): Twenty-five.

BABETTE: This is for you, Grandma. I'm making a bed-jacket. It is nice lace. Papa brought it to me from Spain and I mean for you to have it.

FANNY (*kisses* BABETTE): Thank you, darling. A sequence and three. A pair and five. (*To* TECK, *as they finish the cribbage game*) There. That's two dollars off. I owe you eight-fifty.

TECK: Let us carry it until tomorrow. You shall give it to me as a going-away token.

FANNY (*too pleased*): You're going away?

TECK (*laughs*): Ah, Madame Fanny. Do not sound *that* happy.

FANNY: Did I? That's rude of me. When are you going?

TECK: In a few days, I think. (*Turns to look at* SARA) We're too many refugees, eh, Mrs. Müller?

SARA (*pleasantly*): Perhaps.

TECK: Will you be leaving, also?

SARA: I beg your pardon?

TECK: I thought perhaps you, too, would be moving on. Herr Müller does not give me the feeling of a man who settles down. Men who have done his work, seldom leave it. Not for a quiet country house.

(*All three children look up.*)

SARA (*very quietly*): What work do you think my husband has done, Count de Brancovis?

TECK: Engineering?

SARA (*slowly*): Yes. Engineering.

FANNY (*very deliberately to* TECK): I don't know what you're saying. They shall certainly not be leaving—ever. Is that understood, Sara?

SARA: Well, Mama—

FANNY: There are no wells about it. You've come home to see me die and you will wait until I'm ready.

SARA (*laughs*): Really, Mama, that isn't the reason I came home.

FANNY: It's a good enough reason. I shall do a fine death. I intend to be a great deal of trouble to everybody.

ANISE: I daresay.

FANNY: I shall take to my bed early and stay for years. In great pain.

ANISE: I am sure of it. You will duplicate the disgrace of the birth of Miss Sara.

SARA (*laughs*): Was I born in disgrace?

ANISE: It was not your fault. But it was disgusting. Three weeks before you were to come—all was excellent, of course, in so healthy a woman as Madame Fanny—a great dinner was given here and, most unexpectedly, attended by a beautiful lady from England.

FANNY: Do be still. You are dull and fanciful—

ANISE: Mr. Joshua made the great error of waltzing the beauty for two dances, Madame Fanny being unfitted for the waltz and under no circumstances being the most graceful of dancers.

FANNY (*her voice rising*): Are you crazy? I danced magnificently.

ANISE: It is well you thought so. A minute did not elapse between the second of the waltzes and a scream from Madame Fanny. She was in labor. Two hundred people, and if we had left her alone, she would have remained in the ballroom—

FANNY: How you invent! How you invent!

ANISE: Do not call to me that I am a liar. For three weeks you are in the utmost agony—

FANNY: And so I was. I remember it to this day—

ANISE (*to* SARA, *angrily*): Not a pain. Not a single pain. She would lie up there in state, stealing candy from herself. Then, when your Papa would rest himself for a minute at the dinner or with a book, a scream would dismantle the house—it was revolting. (*Spitefully to* FANNY) And now the years have passed I may disclose to you that Mr. Joshua knew that you were going through the play-acting—

FANNY (*rises*): He did not. You are a malicious—

ANISE: Once he said to me, "Anise, it is well that I am in love. This is of a great strain and her great-uncle Freddie was not right in the head, neither."

FANNY (*screaming*): You will leave this house— You are a liar, a woman of—

SARA: Mama, sit down.

ANISE: I will certainly leave this house. I will—

SARA (*sharply*): Both of you. Sit down. And be still.

ANISE: She has intimated that I lie—

FANNY (*screaming*): Intimated! Is that what I was doing— (ANISE *begins to leave the room*) All right. I beg your pardon. I apologize.

(ANISE *turns*.)

SARA: Both of you. You are acting like children.

BODO: Really, Mama. You insult us.

ANISE: I accept your apology. Seat yourself.

(*They both sit down.*)

FANNY (*after a silence*): I am unloved.

BABETTE: I love you, Grandma.

FANNY: Do you, Babbie?

JOSHUA: And I.

FANNY (*nods, very pleased. To* BODO): And you?

BODO: *I* loved you the primary second I saw you.

FANNY: You are a charlatan.

ANISE: As for me, I am fond of all the living creatures. It is true that the children cause me greater work, which in turn more greatly inconveniences the feet. However, I do not complain. I believe in children.

FANNY: Rather like believing in the weather, isn't it? (DAVID *and* KURT *come in from the terrace. Both are in work clothes, their sleeves rolled up*) Where have you been?

DAVID: Oh, we've been helping Mr. Chabeuf spray the fruit trees.

ANISE: Mr Chabeuf says that Herr Müller has the makings of a good farmer. From a Frenchman that is a large thing to say.

KURT (*who has looked around the room, looked at* TECK, *strolled over to* BODO): Mr. Chabeuf and I have an excellent time exchanging misinformation. My father was a farmer. I have a wide knowledge of farmer's misinformation.

FANNY: This is good farm land. Perhaps, in time—

DAVID (*laughs*): Mama would give you the place, Kurt, if you guaranteed that your great-grandchildren would die here.

KURT (*smiles*): I would like to so guarantee.

TECK: A farmer. That is very interesting. Abandon your ideals, Herr Müller?

KURT: Ideals? (*Carefully*) Sara, heisst das auf deutsch "Ideale"?

SARA: Yes.

KURT: Is that what I have now? I do not like the word. It gives to me the picture of a small, pale man at a seaside resort. (*To* BODO) What are you doing?

BODO: Preparing an elderly electric pad for Miss Anise. I am confused.

KURT (*wanders toward the piano*): So it seems.

BODO: Something has gone wrong with the principle on which I have been working. It is probably that I will ask your assistance.

KURT (*bows to him*): Thank you. Whenever you are ready. (*Begins to pick out notes with one hand.*)

FANNY: We shall have a little concert tomorrow evening. In honor of Babbie's birthday. (*To* KURT) Kurt, you and I will play "The Clock Symphony." Then Joshua and I will play the duet we've learned, and Babbie will sing. And I shall finish with a Chopin Nocturne.

DAVID (*laughs*): I thought you'd be the last on the program.

TECK: Where is Marthe?

FANNY: She'll be back soon. She went into town to do an errand for me. (*To* DAVID) Did you buy presents for everybody?

DAVID: I did.

SARA (*smiles, to* BABETTE): We always did that here. If somebody had a birthday, we all got presents. Nice, isn't it?

DAVID (*to* ANISE): I shall buy you an electric pad. You will need it.

ANISE: Indeed.

FANNY: Did you buy me a good present?

DAVID: Pretty good. (*Pats* BABETTE's *head*) The best present goes to Babbie; it's *her* birthday.

FANNY: Jewelry?

DAVID: No, not jewelry.

FANNY: Oh. Not jewelry.

DAVID: Why?

FANNY (*too casually*): I just asked you.

TECK (*gets up*): It was a natural mistake, David. You see, Mrs. Mellie Sewell told your mother that she had seen you and Marthe in Barstow's. And your mother said you were probably buying her a present, or one for Babbie.

DAVID (*too sharply*): Yes.

TECK (*laughs*): Yes what?

DAVID (*slowly*): Just yes.

FANNY (*too hurriedly*): Mellie gets everything wrong. She's very anxious to meet Marthe because she used to know Francie Cabot, her aunt. Marthe's aunt, I mean, not Mellie's.

SARA (*too hurriedly*): She really came to inspect Kurt and me. But I saw her first. (*She looks anxiously at* DAVID, *who has turned his back on the room and is facing the terrace*) You were lucky to be out, David.

DAVID: Oh, she calls every Saturday afternoon, to bring Mama all the Washington gossip of the preceding week. She gets it all wrong, you understand, but that doesn't make any difference to either Mama or her. Mama then augments it, wits it up, Papa used to say—

FANNY: Certainly. I sharpen it a little. Mellie has no sense of humor.

DAVID: So Mama sharpens it a little, and delivers it tomorrow afternoon to old lady Marcy down the road. Old lady Marcy hasn't heard a word in ten years, so she unsharpens it again, and changes the names. By Wednesday afternoon—

TECK (*smiles*): By Wednesday afternoon it will not be you who were in Barstow's, and it will be a large diamond pin with four sapphires delivered to Gaby Deslys.

DAVID (*turns, looks at him*): Exactly.

FANNY (*very nervously*): Francie Cabot, Marthe's aunt, you understand— (*To* KURT) Did you ever know Paul von Seitz, a German?

KURT: I have heard of him.

FANNY (*speaking very rapidly*): Certainly. He was your Ambassador to somewhere, I've forgotten. Well, Francie Cabot married him. I could have. Any American, not crippled, whose father had money— He was crazy about me. I was better-looking than Francie. Well, years later when he was your Ambassador—my father was, too, as you probably know—not your Ambassador, of course, ours —but I am talking about Von Seitz.

DAVID (*laughs to* KURT): You can understand how it goes. Old lady Marcy is not entirely to blame.

FANNY: Somebody asked me if I didn't regret not marrying him. I said, "Madame, je le regrette tous les jours et j'en suis heureuse chaque soir." (FANNY *turns to* DAVID) That means I regret it every day and am happy about it every night. You understand what I meant, by *night*? Styles in wit change so.

DAVID: I understood it, Mama.

JOSHUA: We, too, Grandma.

BABETTE (*approvingly*): It was most witty.

BODO: I do not know that I understood. You will explain to me, Grandma?

SARA: Later.

FANNY (*turns to look at* TECK): You remember the old Paul von Seitz?

TECK (*nods*): He was stationed in Paris when I first was there.

FANNY: Of course. I always forget you were a diplomat.

TECK: It is just as well.

FANNY: There's something insane about a Roumanian diplomat. Pure insane. I knew another one, once. He wanted to marry me, too.

SARA (*laughs*): All of Europe.

FANNY: Not all. Some. Naturally. I was rich, I was witty, my family was of the best. I was handsome, unaffected—

DAVID: And noble and virtuous and kind and elegant and fashionable and simple—it's hard to remember everything you were. I've often thought it must have been boring for Papa to have owned such perfection.

FANNY (*shrieks*): What! Your father bored with me! Not for a second of our life—

DAVID (*laughs*): Oh God, when will I learn?

BODO: Do not shriek, Grandma. It is an unpleasant sound for the ear.

FANNY: Where was I? Oh, yes. What I started out to say was— (*She turns, speaks carefully to* TECK) Mellie Sewell told me, when you left the room, that she had heard from Louis Chandler's child's governess that you had won quite a bit of money in a poker game with Sam Chandler and some Germans at the Embassy. (KURT, *who has been playing the piano, stops playing very abruptly.* TECK *turns to look at him*) That's how I thought of Von Seitz. His nephew Philip was in on the game.

DAVID (*looks at* TECK): It must have been a big game. Sam Chandler plays in big games.

TECK: Not big enough.

DAVID: Have you known Sam long?

TECK: For years. Every Embassy in Europe knew him.

DAVID (*sharply*): Sam and Nazis must make an unpleasant poker game.

(KURT *begins to play a new melody*.)

TECK (*who has not looked away from* KURT): I do not play poker to be amused.

DAVID (*irritably*): What's Sam selling now?

TECK: Bootleg munitions. He always has.

DAVID: You don't mind?

TECK: Mind? I have not thought about it.

FANNY: Well, you ought to think about it. Sam Chandler has always been a scoundrel. All the Chandlers are. They're cousins of mine. Mama used to say they never should have learned to walk on two feet. They would have been more comfortable on four.

TECK: Do you know the young Von Seitz, Herr Müller? He was your military attaché in Spain.

KURT: He was the German government attaché in Spain. I know his name, of course. He is a famous artillery expert. But the side on which I fought was not where he was stationed, Count de Brancovis.

ANISE (BABETTE *and* JOSHUA *begin to hum the song* KURT *is playing*. SARA *begins to hum*): It is time for the bath and the change of clothes. I will give you five more minutes—

FANNY: What is the song?

TECK: It was a German soldier's song. They sang it as they straggled back in '18. I remember hearing it in Berlin. Were you there then, Herr Müller?

KURT (*the playing and the humming continue*): I was not in Berlin.

TECK: But you were in the war, of course?

KURT: Yes. I was in the war.

FANNY: You didn't think then you'd live to see another war.

KURT: Many of us were afraid we would.

FANNY: What are the words?

SARA: The Germans in Spain, in Kurt's Brigade, wrote new words for the song.

KURT: This was what you heard in Berlin, in 1918. (*Begins to sing.*)

"Wir zieh'n Heim, wir zieh'n Heim,
  Mancher kommt nicht mit,
  Mancher ging verschütt,
  Aber Freunde sind wir stets."
    (*In English.*)
"We come home. We come home.
  Some of us are gone, and some of us are lost, but
    we are friends:
  Our blood is on the earth together.
  Some day. Some day we shall meet again.
  Farewell."

(*Stops singing*) At a quarter before six on the morning of November 7th, 1936, eighteen years later, five hundred Germans walked through the Madrid streets on their way to defend the Manzanares River. We felt good that morning. You know how it is to be good when it is needed to be good? So we had need of new words to say that. I translate with awkwardness, you understand.
(*Begins to sing.*)

"And so we have met again.
  The blood did not have time to dry.
  We lived to stand and fight again.
  This time we fight for people.
  This time the bastards will keep their hands away.
  Those who sell the blood of other men, this time,
  They keep their hands away.
  For us to stand.
  For us to fight.
  This time no farewell, no farewell."

(*Music dies out. There is silence for a minute*) We did not win. (*Looks up, gently*) It would have been a different world if we had.

SARA: Papa said so years ago. Do you remember, Mama? "For every man who lives without freedom, the rest of us must face the guilt."

FANNY: Yes. "We are liable in the conscience-balance for the tailor in Lodz, the black man in our South, the peasant in—" (*Turns to* TECK. *Unpleasantly*) Your country, I think.

ANISE (*rises*): Come. Baths for everybody. (*To* BODO) Gather the wires. You have wrecked my cure.

BODO: If you would allow me a few minutes more—

ANISE: Come along. I have been duped for long enough. Come Joshua. Babette. Baths.

JOSHUA (*starts out after* ANISE. BABETTE *begins to gather up her sewing*): My tub is a thing of glory. But I do not like it so prepared for me and so announced by Miss Anise. (*He exits.*)

BODO (*to* ANISE): You are angry about this. I do not blame you with my heart or my head. I admit I have failed. But Papa will repair it, Anise. Will you not, Papa? In a few minutes—

TECK (*to* BODO): Your father is an expert electrician?

BODO: Oh yes, sir.

TECK: And as good with radio—
(BODO *begins to nod.*)

KURT (*sharply*): Count de Brancovis. Make your questions to me, please. Not to my children.

(*The others look up, surprised.*)

TECK (*pleasantly*): Very well, Herr Müller.

ANISE (*as she exits with* BODO): Nobody can fix it. You have made a pudding of it.

BODO (*as he follows her*): Do not worry. In five minutes tonight, you will have a pad far better— (*As* BODO *reaches the door he bumps into* MARTHE *who is carrying large dress boxes*) Oh. Your pardon. Oh, hello. (*He disappears.*)

MARTHE (*gaily*): Hello. (*To* FANNY) I waited for them. I was afraid they wouldn't deliver this late in the day. (*To* SARA) Come on, Sara. I can't wait to see them.

SARA: What?

MARTHE: Dresses. From Fanny. A tan linen, and a dark green with wonderful buttons, a white net for Babbie, and a suit for you, and play dresses for Babbie, and a dinner dress in gray to wear for Babbie's birthday—gray should be good for you, Sara—all from Savitt's. We sneaked the measurements, Anise and I—

SARA (*she goes toward* FANNY): How nice of you, Mama. How very kind of you. And of you, Marthe, to take so much trouble— (*She leans down, kisses* FANNY) You're a sweet woman, Mama.

DAVID: That's the first time Mama's ever heard that word. (*He takes the boxes from* MARTHE, *puts them near the staircase.* MARTHE *smiles at him, touches his hand, as* TECK *watches them.*)

FANNY (*giggles*): I have a bottom sweetness, if you understand what I mean.

DAVID: I have been too close to the bottom to see it.

FANNY: That should be witty. I don't know why it isn't.

(BABETTE *goes over to stare at the boxes.*)

SARA: From Savitt's. Extravagant of you. They had such lovely clothes. I remember my coming-out dress—(*Goes to* KURT) Do you remember the black suit with the braid, and the Milan hat? Not the *first* day we met, but the picnic day? (*He smiles up at her*) Well, they were from Savitt's. That was over twenty years ago—I've known you a long time. Me, in an evening dress. Now you'll have to take me into Washington. I want to show off. Next week, and we'll dance, maybe— (*Sees that he is not looking at her*) What's the matter, darling? (*No answer. Slowly he turns to look at her*) What's the matter, Kurt? (*Takes his arms, very unhappily*) What have I done? It isn't that dresses have ever mattered to me, it's just that—

KURT: Of course, they have mattered to you. As they should. I do not think of the dresses. (*Draws her to him*) How many years have I loved that face?

SARA (*her face very happy*): So?

KURT: So. (*He leans down, kisses her, as if it were important.*)

SARA (*pleased, unembarrassed*): There are other people here.

MARTHE (*slowly*): And good for us to see.

TECK: Nostalgia?

MARTHE: No. Nostalgia is for something you have known. (FANNY *coughs*.)

BABETTE (*comes to* FANNY): Grandma, is it allowed to look at my dresses?

FANNY: Of course, child. Run along.

BABETTE (*picks up the boxes, goes toward the hall entrance, stops near* FANNY): I love dresses. I have a great fondness for materials and colors. Thank you, Grandma. (*She runs out of the room.*)

(JOSEPH *appears in the doorway.*)

JOSEPH: There is a long-distance operator with a long-distance call for Mr. Müller. She wants to talk with him on the long-distance phone.

KURT: Oh— Excuse me, please—

(KURT *rises quickly.* SARA *turns sharply to look at him.* TECK *looks up.* KURT *goes quickly out.* TECK *watches him go.* SARA *stands staring after him.*)

MARTHE (*laughs*): I feel the same way as Babbie. Come on, Sara. Let's try them on.

(SARA *does not turn.*)

TECK: You also have a new dress?

MARTHE (*looks at him*): Yes. Fanny was kind to me, too.

TECK: You are a very generous woman, Madame Fanny. Did you also give her a sapphire bracelet from Barstow's?

FANNY: I beg your—

DAVID (*slowly*): No. I gave Marthe the bracelet. And I understand that it is not any business of yours.

(FANNY *rises.* SARA *turns.*)

FANNY: Really, David—

DAVID: Be still, Mama.

TECK (*after a second*): Did you tell him that, Marthe?

MARTHE: Yes.

TECK (*looks up at her*): I shall not forgive you for that. (*Looks at* DAVID) It is a statement which no man likes to hear from another man. You understand that? (*Playfully*) That is the type of thing about which we used to play at duels in Europe.

DAVID (*comes toward him*): We are not so musical comedy here. And you are not in Europe.

TECK: Even if I were, I would not suggest any such action. I would have reasons for not wishing it.

DAVID: It would be well for you not to suggest *any* action. And the reason for *that* is you might get hurt.

TECK (*slowly*): That would not be my reason. (*To* MARTHE) Your affair has gone far enough—

MARTHE (*sharply*): It is not an affair—

TECK: I do not care what it is. The time has come to leave here. Go upstairs and pack your things. (*She does not move.* DAVID *turns toward her*) Go on, Marthe.

MARTHE (*to David*): I am not going with him. I told you that.

DAVID: I don't want you to go with him.

FANNY (*carefully*): Really, David, aren't you interfering in all this a good deal—

DAVID (*carefully*): Yes, Mama. I am.

TECK (*to* MARTHE): When you are speaking to me, please say what you have to say to me.

MARTHE (*comes to him*): You are trying to frighten me. But you are not going to frighten me any more. I will say it to you: I am not going with you. I am never going with you again.

TECK (*softly*): If you do not fully mean what you say, or if you might change your mind, you are talking unwisely, Marthe.

MARTHE: I know that.

TECK: Shall we talk about it alone?

MARTHE: You can't make me go, can you, Teck?

TECK: No, I can't make you.

MARTHE: Then there's no sense talking about it.

TECK: Are you in love with him?

MARTHE: Yes.

FANNY (*sharply*): Marthe! What is all this?

MARTHE (*sharply*): I'll tell *you* about it in a minute.

DAVID: You don't have to explain anything to anybody.

TECK (*ignores him*): Is he in love with you?

MARTHE: I don't think so. You won't believe it, because you can't believe anything that hasn't got tricks to it, but David hasn't much to do with this. I told you I would leave some day, and I remember where I said it—(*Slowly*)—and why I said it.

TECK: I also remember. But I did not believe you. I have not had much to offer you these last years. But if now we had some money and could go back—

MARTHE: No. I don't like you, Teck. I never have.

TECK: And I have always known it.

FANNY (*stiffly*): I think your lack of affections should be discussed with more privacy. Perhaps—

DAVID: Mama—

MARTHE: There is nothing to discuss. Strange. I've talked to myself about this scene for almost fifteen years. I knew a lot of things to say to you and I used to lie awake at night or walk along the street and say them. Now I don't want to. I guess you only want to talk that way, when you're not sure what you can do. When you're sure, then what's the sense of saying it? "This is why and this is why and this—" (*Very happily*) But when you know you can do it, you don't have to say anything; you can just go. And I'm going. There is nothing you can do. I would like you to believe that now.

TECK: Very well, Marthe. I think I made a mistake. I should not have brought you here. I believe you now.

MARTHE (*after a pause, she looks at* DAVID): I'll move into Washington, and—

DAVID: Yes. Later. But I'd like you to stay here for a while, with us, if you wouldn't mind.

SARA: It would be better for you, Marthe—

FANNY: It's very interesting that I am not being consulted about this. (*To* MARTHE) I have nothing against you, Marthe. I am sorry for you, but I don't think—

MARTHE: Thank you, Sara, David. But I'd rather move in now. (*Turns, comes toward* FANNY) But perhaps I have something against you. Do you remember my wedding?

FANNY: Yes.

MARTHE: Do you remember how pleased Mama was with herself? Brilliant Mama, handsome Mama—everybody thought so, didn't they? A seventeen-year-old daughter, marrying a pretty good title, about to secure herself in a world that Mama liked—she didn't ask me what I liked. And the one time I tried to tell her, she frightened me— (*Looks up*) Maybe I've always been frightened. All my life.

TECK: Of course.

MARTHE (*to* FANNY, *as if she had not heard* TECK): I remember Mama's face at the wedding—it was *her* wedding, really, not mine.

FANNY (*sharply*): You are very hard on your mother.

MARTHE: Nineteen hundred and twenty-five. No, I'm not hard on her. I only tell the truth. She wanted a life for me, I suppose. It just wasn't the life I wanted for myself. (*Sharply*) And that's what you have tried to do. With your children. In another way. Only Sara got away. And that made you angry—until so many years went by that you forgot.

FANNY: I don't usually mind people saying anything they think, but I find that—

MARTHE: I don't care what you mind or don't mind. I'm in love with your son—

FANNY (*very sharply*): That's unfortunate—

MARTHE: And I'm sick of watching you try to make him into his father. I don't think you even know you do it any more and I don't think he knows it any more, either. And that's what's most dangerous about it.

FANNY (*very angrily*): I don't know what you are talking about.

DAVID: I think you do. (*Smiles*) You shouldn't mind hearing the truth—and neither should I.

FANNY (*worried, sharply*): David! What does all this nonsense mean? I—

MARTHE (*to* FANNY): Look. That pretty world Mama got me into was a tough world, see? I'm used to trouble. So don't try to interfere with me, because I won't let you. (*She goes to* DAVID) Let's just have a good time. (*He leans down, takes both her hands, kisses them. Then slowly, she turns away, starts to exit. To* TECK) You will also be going today?

TECK: Yes.

MARTHE: Then let us make sure we go in different directions, and do not meet again. Good-bye, Teck.

TECK: Good-bye, Marthe. You will not believe me, but I tried my best, and I am now most sorry to lose you.

MARTHE: Yes. I believe you. (*She moves out. There is silence for a minute.*)

FANNY: Well, a great many things have been said in the last few minutes.

DAVID (*crosses to bell cord. To* TECK): I will get Joseph to pack for you.

TECK: Thank you. Do not bother. I will ring for him when I am ready. (KURT *comes in from the study door.* SARA *turns, stares at him, waits. He does not look at her*) It will not take me very long. (*He starts for the door, looking at* KURT.)

SARA: What is it, Kurt?

KURT: It is nothing of importance, darling— (*He looks quickly at* TECK, *who is moving very slowly.*)

SARA: Don't tell me it's nothing. I know the way you look when—

KURT (*sharply*): I said it was of no importance. I must get to California for a few weeks. That is all.

SARA: I—

TECK (*turns*): It is in the afternoon newspaper, Herr Müller. (*Points to paper on table*) I was waiting to find the proper moment to call it to your attention. (*He moves toward the table, as they all turn to watch him. He picks up the paper, turns it over, begins to read*) "Zurich, Switzerland: The Zurich papers today reprinted a despatch from the *Berliner Tageblatt* on the capture of Colonel Max Freidank. Freidank is said—(SARA *begins to move toward him*)—to be the chief of the Anti-Nazi Underground Movement. Colonel Freidank has long been an almost legendary figure. The son of the famous General Freidank, he was a World War officer and a distinguished physicist before the advent of Hitler." That is all.

SARA: Max—

KURT: Be still, Sara.

TECK: They told me of it at the Embassy last night. They also told me that with him they had taken a man who called himself Ebber, and a man who called himself Triste. They could not find a man called Gotter. (*He starts again toward the door*) I shall be a lonely man without Marthe. I am also a very poor one. I should like to have ten thousand dollars before I go.

DAVID (*carefully*): You will make no loans in this house.

TECK: I was not speaking of a loan.

FANNY (*carefully*): God made you not only a scoundrel but a fool. That is a dangerous combination.

DAVID (*suddenly leaps toward* TECK): Damn you, you—

KURT (*suddenly pounds on the top of the piano, as* DAVID *almost reaches* TECK): Leave him alone. (*Moves quickly to stop* DAVID) Leave him alone! *David! Leave him alone!*

DAVID (*angrily to* KURT): Keep out of it. (*Starts toward* TECK *again*) I'm beginning to see what Marthe meant. Blackmailing with your wife— You—

KURT (*very sharply*): He is not speaking of his wife. Or you. He means me. (*Looks at* TECK) Is that correct?

(SARA *moves toward* KURT, DAVID *draws back, bewildered.*)

TECK: Good. It was necessary for me to hear you say it. You understand that?

KURT: I understand it.

SARA (*frightened, softly*): Kurt—

DAVID: What is all this about? What the hell are you talking about?

TECK (*sharply for the first time*): Be still. (*To* KURT) At your convenience. Your hands are shaking, Herr Müller.

KURT (*quietly*): My hands were broken: they are bad when I have fear.

TECK: I am sorry. I can understand that. It is not pleasant. (*Motions toward* FANNY *and* DAVID) Perhaps you would like a little time to— I will go and pack, and be ready to leave. We will all find that more comfortable, I think. You should get yourself a smaller gun, Herr Müller. That pistol you have been carrying is big and awkward.

KURT: You saw the pistol when you examined our bags?

TECK: You knew that?

KURT: Oh, yes. I have the careful eye, through many years of needing it. And then you have not the careful eye. The pistol was lying to the left of a paper package and when you leave, it is to the right of the package.

SARA: Kurt! Do you mean that—

KURT (*sharply*): Please, darling, do not do that.

TECK: It is a German Army Luger?

KURT: Yes.

TECK: Keep it in your pocket, Herr Müller. You will have no need to use it. And, in any case, I am not afraid of it. You understand that?

KURT (*slowly*): I understand that you are not a man of fears. That is strange to me, because I am a man who has so many fears.

TECK (*laughs, as he exits*): Are you? That is most interesting. (*He exits.*)

DAVID (*softly*): What is this about, Kurt?

KURT: He knows who I am and what I do and what I carry with me.

SARA (*carefully*): What about Max?

KURT: The telephone was from Mexico. Ilse received a cable. Early on the morning of Monday, they caught Ebber and Triste. An hour after they took Max in Berlin. (*She looks up at him, begins to shake her head. He presses her arm*) Yes. It is hard.

FANNY (*softly*): You said he knew who you were and what you carried with you. I don't understand.

KURT: I am going to tell you: I am an outlaw. I work with many others in an illegal organization. I have so worked for seven years. I am on what is called a desired list. But I did not know I was worth ten thousand dollars. My price has risen.

DAVID (*slowly*): And what do you carry with you?

KURT: Twenty-three thousand dollars. It has been gathered from the pennies and the nickels of the poor who do not like Fascism, and who believe in the work we do. I came here to bring Sara home and to get the money. I had hopes to rest here for a while, and then—

SARA (*slowly*): And I had hopes someone else would take it back and you would stay with us— (*Shakes her head, then*) Max is not dead?

KURT: No. The left side of his face is dead. (*Softly*) It was a good face.

SARA (*to* FANNY *and* DAVID, *as if she were going to cry*): It was a very good face. He and Kurt—in the old days— (*To* KURT) After so many years. If Max got caught, then nobody's got a chance. Nobody. (*She suddenly sits down.*)

DAVID (*points upstairs*): He wants to sell what he knows to you? Is that right?

KURT: Yes.

FANNY: Wasn't it careless of you to leave twenty-three thousand dollars lying around to be seen?

KURT: No, it was not careless of me. It is in a locked brief-case. I have thus carried money for many years. There seemed no safer place than Sara's home. It was careless of you to have in your house a man who opens baggage and blackmails.

DAVID (*sharply*): Yes. It was very careless.

FANNY: But you said you knew he'd seen it—

KURT: Yes. I knew it the first day we were here. What was I to do about it? He is not a man who steals. This is a safer method. I knew that it would come some other way. I have been waiting to see what the way would be. That is all I could do.

DAVID (*to* FANNY): What's the difference? It's been done. (*To* KURT) If he wants to sell to you, he must have another buyer. Who?

KURT: The Embassy. Von Seitz, I think.

DAVID: You mean he has told Von Seitz about you and—

KURT: No. I do not think he has told him anything. As yet. It would be foolish of him. He has probably only asked most guarded questions.

DAVID: But you're here. You're in this country. They can't do anything to you. They wouldn't be crazy enough to try it. Is your passport all right?

KURT: Not quite.

FANNY: Why not? Why isn't it?

KURT (*wearily, as if he were bored*): Because people like me are not given visas with such ease. And I was in a hurry to bring my wife and my children to safety. (*Sharply*) Madame Fanny, you must come to understand it is no longer the world you once knew.

DAVID: It doesn't matter. You're a political refugee. We don't turn back people like you. People who are in danger. You will give me your passport and tomorrow morning I'll see Barens. We'll tell him the truth— (*Points to the door*) Tell de Brancovis to go to hell. There's not a damn thing he or anybody else can do.

SARA (*looks up at* KURT, *who is staring at her*): You don't understand, David.

DAVID: There's a great deal I don't understand. But there's nothing to worry about.

SARA: Not much to worry about as long as Kurt is in this house. But he's not going to—

KURT: The Count has made the guess that—

SARA: That you will go back to get Ebber and Triste and Max. Is that right, Kurt? Is that right?

KURT: Yes, darling, I will try. They were taken to Sonnenburg. Guards can be bribed— It has been done once before at Sonnenburg. We will try for it again. I must go back, Sara. I must start.

SARA: Of course, you must go back. I guess I was trying to think it wouldn't come. But— (*To* FANNY *and* DAVID) Kurt's got to go back. He's got to go home. He's got to buy them out. He'll do it, too. You'll see. (*She stops, breathes*) It's hard enough to get back. Very hard. But if they knew he was coming— They want Kurt bad. Almost as much as they wanted Max— And then there are hundreds of others, too— (*She gets up, comes to him. He holds her, puts his face in her hair. She stands holding him, trying to speak without crying. She puts her face down on his head*) Don't be scared, darling. You'll get back. You'll see. You've done it before—you'll do it again. Don't be scared. You'll get Max out all right. (*Gasps*) And then you'll do his work, won't you? That's good. That's fine. You'll do a good job, the way you've always done. (*She is crying very hard. To* FANNY) Kurt doesn't feel well. He was wounded and he gets tired— (*To* KURT) You don't feel well, do you? (*Slowly. She is crying too hard now to be heard clearly*) Don't be scared, darling. You'll get home. Don't worry, you'll get home. Yes, you will.

(*The Curtain Falls.*)

# Act Three

SCENE: *The same. A half hour later.*

AT RISE: FANNY *is sitting in a chair.* KURT *is at the piano, his head resting on one hand. He is playing softly with the other hand.* SARA *is sitting very quietly on the couch.* DAVID *is pacing on the terrace.*

FANNY (*to* DAVID): David, would you stop that pacing, please? (DAVID *comes in*) And would you stop that one-hand piano playing? Either play, or get up.

(KURT *gets up, crosses to the couch, sits.* SARA *looks at him, gets up, crosses to the decanters, begins to make a drink.*)

SARA (*to* DAVID): A drink?

DAVID: What? Yes, please. (*To* KURT) Do you intend to buy your friends out of jail?

KURT: I intend to try.

FANNY: It's all very strange to me. I thought things were so well run that bribery and—

KURT (*smiles*): What a magnificent work Fascists have done in convincing the world that they are men from legends.

DAVID: They have done very well for themselves—unfortunately.

KURT: Yes. But not by themselves. Does it make us all uncomfortable to remember that they came in on the shoulders of the most powerful men in the world? Of course. And so we would prefer to believe they are men from the planets. They are not. Let me reassure you. They are smart, they are sick, and they are cruel. But given men who know what they fight for— (*Shrugs*) I will console you. A year ago last month, at three o'clock in the morning, Freidank and I, with two elderly pistols, raided the home of the Gestapo chief in

90

Konstanz, got what we wanted, and the following morning Freidank was eating his breakfast three blocks away, and I was over the Swiss border.

FANNY (*slowly*): You are brave men.

KURT: *I* do not tell you the story to prove we are remarkable, but to prove they are *not*.

(SARA *brings him a drink. Gives one to* DAVID.)

SARA (*softly, touching* KURT's *shoulder*): Kurt loves Max.

KURT: Always since I came here I have a dream: that he will come into this room some day. How he would like it here, eh, Sara? He loves good food and wine, and you have books— (*Laughs happily*) He is fifty-nine years of age. And when he was fifty-seven, he carried me on his back, seven miles across the border. I had been hurt— That takes a man, does it not?

FANNY (*to* KURT): You look like a sick man to me.

KURT: No. I'm only tired. I do not like to wait. It will go. It is the waiting that is always most bad for me.

DAVID (*points upstairs*): Damn him! He's doing it deliberately.

KURT: It is then the corruption begins. Once in Spain I waited for two days until the planes would exhaust themselves. I think then why must our side fight always with naked hands. The spirit and the hands. All is against us but ourselves.

SARA: You will not think that when the time comes. It will go.

KURT: Of a certainty.

FANNY: But does it have to go on being your hands?

KURT: For each man, his own hands. He has to sleep with them.

DAVID (*uncomfortably, as if he did not like to say it*): That's right. I guess it's the way all of us should feel. But—but you have a family. Isn't there somebody else who hasn't a wife and children—

KURT: Each could have his own excuse. Some love for the first time, some have bullet holes, some have fear of the camps, some are sick, many are getting older. (*Shrugs*) Each could find a reason. And many find it. My children are not the only children in the world, even to me.

FANNY: That's noble of you, of course. But they are your children, nevertheless. And Sara, she—

SARA: Mama—

KURT (*after a slight pause*): One means always in English to insult with that word noble?

FANNY: Of course not, I—

KURT: It is not noble. It is the way I must live. Good or bad, it is what I am. (*Turns deliberately to look at* FANNY) And what I am is not what you wanted for your daughter, twenty years ago or now.

FANNY: You are misunderstanding me.

KURT (*smiles*): For our girl, too, we want a safe and happy life. And it is thus I try to make it for her. We each have our way. I do not convert you to mine.

DAVID: You are very certain of your way.

KURT (*smiles*): I seem so to you? Good.

(JOSEPH *appears in the hall doorway. He is carrying valises and overcoats.*)

JOSEPH: What'll I do with these, Miss Fanny?

FANNY: They're too large for eating, aren't they? What were you thinking of doing with them?

JOSEPH: I mean, it's Fred's day off.

DAVID: All right. You drive him into town.

JOSEPH: Then who's going to serve at dinner?

FANNY (*impatiently*): Belle can do it alone tonight.

JOSEPH: No she can't. Belle's upstairs packing with Miss Marthe. My, there's quite a lot of departing, ain't there?

FANNY (*very impatiently*): All right, then cook can bring in dinner.

JOSEPH: I wouldn't ask her to do that, if I were you. She's mighty mad: the sink pipe is leaking again. You just better wait for your dinner till I get back from Washington.

FANNY (*shouting*): We are not cripples and we were eating dinner in this house before you arrived to show us how to use the knife and fork. (JOSEPH *laughs*) Go on. Put his things in the car. I'll ring for you when he's ready.

JOSEPH: You told me the next time you screamed to remind you to ask my pardon.

FANNY: You call that screaming?

JOSEPH: Yes'm.

FANNY: Very well. I ask your pardon. (*Waves him away*) Go on!

JOSEPH: Yes'm. (*Exits.*)

(TECK *appears in the door. He is carrying his hat and the brief-case we have seen in Act One.* SARA, *seeing the brief-case, looks startled, looks quickly at* KURT. KURT *watches* TECK *as he comes toward him.* TECK *throws his hat on a chair, comes to the table at which* KURT *is sitting, puts the brief-case on the table.* KURT *puts out his hand, puts it on the brief-case, leaves it there.*)

TECK (*smiles at the gesture*): Nothing has been touched, Herr Müller. I brought it from your room, for your convenience.

FANNY (*angrily*): Why didn't you steal it? Since you do not seem to—

TECK: That would have been very foolish of me, Madame Fanny.

KURT: Very.

TECK: I hope I have not kept you waiting too long. I wanted to give you an opportunity to make any explanations—

DAVID (*angrily*): Does your price include listening to this tony conversation?

TECK (*turns to look at him*): My price will rise if I have to spend the next few minutes being interrupted by your temper. I will do my business with Herr Müller. And you will understand, I will take from you no interruptions, no exclamations, no lectures, no opinions of what I am or what I am doing.

KURT (*quietly*): You will not be interrupted.

TECK (*sits down at table with* KURT): I have been curious about you, Herr Müller. Even before you came here. Because Fanny and David either knew very little about you, which was strange, or wouldn't talk about you, which was just as strange. Have you ever had come to you one of those insistent half-memories of some person or some place?

KURT (*quietly, without looking up*): You had such a half-memory of me?

TECK: Not even a memory, but something. The curiosity of one European for another, perhaps.

KURT: A most sharp curiosity. You lost no time examining—(*Pats the case*)—this. You are an expert with locks?

TECK: No, indeed. Only when I wish to be.

FANNY (*angrily, to* TECK): I would like you out of this house as quickly as—

TECK (*turns to her*): Madame Fanny, I have just asked Mr. David not to do that. I must now ask you. (*Leans forward to* KURT) Herr Müller, I got one of the desired lists from Von Seitz, without, of course, revealing anything to him. As you probably know, they are quite easy to get. I simply told him that we refugees move in small circles and I might come across somebody on it. If, however, I have to listen to any more of this from any of you, I shall go immediately to him.

KURT (*to* DAVID *and* FANNY): Please allow the Count to do this in his own way. It will be best.

TECK (*takes a sheet of paper from his pocket*): There are sixty-three names on this list. I read them carefully, I narrow the possibilities and under "G" I find Gotter. (*Begins to read*) "Age forty to forty-five. About six feet. One hundred seventy pounds. Birthplace unknown to us. Original occupation unknown to us, although he seems to know Munich and Dresden. Schooling unknown to us. Family unknown to us. No known political connections. No known trade-union connections. Many descriptions, few of them in agreement and none of them of great reliability. Equally unreliable, though often asked for, were Paris, Copenhagen, Brussels police descriptions. Only points on which there is agreement: married to a foreign woman, either American or English; three children; has used name of Gotter, Thomas Bodmer, Karl Francis. Thought to have left Germany in 1933, and to have joined Max Freidank shortly after. Worked closely with Freidank, perhaps directly under his orders. Known to have crossed border in 1934—February, May, June, October. Known to have again crossed border with Max Freidank in 1935—August, twice in October, November, January—"

KURT (*smiles*): The report is unreliable. It would have been impossible for God to have crossed the border that often.

TECK (*looks up, laughs. Then looks back at list*): "In 1934, outlaw radio station announcing itself as Radio European, begins to be heard. Station was located in Düsseldorf: the house of a restaurant waiter was searched, and nothing was found. Radio heard during most of 1934 and 1935. In an attempt to locate it, two probable Communists killed in the tool-house of a farm near Bonn. In three of the broadcasts, Gotter known to have crossed border immediately before and after. Radio again became active in early part of 1936. Active attempt made to locate Freidank. Gotter believed to have then appeared in Spain with Madrid Government army, in one of the German brigades, and to have been a brigade commander under previously used name of Bodmer. Known to have stayed in France the first months of 1938. Again crossed German border some time during week when Hitler's Hamburg radio speech interrupted and went off the air." (*Looks up*) That was a daring deed, Herr Müller. It caused a great scandal. I remember. It amused me.

KURT: It was not done for that reason.

TECK: "Early in 1939, informer in Konstanz reported Gotter's entry, carrying money which had been exchanged in Paris and Brussels. Following day, home of Konstanz Gestapo chief raided for spy list by two men—" (KURT *turns to look at* FANNY *and* DAVID, *smiles*) My God, Herr Müller, that job took two good men.

SARA (*angrily*): Even you admire them.

TECK: Even I. Now I conclude a week ago that you are Gotter, Karl Francis—

KURT: Please. Do not describe me to myself again.

TECK: And that you will be traveling home—(*Points to brief-case*) —with this. But you seem in no hurry, and so I must wait. Last night when I hear that Freidank has been taken, I guess that you will now be leaving. Not for California. I will tell you free of charge, Herr Müller, that they have got no information from Freidank or the others.

KURT: Thank you. But I was sure they would not. I know all three most well. They will take what will be given them.

TECK (*looks down. Softly*): There is a deep sickness in the German character, Herr Müller. A pain-love, a death-love—

DAVID (*very angrily*): Oh, for God's sake, spare us *your* moral judgments.

FANNY (*very sharply*): Yes. They are sickening. Get on!

KURT: Fanny and David are Americans and they do not understand our world—as yet. (*Turns to* DAVID *and* FANNY) All Fascists are not of one mind, one stripe. There are those who give the orders, those who carry out the orders, those who watch the orders being carried out. Then there are those who are half in, half hoping to come in. They are made to do the dishes and clean the boots. Frequently they come in high places and wish now only to survive. They came late: some because they did not jump in time, some because they were stupid, some because they were shocked at the crudity of the *German* evil, and preferred their own evils, and some because they were fastidious men. For those last, we may well some day have pity. They are lost men, their spoils are small, their day is gone. (*To* TECK) Yes?

TECK (*slowly*): Yes. You have the understanding heart. It will get in your way some day.

KURT (*smiles*): I will watch it.

TECK: We are both men in trouble, Herr Müller. The world, ungratefully, seems to like your kind even less than it does mine. (*Leans forward*) Now. Let us do business. You will not get back if Von Seitz knows you are going.

KURT: You are wrong. Instead of crawling a hundred feet an hour in deep night, I will walk across the border with as little trouble as if I were a boy again on a summer walking trip. There are many men they would like to have. I would be allowed to walk directly to them—until they had all the names and all the addresses. (*Laughs, points his finger at* TECK) *Roumanians* would pick me up ahead of time. *Germans* would not.

TECK (*smiles*): Still the national pride?

KURT: Why not? For that which is good.

FANNY (*comes over, very angrily, to* TECK): I have not often in my life felt what I feel now. Whatever you are, and however you became it, the picture of a man selling the lives of other men—

TECK: Is very ugly, Madame Fanny. I do not do it without some shame, and therefore I must sink my shame in large money. (*Puts his hand on the brief-case*) The money is here. For ten thousand, you go back to save your friends, nobody will know that you go, and I will give you my good wishes. (*Slowly, deliberately,* KURT *begins to shake his head.* TECK *waits, then carefully*) No?

KURT: This money is going home with me. It was not given to me to save my life, and I shall not so use it. It is to save the lives and further the work of more than I. It is important to me to carry on that work and to save the lives of three valuable men, and to do that with all speed. But— (*Sharply*) Count de Brancovis, the first morning we arrived in this house, my children wanted their breakfast with great haste. That is because the evening before we had been able only to buy milk and buns for them. If I would not touch this money for them, I would not touch it for you. (*Very sharply*) It goes back with me. The way it is. And if it does not get back, it is because I will not get back.

(*There is a long pause.* SARA *gets up, turns away.*)

TECK: Then I do not think you will get back. You are a brave one, Herr Müller, but you will not get back.

KURT (*as if he were very tired*): I will send to you a postal card and tell you about my bravery.

DAVID (*coming toward* KURT): Is it true that if this swine talks, you and the others will be—

SARA (*very softly*): Caught and killed. Of course. If they're lucky enough to get killed quickly. (*Quietly, points to the table*) You should have seen his hands in 1935.

FANNY (*violently, to* DAVID): We'll give him the money. For God's sake, let's give it to him and get him out of here.

DAVID (*to* SARA): Do you want Kurt to go back?

SARA: Yes. I do.

DAVID: All right. (*Goes to her, lifts her face*) You're a good girl.

KURT: That is true. Brave and good, my Sara. She is everything. She is handsome and gay and— (*Puts his hand over his eyes.* SARA *turns away.*)

DAVID (*after a second, comes to stand near* TECK): If we give you the money, what is to keep you from selling to Von Seitz?

TECK: I do not like your thinking I would do that. But—

DAVID (*tensely*): Look here. I'm sick of what you'd like or wouldn't like. And I'm sick of your talk. We'll get this over with now, without any more fancy talk from you, or as far as I am concerned, you can get out of here without my money and sell to any buyer you can find. I can't take much more of you at any cost.

TECK (*smiles*): It is your anger which delays us. I was about to say that I understood your fear that I would go to Von Seitz, and I would suggest that you give me a small amount of cash now and a check dated a month from now. In a month, Herr Müller should be nearing home, and he can let you know. And if you should not honor the check because Herr Müller is already in Germany, Von Seitz will pay a little something for a reliable description. I will take my chance on that. You will now say that I could do that in any case —and that is the chance you will take.

DAVID (*looks at* KURT, *who does not look up*): Is a month enough? For you to get back?

KURT (*shrugs*): I do not know.

DAVID (*to* TECK): Two months from today. How do you want the cash and how do you want the check?

TECK: *One month from today.* That I will not discuss. One month. Please decide now.

DAVID (*sharply*): All right. (*To* TECK) How do you want it?

TECK: Seventy-five hundred dollars in a check. Twenty-five hundred in cash.

DAVID: I haven't anywhere near that much cash in the house. Leave your address and I'll send it to you in the morning.

TECK (*laughs*): Address? I have no address, and I wish it now. Madame Fanny has cash in her sitting-room safe.

FANNY: Have you investigated that, too?

TECK (*laughs*): No. You once told me you always kept money in the house.

DAVID (*to* FANNY): How much have you got upstairs?

FANNY: I don't know. About fifteen or sixteen hundred.

TECK: Very well. That will do. Make the rest in the check.

DAVID: Get it, Mama, please. (*He starts toward the library door.* FANNY *starts for the hall exit.*)

FANNY (*turns, looks carefully at* TECK): Years ago, I heard somebody say that being Roumanian was not a nationality, but a profession. The years have brought no change.

KURT (*softly*): Being a Roumanian aristocrat is a profession.

(FANNY *exits. After her exit, there is silence.* KURT *does not look up,* SARA *does not move.*)

TECK (*awkwardly*): The new world has left the room. (*Looks up at them*) I feel less discomfort with you. We are Europeans, born to trouble and understanding it.

KURT: My wife is not a European.

TECK: Almost. (*Points upstairs*) They are young. The world has gone well for most of them. For us— (*Smiles*) The three of us—we are like peasants watching the big frost. Work, trouble, ruin— (*Shrugs*) But no need to call curses at the frost. There it is, it will be again, always—for us.

SARA (*gets up, moves to the window, looks out*): You mean my husband and I do not have angry words for you. What for? We know how many there are of you. They don't, yet. My mother and brother feel shocked that you are in their house. For us—we have seen you in so many houses.

TECK: I do not say you *want* to understand me, Mrs. Müller. I say only that you do.

SARA: Yes. You are not difficult to understand.

KURT (*slowly gets up, stands stiffly. Then he moves toward the decanter table*): A whiskey?

TECK: No, thank you. (*He turns his head to watch* KURT *move. He turns back.*)

KURT: Sherry?

TECK (*nods*): Thank you, I will.

KURT (*as he pours*): You, too, wish to go back to Europe.

TECK: Yes.

KURT: But they do not much want you. Not since the Budapest oil deal of '31.

TECK: You seem as well informed about me as I am about you.

KURT: That must have been a conference of high comedy, that one. Everybody trying to guess whether Kessler was working for Fritz Thyssen, and what Thyssen *really* wanted—and whether this "National Socialism" was a smart blind of Thyssen's, and where was Wolff—I should like to have seen you and your friends. It is too bad: you guessed an inch off, eh?

TECK: And Kessler has a memory? (*Almost playfully*) I do not think Von Seitz would pay you money for a description of a man who has a month to travel. But I think he would pay you in a visa and a cable to Kessler. I think you want a visa almost as much as you want money. Therefore, I conclude you will try for the money here, and the visa from Von Seitz. (*He comes toward the table carrying the sherry glass*) I cannot get anywhere near Germany in a month and you know it. (*He is about to place the glass on the table*) I have been bored with this talk of paying you money. If they are willing to try you on this fantasy, I am not. Whatever made you think I would take such a chance? Or *any* chance? You are a gambler. But you should not gamble with your life. (TECK

*has turned to stare at him, made a half motion as if to rise. As he
does so, and on the words, "gamble with your life," KURT drops
the glass, hits TECK in the face. Struggling, TECK makes a violent
effort to rise. KURT throws himself on TECK, knocking him to the
floor. As TECK falls to the floor, KURT hits him on the side of the
head. At the fourth blow, TECK does not move. KURT rises, takes
the gun from his pocket, begins to lift TECK from the floor. As he
does so, JOSHUA appears in the hall entrance. He is washed and
ready for dinner. As he reaches the door, he stops, sees the scene,
stands quietly as if he were waiting for orders. KURT begins to balance TECK, to balance himself. To JOSHUA) Hilf mir. (JOSHUA comes
quickly to KURT) Mach die Tür auf! (JOSHUA runs toward the doors,
opens them, stands waiting) Bleib da! Mach die Tür zu! (KURT
begins to move out through the terrace. When he is outside the
doors, JOSHUA closes them quickly, stands looking at his mother.)*

SARA: There's trouble.

JOSHUA: Do not worry. I will go up now. I will pack. In ten minutes
all will be ready. I will say nothing. I will get the children ready—
(*He starts quickly for the hall, turns for a second to look toward the
terrace doors. Then almost with a sob*) This was a nice house.

SARA (*softly*): We're not going this time, darling. There's no need
to pack.

JOSHUA (*stares at her, puzzled*): But Papa—

SARA: Go upstairs, Joshua. Take Babbie and Bodo in your room,
and close the door. Stay there until I call you. (*He looks at her,
SARA sits down*) There's nothing to be frightened of, darling. Papa
is all right. (*Then very softly*) Papa is going home.

JOSHUA: To Germany?

SARA: Yes.

JOSHUA: Oh. Alone?

SARA: Alone. (*Very softly*) Don't say anything to the children.
He will tell them himself.

JOSHUA: I won't.

SARA (*as he hesitates*): I'm all right. Go upstairs now. (*He moves
slowly out, she watches him, he disappears. For a minute she sits*

*quietly. Then she gets up, moves to the terrace doors, stands with
her hands pressed against them. Then she crosses, picks up the overturned chair, places it by the table, picks up the glass, puts it on the
table. As if without knowing what she is doing, she wipes the table
with her handkerchief.)*

(FANNY *comes in from hall. After a second,* DAVID *comes in from
library. Stops, looks around room.)*

DAVID: Where is he? Upstairs?

SARA: No. They went outside.

FANNY: Outside? They went outside. What are they doing, picking
a bouquet together?

SARA (*without turning*): They just went outside.

DAVID (*looks at her*): What's the matter, Sara?

(SARA *shakes her head. Goes to the desk, opens the telephone book,
looks at a number, begins to dial the telephone.)*

FANNY: Eleven hundred, eleven hundred and fifty, twelve, twelve-
fifty—

DAVID: For God's sake, stop counting that money.

FANNY: All right. I'm nervous. And I don't like to think of giving
him too much.

SARA: It's very nice of you and Mama. All that money— (*Into the
telephone*) Hello. What time is your next plane? Oh. To— South.
To El Paso, or— Brownsville. Yes.

DAVID (*to* FANNY): Is Joseph ready?

FANNY: I don't know. I told him I'd call him.

SARA: To Brownsville? Yes. Yes. That's all right. At what time?
Yes. No. The ticket will be picked up at the airport. (DAVID *begins
to cross to the bell cord. She looks up*) No. David. Don't call
Joseph. *David! Please!* (*He draws back, stares at her. Looking at
him, she goes on with the conversation*) Ritter. R-I-T-T-E-R.
From Chicago. Yes. Yes. (*She hangs up, walks away.)*

DAVID: Sara! What's happening? What is all this? (*She does not answer*) Where is Kurt? What— (*He starts for the terrace door.*)

SARA: David. *Don't go out.*

FANNY (*rises*): Sara! What's happening—

SARA: For seven years now, day in, day out, men have crossed the German border. They are always in danger. They always may be going in to die. Did you ever see the face of a man who never knows if this day will be the last day? (*Softly*) Don't go out on the terrace, David. Leave Kurt alone.

FANNY (*softly*): Sara! What is—

SARA (*quietly*): For them, it may be torture, and it may be death. Some day, when it's all over, maybe there'll be a few of them left to celebrate. There aren't many of Kurt's age left. He couldn't take a chance on them. They wouldn't have liked it. (*Suddenly, violently*) He'd have had a bad time trying to explain to them that because of this house and this nice town and my mother and my brother, he took chances with their work and with their lives. (*Quietly*) Sit down, Mama. I think it's all over now. (*To* DAVID) There's nothing you can do about it. It's the way it had to be.

DAVID: Sara—

FANNY: Do you mean what I think you—(*She sits down.*)

SARA (*she turns, looks out toward the doors. After a pause*): He's going away tonight and he's never coming back any more. (*In a sing-song*) Never, never, never. (*She looks down at her hands, as if she were very interested in them*) I don't like to be alone at night. I guess everybody in the world's got a time they don't like. Me, it's right before I go to sleep. And now it's going to be for always. All the rest of my life. (*She looks up as* KURT *comes in from the terrace*) I've told them. There is an eight-thirty plane going as far south as Brownsville. I've made you a reservation. In the name of Ritter.

KURT (*stands looking at her*): Liebe Sara! (*Then he goes to the table at which* FANNY *is sitting. To* FANNY) It is hard for you, eh? (*He pats her hand*) I am sorry.

FANNY (*without knowing why, she takes her hand away*): Hard? I don't know. I— I don't— I don't know what I want to say.

KURT (*looks at the hand she has touched, then turns to look at* DAVID): Before I come in, I stand and think. I say, I will make Fanny and David understand. I say, how can I? Does one understand a killing? No. To hell with it, I say. I do what must be done. I have long sickened of words when I see the men who live by them. What do you wish to make them understand, I ask myself. Wait. Stand here. Just stand here. What are you thinking? Say it to them just as it comes to you. And this is what came to me. When you kill in a war, it is not so lonely; and I remember a cousin I have not seen for many years; and a melody comes back and I begin to make it with my fingers; a staircase in a house in Bonn years ago; an old dog who used to live in our town; Sara in a hundred places— Shame on us. Thousands of years and we cannot yet make a world. Like a child I am. I have stopped a man's life. (*Points to the place on the couch where he had been sitting opposite* TECK) I sit here. I listen to him. You will not believe—but I pray that I will not have to touch him. Then I know I will have to. I know that if I do not, it is only that I pamper myself, and risk the lives of others. I want you from the room. I know what I must do. (*Loudly*) All right. Do I now pretend sorrow? Do I now pretend it is not I who act thus? No. I do it. I have done it. I will do it again. And I will keep my hope that we may make a world in which all men can die in bed. I have a great hate for the violent. They are the sick of the world. (*Softly*) Maybe I am sick now, too.

SARA: You aren't sick. Stop that. It's late. You must go soon.

KURT (*he puts out his hands, she touches them*): I am going to say good-bye now to my children. Then I am going to take your car— (*Motions with his head*) I will take him with me. After that, it is up to you. Two ways: You can let me go and keep silent. I believe I can hide him and the car. At the end of two days, if they have not been found, you will tell as much of the truth as is safe for you to say. Tell them the last time you saw us we were on our way to Washington. You did not worry at the absence, we might have rested there. Two crazy foreigners fight, one gets killed, you know nothing of the reason. I will have left the gun, there will be no doubt who did the killing. If you will give me those two days, I think I will be far enough away from here. If the car is found before then— (*Shrugs*) I will still try to move with speed. And all that will make you, for yourselves, part of a murder. For the world, I do not think you will be in bad trouble. (*He pauses*) There is another way. You can call your police. You can tell them the truth. I will not get home.

(*To* SARA) I wish to see the children now. (*She goes out into the hall and up the stairs. There is silence.*)

FANNY: What are you thinking, David?

DAVID: I don't know. What are you thinking?

FANNY: Me? Oh, I was thinking about my Joshua. I was thinking that a few months before he died, we were sitting out there. (*Points to terrace*) He said, "Fanny, the Renaissance American is dying, the Renaissance man is dying." I said what do you mean, although I knew what he meant, I always knew. "A Renaissance man," he said, "is a man who wants to know. He wants to know how fast a bird will fly, how thick is the crust of the earth, what made Iago evil, how to plow a field. He knows there is no dignity to a mountain, if there is no dignity to man. You can't put that in a man, but when it's *really* there, and he will fight for it, put your trust in him."

DAVID (*gets up, smiles, looks at* FANNY): You're a smart woman sometimes. (SARA *enters with* JOSHUA. *To* KURT) Don't worry about things here. My soul doesn't have to be so nice and clean. I'll take care of it. You'll have your two days. And good luck to you.

FANNY: You go with my blessing, too. I like you. (BODO *enters.*)

SARA: See? I come from good stock. (KURT *looks at* DAVID. *Then he begins to smile. Nods to* DAVID. *Turns, smiles at* FANNY.)

FANNY: Do you like me?

KURT: I like you, Madame, very much.

FANNY: Would you be able to cash that check?

KURT (*laughs*): Oh, no.

FANNY: Then take the cash. I, too, would like to contribute to your work.

KURT (*slowly*): All right. Thank you. (*He takes the money from the table, puts it in his pocket.*)

BODO (*to* KURT): You like Grandma? I thought you would, with time. I like her, too. Sometimes she dilates with screaming, but— Dilates is correct? (BABETTE *enters.* JOSHUA *stands away from the others, looking at his father.* KURT *turns to look at him.*)

JOSHUA: Alles in Ordnung?

KURT: Alles in Ordnung.

BODO: What? What does that mean, all is well? (*There is an awkward silence.*)

BABETTE (*as if she sensed it*): We are all clean for dinner. But nobody else is clean. And I have on Grandma's dress to me—

FANNY (*very nervously*): Of course. And you look very pretty. You're a pretty little girl, Babbie.

BODO (*looks around the room*): What is the matter? Everybody is acting like such a ninny. I got that word from Grandma.

KURT: Come here. (*They look at him. Then slowly* BABETTE *comes toward him, followed by* BODO. JOSHUA *comes more slowly, to stand at the side of* KURT'S *chair*) We have said many good-byes to each other, eh? We must now say another. (*As they stare at him, he smiles, slowly, as if it were difficult*) This time, I leave you with good people to whom I believe you also will be good. (*Half playfully*) Would you allow me to give away my share in you, until I come back?

BABETTE (*slowly*): If you would like it.

KURT: Good. To your mother, her share. My share, to Fanny and David. It is all that I have to give. (*Laughs*) There. I have made a will, eh? Now. We will not joke. I have something to say to you. It is important for me to say it.

JOSHUA (*softly*): You are talking to us as if we were children.

KURT (*turns to look at him*): Am I, Joshua? I wish you were children. I wish I could say love your mother, do not eat too many sweets, clean your teeth— (*Draws* BODO *to him*) I cannot say these things. You are not children. I took it all away from you.

BABETTE: We have had a most enjoyable life, Papa.

KURT (*smiles*): You are a gallant little liar. And I thank you for it. I have done something bad today—

FANNY (*shocked, sharply*): Kurt—

SARA: Don't, Mama. (BODO *and* BABETTE *have looked at* FANNY *and* SARA, *puzzled. Then they have turned again to look at* KURT.)

KURT: It is not to frighten you. In a few days, your mother and David will tell you.

BODO: You could not do a bad thing.

BABETTE (*proudly*): You could not.

KURT (*shakes his head*): Now let us get straight together. The four of us. Do you remember when we read "Les Misérables"? Do you remember that we talked about it afterward and Bodo got candy on Mama's bed?

BODO: I remember.

KURT: Well. He stole bread. The world is out of shape we said, when there are hungry men. And until it gets in shape, men will steal and lie and—(*A little more slowly*)—kill. But for whatever reason it is done, and whoever does it—you understand me—it is all bad. I want you to remember that. Whoever does it, it is bad. (*Then very gaily*) But you will live to see the day when it will not have to be. All over the world, in every place and every town, there are men who are going to make sure it will not have to be. They want what I want: a childhood for every child. For my children, and I for theirs. (*He picks* BODO *up, rises*) Think of that. It will make you happy. In every town and every village and every mud hut in the world, there is always a man who loves children and who will fight to make a good world for them. And now good-bye. Wait for me. I shall try to come back for you. (*He moves toward the hall, followed by* BAB-ETTE, *and more slowly, by* JOSHUA) Or you shall come to me. At Hamburg, the boat will come in. It will be a fine, safe land— I will be waiting on the dock. And there will be the three of you and Mama and Fanny and David. And I will have ordered an extra big dinner and we will show them what our Germany can be like— (*He has put* BODO *down. He leans down, presses his face in* BABETTE's *hair. Tenderly, as her mother has done earlier, she touches his hair.*)

JOSHUA: Of course. That is the way it will be. Of course. But—but if you should find yourself delayed— (*Very slowly*) Then I will come to you. Mama.

SARA (*she has turned away*): I heard you, Joshua.

KURT (*he kisses* BABETTE): Gute Nacht, Liebling!

BABETTE: Gute Nacht, Papa. Mach's gut!

KURT (*leans to kiss* BODO): Good night, baby.

BODO: Good night, Papa. Mach's gut! (BABETTE *runs up the steps. Slowly* BODO *follows her.*)

KURT (*kisses* JOSHUA): Good night, son.

JOSHUA: Good night, Papa. Mach's gut! (*He begins to climb the steps.* KURT *stands watching them, smiling. When they disappear, he turns to* DAVID.)

KURT: Good-bye, and thank you.

DAVID: Good-bye, and good luck.

KURT (*he moves to* FANNY): Good-bye. I have good children, eh?

FANNY: Yes, you have. (KURT *kisses her hand.*)

KURT (*slowly, he turns toward* SARA): Men who wish to live have the best chance to live. I wish to live. I wish to live with you. (*She comes toward him.*)

SARA: For twenty years. It is as much for me today—(*Takes his arms*) Just once, and for all my life. (*He pulls her toward him*) Come back for me, darling. If you can. (*Takes brief case from table and gives it to him.*)

KURT (*simply*): I will try. (*He turns*) Good-bye, to you all. (*He exits. After a second, there is the sound of a car starting. They sit listening to it. Gradually the noise begins to go off into the distance. A second later,* JOSHUA *appears.*)

JOSHUA: Mama— (*She looks up. He is very tense*) Bodo cries. Babette looks very queer. I think you should come.

SARA (*gets up, slowly*): I'm coming.

JOSHUA (*to* FANNY *and* DAVID. *Still very tense*): Bodo talks so fancy, we forget sometimes he is a baby. (*He waits for* SARA *to come up to him. When she reaches him, she takes his hand, goes up the steps, disappears.* FANNY *and* DAVID *watch them.*)

FANNY (*after a minute*): Well, here we are. We're shaken out of the magnolias, eh?

DAVID: Yes. So we are.

FANNY: Tomorrow will be a hard day. But we'll have Babbie's birthday dinner. And we'll have music afterward. You can be the audience. I think you'd better go up to Marthe now. Be as careful as you can. She'd better stay here for a while. I daresay I can stand it.

DAVID (*turns, smiles*): Even your graciousness is ungracious, Mama.

FANNY: I do my best. Well, I think I shall go and talk to Anise. I like Anise best when I don't feel well. (*She begins to move off.*)

DAVID: Mama. (*She turns*) We are going to be in for trouble. You understand that?

FANNY: I understand it very well. We will manage. You and I. I'm not put together with flour paste. And neither are you—I am happy to learn.

DAVID: Good night, Mama. (*As she moves out, the curtain falls.*)

JOHN M. SYNGE

# The Playboy
## of the
# Western World

*The Playboy of the Western World* was first produced by the National Theater Society at the Abbey
Theater, Dublin, on January 26, 1907.

# CHARACTERS

CHRISTOPHER MAHON
OLD MAHON (*his father, a squatter*)
MICHAEL JAMES FLAHERTY, called MICHAEL JAMES (*a publican*)
MARGARET FLAHERTY, called PEGEEN MIKE (*his daughter*)
WIDOW QUIN (*a woman of about thirty*)
SHAWN KEOGH (*her cousin, a young farmer*)
PHILLY CULLEN and JIMMY FARRELL (*small farmers*)
SARA TANSEY, SUSAN BRADY, and HONOR BLAKE (*village girls*)
A BELLMAN
SOME PEASANTS

*The action takes place near a village, on a wild coast of Mayo. The first Act passes on an evening of autumn, the other two Acts on the following day.*

# Act One

SCENE: *Country public-house or shebeen, very rough and untidy. There is a sort of counter on the right with shelves, holding many bottles and jugs, just seen above it. Empty barrels stand near the counter. At back, a little to left of counter, there is a door into the open air, then, more to the left, there is a settle with shelves above it, with more jugs, and a table beneath a window. At the left there is a large open fire-place, with turf fire, and a small door into inner room. Pegeen, a wild-looking but fine girl of about twenty, is writing at table. She is dressed in the usual peasant dress.*

PEGEEN (*slowly as she writes*): Six yards of stuff for to make a yellow gown. A pair of lace boots with lengthy heels on them and brassy eyes. A hat is suited for a wedding-day. A fine tooth comb. To be sent with three barrels of porter in Jimmy Farrell's creel cart on the evening of the coming Fair to Mister Michael James Flaherty. With the best compliments of this season. Margaret Flaherty.

SHAWN KEOGH (*a fat and fair young man comes in as she signs, looks around awkwardly, when he sees she is alone*): Where's himself?

PEGEEN (*without looking at him*): He's coming. (*She directs the letter*) To Master Sheamus Mulroy, Wine and Spirit Dealer, Castlebar.

SHAWN (*uneasily*): I didn't see him on the road.

PEGEEN: How would you see him (*licks stamp and puts it on letter*) and it dark night this half hour gone by?

SHAWN (*turning towards the door again*): I stood a while outside wondering would I have a right to pass on or to walk in and see you, Pegeen Mike (*comes to fire*), and I could hear the cows breathing, and sighing in the stillness of the air, and not a step moving any place from this gate to the bridge.

PEGEEN (*putting letter in envelope*): It's above at the cross-roads he is, meeting Philly Cullen; and a couple more are going along with him to Kate Cassidy's wake.

SHAWN (*looking at her blankly*): And he's going that length in the dark night?

PEGEEN (*impatiently*): He is surely, and leaving me lonesome on the scruff of the hill. (*She gets up and puts envelope on dresser, then winds clock*) Isn't it long the nights are now, Shawn Keogh, to be leaving a poor girl with her own self counting the hours to the dawn of day?

SHAWN (*with an awkward humour*): If it is, when we're wedded in a short while you'll have no call to complain, for I've little will to be walking off to wakes or weddings in the darkness of the night.

PEGEEN (*with rather scornful good humour*): You're making mighty certain, Shaneen, that I'll wed you now.

SHAWN: Aren't we after making a good bargain, the way we're only waiting these days on Father Reilly's dispensation from the bishops, or the Court of Rome?

PEGEEN (*looking at him teasingly, washing up at dresser*): It's a wonder, Shaneen, the Holy Father'd be taking notice of the likes of you; for if I was him I wouldn't bother with this place where you'll meet none but Red Linahan, has a squint in his eye, and Patcheen is lame in his heel, or the mad Mulrannies were driven from California and they lost in their wits. We're a queer lot these times to go troubling the Holy Father on his sacred seat.

SHAWN (*scandalized*): If we are, we're as good this place as another, maybe, and as good these times as we were for ever.

PEGEEN (*with scorn*): As good, is it? Where now will you meet the like of Daneen Sullivan knocked the eye from a peeler, or Marcus Quin, God rest him, got six months for maiming ewes, and he a great warrant to tell stories of holy Ireland till he'd have the old women shedding down tears about their feet. Where will you find the like of them, I'm saying?

SHAWN (*timidly*): If you don't, it's a good job, maybe; for (*with peculiar emphasis on the words*) Father Reilly has small conceit to have that kind walking around and talking to the girls.

PEGEEN (*impatiently, throwing water from basin out of the door*): Stop tormenting me with Father Reilly (*imitating his voice*) when I'm asking only what way I'll pass these twelve hours of dark, and not take my death with the fear. (*Looking out of door.*)

SHAWN (*timidly*): Would I fetch you the Widow Quin, maybe?

PEGEEN: Is it the like of that murderer? You'll not, surely.

SHAWN (*going to her, soothingly*): Then I'm thinking himself will stop along with you when he sees you taking on, for it'll be a long night-time with great darkness, and I'm after feeling a kind of fellow above in the furzy ditch, groaning wicked like a maddening dog, the way it's good cause you have, maybe, to be fearing now.

PEGEEN (*turning on him sharply*): What's that? Is it a man you seen?

SHAWN (*retreating*): I couldn't see him at all; but I heard him groaning out, and breaking his heart. It should have been a young man from his words speaking.

PEGEEN (*going after him*): And you never went near to see was he hurted or what ailed him at all?

SHAWN: I did not, Pegeen Mike. It was a dark, lonesome place to be hearing the like of him.

PEGEEN: Well, you're a daring fellow, and if they find his corpse stretched above in the dews of dawn, what'll you say then to the peelers, or the Justice of the Peace?

SHAWN (*thunderstruck*): I wasn't thinking of that. For the love of God, Pegeen Mike, don't let on I was speaking of him. Don't tell your father and the men is coming above; for if they heard that story, they'd have great blabbing this night at the wake.

PEGEEN: I'll maybe tell them, and I'll maybe not.

SHAWN: They are coming at the door. Will you whisht, I'm saying?

PEGEEN: Whisht yourself. (*She goes behind counter.* MICHAEL JAMES, *fat jovial publican, comes in followed by* PHILLY CULLEN, *who is thin and mistrusting, and* JIMMY FARRELL, *who is fat and amorous, about forty-five.*)

MEN (*together*): God bless you. The blessing of God on this place.

PEGEEN: God bless you kindly.

MICHAEL (*to men who go to the counter*): Sit down now, and take your rest. (*Crosses to* SHAWN *at the fire*) And how is it you are, Shawn Keogh? Are you coming over the sands to Kate Cassidy's wake?

SHAWN: I am not, Michael James. I'm going home the short cut to my bed.

PEGEEN (*speaking across the counter*): He's right too, and have you no shame, Michael James, to be quitting off for the whole night, and leaving myself lonesome in the shop?

MICHAEL (*good-humouredly*): Isn't it the same whether I go for the whole night or a part only? and I'm thinking it's a queer daughter you are if you'd have me crossing backward through the Stooks of the Dead Women, with a drop taken.

PEGEEN: If I am a queer daughter, it's a queer father'd be leaving me lonesome these twelve hours of dark, and I piling the turf with the dogs barking, and the calves mooing, and my own teeth rattling with the fear.

JIMMY (*flatteringly*): What is there to hurt you, and you a fine, hardy girl would knock the head of any two men in the place?

PEGEEN (*working herself up*): Isn't there the harvest boys with their tongues red for drink, and the ten tinkers is camped in the east glen, and the thousand militia—bad cess to them!—walking idle through the land. There's lots surely to hurt me, and I won't stop alone in it, let himself do what he will.

MICHAEL: If you're that afeard, let Shawn Keogh stop along with you. It's the will of God, I'm thinking, himself should be seeing to you now.

(*They all turn on* SHAWN.)

SHAWN (*in horrified confusion*): I would and welcome, Michael James, but I'm afeard of Father Reilly; and what at all would the Holy Father and the Cardinals of Rome be saying if they heard I did the like of that?

MICHAEL (*with contempt*): God help you! Can't you sit in by the hearth with the light lit and herself beyond in the room? You'll do that surely, for I've heard tell there's a queer fellow above, going mad or getting his death, maybe, in the gripe of the ditch, so she'd be safer this night with a person here.

SHAWN (*with plaintive despair*): I'm afeard of Father Reilly, I'm saying. Let you not be tempting me, and we near married itself.

PHILLY (*with cold contempt*): Lock him in the west room. He'll stay then and have no sin to be telling to the priest.

MICHAEL (*to* SHAWN, *getting between him and the door*): Go up now.

SHAWN (*at the top of his voice*): Don't stop me, Michael James. Let me out of the door, I'm saying, for the love of the Almighty God. Let me out. (*Trying to dodge past him*) Let me out of it, and may God grant you His indulgence in the hour of need.

MICHAEL (*loudly*): Stop your noising, and sit down by the hearth. (*Gives him a push and goes to counter laughing.*)

SHAWN (*turning back, wringing his hands*): Oh, Father Reilly and the saints of God, where will I hide myself today? Oh, St. Joseph and St. Patrick and St. Brigid, and St. James, have mercy on me now! (SHAWN *turns round, sees door clear, and makes a rush for it.*)

MICHAEL (*catching him by the coat-tail*): You'd be going, is it?

SHAWN (*screaming*): Leave me go, Michael James, leave me go, you old Pagan, leave me go, or I'll get the curse of the priests on you, and of the scarlet-coated bishops of the courts of Rome. (*With a sudden movement he pulls himself out of his coat, and disappears out of the door, leaving his coat in* MICHAEL'S *hands.*)

MICHAEL (*turning round, and holding up coat*): Well, there's the coat of a Christian man. Oh, there's sainted glory this day in the lonesome west; and by the will of God I've got you a decent man, Pegeen, you'll have no call to be spying after if you've a score of young girls, maybe, weeding in your fields.

PEGEEN (*taking up the defense of her property*): What right have you to be making game of a poor fellow for minding the priest, when it's your own the fault is, not paying a penny pot-boy to stand along with me and give me courage in the doing of my work? (*She snaps the coat away from him, and goes behind counter with it.*)

MICHAEL (*taken aback*): Where would I get a pot-boy? Would you have me send the bellman screaming in the streets of Castlebar?

SHAWN (*opening the door a chink and putting in his head, in a small voice*): Michael James!

MICHAEL (*imitating him*): What ails you?

SHAWN: The queer dying fellow's beyond looking over the ditch. He's come up, I'm thinking, stealing your hens. (*Looks over his shoulder*) God help me, he's following me now (*he runs into room*), and if he's heard what I said, he'll be having my life, and I going home lonesome in the darkness of the night.

(*For a perceptible moment they watch the door with curiosity. Some one coughs outside. Then* CHRISTY MAHON, *a slight young man, comes in very tired and frightened and dirty.*)

CHRISTY (*in a small voice*): God save all here!

MEN: God save you kindly.

CHRISTY (*going to the counter*): I'd trouble you for a glass of porter, woman of the house. (*He puts down coin.*)

PEGEEN (*serving him*): You're one of the tinkers, young fellow, is beyond camped in the glen?

CHRISTY: I am not; but I'm destroyed walking.

MICHAEL (*patronizingly*): Let you come up then to the fire. You're looking famished with the cold.

CHRISTY: God reward you. (*He takes up his glass and goes a little way across to the left, then stops and looks about him*) Is it often the police do be coming into this place, master of the house?

MICHAEL: If you'd come in better hours, you'd have seen "Licensed for the sale of Beer and Spirits, to be consumed on the premises," written in white letters above the door, and what would the polis want spying on me, and not a decent house within four miles, the way every living Christian is a bona fide, saving one widow alone?

CHRISTY (*with relief*): It's a safe house, so. (*He goes over to the fire, sighing and moaning. Then he sits down, putting his glass beside him and begins gnawing a turnip, too miserable to feel the others staring at him with curiosity.*)

MICHAEL (*going after him*): Is it yourself is fearing the polis? You're wanting, maybe?

CHRISTY: There's many wanting.

MICHAEL: Many surely, with the broken harvest and the ended wars. (*He picks up some stockings, etc., that are near the fire, and carries them away furtively*) It should be larceny, I'm thinking.

CHRISTY (*dolefully*): I had it in my mind it was a different word and a bigger.

PEGEEN: There's a queer lad. Were you never slapped in school, young fellow, that you don't know the name of your deed?

CHRISTY (*bashfully*): I'm slow at learning, a middling scholar only.

MICHAEL: If you're a dunce itself, you'd have a right to know that larceny's robbing and stealing. Is it for the like of that you're wanting?

CHRISTY (*with a flash of family pride*): And I the son of a strong farmer (*with a sudden qualm*), God rest his soul, could have bought up the whole of your old house awhile since, from the butt of his tailpocket, and not have missed the weight of it gone.

MICHAEL (*impressed*): If it's not stealing, it's maybe something big.

CHRISTY (*flattered*): Aye; it's maybe something big.

JIMMY: He's a wicked-looking young fellow. Maybe he followed after a young woman on a lonesome night.

CHRISTY (*shocked*): Oh, the saints forbid, mister; I was all times a decent lad.

PHILLY (*turning on* JIMMY): You're a silly man, Jimmy Farrell. He said his father was a farmer a while since, and there's himself now in a poor state. Maybe the land was grabbed from him, and he did what any decent man would do.

MICHAEL (*to* CHRISTY, *mysteriously*): Was it bailiffs?

CHRISTY: The divil a one.

MICHAEL: Agents?

CHRISTY: The divil a one.

MICHAEL: Landlords?

CHRISTY (*peevishly*): Ah, not at all, I'm saying. You'd see the like of them stories on any little paper of a Munster town. But I'm not calling to mind any person, gentle, simple, judge or jury, did the like of me.

(*They all draw nearer with delighted curiosity.*)

PHILLY: Well, that lad's a puzzle-the-world.

JIMMY: He'd beat Dan Davies' circus, or the holy missioners making sermons on the villainy of man. Try him again, Philly.

PHILLY: Did you strike golden guineas out of solder, young fellow, or shilling coins itself?

CHRISTY: I did not, mister, not sixpence nor a farthing coin.

JIMMY: Did you marry three wives maybe? I'm told there's a sprinkling have done that among the holy Luthers of the preaching north.

CHRISTY (*shyly*): I never married with one, let alone with a couple or three.

PHILLY: Maybe he went fighting for the Boers, the like of the man beyond, was judged to be hanged, quartered and drawn. Were you off east, young fellow, fighting bloody wars for Kruger and the freedom of the Boers?

CHRISTY: I never left my own parish till Tuesday was a week.

PEGEEN (*coming from counter*): He's done nothing, so. (*To* CHRISTY) If you didn't commit murder or a bad, nasty thing, or false coining, or robbery, or butchery, or the like of them, there isn't anything that would be worth your troubling for to run from now. You did nothing at all.

CHRISTY (*his feelings hurt*): That's an unkindly thing to be saying to a poor orphaned traveller, has a prison behind him, and hanging before, and hell's gap gaping below.

PEGEEN (*with a sign to the men to be quiet*): You're only saying it. You did nothing at all. A soft lad the like of you wouldn't slit the windpipe of a screeching sow.

CHRISTY (*offended*): You're not speaking the truth.

PEGEEN (*in mock rage*): Not speaking the truth, is it? Would you have me knock the head off you with the butt of the broom?

CHRISTY (*twisting round on her with a sharp cry of horror*): Don't strike me. I killed my poor father, Tuesday was a week, for doing the like of that.

PEGEEN (*with blank amazement*): Is it killed your father?

CHRISTY (*subsiding*): With the help of God I did surely, and that the Holy Immaculate Mother may intercede for his soul.

PHILLY (*retreating with* JIMMY): There's a daring fellow.

JIMMY: Oh, glory be to God!

MICHAEL (*with great respect*): That was a hanging crime, mister honey. You should have had good reason for doing the like of that.

CHRISTY (*in a very reasonable tone*): He was a dirty man, God forgive him, and he getting old and crusty, the way I couldn't put up with him at all.

PEGEEN: And you shot him dead?

CHRISTY (*shaking his head*): I never used weapons. I've no license, and I'm a law-fearing man.

MICHAEL: It was with a hilted knife maybe? I'm told, in the big world it's bloody knives they use.

CHRISTY (*loudly, scandalized*): Do you take me for a slaughter-boy?

PEGEEN: You never hanged him, the way Jimmy Farrell hanged his dog from the license, and had it screeching and wriggling three hours at the butt of a string, and himself swearing it was a dead dog, and the peelers swearing it had life?

CHRISTY: I did not then. I just riz the loy and let fall the edge of it on the ridge of his skull, and he went down at my feet like an empty sack, and never let a grunt or groan from him at all.

MICHAEL (*making a sign to* PEGEEN *to fill* CHRISTY's *glass*): And what way weren't you hanged, mister? Did you bury him then?

CHRISTY (*considering*): Aye. I buried him then. Wasn't I digging spuds in the field?

MICHAEL: And the peelers never followed after you the eleven days that you're out?

CHRISTY (*shaking his head*): Never a one of them, and I walking forward facing hog, dog, or divil on the highway of the road.

PHILLY (*nodding wisely*): It's only with a common week-day kind of a murderer them lads would be trusting their carcase, and that man should be a great terror when his temper's roused.

MICHAEL: He should then. (*To* CHRISTY) And where was it, mister honey, that you did the deed?

CHRISTY (*looking at him with suspicion*): Oh, a distant place, master of the house, a windy corner of high, distant hills.

PHILLY (*nodding with approval*): He's a close man, and he's right, surely.

PEGEEN: That'd be a lad with the sense of Solomon to have for a pot-boy, Michael James, if it's the truth you're seeking one at all.

PHILLY: The peelers is fearing him, and if you'd that lad in the house there isn't one of them would come smelling around if the dogs itself were lapping poteen from the dung-pit of the yard.

JIMMY: Bravery's a treasure in a lonesome place, and a lad would kill his father, I'm thinking, would face a foxy divil with a pitchpike on the flags of hell.

PEGEEN: It's the truth they're saying, and if I'd that lad in the house, I wouldn't be fearing the looséd kharki cut-throats, or the walking dead.

CHRISTY (*swelling with surprise and triumph*): Well, glory be to God!

MICHAEL (*with deference*): Would you think well to stop here and be pot-boy, mister honey, if we gave you good wages, and didn't destroy you with the weight of work?

SHAWN (*coming forward uneasily*): That'd be a queer kind to bring into a decent quiet household with the like of Pegeen Mike.

PEGEEN (*very sharply*): Will you whisht? Who's speaking to you?

SHAWN (*retreating*): A bloody-handed murderer the like of . . .

PEGEEN (*snapping at him*): Whisht I am saying; we'll take no fooling from your like at all. (*To* CHRISTY *with a honeyed voice*) And you, young fellow, you'd have a right to stop, I'm thinking, for we'd do our all and utmost to content your needs.

CHRISTY (*overcome with wonder*): And I'd be safe in this place from the searching law?

MICHAEL: You would, surely. If they're not fearing you, itself, the peelers in this place is decent droughty poor fellows, wouldn't touch a cur dog and not give warning in the dead of night.

PEGEEN (*very kindly and persuasively*): Let you stop a short while anyhow. Aren't you destroyed walking with your feet in bleeding blisters, and your whole skin needing washing like a Wicklow sheep?

CHRISTY (*looking round with satisfaction*): It's a nice room, and if it's not humbugging me you are, I'm thinking that I'll surely stay.

JIMMY (*jumps up*): Now, by the grace of God, herself will be safe this night, with a man killed his father holding danger from the door, and let you come on, Michael James, or they'll have the best stuff drunk at the wake.

MICHAEL (*going to the door with men*): And begging your pardon, mister, what name will we call you, for we'd like to know?

CHRISTY: Christopher Mahon.

MICHAEL: Well, God bless you, Christy, and a good rest till we meet again when the sun'll be rising to the noon of day.

CHRISTY: God bless you all.

MEN: God bless you.

(*They go out except* SHAWN, *who lingers at door.*)

SHAWN (*to* PEGEEN): Are you wanting me to stop along with you and keep you from harm?

PEGEEN (*gruffly*): Didn't you say you were fearing Father Reilly?

SHAWN: There'd be no harm staying now, I'm thinking, and himself in it too.

PEGEEN: You wouldn't stay when there was need for you, and let you step off nimble this time when there's none.

SHAWN: Didn't I say it was Father Reilly . . .

PEGEEN: Go on, then, to Father Reilly (*in a jeering tone*), and let him put you in the holy brotherhoods, and leave that lad to me.

SHAWN: If I meet the Widow Quin . . .

PEGEEN: Go on, I'm saying, and don't be waking this place with your noise. (*She hustles him out and bolts the door*) That lad would wear the spirits from the saints of peace. (*Bustles about, then takes off her apron and pins it up in the window as a blind.* CHRISTY *watching her timidly. Then she comes to him and speaks with bland good-humour*) Let you stretch out now by the fire, young fellow. You should be destroyed travelling.

CHRISTY (*shyly again, drawing off his boots*): I'm tired, surely, walking wild eleven days, and waking fearful in the night. (*He holds up one of his feet, feeling his blisters, and looking at them with compassion.*)

PEGEEN (*standing beside him, watching him with delight*): You should have had great people in your family, I'm thinking, with the little, small feet you have, and you with a kind of a quality name, the like of what you'd find on the great powers and potentates of France and Spain.

CHRISTY (*with pride*): We were great surely, with wide and windy acres of rich Munster land.

PEGEEN: Wasn't I telling you, and you a fine, handsome young fellow with a noble brow?

CHRISTY (*with a flash of delighted surprise*): Is it me?

PEGEEN: Aye. Did you never hear that from the young girls where you come from in the west or south?

CHRISTY (*with venom*): I did not then. Oh, they're bloody liars in the naked parish where I grew a man.

PEGEEN: If they are itself, you've heard it these days, I'm thinking, and you walking the world telling out your story to young girls or old.

CHRISTY: I've told my story no place till this night, Pegeen Mike, and it's foolish I was here, maybe, to be talking free, but you're decent people, I'm thinking, and yourself a kindly woman, the way I wasn't fearing you at all.

PEGEEN (*filling a sack with straw*): You've said the like of that, maybe, in every cot and cabin where you've met a young girl on your way.

CHRISTY (*going over to her, gradually raising his voice*): I've said it nowhere till this night, I'm telling you, for I've seen none the like of you the eleven long days I am walking the world, looking over a low ditch or a high ditch on my north or my south, into stony scattered fields, or scribes of bog, where you'd see young, limber girls, and fine prancing women making laughter with the men.

PEGEEN: If you weren't destroyed travelling, you'd have as much talk and streeleen, I'm thinking, as Owen Roe O'Sullivan or the poets of the Dingle Bay, and I've heard all times it's the poets are your like, fine fiery fellows with great rages when their temper's roused.

CHRISTY (*drawing a little nearer to her*): You've a power of rings, God bless you, and would there be any offense if I was asking are you single now?

PEGEEN: What would I want wedding so young?

CHRISTY (*with relief*): We're alike, so.

PEGEEN (*she puts sack on settle and beats it up*): I never killed my father. I'd be afeard to do that, except I was the like of yourself with blind rages tearing me within, for I'm thinking you should have had great tussling when the end was come.

CHRISTY (*expanding with delight at the first confidential talk he has ever had with a woman*): We had not then. It was a hard woman was come over the hill, and if he was always a crusty kind when he'd a hard woman setting him on, not the divil himself or his four fathers could put up with him at all.

PEGEEN (*with curiosity*): And isn't it a great wonder that one wasn't fearing you?

CHRISTY (*very confidentially*): Up to the day I killed my father, there wasn't a person in Ireland knew the kind I was, and I there drinking, waking, eating, sleeping, a quiet, simple poor fellow with no man giving me heed.

PEGEEN (*getting a quilt out of the cupboard and putting it on the sack*): It was the girls were giving you heed maybe, and I'm thinking it's most conceit you'd have to be gaming with their like.

CHRISTY (*shaking his head, with simplicity*): Not the girls itself, and I won't tell you a lie. There wasn't anyone heeding me in that place saving only the dumb beasts of the field. (*He sits down at fire.*)

PEGEEN (*with disappointment*): And I thinking you should have been living the like of a king of Norway or the Eastern world. (*She comes and sits beside him after placing bread and mug of milk on the table.*)

CHRISTY (*laughing piteously*): The like of a king, is it? And I after toiling, moiling, digging, dodging from the dawn till dusk with never a sight of joy or sport saving only when I'd be abroad in the dark night poaching rabbits on hills, for I was a divil to poach, God forgive me, (*very naïvely*) and I near got six months for going with a dung fork and stabbing a fish.

PEGEEN: And it's that you'd call sport, is it, to be abroad in the darkness with yourself alone?

CHRISTY: I did, God help me, and there I'd be as happy as the sunshine of St. Martin's Day, watching the light passing the north or the patches of fog, till I'd hear a rabbit starting to screech and I'd go running in the furze. Then when I'd my full share I'd come walking down where you'd see the ducks and geese stretched sleeping on the highway of the road, and before I'd pass the dunghill, I'd hear himself snoring out, a loud lonesome snore he'd be making all times, the while he was sleeping, and he a man 'd be raging all times, the while he was waking, like a gaudy officer you'd hear cursing and damning and swearing oaths.

PEGEEN: Providence and Mercy, spare us all!

CHRISTY: It's that you'd say surely if you seen him and he after drinking for weeks, rising up in the red dawn, or before it maybe, and going out into the yard as naked as an ash tree in the moon of May, and shying clods against the visage of the stars till he'd put the fear of death into the banbhs and the screeching sows.

PEGEEN: I'd be well-nigh afeard of that lad myself, I'm thinking. And there was no one in it but the two of you alone?

CHRISTY: The divil a one, though he'd sons and daughters walking all great states and territories of the world, and not a one of them, to this day, but would say their seven curses on him, and they rousing up to let a cough or sneeze, maybe, in the deadness of the night.

PEGEEN (*nodding her head*): Well, you should have been a queer lot. I never cursed my father the like of that, though I'm twenty and more years of age.

CHRISTY: Then you'd have cursed mine, I'm telling you, and he a man never gave peace to any, saving when he'd get two months or three, or be locked in the asylums for battering peelers or assaulting men (*with depression*) the way it was a bitter life he led me till I did up a Tuesday and halve his skull.

PEGEEN (*putting her hand on his shoulder*): Well, you'll have peace in this place, Christy Mahon, and none to trouble you, and it's near time a fine lad like you should have your good share of the earth.

CHRISTY: It's time surely, and I a seemly fellow with great strength in me and bravery of . . .

(*Someone knocks.*)

CHRISTY (*clinging to* PEGEEN): Oh, glory! it's late for knocking, and this last while I'm in terror of the peelers, and the walking dead.

(*Knocking again.*)

PEGEEN: Who's there?

VOICE (*outside*): Me.

PEGEEN: Who's me?

VOICE: The Widow Quin.

PEGEEN (*jumping up and giving him the bread and milk*): Go on now with your supper, and let on to be sleepy, for if she found you were such a warrant to talk, she'd be stringing gabble till the dawn of day. (*He takes bread and sits shyly with his back to the door.*)

PEGEEN (*opening door, with temper*): What ails you, or what is it you're wanting at this hour of the night?

WIDOW QUIN (*coming in a step and peering at* CHRISTY): I'm after meeting Shawn Keogh and Father Reilly below, who told me of your curiosity man, and they fearing by this time he was maybe roaring, romping on your hands with drink.

PEGEEN (*pointing to* CHRISTY): Look now is he roaring, and he stretched away drowsy with his supper and his mug of milk. Walk down and tell that to Father Reilly and to Shaneen Keogh.

WIDOW QUINN (*coming forward*): I'll not see them again, for I've their word to lead that lad forward for to lodge with me.

PEGEEN (*in blank amazement*): This night, is it?

WIDOW QUIN (*going over*): This night. "It isn't fitting," says the priesteen, "to have his likeness lodging with an orphaned girl." (*To* CHRISTY) God save you, mister!

CHRISTY (*shyly*): God save you kindly.

WIDOW QUIN (*looking at him with half-amazed curiosity*): Well, aren't you a little smiling fellow? It should have been great and bitter torments did rouse your spirits to a deed of blood.

CHRISTY (*doubtfully*): It should, maybe.

WIDOW QUIN: It's more than "maybe" I'm saying, and it'd soften my heart to see you sitting so simple with your cup and cake, and you fitter to be saying your catechism than slaying your da.

PEGEEN (*at counter, washing glasses*): There's talking when any'd see he's fit to be holding his head high with the wonders of the world. Walk on from this, for I'll not have him tormented and he destroyed travelling since Tuesday was a week.

WIDOW QUIN (*peaceably*): We'll be walking surely when his supper's done, and you'll find we're great company, young fellow, when it's of the like of you and me you'd hear the penny poets singing in an August Fair.

CHRISTY (*innocently*): Did you kill your father?

PEGEEN (*contemptuously*): She did not. She hit himself with a worn pick, and the rusted poison did corrode his blood the way he never overed it, and died after. That was a sneaky kind of murder did win small glory with the boys itself. (*She crosses to* CHRISTY's *left.*)

WIDOW QUIN (*with good-humour*): If it didn't, maybe all knows a widow woman has buried her children and destroyed her man is a wiser comrade for a young lad than a girl, the like of you, who'd go helter-skeltering after any man would let you a wink upon the road.

PEGEEN (*breaking out into wild rage*): And you'll say that, Widow Quin, and you gasping with the rage you had racing the hill beyond to look on his face.

WIDOW QUIN (*laughing derisively*): Me, is it? Well, Father Reilly has cuteness to divide you now. (*She pulls* CHRISTY *up*) There's great temptation in a man did slay his da, and we'd best be going, young fellow; so rise up and come with me.

PEGEEN (*seizing his arm*): He'll not stir. He's pot-boy in this place, and I'll not have him stolen off and kidnabbed while himself's abroad.

WIDOW QUIN: It'd be a crazy pot-boy'd lodge him in the shebeen where he works by day, so you'd have a right to come on, young fellow, till you see my little houseen, a perch off on the rising hill.

PEGEEN: Wait till morning, Christy Mahon. Wait till you lay eyes on her leaky thatch is growing more pasture for her buck goat than her square of fields, and she without a tramp itself to keep in order her place at all.

WIDOW QUIN: When you see me contriving in my little gardens, Christy Mahon, you'll swear the Lord God formed me to be living lone, and that there isn't my match in Mayo for thatching, or mowing, or shearing a sheep.

PEGEEN (*with noisy scorn*): It's true the Lord God formed you to contrive indeed. Doesn't the world know you reared a black lamb at your own breast, so that the Lord Bishop of Connaught felt the elements of a Christian, and he eating it after in a kidney stew? Doesn't the world know you've been seen shaving the foxy skipper from France for a threepenny bit and a sop of grass tobacco would wring the liver from a mountain goat you'd meet leaping the hills?

WIDOW QUIN (*with amusement*): Do you hear her now, young fellow? Do you hear the way she'll be rating at your own self when a week is by?

PEGEEN (*to* CHRISTY): Don't heed her. Tell her to go into her pigsty and not plague us here.

WIDOW QUIN: I'm going; but he'll come with me.

PEGEEN (*shaking him*): Are you dumb, young fellow?

CHRISTY (*timidly, to* WIDOW QUIN): God increase you; but I'm pot-boy in this place, and it's here I'd liefer stay.

PEGEEN (*triumphantly*): Now you have heard him, and go on from this.

WIDOW QUIN (*looking round the room*): It's lonesome this hour crossing the hill, and if he won't come along with me, I'd have a right maybe to stop this night with yourselves. Let me stretch out on the settle, Pegeen Mike; and himself can lie by the hearth.

PEGEEN (*short and fiercely*): Faith, I won't. Quit off or I will send you now.

WIDOW QUIN (*gathering her shawl up*): Well, it's a terror to be aged a score. (*To* CHRISTY) God bless you now, young fellow, and let you be wary, or there's right torment will await you here if you go romancing with her like, and she waiting only, as they bade me say, on a sheepskin parchment to be wed with Shawn Keogh of Killakeen.

CHRISTY (*going to* PEGEEN *as she bolts the door*): What's that she's after saying?

PEGEEN: Lies and blather, you've no call to mind. Well, isn't Shawn Keogh an impudent fellow to send up spying on me? Wait till I lay hands on him. Let him wait, I'm saying.

CHRISTY: And you're not wedding him at all?

PEGEEN: I wouldn't wed him if a bishop came walking for to join us here.

CHRISTY: That God in glory may be thanked for that.

PEGEEN: There's your bed now. I've put a quilt upon you I'm after quilting a while since with my own two hands, and you'd best stretch out now for your sleep, and may God give you a good rest till I call you in the morning when the cocks will crow.

CHRISTY (*as she goes to inner room*): May God and Mary and St. Patrick bless you and reward you, for your kindly talk. (*She shuts the door behind her. He settles his bed slowly, feeling the quilt with immense satisfaction*) Well, it's a clean bed and soft with it, and it's great luck and company I've won me in the end of time—two fine women fighting for the likes of me—till I'm thinking this night wasn't I a foolish fellow not to kill my father in the years gone by.

(*The Curtain Falls.*)

# Act Two

SCENE, *as before. Brilliant morning light.* CHRISTY, *looking bright and cheerful, is cleaning a girl's boots.*

CHRISTY (*to himself, counting jugs on dresser*): Half a hundred beyond. Ten there. A score that's above. Eighty jugs. Six cups and a broken one. Two plates. A power of glasses. Bottles, a schoolmaster'd be hard set to count, and enough in them, I'm thinking, to drunken all the wealth and wisdom of the County Clare. (*He puts down the boot carefully*) There's her boots now, nice and decent for evening use, and isn't it grand brushes she has? (*He puts them down and goes by degrees to the looking-glass*) Well, this'd be a fine place to be my whole life talking out with swearing Christians, in place of my old dogs and cat, and I stalking around, smoking my pipe and drinking my fill, and never a day's work but drawing a cork an odd time, or wiping a glass, or rinsing out a shiny tumbler for a decent man. (*He takes the looking-glass from the wall and puts it on the back of a chair; then sits down in front of it and begins washing his face*) Didn't I know rightly I was handsome, though it was the divil's own mirror we had beyond, would twist a squint across an angel's brow; and I'll be growing fine from this day, the way I'll have a soft lovely skin on me and won't be the like of the clumsy young fellows do be ploughing all times in the earth and dung. (*He starts*) Is she coming again? (*He looks out*) Stranger girls. God help me, where'll I hide myself away and my long neck naked to the world? (*He looks out*) I'd best go to the room maybe till I'm dressed again. (*He gathers up his coat and the looking-glass, and runs into the inner room. The door is pushed open, and* SUSAN BRADY *looks in, and knocks on door.*)

SUSAN: There's nobody in it. (*Knocks again*)

NELLY (*pushing her in and following her, with* HONOR BLAKE *and* SARA TANSEY): It'd be early for them both to be out walking the hill.

SUSAN: I'm thinking Shawn Keogh was making game of us and there's no such man in it at all.

HONOR (*pointing to straw and quilt*): Look at that. He's been sleeping there in the night. Well, it'll be a hard case if he's gone off now, the way we'll never set eyes on a man killed his father, and we after rising early and destroying ourselves running fast on the hill.

NELLY: Are you thinking them's his boots?

SARA (*taking them up*): If they are, there should be his father's track on them. Did you never read in the papers the way murdered men do bleed and drip?

SUSAN: Is that blood there, Sara Tansey?

SARA (*smelling it*): That's bog water, I'm thinking, but it's his own they are surely, for I never seen the like of them for whity mud, and red mud, and turf on them, and the fine sands of the sea. That man's been walking, I'm telling you. (*She goes down right, putting on one of his boots.*)

SUSAN (*going to window*): Maybe he's stolen off to Belmullet with the boots of Michael James, and you'd have a right so to follow after him, Sara Tansey, and you the one yoked the ass cart and drove ten miles to set your eyes on the man bit the yellow lady's nostril on the northern shore. (*She looks out.*)

SARA (*running to window with one boot on*): Don't be talking, and we fooled to-day. (*Putting on other boot*) There's a pair do fit me well, and I'll be keeping them for walking to the priest, when you'd be ashamed this place, going up winter and summer with nothing worth while to confess at all.

HONOR (*who has been listening at the door*): Whisht! there's someone inside the room. (*She pushes door a chink open*) It's a man.

(SARA *kicks off boots and puts them where they were. They all stand in a line looking through chink.*)

SARA: I'll call him. Mister! Mister! (*He puts in his head*) Is Pegeen within?

CHRISTY (*coming in as meek as a mouse, with the looking-glass held behind his back*): She's above on the cnuceen, seeking the nanny goats, the way she'd have a sup of goat's milk for to colour my tea.

SARA: And asking your pardon, is it you's the man killed his father?

CHRISTY (*sidling toward the nail where the glass was hanging*): I am, God help me!

SARA (*taking eggs she has brought*): Then my thousand welcomes to you, and I've run up with a brace of duck's eggs for your food today. Pegeen's ducks is no use, but these are the real rich sort. Hold out your hand and you'll see it's no lie I'm telling you.

CHRISTY (*coming forward shyly, and holding out his left hand*): They're a great and weighty size.

SUSAN: And I run up with a pat of butter, for it'd be a poor thing to have you eating your spuds dry, and you after running a great way since you did destroy your da.

CHRISTY: Thank you kindly.

HONOR: And I brought you a little cut of cake, for you should have a thin stomach on you, and you that length walking the world.

NELLY: And I brought you a little laying pullet—boiled and all she is—was crushed at the fall of night by the curate's car. Feel the fat of that breast, mister.

CHRISTY: It's bursting, surely. (*He feels it with the back of his hand, in which he holds the presents.*)

SARA: Will you pinch it? Is your right hand too sacred for to use at all? (*She slips round behind him*) It's a glass he has. Well, I never seen to this day a man with a looking-glass held to his back. Them that kills their fathers is a vain lot surely.

(*Girls giggle.*)

CHRISTY (*smiling innocently and piling presents on glass*): I'm very thankful to you all today . . .

WIDOW QUIN (*coming in quickly, at door*): Sara Tansey, Susan Brady, Honor Blake! What in glory has you here at this hour of day?

GIRLS (*giggling*): That's the man killed his father.

WIDOW QUIN (*coming to them*): I know well it's the man; and I'm after putting him down in the sports below for racing, leaping, pitching, and the Lord knows what.

SARA (*exuberantly*): That's right, Widow Quin. I'll bet my dowry that he'll lick the world.

WIDOW QUIN: If you will, you'd have a right to have him fresh and nourished in place of nursing a feast. (*Taking presents*) Are you fasting or fed, young fellow?

CHRISTY: Fasting, if you please.

WIDOW QUIN (*loudly*): Well, you're the lot. Stir up now and give him his breakfast. (*To* CHRISTY) Come here to me (*she puts him on bench beside her while the girls make tea and get his breakfast*) and let you tell us your story before Pegeen will come, in place of grinning your ears off like the moon of May.

CHRISTY (*beginning to be pleased*): It's a long story; you'd be destroyed listening.

WIDOW QUIN: Don't be letting on to be shy, a fine, gamey, treacherous lad the like of you. Was it in your house beyond you cracked his skull?

CHRISTY (*shy but flattered*): It was not. We were digging spuds in his cold, sloping, stony, divil's patch of a field.

WIDOW QUIN: And you went asking money of him, or making talk of getting a wife would drive him from his farm?

CHRISTY: I did not, then; but there I was, digging and digging, and "You squinting idiot," says he, "let you walk down now and tell the priest you'll wed the Widow Casey in a score of days."

WIDOW QUIN: And what kind was she?

CHRISTY (*with horror*): A walking terror from beyond the hills, and she two score and five years, and two hundredweights and five pounds in the weighing scales, with a limping leg on her, and a blinded eye, and she a woman of noted misbehavior with the old and young.

GIRLS (*clustering round him, serving him*): Glory be.

WIDOW QUIN: And what did he want driving you to wed with her? (*She takes a bit of the chicken.*)

CHRISTY (*eating with growing satisfaction*): He was letting on I was wanting a protector from the harshness of the world, and he without a thought the whole while but how he'd have her hut to live in and her gold to drink.

WIDOW QUIN: There's maybe worse than a dry hearth and a widow woman and your glass at night. So you hit him then?

CHRISTY (*getting almost excited*): I did not. "I won't wed her," says I, "when all know she did suckle me for six weeks when I came into the world, and she a hag this day with a tongue on her has the crows and seabirds scattered, the way they would cast a shadow on her garden with the dread of her curse."

WIDOW QUIN (*teasingly*): That one should be right company.

SARA (*eagerly*): Don't mind her. Did you kill him then?

CHRISTY: "She's too good for the like of you," says he, "and go on now or I'll flatten you out like a crawling beast has passed under a dray." "You will not if I can help it," says I. "Go on," says he, "or I'll have the divil making garters of your limbs tonight." "You will not if I can help it," says I. (*He sits up, brandishing his mug.*)

SARA: You were right surely.

CHRISTY (*impressively*): With that the sun came out between the cloud and the hill, and it shining green in my face. "God have mercy on your soul," says he, lifting a scythe; "or on your own," says I, raising the loy.

SUSAN: That's a grand story.

HONOR: He tells it lovely.

CHRISTY (*flattered and confident, waving bone*): He gave a drive with the scythe, and I gave a lep to the east. Then I turned around with my back to the north, and I hit a blow on the ridge of his skull, laid him stretched out, and he split to the knob of his gullet. (*He raises the chicken bone to his Adam's apple.*)

GIRLS (*together*): Well, you're a marvel! Oh, God bless you! You're the lad surely!

SUSAN: I'm thinking the Lord God sent him this road to make a second husband to the Widow Quin, and she with a great yearning to be wedded, though all dread her here. Lift him on her knee, Sara Tansey.

WIDOW QUIN: Don't tease him.

SARA (*going over to dresser and counter very quickly, and getting two glasses and porter*): You're heroes surely, and let you drink a supeen with your arms linked like the outlandish lovers in the sailor's song. (*She links their arms and gives them the glasses*) There now. Drink a health to the wonders of the western world, the pirates, preachers, poteen-makers, with the jobbing jockies; parching peelers, and the juries fill their stomachs selling judgments of the English law. (*Brandishing the bottle.*)

WIDOW QUIN: That's a right toast, Sara Tansey. Now, Christy.

(*They drink with their arms linked, he drinking with his left hand, she with her right. As they are drinking,* PEGEEN MIKE *comes in with a milk can and stands aghast. They all spring away from* CHRISTY. *He goes down left.* WIDOW QUIN *remains seated.*)

PEGEEN (*angrily, to* SARA): What is it you're wanting?

SARA (*twisting her apron*): An ounce of tobacco.

PEGEEN: Have you tuppence?

SARA: I've forgotten my purse.

PEGEEN: Then you'd best be getting it and not fooling us here. (*To the* WIDOW QUIN, *with more elaborate scorn*) And what is it you're wanting, Widow Quin?

WIDOW QUIN (*insolently*): A penn'orth of starch.

PEGEEN (*breaking out*): And you without a white shift or a shirt in your whole family since the drying of the flood. I've no starch for the like of you, and let you walk on now to Killamuck.

WIDOW QUIN (*turning to* CHRISTY, *as she goes out with the girls*): Well, you're mighty huffy this day, Pegeen Mike, and, you young fellow, let you not forget the sports and racing when the noon is by.

(*They go out.*)

PEGEEN (*imperiously*): Fling out that rubbish and put them cups away. (CHRISTY *tidies away in great haste*) Shove in the bench by the wall. (*He does so*) And hang that glass on the nail. What disturbed it at all?

CHRISTY (*very meekly*): I was making myself decent only, and this a fine country for young lovely girls.

PEGEEN (*sharply*): Whisht your talking of girls. (*Goes to counter —right.*)

CHRISTY: Wouldn't any wish to be decent in a place . . .

PEGEEN: Whisht I'm saying.

CHRISTY (*looks at her face for a moment with great misgivings, then as a last effort, takes up a loy, and goes towards her, with feigned assurance*): It was with a loy the like of that I killed my father.

PEGEEN (*still sharply*): You've told me that story six times since the dawn of day.

CHRISTY (*reproachfully*): It's a queer thing you wouldn't care to be hearing it and them girls after walking four miles to be listening to me now.

PEGEEN (*turning around astonished*): Four miles.

CHRISTY (*apologetically*): Didn't himself say there were only four bona fides living in the place?

PEGEEN: It's bona fides by the road they are, but that lot came over the river lepping the stones. It's not three perches when you go like that, and I was down this morning looking on the papers the postboy does have in his bag. (*With meaning and emphasis*) For there was great news this day, Christopher Mahon. (*She goes into room left.*)

CHRISTY (*suspiciously*): Is it news of my murder?

PEGEEN (*inside*): Murder, indeed.

CHRISTY (*loudly*): A murdered da?

PEGEEN (*coming in again and crossing right*): There was not, but a story filled half a page of the hanging of a man. Ah, that should be a fearful end, young fellow, and it worst of all for a man who destroyed his da, for the like of him would get small mercies, and when it's dead he is, they'd put him in a narrow grave, with cheap sacking wrapping him round, and pour down quicklime on his head, the way you'd see a woman pouring any frish-frash from a cup.

CHRISTY (*very miserably*): Oh, God help me. Are you thinking I'm safe? You were saying at the fall of night, I was shut of jeopardy and I here with yourselves.

PEGEEN (*severely*): You'll be shut of jeopardy in no place if you go talking with a pack of wild girls the like of them do be walking abroad with the peelers, talking whispers at the fall of night.

CHRISTY (*with terror*): And you're thinking they'd tell?

PEGEEN (*with mock sympathy*): Who knows, God help you.

CHRISTY (*loudly*): What joy would they have to bring hanging to the likes of me?

PEGEEN: It's queer joys they have, and who knows the thing they'd do, if it'd make the green stones cry itself to think of you swaying and swiggling at the butt of a rope, and you with a fine, stout neck, God bless you! the way you'd be a half an hour, in great anguish, getting your death.

CHRISTY (*getting his boots and putting them on*): If there's that terror of them, it'd be best, maybe, I went on wandering like Esau or Cain and Abel on the other sides of Neifin or the Erris plain.

PEGEEN (*beginning to play with him*): It would, maybe, for I've heard the Circuit Judges this place is a heartless crew.

CHRISTY (*bitterly*): It's more than Judges this place is a heartless crew. (*Looking up at her*) And isn't it a poor thing to be starting again and I a lonesome fellow will be looking out on women and girls the way the needy fallen spirits do be looking on the Lord?

PEGEEN: What call have you to be that lonesome when there's poor girls walking Mayo in their thousands now?

CHRISTY (*grimly*): It's well you know what call I have. It's well you know it's a lonesome thing to be passing small towns with the lights shining sideways when the night is down, or going in strange places with a dog noising before you and a dog noising behind, or drawn to the cities where you'd hear a voice kissing and talking deep love in every shadow of the ditch, and you passing on with an empty, hungry stomach failing from your heart.

PEGEEN: I'm thinking you're an odd man, Christy Mahon. The oddest walking fellow I ever set my eyes on to this hour today.

CHRISTY: What would any be but odd men and they living lonesome in the world?

PEGEEN: I'm not odd, and I'm my whole life with my father only.

CHRISTY (*with infinite admiration*): How would a lovely handsome woman the like of you be lonesome when all men should be thronging around to hear the sweetness of your voice, and the little infant children should be pestering your steps I'm thinking, and you walking the roads.

PEGEEN: I'm hard set to know what way a coaxing fellow the like of yourself should be lonesome either.

CHRISTY: Coaxing?

PEGEEN: Would you have me think a man never talked with the girls would have the words you've spoken today? It's only letting on you are to be lonesome, the way you'd get around me now.

CHRISTY: I wish to God I was letting on; but I was lonesome all times, and born lonesome, I'm thinking, as the moon of dawn. (*Going to door.*)

PEGEEN (*puzzled by his talk*): Well, it's a story I'm not understanding at all why you'd be worse than another, Christy Mahon, and you a fine lad with the great savagery to destroy your da.

CHRISTY: It's little I'm understanding myself, saving only that my heart's scalded this day, and I am going off stretching out the earth between us, the way I'll not be walking near you another dawn of the year till the two of us do arise to hope or judgment with the saints of God, and now I'd best be going with my wattle in my hand, for hanging is a poor thing (*turning to go*), and it's little welcome only is left me in this house today.

PEGEEN (*sharply*): Christy! (*He turns round*) Come here to me. (*He goes towards her*) Lay down that switch and throw some sods on the fire. You're pot-boy in this place, and I'll not have you mitch off from us now.

CHRISTY: You were saying I'd be hanged if I stay.

PEGEEN (*quite kindly at last*): I'm after going down and reading the fearful crimes of Ireland for two weeks or three, and there wasn't a word of your murder. (*Getting up and going over to the counter*) They've likely not found the body. You're safe so with ourselves.

CHRISTY (*astonished, slowly*): It's making game of me you were (*following her with fearful joy*), and I can stay so, working at your side, and I not lonesome from this mortal day.

PEGEEN: What's to hinder you from staying, except the widow woman or the young girls would inveigle you off?

CHRISTY (*with rapture*): And I'll have your words from this day filling my ears, and that look is come upon you meeting my two eyes, and I watching you loafing around in the warm sun, or rinsing your ankles when the night is come.

PEGEEN (*kindly, but a little embarrassed*): I'm thinking you'll be a loyal young lad to have working around, and if you vexed me a while since with your leaguing with the girls, I wouldn't give a thraneen for a lad hadn't a mighty spirit in him and a gamey heart.

(SHAWN KEOGH *runs in carrying a cleeve on his back, followed by the* WIDOW QUIN.)

SHAWN (*to* PEGEEN): I was passing below, and I seen your mountainy sheep eating cabbages in Jimmy's field. Run up or they'll be bursting surely.

PEGEEN: Oh, God mend them! (*She puts a shawl over her head and runs out.*)

CHRISTY (*looking from one to the other. Still in high spirits*): I'd best go to her aid maybe. I'm handy with ewes.

WIDOW QUIN (*closing the door*): She can do that much, and there is Shaneen has long speeches for to tell you now. (*She sits down with an amused smile.*)

SHAWN (*taking something from his pocket and offering it to* CHRISTY): Do you see that, mister?

CHRISTY (*looking at it*): The half of a ticket to the Western States!

SHAWN (*trembling with anxiety*): I'll give it to you and my new hat (*pulling it out of hamper*); and my breeches with the double seat (*pulling it off*); and my new coat is woven from the blackest shearings for three miles around (*giving him the coat*); I'll give you the whole of them, and my blessing, and the blessing of Father Reilly itself, maybe, if you'll quit from this and leave us in the peace we had till last night at the fall of dark.

CHRISTY (*with a new arrogance*): And for what is it you're wanting to get shut of me?

SHAWN (*looking to the* WIDOW *for help*): I'm a poor scholar with middling faculties to coin a lie, so I'll tell you the truth, Christy Mahon. I'm wedding with Pegeen beyond, and I don't think well of having a clever fearless man the like of you dwelling in her house.

CHRISTY (*almost pugnaciously*): And you'd be using bribery for to banish me?

SHAWN (*in an imploring voice*): Let you not take it badly, mister honey, isn't beyond the best place for you where you'll have golden chains and shiny coats and you riding upon hunters with the ladies of the land. (*He makes an eager sign to the* WIDOW QUIN *to come to help him.*)

WIDOW QUIN (*coming over*): It's true for him, and you'd best quit off and not have that poor girl setting her mind on you, for there's Shaneen thinks she wouldn't suit you though all is saying that she'll wed you now.

(CHRISTY *beams with delight.*)

SHAWN (*in terrified earnest*): She wouldn't suit you, and she with the divil's own temper the way you'd be strangling one another in a score of days. (*He makes the movement of strangling with his hands*) It's the like of me only that she's fit for, a quiet simple fellow wouldn't raise a hand upon her if she scratched itself.

WIDOW QUIN (*putting* SHAWN's *hat on* CHRISTY): Fit them clothes on you anyhow, young fellow, and he'd maybe loan them to you for the sports. (*Pushing him towards inner door*) Fit them on and you can give your answer when you have them tried.

CHRISTY (*beaming, delighted with the clothes*): I will then. I'd like herself to see me in them tweeds and hat. (*He goes into room and shuts the door.*)

SHAWN (*in great anxiety*): He'd like herself to see them. He'll not leave us, Widow Quin. He's a score of divils in him the way it's well nigh certain he will wed Pegeen.

WIDOW QUIN (*jeeringly*): It's true all girls are fond of courage and do hate the like of you.

SHAWN (*walking about in desperation*): Oh, Widow Quin, what'll I be doing now? I'd inform again him, but he'd burst from Kilmainham and he'd be sure and certain to destroy me. If I wasn't so God-fearing, I'd near have courage to come behind him and run a pike into his side. Oh, it's a hard case to be an orphan and not to have your father that you're used to, and you'd easy kill and make yourself a hero in the sight of all. (*Coming up to her*) Oh, Widow Quin, will you find me some contrivance when I've promised you a ewe?

WIDOW QUIN: A ewe's a small thing, but what would you give me if I did wed him and did save you so?

SHAWN (*with astonishment*): You?

WIDOW QUIN: Aye. Would you give me the red cow you have and the mountainy ram, and the right of way across your rye path, and a load of dung at Michaelmas, and turbary upon the western hill?

SHAWN (*radiant with hope*): I would surely, and I'd give you the wedding-ring I have, and the loan of a new suit, the way you'd have him decent on the wedding-day. I'd give you two kids for your dinner, and a gallon of poteen, and I'd call the piper on the long car to your wedding from Crossmolina or from Ballina. I'd give you . . .

WIDOW QUIN: That'll do so, and let you whisht, for he's coming now again.

(CHRISTY *comes in very natty in the new clothes.* WIDOW QUIN *goes to him admiringly.*)

WIDOW QUIN: If you seen yourself now, I'm thinking you'd be too proud to speak to us at all, and it'd be a pity surely to have your like sailing from Mayo to the Western World.

CHRISTY (*as proud as a peacock*): I'm not going. If this is a poor place itself, I'll make myself contented to be lodging here.

(WIDOW QUIN *makes a sign to* SHAWN *to leave them.*)

SHAWN: Well, I'm going measuring the race-course while the tide is low, so I'll leave you the garments and my blessing for the sports today. God bless you! (*He wriggles out.*)

WIDOW QUIN (*admiring* CHRISTY): Well, you're mighty spruce, young fellow. Sit down now while you're quiet till you talk with me.

CHRISTY (*swaggering*): I'm going abroad on the hillside for to seek Pegeen.

WIDOW QUIN: You'll have time and plenty for to seek Pegeen, and you heard me saying at the fall of night the two of us should be great company.

CHRISTY: From this out I'll have no want of company when all sorts is bringing me their food and clothing (*he swaggers to the door, tightening his belt*), the way they'd set their eyes upon a gallant orphan cleft his father with one blow to the breeches belt. (*He opens door, then staggers back*) Saints of glory! Holy angels from the throne of light!

WIDOW QUIN (*going over*): What ails you?

CHRISTY: It's the walking spirit of my murdered da?

WIDOW QUIN (*looking out*): Is it that tramper?

CHRISTY (*wildly*): Where'll I hide my poor body from that ghost of hell?

(*The door is pushed open, and old* MAHON *appears on threshold.* CHRISTY *darts in behind door.*)

WIDOW QUIN (*in great amusement*): God save you, my poor man.

MAHON (*gruffly*): Did you see a young lad passing this way in the early morning or the fall of night?

WIDOW QUIN: You're a queer kind to walk in not saluting at all.

MAHON: Did you see the young lad?

WIDOW QUIN (*stiffly*): What kind was he?

MAHON: An ugly young streeler with a murderous gob on him, and a little switch in his hand. I met a tramper seen him coming this way at the fall of night.

WIDOW QUIN: There's harvest hundreds do be passing these days for the Sligo boat. For what is it you're wanting him, my poor man?

MAHON: I want to destroy him for breaking the head on me with the clout of a loy. (*He takes off a big hat, and shows his head in a mass of bandages and plaster, with some pride*) It was he did that, and amn't I a great wonder to think I've traced him ten days with that rent in my crown?

WIDOW QUIN (*taking his head in both hands and examining it with extreme delight*): That was a great blow. And who hit you? A robber maybe?

MAHON: It was my own son hit me, and he the divil a robber, or anything else, but a dirty, stuttering lout.

WIDOW QUIN (*letting go his skull and wiping her hands in her apron*): You'd best be wary of a mortified scalp, I think they call it, lepping around with that wound in the splendour of the sun. It was a bad blow surely, and you should have vexed him fearful to make him strike that gash in his da.

MAHON: Is it me?

WIDOW QUIN (*amusing herself*): Aye. And isn't it a great shame when the old and hardened do torment the young?

MAHON (*raging*): Torment him is it? And I after holding out with the patience of a martyred saint till there's nothing but destruction on, and I'm driven out in my old age with none to aid me.

WIDOW QUIN (*greatly amused*): It's a sacred wonder the way that wickedness will spoil a man.

MAHON: My wickedness, is it? Amn't I after saying it is himself has me destroyed, and he a liar on walls, a talker of folly, a man you'd see stretched the half of the day in the brown ferns with his belly to the sun.

WIDOW QUIN: Not working at all?

MAHON: The divil a work, or if he did itself, you'd see him raising up a haystack like the stalk of a rush, or driving our last cow till he broke her leg at the hip, and when he wasn't at that he'd be fooling over little birds he had—finches and felts—or making mugs at his own self in the bit of a glass we had hung on the wall.

WIDOW QUIN (*looking at* CHRISTY): What way was he so foolish? It was running wild after the girls maybe?

MAHON (*with a shout of derision*): Running wild, is it? If he seen a red petticoat coming swinging over the hill, he'd be off to hide in the sticks, and you'd see him shooting out his sheep's eyes between the little twigs and the leaves, and his two ears rising like a hare looking out through a gap. Girls, indeed!

WIDOW QUIN: It was drink maybe?

MAHON: And he a poor fellow would get drunk on the smell of a pint. He'd a queer rotten stomach, I'm telling you, and when I gave him three pulls from my pipe a while since, he was taken with contortions till I had to send him in the ass cart to the females' nurse.

WIDOW QUIN (*clasping her hands*): Well, I never till this day heard tell of a man the like of that!

MAHON: I'd take a mighty oath you didn't surely, and wasn't he the laughing joke of every female woman where four baronies meet, the way the girls would stop their weeding if they seen him coming the road to let a roar at him, and call him the looney of Mahon's.

WIDOW QUIN: I'd give the world and all to see the like of him. What kind was he?

MAHON: A small low fellow.

WIDOW QUIN: And dark?

MAHON: Dark and dirty.

WIDOW QUIN (*considering*): I'm thinking I seen him.

MAHON (*eagerly*): An ugly young blackguard.

WIDOW QUIN: A hideous, fearful villain, and the spit of you.

MAHON: What way is he fled?

WIDOW QUIN: Gone over the hills to catch a coasting steamer to the north or south.

MAHON: Could I pull up on him now?

WIDOW QUIN: If you'll cross the sands below where the tide is out, you'll be in it as soon as himself, for he had to go round ten miles by the top of the bay. (*She points to the door*) Strike down by the head beyond and then follow on the roadway to the north and east.

(MAHON *goes abruptly*.)

WIDOW QUIN (*shouting after him*): Let you give him a good vengeance when you come up with him, but don't put yourself in the power of the law, for it'd be a poor thing to see a judge in his black cap reading out his sentence on a civil warrior the like of you. (*She swings the door to and looks at* CHRISTY, *who is cowering in terror, for a moment, then she bursts into a laugh.*)

WIDOW QUIN: Well, you're the walking Playboy of the Western World, and that's the poor man you had divided to his breeches belt.

CHRISTY (*looking out: then, to her*): What'll Pegeen say when she hears that story? What'll she be saying to me now?

WIDOW QUIN: She'll knock the head of you, I'm thinking, and drive you from the door. God help her to be taking you for a wonder, and you a little schemer making up the story you destroyed your da.

CHRISTY (*turning to the door, nearly speechless with rage, half to himself*): To be letting on he was dead, and coming back to his life, and following after me like an old weasel tracing a rat, and coming in here laying desolation between my own self and the fine women of Ireland, and he a kind of carcase that you'd fling upon the sea . . .

WIDOW QUIN (*more soberly*): There's talking for a man's one only son.

CHRISTY (*breaking out*): His one son, is it? May I meet him with one tooth and it aching, and one eye to be seeing seven and seventy divils in the twists of the road, and one old timber leg on him to limp into the scalding grave. (*Looking out*) There he is now crossing the strands, and that the Lord God would send a high wave to wash him from the world.

WIDOW QUIN (*scandalized*): Have you no shame? (*Putting her hand on his shoulder and turning him round*) What ails you? Near crying, is it?

CHRISTY (*in despair and grief*): Amn't I after seeing the lovelight of the star of knowledge shining from her brow, and hearing words would put you thinking on the holy Brigid speaking to the infant saints, and now she'll be turning again, and speaking hard words to me, like an old woman with a spavindy ass she'd have, urging on a hill.

WIDOW QUIN: There's poetry talk for a girl you'd see itching and scratching, and she with a stale stink of poteen on her from selling in the shop.

CHRISTY (*impatiently*): It's her like is fitted to be handling merchandise in the heavens above, and what'll I be doing now, I ask you, and I a kind of wonder was jilted by the heavens when a day was by.

(*There is a distant noise of girls' voices.* WIDOW QUIN *looks from window and comes to him, hurriedly.*)

WIDOW QUIN: You'll be doing like myself, I'm thinking, when I did destroy my man, for I'm above many's the day, odd times in great spirits, abroad in the sunshine, darning a stocking or stitching a shift; and odd times again looking out on the schooners, hookers, trawlers is sailing the sea, and I thinking on the gallant hairy fellows are drifting beyond, and myself long years living alone.

CHRISTY (*interested*): You're like me, so.

WIDOW QUIN: I am your like, and it's for that I'm taking a fancy to you, and I with my little houseen above where there'd be myself to tend you, and none to ask were you a murderer or what at all.

CHRISTY: And what would I be doing if I left Pegeen?

WIDOW QUIN: I've nice jobs you could be doing, gathering shells to make a whitewash for our hut within, building up a little goosehouse, or stretching a new skin on an old curragh I have, and if my hut is far from all sides, it's there you'll meet the wisest old men, I tell you, at the corner of my wheel, and it's there yourself and me will have great times whispering and hugging. . . .

VOICES (*outside, calling far away*): Christy! Christy Mahon! Christy!

CHRISTY: Is it Pegeen Mike?

WIDOW QUIN: It's the young girls, I'm thinking, coming to bring you to the sports below, and what is it you'll have me to tell them now?

CHRISTY: Aid me for to win Pegeen. It's herself only that I'm seeking now. (WIDOW QUIN *gets up and goes to window*) Aid me for to win her, and I'll be asking God to stretch a hand to you in the hour of death, and lead you short cuts through the Meadows of Ease, and up the floor of Heaven to the Footstool of the Virgin's Son.

WIDOW QUIN: There's praying.

VOICES (*nearer*): Christy! Christy Mahon!

CHRISTY (*with agitation*): They're coming. Will you swear to aid and save me for the love of Christ?

WIDOW QUIN (*looks at him for a moment*): If I aid you, will you swear to give me a right of way I want, and a mountainy ram, and a load of dung at Michaelmas, the time that you'll be master here?

CHRISTY: I will, by the elements and stars of night.

WIDOW QUIN: Then we'll not say a word of the old fellow, the way Pegeen won't know your story till the end of time.

CHRISTY: And if he chances to return again?

WIDOW QUIN: We'll swear he's a maniac and not your da. I could take an oath I seen him raving on the sands today.

(*Girls run in.*)

SUSAN: Come on to the sports below. Pegeen says you're to come.

SARA TANSEY: The lepping's beginning, and we've a jockey's suit to fit upon you for the mule race on the sands below.

HONOR: Come on, will you?

CHRISTY: I will then if Pegeen's beyond.

SARA TANSEY: She's in the boreen making game of Shaneen Keogh.

CHRISTY: Then I'll be going to her now. (*He runs out followed by the girls.*)

WIDOW QUIN: Well, if the worst comes in the end of all, it'll be great game to see there's none to pity him but a widow woman, the like of me, has buried her children and destroyed her man. (*She goes out.*)

(*The Curtain Falls.*)

# Act Three

SCENE, *as before. Later in the day.* JIMMY *comes in, slightly drunk.*

JIMMY (*calls*): Pegeen! (*Crosses to inner door*) Pegeen Mike! (*Comes back again into the room*) Pegeen! (PHILLY *comes in in the same state*) (*To* PHILLY) Did you see herself?

PHILLY: I did not; but I sent Shawn Keogh with the ass cart for to bear him home. (*Trying cupboards which are locked*) Well, isn't he a nasty man to get into such staggers at a morning wake? and isn't herself the divil's daughter for locking, and she so fussy after that young gaffer, you might take your death with drought and none to heed you?

JIMMY: It's little wonder she'd be fussy, and he after bringing bankrupt ruin on the roulette man, and the trick-o'-the-loop man, and breaking the nose of the cockshot-man, and winning all in the sports below, racing, lepping, dancing, and the Lord knows what! He's right luck, I'm telling you.

PHILLY: If he has, he'll be rightly hobbled yet, and he not able to say ten words without making a brag of the way he killed his father, and the great blow he hit with the loy.

JIMMY: A man can't hang by his own informing, and his father should be rotten by now.

(OLD MAHON *passes window slowly.*)

PHILLY: Supposing a man's digging spuds in that field with a long spade, and supposing he flings up the two halves of that skull, what'll be said then in the papers and the courts of law?

JIMMY: They'd say it was an old Dane, maybe, was drowned in the flood. (OLD MAHON *comes in and sits down near door listening*) Did you never hear tell of the skulls they have in the city of Dublin, ranged out like blue jugs in a cabin of Connaught?

PHILLY: And you believe that?

JIMMY (*pugnaciously*): Didn't a lad see them and he after coming from harvesting in the Liverpool boat? "They have them there," says he, "making a show of the great people there was one time walking the world. White skulls and black skulls and yellow skulls, and some with full teeth, and some haven't only but one."

PHILLY: It was no lie, maybe, for when I was a young lad there was a graveyard beyond the house with the remnants of a man who had thighs as long as your arm. He was a horrid man, I'm telling you, and there was many a fine Sunday I'd put him together for fun, and he with shiny bones, you wouldn't meet the like of these days in the cities of the world.

MAHON (*getting up*): You wouldn't, is it? Lay your eyes on that skull, and tell me where and when there was another the like of it, is splintered only from the blow of a loy.

PHILLY: Glory be to God! And who hit you at all?

MAHON (*triumphantly*): It was my own son hit me. Would you believe that?

JIMMY: Well, there's wonders hidden in the heart of man!

PHILLY (*suspiciously*): And what way was it done?

MAHON (*wandering about the room*): I'm after walking hundreds and long scores of miles, winning clean beds and the fill of my belly four times in the day, and I doing nothing but telling stories of that naked truth. (*He comes to them a little aggressively*) Give me a supeen and I'll tell you now.

(WIDOW QUIN *comes in and stands aghast behind him. He is facing* JIMMY *and* PHILLY, *who are on the left.*)

JIMMY: Ask herself beyond. She's the stuff hidden in her shawl.

WIDOW QUIN (*coming to* MAHON *quickly*): You here, is it? You didn't go far at all?

MAHON: I seen the coasting steamer passing, and I got a drought upon me and a cramping leg, so I said, "The divil go along with him," and turned again. (*Looking under her shawl*) And let you give me a supeen, for I'm destroyed travelling since Tuesday was a week.

WIDOW QUIN (*getting a glass, in a cajoling tone*): Sit down then by the fire and take your ease for a space. You've a right to be destroyed indeed, with your walking, and fighting, and facing the sun. (*Giving him poteen from a stone jar she has brought in*) There now is a drink for you, and may it be to your happiness and length of life.

MAHON (*taking glass greedily and sitting down by fire*): God increase you!

WIDOW QUIN (*taking men to the right stealthily*): Do you know what? That man's raving from his wound today, for I met him a while since telling a rambling tale of a tinker had him destroyed. Then he heard of Christy's deed, and he up and says it was his son had cracked his skull. O isn't madness a fright, for he'll go killing someone yet, and he thinking it's the man has struck him so?

JIMMY (*entirely convinced*): It's a fright, surely. I knew a party was kicked in the head by a red mare, and he went killing horses a great while, till he eat the insides of a clock and died after.

PHILLY (*with suspicion*): Did he see Christy?

WIDOW QUIN: He didn't. (*With a warning gesture*) Let you not be putting him in mind of him, or you'll be likely summoned if there's murder done. (*Looking round at* MAHON) Whisht! He's listening. Wait now till you hear me taking him easy and unravelling all. (*She goes to* MAHON) And what way are you feeling, mister? Are you in contentment now?

MAHON (*slightly emotional from his drink*): I'm poorly only, for it's a hard story the way I'm left today, when it was I did tend him from his hour of birth, and he a dunce never reached his second book, the way he'd come from school, many's the day, with his legs lamed under him, and he blackened with his beatings like a tinker's ass. It's a hard story, I'm saying, the way some do have their next and nighest raising up a hand of murder on them, and some is lonesome getting their death with lamentation in the dead of night.

WIDOW QUIN (*not knowing what to say*): To hear you talking so quiet, who'd know you were the same fellow we seen pass today?

MAHON: I'm the same surely. The wrack and ruin of three score years; and it's a terror to live that length, I tell you, and to have your sons going to the dogs against you, and you wore out scolding them, and skelping them, and God knows what.

PHILLY (*to* JIMMY): He's not raving. (*To* WIDOW QUIN) Will you ask him what kind was his son?

WIDOW QUIN (*to* MAHON, *with a peculiar look*): Was your son that hit you a lad of one year and a score maybe, a great hand at racing and lepping and licking the world?

MAHON (*turning on her with a roar of rage*): Didn't you hear me say he was the fool of men, the way from this out he'll know the orphan's lot with old and young making game of him and they swearing, raging, kicking at him like a mangy cur.

(*A great burst of cheering outside, some way off.*)

MAHON (*putting his hands to his ears*): What in the name of God do they want roaring below?

WIDOW QUIN (*with the shade of a smile*): They're cheering a young lad, the champion Playboy of the Western World.

(*More cheering.*)

MAHON (*going to window*): It'd split my heart to hear them, and I with pulses in my brain-pan for a week gone by. Is it racing they are?

JIMMY (*looking from door*): It is then. They are mounting him for the mule race will be run upon the sands. That's the playboy on the winkered mule.

MAHON (*puzzled*): That lad, is it? If you said it was a fool he was, I'd have laid a mighty oath he was the likeness of my wandering son. (*Uneasily, putting his hand to his head*) Faith, I'm thinking I'll go walking for to view the race.

WIDOW QUIN (*stopping him, sharply*): You will not. You'd best take the road to Belmullet, and not be dilly-dallying in this place where there isn't a spot you could sleep.

PHILLY (*coming forward*): Don't mind her. Mount there on the bench and you'll have a view of the whole. They're hurrying before the tide will rise, and it'd be near over if you went down the pathway through the crags below.

MAHON (*mounts on bench,* WIDOW QUIN *beside him*): That's a right view again the edge of the sea. They're coming now from the point. He's leading. Who is he at all?

WIDOW QUIN: He's the champion of the world, I tell you, and there isn't a hop'orth isn't falling lucky to his hands today.

PHILLY (*looking out, interested in the race*): Look at that. They're pressing him now.

JIMMY: He'll win it yet.

PHILLY: Take your time, Jimmy Farrell. It's too soon to say.

WIDOW QUIN (*shouting*): Watch him taking the gate. There's riding.

JIMMY (*cheering*): More power to the young lad!

MAHON: He's passing the third.

JIMMY: He'll lick them yet!

WIDOW QUIN: He'd lick them if he was running races with a score itself.

MAHON: Look at the mule he has, kicking the stars.

WIDOW QUIN: There was a lep! (*Catching hold of* MAHON *in her excitement*) He's fallen! He's mounted again! Faith, he's passing them all!

JIMMY: Look at him skelping her!

PHILLY: And the mountain girls hooshing him on!

JIMMY: It's the last turn! The post's cleared for them now!

MAHON: Look at the narrow place. He'll be into the bogs! (*With a yell*) Good rider! He's through it again!

JIMMY: He's neck and neck!

MAHON: Good boy to him! Flames, but he's in!

(*Great cheering, in which all join.*)

MAHON (*with hesitation*): What's that? They're raising him up. They're coming this way. (*With a roar of rage and astonishment*)

It's Christy! by the stars of God! I'd know his way of spitting and he astride the moon.

(*He jumps down and makes for the door, but* WIDOW QUIN *catches him and pulls him back.*)

WIDOW QUIN: Stay quiet, will you? That's not your son. (*To* JIMMY) Stop him, or you'll get a month for the abetting of manslaughter and be fined as well.

JIMMY: I'll hold him.

MAHON (*struggling*): Let me out! Let me out, the lot of you! till I have my vengeance on his head today.

WIDOW QUIN (*shaking him, vehemently*): That's not your son. That's a man is going to make a marriage with the daughter of this house, a place with fine trade, with a license, and with poteen too.

MAHON (*amazed*): That man marrying a decent and a moneyed girl! Is it mad yous are? Is it in a crazy-house for females that I'm landed now?

WIDOW QUIN: It's mad yourself is with the blow upon your head. That lad is the wonder of the Western World.

MAHON: I seen it's my son.

WIDOW QUIN: You seen that you're mad. (*Cheering outside*) Do you hear them cheering him in the zig-zags of the road? Aren't you after saying that your son's a fool, and how would they be cheering a true idiot born?

MAHON (*getting distressed*): It's maybe out of reason that that man's himself. (*Cheering again*) There's none surely will go cheering him. Oh, I'm raving with a madness that would fright the world! (*He sits down with his hand to his head*) There was one time I seen ten scarlet divils letting on they'd cork my spirit in a gallon can; and one time I seen rats as big as badgers sucking the life blood from the butt of my lug; but I never till this day confused that dribbling idiot with a likely man. I'm destroyed surely.

WIDOW QUIN: And who'd wonder when it's your brain-pan that is gaping now?

MAHON: Then the blight of the sacred drought upon myself and him, for I never went mad to this day, and I not three weeks with the Limerick girls drinking myself silly, and parlatic from the dusk to dawn. (*To* WIDOW QUIN, *suddenly*) Is my visage astray?

WIDOW QUIN: It is then. You're a sniggering maniac, a child could see.

MAHON (*getting up more cheerfully*): Then I'd best be going to the union beyond, and there'll be a welcome before me, I tell you (*with great pride*), and I a terrible and fearful case, the way that there I was one time, screeching in a straitened waistcoat, with seven doctors writing out my sayings in a printed book. Would you believe that?

WIDOW QUIN: If you're a wonder itself, you'd best be hasty, for them lads caught a maniac one time and pelted the poor creature till he ran out, raving and foaming, and was drowned in the sea.

MAHON (*with philosophy*): It's true mankind is the divil when your head's astray. Let me out now and I'll slip down the boreen, and not see them so.

WIDOW QUIN (*showing him out*): That's it. Run to the right, and not a one will see.

(*He runs off.*)

PHILLY (*wisely*): You're at some gaming, Widow Quin; but I'll walk after him and give him his dinner and a time to rest, and I'll see then if he's raving or as sane as you.

WIDOW QUIN (*annoyed*): If you go near that lad, let you be wary of your head, I'm saying. Didn't you hear him telling he was crazed at times?

PHILLY: I heard him telling a power; and I'm thinking we'll have right sport, before night will fall. (*He goes out.*)

JIMMY: Well, Philly's a conceited and foolish man. How could that madman have his senses and his brain-pan slit? I'll go after them and see him turn on Philly now.

(*He goes;* WIDOW QUIN *hides poteen behind counter. Then hubbub outside.*)

VOICES: There you are! Good jumper! Grand lepper! Darlint boy! He's the racer! Bear him on, will you!

(*Christy comes in, in* JOCKEY'S *dress, with* PEGEEN MIKE, SARA, *and other girls, and men.*)

PEGEEN (*to crowd*): Go on now and don't destroy him and he drenching with sweat. Go along, I'm saying, and have your tug-of-warring till he's dried his skin.

CROWD: Here's his prizes! A bagpipes! A fiddle was played by a poet in the years gone by! A flat and three-thorned blackthorn would lick the scholars out of Dublin town!

CHRISTY (*taking prizes from the men*): Thank you kindly, the lot of you. But you'd say it was little only I did this day if you'd seen me a while since striking my one single blow.

TOWN CRIER (*outside, ringing a bell*): Take notice, last event of this day! Tug-of-warring on the green below! Come on, the lot of you! Great achievement for all Mayo men!

PEGEEN: Go on, and leave him for to rest and dry. Go on, I tell you, for he'll do no more. (*She hustles crowd out;* WIDOW QUIN *following them.*)

MEN (*going*): Come on, then. Good luck for the while!

PEGEEN (*radiantly, wiping his face with her shawl*): Well, you're the lad, and you'll have great times from this out when you could win that wealth of prizes, and you sweating in the heat of noon!

CHRISTY (*looking at her with delight*): I'll have great times if I win the crowning prize I'm seeking now, and that's your promise that you'll wed me in a fortnight, when our banns is called.

PEGEEN (*backing away from him*): You've right daring to go ask me that, when all knows you'll be starting to some girl in your own townland, when your father's rotten in four months, or five.

CHRISTY (*indignantly*): Starting from you, is it? (*He follows her*) I will not, then, and when the airs is warming in four months, or five, it's then yourself and me should be pacing Neifin in the dews of night, the times sweet smells do be rising, and you'd see a little shiny new moon, maybe, sinking on the hills.

PEGEEN (*looking at him playfully*): And it's that kind of a poacher's love you'd make, Christy Mahon, on the sides of Neifin, when the night is down?

CHRISTY: It's little you'll think if my love's a poacher's, or an earl's itself, when you'll feel my two hands stretched around you, and I squeezing kisses on your puckered lips, till I'd feel a kind of pity for the Lord God in all ages sitting lonesome in his golden chair.

PEGEEN: That'll be right fun, Christy Mahon, and any girl would walk her heart out before she'd meet a young man was your like for eloquence, or talk, at all.

CHRISTY (*encouraged*): Let you wait, to hear me talking, till we're astray in Erris, when Good Friday's by, drinking a sup from a well, and making mighty kisses with our wetted mouths, or gaming in a gap or sunshine, with yourself stretched back unto your necklace, in the flowers of the earth.

PEGEEN (*in a lower voice, moved by his tone*): I'd be nice so, is it?

CHRISTY (*with rapture*): If the mitred bishops seen you that time, they'd be the like of the holy prophets, I'm thinking, do be straining the bars of Paradise to lay eyes on the Lady Helen of Troy, and she abroad, pacing back and forward, with a nosegay in her golden shawl.

PEGEEN (*with real tenderness*): And what is it I have, Christy Mahon, to make me fitting entertainment for the like of you, that has such poet's talking, and such bravery of heart?

CHRISTY (*in a low voice*): Isn't there the light of seven heavens in your heart alone, the way you'll be an angel's lamp to me from this out, and I abroad in the darkness, spearing salmons in the Owens, or the Carrowmore?

PEGEEN: If I was your wife, I'd be along with you those nights, Christy Mahon, the way you'd see I was a great hand at coaxing bailiffs, or coining funny nick-names for the stars of night.

CHRISTY: You, is it? Taking your death in the hailstones, or in the fogs of dawn.

PEGEEN: Yourself and me would shelter easy in a narrow bush, (*with a qualm of dread*) but we're only talking, maybe, for this would be a poor, thatched place to hold a fine lad is the like of you.

CHRISTY (*putting his arm around her*): If I wasn't a good Christian, it's on my naked knees I'd be saying my prayers and paters to every jackstraw you have roofing your head, and every stony pebble is paving the laneway to your door.

PEGEEN (*radiantly*): If that's the truth, I'll be burning candles from this out to the miracles of God that have brought you from the south today, and I, with my gowns bought ready, the way that I can wed you, and not wait at all.

CHRISTY: It's miracles, and that's the truth. Me there toiling a long while, and walking a long while, not knowing at all I was drawing all times nearer to this holy day.

PEGEEN: And myself, a girl, was tempted often to go sailing the seas till I'd marry a Jew-man, with ten kegs of gold, and I not knowing at all there was the like of you drawing nearer, like the stars of God.

CHRISTY: And to think I'm long years hearing women talking that talk, to all bloody fools, and this the first time I've heard the like of your voice talking sweetly for my own delight.

PEGEEN: And to think it's me is talking sweetly, Christy Mahon, and I the fright of seven townlands for my biting tongue. Well, the heart's a wonder; and, I'm thinking, there won't be our like in Mayo, for gallant lovers, from this hour, today. (*Drunken singing is heard outside*) There's my father coming from the wake, and when he's had his sleep we'll tell him, for he's peaceful then.

(*They separate.*)

MICHAEL (*singing outside*):
> The jailor and the turnkey
>   They quickly ran us down,
> And brought us back as prisoners
>   Once more to Cavan town.

(*He comes in supported by* SHAWN.)
> There we lay bewailing
>   All in a prison bound. . . .

(*He sees* CHRISTY. *Goes and shakes him drunkenly by the hand, while* PEGEEN *and* SHAWN *talk on the left.*)

MICHAEL (*to* CHRISTY): The blessing of God and the holy angels on your head, young fellow. I hear tell you're after winning all in the sports below; and wasn't it a shame I didn't bear you along with me to Kate Cassidy's wake, a fine, stout lad, the like of you, for you'd never see the match of it for flows of drink, the way when we sunk her bones at noonday in her narrow grave, there were five men, aye, and six men, stretched out retching speechless on the holy stones.

CHRISTY (*uneasily, watching* PEGEEN): Is that the truth?

MICHAEL: It is then, and aren't you a louty schemer to go burying your poor father unbeknownst when you'd a right to throw him on the crupper of a Kerry mule and drive him westwards, like holy Joseph in the days gone by, the way we could have given him a decent burial, and not have him rotting beyond, and not a Christian drinking a smart drop to the glory of his soul?

CHRISTY (*gruffly*): It's well enough he's lying, for the likes of him.

MICHAEL (*slapping him on the back*): Well, aren't you a hardened slayer? It'll be a poor thing for the household man where you go sniffing for a female wife; and (*pointing to* SHAWN) look beyond at that shy and decent Christian I have chosen for my daughter's hand, and I after getting the gilded dispensation this day for to wed them now.

CHRISTY: And you'll be wedding them this day, is it?

MICHAEL (*drawing himself up*): Aye. Are you thinking, if I'm drunk itself, I'd leave my daughter living single with a little frisky rascal is the like of you?

PEGEEN (*breaking away from* SHAWN): Is it the truth the dispensation's come?

MICHAEL (*triumphantly*): Father Reilly's after reading it in gallous Latin, and "It's come in the nick of time," says he; "so I'll wed them in a hurry, dreading that young gaffer who'd capsize the stars."

PEGEEN (*fiercely*): He's missed his nick of time, for it's that lad, Christy Mahon, that I'm wedding now.

MICHAEL (*loudly with horror*): You'd be making him a son to me, and he wet and crusted with his father's blood?

PEGEEN: Aye. Wouldn't it be a bitter thing for a girl to go marrying the like of Shaneen, and he a middling kind of a scarecrow, with no savagery or fine words in him at all?

MICHAEL (*gasping and sinking on a chair*): Oh, aren't you a heathen daughter to go shaking the fat of my heart, and I swamped and drownded with the weight of drink? Would you have them turning on me the way that I'd be roaring to the dawn of day with the wind upon my heart? Have you not a word to aid me, Shaneen? Are you not jealous at all?

SHAWN (*in great misery*): I'd be afeard to be jealous of a man did slay his da.

PEGEEN: Well, it'd be a poor thing to go marrying your like. I'm seeing there's a world of peril for an orphan girl, and isn't it a great blessing I didn't wed you, before himself came walking from the west or south?

SHAWN: It's a queer story you'd go picking a dirty tramp up from the highways of the world.

PEGEEN (*playfully*): And you think you're a likely beau to go straying along with, the shiny Sundays of the opening year, when it's sooner on a bullock's liver you'd put a poor girl thinking than on the lily or the rose?

SHAWN: And have you no mind of my weight of passion, and the holy dispensation, and the drift of heifers I am giving, and the golden ring?

PEGEEN: I'm thinking you're too fine for the like of me, Shawn Keogh of Killakeen, and let you go off till you'd find a radiant lady with droves of bullocks on the plains of Meath, and herself bedizened in the diamond jewelries of Pharaoh's ma. That'd be your match, Shaneen. So God save you now! (*She retreats behind* CHRISTY.)

SHAWN: Won't you hear me telling you . . . ?

CHRISTY (*with ferocity*): Take yourself from this, young fellow, or I'll maybe add a murder to my deeds today.

MICHAEL (*springing up with a shriek*): Murder is it? Is it mad yous are? Would you go making murder in this place, and it piled with poteen for our drink tonight? Go on to the foreshore if it's fighting you want, where the rising tide will wash all traces from the memory of man. (*Pushing* SHAWN *towards* CHRISTY.)

SHAWN (*shaking himself free, and getting behind* MICHAEL): I'll not fight him, Michael James. I'd liefer live a bachelor, simmering in passions to the end of time, than face a lepping savage the like of him has descended from the Lord knows where. Strike him yourself, Michael James, or you'll lose my drift of heifers and my blue bull from Sneem.

MICHAEL: Is it me fight him, when it's father-slaying he's bred to now? (*Pushing* SHAWN) Go on you fool and fight him now.

SHAWN (*coming forward a little*): Will I strike him with my hand?

MICHAEL: Take the loy is on your western side.

SHAWN: I'd be afeard of the gallows if I struck him with that.

CHRISTY (*taking up the loy*): Then I'll make you face the gallows or quit off from this.

(SHAWN *flies out of the door.*)

CHRISTY: Well, fine weather be after him, (*going to* MICHAEL, *coaxingly*) and I'm thinking you wouldn't wish to have that quaking blackguard in your house at all. Let you give us your blessing and hear her swear her faith to me, for I'm mounted on the springtide of the stars of luck, the way it'll be good for any to have me in the house.

PEGEEN (*at the other side of* MICHAEL): Bless us now, for I swear to God I'll wed him, and I'll not renege.

MICHAEL (*standing up in the centre, holding on to both of them*): It's the will of God, I'm thinking, that all should win an easy or a cruel end, and it's the will of God that all should rear up lengthy families for the nuture of the earth. What's a single man, I ask you, eating a bit in one house and drinking a sup in another, and he with no place of his own, like an old braying jackass strayed upon the rocks? (*To* CHRISTY) It's many would be in dread to bring your like into their house for to end them, maybe, with a sudden end; but I'm a decent man of Ireland, and I liefer face the grave untimely and I seeing a score of grandsons growing up little gallant swearers by the name of God, than go peopling my bedside with puny weeds the like of what you'd breed, I'm thinking, out of Shaneen Keogh. (*He joins their hands*) A daring fellow is the jewel of the world, and a man did split his father's middle with a single clout, should have the bravery of ten, so may God and Mary and St. Patrick bless you, and increase you from this mortal day.

CHRISTY AND PEGEEN: Amen, O Lord!

(*Hubbub outside.*)

(OLD MAHON *rushes in, followed by all the crowd, and* WIDOW QUIN. *He makes a rush at* CHRISTY, *knocks him down, and begins to beat him.*)

PEGEEN (*dragging back his arm*): Stop that, will you? Who are you at all?

MAHON: His father, God forgive me!

PEGEEN (*drawing back*): Is it rose from the dead?

MAHON: Do you think I look so easy quenched with the tap of a loy? (*Beats* CHRISTY *again.*)

PEGEEN (*glaring at* CHRISTY): And it's lies you told, letting on you had him slitted, and you nothing at all.

CHRISTY (*catching* MAHON's *stick*): He's not my father. He's a raving maniac would scare the world. (*Pointing to* WIDOW QUIN) Herself knows it's true.

CROWD: You're fooling Pegeen! The Widow Quin seen him this day, and you likely knew! You're a liar!

CHRISTY (*dumbfounded*): It's himself was a liar, lying stretched out with an open head on him, letting on he was dead.

MAHON: Weren't you off racing the hills before I got my breath with the start I had seeing you turn on me at all?

PEGEEN: And to think of the coaxing glory we had given him, and he after doing nothing but hitting a soft blow and chasing northward in a sweat of fear. Quit off from this.

CHRISTY (*piteously*): You've seen my doings this day, and let you save me from the old man; for why would you be in such a scorch of haste to spur me to destruction now?

PEGEEN: It's there your treachery is spurring me, till I'm hard set to think you're the one I'm after lacing in my heart-strings half-an-hour gone by. (*To* MAHON) Take him on from this, for I think bad the world should see me raging for a Munster liar, and the fool of men.

MAHON: Rise up now to retribution, and come on with me.

CROWD (*jeeringly*): There's the playboy! There's the lad thought he'd rule the roost in Mayo. Slate him now, mister.

CHRISTY (*getting up in shy terror*): What is it drives you to torment me here, when I'd asked the thunders of the might of God to blast me if I ever did hurt to any saving only that one single blow?

MAHON (*loudly*): If you didn't, you're a poor good-for-nothing, and isn't it by the like of you the sins of the whole world are committed?

CHRISTY (*raising his hands*): In the name of the Almighty God. . . .

MAHON: Leave troubling the Lord God. Would you have him sending down droughts, and fevers, and the old hen and the cholera morbus?

CHRISTY (*to* WIDOW QUIN): Will you come between us and protect me now?

WIDOW QUIN: I've tried a lot, God help me, and my share is done.

CHRISTY (*looking round in desperation*): And I must go back into my torment is it, or run off like a vagabond straying through the Unions with the dusts of August making mud-stains in the gullet of my throat, or the winds of March blowing on me till I'd take an oath I felt them making whistles of my ribs within?

SARA: Ask Pegeen to aid you. Her like does often change.

CHRISTY: I will not then, for there's torment in the splendour of her like, and she a girl any moon of midnight would take pride to meet, facing southwards on the heaths of Keel. But what did I want crawling forward to scorch my understanding at her flaming brow?

PEGEEN (*to* MAHON, *vehemently, fearing she will break into tears*): Take him on from this or I'll set the young lads to destroy him here.

MAHON (*going to him, shaking his stick*): Come on now if you wouldn't have the company to see you skelped.

PEGEEN (*half laughing, through her tears*): That's it, now the world will see him pandied, and he an ugly liar was playing off the hero, and the fright of men.

CHRISTY (*to* MAHON, *very sharply*): Leave me go!

CROWD: That's it. Now, Christy. If them two set fighting, it will lick the world.

MAHON (*making a grab at* Christy): Come here to me.

CHRISTY (*more threateningly*): Leave me go, I'm saying.

MAHON: I will maybe, when your legs is limping, and your back is blue.

CROWD: Keep it up, the two of you. I'll back the old man. Now the playboy.

CHRISTY (*in low and intense voice*): Shut your yelling, for if you're after making a mighty man of me this day by the power of a lie, you're setting me now to think if it's a poor thing to be lonesome, it's worse maybe to go mixing with the fools of earth.

(MAHON *makes a movement towards him.*)

CHRISTY (*almost shouting*): Keep off . . . lest I do show a blow unto the lot of you would set the guardian angels winking in the clouds above. (*He swings round with a sudden rapid movement and picks up a loy.*)

CROWD (*half frightened, half amused*): He's going mad! Mind yourselves! Run from the idiot!

CHRISTY: If I am an idiot, I'm after hearing my voice this day saying words would raise the topknot on a poet in a merchant's town. I've won your racing, your lepping, and . . .

MAHON: Shut your gullet and come on with me.

CHRISTY: I'm going, but I'll stretch you first.

(*He runs at old* MAHON *with the loy, chases him out of the door, followed by crowd and* WIDOW QUIN. *There is a great noise outside, then a yell, and dead silence for a moment.* CHRISTY *comes in, half dazed, and goes to fire.*)

WIDOW QUIN (*coming in, hurriedly, and going to him*): They're turning again you. Come on, or you'll be hanged, indeed.

CHRISTY: I'm thinking, from this out, Pegeen'll be giving me praises the same as in the hours gone by.

WIDOW QUIN (*impatiently*): Come by the back-door. I'd think bad to have you stifled on the gallows tree.

CHRISTY (*indignantly*): I will not, then. What good'd be my life-time, if I left Pegeen?

WIDOW QUIN: Come on, and you'll be no worse than you were last night; and you with a double murder this time to be telling to the girls.

CHRISTY: I'll not leave Pegeen Mike.

WIDOW QUIN (*impatiently*): Isn't there the match of her in every parish public, from Binghamstown unto the plain of Meath? Come on, I tell you, and I'll find you finer sweethearts at each waning moon.

CHRISTY: It's Pegeen I'm seeking only, and what'd I care if you brought me a drift of chosen females, standing in their shifts itself, maybe, from this place to the Eastern World?

SARA (*runs in, pulling off one of her petticoats*): They're going to hang him. (*Holding out petticoat and shawl*) Fit these upon him, and let him run off to the east.

WIDOW QUIN: He's raving now; but we'll fit them on him, and I'll take him, in the ferry, to the Achill boat.

CHRISTY (*struggling feebly*): Leave me go, will you? when I'm thinking of my luck today, for she will wed me surely, and I a proven hero in the end of all.

(*They try to fasten petticoat round him.*)

WIDOW QUIN: Take his left hand, and we'll pull him now. Come on, young fellow.

CHRISTY (*suddenly starting up*): You'll be taking me from her? You're jealous, is it, of her wedding me? Go on from this. (*He snatches up a stool, and threatens them with it.*)

WIDOW QUIN (*going*): It's in the mad-house they should put him, not in jail, at all. We'll go by the back-door, to call the doctor, and we'll save him so.

(*She goes out, with* SARA, *through inner room. Men crowd in the doorway.* CHRISTY *sits down again by the fire.*)

MICHAEL (*in a terrified whisper*): Is the old lad killed surely?

PHILLY: I'm after feeling the last gasps quitting his heart.

(*They peer in at* CHRISTY.)

MICHAEL (*with a rope*): Look at the way he is. Twist a hangman's knot on it, and slip it over his head, while he's not minding at all.

PHILLY: Let you take it, Shaneen. You're the soberest of all that's here.

SHAWN: Is it me to go near him, and he the wickedest and worst with me? Let you take it, Pegeen Mike.

PEGEEN: Come on, so.

(*She goes forward with the others, and they drop the double hitch over his head.*)

CHRISTY: What ails you?

SHAWN (*triumphantly, as they pull the rope tight on his arms*): Come on to the peelers, till they stretch you now.

CHRISTY: Me!

MICHAEL: If we took pity on you, the Lord God would, maybe, bring us ruin from the law today, so you'd best come easy, for hanging is an easy and a speedy end.

CHRISTY: I'll not stir. (*To* PEGEEN) And what is it you'll say to me, and I after doing it this time in the face of all?

PEGEEN: I'll say, a strange man is a marvel, with his mighty talk; but what's a squabble in your back-yard, and the blow of a loy, have taught me that there's a great gap between a gallous story and a dirty deed. (*To* MEN) Take him on from this, or the lot of us will be likely put on trial for his deed today.

CHRISTY (*with horror in his voice*): And it's yourself will send me off, to have a horny-fingered hangman hitching his bloody slip-knots at the butt of my ear.

MEN (*pulling rope*): Come on, will you?

(*He is pulled down on the floor.*)

CHRISTY (*twisting his legs round the table*): Cut the rope, Pegeen, and I'll quit the lot of you, and live from this out, like the madmen of Keel, eating muck and green weeds, on the faces of the cliffs.

PEGEEN: And leave us to hang, is it, for a saucy liar, the like of you? (*To* MEN) Take him on, out from this.

SHAWN: Pull a twist on his neck, and squeeze him so.

PHILLY: Twist yourself. Sure he cannot hurt you, if you keep your distance from his teeth alone.

SHAWN: I'm afeard of him. (*To* PEGEEN) Lift a lighted sod, will you, and scorch his leg.

PEGEEN (*blowing the fire, with a bellows*): Leave go now, young fellow, or I'll scorch your shins.

CHRISTY: You're blowing for to torture me. (*His voice rising and growing stronger*) That's your kind, is it? Then let the lot of you be wary, for, if I've to face the gallows, I'll have a gay march down, I tell you, and shed the blood of some of you before I die.

SHAWN (*in terror*): Keep a good hold, Philly. Be wary, for the love of God. For I'm thinking he would liefest wreak his pains on me.

CHRISTY (*almost gaily*): If I do lay my hands on you, it's the way you'll be at the fall of night, hanging as a scarecrow for the fowls of hell. Ah, you'll have a gallous jaunt I'm saying, coaching out through Limbo with my father's ghost.

SHAWN (*to* PEGEEN): Make haste, will you? Oh, isn't he a holy terror, and isn't it true for Father Reilly, that all drink's a curse that has the lot of you so shaky and uncertain now?

CHRISTY: If I can wring a neck among you, I'll have a royal judgment looking on the trembling jury in the courts of law. And won't there be crying out in Mayo the day I'm stretched upon the rope with ladies in their silks and satins snivelling in their lacy kerchiefs, and they rhyming songs and ballads on the terror of my fate? (*He squirms round on the floor and bites* SHAWN's *leg.*)

SHAWN (*shrieking*): My leg's bit on me. He's the like of a mad dog, I'm thinking, the way that I will surely die.

CHRISTY (*delighted with himself*): You will then, the way you can shake out hell's flags of welcome for my coming in two weeks or three, for I'm thinking Satan hasn't many have killed their da in Kerry, and in Mayo too.

(OLD MAHON *comes in behind on all fours and looks on unnoticed.*)

MEN (*to* PEGEEN): Bring the sod, will you?

PEGEEN (*coming over*): God help him so. (*Burns his leg.*)

CHRISTY (*kicking and screaming*): O, glory be to God!

(*He kicks loose from the table, and they all drag him towards the door.*)

JIMMY (*seeing old* MAHON): Will you look what's come in?

(*They all drop* CHRISTY *and run left.*)

CHRISTY (*scrambling on his knees face to face with old* MAHON): Are you coming to be killed a third time, or what ails you now?

MAHON: For what is it they have you tied?

CHRISTY: They're taking me to the peelers to have me hanged for slaying you.

MICHAEL (*apologetically*): It is the will of God that all should guard their little cabins from the treachery of law, and what would my daughter be doing if I was ruined or was hanged itself?

MAHON (*grimly, loosening* CHRISTY): It's little I care if you put a bag on her neck, and went picking cockles till the hour of death; but my son and myself will be going our own way, and we'll have great times from this out telling stories of the villany of Mayo, and the fools is here. (*To* CHRISTY, *who is freed*) Come on now.

CHRISTY: Go with you, is it? I will then, like a gallant captain with his heathen slave. Go on now and I'll see you from this day stewing my oatmeal and washing my spuds, for I'm master of all fights from now. (*Pushing* MAHON) Go on, I'm saying.

MAHON: Is it me?

CHRISTY: Not a word out of you. Go on from this.

MAHON (*walking out and looking back at* CHRISTY *over his shoulder*): Glory be to God! (*With a broad smile*) I am crazy again! (*Goes.*)

CHRISTY: Ten thousand blessings upon all that's here, for you've turned me a likely gaffer in the end of all, the way I'll go romancing through a romping lifetime from this hour to the dawning of the judgment day. (*He goes out.*)

MICHAEL: By the will of God, we'll have peace now for our drinks. Will you draw the porter, Pegeen?

SHAWN (*going up to her*): It's a miracle Father Reilly can wed us in the end of all, and we'll have none to trouble us when his vicious bite is healed.

PEGEEN (*hitting him a box on the ear*): Quit my sight. (*Putting her shawl over her head and breaking out into wild lamentations*) Oh my grief, I've lost him surely. I've lost the only Playboy of the Western World.

(*The Curtain Falls.*)

# HENRIK IBSEN

# The Wild Duck

Translated by

FRANCES E. ARCHER

*The Wild Duck* was published on November 11, 1884, and produced in many leading theaters in Norway in January, 1885.

# CHARACTERS

WERLE, *a merchant, manufacturer, etc.*

GREGERS WERLE, *his son.*

OLD EKDAL.

HIALMAR EKDAL, *his son, a photographer.*

GINA EKDAL, *Hialmar's wife.*

HEDVIG, *their daughter, a girl of fourteen.*

MRS. SÖRBY, *Werle's housekeeper.*

RELLING, *a doctor.*

MOLVIK, *student of theology.*

GRÅBERG, *Werle's bookkeeper.*

PETTERSEN, *Werle's servant.*

JENSEN, *a hired waiter.*

A FLABBY GENTLEMAN.

A THIN-HAIRED GENTLEMAN.

A SHORT-SIGHTED GENTLEMAN.

SIX OTHER GENTLEMEN, *guests at Werle's dinner-party.*

SEVERAL HIRED WAITERS.

*The first act passes in* WERLE'S *house, the remaining acts at* HIALMAR EKDAL'S.

Pronunciation of Names: GREGERS WERLE = Grayghers Verlë; HIALMAR EKDAL = Yalmar Aykdal; GINA = Cheena; GRÅBERG = Groberg; JENSEN = Yensen.

# Act One

AT WERLE'S *house. A richly and comfortably furnished study; bookcases and upholstered furniture; a writing-table, with papers and documents, in the centre of the room; lighted lamps with green shades, giving a subdued light. At the back, open folding-doors with curtains drawn back. Within is seen a large and handsome room, brilliantly lighted with lamps and branching candlesticks. In front, on the right (in the study), a small baize door leads into* WERLE'S *office. On the left, in front, a fireplace with a glowing coal fire, and farther back a double door leading into the dining-room.*

WERLE'S *servant,* PETTERSEN, *in livery, and* JENSEN, *the hired waiter, in black, are putting the study in order. In the large room, two or three other hired waiters are moving about, arranging things and lighting more candles. From the dining-room, the hum of conversation and laughter of many voices are heard; a glass is tapped with a knife; silence follows, and a toast is proposed; shouts of "Bravo!" and then again a buzz of conversation.*

PETTERSEN (*lights a lamp on the chimney-place and places a shade over it*): Hark to them, Jensen! now the old man's on his legs holding a long palaver about Mrs. Sörby.

JENSEN (*pushing forward an armchair*): Is it true, what folks say, that they're—very good friends, eh?

PETTERSEN: Lord knows.

JENSEN: I've heard tell as he's been a lively customer in his day.

PETTERSEN: May be.

JENSEN: And he's giving this spread in honour of his son, they say.

PETTERSEN: Yes. His son came home yesterday.

JENSEN: This is the first time I ever heard as Mr. Werle had a son.

173

PETTERSEN: Oh, yes, he has a son, right enough. But he's a fixture, as you might say, up at the Höidal works. He's never once come to town all the years I've been in service here.

A WAITER (*in the doorway of the other room*): Pettersen, here's an old fellow wanting . . .

PETTERSEN (*mutters*): The devil—who's this now?

(OLD EKDAL *appears from the right, in the inner room. He is dressed in a threadbare overcoat with a high collar; he wears woollen mittens and carries in his hand a stick and a fur cap. Under his arm, a brown paper parcel. Dirty red-brown wig and small grey moustache.*)

PETTERSEN (*goes towards him*): Good Lord—what do you want here?

EKDAL (*in the doorway*): Must get into the office, Pettersen.

PETTERSEN: The office was closed an hour ago, and . . .

EKDAL: So they told me at the front door. But Gråberg's in there still. Let me slip in this way, Pettersen; there's a good fellow. (*Points towards the baize door*) It's not the first time I've come this way.

PETTERSEN: Well, you may pass. (*Opens the door*) But mind you go out again the proper way, for we've got company.

EKDAL: I know, I know—h'm! Thanks, Pettersen, good old friend! Thanks! (*Mutters softly*) Ass!

(*He goes into the office;* PETTERSEN *shuts the door after him.*)

JENSEN: Is he one of the office people?

PETTERSEN: No, he's only an outside hand that does odd jobs of copying. But he's been a tip-topper in his day, has old Ekdal.

JENSEN: You can see he's been through a lot.

PETTERSEN: Yes; he was an army officer, you know.

JENSEN: You don't say so?

PETTERSEN: No mistake about it. But then he went into the timber trade or something of the sort. They say he once played Mr. Werle a very nasty trick. They were partners in the Höidal works at the time. Oh, I know old Ekdal well, I do. Many a nip of bitters and bottle of ale we two have drunk at Madam Eriksen's.

JENSEN: He don't look as if he'd much to stand treat with.

PETTERSEN: Why, bless you, Jensen, it's me that stands treat. I always think there's no harm in being a bit civil to folks that have seen better days.

JENSEN: Did he go bankrupt, then?

PETTERSEN: Worse than that. He went to prison.

JENSEN: To prison!

PETTERSEN: Or perhaps it was the Penitentiary. (*Listens*) Sh! They're leaving the table.

(*The dining-room door is thrown open from within by a couple of waiters.* MRS. SÖRBY *comes out conversing with two gentlemen. Gradually the whole company follows, amongst them* WERLE. *Last come* HIALMAR EKDAL *and* GREGERS WERLE.)

MRS. SÖRBY (*in passing, to the servant*): Tell them to serve the coffee in the music-room, Pettersen.

PETTERSEN: Very well, Madam.

(*She goes with the two gentlemen into the inner room and thence out to the right.* PETTERSEN *and* JENSEN *go out the same way.*)

A FLABBY GENTLEMAN (*to a* THIN-HAIRED GENTLEMAN): Whew! What a dinner!—It was no joke to do it justice!

THE THIN-HAIRED GENTLEMAN: Oh, with a little good-will one can get through a lot in three hours.

THE FLABBY GENTLEMAN: Yes, but afterwards, afterwards, my dear Chamberlain!

A THIRD GENTLEMAN: I hear the coffee and maraschino are to be served in the music-room.

THE FLABBY GENTLEMAN: Bravo! Then perhaps Mrs. Sörby will play us something.

THE THIN-HAIRED GENTLEMAN (*in a low voice*): I hope Mrs. Sörby mayn't play us a tune we don't like, one of these days!

THE FLABBY GENTLEMAN: Oh, no, not she! Bertha will never turn against her old friends.

(*They laugh and pass into the inner room.*)

WERLE (*in a low voice, dejectedly*): I don't think anybody noticed it, Gregers.

GREGERS (*looks at him*): Noticed what?

WERLE: Did you not notice it either?

GREGERS: What do you mean?

WERLE: We were thirteen at table.

GREGERS: Indeed? Were there thirteen of us?

WERLE (*glances towards* HIALMAR EKDAL): Our usual party is twelve. (*To the others*) This way, gentlemen!

(WERLE *and the others, all except* HIALMAR *and* GREGERS, *go out by the back, to the right.*)

HIALMAR (*who has overheard the conversation*): You ought not to have invited me, Gregers.

GREGERS: What! Not ask my best and only friend to a party supposed to be in my honour . . . ?

HIALMAR: But I don't think your father likes it. You see I am quite outside his circle.

GREGERS: So I hear. But I wanted to see you and have a talk with you, and I certainly shan't be staying long.—Ah, we two old schoolfellows have drifted far apart from each other. It must be sixteen or seventeen years since we met.

HIALMAR: Is it so long?

GREGERS: It is indeed. Well, how goes it with you? You look well. You have put on flesh and grown almost stout.

HIALMAR: Well, "stout" is scarcely the word; but I daresay I look a little more of a man than I used to.

GREGERS: Yes, you do; your outer man is in first-rate condition.

HIALMAR (*in a tone of gloom*): Ah, but the inner man! That is a very different matter, I can tell you! Of course you know of the terrible catastrophe that has befallen me and mine since last we met.

GREGERS (*more softly*): How are things going with your father now?

HIALMAR: Don't let us talk of it, old fellow. Of course my poor unhappy father lives with me. He hasn't another soul in the world to care for him. But you can understand that this is a miserable subject for me.—Tell me, rather, how you have been getting on up at the works.

GREGERS: I have had a delightfully lonely time of it—plenty of leisure to think and think about things. Come over here; we may as well make ourselves comfortable.

(*He seats himself in an armchair by the fire and draws* HIALMAR *down into another alongside of it.*)

HIALMAR (*sentimentally*): After all, Gregers, I thank you for inviting me to your father's table; for I take it as a sign that you have got over your feeling against me.

GREGERS (*surprised*): How could you imagine I had any feeling against you?

HIALMAR: You had at first, you know.

GREGERS: How at first?

HIALMAR: After the great misfortune. It was natural enough that you should. Your father was within an ace of being drawn into that—well, that terrible business.

GREGERS: Why should that give me any feeling against you? Who can have put that into your head?

HIALMAR: I know it did, Gregers; your father told me so himself.

GREGERS (*starts*): My father! Oh, indeed. H'm.—Was that why you never let me hear from you?—not a single word.

HIALMAR: Yes.

GREGERS: Not even when you made up your mind to become a photographer?

HIALMAR: Your father said I had better not write to you at all, about anything.

GREGERS (*looking straight before him*): Well, well, perhaps he was right.—But tell me now, Hialmar: are you pretty well satisfied with your present position?

HIALMAR (*with a little sigh*): Oh, yes, I am; I have really no cause to complain. At first, as you may guess, I felt it a little strange. It was such a totally new state of things for me. But of course my whole circumstances were totally changed. Father's utter, irretrievable ruin,—the shame and disgrace of it, Gregers . . .

GREGERS (*affected*): Yes, yes; I understand.

HIALMAR: I couldn't think of remaining at college; there wasn't a shilling to spare; on the contrary, there were debts—mainly to your father, I believe . . .

GREGERS: H'm . . .

HIALMAR: In short, I thought it best to break, once for all, with my old surroundings and associations. It was your father that specially urged me to it; and since he interested himself so much in me . . .

GREGERS: My father did?

HIALMAR: Yes, you surely knew that, didn't you? Where do you suppose I found the money to learn photography, and to furnish a studio and make a start? All that cost a pretty penny, I can tell you.

GREGERS: And my father provided the money?

HIALMAR: Yes, my dear fellow, didn't you know? I understood him to say he had written to you about it.

GREGERS: Not a word about his part in the business. He must have forgotten it. Our correspondence has always been purely a business one. So it was my father that . . . !

HIALMAR: Yes, certainly. He didn't wish it to be generally known; but he it was. And of course it was he, too, that put me in a position to marry. Don't you—don't you know about that either?

GREGERS: No, I haven't heard a word of it. (*Shakes him by the arm*) But, my dear Hialmar, I can't tell you what pleasure all this gives

me—pleasure, and self-reproach. I have perhaps done my father in-
justice after all—in some things. This proves that he has a heart. It
shows a sort of compunction . . .

HIALMAR: Compunction . . . ?

GREGERS: Yes, yes—whatever you like to call it. Oh, I can't tell you
how glad I am to hear this of father.—So you are a married man,
Hialmar! That is further than I shall ever get. Well, I hope you are
happy in your married life?

HIALMAR: Yes, thoroughly happy. She is as good and capable a wife
as any man could wish for. And she is by no means without culture.

GREGERS (*rather surprised*): No, of course not.

HIALMAR: You see, life is itself an education. Her daily intercourse
with me . . . And then we know one or two rather remarkable men,
who come a good deal about us. I assure you, you would hardly
know Gina again.

GREGERS: Gina?

HIALMAR: Yes; had you forgotten that her name was Gina?

GREGERS: Whose name? I haven't the slightest idea . . .

HIALMAR: Don't you remember that she used to be in service here?

GREGERS (*looks at him*): Is it Gina Hansen . . . ?

HIALMAR: Yes, of course it is Gina Hansen.

GREGERS: . . . who kept house for us during the last year of my
mother's illness?

HIALMAR: Yes, exactly. But, my dear friend, I'm quite sure your
father told you that I was married.

GREGERS (*who has risen*): Oh, yes, he mentioned it; but not that . . .
(*Walking about the room*) Stay—perhaps he did—now that I think
of it. My father always writes such short letters. (*Half seats himself
on the arm of the chair*) Now tell me, Hialmar—this is interesting—
how did you come to know Gina—your wife?

HIALMAR: The simplest thing in the world. You know Gina did not
stay here long; everything was so much upset at that time, owing to

your mother's illness and so forth, that Gina was not equal to it all;
so she gave notice and left. That was the year before your mother
died—or it may have been the same year.

GREGERS: It was the same year. I was up at the works then. But
afterwards . . . ?

HIALMAR: Well, Gina lived at home with her mother, Madam Hansen, an excellent hard-working woman, who kept a little eating-
house. She had a room to let, too; a very nice comfortable room.

GREGERS: And I suppose you were lucky enough to secure it?

HIALMAR: Yes; in fact, it was your father that recommended it to
me. So it was there, you see, that I really came to know Gina.

GREGERS: And then you got engaged?

HIALMAR: Yes. It doesn't take young people long to fall in love . . . ;
h'm . . .

GREGERS (*rises and moves about a little*): Tell me: was it after your
engagement—was it then that my father—I mean was it then that
you began to take up photography?

HIALMAR: Yes, precisely. I wanted to make a start and to set up house
as soon as possible; and your father and I agreed that this photography business was the readiest way. Gina thought so, too. Oh, and
there was another thing in its favour, by-the-bye; it happened,
luckily, that Gina had learnt to retouch.

GREGERS: That chimed in marvellously.

HIALMAR (*pleased, rises*): Yes, didn't it? Don't you think it was a
marvellous piece of luck?

GREGERS: Oh, unquestionably. My father seems to have been almost
a kind of providence for you.

HIALMAR (*with emotion*): He did not forsake his old friend's son
in the hour of his need. For he has a heart, you see.

MRS. SÖRBY (*enters, arm-in-arm with* WERLE): Nonsense, my dear
Mr. Werle; you mustn't stop there any longer staring at all the lights.
It's very bad for you.

WERLE (*lets go her arm and passes his hand over his eyes*): I daresay you are right.

(PETTERSEN *and* JENSEN *carry round refreshment trays.*)

MRS. SÖRBY (*to the guests in the other room*): This way, if you please, gentlemen. Whoever wants a glass of punch must be so good as to come in here.

THE FLABBY GENTLEMAN (*comes up to* MRS. SÖRBY): Surely, it isn't possible that you have suspended our cherished right to smoke?

MRS. SÖRBY: Yes. No smoking here, in Mr. Werle's sanctum, Chamberlain.

THE THIN-HAIRED GENTLEMAN: When did you enact these stringent amendments on the cigar law, Mrs. Sörby?

MRS. SÖRBY: After the last dinner, Chamberlain, when certain persons permitted themselves to overstep the mark.

THE THIN-HAIRED GENTLEMAN: And may one never overstep the mark a little bit, Madame Bertha? Not the least little bit?

MRS. SÖRBY: Not in any respect whatsoever, Mr. Balle.

(*Most of the guests have assembled in the study; servants hand round glasses of punch.*)

WERLE (*to* HIALMAR, *who is standing beside a table*): What are you studying so intensely, Ekdal?

HIALMAR: Only an album, Mr. Werle.

THE THIN-HAIRED GENTLEMAN (*who is wandering about*): Ah, photographs! They are quite in your line, of course.

THE FLABBY GENTLEMAN (*in an armchair*): Haven't you brought any of your own with you?

HIALMAR: No, I haven't.

THE FLABBY GENTLEMAN: You ought to have; it's very good for the digestion to sit and look at pictures.

THE THIN-HAIRED GENTLEMAN: And it contributes to the entertainment, you know.

THE SHORT-SIGHTED GENTLEMAN: And all contributions are thankfully received.

MRS. SÖRBY: The Chamberlains think that when one is invited out to dinner, one ought to exert oneself a little in return, Mr. Ekdal.

THE FLABBY GENTLEMAN: Where one dines so well, that duty becomes a pleasure.

THE THIN-HAIRED GENTLEMAN: And when it's a case of the struggle for existence, you know . . .

MRS. SÖRBY: I quite agree with you!

(*They continue the conversation, with laughter and joking.*)

GREGERS (*softly*): You must join in, Hialmar.

HIALMAR (*writhing*): What am I to talk about?

THE FLABBY GENTLEMAN: Don't you think, Mr. Werle, that Tokay may be considered one of the more wholesome sorts of wine?

WERLE (*by the fire*): I can answer for the Tokay you had today, at any rate; it's one of the very finest seasons. Of course you would notice that.

THE FLABBY GENTLEMAN: Yes, it had a remarkably delicate flavour.

HIALMAR (*shyly*): Is there any difference between the seasons?

THE FLABBY GENTLEMAN (*laughs*): Come! That's good!

WERLE (*smiles*): It really doesn't pay to set fine wine before you.

THE THIN-HAIRED GENTLEMAN: Tokay is like photographs, Mr. Ekdal: they both need sunshine. Am I not right?

HIALMAR: Yes, light is important no doubt.

MRS. SÖRBY: And it's exactly the same with Chamberlains—they, too, depend very much on sunshine,* as the saying is.

THE THIN-HAIRED GENTLEMAN: Oh, fie! That's a very threadbare sarcasm!

THE SHORT-SIGHTED GENTLEMAN: Mrs. Sörby is coming out . . .

* The "sunshine" of court favour.

THE FLABBY GENTLEMAN: . . . and at our expense, too. (*Holds up his finger reprovingly*) Oh, Madame Bertha, Madame Bertha!

MRS. SÖRBY: Yes, and there's not the least doubt that the seasons differ greatly. The old vintages are the finest.

THE SHORT-SIGHTED GENTLEMAN: Do you reckon me among the old vintages?

MRS. SÖRBY: Oh, far from it.

THE THIN-HAIRED GENTLEMAN: There now! But me, dear Mrs. Sörby . . . ?

THE FLABBY GENTLEMAN: Yes, and me? What vintage should you say that we belong to?

MRS. SÖRBY: Why, to the sweet vintage, gentlemen.

(*She sips a glass of punch. The gentlemen laugh and flirt with her.*)

WERLE: Mrs. Sörby can always find a loop-hole—when she wants to. Fill your glasses, gentlemen! Pettersen, will you see to it . . . ! Gregers, suppose we have a glass together. (GREGERS *does not move*) Won't you join us, Ekdal? I found no opportunity of drinking with you at table.

(GRÅBERG, *the bookkeeper, looks in at the baize door.*)

GRÅBERG: Excuse me, sir, but I can't get out.

WERLE: Have you been locked in again?

GRÅBERG: Yes, and Flakstad has carried off the keys.

WERLE: Well, you can pass out this way.

GRÅBERG: But there's some one else . . .

WERLE: All right; come through, both of you. Don't be afraid.

(GRÅBERG *and* OLD EKDAL *come out of the office.*)

WERLE (*involuntarily*): Ugh!

(*The laughter and talk among the guests cease.* HIALMAR *starts at the sight of his father, puts down his glass and turns towards the fireplace.*)

EKDAL (*does not look up, but makes little bows to both sides as he passes, murmuring*): Beg pardon, come the wrong way. Door locked—door locked. Beg pardon.

(*He and* GRÅBERG *go out by the back, to the right.*)

WERLE (*between his teeth*): That idiot Gråberg.

GREGERS (*open-mouthed and staring, to* HIALMAR): Why surely that wasn't . . . !

THE FLABBY GENTLEMAN: What's the matter? Who was it?

GREGERS: Oh, nobody, only the bookkeeper and some one with him.

THE SHORT-SIGHTED GENTLEMAN (*to* HIALMAR): Did you know that man?

HIALMAR: I don't know—I didn't notice . . .

THE FLABBY GENTLEMAN: What the deuce has come over every one?

(*He joins another group who are talking softly.*)

MRS. SÖRBY (*whispers to the servant*): Give him something to take with him;—something good, mind.

PETTERSEN (*nods*): I'll see to it. (*Goes out.*)

GREGERS (*softly and with emotion, to* HIALMAR): So that was really he!

HIALMAR: Yes.

GREGERS: And you could stand there and deny that you knew him!

HIALMAR (*whispers vehemently*): But how could I . . . !

GREGERS: . . . acknowledge your own father?

HIALMAR (*with pain*): Oh, if you were in my place . . .

(*The conversation amongst the guests, which has been carried on in a low tone, now swells into constrained joviality.*)

THE THIN-HAIRED GENTLEMAN (*approaching* HIALMAR *and* GREGERS *in a friendly manner*): Aha! Reviving old college memories, eh? Don't you smoke, Mr. Ekdal? May I give you a light? Oh, by-the-bye, we mustn't . . .

HIALMAR: No, thank you, I won't . . .

THE FLABBY GENTLEMAN: Haven't you a nice little poem you could recite to us, Mr. Ekdal? You used to recite so charmingly.

HIALMAR: I am sorry I can't remember anything.

THE FLABBY GENTLEMAN: Oh, that's a pity. Well, what shall we do, Balle?

(*Both gentlemen move away and pass into the other room.*)

HIALMAR (*gloomily*): Gregers—I am going! When a man has felt the crushing hand of Fate, you see . . . Say good-bye to your father for me.

GREGERS: Yes, yes. Are you going straight home?

HIALMAR: Yes. Why?

GREGERS: Oh, because I may perhaps look in on you later.

HIALMAR: No, you mustn't do that. You must not come to my home. Mine is a melancholy abode, Gregers; especially after a splendid banquet like this. We can always arrange to meet somewhere in the town.

MRS. SÖRBY (*who has quietly approached*): Are you going, Ekdal?

HIALMAR: Yes.

MRS. SÖRBY: Remember me to Gina.

HIALMAR: Thanks.

MRS. SÖRBY: And say I am coming up to see her one of these days.

HIALMAR: Yes, thank you. (*To* GREGERS) Stay here; I will slip out unobserved.

(*He saunters away, then into the other room, and so out to the right.*)

MRS. SÖRBY (*softly to the servant, who has come back*): Well, did you give the old man something?

PETTERSEN: Yes; I sent him off with a bottle of cognac.

MRS. SÖRBY: Oh, you might have thought of something better than that.

PETTERSEN: Oh, no, Mrs. Sörby; cognac is what he likes best in the world.

THE FLABBY GENTLEMAN (*in the doorway with a sheet of music in his hand*): Shall we play a duet, Mrs. Sörby?

MRS. SÖRBY: Yes, suppose we do.

THE GUESTS: Bravo, bravo!

(*She goes with all the guests through the back room, out to the right.* GREGERS *remains standing by the fire.* WERLE *is looking for something on the writing-table and appears to wish that* GREGERS *would go; as* GREGERS *does not move,* WERLE *goes towards the door.*)

GREGERS: Father, won't you stay a moment?

WERLE (*stops*): What is it?

GREGERS: I must have a word with you.

WERLE: Can it not wait till we are alone?

GREGERS: No, it cannot; for perhaps we shall never be alone together.

WERLE (*drawing nearer*): What do you mean by that?

(*During what follows, the pianoforte is faintly heard from the distant music-room.*)

GREGERS: How has that family been allowed to go so miserably to the wall?

WERLE: You mean the Ekdals, I suppose.

GREGERS: Yes, I mean the Ekdals. Lieutenant Ekdal was once so closely associated with you.

WERLE: Much too closely; I have felt that to my cost for many a year. It is thanks to him that I—yes I—have had a kind of slur cast upon my reputation.

GREGERS (*softly*): Are you sure that he alone was to blame?

WERLE: Who else do you suppose . . . ?

GREGERS: You and he acted together in that affair of the forests . . .

WERLE: But was it not Ekdal that drew the map of the tracts we had bought—that fraudulent map! It was he who felled all that timber illegally on Government ground. In fact, the whole management was in his hands. I was quite in the dark as to what Lieutenant Ekdal was doing.

GREGERS: Lieutenant Ekdal himself seems to have been very much in the dark as to what he was doing.

WERLE: That may be. But the fact remains that he was found guilty and I acquitted.

GREGERS: Yes, I know that nothing was proved against you.

WERLE: Acquittal is acquittal. Why do you rake up these old miseries that turned my hair grey before its time? Is that the sort of thing you have been brooding over up there, all these years? I can assure you, Gregers, here in the town the whole story has been forgotten long ago—so far as *I* am concerned.

GREGERS: But that unhappy Ekdal family . . .

WERLE: What would you have had me do for the people? When Ekdal came out of prison he was a broken-down being, past all help. There are people in the world who dive to the bottom the moment they get a couple of slugs in their body and never come to the surface again. You may take my word for it, Gregers, I have done all I could without positively laying myself open to all sorts of suspicion and gossip . . .

GREGERS: Suspicion . . . ? Oh, I see.

WERLE: I have given Ekdal copying to do for the office, and I pay him far, far more for it than his work is worth . . .

GREGERS (*without looking at him*): H'm; that I don't doubt.

WERLE: You laugh? Do you think I am not telling you the truth? Well, I certainly can't refer you to my books, for I never enter payments of that sort.

GREGERS (*smiles coldly*): No, there are certain payments it is best to keep no account of.

WERLE (*taken aback*): What do you mean by that?

GREGERS (*mustering up courage*): Have you entered what it cost you to have Hialmar Ekdal taught photography?

WERLE: I? How "entered" it?

GREGERS: I have learnt that it was you who paid for his training. And I have learnt, too, that it was you who enabled him to set up house so comfortably.

WERLE: Well, and yet you talk as though I had done nothing for the Ekdals! I can assure you these people have cost me enough in all conscience.

GREGERS: Have you entered any of these expenses in your books?

WERLE: Why do you ask?

GREGERS: Oh, I have my reasons. Now tell me: when you interested yourself so warmly in your old friend's son—it was just before his marriage, was it not?

WERLE: Why, deuce take it—after all these years, how can I . . . ?

GREGERS: You wrote me a letter about that time—a business letter, of course; and in a postscript you mentioned—quite briefly—that Hialmar Ekdal had married a Miss Hansen.

WERLE: Yes, that was quite right. That was her name.

GREGERS: But you did not mention that this Miss Hansen was Gina Hansen—our former housekeeper.

WERLE (*with a forced laugh of derision*): No; to tell the truth, it didn't occur to me that you were so particularly interested in our former housekeeper.

GREGERS: No more I was. But (*lowers his voice*) there were others in this house who were particularly interested in her.

WERLE: What do you mean by that? (*Flaring up*) You are not alluding to me, I hope?

GREGERS (*softly but firmly*): Yes, I am alluding to you.

WERLE: And you dare . . . ! You presume to . . . ! How can that ungrateful hound—that photographer fellow—how dare he go making such insinuations!

GREGERS: Hialmar has never breathed a word about this. I don't believe he has the faintest suspicion of such a thing.

WERLE: Then where have you got it from? Who can have put such notions in your head?

GREGERS: My poor unhappy mother told me; and that the very last time I saw her.

WERLE: Your mother! I might have known as much! You and she—you always held together. It was she who turned you against me, from the first.

GREGERS: No, it was all that she had to suffer and submit to, until she broke down and came to such a pitiful end.

WERLE: Oh, she had nothing to suffer or submit to; not more than most people, at all events. But there's no getting on with morbid, overstrained creatures—that I have learnt to my cost.—And you could go on nursing such a suspicion—burrowing into all sorts of old rumours and slanders against your own father! I must say, Gregers, I really think that at your age you might find something more useful to do.

GREGERS: Yes, it is high time.

WERLE: Then perhaps your mind would be easier than it seems to be now. What can be your object in remaining up at the works, year out and year in, drudging away like a common clerk, and not drawing a farthing more than the ordinary monthly wage? It is downright folly.

GREGERS: Ah, if I were only sure of that.

WERLE: I understand you well enough. You want to be independent; you won't be beholden to me for anything. Well, now there happens to be an opportunity for you to become independent, your own master in everything.

GREGERS: Indeed? In what way . . . ?

WERLE: When I wrote you insisting on your coming to town at once—h'm . . .

GREGERS: Yes, what is it you really want of me? I have been waiting all day to know.

WERLE: I want to propose that you should enter the firm, as partner.

GREGERS: I! Join your firm? As partner?

WERLE: Yes. It would not involve our being constantly together. You could take over the business here in town, and I should move up to the works.

GREGERS: You would?

WERLE: The fact is, I am not so fit for work as I once was. I am obliged to spare my eyes, Gregers; they have begun to trouble me.

GREGERS: They have always been weak.

WERLE: Not as they are now. And besides, circumstances might possibly make it desirable for me to live up there—for a time, at any rate.

GREGERS: That is certainly quite a new idea to me.

WERLE: Listen, Gregers: there are many things that stand between us; but we are father and son after all. We ought surely to be able to come to some sort of understanding with each other.

GREGERS: Outwardly, you mean, of course?

WERLE: Well, even that would be something. Think it over, Gregers. Don't you think it ought to be possible? Eh?

GREGERS (*looking at him coldly*): There is something behind all this.

WERLE: How so?

GREGERS: You want to make use of me in some way.

WERLE: In such a close relationship as ours, the one can always be useful to the other.

GREGERS: Yes, so people say.

WERLE: I want very much to have you at home with me for a time. I am a lonely man, Gregers; I have always felt lonely, all my life through; but most of all now that I am getting up in years. I feel the need of some one about me . . .

GREGERS: You have Mrs. Sörby.

WERLE: Yes, I have her; and she has become, I may say, almost indispensable to me. She is lively and even-tempered; she brightens up the house; and that is a very great thing for me.

GREGERS: Well, then, you have everything just as you wish it.

WERLE: Yes, but I am afraid it can't last. A woman so situated may easily find herself in a false position, in the eyes of the world. For that matter it does a man no good, either.

GREGERS: Oh, when a man gives such dinners as you give, he can risk a great deal.

WERLE: Yes, but how about the woman, Gregers? I fear she won't accept the situation much longer; and even if she did—even if, out of attachment to me, she were to take her chance of gossip and scandal and all that . . . ? Do you think, Gregers—you with your strong sense of justice . . .

GREGERS (*interrupts him*): Tell me in one word: are you thinking of marrying her?

WERLE: Suppose I were thinking of it? What then?

GREGERS: That's what I say: what then?

WERLE: Should you be inflexibly opposed to it!

GREGERS: Not at all. Not by any means.

WERLE: I was not sure whether your devotion to your mother's memory . . .

GREGERS: I am not overstrained.

WERLE: Well, whatever you may or may not be, at all events you have lifted a great weight from my mind. I am extremely pleased that I can reckon on your concurrence in this matter.

GREGERS (*looking intently at him*): Now I see the use you want to put me to.

WERLE: Use to put you to? What an expression!

GREGERS: Oh, don't let us be nice in our choice of words—not when we are alone together, at any rate. (*With a short laugh*) Well, well! So this is what made it absolutely essential that I should come to town in person. For the sake of Mrs. Sörby, we are to get up a pretence at family life in the house—a tableau of filial affection! That will be something new indeed.

WERLE: How dare you speak in that tone!

GREGERS: Was there ever any family life here? Never since I can remember. But now, forsooth, your plans demand something of the sort. No doubt it will have an excellent effect when it is reported that the son has hastened home, on the wings of filial piety, to the grey-haired father's wedding-feast. What will then remain of all the rumours as to the wrongs the poor dead mother had to submit to? Not a vestige. Her son annihilates them at one stroke.

WERLE: Gregers—I believe there is no one in the world you detest as you do me.

GREGERS (*softly*): I have seen you at too close quarters.

WERLE: You have seen me with your mother's eyes. (*Lowers his voice a little*) But you should remember that her eyes were—clouded now and then.

GREGERS (*quivering*): I see what you are hinting at. But who was to blame for mother's unfortunate weakness? Why you, and all those . . . ! The last of them was this woman that you palmed off upon Hialmar Ekdal, when you were . . . Ugh!

WERLE (*shrugs his shoulders*): Word for word as if it were your mother speaking!

GREGERS (*without heeding*): And there he is now, with his great, confiding, childlike mind, compassed about with all this treachery—living under the same roof with such a creature and never dreaming that what he calls his home is built upon a lie! (*Comes a step nearer*) When I look back upon your past, I seem to see a battle-field with shattered lives on every hand.

WERLE: I begin to think the chasm that divides us is too wide.

GREGERS (*bowing, with self-command*): So I have observed; and therefore I take my hat and go.

WERLE: You are going! Out of the house?

GREGERS: Yes. For at last I see my mission in life.

WERLE: What mission?

GREGERS: You would only laugh if I told you.

WERLE: A lonely man doesn't laugh so easily, Gregers.

GREGERS: (*pointing towards the background*): Look, father,—the Chamberlains are playing blind-man's-buff with Mrs. Sörby.—Good-night and good-bye.

(*He goes out by the back to the right. Sounds of laughter and merriment from the company, who are now visible in the outer room.*)

WERLE (*muttering contemptuously after* GREGERS): Ha . . . ! Poor wretch—and he says he is not overstrained!

(*The Curtain Falls.*)

# Act Two

HIALMAR EKDAL'S *studio, a good-sized room, evidently in the top story of the building. On the right, a sloping roof of large panes of glass, half-covered by a blue curtain. In the right-hand corner, at the back, the entrance door; farther forward, on the same side, a door leading to the sitting-room. Two doors on the opposite side, and between them an iron stove. At the back, a wide double sliding-door. The studio is plainly but comfortably fitted up and furnished. Between the doors on the right, standing out a little from the wall, a sofa with a table and some chairs; on the table a lighted lamp with a shade; beside the stove an old armchair. Photographic instruments and apparatus of different kinds lying about the room. Against the back wall, to the left of the double door, stands a bookcase containing a few books, boxes, and bottles of chemicals, instruments, tools, and other objects. Photographs and small articles, such as camel's-hair pencils, paper, and so forth, lie on the table.*

GINA EKDAL *sits on a chair by the table, sewing.* HEDVIG *is sitting on the sofa, with her hands shading her eyes and her thumbs in her ears, reading a book.*

GINA (*glances once or twice at* HEDVIG, *as if with secret anxiety; then says*): Hedvig!

(HEDVIG *does not hear.*)

GINA (*repeats more loudly*): Hedvig!

HEDVIG (*takes away her hands and looks up*): Yes, mother?

GINA: Hedvig dear, you mustn't sit reading any longer now.

HEDVIG: Oh, mother, mayn't I read a little more? Just a little bit?

GINA: No, no, you must put away your book now. Father doesn't like it; he never reads hisself in the evening.

HEDVIG (*shuts the book*): No, father doesn't care much about reading.

GINA (*puts aside her sewing and takes up a lead pencil and a little account-book from the table*): Can you remember how much we paid for the butter today?

HEDVIG: It was one crown sixty-five.

GINA: That's right. (*Puts it down*) It's terrible what a lot of butter we get through in this house. Then there was the smoked sausage, and the cheese—let me see—(*Writes*)—and the ham—(*Adds up*) Yes, that makes just . . .

HEDVIG: And then the beer.

GINA: Yes, to be sure. (*Writes*) How it do mount up! But we can't manage with no less.

HEDVIG: And then you and I didn't need anything hot for dinner, as father was out.

GINA: No; that was so much to the good. And then I took eight crowns fifty for the photographs.

HEDVIG: Really! So much as that?

GINA: Exactly eight crowns fifty.

(*Silence.* GINA *takes up her sewing again,* HEDVIG *takes paper and pencil and begins to draw, shading her eyes with her left hand.*)

HEDVIG: Isn't it jolly to think that father is at Mr. Werle's big dinner-party?

GINA: You know he's not really Mr. Werle's guest. It was the son invited him. (*After a pause*) We have nothing to do with that Mr. Werle.

HEDVIG: I'm longing for father to come home. He promised to ask Mrs. Sörby for something nice for me.

GINA: Yes, there's plenty of good things going in that house, I can tell you.

HEDVIG (*goes on drawing*): And I believe I'm a little hungry, too.

(OLD EKDAL, *with the paper parcel under his arm and another parcel in his coat pocket, comes in by the entrance door.*)

GINA: How late you are today, grandfather!

EKDAL: They had locked the office door. Had to wait in Gråberg's room. And then they let me through—h'm.

HEDVIG: Did you get some more copying to do, grandfather?

EKDAL: This whole packet. Just look.

GINA: That's capital.

HEDVIG: And you have another parcel in your pocket.

EKDAL: Eh? Oh, never mind, that's nothing. (*Puts his stick away in a corner*) This work will keep me going a long time, Gina. (*Opens one of the sliding-doors in the back wall a little*) Hush! (*Peeps into the room for a moment, then pushes the door carefully to again*) Hee-hee! They're fast asleep, all the lot of them. And she's gone into the basket herself. Hee-hee!

HEDVIG: Are you sure she isn't cold in that basket, grandfather?

EKDAL: Not a bit of it! Cold? With all that straw? (*Goes towards the farther door on the left*) There are matches in here, I suppose.

GINA: The matches is on the drawers.

(EKDAL *goes into his room.*)

HEDVIG: It's nice that grandfather has got all that copying.

GINA: Yes, poor old father; it means a bit of pocket-money for him.

HEDVIG: And he won't be able to sit the whole forenoon down at that horrid Madam Eriksen's.

GINA: No more he won't. (*Short silence.*)

HEDVIG: Do you suppose they are still at the dinner-table?

GINA: Goodness knows; as like as not.

HEDVIG: Think of all the delicious things father is having to eat! I'm certain he'll be in splendid spirits when he comes. Don't you think so, mother?

GINA: Yes; and if only we could tell him that we'd got the room let . . .

HEDVIG: But we don't need that this evening.

GINA: Oh, we'd be none the worst of it, I can tell you. It's no use to us as it is.

HEDVIG: I mean we don't need it this evening, for father will be in a good humour at any rate. It is best to keep the letting of the room for another time.

GINA (*looks across at her*): You like having some good news to tell father when he comes home in the evening?

HEDVIG: Yes; for then things are pleasanter somehow.

GINA (*thinking to herself*): Yes, yes, there's something in that.

(OLD EKDAL *comes in again and is going out by the foremost door to the left.*)

GINA (*half turning in her chair*): Do you want something out of the kitchen, grandfather?

EKDAL: Yes, yes, I do. Don't you trouble. (*Goes out.*)

GINA: He's not poking away at the fire, is he? (*Waits a moment*) Hedvig, go and see what he's about.

(EKDAL *comes in again with a small jug of steaming hot water.*)

HEDVIG: Have you been getting some hot water, grandfather?

EKDAL: Yes, hot water. Want it for something. Want to write, and the ink has got as thick as porridge—h'm.

GINA: But you'd best have your supper first, grandfather. It's laid in there.

EKDAL: Can't be bothered with supper, Gina. Very busy, I tell you. No one's to come to my room. No one—h'm.

(*He goes into his room;* GINA *and* HEDVIG *look at each other.*)

GINA (*softly*): Can you imagine where he's got money from?

HEDVIG: From Gråberg, perhaps.

GINA: Not a bit of it. Gråberg always sends the money to me.

HEDVIG: Then he must have got a bottle on credit somewhere.

GINA: Poor grandfather, who'd give him credit?

(HIALMAR EKDAL, *in an overcoat and grey felt hat, comes in from the right.*)

GINA (*throws down her sewing and rises*): Why, Ekdal, is that you already?

HEDVIG (*at the same time jumping up*): Fancy your coming so soon, father!

HIALMAR (*taking off his hat*): Yes, most of the people were coming away.

HEDVIG: So early?

HIALMAR: Yes, it was a dinner-party, you know. (*Is taking off his overcoat.*)

GINA: Let me help you.

HEDVIG: Me, too.

(*They draw off his coat;* GINA *hangs it up on the back wall.*)

HEDVIG: Were there many people there, father?

HIALMAR: Oh, no, not many. We were about twelve or fourteen at table.

GINA: And you had some talk with them all?

HIALMAR: Oh, yes, a little; but Gregers took me up most of the time.

GINA: Is Gregers as ugly as ever?

HIALMAR: Well, he's not very much to look at. Hasn't the old man come home?

HEDVIG: Yes, grandfather is in his room, writing.

HIALMAR: Did he say anything?

GINA: No, what should he say?

HIALMAR: Didn't he say anything about . . . ? I heard something about his having been with Gråberg. I'll go in and see him for a moment.

GINA: No, no, better not.

HIALMAR: Why not? Did he say he didn't want me to go in?

GINA: I don't think he wants to see nobody this evening . . .

HEDVIG (*making signs*): H'm—h'm!

GINA (*not noticing*): . . . he has been in to fetch hot water . . .

HIALMAR: Aha! Then he's . . .

GINA: Yes, I suppose so.

HIALMAR: Oh, God! my poor old white-haired father! . . . Well, well; there let him sit and get all the enjoyment he can.

(OLD EKDAL, *in an indoor coat and with a lighted pipe, comes from his room.*)

EKDAL: Got home? Thought it was you I heard talking.

HIALMAR: Yes, I have just come.

EKDAL: You didn't see me, did you?

HIALMAR: No, but they told me you had passed through—so I thought I would follow you.

EKDAL: H'm, good of you, Hialmar.—Who were they, all those fellows?

HIALMAR: Oh, all sorts of people. There was Chamberlain Flor, and Chamberlain Balle, and Chamberlain Kaspersen and Chamberlain—this, that, and the other—I don't know who all . . .

EKDAL (*nodding*): Hear that, Gina! Chamberlains every one of them!

GINA: Yes, I hear as they're terrible genteel in that house nowadays.

HEDVIG: Did the Chamberlains sing, father? Or did they read aloud?

HIALMAR: No, they only talked nonsense. They wanted me to recite something for them; but I knew better than that.

EKDAL: You weren't to be persuaded, eh?

GINA: Oh, you might have done it.

HIALMAR: No; one mustn't be at everybody's beck and call. (*Walks about the room*) That's not my way, at any rate.

EKDAL: No, no; Hialmar's not to be had for the asking, he isn't.

HIALMAR: I don't see why *I* should bother myself to entertain people on the rare occasions when I go into society. Let the others exert themselves. These fellows go from one great dinner-table to the next and gorge and guzzle day out and day in. It's for them to bestir themselves and do something in return for all the good feeding they get.

GINA: But you didn't say that?

HIALMAR (*humming*): Ho-ho-ho . . . ; faith, I gave them a bit of my mind.

EKDAL: Not the Chamberlains?

HIALMAR: Oh, why not? (*Lightly*) After that, we had a little discussion about Tokay.

EKDAL: Tokay! There's a fine wine for you!

HIALMAR (*comes to a standstill*): It may be a fine wine. But of course you know the vintages differ; it all depends on how much sunshine the grapes have had.

GINA: Why, you know everything, Ekdal.

EKDAL: And did they dispute that?

HIALMAR: They tried to; but they were requested to observe that it was just the same with Chamberlains—that with them, too, different batches were of different qualities.

GINA: What things you do think of!

EKDAL: Hee-hee! So they got that in their pipes, too?

HIALMAR: Right in their teeth.

EKDAL: Do you hear that, Gina? He said it right in the very teeth of all the Chamberlains.

GINA: Fancy . . . ! Right in their teeth!

HIALMAR: Yes, but I don't want it talked about. One doesn't speak of such things. The whole affair passed off quite amicably of course. They were nice, genial fellows; I didn't want to wound them—not I!

EKDAL: Right in their teeth, though . . . !

HEDVIG (*caressingly*): How nice it is to see you in a dress-coat! It suits you so well, father.

HIALMAR: Yes, don't you think so? And this one really fits to perfection. It fits almost as if it had been made for me;—a little tight in the arm-holes perhaps;—help me, Hedvig (*takes off the coat*). I think I'll put on my jacket. Where is my jacket, Gina?

GINA: Here it is. (*Brings the jacket and helps him.*)

HIALMAR: That's it! Don't forget to send the coat back to Molvik first thing tomorrow morning.

GINA (*laying it away*): I'll be sure and see to it.

HIALMAR (*stretching himself*): After all, there's a more homely feeling about this. A free-and-easy indoor costume suits my whole personality better. Don't you think so, Hedvig?

HEDVIG: Yes, father.

HIALMAR: When I loosen my necktie into a pair of flowing ends— like this—eh?

HEDVIG: Yes, that goes so well with your moustache and the sweep of your curls.

HIALMAR: I should not call them curls exactly; I should rather say locks.

HEDVIG: Yes, they are too big for curls.

HIALMAR: Locks describes them better.

HEDVIG (*after a pause, twitching his jacket*): Father.

HIALMAR: Well, what is it?

HEDVIG: Oh, you know very well.

HIALMAR: No, really I don't . . .

HEDVIG (*half laughing, half whimpering*): Oh, yes, father; now don't tease me any longer!

HIALMAR: Why, what do you mean?

HEDVIG (*shaking him*): Oh, what nonsense; come, where are they, father? All the good things you promised me, you know?

HIALMAR: Oh—if I haven't forgotten all about them!

HEDVIG: Now you're only teasing me, father! Oh, it's too bad of you! Where have you put them?

HIALMAR: No, I positively forgot to get anything. But wait a little! I have something else for you, Hedvig. (*Goes and searches in the pockets of the coat.*)

HEDVIG (*skipping and clapping her hands*): Oh, mother, mother!

GINA: There, you see; if you only give him time . . .

HIALMAR (*with a paper*): Look, here it is.

HEDVIG: That? Why, that's only a paper.

HIALMAR: That is the bill of fare, my dear; the whole bill of fare. Here you see: "Menu"—that means bill of fare.

HEDVIG: Haven't you anything else?

HIALMAR: I forgot the other things, I tell you. But you may take my word for it, these dainties are very unsatisfying. Sit down at the table and read the bill of fare, and then I'll describe to you how the dishes taste. Here you are, Hedvig.

HEDVIG (*gulping down her tears*): Thank you. (*She seats herself, but does not read;* GINA *makes signs to her;* HIALMAR *notices it.*)

HIALMAR (*pacing up and down the room*): It's monstrous what absurd things the father of a family is expected to think of; and if he forgets the smallest trifle, he is treated to sour faces at once. Well, well, one gets used to that, too. (*Stops near the stove, by the old man's chair*) Have you peeped in there this evening, father?

EKDAL: Yes, to be sure I have. She's gone into the basket.

HIALMAR: Ah, she has gone into the basket. Then she's beginning to get used to it.

EKDAL: Yes; just as I prophesied. But you know there are still a few little things . . .

HIALMAR: A few improvements, yes.

EKDAL: They've got to be made, you know.

HIALMAR: Yes, let us have a talk about the improvements, father. Come, let us sit on the sofa.

EKDAL: All right. H'm—think I'll just fill my pipe first. Must clean it out, too. H'm. (*He goes into his room.*)

GINA (*smiling to* HIALMAR): His pipe!

HIALMAR: Oh, yes, yes, Gina; let him alone—the poor, shipwrecked old man.—Yes, these improvements—we had better get them out of hand tomorrow.

GINA: You'll hardly have time tomorrow, Ekdal.

HEDVIG (*interposing*): Oh, yes he will, mother!

GINA: . . . for remember them prints that has to be retouched; they've sent for them time after time.

HIALMAR: There now! those prints again! I shall get them finished all right! Have any new orders come in?

GINA: No, worse luck; tomorrow I have nothing but those two sittings, you know.

HIALMAR: Nothing else? Oh, no, if people won't set about things with a will . . .

GINA: But what more can I do? Don't I advertise in the papers as much as we can afford?

HIALMAR: Yes, the papers, the papers; you see how much good they do. And I suppose no one has been to look at the room either?

GINA: No, not yet.

HIALMAR: That was only to be expected. If people won't keep their eyes open. . . . Nothing can be done without a real effort, Gina!

HEDVIG (*going towards him*): Shall I fetch you the flute, father?

HIALMAR: No; no flute for me; *I* want no pleasures in this world. (*Pacing about*) Yes, indeed I will work tomorrow; you shall see if I don't. You may be sure I shall work as long as my strength holds out.

GINA: But my dear, good Ekdal, I didn't mean it in that way.

HEDVIG: Father, mayn't I bring in a bottle of beer?

HIALMAR: No, certainly not. I require nothing, nothing . . . (*Comes to a standstill*) Beer? Was it beer you were talking about?

HEDVIG (*cheerfully*): Yes, father; beautiful, fresh beer.

HIALMAR: Well—since you insist upon it, you may bring in a bottle.

GINA: Yes, do; and we'll be nice and cosy.

(HEDVIG *runs towards the kitchen door.*)

HIALMAR (*by the stove, stops her, looks at her, puts his arm round her neck and presses her to him*): Hedvig, Hedvig!

HEDVIG (*with tears of joy*): My dear, kind father!

HIALMAR: No, don't call me that. Here have I been feasting at the rich man's table,—battening at the groaning board . . . ! And I couldn't even . . . !

GINA (*sitting at the table*): Oh, nonsense, nonsense, Ekdal.

HIALMAR: It's not nonsense! And yet you mustn't be too hard upon me. You know that I love you for all that.

HEDVIG (*throwing her arms round him*): And we love you, oh so dearly, father!

HIALMAR: And if I am unreasonable once in a while,—why then— you must remember that I am a man beset by a host of cares. There, there! (*Dries his eyes*) No beer at such a moment as this. Give me the flute.

(HEDVIG *runs to the bookcase and fetches it.*)

HIALMAR: Thanks! That's right. With my flute in my hand and you two at my side . . . ah . . . !

(HEDVIG *seats herself at the table near* GINA; HIALMAR *paces back-wards and forwards, pipes up vigorously and plays a Bohemian peasant dance, but in a slow plaintive tempo, and with sentimental expression.*)

HIALMAR (*breaking off the melody, holds out his left hand to* GINA *and says with emotion*): Our roof may be poor and humble, Gina; but it is home. And with all my heart I say: here dwells my happiness.

(*He begins to play again; almost immediately after, a knocking is heard at the entrance door.*)

GINA (*rising*): Hush, Ekdal,—I think there's some one at the door.

HIALMAR (*laying the flute on the bookcase*): There! Again!

(GINA *goes and opens the door.*)

GREGERS WERLE (*in the passage*): Excuse me . . .

GINA (*starting back slightly*): Oh!

GREGERS: . . . does not Mr. Ekdal, the photographer, live here?

GINA: Yes, he does.

HIALMAR (*going towards the door*): Gregers! You here after all? Well, come in then.

GREGERS (*coming in*): I told you I would come and look you up.

HIALMAR: But this evening . . . ? Have you left the party?

GREGERS: I have left both the party and my father's house.—Good evening, Mrs. Ekdal. I don't know whether you recognize me?

GINA: Oh, yes; it's not difficult to know young Mr. Werle again.

GREGERS: No, I am like my mother; and no doubt you remember her.

HIALMAR: Left your father's house, did you say?

GREGERS: Yes, I have gone to a hotel.

HIALMAR: Indeed. Well, since you're here, take off your coat and sit down.

GREGERS: Thanks.

(*He takes off his overcoat. He is now dressed in a plain grey suit of a countrified cut.*)

HIALMAR: Here, on the sofa. Make yourself comfortable.

(GREGERS *seats himself on the sofa;* HIALMAR *takes a chair at the table.*)

GREGERS (*looking around him*): So these are your quarters, Hialmar —this is your home.

HIALMAR: This is the studio, as you see . . .

GINA: But it's the largest of our rooms, so we generally sit here.

HIALMAR: We used to live in a better place; but this flat has one great advantage: there are such capital outer rooms . . .

GINA: And we have a room on the other side of the passage that we can let.

GREGERS (*to* HIALMAR): Ah—so you have lodgers, too?

HIALMAR: No, not yet. They're not so easy to find, you see; you have to keep your eyes open. (*To* HEDVIG) What about the beer, eh?

(HEDVIG *nods and goes out into the kitchen.*)

GREGERS: So that is your daughter?

HIALMAR: Yes, that is Hedvig.

GREGERS: And she is your only child?

HIALMAR: Yes, the only one. She is the joy of our lives, and—(*lowering his voice*)—at the same time our deepest sorrow, Gregers.

GREGERS: What do you mean?

HIALMAR: She is in serious danger of losing her eyesight.

GREGERS: Becoming blind?

HIALMAR: Yes. Only the first symptoms have appeared as yet, and she may not feel it much for some time. But the doctor has warned us. It is coming, inexorably.

GREGERS: What a terrible misfortune! How do you account for it?

HIALMAR (*sighs*): Hereditary, no doubt.

GREGERS (*starting*): Hereditary?

GINA: Ekdal's mother had weak eyes.

HIALMAR: Yes, so my father says; I can't remember her.

GREGERS: Poor child! And how does she take it?

HIALMAR: Oh, you can imagine we haven't the heart to tell her of it. She dreams of no danger. Gay and careless and chirping like a little bird, she flutters onward into a life of endless night. (*Overcome*) Oh, it is cruelly hard on me, Gregers.

(HEDVIG *brings a tray with beer and glasses, which she sets upon the table.*)

HIALMAR (*stroking her hair*): Thanks, thanks, Hedvig.

(HEDVIG *puts her arm around his neck and whispers in his ear.*)

HIALMAR: No, no bread and butter just now. (*Looks up*) But perhaps you would like some, Gregers.

GREGERS (*with a gesture of refusal*): No, no thank you.

HIALMAR (*still melancholy*): Well, you can bring in a little all the same. If you have a crust, that is all I want. And plenty of butter on it, mind.

(HEDVIG *nods gaily and goes out into the kitchen again.*)

GREGERS (*who has been following her with his eyes*): She seems quite strong and healthy otherwise.

GINA: Yes. In other ways there's nothing amiss with her, thank goodness.

GREGERS: She promises to be very like you, Mrs. Ekdal. How old is she now?

GINA: Hedvig is close on fourteen; her birthday is the day after tomorrow.

GREGERS: She is pretty tall for her age, then.

GINA: Yes, she's shot up wonderful this last year.

GREGERS: It makes one realize one's own age to see these young people growing up.—How long is it now since you were married?

GINA: We've been married—let me see— just on fifteen years.

GREGERS: Is it so long as that?

GINA (*becomes attentive; looks at him*): Yes, it is indeed.

HIALMAR: Yes, so it is. Fifteen years all but a few months. (*Changing his tone*) They must have been long years for you, up at the works, Gregers.

GREGERS: They seemed long while I was living them; now they are over, I hardly know how the time has gone.

(OLD EKDAL *comes from his room without his pipe, but with his old-fashioned uniform cap on his head; his gait is somewhat unsteady.*)

EKDAL: Come now, Hialmar, let's sit down and have a good talk about this—h'm—what was it again?

HIALMAR (*going towards him*): Father, we have a visitor here—Gregers Werle.—I don't know if you remember him.

EKDAL (*looking at* GREGERS, *who has risen*): Werle? Is that the son? What does he want with me?

HIALMAR: Nothing; it's me he has come to see.

EKDAL: Oh! Then there's nothing wrong?

HIALMAR: No, no, of course not.

EKDAL (*with a large gesture*): Not that I'm afraid, you know; but . . .

GREGERS (*goes over to him*): I bring you a greeting from your old hunting-grounds, Lieutenant Ekdal.

EKDAL: Hunting-grounds?

GREGERS: Yes, up in Höidal, about the works, you know.

EKDAL: Oh, up there. Yes, I knew all those places well in the old days.

GREGERS: You were a great sportsman then.

EKDAL: So I was, I don't deny it. You're looking at my uniform cap. I don't ask anybody's leave to wear it in the house. So long as I don't go out in the streets with it . . .

(HEDVIG *brings a plate of bread and butter, which she puts upon the table.*)

HIALMAR: Sit down, father, and have a glass of beer. Help yourself, Gregers.

(EKDAL *mutters and stumbles over to the sofa.* GREGERS *seats himself on the chair nearest to him,* HIALMAR *on the other side of* GREGERS. GINA *sits a little way from the table, sewing;* HEDVIG *stands beside her father.*)

GREGERS: Can you remember, Lieutenant Ekdal, how Hialmar and I used to come up and visit you in the summer and at Christmas?

EKDAL: Did you? No, no, no; I don't remember it. But sure enough I've been a tidy bit of a sportsman in my day. I've shot bears, too. I've shot nine of 'em, no less.

GREGERS (*looking sympathetically at him*): And now you never get any shooting?

EKDAL: Can't just say that, sir. Get a shot now and then perhaps. Of course not in the old way. For the woods you see—the woods, the woods . . . ! (*Drinks*) Are the woods fine up there now?

GREGERS: Not so fine as in your time. They have been thinned a good deal.

EKDAL: Thinned? (*More softly, and as if afraid*) It's dangerous work that. Bad things come of it. The woods revenge themselves.

HIALMAR (*filling up his glass*): Come—a little more, father.

GREGERS: How can a man like you—such a man for the open air—live in the midst of a stuffy town, boxed within four walls?

EKDAL (*laughs quietly and glances at* HIALMAR): Oh, it's not bad here. Not at all so bad.

GREGERS: But don't you miss all the things that used to be a part of your very being—the cool sweeping breezes, the free life in the woods and on the uplands, among beasts and birds . . . ?

EKDAL (*smiling*): Hialmar, shall we let him see it?

HIALMAR (*hastily and a little embarrassed*): Oh, no, no, father; not this evening.

GREGERS: What does he want to show me?

HIALMAR: Oh, it's only something—you can see it another time.

GREGERS (*continues, to the old man*): You see I have been thinking, Lieutenant Ekdal, that you should come up with me to the works; I am sure to be going back soon. No doubt you could get some copying there, too. And here, you have nothing on earth to interest you—nothing to liven you up.

EKDAL (*stares in astonishment at him*): Have *I* nothing on earth to . . . !

GREGERS: Of course you have Hialmar; but then he has his own family. And a man like you, who has always had such a passion for what is free and wild . . .

EKDAL (*thumps the table*): Hialmar, he shall see it!

HIALMAR: Oh, do you think it's worth while, father? It's all dark.

EKDAL: Nonsense; it's moonlight. (*Rises*) He shall see it, I tell you. Let me pass! Come and help me, Hialmar.

HEDVIG: Oh, yes, do, father!

HIALMAR (*rising*): Very well then.

GREGERS (*to* GINA): What is it?

GINA: Oh, nothing so very wonderful, after all.

(EKDAL *and* HIALMAR *have gone to the back wall and are each push-ing back a side of the sliding door;* HEDVIG *helps the old man;* GREGERS *remains standing by the sofa;* GINA *sits still and sews. Through the open doorway a large, deep irregular garret is seen with odd nooks and corners; a couple of stove-pipes running through it, from rooms below. There are skylights through which clear moonbeams shine in on some parts of the great room; others lie in deep shadow.*)

EKDAL (*to* GREGERS): You may come close up if you like.

GREGERS (*going over to them*): Why, what is it?

EKDAL: Look for yourself. H'm.

HIALMAR (*somewhat embarrassed*): This belongs to father, you understand.

GREGERS (*at the door, looks into the garret*): Why, you keep poultry, Lieutenant Ekdal.

EKDAL: Should think we did keep poultry. They've gone to roost now. But you should just see our fowls by daylight, sir!

HEDVIG: And there's a . . .

EKDAL: Sh—sh! don't say anything about it yet.

GREGERS: And you have pigeons, too, I see.

EKDAL: Oh, yes, haven't we just got pigeons! They have their nest-boxes up there under the roof-tree; for pigeons like to roost high, you see.

HIALMAR: They aren't all common pigeons.

EKDAL: Common! Should think not indeed! We have tumblers and a pair of pouters, too. But come here! Can you see that hutch down there by the wall?

GREGERS: Yes; what do you use it for?

EKDAL: That's where the rabbits sleep, sir.

GREGERS: Dear me; so you have rabbits, too?

EKDAL: Yes, you may take my word for it, we have rabbits! He wants to know if we have rabbits, Hialmar! H'm! But now comes the thing, let me tell you! Here we have it! Move away, Hedvig. Stand here; that's right,—and now look down there.—Don't you see a basket with straw in it?

GREGERS: Yes. And I can see a fowl lying in the basket.

EKDAL: H'm—"a fowl" . . .

GREGERS: Isn't it a duck?

EKDAL (*hurt*): Why, of course it's a duck.

HIALMAR: But what kind of duck, do you think?

HEDVIG: It's not just a common duck . . .

EKDAL: Sh!

GREGERS: And it's not a Muscovy duck either.

EKDAL: No, Mr.—Werle; it's not a Muscovy duck; for it's a wild duck!

GREGERS: Is it really? A wild duck?

EKDAL: Yes, that's what it is. That "fowl" as you call it—is the wild duck. It's our wild duck, sir.

HEDVIG: My wild duck. It belongs to me.

GREGERS: And can it live up here in the garret? Does it thrive?

EKDAL: Of course it has a trough of water to splash about in, you know.

HIALMAR: Fresh water every other day.

GINA (*turning towards* HIALMAR): But my dear Ekdal, it's getting icy cold here.

EKDAL: H'm, we had better shut up then. It's as well not to disturb their night's rest, too. Close up, Hedvig.

(HIALMAR *and* HEDVIG *push the garret doors together.*)

EKDAL: Another time you shall see her properly. (*Seats himself in the armchair by the stove*) Oh, they're curious things, these wild ducks. I can tell you.

GREGERS: How did you manage to catch it, Lieutenant Ekdal?

EKDAL: *I* didn't catch it. There's a certain man in this town whom we have to thank for it.

GREGERS (*starts slightly*): That man was not my father, was he?

EKDAL: You've hit it. Your father and no one else. H'm.

HIALMAR: Strange that you should guess that, Gregers.

GREGERS: You were telling me that you owed so many things to my father; and so I thought perhaps . . .

GINA: But we didn't get the duck from Mr. Werle himself . . .

EKDAL: It's Håkon Werle we have to thank for her, all the same, Gina. (*To* GREGERS) He was shooting from a boat, you see, and he brought her down. But your father's sight is not very good now. H'm; she was only wounded.

GREGERS: Ah! She got a couple of slugs in her body, I suppose.

HIALMAR: Yes, two or three.

HEDVIG: She was hit under the wing, so that she couldn't fly.

GREGERS: And I suppose she dived to the bottom, eh?

EKDAL (*sleepily, in a thick voice*): Of course. Always do that, wild ducks do. They shoot to the bottom as deep as they can get, sir—and bite themselves fast in the tangle and seaweed—and all the devil's own mess that grows down there. And they never come up again.

GREGERS: But your wild duck came up again, Lieutenant Ekdal.

EKDAL: He had such an amazingly clever dog, your father had. And that dog—he dived in after the duck and fetched her up again.

GREGERS (*who has turned to* HIALMAR): And then she was sent to you here?

HIALMAR: Not at once; at first your father took her home. But she wouldn't thrive there; so Pettersen was told to put an end to her . . .

EKDAL (*half asleep*): H'm—yes—Pettersen—that ass . . .

HIALMAR (*speaking more softly*): That was how we got her, you see; for father knows Pettersen a little; and when he heard about the wild duck he got him to hand her over to us.

GREGERS: And now she thrives as well as possible in the garret there?

HIALMAR: Yes, wonderfully well. She has got fat. You see, she has lived in there so long now that she has forgotten her natural wild life; and it all depends on that.

GREGERS: You are right there, Hialmar. Be sure you never let her get a glimpse of the sky and the sea. . . . But I mustn't stay any longer; I think your father is asleep.

HIALMAR: Oh, as for that . . .

GREGERS: But, by-the-bye—you said you had a room to let—a spare room?

HIALMAR: Yes; what then? Do you know of anybody . . . ?

GREGERS: Can I have that room?

HIALMAR: You?

GINA: Oh, no, Mr. Werle, you . . .

GREGERS: May I have the room? If so, I'll take possession first thing tomorrow morning.

HIALMAR: Yes, with the greatest pleasure . . .

GINA: But, Mr. Werle, I'm sure it's not at all the sort of room for you.

HIALMAR: Why, Gina! how can you say that?

GINA: Why, because the room's neither large enough nor light enough, and . . .

GREGERS: That really doesn't matter, Mrs. Ekdal.

HIALMAR: I call it quite a nice room, and not at all badly furnished either.

GINA: But remember the pair of them underneath.

GREGERS: What pair?

GINA: Well, there's one as has been a tutor . . .

HIALMAR: That's Molvik—Mr. Molvik, B.A.

GINA: And then there's a doctor, by the name of Relling.

GREGERS: Relling? I know him a little; he practised for a time up in Höidal.

GINA: They're a regular rackety pair, they are. As often as not, they're out on the loose in the evenings; and then they come home at all hours, and they're not always just . . .

GREGERS: One soon gets used to that sort of thing. I daresay I shall be like the wild duck . . .

GINA: H'm; I think you ought to sleep upon it first, anyway.

GREGERS: You seem very unwilling to have me in the house, Mrs. Ekdal.

GINA: Oh, no! What makes you think that?

HIALMAR: Well, you really behave strangely about it, Gina. (*To* GREGERS) Then I suppose you intend to remain in the town for the present?

GREGERS (*putting on his overcoat*): Yes, now I intend to remain here.

HIALMAR: And yet not at your father's? What do you propose to do, then?

GREGERS: Ah, if I only knew that, Hialmar, I shouldn't be so badly off! But when one has the misfortune to be called Gregers—! "Gregers"—and then "Werle" after it; did you ever hear anything so hideous?

HIALMAR: Oh, I don't think so at all.

GREGERS: Ugh! Bah! I feel I should like to spit upon the fellow that answers to such a name. But when a man is once for all doomed to be Gregers—Werle in this world, as I am . . .

HIALMAR (*laughs*): Ha, ha! If you weren't Gregers Werle, what would you like to be?

GREGERS: If I should choose, I should like best to be a clever dog.

GINA: A dog!

HEDVIG (*involuntarily*): Oh, no!

GREGERS: Yes, an amazingly clever dog; one that goes to the bottom after wild ducks when they dive and bite themselves fast in tangle and sea-weed, down among the ooze.

HIALMAR: Upon my word now, Gregers—I don't in the least know what you're driving at.

GREGERS: Oh, well, you might not be much the wiser if you did. It's understood, then, that I move in early tomorrow morning. (*To*

GINA) I won't give you any trouble; I do everything for myself. (*To* HIALMAR) We can talk about the rest tomorrow.—Good-night, Mrs. Ekdal. (*Nods to* HEDVIG) Good-night.

GINA: Good-night, Mr. Werle.

HEDVIG: Good-night.

HIALMAR (*who has lighted a candle*): Wait a moment; I must show you a light; the stairs are sure to be dark.

(GREGERS *and* HIALMAR *go out by the passage door.*)

GINA (*looking straight before her, with her sewing in her lap*): Wasn't that queer-like talk about wanting to be a dog?

HEDVIG: Do you know, mother—I believe he meant something quite different by that.

GINA: Why, what should he mean?

HEDVIG: Oh, I don't know; but it seemed to me he meant something different from what he said—all the time.

GINA: Do you think so? Yes, it was sort of queer.

HIALMAR (*comes back*): The lamp was still burning. (*Puts out the candle and sets it down*) Ah, now one can get a mouthful of food at last. (*Begins to eat the bread and butter*) Well, you see, Gina— if only you keep your eyes open . . .

GINA: How, keep your eyes open . . . ?

HIALMAR: Why, haven't we at last had the luck to get the room let? And just think—to a person like Gregers—a good old friend.

GINA: Well, I don't know what to say about it.

HEDVIG: Oh, mother, you'll see; it'll be such fun!

HIALMAR: You're very strange. You were so bent upon getting the room let before; and now you don't like it.

GINA: Yes, I do, Ekdal; if it had only been to some one else . . . But what do you suppose Mr. Werle will say?

HIALMAR: Old Werle? It doesn't concern him.

GINA: But surely you can see that there's something amiss between them again, or the young man wouldn't be leaving home. You know very well those two can't get on with each other.

HIALMAR: Very likely not, but . . .

GINA: And now Mr. Werle may fancy it's you that has egged him on . . .

HIALMAR: Let him fancy so, then! Mr. Werle has done a great deal for me; far be it from me to deny it. But that doesn't make me ever-lastingly dependent upon him.

GINA: But, my dear Ekdal, maybe grandfather'll suffer for it. He may lose the little bit of work he gets from Gråberg.

HIALMAR: I could almost say: so much the better! Is it not humiliating for a man like me to see his grey-haired father treated as a pariah? But now I believe the fulness of time is at hand. (*Takes a fresh piece of bread and butter*) As sure as I have a mission in life, I mean to fulfil it now!

HEDVIG: Oh, yes, father, do!

GINA: Hush! Don't wake him!

HIALMAR (*more softly*): I will fulfil it, I say. The day shall come when . . . And that is why I say it's a good thing we have let the room; for that makes me more independent. The man who has a mission in life must be independent. (*By the armchair, with emotion*) Poor old white-haired father! Rely on your Hialmar. He has broad shoulders—strong shoulders, at any rate. You shall yet wake up some fine day and . . . (*To* GINA) Do you not believe it?

GINA (*rising*): Yes, of course I do; but in the meantime suppose we see about getting him to bed.

HIALMAR: Yes, come.

(*They take hold of the old man carefully.*)

(*The Curtain Falls.*)

# Act Three

*H*IALMAR EKDAL'S *studio. It is morning: the daylight shines through the large window in the slanting roof; the curtain is drawn back.*

*HIALMAR is sitting at the table, busy retouching a photograph; several others lie before him. Presently GINA, wearing her hat and cloak, enters by the passage door; she has a covered basket on her arm.*

HIALMAR: Back already, Gina?

GINA: Oh, yes, one can't let the grass grow under one's feet. (*Sets her basket on a chair and takes off her things.*)

HIALMAR: Did you look in at Gregers' room?

GINA: Yes, that I did. It's a rare sight, I can tell you; he's made a pretty mess to start off with.

HIALMAR: How so?

GINA: He was determined to do everything for himself, he said; so he sets to work to light the stove, and what must he do but screw down the damper till the whole room is full of smoke. Ugh! There was a smell fit to . . .

HIALMAR: Well, really!

GINA: But that's not the worst of it; for then he thinks he'll put out the fire, and goes and empties his water-jug into the stove and so makes the whole floor one filthy puddle.

HIALMAR: How annoying!

GINA: I've got the porter's wife to clear up after him, pig that he is! But the room won't be fit to live in till the afternoon.

HIALMAR: What's he doing with himself in the meantime?

GINA: He said he was going out for a little while.

HIALMAR: I looked in upon him, too, for a moment—after you had gone.

GINA: So I heard. You've asked him to lunch.

HIALMAR: Just to a little bit of early lunch, you know. It's his first day—we can hardly do less. You've got something in the house, I suppose?

GINA: I shall have to find something or other.

HIALMAR: And don't cut it too fine, for I fancy Relling and Molvik are coming up, too. I just happened to meet Relling on the stairs, you see; so I had to . . .

GINA: Oh, are we to have those two as well?

HIALMAR: Good Lord—a couple more or less can't make any difference.

OLD EKDAL (*opens his door and looks in*): I say, Hialmar . . . (*Sees* GINA) Oh!

GINA: Do you want anything, grandfather?

EKDAL: Oh, no, it doesn't matter. H'm! (*Retires again.*)

GINA (*takes up the basket*): Be sure you see that he doesn't go out.

HIALMAR: All right, all right. And, Gina, a little herring-salad wouldn't be a bad idea; Relling and Molvik were out on the loose again last night.

GINA: If only they don't come before I'm ready for them . . .

HIALMAR: No, of course they won't; take your own time.

GINA: Very well; and meanwhile you can be working a bit.

HIALMAR: Well, I am working! I am working as hard as I can!

GINA: Then you'll have that job off your hands, you see.

(*She goes out to the kitchen with her basket.* HIALMAR *sits for a time pencilling away at the photograph, in an indolent and listless manner.*)

EKDAL (*peeps in, looks round the studio and says softly*): Are you busy?

HIALMAR: Yes, I'm toiling at these wretched pictures . . .

EKDAL: Well, well, never mind,—since you're so busy— h'm! (*He goes out again; the door stands open.*)

HIALMAR (*continues for some time in silence; then he lays down his brush and goes over to the door*): Are you busy, father?

EKDAL (*in a grumbling tone, within*): If you're busy, I'm busy, too. H'm!

HIALMAR: Oh, very well, then. (*Goes to his work again.*)

EKDAL (*presently, coming to the door again*): H'm; I say, Hialmar, I'm not so very busy, you know.

HIALMAR: I thought you were writing.

EKDAL: Oh, the devil take it! can't Gråberg wait a day or two? After all, it's not a matter of life and death.

HIALMAR: No; and you're not his slave either.

EKDAL: And about that other business in there . . .

HIALMAR: Just what I was thinking of. Do you want to go in? Shall I open the door for you?

EKDAL: Well, it wouldn't be a bad notion.

HIALMAR (*rises*): Then we'd have that off our hands.

EKDAL: Yes, exactly. It's got to be ready first thing tomorrow. It is tomorrow, isn't it? H'm?

HIALMAR: Yes, of course it's tomorrow.

(HIALMAR *and* EKDAL *push aside each his half of the sliding door. The morning sun is shining in through the skylights; some doves are flying about; others sit cooing, upon the perches; the hens are heard clucking now and then, further back in the garret.*)

HIALMAR: There; now you can get to work, father.

EKDAL (*goes in*): Aren't you coming, too?

HIALMAR: Well, really, do you know . . . ; I almost think . . . (*Sees* GINA *at the kitchen door*) I? No; I haven't time; I must work. —But now for our new contrivance . . .

(*He pulls a cord, a curtain slips down inside, the lower part con-
sisting of a piece of old sailcloth, the upper part of a stretched fish-
ing net. The floor of the garret is thus no longer visible.*)

HIALMAR (*goes to the table*): So! Now, perhaps I can sit in peace for
a little while.

GINA: Is he rampaging in there again?

HIALMAR: Would you rather have had him slip down to Madam
Eriksen's? (*Seats himself*) Do you want anything? You know you
said . . .

GINA: I only wanted to ask if you think we can lay the table for
lunch here?

HIALMAR: Yes; we have no early appointment, I suppose?

GINA: No, I expect no one today except those two sweethearts that
are to be taken together.

HIALMAR: Why the deuce couldn't they be taken together another
day!

GINA: Don't you know, I told them to come in the afternoon, when
you are having your nap.

HIALMAR: Oh, that's capital. Very well, let us have lunch here then.

GINA: All right; but there's no hurry about laying the cloth; you
can have the table for a good while yet.

HIALMAR: Do you think I am not sticking at my work? I'm at it as
hard as I can!

GINA: Then you'll be free later on, you know. (*Goes out into the
kitchen again. Short pause.*)

EKDAL (*in the garret doorway, behind the net*). Hialmar!

HIALMAR: Well?

EKDAL: Afraid we shall have to move the water-trough, after all.

HIALMAR: What else have I been saying all along?

EKDAL: H'm—h'm—h'm. (*Goes away from the door again.* HIAL-
MAR *goes on working a little; glances towards the garret and half
rises.* HEDVIG *comes in from the kitchen.*)

HIALMAR (*sits down again hurriedly*): What do you want?

HEDVIG: I only wanted to come in beside you, father.

HIALMAR (*after a pause*): What makes you go prying around like that? Perhaps you are told off to watch me?

HEDVIG: No, no.

HIALMAR: What is your mother doing out there?

HEDVIG: Oh, mother's in the middle of making the herring-salad. (*Goes to the table*) Isn't there any little thing I could help you with, father?

HIALMAR: Oh, no. It is right that I should bear the whole burden—so long as my strength holds out. Set your mind at rest, Hedvig; if only your father keeps his health . . .

HEDVIG: Oh, no, father! You mustn't talk in that horrid way.

(*She wanders about a little, stops by the doorway and looks into the garret.*)

HIALMAR: Tell me, what is he doing?

HEDVIG: I think he's making a new path to the water-trough.

HIALMAR: He can never manage that by himself! And here am I doomed to sit . . . !

HEDVIG (*goes to him*): Let me take the brush, father; I can do it, quite well.

HIALMAR: Oh, nonsense; you will only hurt your eyes.

HEDVIG: Not a bit. Give me the brush.

HIALMAR (*rising*): Well, it won't take more than a minute or two.

HEDVIG: Pooh, what harm can it do then? (*Takes the brush*) There! (*Seats herself*) I can begin upon this one.

HIALMAR: But mind you don't hurt your eyes! Do you hear? *I* won't be answerable; you do it on your own responsibility—understand that.

HEDVIG (*retouching*): Yes, yes, I understand.

HIALMAR: You are quite clever at it, Hedvig. Only a minute or two, you know.

(*He slips through by the edge of the curtain into the garret.* HEDVIG *sits at her work.* HIALMAR *and* EKDAL *are heard disputing inside.*)

HIALMAR (*appears behind the net*): I say, Hedvig—give me those pincers that are lying on the shelf. And the chisel. (*Turns away inside*) Now you shall see, father. Just let me show you first what I mean!

(HEDVIG *has fetched the required tools from the shelf and hands them to him through the net.*)

HIALMAR: Ah, thanks. I didn't come a moment too soon. (*Goes back from the curtain again; they are heard carpentering and talking inside.* HEDVIG *stands looking in at them. A moment later there is a knock at the passage door; she does not notice it.*)

GREGERS WERLE (*bareheaded, in indoor dress, enters and stops near the door*): H'm . . . !

HEDVIG (*turns and goes towards him*): Good morning. Please come in.

GREGERS: Thank you. (*Looking towards the garret*) You seem to have workpeople in the house.

HEDVIG: No, it is only father and grandfather. I'll tell them you are here.

GREGERS: No, no, don't do that; I would rather wait a little. (*Seats himself on the sofa.*)

HEDVIG: It looks so untidy here . . . (*Begins to clear away the photographs.*)

GREGERS: Oh, don't take them away. Are those prints that have to be finished off?

HEDVIG: Yes, they are a few I was helping father with.

GREGERS: Please don't let me disturb you.

HEDVIG: Oh, no.

(*She gathers the things to her and sits down to work;* GREGERS *looks at her, meanwhile, in silence.*)

GREGERS: Did the wild duck sleep well last night?

HEDVIG: Yes, I think so, thanks.

GREGERS (*turning towards the garret*): It looks quite different by day from what it did last night in the moonlight.

HEDVIG: Yes, it changes ever so much. It looks different in the morning and in the afternoon; and it's different on rainy days from what it is in fine weather.

GREGERS: Have you noticed that?

HEDVIG: Yes, how could I help it?

GREGERS: Are you, too, fond of being in there with the wild duck?

HEDVIG: Yes, when I can manage it . . .

GREGERS: But I suppose you haven't much spare time; you go to school, no doubt.

HEDVIG: No, not now; father is afraid of my hurting my eyes.

GREGERS: Oh; then he reads with you himself?

HEDVIG: Father has promised to read with me; but he has never had time yet.

GREGERS: Then is there nobody else to give you a little help?

HEDVIG: Yes, there is Mr. Molvik; but he is not always exactly— quite . . .

GREGERS: Sober?

HEDVIG: Yes, I suppose that's it!

GREGERS: Why, then you must have any amount of time on your hands. And in there I suppose it is a sort of world by itself?

HEDVIG: Oh, yes, quite. And there are such lots of wonderful things.

GREGERS: Indeed?

HEDVIG: Yes, there are big cupboards full of books; and a great many of the books have pictures in them.

GREGERS: Aha!

HEDVIG: And there's an old bureau with drawers and flaps, and a big clock with figures that go out and in. But the clock isn't going now.

GREGERS: So time has come to a standstill in there— in the wild duck's domain.

HEDVIG: Yes. And then there's an old paint-box and things of that sort; and all the books.

GREGERS: And you read the books, I suppose?

HEDVIG: Oh, yes, when I get the chance. Most of them are English though, and I don't understand English. But then I look at the pictures.—There is one great big book called "Harrison's History of London."* It must be a hundred years old; and there are such heaps of pictures in it. At the beginning there is Death with an hour-glass and a woman. I think that is horrid. But then there are all the other pictures of churches and castles and streets and great ships sailing on the sea.

GREGERS: But tell me, where did all those wonderful things come from?

HEDVIG: Oh, an old sea captain once lived here, and he brought them home with him. They used to call him "The Flying Dutchman." That was curious, because he wasn't a Dutchman at all.

GREGERS: Was he not?

HEDVIG: No. But at last he was drowned at sea; and so he left all those things behind him.

GREGERS: Tell me now—when you are sitting in there looking at the pictures, don't you wish you could travel and see the real world for yourself?

HEDVIG: Oh, no! I mean always to stay at home and help father and mother.

GREGERS: To retouch photographs?

HEDVIG: No, not only that. I should love above everything to learn to engrave pictures like those in the English books.

GREGERS: H'm. What does you father say to that?

* A *New and Universal History of the Cities of London and Westminster*, by Walter Harrison. London, 1775, folio.

HEDVIG: I don't think father likes it; father is strange about such things. Only think, he talks of my learning basket-making and straw-plaiting! But I don't think that would be much good.

GREGERS: Oh, no, I don't think so either.

HEDVIG: But father was right in saying that if I had learnt basket-making I could have made the new basket for the wild duck.

GREGERS: So you could; and it was you that ought to have done it, wasn't it?

HEDVIG: Yes, for it's my wild duck.

GREGERS: Of course it is.

HEDVIG: Yes, it belongs to me. But I lend it to father and grandfather as often as they please.

GREGERS: Indeed? What do they do with it?

HEDVIG: Oh, they look after it, and build places for it, and so on.

GREGERS: I see; for no doubt the wild duck is by far the most distinguished inhabitant of the garret?

HEDVIG: Yes, indeed she is; for she is a real wild fowl, you know. And then she is so much to be pitied; she has no one to care for, poor thing.

GREGERS: She has no family, as the rabbits have . . .

HEDVIG: No. The hens, too, many of them, were chickens together; but she has been taken right away from all her friends. And then there is so much that is strange about the wild duck. Nobody knows her, and nobody knows where she came from either.

GREGERS: And she has been down in the depths of the sea.

HEDVIG (with a quick glance at him, represses a smile and asks). Why do you say "the depths of the sea"?

GREGERS: What else should I say?

HEDVIG: You could say "the bottom of the sea."*

* Gregers here uses the old-fashioned expression "havsens bund," while Hedvig would have him use the more commonplace "havets bund" or "havbunden."

GREGERS: Oh, mayn't I just as well say the depths of the sea?

HEDVIG: Yes; but it sounds so strange to me when other people speak of the depths of the sea.

GREGERS: Why so? Tell me why?

HEDVIG: No, I won't; it's so stupid.

GREGERS: Oh, no, I am sure it's not. Do tell me why you smiled.

HEDVIG: Well, this is the reason: whenever I come to realize suddenly —in a flash—what is in there, it always seems to me that the whole room and everything in it should be called "the depths of the sea."— But that is so stupid.

GREGERS: You mustn't say that.

HEDVIG: Oh, yes, for you know it is only a garret.

GREGERS (*looks fixedly at her*): Are you so sure of that?

HEDVIG (*astonished*): That it's a garret?

GREGERS: Are you quite certain of it?

(HEDVIG *is silent, and looks at him open-mouthed.* GINA *comes in from the kitchen with the table things.*)

GREGERS (*rising*): I have come in upon you too early.

GINA: Oh, you must be somewhere; and we're nearly ready now, anyway. Clear the table, Hedvig.

(HEDVIG *clears away her things; she and* GINA *lay the cloth during what follows.* GREGERS *seats himself in the armchair and turns over an album.*)

GREGERS: I hear you can retouch, Mrs. Ekdal.

GINA (*with a side glance*): Yes, I can.

GREGERS: That was exceedingly lucky.

GINA: How—lucky?

GREGERS: Since Ekdal took to photography, I mean.

HEDVIG: Mother can take photographs, too.

GINA: Oh, yes; I was bound to learn that.

GREGERS: So it is really you that carry on the business, I suppose?

GINA: Yes, when Ekdal hasn't time himself . . .

GREGERS: He is a great deal taken up with his old father, I daresay.

GINA: Yes; and then you can't expect a man like Ekdal to do nothing but take car-de-visits of Dick, Tom and Harry.

GREGERS: I quite agree with you; but having once gone in for the thing . . .

GINA: You can surely understand, Mr. Werle, that Ekdal's not like one of your common photographers.

GREGERS: Of course not; but still . . .

(*A shot is fired within the garret.*)

GREGERS (*starting up*): What's that?

GINA: Ugh! now they're firing again!

GREGERS: Have they firearms in there?

HEDVIG: They are out shooting.

GREGERS: What! (*At the door of the garret*) Are you shooting, Hialmar?

HIALMAR (*inside the net*): Are you there? I didn't know; I was so taken up . . . (*To* HEDVIG) Why did you not let us know? (*Comes into the studio.*)

GREGERS: Do you go shooting in the garret?

HIALMAR (*showing a double-barrelled pistol*): Oh, only with this thing.

GINA: Yes, you and grandfather will do yourselves a mischief some day with that there pigstol.

HIALMAR (*with irritation*): I believe I have told you that this kind of firearm is called a pistol.

GINA: Oh, that doesn't make it much better, that I can see.

GREGERS: So you have become a sportsman, too, Hialmar?

HIALMAR: Only a little rabbit-shooting now and then. Mostly to please father, you understand.

GINA: Men are strange beings; they must always have something to pervert theirselves with.

HIALMAR (*snappishly*): Just so; we must always have something to divert ourselves with.

GINA: Yes, that's just what I say.

HIALMAR: H'm (*To* GREGERS) You see the garret is fortunately so situated that no one can hear us shooting. (*Lays the pistol on the top shelf of the bookcase*) Don't touch the pistol, Hedvig! One of the barrels is loaded; remember that.

GREGERS (*looking through the net*): You have a fowling-piece, too, I see.

HIALMAR: That is father's old gun. It's of no use now; something has gone wrong with the lock. But it's fun to have it all the same; for we can take it to pieces now and then, and clean and grease it, and screw it together again.—Of course, it's mostly father that fiddle-faddles with all that sort of thing.

HEDVIG (*beside* GREGERS): Now you can see the wild duck properly.

GREGERS: I was just looking at her. One of her wings seems to me to droop a bit.

HEDVIG: Well, no wonder; her wing was broken, you know.

GREGERS: And she trails one foot a little. Isn't that so?

HIALMAR: Perhaps a very little bit.

HEDVIG: Yes, it was by that foot the dog took hold of her.

HIALMAR: But otherwise she hasn't the least thing the matter with her; and that is simply marvellous for a creature that has a charge of shot in her body and has been between a dog's teeth . . .

GREGERS (*with a glance at* HEDVIG): . . . and that has lain in the depths of the sea—so long.

HEDVIG (*smiling*): Yes.

GINA (*laying the table*): That blessed wild duck! What a lot of fuss you do make over her.

HIALMAR: H'm;—will lunch soon be ready?

GINA: Yes, directly. Hedvig, you must come and help me now.

(GINA *and* HEDVIG *go out into the kitchen.*)

HIALMAR (*in a low voice*): I think you had better not stand there looking in at father; he doesn't like it. (GREGERS *moves away from the garret door.*) Besides, I may as well shut up before the others come. (*Claps his hands to drive the fowls back*) Shh-shh, in with you! (*Draws up the curtain and pulls the doors together*) All the contrivances are my own invention. It's really quite amusing to have things of this sort to potter with and to put to rights when they get out of order. And it's absolutely necessary, too; for Gina objects to having rabbits and fowls in the studio.

GREGERS: To be sure; and I suppose the studio is your wife's special department?

HIALMAR: As a rule, I leave the everyday details of business to her; for then I can take refuge in the parlour and give my mind to more important things.

GREGERS: What things may they be, Hialmar?

HIALMAR: I wonder you have not asked that question sooner. But perhaps you haven't heard of the invention?

GREGERS: The invention? No.

HIALMAR: Really? Have you not? Oh, no, out there in the wilds . . .

GREGERS: So you have invented something, have you?

HIALMAR: It is not quite completed yet; but I am working at it. You can easily imagine that when I resolved to devote myself to photography, it wasn't simply with the idea of taking likenesses of all sorts of commonplace people.

GREGERS: No; your wife was saying the same thing just now.

HIALMAR: I swore that if I consecrated my powers to this handicraft, I would so exalt it that it should become both an art and a science. And to that end I determined to make this great invention.

GREGERS: And what is the nature of the invention? What purpose does it serve?

HIALMAR: Oh, my dear fellow, you mustn't ask for details yet. It takes time, you see. And you must not think that my motive is vanity. It is not for my own sake that I am working. Oh, no; it is my life's mission that stands before me night and day.

GREGERS: What is your life's mission?

HIALMAR: Do you forget the old man with the silver hair?

GREGERS: Your poor father? Well, but what can you do for him?

HIALMAR: I can raise up his self-respect from the dead, by restoring the name of Ekdal to honour and dignity.

GREGERS: Then that is your life's mission?

HIALMAR: Yes. I will rescue the shipwrecked man. For shipwrecked he was, by the very first blast of the storm. Even while those terrible investigations were going on, he was no longer himself. That pistol there—the one we use to shoot rabbits with—has played its part in the tragedy of the house of Ekdal.

GREGERS: The pistol? Indeed?

HIALMAR: When the sentence of imprisonment was passed—he had the pistol in his hand . . .

GREGERS: Had he . . . ?

HIALMAR: Yes; but he dared not use it. His courage failed him. So broken, so demoralized was he even then! Oh, can you understand it? He, a soldier; he, who had shot nine bears, and who was descended from two lieutenant-colonels—one after the other, of course. Can you understand it, Gregers?

GREGERS: Yes, I understand it well enough.

HIALMAR: I cannot. And once more the pistol played a part in the history of our house. When he had put on the grey clothes and was under lock and key—oh, that was a terrible time for me, I can tell you. I kept the blinds drawn down over both my windows. When I peeped out, I saw the sun shining as if nothing had happened. I could not understand it. I saw people going along the street, laughing and talking about indifferent things. I could not understand it. It seemed to me that the whole of existence must be at a standstill—as if under an eclipse.

GREGERS: I felt that, too, when my mother died.

HIALMAR: It was in such an hour that Hialmar Ekdal pointed the pistol at his own breast.

GREGERS: You, too, thought of . . . !

HIALMAR: Yes.

GREGERS: But you did not fire?

HIALMAR: No. At the decisive moment I won the victory over myself. I remained in life. But I can assure you it takes some courage to choose life under circumstances like those.

GREGERS: Well, that depends on how you look at it.

HIALMAR: Yes, indeed, it takes courage. But I am glad I was firm; for now I shall soon perfect my invention; and Dr. Relling thinks, as I do myself, that father may be allowed to wear his uniform again. I will demand that as my sole reward.

GREGERS: So that is what he meant about his uniform . . . ?

HIALMAR: Yes, that is what he most yearns for. You can't think how my heart bleeds for him. Every time we celebrate any little family festival—Gina's and my wedding-day, or whatever it may be—in comes the old man in the lieutenant's uniform of happier days. But if he only hears a knock at the door—for he daren't show himself to strangers, you know—he hurries back to his room again as fast as his old legs can carry him. Oh, it's heart-rending for a son to see such things!

GREGERS: How long do you think it will take you to finish your invention?

HIALMAR: Come now, you mustn't expect me to enter into particulars like that. An invention is not a thing completely under one's own control. It depends largely on inspiration—on intuition—and it is almost impossible to predict when the inspiration may come.

GREGERS: But it's advancing?

HIALMAR: Yes, certainly, it is advancing. I turn it over in my mind every day; I am full of it. Every afternoon, when I have had my dinner, I shut myself up in the parlour, where I can ponder undisturbed. But I can't be goaded to it; it's not a bit of good; Relling says so, too.

GREGERS: And you don't think that all that business in the garret draws you off and distracts you too much?

HIALMAR: No, no, no; quite the contrary. You mustn't say that. I cannot be everlastingly absorbed in the same laborious train of thought. I must have something alongside of it to fill up the time of waiting. The inspiration, the intuition, you see—when it comes, it comes, and there's an end of it.

GREGERS: My dear Hialmar, I almost think you have something of the wild duck in you.

HIALMAR: Something of the wild duck? How do you mean?

GREGERS: You have dived down and bitten yourself fast in the undergrowth.

HIALMAR: Are you alluding to the well-nigh fatal shot that has broken my father's wing—and mine, too?

GREGERS: Not exactly to that. I don't say that your wing has been broken; but you have strayed into a poisonous marsh, Hialmar; an insidious disease has taken hold of you, and you have sunk down to die in the dark.

HIALMAR: I? To die in the dark? Look here, Gregers, you must really leave off talking such nonsense.

GREGERS: Don't be afraid; I shall find a way to help you up again. I, too, have a mission in life now; I found it yesterday.

HIALMAR: That's all very well; but you will please leave me out of it. I can assure you that—apart from my very natural melancholy, of course—I am as contented as any one can wish to be.

GREGERS: Your contentment is an effect of the marsh poison.

HIALMAR: Now, my dear Gregers, pray do not go on about disease and poison; I am not used to that sort of talk. In my house nobody ever speaks to me about unpleasant things.

GREGERS: Ah, that I can easily believe.

HIALMAR: It's not good for me, you see. And there are no marsh poisons here, as you express it. The poor photographer's roof is lowly, I know—and my circumstances are narrow. But I am an inventor, and I am the breadwinner of a family. That exalts me above my mean surroundings.—Ah, here comes lunch!

(GINA *and* HEDVIG *bring bottles of ale, a decanter of brandy, glasses, etc. At the same time,* RELLING *and* MOLVIK *enter from the passage; they are both without hat or overcoat.* MOLVIK *is dressed in black.*)

GINA (*placing the things upon the table*): Ah, you two have come in the nick of time.

RELLING: Molvik got it into his head that he could smell herring-salad, and then there was no holding him.—Good morning again, Ekdal.

HIALMAR: Gregers, let me introduce you to Mr. Molvik. Doctor . . . Oh, you know Relling, don't you?

GREGERS: Yes, slightly.

RELLING: Oh, Mr. Werle, junior! Yes, we two have had one or two little skirmishes up at the Höidal works. You've just moved in?

GREGERS: I moved in this morning.

RELLING: Molvik and I live right under you; so you haven't far to go for the doctor and the clergyman, if you should need anything in that line.

GREGERS: Thanks, it's not quite unlikely; for yesterday we were thirteen at table.

HIALMAR: Oh, come now, don't let us get upon unpleasant subjects again!

RELLING: You may make your mind easy, Ekdal; I'll be hanged if the finger of fate points to you.

HIALMAR: I should hope not, for the sake of my family. But let us sit down now, and eat and drink and be merry.

GREGERS: Shall we not wait for your father?

HIALMAR: No, his lunch will be taken in to him later. Come along!

(*The men seat themselves at table, and eat and drink.* GINA *and* HEDVIG *go in and out and wait upon them.*)

RELLING: Molvik was frightfully screwed yesterday, Mrs. Ekdal.

GINA: Really? Yesterday again?

RELLING: Didn't you hear him when I brought him home last night?

GINA: No, I can't say I did.

RELLING: That was a good thing, for Molvik was disgusting last night.

GINA: Is that true, Molvik?

MOLVIK: Let us draw a veil over last night's proceedings. That sort of thing is totally foreign to my better self.

RELLING (*to* GREGERS): It comes over him like a sort of possession, and then I have to go out on the loose with him. Mr. Molvik is dæmonic, you see.

GREGERS: Dæmonic?

RELLING: Molvik is dæmonic, yes.

GREGERS: H'm.

RELLING: And dæmonic natures are not made to walk straight through the world; they must meander a little now and then.—Well, so you still stick up there at those horrible grimy works?

GREGERS: I have stuck there until now.

RELLING: And did you ever manage to collect that claim you went about presenting?

GREGERS: Claim? (*Understands him*) Ah, I see.

HIALMAR: Have you been presenting claims, Gregers?

GREGERS: Oh, nonsense.

RELLING: Faith, but he has, though! He went around to all the cottars' cabins presenting something he called "the claim of the ideal."

GREGERS: I was young then.

RELLING: You're right; you were very young. And as for the claim of the ideal—you never got it honoured while *I* was up there.

GREGERS: Nor since either.

RELLING: Ah, then you've learnt to knock a little discount off, I expect.

GREGERS: Never, when I have a true man to deal with.

HIALMAR: No, I should think not, indeed. A little butter, Gina.

RELLING: And a slice of bacon for Molvik.

MOLVIK: Ugh, not bacon! (*A knock at the garret door.*)

HIALMAR: Open the door, Hedvig; father wants to come out.

(HEDVIG *goes and opens the door a little way;* EKDAL *enters with a fresh rabbit-skin; she closes the door after him.*)

EKDAL: Good morning, gentlemen! Good sport today. Shot a big one.

HIALMAR: And you've gone and skinned it without waiting for me . . . !

EKDAL: Salted it, too. It's good tender meat, is rabbit; it's sweet; it tastes like sugar. Good appetite to you, gentlemen. (*Goes into his room.*)

MOLVIK (*rising*): Excuse me . . . ; I can't . . . ; I must get downstairs immediately . . .

RELLING: Drink some soda water, man!

MOLVIK (*hurrying away*): Ugh—ugh! (*Goes out by the passage door.*)

RELLING (*to* HIALMAR): Let us drain a glass to the old hunter.

HIALMAR (*clinks glasses with him*): To the undaunted sportsman who has looked death in the face!

RELLING: To the grey-haired . . . (*Drinks*) By-the-bye, is his hair grey or white?

HIALMAR: Something between the two, I fancy; for that matter, he has very few hairs left of any colour.

RELLING: Well, well, one can get through the world with a wig. After all, you are a happy man, Ekdal; you have your noble mission to labour for . . .

HIALMAR: And I do labour, I can tell you.

RELLING: And then you have your excellent wife, shuffling quietly in and out in her felt slippers, and that see-saw walk of hers, and making everything cosy and comfortable about you.

HIALMAR: Yes, Gina—(*nods to her*)—you are a good helpmate on the path of life.

GINA: Oh, don't sit there cricketizing me.

RELLING: And your Hedvig, too, Ekdal!

HIALMAR (*affected*): The child, yes! The child before everything! Hedvig, come here to me. (*Strokes her hair*) What day is it to-morrow, eh?

HEDVIG (*shaking him*): Oh, no, you're not to say anything, father.

HIALMAR: It cuts me to the heart when I think what a poor affair it will be; only a little festivity in the garret . . .

HEDVIG: Oh, but that's just what I like!

RELLING: Just you wait till the wonderful invention sees the light, Hedvig!

HIALMAR: Yes, indeed—then you shall see . . . ! Hedvig, I have re-solved to make your future secure. You shall live in comfort all your days. I will demand—something or other—on your behalf. That shall be the poor inventor's sole reward.

HEDVIG (*whispering, with her arms round his neck*): Oh, you dear, kind father!

RELLING (*to* GREGERS): Come now, don't you find it pleasant, for once in a way, to sit at a well-spread table in a happy family circle?

HIALMAR: Ah, yes, I really prize these social hours.

GREGERS: For my part, I don't thrive in marsh vapours.

RELLING: Marsh vapours?

HIALMAR: Oh, don't begin with that stuff again!

GINA: Goodness knows there's no marsh vapours in this house, Mr. Werle; I give the place a good airing every blessed day.

GREGERS (*leaves the table*): No airing you can give will drive out the taint I mean.

HIALMAR: Taint!

GINA: Yes, what do you say to that, Ekdal!

RELLING: Excuse me—may it not be you yourself that have brought the taint from those mines up there?

GREGERS: It is like you to call what I bring into this house a taint.

RELLING (*goes up to him*): Look here, Mr. Werle, junior: I have a strong suspicion that you are still carrying about that "claim of the ideal" large as life, in your coat-tail pocket.

GREGERS: I carry it in my breast.

RELLING: Well, wherever you carry it, I advise you not to come dunning us with it here, so long as *I* am on the premises.

GREGERS: And if I do so nonetheless?

RELLING: Then you'll go head-foremost down the stairs; now I've warned you.

HIALMAR (*rising*): Oh, but Relling . . . !

GREGERS: Yes, you may turn me out . . .

GINA (*interposing between them*): We can't have that, Relling. But I must say, Mr. Werle, it ill becomes you to talk about vapours and taints, after all the mess you made with your stove. (*A knock at the passage door.*)

HEDVIG: Mother, there's somebody knocking.

HIALMAR: There now, we're going to have a whole lot of people!

GINA: I'll go . . . (*Goes over and opens the door, starts, and draws back*) Oh—oh, dear!

(WERLE, *in a fur coat, advances one step into the room.*)

WERLE: Excuse me; but I think my son is staying here.

GINA (*with a gulp*): Yes.

HIALMAR (*approaching him*): Won't you do us the honour to . . . ?

WERLE: Thank you, I merely wish to speak to my son.

GREGERS: What is it? Here I am.

WERLE: I want a few words with you, in your room.

GREGERS: In my room? Very well . . . (*About to go.*)

GINA: No, no, your room's not in a fit state . . .

WERLE: Well then, out in the passage here; I want to have a few words with you alone.

HIALMAR: You can have them here, sir. Come into the parlour, Relling.

(HIALMAR *and* RELLING *go off to the right.* GINA *takes* HEDVIG *with her into the kitchen.*)

GREGERS (*after a short pause*): Well, now we are alone.

WERLE: From something you let fall last evening, and from your coming to lodge with the Ekdals, I can't help inferring that you intend to make yourself unpleasant to me, in one way or another.

GREGERS: I intend to open Hialmar Ekdal's eyes. He shall see his position as it really is—that is all.

WERLE: Is that the mission in life you spoke of yesterday?

GREGERS: Yes. You have left me no other.

WERLE: Is it I, then, that crippled your mind, Gregers?

GREGERS: You have crippled my whole life. I am not thinking of all that about mother . . . But it's thanks to you that I am continually haunted and harassed by a guilty conscience.

WERLE: Indeed! It is your conscience that troubles you, is it?

GREGERS: I ought to have taken a stand against you when the trap was set for Lieutenant Ekdal. I ought to have cautioned him; for I had a misgiving as to what was in the wind.

WERLE: Yes, that was the time to have spoken.

GREGERS: I did not dare to, I was so cowed and spiritless. I was mortally afraid of you—not only then, but long afterwards.

WERLE: You have got over that fear now, it appears.

GREGERS: Yes, fortunately. The wrong done to old Ekdal, both by me and by —others, can never be undone; but Hialmar I can rescue from all the falsehood and deception that are bringing him to ruin.

WERLE: Do you think that will be doing him a kindness?

GREGERS: I have not the least doubt of it.

WERLE: You think our worthy photographer is the sort of man to appreciate such friendly offices?

GREGERS: Yes, I do.

WERLE: H'm—we shall see.

GREGERS: Besides, if I am to go on living, I must try to find some cure for my sick conscience.

WERLE: It will never be sound. Your conscience has been sickly from childhood. That is a legacy from your mother, Gregers—the only one she left you.

GREGERS (*with a scornful half-smile*): Have you not yet forgiven her for the mistake you made in supposing she would bring you a fortune?

WERLE: Don't let us wander from the point.—Then you hold to your purpose of setting young Ekdal upon what you imagine to be the right scent?

GREGERS: Yes, that is my fixed resolve.

WERLE: Well, in that case I might have spared myself this visit; for, of course, it is useless to ask whether you will return home with me?

GREGERS: Quite useless.

WERLE: And I suppose you won't enter the firm either?

GREGERS: No.

WERLE: Very good. But as I am thinking of marrying again, your share in the property will fall to you at once.*

GREGERS (*quickly*): No, I do not want that.

WERLE: You don't want it?

GREGERS: No, I dare not take it, for conscience' sake.

WERLE (*after a pause*): Are you going up to the works again?

GREGERS: No; I consider myself released from your service.

WERLE: But what are you going to do?

GREGERS: Only to fulfill my mission; nothing more.

WERLE: Well, but afterwards? What are you going to live upon?

GREGERS: I have laid by a little out of my salary.

WERLE: How long will that last?

GREGERS: I think it will last my time.

WERLE: What do you mean?

GREGERS: I shall answer no more questions.

WERLE: Good-bye then, Gregers.

GREGERS: Good-bye (WERLE *goes.*)

HIALMAR (*peeping in*): He's gone, isn't he?

GREGERS: Yes.

(HIALMAR *and* RELLING *enter; also* GINA *and* HEDVIG *from the kitchen.*)

RELLING: That luncheon-party was a failure.

GREGERS: Put on your coat, Hialmar; I want you to come for a long walk with me.

HIALMAR: With pleasure. What was it your father wanted? Had it anything to do with me?

GREGERS: Come along. We must have a talk. I'll go and put on my overcoat. (*Goes out by the passage door.*)

* By Norwegian law, before a widower can marry again, a certain proportion of his property must be settled on his children by his former marriage.

GINA: You shouldn't go out with him, Ekdal.

RELLING: No, don't you do it. Stay where you are.

HIALMAR (*gets his hat and overcoat*): Oh, nonsense! When a friend of my youth feels impelled to open his mind to me in private . . .

RELLING: But devil take it—don't you see that the fellow's mad, cracked, demented!

GINA: There, what did I tell you! His mother before him had crazy fits like that sometimes.

HIALMAR: The more need for a friend's watchful eye. (*To* GINA) Be sure you have dinner ready in good time. Good-bye for the present. (*Goes out by the passage door.*)

RELLING: It's a thousand pities the fellow didn't go to hell through one of the Höidal mines.

GINA: Good Lord! what makes you say that?

RELLING (*muttering*): Oh, I have my own reasons.

GINA: Do you think young Werle is really mad?

RELLING: No, worse luck; he's no madder than most other people. But one disease he has certainly got in his system.

GINA: What is it that's the matter with him?

RELLING: Well, I'll tell you, Mrs. Ekdal. He is suffering from an acute attack of integrity.

GINA: Integrity?

HEDVIG: Is that a kind of disease?

RELLING: Yes, it's a national disease; but it only appears sporadically. (*Nods to* GINA) Thanks for your hospitality. (*He goes out by the passage door.*)

GINA (*moving restlessly to and fro*): Ugh, that Gregers Werle—he was always a wretched creature.

HEDVIG (*standing by the table and looking searchingly at her*): I think all this is very strange.

(*The Curtain Falls.*)

# Act Four

HIALMAR EKDAL'S *studio. A photograph has just been taken; a camera with the cloth over it, a pedestal, two chairs, a folding table, etc., are standing out in the room. Afternoon light; the sun is going down; a little later it begins to grow dusk.*

GINA *stands in the passage doorway, with a little box and a wet glass plate in her hand, and is speaking to somebody outside.*

GINA: Yes, certainly. When I make a promise I keep it. The first dozen shall be ready on Monday. Good afternoon.

(*Someone is heard going downstairs.* GINA *shuts the door, slips the plate into the box and puts it into the covered camera.*)

HEDVIG (*comes in from the kitchen*): Are they gone?

GINA (*tidying up*): Yes, thank goodness, I've got rid of them at last.

HEDVIG: But can you imagine why father hasn't come home yet?

GINA: Are you sure he's not down in Relling's room?

HEDVIG: No, he's not; I ran down the kitchen stair just now and asked.

GINA: And his dinner standing and getting cold, too.

HEDVIG: Yes, I can't understand it. Father's always so careful to be home to dinner!

GINA: Oh, he'll be here directly, you'll see.

HEDVIG: I wish he would come; everything seems so queer today

GINA (*calls out*): There he is!

(HIALMAR EKDAL *comes in at the passage door.*)

HEDVIG (*going to him*): Father! Oh, what a time we've been waiting for you!

GINA (*glancing sidelong at him*): You've been out a long time, Ekdal.

HIALMAR (*without looking at her*): Rather long, yes.

(*He takes off his overcoat;* GINA *and* HEDVIG *go to help him; he motions them away.*)

GINA: Perhaps you've had dinner with Werle?

HIALMAR (*hanging up his coat*): No.

GINA (*going towards the kitchen door*): Then I'll bring some in for you.

HIALMAR: No; let the dinner alone. I want nothing to eat.

HEDVIG (*going nearer to him*): Are you not well, father?

HIALMAR: Well? Oh, yes, well enough. We have had a tiring walk, Gregers and I.

GINA: You didn't ought to have gone so far, Ekdal; you're not used to it.

HIALMAR: H'm; there's many a thing a man must get used to in this world. (*Wanders about the room*) Has any one been here whilst I was out?

GINA: Nobody but the two sweethearts.

HIALMAR: No new orders?

GINA: No, not today.

HEDVIG: There will be some tomorrow, father, you'll see.

HIALMAR: I hope there will; for tomorrow I am going to set to work in real earnest.

HEDVIG: Tomorrow! Don't you remember what day it is tomorrow?

HIALMAR: Oh, yes, by-the-bye. . . . Well, the day after, then. Henceforth I mean to do everything myself; I shall take all the work into my own hands.

GINA: Why, what can be the good of that, Ekdal? It'll only make your life a burden to you. I can manage the photography all right; and you can go on working at your invention.

HEDVIG: And think of the wild duck, father,—and all the hens and rabbits and . . . !

HIALMAR: Don't talk to me of all that trash! From tomorrow I will never set foot in the garret again.

HEDVIG: Oh, but father, you promised that we should have a little party . . .

HIALMAR: H'm, true. Well, then, from the day after tomorrow. I should almost like to wring that cursed wild duck's neck!

HEDVIG (*shrieks*): The wild duck!

GINA: Well, I never!

HEDVIG (*shaking him*): Oh, no, father; you know it's my wild duck!

HIALMAR: That is why I don't do it. I haven't the heart to—for your sake, Hedvig. But in my inmost soul I feel that I ought to do it. I ought not to tolerate under my roof a creature that has been through those hands.

GINA: Why, good gracious, even if grandfather did get it from that poor creature, Pettersen . . .

HIALMAR (*wandering about*): There are certain claims—what shall I call them?—let me say claims of the ideal—certain obligations, which a man cannot disregard without injury to his soul.

HEDVIG (*going after him*): But think of the wild duck,—the poor wild duck!

HIALMAR (*stops*): I tell you I will spare it—for your sake. Not a hair of its head shall be—I mean, it shall be spared. There are greater problems than that to be dealt with. But you should go out a little now, Hedvig, as usual; it is getting dusk enough for you now.

HEDVIG: No, I don't care about going out now.

HIALMAR: Yes, do; it seems to me your eyes are blinking a great deal; all these vapours in here are bad for you. The air is heavy under this roof.

HEDVIG: Very well, then, I'll run down the kitchen stair and go for a little walk. My cloak and hat?—oh, they're in my own room. Father —be sure you don't do the wild duck any harm whilst I'm out.

HIALMAR: Not a feather of its head shall be touched. (*Draws her to him*) You and I, Hedvig—we two . . . ! Well, go along.

(HEDVIG *nods to her parents and goes out through the kitchen.*)

HIALMAR (*walks about without looking up*): Gina.

GINA: Yes?

HIALMAR: From tomorrow—or, say, from the day after tomorrow —I should like to keep the household account-book myself.

GINA: Do you want to keep the accounts, too, now?

HIALMAR: Yes; or to check the receipts at any rate.

GINA: Lord help us! that's soon done.

HIALMAR: One would hardly think so; at any rate, you seem to make the money go a very long way. (*Stops and looks at her*) How do you manage it?

GINA: It's because me and Hedvig, we need so little.

HIALMAR: Is it the case that father is very liberally paid for the copying he does for Mr. Werle?

GINA: I don't know as he gets anything out of the way. I don't know the rates for that sort of work.

HIALMAR: Well, what does he get, about? Let me hear!

GINA: Oh, it varies; I daresay it'll come to about as much as he costs us, with a little pocket-money over.

HIALMAR: As much as he costs us! And you have never told me this before!

GINA: No, how could I tell you? It pleased you so much to think he got everything from you.

HIALMAR: And he gets it from Mr. Werle.

GINA: Oh, well, he has plenty and to spare, he has.

HIALMAR: Light the lamp for me, please!

GINA (*lighting the lamp*): And, of course, we don't know as it's Mr. Werle himself; it may be Gråberg . . .

HIALMAR: Why attempt such an evasion?

GINA: I don't know; I only thought . . .

HIALMAR: H'm.

GINA: It wasn't me that got grandfather that copying. It was Bertha, when she used to come about us.

HIALMAR: It seems to me your voice is trembling.

GINA (*putting the lamp-shade on*): Is it?

HIALMAR: And your hands are shaking, are they not?

GINA (*firmly*): Come right out with it, Ekdal. What has he been saying about me?

HIALMAR: Is it true—can it be true that—that there was an—an under-standing between you and Mr. Werle, while you were in service there?

GINA: That's not true. Not at that time. Mr. Werle did come after me, that's a fact. And his wife thought there was something in it, and then she made such a hocus-pocus and hurly-burly, and she hustled me and bustled me about so, that I left her service.

HIALMAR: But afterwards, then?

GINA: Well, then I went home. And mother—well, she wasn't the woman you took her for, Ekdal; she kept on worrying and worrying at me about one thing and another—for Mr. Werle was a widower by that time.

HIALMAR: Well, and then?

GINA: I suppose you've got to know it. He gave me no peace until he'd had his way.

HIALMAR (*striking his hands together*): And this is the mother of my child! How could you hide this from me?

GINA: Yes, it was wrong of me; I ought certainly to have told you long ago.

HIALMAR: You should have told me at the very first;—then I should have known the sort of woman you were.

GINA: But would you have married me all the same?

HIALMAR: How can you dream that I would?

GINA: That's just why I didn't dare tell you anything, then. For I'd come to care for you so much, you see; and I couldn't go and make myself utterly miserable . . .

HIALMAR (*walks about*): And this is my Hedvig's mother. And to know that all I see before me—(*kicks a chair*)—all that I call my home—I owe to a favoured predecessor! Oh, that scoundrel Werle!

GINA: Do you repent of the fourteen—the fifteen years we've lived together?

HIALMAR (*placing himself in front of her*): Have you not every day, every hour, repented of the spider's-web of deceit you have spun around me? Answer me that! How could you help writhing with penitence and remorse?

GINA: Oh, my dear Ekdal, I've had all I could do to look after the house and get through the day's work . . .

HIALMAR: Then you never think of reviewing your past?

GINA: No; Heaven knows I'd almost forgotten those old stories.

HIALMAR: Oh, this dull, callous contentment! To me there is something revolting about it. Think of it—never so much as a twinge of remorse!

GINA: But tell me, Ekdal—what would have become of you if you hadn't had a wife like me?

HIALMAR: Like you . . . !

GINA: Yes; for you know I've always been a bit more practical and wide-awake than you. Of course I'm a year or two older.

HIALMAR: What would have become of me!

GINA: You'd got into all sorts of bad ways when first you met me; that you can't deny.

HIALMAR: "Bad ways" do you call them? Little do you know what a man goes through when he is in grief and despair—especially a man of my fiery temperament.

GINA: Well, well, that may be so. And I've no reason to crow over you, neither; for you turned a moral of a husband, that you did, as soon as ever you had a house and home of your own.—And now we'd got everything so nice and cosy about us; and me and Hedvig was just thinking we'd soon be able to let ourselves go a bit, in the way of both food and clothes.

HIALMAR: In the swamp of deceit, yes.

GINA: I wish to goodness that detestable thing had never set his foot inside our doors!

HIALMAR: And I, too, thought my home such a pleasant one. That was a delusion. Where shall I now find the elasticity of spirit to bring my invention into the world of reality? Perhaps it will die with me; and then it will be your past, Gina, that will have killed it.

GINA (*nearly crying*): You mustn't say such things, Ekdal. Me, that has only wanted to do the best I could for you, all my days!

HIALMAR: I ask you, what becomes of the breadwinner's dream? When I used to lie in there on the sofa and brood over my invention, I had a clear enough presentiment that it would sap my vitality to the last drop. I felt even then that the day when I held the patent in my hand—that day—would bring my—release. And then it was my dream that you should live on after me, the dead inventor's well-to-do widow.

GINA (*drying her tears*): No, you mustn't talk like that, Ekdal. May the Lord never let me see the day I am left a widow!

HIALMAR: Oh, the whole dream has vanished. It is all over now. All over!

(GREGERS WERLE *opens the passage door cautiously and looks in.*)

GREGERS: May I come in?

HIALMAR: Yes, come in.

GREGERS (*comes forward, his face beaming with satisfaction, and holds out both his hands to them*): Well, dear friends . . . ! (*Looks from one to the other and whispers to* HIALMAR) Have you not done it yet?

HIALMAR (*aloud*): It is done.

GREGERS: It is?

HIALMAR: I have passed through the bitterest moments of my life.

GREGERS: But also, I trust, the most ennobling.

HIALMAR: Well, at any rate, we have got through it for the present.

GINA: God forgive you, Mr. Werle.

GREGERS (*in great surprise*): But I don't understand this.

HIALMAR: What don't you understand?

GREGERS: After so great a crisis—a crisis that is to be the starting-point of an entirely new life—of a communion founded on truth, and free from all taint of deception . . .

HIALMAR: Yes, yes, I know; I know that quite well.

GREGERS: I confidently expected, when I entered the room, to find the light of transfiguration shining upon me from both husband and wife. And now I see nothing but dulness, oppression, gloom . . .

GINA: Oh, is that it? (*Takes off the lamp-shade.*)

GREGERS: You will not understand me, Mrs. Ekdal. Ah, well, you, I suppose, need time to. . . . But you, Hialmar? Surely you feel a new consecration after the great crisis.

HIALMAR: Yes, of course I do. That is—in a sort of way.

GREGERS: For surely nothing in the world can compare with the joy of forgiving one who has erred and raising her up to oneself in love.

HIALMAR: Do you think a man can so easily throw off the bitter cup I have drained?

GREGERS: No, not a common man, perhaps. But a man like you . . . !

HIALMAR: Good God! I know that well enough. But you must keep me up to it, Gregers. It takes time, you know.

GREGERS: You have much of the wild duck in you, Hialmar. (RELLING *has come in at the passage door.*)

RELLING: Oho! is the wild duck to the fore again?

HIALMAR: Yes; Mr. Werle's wing-broken victim.

RELLING: Mr. Werle's . . . ? So it's him you are talking about?

HIALMAR: Him and—ourselves.

RELLING (*in an undertone to* GREGERS): May the devil fly away with you!

HIALMAR: What is that you are saying?

RELLING: Only uttering a heartfelt wish that this quack-salver would take himself off. If he stays here, he is quite equal to making an utter mess of life, for both of you.

GREGERS: These two will not make a mess of life, Mr. Relling. Of course I won't speak of Hialmar—him we know. But she, too, in her innermost heart, has certainly something loyal and sincere . . .

GINA (*almost crying*): You might have let me alone for what I was, then.

RELLING (*to* GREGERS): Is it rude to ask what you really want in this house?

GREGERS: To lay the foundations of a true marriage.

RELLING: So you don't think Ekdal's marriage is good enough as it is?

GREGERS: No doubt it is as good a marriage as most others, worse luck. But a true marriage it has yet to become.

HIALMAR: You have never had eyes for the claims of the ideal, Relling.

RELLING: Rubbish, my boy!—but excuse me, Mr. Werle: how many —in round numbers—how many true marriages have you seen in the course of your life?

GREGERS: Scarcely a single one.

RELLING: Nor I either.

GREGERS: But I have seen innumerable marriages of the opposite kind. And it has been my fate to see at close quarters what ruin such a marriage can work in two human souls.

HIALMAR: A man's whole moral basis may give away beneath his feet; that is the terrible part of it.

RELLING: Well, I can't say I've ever been exactly married, so I don't pretend to speak with authority. But this I know, that the child enters into the marriage problem. And you must leave the child in peace.

HIALMAR: Oh—Hedvig! my poor Hedvig!

RELLING: Yes, you must be good enough to keep Hedvig outside of all this. You two are grown-up people; you are free, in God's name, to make what mess and muddle you please of your life. But you must deal cautiously with Hedvig, I tell you; else you may do her a great injury.

HIALMAR: An injury!

RELLING: Yes, or she may do herself an injury—and perhaps others, too.

GINA: How can you know that, Relling?

HIALMAR: Her sight is in no immediate danger, is it?

RELLING: I am not talking about her sight. Hedvig is at a critical age. She may be getting all sorts of mischief into her head.

GINA: That's true—I've noticed it already! She's taken to carrying on with the fire, out in the kitchen. She calls it playing at house-on-fire. I'm often scared for fear she really sets fire to the house.

RELLING: You see; I thought as much.

GREGERS (to RELLING): But how do you account for that?

RELLING (sullenly): Her constitution's changing, sir.

HIALMAR: So long as the child has me . . . ! So long as I am above ground . . . ! (A knock at the door.)

GINA: Hush, Ekdal; there's some one in the passage. (Calls out) Come in!

(MRS. SÖRBY, in walking dress, comes in.)

MRS. SÖRBY: Good evening.

GINA (*going towards her*): Is it really you, Bertha?

MRS. SÖRBY: Yes, of course it is. But I'm disturbing you, I'm afraid?

HIALMAR: No, not at all; an emissary from that house . . .

MRS. SÖRBY (*to* GINA): To tell the truth, I hoped your men-folk would be out at this time. I just ran up to have a little chat with you, and to say good-bye.

GINA: Good-bye? Are you going away, then?

MRS. SÖRBY: Yes, tomorrow morning,—up to Höidal. Mr. Werle started this afternoon. (*Lightly to* GREGERS) He asked me to say good-bye for him.

GINA: Only fancy . . . !

HIALMAR: So Mr. Werle has gone? And now you are going after him?

MRS. SÖRBY: Yes, what do you say to that, Ekdal?

HIALMAR: I say: beware!

GREGERS: I must explain the situation. My father and Mrs. Sörby are going to be married.

HIALMAR: Going to be married!

GINA: Oh, Bertha! So it's come to that at last!

RELLING (*his voice quivering a little*): This is surely not true?

MRS. SÖRBY: Yes, my dear Relling, it's true enough.

RELLING: You are going to marry again?

MRS. SÖRBY: Yes, it looks like it. Werle has got a special license, and we are going to be married quite quietly, up at the works.

GREGERS: Then I must wish you all happiness, like a dutiful stepson.

MRS. SÖRBY: Thank you very much—if you mean what you say. I certainly hope it will lead to happiness, both for Werle and for me.

RELLING: You have every reason to hope that. Mr. Werle never gets drunk—so far as I know; and I don't suppose he's in the habit of thrashing his wives, like the late lamented horse-doctor.

MRS. SÖRBY: Come now, let Sörby rest in peace. He had his good points, too.

RELLING: Mr. Werle has better ones, I have no doubt.

MRS. SÖRBY: He hasn't frittered away all that was good in him, at any rate. The man who does that must take the consequences.

RELLING: I shall go out with Molvik this evening.

MRS. SÖRBY: You mustn't do that, Relling. Don't do it—for my sake.

RELLING: There's nothing else for it. (*To* HIALMAR) If you're going with us, come along.

GINA: No, thank you. Ekdal doesn't go in for that sort of dissertation.

HIALMAR (*half aloud, in vexation*): Oh, do hold your tongue!

RELLING: Good-bye, Mrs.—Werle. (*Goes out through the passage door.*)

GREGERS (*to* MRS. SÖRBY): You seem to know Dr. Relling pretty intimately.

MRS. SÖRBY: Yes, we have known each other for many years. At one time it seemed as if things might have gone further between us.

GREGERS: It was surely lucky for you that they did not.

MRS. SÖRBY: You may well say that. But I have always been wary of acting on impulse. A woman can't afford absolutely to throw herself away.

GREGERS: Are you not in the least afraid that I may let my father know about this old friendship?

MRS. SÖRBY: Why, of course, I have told him all about it myself.

GREGERS: Indeed?

MRS. SÖRBY: Your father knows every single thing that can, with any truth, be said about me. I have told him all; it was the first thing I did when I saw what was in his mind.

GREGERS: Then you have been franker than most people, I think.

MRS. SÖRBY: I have always been frank. We women find that the best policy.

HIALMAR: What do you say to that, Gina?

GINA: Oh, we're not all alike, us women aren't. Some are made one way, some another.

MRS. SÖRBY: Well, for my part, Gina, I believe it's wisest to do as I've done. And Werle has no secrets either, on his side. That's really the great bond between us, you see. Now he can talk to me as openly as a child. He has never had the chance to do that before. Fancy a man like him, full of health and vigour, passing his whole youth and the best years of his life in listening to nothing but penitential sermons! And very often the sermons had for their text the most imaginary offenses—at least so I understand.

GINA: That's true enough.

GREGERS: If you ladies are going to follow up this topic, I had better withdraw.

MRS. SÖRBY: You can stay as far as that's concerned. I shan't say a word more. But I wanted you to know that I had done nothing secretly or in an underhand way. I may seem to have come in for a great piece of luck; and so I have, in a sense. But after all, I don't think I am getting any more than I am giving. I shall stand by him always, and I can tend and care for him as no one else can, now that he is getting helpless.

HIALMAR: Getting helpless?

GREGERS (to MRS. SÖRBY): Hush, don't speak of that here.

MRS. SÖRBY: There is no disguising it any longer, however much he would like to. He is going blind.

HIALMAR (starts): Going blind? That's strange. He, too, going blind!

GINA: Lots of people do.

MRS. SÖRBY: And you can imagine what that means to a business man. Well, I shall try as well as I can to make my eyes take the place of his. But I mustn't stay any longer; I have such heaps of things to do. —Oh, by-the-bye, Ekdal, I was to tell you that if there is anything Werle can do for you, you must just apply to Gråberg.

GREGERS: That offer I am sure Hialmar Ekdal will decline with thanks.

MRS. SÖRBY: Indeed? I don't think he used to be so . . .

GINA: No, Bertha, Ekdal doesn't need anything from Mr. Werle now.

HIALMAR (*slowly, and with emphasis*): Will you present my compliments to your future husband and say that I intend very shortly to call upon Mr. Gråberg . . .

GREGERS: What! You don't really mean that?

HIALMAR: To call upon Mr. Gråberg, I say, and obtain an account of the sum I owe his principal. I will pay that debt of honour—ha ha ha! a debt of honour, let us call it! In any case, I will pay the whole with five per cent. interest.

GINA: But, my dear Ekdal, God knows we haven't got the money to do it.

HIALMAR: Be good enough to tell your future husband that I am working assiduously at my invention. Please tell him that what sustains me in this laborious task is the wish to free myself from a torturing burden of debt. That is my reason for proceeding with the invention. The entire profits shall be devoted to releasing me from my pecuniary obligations to your future husband.

MRS. SÖRBY: Something has happened here.

HIALMAR: Yes, you are right.

MRS. SÖRBY: Well, good-bye. I had something else to speak to you about, Gina; but it must keep till another time. Good-bye.

(HIALMAR *and* GREGERS *bow silently.* GINA *follows* MRS. SÖRBY *to the door.*)

HIALMAR: Not beyond the threshold, Gina!

(MRS. SÖRBY *goes;* GINA *shuts the door after her.*)

HIALMAR: There now, Gregers, I have got that burden of debt off my mind.

GREGERS: You soon will, at all events.

HIALMAR: I think my attitude may be called correct.

GREGERS: You are the man I have always taken you for.

HIALMAR: In certain cases, it is impossible to disregard the claim of the ideal. Yet, as the breadwinner of a family, I cannot but writhe and groan under it. I can tell you it is no joke for a man without capital to attempt the repayment of a long-standing obligation, over which, so to speak, the dust of oblivion had gathered. But it cannot be helped: the Man in me demands his rights.

GREGERS (*laying his hand on* HIALMAR's *shoulder*): My dear Hialmar —was it not a good thing I came?

HIALMAR: Yes.

GREGERS: Are you not glad to have had your true position made clear to you?

HIALMAR (*somewhat impatiently*): Yes, of course I am. But there is one thing that is revolting to my sense of justice.

GREGERS: And what is that?

HIALMAR: It is that—but I don't know whether I ought to express myself so unreservedly about your father.

GREGERS: Say what you please, so far as I am concerned.

HIALMAR: Well, then, is it not exasperating to think that it is not I, but he, who will realize the true marriage?

GREGERS: How can you say such a thing?

HIALMAR: Because it is clearly the case. Isn't the marriage between your father and Mrs. Sörby founded upon complete confidence, upon entire and unreserved candour on both sides? They hide nothing from each other, they keep no secrets in the background; their relation is based, if I may put it so, on mutual confession and absolution.

GREGERS: Well, what then?

HIALMAR: Well, is not that the whole thing? Did you not yourself say that this was precisely the difficulty that had to be overcome in order to found a true marriage?

GREGERS: But this is a totally different matter, Hialmar. You surely don't compare either yourself or your wife with those two . . . ? Oh, you understand me well enough.

HIALMAR: Say what you like, there is something in all this that hurts and offends my sense of justice. It really looks as if there were no just providence to rule the world.

GINA: Oh, no, Ekdal; for God's sake don't say such things.

GREGERS: H'm; don't let us get upon those questions.

HIALMAR: And yet, after all, I cannot but recognize the guiding finger of fate. He is going blind.

GINA: Oh, you can't be sure of that.

HIALMAR: There is no doubt about it. At all events there ought not to be; for in that very fact lies the righteous retribution. He has hoodwinked a confiding fellow creature in days gone by . . .

GREGERS: I fear he has hoodwinked many.

HIALMAR: And now comes inexorable, mysterious Fate and demands Werle's own eyes.

GINA: Oh, how dare you say such dreadful things! You make me quite scared.

HIALMAR: It is profitable, now and then, to plunge deep into the night side of existence.

(HEDVIG, *in her hat and cloak, comes in by the passage door. She is pleasurably excited and out of breath.*)

GINA: Are you back already?

HEDVIG: Yes, I didn't care to go any farther. It was a good thing, too; for I've just met some one at the door.

HIALMAR: It must have been that Mrs. Sörby.

HEDVIG: Yes.

HIALMAR (*walks up and down*): I hope you have seen her for the last time.

(*Silence,* HEDVIG, *discouraged, looks first at one and then at the other, trying to divine their frame of mind.*)

HEDVIG (*approaching, coaxingly*): Father.

HIALMAR: Well—what is it, Hedvig?

HEDVIG: Mrs. Sörby had something with her for me.

HIALMAR (*stops*): For you?

HEDVIG: Yes. something for tomorrow.

GINA: Bertha has always given you some little thing on your birth-day.

HIALMAR: What is it?

HEDVIG: Oh, you mustn't see it now. Mother is to give it to me to-morrow morning before I'm up.

HIALMAR: What is all this hocus-pocus that I am to be in the dark about!

HEDVIG (*quickly*): Oh, no, you may see it if you like. It's a big letter. (*Takes the letter out of her cloak pocket.*)

HIALMAR: A letter, too?

HEDVIG: Yes, it is only a letter. The rest will come afterwards, I sup-pose. But fancy—a letter! I've never had a letter before. And there's "Miss" written upon it. (*Reads*) "Miss Hedvig Ekdal." Only fancy —that's me!

HIALMAR: Let me see that letter.

HEDVIG (*hands it to him*): There it is.

HIALMAR: That is Mr. Werle's hand.

GINA: Are you sure of that, Ekdal?

HIALMAR: Look for yourself.

GINA: Oh, what do *I* know about such-like things?

HIALMAR: Hedvig, may I open the letter—and read it?

HEDVIG: Yes, of course you may, if you want to.

GINA: No, not tonight, Ekdal; it's to be kept till tomorrow.

HEDVIG (*softly*): Oh can't you let him read it! It's sure to be something good; and then father will be glad, and everything will be nice again.

HIALMAR: I may open it, then?

HEDVIG: Yes, do, father. I'm so anxious to know what it is.

HIALMAR: Well and good. (*Opens the letter, takes out a paper, reads it through and appears bewildered*) What is this . . . !

GINA: What does it say?

HEDVIG: Oh, yes, father—tell us!

HIALMAR: Be quiet. (*Reads it through again; he has turned pale, but says with self-control:*) It is a deed of gift, Hedvig.

HEDVIG: Is it? What sort of gift am I to have?

HIALMAR: Read for yourself.

(HEDVIG *goes over and reads for a time by the lamp.*)

HIALMAR (*half-aloud, clenching his hands*): The eyes! The eyes—and then that letter!

HEDVIG (*leaves off reading*): Yes, but it seems to me that it's grandfather that's to have it.

HIALMAR (*takes letter from her*): Gina—can you understand this?

GINA: I know nothing whatever about it; tell me what's the matter.

HIALMAR: Mr. Werle writes to Hedvig that her old grandfather need not trouble himself any longer with the copying, but that he can henceforth draw on the office for a hundred crowns a month . . .

GREGERS: Aha!

HEDVIG: A hundred crowns, mother! I read that.

GINA: What a good thing for grandfather!

HIALMAR: . . . a hundred crowns a month so long as he needs it—that means, of course, so long as he lives.

GINA: Well, so he's provided for, poor dear.

HIALMAR: But there is more to come. You didn't read that, Hedvig. Afterwards this gift is to pass on to you.

HEDVIG: To me! The whole of it?

HIALMAR: He says that the same amount is assured to you for the whole of your life. Do you hear that, Gina?

GINA: Yes, I hear.

HEDVIG: Fancy—all that money for me! (*Shakes him*) Father, father, aren't you glad . . . ?

HIALMAR (*eluding her*): Glad! (*Walks about*) Oh what vistas—what perspectives open up before me! It is Hedvig, Hedvig that he showers these benefactions upon!

GINA: Yes, because it's Hedvig's birthday . . .

HEDVIG: And you'll get it all the same, father! You know quite well I shall give all the money to you and mother.

HIALMAR: To mother, yes! There we have it.

GREGERS: Hialmar, this is a trap he is setting for you.

HIALMAR: Do you think it's another trap?

GREGERS: When he was here this morning he said: Hialmar Ekdal is not the man you imagine him to be.

HIALMAR: Not the man . . . !

GREGERS: That you shall see, he said.

HIALMAR: He meant you should see that I would let myself be bought off . . . !

HEDVIG: Oh, mother, what does all this mean?

GINA: Go and take off your things.

(HEDVIG *goes out by the kitchen door, half-crying*.)

GREGERS: Yes, Hialmar—now is the time to show who was right, he or I.

HIALMAR (*slowly tears the paper across, lays both pieces on the table and says*): Here is my answer.

GREGERS: Just what I expected.

HIALMAR (*goes over to* GINA, *who stands by the stove, and says in a low voice*): Now please make a clean breast of it. If the connection between you and him was quite over when you—came to care for me, as you call it—why did he place us in a position to marry?

GINA: I suppose he thought as he could come and go in our house.

HIALMAR: Only that? Was not he afraid of a possible contingency?

GINA: I don't know what you mean.

HIALMAR: I want to know whether—your child has the right to live under my roof.

GINA (*draws herself up; her eyes flash*): You ask that!

HIALMAR: You shall answer me this one question: Does Hedvig belong to me—or. . . ? Well!

GINA (*looking at him with cold defiance*): I don't know.

HIALMAR (*quivering a little*): You don't know!

GINA: How should *I* know. A creature like me . . .

HIALMAR (*quietly turning away from her*): Then I have nothing more to do in this house.

GREGERS: Take care, Hialmar! Think what you are doing!

HIALMAR (*puts on his overcoat*): In this case, there is nothing for a man like me to think twice about.

GREGERS: Yes, indeed, there are endless things to be considered. You three must be together if you are to attain the true frame of mind for self-sacrifice and forgiveness.

HIALMAR: I don't want to attain it. Never, never! My hat! (*Takes his hat*) My home has fallen in ruins about me. (*Bursts into tears*) Gregers, I have no child!

HEDVIG (*who has opened the kitchen door*): What is that you're saying? (*Coming to him*) Father, father!

GINA: There, you see!

HIALMAR: Don't come near me, Hedvig! Keep far away. I cannot bear to see you. Oh! those eyes . . . ! Good-bye. (*Makes for the door.*)

HEDVIG (*clinging close to him and screaming loudly*): No! no! Don't leave me!

GINA (*cries out*): Look at the child, Ekdal! Look at the child!

HIALMAR: I will not! I cannot! I must get out—away from all this!

(*He tears himself away from* HEDVIG *and goes out by the passage door.*)

HEDVIG (*with despairing eyes*): He is going away from us, mother! He is going away from us! He will never come back again!

GINA: Don't cry, Hedvig. Father's sure to come back again.

HEDVIG (*throws herself sobbing on the sofa*): No, no, he'll never come home to us any more.

GREGERS: Do you believe I meant all for the best, Mrs. Ekdal?

GINA: Yes, I daresay you did; but God forgive you, all the same.

HEDVIG (*lying on the sofa*): Oh, this will kill me! What have I done to him? Mother, you must fetch him home again!

GINA: Yes, yes, yes; only be quiet, and I'll go out and look for him. (*Puts on her outdoor things*) Perhaps he's gone in to Relling's. But you mustn't lie there and cry. Promise me!

HEDVIG (*weeping convulsively*): Yes, I'll stop, I'll stop; if only father comes back!

GREGERS (*to Gina, who is going*): After all, had you not better leave him to fight out his bitter fight to the end?

GINA: Oh, he can do that afterwards. First of all, we must get the child quieted. (*Goes out by the passage door.*)

HEDVIG (*sits up and dries her tears*): Now you must tell me what all this means. Why doesn't father want me any more?

GREGERS: You mustn't ask that till you are a big girl—quite grown-up.

HEDVIG (*sobs*): But I can't go on being as miserable as this till I'm grown-up.—I think I know what it is.—Perhaps I'm not really father's child.

GREGERS (*uneasily*): How could that be?

HEDVIG: Mother might have found me. And perhaps father has just got to know it; I've read of such things.

GREGERS: Well, but if it were so . . .

HEDVIG: I think he might be just as fond of me for all that. Yes, fonder almost. We got the wild duck in a present, you know, and I love it so dearly all the same.

GREGERS (*turning the conversation*): Ah, the wild duck, by-the-bye! Let us talk about the wild duck a little, Hedvig.

HEDVIG: The poor wild duck! He doesn't want to see it any more either. Only think, he wanted to wring its neck!

GREGERS: Oh, he won't do that.

HEDVIG: No; but he said he would like to. And I think it was horrid of father to say it; for I pray for the wild duck every night and ask that it may be preserved from death and all that is evil.

GREGERS (*looking at her*): Do you say your prayers every night?

HEDVIG: Yes.

GREGERS: Who taught you to do that?

HEDVIG: I myself; one time when father was very ill, and had leeches on his neck and said that death was staring him in the face.

GREGERS: Well?

HEDVIG: Then I prayed for him as I lay in bed; and since then I have always kept it up.

GREGERS: And now you pray for the wild duck, too?

HEDVIG: I thought it was best to bring in the wild duck; for she was so weakly at first.

GREGERS: Do you pray in the morning, too?

HEDVIG: No, of course not.

GREGERS: Why not in the morning as well?

HEDVIG: In the morning it's light, you know, and there's nothing in particular to be afraid of.

GREGERS: And your father was going to wring the neck of the wild duck that you love so dearly?

HEDVIG: No; he said he ought to wring its neck, but he would spare it for my sake; and that was kind of father.

GREGERS (*coming a little nearer*): But suppose you were to sacrifice the wild duck of your own free will for his sake.

HEDVIG (*rising*): The wild duck!

GREGERS: Suppose you were to make a free-will offering, for his sake, of the dearest treasure you have in the world!

HEDVIG: Do you think that would do any good?

GREGERS: Try it, Hedvig.

HEDVIG (*softly, with flashing eyes*): Yes, I will try it.

GREGERS: Have you really the courage for it, do you think?

HEDVIG: I'll ask grandfather to shoot the wild duck for me.

GREGERS: Yes, do. But not a word to your mother about it.

HEDVIG: Why not?

GREGERS: She doesn't understand us.

HEDVIG: The wild duck! I'll try it tomorrow morning.

(GINA *comes in by the passage door.*)

HEDVIG (*going towards her*): Did you find him, mother?

GINA: No, but I heard as he had called and taken Relling with him.

GREGERS: Are you sure of that?

GINA: Yes, the porter's wife said so. Molvik went with them, too, she said.

GREGERS: This evening, when his mind so sorely needs to wrestle in solitude . . . !

GINA (*takes off her things*): Yes, men are strange creatures, so they are. The Lord only knows where Relling has dragged him to! I ran over to Madam Eriksen's, but they weren't there.

HEDVIG (*struggling to keep back her tears*): Oh, if he should never come home any more!

GREGERS: He will come home again. I shall have news to give him tomorrow; and then you shall see how he comes home. You may rely upon that, Hedvig, and sleep in peace. Good-night.

(*He goes out by the passage door.*)

HEDVIG (*throws herself sobbing on* GINA's *neck*): Mother, mother!

GINA (*pats her shoulder and sighs*): Ah, yes; Relling was right, he was. That's what comes of it when crazy creatures go about presenting the claims of the—what-you-may-call-it.

(The Curtain Falls.)

# Act Five

HIALMAR EKDAL's *studio. Cold, grey morning light. Wet snow lies upon the large panes of the sloping roof-window.*

GINA *comes from the kitchen with an apron and bib on, and carrying a dusting-brush and a duster; she goes towards the sitting-room door. At the same moment* HEDVIG *comes hurriedly in from the passage.*

GINA (*stops*): Well?

HEDVIG: Oh, mother, I almost think he's down at Relling's . . .

GINA: There, you see!

HEDVIG: . . . because the porter's wife says she could hear that Relling had two people with him when he came home last night.

GINA: That's just what I thought.

HEDVIG: But it's no use his being there, if he won't come up to us.

GINA: I'll go down and speak to him at all events.

(OLD EKDAL, *in dressing-gown and slippers, and with a lighted pipe, appears at the door of his room.*)

EKDAL: Hialmar . . . Isn't Hialmar at home?

GINA: No, he's gone out.

EKDAL: So early? And in such a tearing snowstorm? Well, well; just as he pleases; I can take my morning walk alone.

(*He slides the garret door aside;* HEDVIG *helps him; he goes in; she closes it after him.*)

HEDVIG (*in an undertone*): Only think, mother, when poor grandfather hears that father is going to leave us.

GINA: Oh, nonsense; grandfather mustn't hear anything about it. It was a heaven's mercy he wasn't at home yesterday in all that hurly-burly.

HEDVIG: Yes, but . . .

(GREGERS *comes in by the passage door.*)

GREGERS: Well, have you any news of him?

GINA: They say he's down at Relling's.

GREGERS: At Relling's! Has he really been out with those creatures?

GINA: Yes, like enough.

GREGERS: When he ought to have been yearning for solitude, to collect and clear his thoughts . . .

GINA: Yes, you may well say so.

(RELLING *enters from the passage.*)

HEDVIG (*going to him*): Is father in your room?

GINA (*at the same time*): Is he there?

RELLING: Yes, to be sure he is.

HEDVIG: And you never let us know!

RELLING: Yes, I'm a brute. But in the first place I had to look after the other brute; I mean our dæmonic friend, of course; and then I fell so dead asleep that . . .

GINA: What does Ekdal say today?

RELLING: He says nothing whatever.

HEDVIG: Doesn't he speak?

RELLING: Not a blessed word.

GREGERS: No, no; I can understand that very well.

GINA: But what's he doing then?

RELLING: He's lying on the sofa, snoring.

GINA: Oh, is he? Yes, Ekdal's a rare one to snore.

HEDVIG: Asleep? Can he sleep?

RELLING: Well it certainly looks like it.

GREGERS: No wonder, after the spiritual conflict that has rent him . . .

GINA: And then he's never been used to gadding about out of doors at night.

HEDVIG: Perhaps it's a good thing that he's getting sleep, mother.

GINA: Of course it is; and we must take care we don't wake him up too early. Thank you, Relling. I must get the house cleaned up a bit now, and then . . . Come and help me, Hedvig.

(GINA *and* HEDVIG *go into the sitting-room.*)

GREGERS (*turning to* RELLING): What is your explanation of the spiritual tumult that is now going on in Hialmar Ekdal?

RELLING: Devil a bit of a spiritual tumult have *I* noticed in him.

GREGERS: What! Not at such a crisis, when his whole life has been placed on a new foundation . . . ? How can you think that such an individuality as Hialmar's . . . ?

RELLING: Oh, individuality—he! If he ever had any tendency to the abnormal developments you call individuality, I can assure you it was rooted out of him while he was still in his teens.

GREGERS: That would be strange indeed,—considering the loving care with which he was brought up.

RELLING: By those two high-flown, hysterical maiden aunts, you mean?

GREGERS: Let me tell you that they were women who never forgot the claim of the ideal—but of course you will only jeer at me again.

RELLING: No, I'm in no humour for that. I know all about those ladies; for he has ladled out no end of rhetoric on the subject of his "two soul-mothers." But I don't think he has much to thank them for. Ekdal's misfortune is that in his own circle he has always been looked upon as a shining light . . .

GREGERS: Not without reason, surely. Look at the depth of his mind!

RELLING: *I* have never discovered it. That his father believed in it I don't so much wonder; the old lieutenant has been an ass all his days.

GREGERS: He has had a child-like mind all his days; that is what you cannot understand.

RELLING: Well, so be it. But then, when our dear, sweet Hialmar went to college, he at once passed for the great light of the future amongst his comrades, too! He was handsome, the rascal—red and white—a shop-girl's dream of manly beauty; and with his superficially emotional temperament, and his sympathetic voice and his talent for declaiming other people's verses and other people's thoughts . . .

GREGERS (*indignantly*): Is it Hialmar Ekdal you are talking about in this strain?

RELLING: Yes, with your permission; I am simply giving you an inside view of the idol you are grovelling before.

GREGERS: I should hardly have thought I was quite stone blind.

RELLING: Yes, you are—or not far from it. You are a sick man, too, you see.

GREGERS: You are right there.

RELLING: Yes. Yours is a complicated case. First of all there is that plaguy integrity-fever; and then—what's worse—you are always in a delirium of hero-worship; you must always have something to adore, outside yourself.

GREGERS: Yes, I must certainly seek it outside myself.

RELLING: But you make such shocking mistakes about every new phœnix you think you have discovered. Here again you have come to a cotter's cabin with your claim of the ideal; and the people of the house are insolvent.

GREGERS: If you don't think better than that of Hialmar Ekdal, what pleasure can you find in being everlastingly with him?

RELLING: Well, you see, I'm supposed to be a sort of a doctor—save the mark! I can't but give a hand to the poor sick folk who live under the same roof with me.

GREGERS: Oh, indeed! Hialmar Ekdal is sick, too, is he!

RELLING: Most people are, worse luck.

GREGERS: And what remedy are you applying in Hialmar's case?

RELLING: My usual one. I am cultivating the life-illusion* in him.

GREGERS: Life—illusion? I didn't catch what you said.

RELLING: Yes, I said illusion. For illusion, you know, is the stimulating principle.

GREGERS: May I ask with what illusion Hialmar is inoculated?

RELLING: No, thank you; I don't betray professional secrets to quack-salvers. You would probably go and muddle his case still more than you have already. But my method is infallible. I have applied it to Molvik as well. I have made him "dæmonic." That's the blister I have to put on his neck.

GREGERS: Is he not really dæmonic, then?

RELLING: What the devil do you mean by dæmonic! It's only a piece of gibberish I've invented to keep up a spark of life in him. But for that, the poor harmless creature would have succumbed to self-contempt and despair many a long year ago. And then the old lieutenant! But he has hit upon his own cure, you see.

GREGERS: Lieutenant Ekdal? What of him?

RELLING: Just think of the old bear-hunter shutting himself up in that dark garret to shoot rabbits! I tell you there is not a happier sportsman in the world than that old man pottering about in there among all that rubbish. The four or five withered Christmas trees he has saved up are the same to him as the whole great fresh Höidal forest; the cock and the hens are big game-birds in the fir-tops; and the rabbits that flop about the garret floor are the bears he has to battle with—the mighty hunter of the mountains!

GREGERS: Poor unfortunate old man! Yes; he has indeed had to narrow the ideals of his youth.

RELLING: While I think of it, Mr. Werle, junior—don't use that foreign word: ideals. We have the excellent native word: lies.

GREGERS: Do you think the two things are related?

RELLING: Yes, just about as closely as typhus and putrid fever.

* "Livslögnen," literally "the life-lie."

GREGERS: Dr. Relling, I shall not give up the struggle until I have rescued Hialmar from your clutches!

RELLING: So much the worse for him. Rob the average man of his life-illusion, and you rob him of his happiness at the same stroke. (*To* HEDVIG, *who comes in from the sitting-room*) Well, little wild-duck-mother, I'm just going down to see whether papa is still lying meditating upon that wonderful invention of his. (*Goes out by passage door.*)

GREGERS (*approaches* HEDVIG): I can see by your face that you have not yet done it.

HEDVIG: What? Oh, that about the wild duck! No.

GREGERS: I suppose your courage failed when the time came.

HEDVIG: No, that wasn't it. But when I awoke this morning and remembered what we had been talking about, it seemed so strange.

GREGERS: Strange?

HEDVIG: Yes, I don't know . . . Yesterday evening, at the moment, I thought there was something so delightful about it; but since I have slept and thought of it again, it somehow doesn't seem worth while.

GREGERS: Ah, I thought you could not have grown up quite unharmed in this house.

HEDVIG: I don't care about that, if only father would come up . . .

GREGERS: Oh, if only your eyes had been opened to that which gives life it's value—if you possessed the true, joyous, fearless spirit of sacrifice, you would soon see how he would come up to you.—But I believe in you still, Hedvig.

(*He goes out by the passage door.* HEDVIG *wanders about the room for a time; she is on the point of going into the kitchen when a knock is heard at the garret door.* HEDVIG *goes over and opens it a little; old* EKDAL *comes out; she pushes the door to again.*)

EKDAL: H'm, it's not much fun to take one's morning walk alone.

HEDVIG: Wouldn't you like to go shooting, grandfather?

EKDAL: It's not the weather for it today. It's so dark there, you can scarcely see where you're going.

HEDVIG: Do you never want to shoot anything besides the rabbits?

EKDAL: Do you think the rabbits aren't good enough?

HEDVIG: Yes, but what about the wild duck?

EKDAL: Ho-ho! are you afraid I shall shoot your wild duck? Never in the world. Never.

HEDVIG: No, I suppose you couldn't; they say it's very difficult to shoot wild ducks.

EKDAL: Couldn't! Should rather think I could.

HEDVIG: How would you set about it, grandfather?—I don't mean with my wild duck, but with others?

EKDAL: I should take care to shoot them in the breast, you know; that's the surest place. And then you must shoot against the feathers, you see—not the way of the feathers.

HEDVIG: Do they die then, grandfather?

EKDAL: Yes, they die right enough—when you shoot properly. Well, I must go and brush up a bit. H'm—understand—h'm (*Goes into his room.*)

(HEDVIG *waits a little, glances towards the sitting-room door, goes over to the book-case, stands on tip-toe, takes the double-barrelled pistol down from the shelf and looks at it.* GINA, *with brush and duster, comes from the sitting-room.* HEDVIG *hastily lays down the pistol, unobserved.*)

GINA: Don't stand raking amongst father's things, Hedvig.

HEDVIG (*goes away from the bookcase*): I was only going to tidy up a little.

GINA: You'd better go into the kitchen and see if the coffee's keeping hot; I'll take his breakfast on a tray, when I go down to him.

(HEDVIG *goes out.* GINA *begins to sweep and clean up the studio. Presently the passage door is opened with hesitation, and* HIALMAR EKDAL *looks in. He has on his overcoat, but not his hat; he is unwashed, and his hair is dishevelled and unkempt. His eyes are dull and heavy.*)

GINA (*standing with the brush in her hand and looking at him*): Oh, there now, Ekdal—so you've come after all!

HIALMAR (*comes in and answers in a toneless voice*): I come—only to depart again immediately.

GINA: Yes, yes, I suppose so. But, Lord help us! what a sight you are!

HIALMAR: A sight?

GINA: And your nice winter coat, too! Well, that's done for.

HEDVIG (*at the kitchen door*): Mother, hadn't I better . . . ? (*Sees* HIALMAR, *gives a loud scream of joy and runs to him.*) Oh, father, father!

HIALMAR (*turns away and makes a gesture of repulsion*): Away, away, away! (*To* GINA) Keep her away from me, I say!

GINA (*in a low tone*): Go into the sitting-room, Hedvig.

(HEDVIG *does so without a word.*)

HIALMAR (*fussily pulls out the table-drawer*): I must have my books with me. Where are my books?

GINA: Which books?

HIALMAR: My scientific books, of course; the technical magazines I require for my invention.

GINA (*searches in the bookcase*): Is it these here paper-covered ones?

HIALMAR: Yes, of course.

GINA (*lays a heap of magazines on the table*): Shan't I get Hedvig to cut them for you?

HIALMAR: I don't require to have them cut for me. (*Short silence.*)

GINA: Then you're still set on leaving us, Ekdal?

HIALMAR (*rummaging amongst the books*): Yes, that is a matter of course, I should think.

GINA: Well, well.

HIALMAR (*vehemently*): How can I live here, to be stabbed to the heart every hour of the day?

GINA: God forgive you for thinking such vile things of me.

HIALMAR: Prove . . . !

GINA: I think it's you as has got to prove.

HIALMAR: After a past like yours? There are certain claims—I may almost call them claims of the ideal . . .

GINA: But what about grandfather? What's to become of him, poor dear!

HIALMAR: I know my duty; my helpless father will come with me. I am going out into the town to make arrangements . . . H'm— (*hesitatingly*)—has any one found my hat on the stairs?

GINA: No. Have you lost your hat?

HIALMAR: Of course I had it on when I came in last night; there's no doubt about that; but I couldn't find it this morning.

GINA: Lord help us! where have you been to with those two ne'er-do-wells?

HIALMAR: Oh, don't bother me about trifles. Do you suppose I am in the mood to remember details?

GINA: If only you haven't caught cold, Ekdal . . . (*Goes out into the kitchen.*)

HIALMAR (*talks to himself in a low tone of irritation, whilst he empties the table-drawer*): You're a scoundrel, Relling!—You're a low fellow!—Ah, you shameless tempter!—I wish I could get some one to stick a knife into you!

(*He lays some old letters on one side, finds the torn document of yesterday, takes it up and looks at the pieces; puts it down hurriedly as* GINA *enters.*)

GINA (*sets a tray with coffee, etc., on the table*): Here's a drop of something hot, if you'd fancy it. And there's some bread and butter and a snack of salt meat.

HIALMAR (*glancing at the tray*): Salt meat? Never under this roof! It's true I have not had a mouthful of solid food for nearly twenty-four hours; but no matter.—My memoranda! The commencement of my autobiography! What has become of my diary, and all my important papers? (*Opens the sitting-room door but draws back*) She is there, too!

GINA: Good Lord! the child must be somewhere!

HIALMAR: Come out.

(*He makes room,* HEDVIG *comes, scared, into the studio.*)

HIALMAR (*with his hand upon the door-handle, says to* GINA): In these, the last moments I spend in my former home, I wish to be spared from interlopers . . . (*Goes into the room.*)

HEDVIG (*with a bound towards her mother, asks softly, trembling*): Does that mean me?

GINA: Stay out in the kitchen, Hedvig; or, no—you'd best go into your own room. (*Speaks to* HIALMAR *as she goes in to him*) Wait a bit, Ekdal; don't rummage so in the drawers; *I* know where everything is.

HEDVIG (*stands a moment immovable, in terror and perplexity, biting her lips to keep back the tears; then she clenches her hands convulsively and says softly*): The wild duck.

(*She steals over and takes the pistol from the shelf, opens the garret door a little way, creeps in and draws the door to after her.* HIALMAR *and* GINA *can be heard disputing in the sitting-room.*)

HIALMAR (*comes in with some manuscript books and old loose papers, which he lays upon the table*): That portmanteau is of no use! There are a thousand and one things I must drag with me.

GINA (*following with the portmanteau*): Why not leave all the rest for the present and only take a shirt and a pair of woollen drawers with you?

HIALMAR: Whew!—all these exhausting preparations . . . ! (*Pulls off his overcoat and throws it upon the sofa.*)

GINA: And there's the coffee getting cold.

HIALMAR: H'm. (*Drinks a mouthful without thinking of it and then another.*)

GINA (*dusting the backs of the chairs*): A nice job you'll have to find such another big garret for the rabbits.

HIALMAR: What! Am I to drag all those rabbits with me, too?

GINA: You don't suppose grandfather can get on without his rabbits.

HIALMAR: He must just get used to doing without them. Have not *I* to sacrifice very much greater things than rabbits!

GINA (*dusting the bookcase*): Shall I put the flute in the portmanteau for you?

HIALMAR: No. No flute for me. But give me the pistol!

GINA: Do you want to take the pistol with you?

HIALMAR: Yes. My loaded pistol.

GINA (*searching for it*): It's gone. He must have taken it in with him.

HIALMAR: Is he in the garret?

GINA: Yes, of course he's in the garret.

HIALMAR: H'm—poor lonely old man.

(*He takes a piece of bread and butter, eats it and finishes his cup of coffee.*)

GINA: If we hadn't have let that room, you could have moved in there.

HIALMAR: And continued to live under the same roof with . . . ! Never,—never!

GINA: But couldn't you put up with the sitting-room for a day or two? You could have it all to yourself.

HIALMAR: Never within these walls!

GINA: Well, then, down with Relling and Molvik.

HIALMAR: Don't mention those wretches' names to me! The very thought of them almost takes away my appetite.—Oh, no, I must go out into the storm and the snow-drift,—go from house to house and seek shelter for my father and myself.

GINA: But you've got no hat, Ekdal! You've been and lost your hat, you know.

HIALMAR: Oh, those two brutes, those slaves of all the vices! A hat must be procured. (*Takes another piece of bread and butter*) Some arrangements must be made. For I have no mind to throw away my life, either. (*Looks for something on the tray.*)

GINA: What are you looking for?

HIALMAR: Butter.

GINA: I'll get some at once. (*Goes into the kitchen.*)

HIALMAR (*calls after her*): Oh, it doesn't matter; dry bread is good enough for me.

GINA (*brings a dish of butter*): Look here; this is fresh churned.

(*She pours out another cup of coffee for him; he seats himself on the sofa, spreads more butter on the already buttered bread and eats and drinks awhile in silence.*)

HIALMAR: Could I, without being subject to intrusion—intrusion of any sort—could I live in the sitting-room there for a day or two?

GINA: Yes, to be sure you could, if you only would.

HIALMAR: For I see no possibility of getting all father's things out in such a hurry.

GINA: And, besides, you've surely got to tell him first as you don't mean to live with us others no more.

HIALMAR (*pushes away his coffee cup*): Yes, there is that, too; I shall have to lay bare the whole tangled story to him . . . I must turn matters over; I must have breathing-time; I cannot take all these burdens on my shoulders in a single day.

GINA: No, especially in such horrible weather as it is outside.

HIALMAR (*touching* WERLE's *letter*): I see that paper is still lying about here.

GINA: Yes, *I* haven't touched it.

HIALMAR: So far as I am concerned it is mere waste paper . . .

GINA: Well, *I* have certainly no notion of making any use of it.

HIALMAR: . . . but we had better not let it get lost all the same;—in all the upset when I move, it might easily . . .

GINA: I'll take good care of it, Ekdal.

HIALMAR: The donation is in the first instance made to father, and it rests with him to accept or decline it.

GINA (*sighs*): Yes, poor old father . . .

HIALMAR: To make quite safe . . . Where shall I find some gum?

GINA (*goes to the bookcase*): Here's the gum-pot.

HIALMAR: And a brush?

GINA: The brush is here, too. (*Brings him the things.*)

HIALMAR (*takes a pair of scissors*): Just a strip of paper at the back . . . (*Clips and gums*) Far be it from me to lay hands upon what is not my own—and least of all upon what belongs to a destitute old man—and to—the other as well.—There now. Let it lie there for a time; and when it is dry, take it away. I wish never to see that document again. Never!

(GREGERS WERLE *enters from the passage.*)

GREGERS (*somewhat surprised*): What,—are you sitting here, Hialmar?

HIALMAR (*rises hurriedly*): I had sunk down from fatigue.

GREGERS: You have been having breakfast, I see.

HIALMAR: The body sometimes makes its claims felt, too.

GREGERS: What have you decided to do?

HIALMAR: For a man like me, there is only one course possible. I am just putting my most important things together. But it takes time, you know.

GINA (*with a touch of impatience*): Am I to get the room ready for you, or am I to pack your portmanteau?

HIALMAR (*after a glance of annoyance at* GREGERS): Pack—and get the room ready!

GINA (*takes the portmanteau*): Very well; then I'll put in the shirt and the other things. (*Goes into the sitting-room and draws the door to after her.*)

GREGERS (*after a short silence*): I never dreamed that this would be the end of it. Do you really feel it a necessity to leave house and home?

HIALMAR (*wanders about restlessly*): What would you have me do? —I am not fitted to bear unhappiness, Gregers. I must feel secure and at peace in my surroundings.

GREGERS: But can you not feel that here? Just try it. I should have thought you had firm ground to build upon now—if only you start afresh. And remember, you have your invention to live for.

HIALMAR: Oh, don't talk about my invention. It's perhaps still in the dim distance.

GREGERS: Indeed!

HIALMAR: Why, great heavens, what would you have me invent? Other people have invented almost everything already. It becomes more and more difficult every day . . .

GREGERS: And you have devoted so much labour to it.

HIALMAR: It was that blackguard Relling that urged me to it.

GREGERS: Relling?

HIALMAR: Yes, it was he that first made me realize my aptitude for making some notable discovery in photography.

GREGERS: Aha—it was Relling!

HIALMAR: Oh, I have been so truly happy over it! Not so much for the sake of the invention itself, as because Hedvig believed in it— believed in it with a child's whole eagerness of faith.—At least, I have been fool enough to go and imagine that she believed in it.

GREGERS: Can you really think Hedvig has been false to you?

HIALMAR: I can think anything now. It is Hedvig that stands in my way. She will blot out the sunlight from my whole life.

GREGERS: Hedvig! Is it Hedvig you are talking of? How should she blot out your sunlight?

HIALMAR (*without answering*): How unutterably I have loved that child! How unutterably happy I have felt every time I came home to my humble room, and she flew to meet me, with her sweet little blinking eyes. Oh, confiding fool that I have been! I loved her un-utterably;—and I yielded myself up to the dream, the delusion, that she loved me unutterably in return.

GREGERS: Do you call that a delusion?

HIALMAR: How should I know? I can get nothing out of Gina; and besides, she is totally blind to the ideal side of these complications. But to you I feel impelled to open my mind, Gregers. I cannot shake off this frightful doubt—perhaps Hedvig has never really and honestly loved me.

GREGERS: What would you say if she were to give you a proof of her love? (*Listens.*) What's that? I thought I heard the wild duck . . . ?

HIALMAR: It's the wild duck quacking. Father's in the garret.

GREGERS: Is he? (*His face lights up with joy*): I say, you may yet have proof that your poor misunderstood Hedvig loves you!

HIALMAR: Oh, what proof can she give me? I dare not believe in any assurance from that quarter.

GREGERS: Hedvig does not know what deceit means.

HIALMAR: Oh, Gregers, that is just what I cannot be sure of. Who knows what Gina and that Mrs. Sörby may many a time have sat here whispering and tattling about? And Hedvig usually has her ears open, I can tell you. Perhaps the deed of gift was not such a surprise to her, after all. In fact, I'm not sure but that I noticed something of the sort.

GREGERS: What spirit is this that has taken possession of you?

HIALMAR: I have had my eyes opened. Just you notice;—you'll see, the deed of gift is only a beginning. Mrs. Sörby has always been a good deal taken up with Hedvig; and now she has the power to do whatever she likes for the child. They can take her from me when-ever they please.

GREGERS: Hedvig will never, never leave you.

HIALMAR: Don't be so sure of that. If only they beckon to her and throw out a golden bait . . . ! And, oh! I have loved her so unspeakably! I would have counted it my highest happiness to take her tenderly by the hand and lead her, as one leads a timid child through a great dark empty room!—I am cruelly certain now that the poor photographer in his humble attic has never really and truly been anything to her. She has only cunningly contrived to keep on a good footing with him until the time came.

GREGERS: You don't believe that yourself, Hialmar.

HIALMAR: That is just the terrible part of it—I don't know what to believe,—I never can know it. But can you really doubt that it must be as I say? Ho-ho, you have far too much faith in the claim of the ideal, my good Gregers! If those others came, with the glamour of wealth about them, and called to the child:—"Leave him: come to us: here life awaits you . . . !"

GREGERS (*quickly*): Well, what then?

HIALMAR: If I then asked her: Hedvig, are you willing to renounce that life for me? (*Laughs scornfully*) No, thank  you! You would soon hear what answer I should get. (*A pistol shot is heard from within the garret.*)

GREGERS (*loudly and joyfully*): Hialmar!

HIALMAR: There now; he must needs go shooting, too.

GINA (*comes in*): Oh, Ekdal, I can hear grandfather blazing away in the garret by hisself.

HIALMAR: I'll look in . . .

GREGERS (*eagerly, with emotion*): Wait a moment! Do you know what that was?

HIALMAR: Yes, of course I know.

GREGERS: No, you don't know. But *I* do. That was the proof!

HIALMAR: What proof?

GREGERS: It was a child's free-will offering. She has got your father to shoot the wild duck.

HIALMAR: To shoot the wild duck!

GINA: Oh, think of that . . . !

HIALMAR: What was that for?

GREGERS: She wanted to sacrifice to you her most cherished possession; for then she thought you would surely come to love her again.

HIALMAR (*tenderly, with emotion*): Oh, poor child!

GINA: What things she does think of!

GREGERS: She only wanted your love again, Hialmar. She could not live without it.

GINA (*struggling with her tears*): There, you can see for yourself, Ekdal.

HIALMAR: Gina, where is she?

GINA (*sniffs*): Poor dear, she's sitting out in the kitchen, I dare say.

HIALMAR (*goes over, tears open the kitchen door and says*): Hedvig, come, come in to me! (*Looks around*) No, she's not here.

GINA: Then she must be in her own little room.

HIALMAR (*without*): No, she's not here either. (*Comes in*) She must have gone out.

GINA: Yes, you wouldn't have her anywheres in the house.

HIALMAR: Oh, if she would only come home quickly, so that I can tell her . . . Everything will come right now, Gregers; now I believe we can begin life afresh.

GREGERS (*quietly*): I knew it; I knew the child would make amends.

(OLD EKDAL *appears at the door of his room; he is in full uniform and is busy buckling on his sword.*)

HIALMAR (*astonished*): Father! Are you there?

GINA: Have you been firing in your room?

EKDAL (*resentfully, approaching*): So you go shooting alone, do you, Hialmar?

HIALMAR (*excited and confused*): Then it wasn't you that fired that shot in the garret?

EKDAL: Me that fired? H'm.

GREGERS (*calls out to* HIALMAR): She has shot the wild duck herself!

HIALMAR: What can it mean? (*Hastens to the garret door, tears it aside, looks in and calls loudly*): Hedvig!

GINA (*runs to the door*): Good God, what's that!

HIALMAR (*goes in*): She's lying on the floor!

GREGERS: Hedvig! lying on the floor! (*Goes in to* HIALMAR)

GINA (*at the same time*): Hedvig! (*Inside the garret*) No, no, no!

EKDAL: Ho-ho! does she go shooting, too, now?

(HIALMAR, GINA *and* GREGERS *carry* HEDVIG *into the studio; in her dangling right hand she holds the pistol fast clasped in her fingers.*)

HIALMAR (*distracted*): The pistol has gone off. She has wounded herself. Call for help! Help!

GINA (*runs into the passage and calls down*): Relling! Relling! Doctor Relling; come up as quick as you can!

(HIALMAR *and* GREGERS *lay* HEDVIG *down on the sofa.*)

EKDAL (*quietly*): The woods avenge themselves.

HIALMAR (*on his knees beside* HEDVIG): She'll soon come to now. She's coming to . . . ; yes, yes, yes.

GINA (*who has come in again*): Where has she hurt herself? I can't see anything . . .

(RELLING *comes hurriedly, and immediately after him* MOLVIK; *the latter without his waistcoat and necktie, and with his coat open.*)

RELLING: What's the matter here?

GINA: They say Hedvig has shot herself.

HIALMAR: Come and help us!

RELLING: Shot herself!

(*He pushes the table aside and begins to examine her.*)

HIALMAR (*kneeling and looking anxiously up at him*): It can't be dangerous? Speak, Relling! She is scarcely bleeding at all. It can't be dangerous?

RELLING: How did it happen?

HIALMAR: Oh, we don't know . . .

GINA: She wanted to shoot the wild duck.

RELLING: The wild duck?

HIALMAR: The pistol must have gone off.

RELLING: H'm. Indeed.

EKDAL: The woods avenge themselves. But I'm not afraid, all the same. (*Goes into the garret and closes the door after him.*)

HIALMAR: Well, Relling,—why don't you say something?

RELLING: The ball has entered the breast.

HIALMAR: Yes, but she's coming to!

RELLING: Surely you can see that Hedvig is dead.

GINA (*bursts into tears*): Oh, my child, my child . . .

GREGERS (*huskily*): In the depths of the sea . . .

HIALMAR (*jumps up*): No, no, she must live! Oh, for God's sake, Relling—only a moment—only just till I can tell her how unspeakably I loved her all the time!

RELLING: The bullet has gone through her heart. Internal hemorrhage. Death must have been instantaneous.

HIALMAR: And I! I hunted her from me like an animal! And she crept terrified into the garret and died for love of me! (*Sobbing*) I can never atone to her! I can never tell her . . . ! (*Clenches his hands and cries, upwards*) O thou above . . . ! If thou be indeed! Why hast thou done this thing to me?

GINA: Hush, hush, you mustn't go on that awful way. We had no right to keep her, I suppose.

MOLVIK: The child is not dead, but sleepeth.

RELLING: Bosh!

HIALMAR (*becomes calm, goes over to the sofa, folds his arms and looks at* HEDVIG): There she lies so stiff and still.

RELLING (*tries to loosen the pistol*): She's holding it so tight, so tight.

GINA: No, no, Relling, don't break her fingers; let the pistol be.

HIALMAR: She shall take it with her.

GINA: Yes, let her. But the child mustn't lie here for a show. She shall go to her own room, so she shall. Help me, Ekdal. (HIALMAR *and* GINA *take* HEDVIG *between them.*)

HIALMAR (*as they are carrying her*): Oh, Gina, Gina, can you survive this!

GINA: We must help each other to bear it. For now at least she belongs to both of us.

MOLVIK (*stretches out his arms and mumbles*): Blessed be the Lord; to earth thou shalt return; to earth thou shalt return . . .

RELLING (*whispers*): Hold your tongue, you fool; you're drunk.

(HIALMAR *and* GINA *carry the body out through the kitchen door.* RELLING *shuts it after them.* MOLVIK *slinks out into the passage.*)

RELLING (*goes over to* GREGERS *and says*): No one shall ever convince me that the pistol went off by accident.

GREGERS (*who has stood terrified, with convulsive twitchings*): Who can say how the dreadful thing happened?

RELLING: The powder has burnt the body of her dress. She must have pressed the pistol right against her breast and fired.

GREGERS: Hedvig has not died in vain. Did you not see how sorrow set free what is noble in him?

RELLING: Most people are ennobled by the actual presence of death. But how long do you suppose this nobility will last in him?

GREGERS: Why should it not endure and increase throughout his life?

RELLING: Before a year is over, little Hedvig will be nothing to him but a pretty theme for declamation.

GREGERS: How dare you say that of Hialmar Edkal?

RELLING: We will talk of this again, when the grass has first withered on her grave. Then you'll hear him spouting about "the child too early torn from her father's heart"; then you'll see him steep himself in a syrup of sentiment and self-admiration and self-pity. Just you wait!

GREGERS: If you are right and I am wrong, then life is not worth living.

RELLING: Oh, life would be quite tolerable, after all, if only we could be rid of the confounded duns that keep on pestering us, in our poverty, with the claim of the ideal.

GREGERS (*looking straight before him*): In that case, I am glad that my destiny is what is.

RELLING: May I inquire,—what is your destiny?

GREGERS (*going*): To be the thirteenth at table.

RELLING: The devil it is.

(*The Curtain Falls.*)

# TENNESSEE WILLIAMS

# The
# Glass Menagerie

*The Glass Menagerie* was first produced at the Civic Theater, Chicago, Illinois, on December 26, 1944, and then at the Playhouse Theater, New York City, on March 31, 1945.

# CHARACTERS

**AMANDA WINGFIELD** (*the mother*)

A little woman of great but confused vitality clinging frantically to another time and place. Her characterization must be carefully created, not copied from type. She is not paranoiac, but her life is paranoia. There is much to admire in Amanda, and as much to love and pity as there is to laugh at. Certainly she has endurance and a kind of heroism, and though her foolishness makes her unwittingly cruel at times, there is tenderness in her slight person.

**LAURA WINGFIELD** (*her daughter*)

Amanda, having failed to establish contact with reality, continues to live vitally in her illusions, but Laura's situation is even graver. A childhood illness has left her crippled, one leg slightly shorter than the other, and held in a brace. This defect need not be more than suggested on the stage. Stemming from this, Laura's separation increases till she is like a piece of her own glass collection, too exquisitely fragile to move from the shelf.

**TOM WINGFIELD** (*her son*)

And the narrator of the play. A poet with a job in a warehouse. His nature is not remorseless, but to escape from a trap he has to act without pity.

**JIM O'CONNOR** (*the gentleman caller*)

A nice, ordinary, young man.

SCENE: An Alley in St. Louis.

TIME: Now and the Past.

# Scene One

The Wingfield apartment is in the rear of the building, one of those vast hive-like conglomerations of cellular living-units that flower as warty growths in overcrowded urban centers of lower middle-class population and are symptomatic of the impulse of this largest and fundamentally enslaved section of American society to avoid fluidity and differentiation and to exist and function as one interfused mass of automatism.

The apartment faces an alley and is entered by a fire-escape, a structure whose name is a touch of accidental poetic truth, for all of these huge buildings are always burning with the slow and implacable fires of human desperation. The fire-escape is included in the set—that is, the landing of it and steps descending from it.

The scene is memory and is therefore nonrealistic. Memory takes a lot of poetic license. It omits some details; others are exaggerated, according to the emotional value of the articles it touchs, for memory is seated predominantly in the heart. The interior is therefore rather dim and poetic.

At the rise of the curtain, the audience is faced with the dark, grim rear wall of the Wingfield tenement. This building, which runs parallel to the footlights, is flanked on both sides by dark, narrow alleys which run into murky canyons of tangled clotheslines, garbage cans and the sinister latticework of neighboring fire-escapes. It is up and down these side alleys that exterior entrances and exits are made, during the play. At the end of TOM's opening commentary, the dark tenement wall slowly reveals (by means of a transparency) the interior of the ground floor Wingfield apartment.

Downstage is the living room, which also serves as a sleeping room for LAURA, the sofa unfolding to make her bed. Upstage, center, and divided by a wide arch or second proscenium with transparent faded portieres (or second curtain), is the dining room. In an old-fashioned what-not in the living room are seen scores of transparent glass animals. A blown-up photograph of the father hangs on the wall of the living room, facing the audience, to the left of the archway. It is the face of a very handsome young man in a *doughboy's First World War cap. He is gallantly smiling, ineluctably smiling, as if to say, "I will be smiling forever."*

*The audience hears and sees the opening scene in the dining room through both the transparent fourth wall of the building and the transparent gauze portieres of the dining-room arch. It is during this revealing scene that the fourth wall slowly ascends, out of sight. This transparent exterior wall is not brought down again until the very end of the play, during* TOM's *final speech.*

*The narrator is an undisguised convention of the play. He takes whatever license with dramatic convention as is convenient to his purposes.*

TOM *enters dressed as a merchant sailor from alley, stage left, and strolls across the front of the stage to the fire-escape. There he stops and lights a cigarette. He addresses the audience.*

TOM: Yes, I have tricks in my pocket, I have things up my sleeve. But I am the opposite of a stage magician. He gives you illusion that has the appearance of truth. I give you truth in the pleasant disguise of illusion.

To begin with, I turn back time. I reverse it to that quaint period, the thirties, when the huge middle class of America was matriculating in a school for the blind. Their eyes had failed them, or they had failed their eyes, and so they were having their fingers pressed forcibly down on the fiery Braille alphabet of a dissolving economy.

In Spain there was revolution. Here there was only shouting and confusion.

In Spain there was Guernica. Here there were disturbances of labor, sometimes pretty violent, in otherwise peaceful cities such as Chicago, Cleveland, Saint Louis . . .

This is the social background of the play.

(MUSIC.)

The play is memory.

Being a memory play, it is dimly lighted, it is sentimental, it is not realistic.

In memory everything seems to happen to music. That explains the fiddle in the wings.

I am the narrator of the play, and also a character in it.

The other characters are my mother, Amanda, my sister, Laura, and a gentleman caller who appears in the final scenes.

He is the most realistic character in the play, being an emissary from a world of reality that we were somehow set apart from.

But since I have a poet's weakness for symbols, I am using this character also as a symbol; he is the long delayed but always expected something that we live for.

There is a fifth character in the play who doesn't appear except in this larger-than-life-size photograph over the mantel.

This is our father who left us a long time ago.

He was a telephone man who fell in love with long distances; he gave up his job with the telephone company and skipped the light fantastic out of town . . .

The last we heard of him was a picture post-card from Mazatlan, on the Pacific coast of Mexico, containing a message of two words—

"Hello— Good-bye!" and no address.

I think the rest of the play will explain itself. . . .

(AMANDA's *voice becomes audible through the portieres.*)
(LEGEND ON SCREEN: "OU SONT LES NEIGES.")
(*He divides the portieres and enters the upstage area.*)
(AMANDA *and* LAURA *are seated at a drop-leaf table. Eating is indicated by gestures without food or utensils.* AMANDA *faces the audience,* TOM *and* LAURA *are seated in profile. The interior has lit up softly and through the scrim we see* AMANDA *and* LAURA *seated at the table in the upstage area.*)

AMANDA (*calling*): Tom?

TOM: Yes, Mother.

AMANDA: We can't say grace until you come to the table!

TOM: Coming, Mother. (*He bows slightly and withdraws, reappearing a few moments later in his place at the table.*)

AMANDA (*to her son*): Honey, don't *push* with your *fingers*. If you have to push with something, the thing to push with is a crust of bread. And chew—chew! Animals have sections in their stomachs which enable them to digest food without mastication, but human beings are supposed to chew their food before they swallow it down. Eat food leisurely, son, and really enjoy it. A well-cooked meal has lots of delicate flavors that have to be held in the mouth for appreciation. So chew your food and give your salivary glands a chance to function!

(TOM *deliberately lays his imaginary fork down and pushes his chair back from the table.*)

TOM: I haven't enjoyed one bite of this dinner because of your constant directions on how to eat it. It's you that make me rush through meals with your hawk-like attention to every bite I take. Sickening—spoils my appetite—all this discussion of—animals' secretion—salivary glands—mastication!

AMANDA (*lightly*): Temperament like a Metropolitan star! (*He rises and crosses downstage*) You're not excused from the table.

TOM: I'm getting a cigarette.

AMANDA: You smoke too much.

(LAURA *rises.*)

LAURA: I'll bring in the blanc mange.

(*He remains standing with his cigarette by the portieres during the following.*)

AMANDA (*rising*): No, sister, no, sister—you be the lady this time and I'll be the darky.

LAURA: I'm already up.

AMANDA: Resume your seat, little sister—I want you to stay fresh and pretty—for gentlemen callers!

LAURA: I'm not expecting any gentlemen callers.

AMANDA (*crossing out to kitchenette. Airily*): Sometimes they come when they are least expected! Why, I remember one Sunday afternoon in Blue Mountain—(*Enters kitchenette.*)

TOM: I know what's coming!

LAURA: Yes. But let her tell it.

TOM: Again?

LAURA: She loves to tell it.

(AMANDA *returns with bowl of dessert.*)

AMANDA: One Sunday afternoon in Blue Mountain—your mother received—*seventeen!*—gentlemen callers! Why, sometimes there weren't chairs enough to accommodate them all. We had to send the nigger over to bring in folding chairs from the parish house.

TOM (*remaining at portieres*): How did you entertain those gentlemen callers?

AMANDA: I understood the art of conversation!

TOM: I bet you could talk.

AMANDA: Girls in those days *knew* how to talk, I can tell you.

TOM: Yes?

(IMAGE: AMANDA AS A GIRL ON A PORCH, GREETING CALLERS.)

AMANDA: They knew how to entertain their gentlemen callers. It wasn't enough for a girl to be possessed of a pretty face and a graceful figure—although I wasn't slighted in either respect. She also needed to have a nimble wit and a tongue to meet all occasions.

TOM: What did you talk about?

AMANDA: Things of importance going on in the world! Never anything coarse or common or vulgar. (*She addresses* TOM *as though he were seated in the vacant chair at the table though he remains by portieres. He plays this scene as though he held the book*) My callers were gentlemen—all! Among my callers were some of the most prominent young planters of the Mississippi Delta—planters and sons of planters!

(TOM *motions for music and a spot of light on* AMANDA.)
(*Her eyes lift, her face glows, her voice becomes rich and elegiac.*)
(SCREEN LEGEND: "OU SONT LES NEIGES.")

There was young Champ Laughlin who later became vice-president of the Delta Planters Bank.

Hadley Stevenson who was drowned in Moon Lake and left his widow one hundred and fifty thousand in Government bonds.

There were the Cutrere brothers, Wesley and Bates. Bates was one of my bright particular beaux! He got in a quarrel with that wild Wainwright boy. They shot it out on the floor of Moon Lake Casino. Bates was shot through the stomach. Died in the ambulance on his way to Memphis. His widow was also well-provided for, came into eight or ten thousand acres, that's all. She married him on the rebound—never loved her—carried my picture on him the night he died!

And there was that boy that every girl in the Delta had set her cap for! That beautiful, brilliant young Fitzhugh boy from Greene County!

TOM: What did he leave his widow?

AMANDA: He never married! Gracious, you talk as though all of my old admirers had turned up their toes to the daisies!

TOM: Isn't this the first you've mentioned that still survives?

AMANDA: That Fitzhugh boy went North and made a fortune—came to be known as the Wolf of Wall Street! He had the Midas touch, whatever he touched turned to gold!

And I could have been Mrs. Duncan J. Fitzhugh, mind you! But —I picked your *father!*

LAURA (*rising*): Mother, let me clear the table.

AMANDA: No, dear, you go in front and study your typewriter chart. Or practice your shorthand a little. Stay fresh and pretty!—It's almost time for our gentlemen callers to start arriving. (*She flounces girlishly toward the kitchenette*) How many do you suppose we're going to entertain this afternoon?

(TOM *throws down the paper and jumps up with a groan.*)

LAURA (*alone in the dining room*): I don't believe we're going to receive any, Mother.

AMANDA (*reappearing, airily*): What? No one—not one? You must be joking! (LAURA *nervously echoes her laugh. She slips in a fugitive manner through the half-open portieres and draws them gently behind her. A shaft of very clear light is thrown on her face against the faded tapestry of the curtains.* MUSIC: "THE GLASS MENAGERIE" UNDER FAINTLY. *Lightly*) Not one gentleman caller? It can't be true! There must be a flood, there must have been a tornado!

LAURA: It isn't a flood, it's not a tornado, Mother. I'm just not popular like you were in Blue Mountain. . . . (TOM *utters another groan.* LAURA *glances at him with a faint, apologetic smile. Her voice catching a little*) Mother's afraid I'm going to be an old maid.

(*The Scene Dims Out with "Glass Menagerie" Music.*)

# Scene Two

L *aura, Haven't You Ever Liked Some Boy?"*
*On the dark stage the screen is lighted with the image of blue roses.*

*Gradually* LAURA's *figure becomes apparent and the screen goes out.*

*The music subsides.*

LAURA *is seated in the delicate ivory chair at the small clawfoot table.*

*She wears a dress of soft violet material for a kimono—her hair tied back from her forehead with a ribbon.*

*She is washing and polishing her collection of glass.*

AMANDA *appears on the fire-escape steps. At the sound of her ascent,* LAURA *catches her breath, thrusts the bowl of ornaments away and seats herself stiffly before the diagram of the typewriter keyboard as though it held her spellbound.*

*Something has happened to* AMANDA. *It is written in her face as she climbs to the landing: a look that is grim and hopeless and a little absurd.*

*She has on one of those cheap or imitation velvety-looking cloth coats with imitation fur collar. Her hat is five or six years old, one of those dreadful cloche hats that were worn in the late twenties and she is clasping an enormous black patent-leather pocketbook with nickel clasps and initials. This is her full-dress outfit, the one she usually wears to the D.A.R.*

*Before entering she looks through the door.*

*She purses her lips, opens her eyes very wide, rolls them upward and shakes her head.*

*Then she slowly lets herself in the door. Seeing her mother's expression* LAURA *touches her lips with a nervous gesture.*

LAURA: Hello, Mother, I was— (*She makes a nervous gesture toward the chart on the wall.* AMANDA *leans against the shut door and stares at* LAURA *with a martyred look.*)

AMANDA: Deception? Deception? (*She slowly removes her hat and gloves, continuing the sweet suffering stare. She lets the hat and gloves fall on the floor—a bit of acting.*)

LAURA (*shakily*): How was the D.A.R. meeting? (AMANDA *slowly opens her purse and removes a dainty white handkerchief which she shakes out delicately and delicately touches to her lips and nostrils*) Didn't you go to the D.A.R. meeting, Mother?

AMANDA (*faintly, almost inaudibly*): —No.—No. (*Then more forcibly*) I did not have the strength—to go to the D.A.R. In fact, I did not have the courage! I wanted to find a hole in the ground and hide myself in it forever! (*She crosses slowly to the wall and removes the diagram of the typewriter keyboard. She holds it in front of her for a second, staring at it sweetly and sorrowfully—then bites her lips and tears it in two pieces.*)

LAURA (*faintly*): Why did you do that, Mother? (AMANDA *repeats the same procedure with the chart of the Gregg Alphabet*) Why are you—

AMANDA: Why? Why? How old are you, Laura?

LAURA: Mother, you know my age.

AMANDA: I thought that you were an adult; it seems that I was mistaken. (*She crosses slowly to the sofa and sinks down and stares at* LAURA.)

LAURA: Please don't stare at me, Mother.

(AMANDA *closes her eyes and lowers her head. Count ten.*)

AMANDA: What are we going to do, what is going to become of us, what is the future?

(*Count ten.*)

LAURA: Has something happened, Mother? (AMANDA *draws a long breath and takes out the handkerchief again. Dabbing process*) Mother, has—something happened?

AMANDA: I'll be all right in a minute, I'm just bewildered—(*Count five*)—by life. . . .

LAURA: Mother, I wish that you would tell me what's happened!

AMANDA: As you know, I was supposed to be inducted into my office at the D.A.R. this afternoon. (IMAGE: A SWARM OF TYPEWRITERS) But I stopped off at Rubicam's Business College to speak to your teachers about your having a cold and ask them what progress they thought you were making down there.

LAURA: Oh. . . .

AMANDA: I went to the typing instructor and introduced myself as your mother. She didn't know who you were. Wingfield, she said. We don't have any such student enrolled at the school!

I assured her she did, that you had been going to classes since early in January.

"I wonder," she said, "if you could be talking about that terribly shy little girl who dropped out of school after only a few days' attendance?"

"No," I said, "Laura, my daughter, has been going to school every day for the past six weeks!"

"Excuse me," she said. She took the attendance book out and there was your name, unmistakably printed, and all the dates you were absent until they decided that you had dropped out of school.

I still said, "No, there must have been some mistake! There must have been some mix-up in the records!"

And she said, "No—I remember her perfectly now. Her hands shook so that she couldn't hit the right keys! The first time we gave a speed-test, she broke down completely—was sick at the stomach and almost had to be carried into the wash-room! After that morning she never showed up any more. We phoned the house but never got any answer"—while I was working at Famous and Barr, I suppose, demonstrating those— Oh!

I felt so weak I could barely keep on my feet!

I had to sit down while they got me a glass of water!

Fifty dollars' tuition, all of our plans—my hopes and ambitions for you—just gone up the spout, just gone up the spout like that.

(LAURA *draws a long breath and gets awkwardly to her feet. She crosses to the victrola and winds it up.*)

What are you doing?

LAURA: Oh! (*She releases the handle and returns to her seat.*)

AMANDA: Laura, where have you been going when you've gone out pretending that you were going to business college?

LAURA: I've just been going out walking.

AMANDA: That's not true.

LAURA: It is. I just went walking.

AMANDA: Walking? Walking? In winter? Deliberately courting pneumonia in that light coat? Where did you walk to, Laura?

LAURA: All sorts of places—mostly in the park.

AMANDA: Even after you'd started catching that cold?

LAURA: It was the lesser of two evils, Mother. (IMAGE: WINTER SCENE IN PARK) I couldn't go back up. I—threw up—on the floor!

AMANDA: From half past seven till after five every day you mean to tell me you walked around in the park, because you wanted to make me think that you were still going to Rubicam's Business College?

LAURA: It wasn't as bad as it sounds. I went inside places to get warmed up.

AMANDA: Inside where?

LAURA: I went in the art museum and the bird-houses at the Zoo. I visited the penguins every day! Sometimes I did without lunch and went to the movies. Lately I've been spending most of my afternoons in the Jewel-box, that big glass house where they raise the tropical flowers.

AMANDA: You did all this to deceive me, just for deception? (LAURA *looks down*) Why?

LAURA: Mother, when you're disappointed, you get that awful suffering look on your face, like the picture of Jesus' mother in the museum!

AMANDA: Hush!

LAURA: I couldn't face it.

(*Pause. A whisper of strings.*)
(LEGEND: "THE CRUST OF HUMILITY.")

AMANDA (*hopelessly fingering the huge pocketbook*): So what are we going to do the rest of our lives? Stay home and watch the parades go by? Amuse ourselves with the glass menagerie, darling? Eternally play those worn-out phonograph records your father left as a painful reminder of him?

We won't have a business career—we've given that up because it gave us nervous indigestion! (*Laughs wearily*) What is there left but dependency all our lives? I know so well what becomes of unmarried women who aren't prepared to occupy a position. I've seen such pitiful cases in the South—barely tolerated spinsters living upon the grudging patronage of sister's husband or brother's wife!—stuck away in some little mouse-trap of a room—encouraged by one in-law to visit another—little birdlike women without any nest—eating the crust of humility all their life!

Is that the future that we've mapped out for ourselves?

I swear it's the only alternative I can think of!

It isn't a very pleasant alternative, is it?

Of course—some girls *do marry*.

(LAURA *twists her hands nervously*.)

Haven't you ever liked some boy?

LAURA: Yes. I liked one once. (*Rises*) I came across his picture a while ago.

AMANDA (*with some interest*): He gave you his picture?

LAURA: No, it's in the year-book.

AMANDA (*disappointed*): Oh—a high-school boy.

(SCREEN IMAGE: JIM AS HIGH-SCHOOL HERO BEARING A SILVER CUP.)

LAURA: Yes. His name was Jim. (LAURA *lifts the heavy annual from the claw-foot table*) Here he is in *The Pirates of Penzance*.

AMANDA (*absently*): The what?

LAURA: The operetta the senior class put on. He had a wonderful voice and we sat across the aisle from each other Mondays, Wednesdays and Fridays in the Aud. Here he is with the silver cup for debating! See his grin?

AMANDA (*absently*): He must have had a jolly disposition.

LAURA: He used to call me—Blue Roses.

(IMAGE: BLUE ROSES.)

AMANDA: Why did he call you such a name as that?

LAURA: When I had that attack of pleurosis—he asked me what was the matter when I came back. I said pleurosis—he thought that I said Blue Roses! So that's what he always called me after that. Whenever he saw me, he'd holler, "Hello, Blue Roses!" I didn't care for the girl that he went out with. Emily Meisenbach. Emily was the best-dressed girl at Soldan. She never struck me, though, as being sincere . . . It says in the Personal Section—they're engaged. That's —six years ago! They must be married by now.

AMANDA: Girls that aren't cut out for business careers usually wind up married to some nice man. (*Gets up with a spark of revival*) Sister, that's what you'll do!

(LAURA *utters a startled, doubtful laugh. She reaches quickly for a piece of glass.*)

LAURA: But, Mother—

AMANDA: Yes? (*Crossing to photograph.*)

LAURA (*in a tone of frightened apology*): I'm—crippled!

(IMAGE: SCREEN.)

AMANDA: Nonsense! Laura, I've told you never, never to use that word. Why, you're not crippled, you just have a little defect— hardly noticeable, even! When people have some slight disadvantage like that, they cultivate other things to make up for it—develop charm—and vivacity—and—*charm!* That's all you have to do! (*She turns again to the photograph*) One thing your father had *plenty* of—was *charm!*

(TOM *motions to the fiddle in the wings.*)

(*The Scene Fades Out with Music.*)

# Scene Three

LEGEND ON SCREEN: "AFTER THE FIASCO—"
TOM *speaks from the fire-escape landing.*

TOM: After the fiasco at Rubicam's Business College, the idea of getting a gentleman caller for Laura began to play a more and more important part in Mother's calculations.

It became an obsession. Like some archetype of the universal unconscious, the image of the gentleman caller haunted our small apartment. . . .

(IMAGE: YOUNG MAN AT DOOR WITH FLOWERS.)

An evening at home rarely passed without some allusion to this image, this spectre, this hope. . . .

Even when he wasn't mentioned, his presence hung in Mother's preoccupied look and in my sister's frightened, apologetic manner—hung like a sentence passed upon the Wingfields!

Mother was a woman of action as well as words.

She began to take logical steps in the planned direction.

Late that winter and in the early spring—realizing that extra money would be needed to properly feather the nest and plume the bird—she conducted a vigorous campaign on the telephone, roping in subscribers to one of those magazines for matrons called *The Homemaker's Companion*, the type of journal that features the serialized sublimations of ladies of letters who think in terms of delicate cup-like breasts, slim, tapering waists, rich, creamy thighs, eyes like wood-smoke in autumn, fingers that soothe and caress like strains of music, bodies as powerful as Etruscan sculpture.

(SCREEN IMAGE: GLAMOR MAGAZINE COVER.)

(AMANDA *enters with phone on long extension cord. She is spotted in the dim stage.*)

AMANDA: Ida Scott? This is Amanda Wingfield!

We *missed* you at the D.A.R. last Monday!

I said to myself: She's probably suffering with that sinus condition! How is that sinus condition?

Horrors! Heaven have mercy!—You're a Christian martyr, yes, that's what you are, a Christian martyr!

Well, I just now happened to notice that your subscription to the *Companion's* about to expire! Yes, it expires with the next issue, honey!—just when that wonderful new serial by Bessie Mae Hopper is getting off to such an exciting start. Oh, honey, it's something that you can't miss! You remember how *Gone With the Wind* took everybody by storm? You simply couldn't go out if you hadn't read it. All everybody *talked* was Scarlett O'Hara. Well, this is a book that critics already compare to *Gone With the Wind*. It's the *Gone With the Wind* of the post-World War generation!—What?—Burning?—Oh, honey, don't let them burn, go take a look in the oven and I'll hold the wire! Heavens—I think she's hung up!

### DIM OUT

(LEGEND ON SCREEN: "YOU THINK I'M IN LOVE WITH CONTINENTAL SHOEMAKERS?")

(*Before the stage is lighted, the violent voices of* TOM *and* AMANDA *are heard.*)

(*They are quarreling behind the portieres. In front of them stands* LAURA *with clenched hands and panicky expression.*)

(*A clear pool of light on her figure throughout this scene.*)

TOM: What in Christ's name am I—

AMANDA (*shrilly*): Don't you use that—

TOM: Supposed to do!

AMANDA: Expression! Not in my—

TOM: Ohhh!

AMANDA: Presence! Have you gone out of your senses?

TOM: I have, that's true, *driven* out!

AMANDA: What is the matter with you, you—big—big—IDIOT!

TOM: Look!—I've got *no thing*, no single thing—

AMANDA: Lower your voice!

TOM: In my life here that I can call my own! Everything is—

AMANDA: Stop that shouting!

TOM: Yesterday you confiscated my books! You had the nerve to—

AMANDA: I took that horrible novel back to the library—yes! That hideous book by that insane Mr. Lawrence. (TOM *laughs wildly*) I cannot control the output of diseased minds or people who cater to them— (TOM *laughs still more wildly*) BUT I WON'T ALLOW SUCH FILTH BROUGHT INTO MY HOUSE! No, no, no, no, no!

TOM: House, house! Who pays rent on it, who makes a slave of himself to—

AMANDA (*fairly screeching*): Don't you DARE to—

TOM: No, no, *I* mustn't say things! *I've* got to just—

AMANDA: Let me tell you—

TOM: I don't want to hear any more! (*He tears the portieres open. The upstage area is lit with a turgid smoky red glow.*)

(AMANDA's *hair is in metal curlers and she wears a very old bathrobe, much too large for her slight figure, a relic of the faithless Mr. Wingfield.*)
(*An upright typewriter and a wild disarray of manuscripts is on the drop-leaf table. The quarrel was probably precipitated by* AMANDA'S *interruption of his creative labor. A chair lying overthrown on the floor.*)
(*Their gesticulating shadows are cast on the ceiling by the fiery glow.*)

AMANDA: You *will* hear more, you—

TOM: No, I won't hear more, I'm going out!

AMANDA: You come right back in—

TOM: Out, out, out! Because I'm—

AMANDA: Come back here, Tom Wingfield! I'm not through talking to you!

TOM: Oh, go—

LAURA (*desperately*): —Tom!

AMANDA: You're going to listen, and no more insolence from you! I'm at the end of my patience!

(*He comes back toward her.*)

TOM: What do you think I'm at? Aren't I supposed to have any patience to reach the end of, Mother? I know, I know. It seems unimportant to you, what I'm *doing*—what I *want* to do—having a little *difference* between them! You don't think that—

AMANDA: I think you've been doing things that you're ashamed of. That's why you act like this. I don't believe that you go every night to the movies. Nobody goes to the movies night after night. Nobody in their right minds goes to the movies as often as you pretend to. People don't go to the movies at nearly midnight, and movies don't let out at two A.M. Come in stumbling. Muttering to yourself like a maniac! You get three hours' sleep and then go to work. Oh, I can picture the way you're doing down there. Moping, doping, because you're in no condition.

TOM (*wildly*): No, I'm in no condition!

AMANDA: What right have you got to jeopardize your job? Jeopardize the security of us all? How do you think we'd manage if you were—

TOM: Listen! You think I'm crazy *about the warehouse?* (*He bends fiercely toward her slight figure*) You think I'm in love with the Continental Shoemakers? You think I want to spend fifty-five *years* down there in that—*celotex interior!* with—*fluorescent—tubes!* Look! I'd rather somebody picked up a crowbar and battered out my brains —than go back mornings! I *go!* Every time you come in yelling that God damn "*Rise and Shine!*" "*Rise and Shine!*" I say to myself, "How *lucky dead* people are!" But I get up. I *go!* For sixty-five dollars a month I give up all that I dream of doing and being *ever!* And you say self—*self's* all I ever think of. Why, listen, if self is what I thought of, Mother, I'd be where he is—GONE! (*Pointing to father's picture*) As far as the system of transportation reaches! (*He starts past her. She grabs his arm*) Don't grab at me, Mother!

AMANDA: Where are you going?

TOM: I'm going to the *movies!*

AMANDA: I don't believe that lie!

TOM (*crouching toward her, overtowering her tiny figure. She backs away, gasping*): I'm going to opium dens! Yes, opium dens, dens of vice and criminals' hang-outs, Mother. I've joined the Hogan gang, I'm a hired assassin, I carry a tommy-gun in a violin case! I run a string of cat-houses in the Valley! They call me Killer, Killer Wingfield, I'm leading a double-life, a simple, honest warehouse worker by day, by night a dynamic *czar* of the *underworld, Mother.* I go to gambling casinos, I spin away fortunes on the roulette table! I wear a patch over one eye and a false mustache, sometimes I put on green whiskers. On those occasions they call me—*El Diablo!* Oh, I could tell you things to make you sleepless! My enemies plan to dynamite this place. They're going to blow us all sky-high some night! I'll be glad, very happy, and so will you! You'll go up, up on a broomstick, over Blue Mountain with seventeen gentlemen callers! You ugly—babbling old—*witch.* . . . (*He goes through a series of violent, clumsy movements, seizing his overcoat, lunging to the door, pulling it fiercely open. The women watch him, aghast. His arm catches in the sleeve of the coat as he struggles to pull it on. For a moment he is pinioned by the bulky garment. With an outraged groan he tears the coat off again, splitting the shoulder of it, and hurls it across the room. It strikes against the shelf of* LAURA'S *glass collection, there is a tinkle of shattering glass.* LAURA *cries out as if wounded.*)

(MUSIC. LEGEND: "THE GLASS MENAGERIE.")

LAURA (*shrilly*): My glass!—menagerie. . . . (*She covers her face and turns away.*)

(*But* AMANDA *is still stunned and stupefied by the "ugly witch" so that she barely notices this occurrence. Now she recovers her speech.*)

AMANDA (*in an awful voice*): I won't speak to you—until you apologize! (*She crosses through portieres and draws them together behind her.* TOM *is left with* LAURA. LAURA *clings weakly to the mantel with her face averted.* TOM *stares at her stupidly for a moment. Then he crosses to shelf. Drops awkwardly on his knees to collect the fallen glass, glancing at* LAURA *as if he would speak but couldn't.*)

    ("*The Glass Menagerie*" steals in as

*The Scene Dims Out.*)

# Scene Four

*The interior is dark. Faint light in the alley.*
*A deep-voiced bell in a church is tolling the hour of five as the scene commences.*

*TOM appears at the top of the alley. After each solemn boom of the bell in the tower, he shakes a little noise-maker or rattle as if to express the tiny spasm of man in contrast to the sustained power and dignity of the Almighty. This and the unsteadiness of his advance make it evident that he has been drinking.*

*As he climbs the few steps to the fire-escape landing light steals up inside. LAURA appears in night-dress, observing TOM's empty bed in the front room.*

*TOM fishes in his pockets for door-key, removing a motley assortment of articles in the search, including a perfect shower of movie-ticket stubs and an empty bottle. At last he finds the key, but just as he is about to insert it, it slips from his fingers. He strikes a match and crouches below the door.*

TOM (*bitterly*): One crack—and it falls through!

(LAURA *opens the door.*)

LAURA: Tom, Tom, what are you doing?

TOM: Looking for a door-key.

LAURA: Where have you been all this time?

TOM: I have been to the movies.

LAURA: All this time at the movies?

TOM: There was a very long program. There was a Garbo picture and a Mickey Mouse and a travelogue and a newsreel and a preview of coming attractions. And there was an organ solo and a collection for the milk-fund—simultaneously—which ended up in a terrible fight between a fat lady and an usher!

LAURA (*innocently*): Did you have to stay through everything?

TOM: Of course! And, oh, I forgot! There was a big stage show! The headliner on this stage show was Malvolio the Magician. He performed wonderful tricks, many of them, such as pouring water back and forth between pitchers. First it turned to wine and then it turned to beer and then it turned to whiskey. I know it was whiskey it finally turned into because he needed somebody to come up out of the audience to help him, and I came up—both shows! It was Kentucky Straight Bourbon. A very generous fellow, he gave souvenirs. (*He pulls from his back pocket a shimmering rainbow-colored scarf*) He gave me this. This is his magic scarf. You can have it, Laura. You wave it over a canary cage and you get a bowl of gold-fish. You wave it over the gold-fish bowl and they fly away canaries. . . . But the wonderfullest trick of all was the coffin trick. We nailed him into a coffin and he got out of the coffin without removing one nail. (*He has come inside*) There is a trick that would come in handy for me—get me out of this 2 by 4 situation! (*Flops onto bed and starts removing shoes.*)

LAURA: Tom—Shhh!

TOM: What're you shushing me for?

LAURA: You'll wake up Mother.

TOM: Goody, goody! Pay 'er back for all those "Rise an' Shines." (*Lies down, groaning*) You know it don't take much intelligence to get yourself into a nailed-up coffin, Laura. But who in hell ever got himself out of one without removing one nail?

(*As if in answer, the father's grinning photograph lights up.*)

### SCENE DIMS OUT

(*Immediately following: The church bell is heard striking six. At the sixth stroke the alarm clock goes off in* AMANDA'S *room, and after a few moments we hear her calling: "Rise and Shine! Rise and Shine! Laura, go tell your brother to rise and shine!"*)

TOM (*sitting up slowly*): I'll rise—but I won't shine.

(*The light increases.*)

AMANDA: Laura, tell your brother his coffee is ready.

(LAURA *slips into front room.*)

LAURA: Tom!—It's nearly seven. Don't make Mother nervous. (*He stares at her stupidly. Beseechingly*) Tom, speak to Mother this morning. Make up with her, apologize, speak to her!

TOM: She won't to me. It's her that started not speaking.

LAURA: If you just say you're sorry she'll start speaking.

TOM: Her not speaking—is that such a tragedy?

LAURA: Please—please!

AMANDA (*calling from kitchenette*): Laura, are you going to do what I asked you to do, or do I have to get dressed and go out myself?

LAURA: Going, going—soon as I get on my coat! (*She pulls on a shapeless felt hat with nervous, jerky movement, pleadingly glancing at* TOM. *Rushes awkwardly for coat. The coat is one of* AMANDA's, *inaccurately made-over, the sleeves too short for* LAURA) Butter and what else?

AMANDA (*entering upstage*): Just butter. Tell them to charge it.

LAURA: Mother, they make such faces when I do that.

AMANDA: Sticks and stones can break our bones, but the expression on Mr. Garfinkel's face won't harm us! Tell your brother his coffee is getting cold.

LAURA (*at door*): Do what I asked you, will you, will you, Tom?

(*He looks sullenly away.*)

AMANDA: Laura, go now or just don't go at all!

LAURA (*rushing out*): Going—going! (*A second later she cries out.* TOM *springs up and crosses to door.* AMANDA *rushes anxiously in.* TOM *opens the door.*)

TOM: Laura?

LAURA: I'm all right. I slipped, but I'm all right.

AMANDA (*peering anxiously after her*): If anyone breaks a leg on those fire-escape steps, the landlord ought to be sued for every cent he possesses! (*She shuts door. Remembers she isn't speaking and returns to other room.*)

(*As* TOM *enters listlessly for his coffee, she turns her back to him and stands rigidly facing the window on the gloomy gray vault of the areaway. Its light on her face with its aged but childish features is cruelly sharp, satirical as a Daumier print.*)

(MUSIC UNDER: "AVE MARIA.")

(TOM *glances sheepishly but sullenly at her averted figure and slumps at the table. The coffee is scalding hot; he sips it and gasps and spits it back in the cup. At his gasp,* AMANDA *catches her breath and half turns. Then catches herself and turns back to window.*)

(TOM *blows on his coffee, glancing sidewise at his mother. She clears her throat.* TOM *clears his. He starts to rise. Sinks back down again, scratches his head, clears his throat again.* AMANDA *coughs.* TOM *raises his cup in both hands to blow on it, his eyes staring over the rim of it at his mother for several moments. Then he slowly sets the cup down and awkwardly and hesitantly rises from the chair.*)

TOM (*hoarsely*): Mother. I—I apologize, Mother. (AMANDA *draws a quick, shuddering breath. Her face works grotesquely. She breaks into childlike tears*) I'm sorry for what I said, for everything that I said, I didn't mean it.

AMANDA (*sobbingly*): My devotion has made me a witch and so I make myself hateful to my children!

TOM: *No*, you *don't*.

AMANDA: I worry so much, don't sleep, it makes me nervous!

TOM (*gently*): I understand that.

AMANDA: I've had to put up a solitary battle all these years. But you're my right-hand bower! Don't fall down, don't fail!

TOM (*gently*): I try, Mother.

AMANDA (*with great enthusiasm*): Try and you will SUCCEED! (*The notion makes her breathless*) Why, you—you're just *full* of natural endowments! Both my children—they're *unusual* children! Don't you think I know it? I'm so—*proud!* Happy and—feel I've—so much to be thankful for but— Promise me one thing, Son!

TOM: What, Mother?

AMANDA: Promise, son, you'll—never be a drunkard!

TOM (*turns to her grinning*): I will never be a drunkard, Mother.

AMANDA: That's what frightened me so, that you'd be drinking! Eat a bowl of Purina!

TOM: Just coffee, Mother.

AMANDA: Shredded wheat biscuit?

TOM: No. No, Mother, just coffee.

AMANDA: You can't put in a day's work on an empty stomach. You've got ten minutes—don't gulp! Drinking too-hot liquids makes cancer of the stomach. . . . Put cream in.

TOM: No, thank you.

AMANDA: To cool it.

TOM: No! No, thank you, I want it black.

AMANDA: I know, but it's not good for you. We have to do all that we can to build ourselves up. In these trying times we live in, all that we have to cling to is—each other. . . . That's why it's so important to— Tom, I— I sent out your sister so I could discuss something with you. If you hadn't spoken I would have spoken to you. (*Sits down.*)

TOM (*gently*): What is it, Mother, that you want to discuss?

AMANDA: *Laura!*

(TOM *puts his cup down slowly.*)
(LEGEND ON SCREEN: "LAURA.")
(MUSIC: "THE GLASS MENAGERIE.")

TOM: —Oh.—Laura . . .

AMANDA (*touching his sleeve*): You know how Laura is. So quiet but—still water runs deep! She notices things and I think she—broods about them. (TOM *looks up*) A few days ago I came in and she was crying.

TOM: What about?

AMANDA: You.

TOM: Me?

AMANDA: She has an idea that you're not happy here.

TOM: What gave her that idea?

AMANDA: What gives her any idea? However, you do act strangely. I—I'm not criticizing, understand *that!* I know your ambitions do not lie in the warehouse, that like everybody in the whole wide world—you've had to—make sacrifices, but—Tom—Tom—life's not easy, it calls for—Spartan endurance! There's so many things in my heart that I cannot describe to you! I've never told you but I—*loved* your father. . . .

TOM (*gently*): I know that, Mother.

AMANDA: And you—when I see you taking after his ways! Staying out late—and—well, you *had* been drinking the night you were in that—terrifying condition! Laura says that you hate the apartment and that you go out nights to get away from it! Is that true, Tom?

TOM: No. You say there's so much in your heart that you can't describe to me. That's true of me, too. There's so much in my heart that I can't describe to *you!* So let's respect each other's—

AMANDA: But, why—*why*, Tom—are you always so *restless?* Where do you *go* to, nights?

TOM: I—go to the movies.

AMANDA: Why do you go to the movies so much, Tom?

TOM: I go to the movies because—I like adventure. Adventure is something I don't have much of at work, so I go to the movies.

AMANDA: But, Tom, you go to the movies *entirely* too *much!*

TOM: I like a lot of adventure.

(AMANDA *looks baffled, then hurt. As the familiar inquisition resumes he becomes hard and impatient again.* AMANDA *slips back into her querulous attitude toward him.*)
(IMAGE ON SCREEN: SAILING VESSEL WITH JOLLY ROGER.)

AMANDA: Most young men find adventure in their careers.

TOM: Then most young men are not employed in a warehouse.

AMANDA: The world is full of young men employed in warehouses and offices and factories.

TOM: Do all of them find adventure in their careers?

AMANDA: They do or they do without it! Not everybody has a craze for adventure.

TOM: Man is by instinct a lover, a hunter, a fighter, and none of those instincts are given much play at the warehouse!

AMANDA: Man is by instinct! Don't quote instinct to me! Instinct is something that people have got away from! It belongs to animals! Christian adults don't want it!

TOM: What do Christian adults want, then, Mother?

AMANDA: Superior things! Things of the mind and the spirit! Only animals have to satisfy instincts! Surely your aims are somewhat higher than theirs! Than monkeys—pigs—

TOM: I reckon they're not.

AMANDA: You're joking! However, that isn't what I wanted to discuss.

TOM (*rising*): I haven't much time.

AMANDA (*pushing his shoulders*): Sit down.

TOM: You want me to punch in red at the warehouse, Mother?

AMANDA: You have five minutes. I want to talk about Laura.

(LEGEND: "PLANS AND PROVISIONS.")

TOM: All right! What about Laura?

AMANDA: We have to be making some plans and provisions for her. She's older than you, two years, and nothing has happened. She just drifts along doing nothing. It frightens me terribly how she just drifts along.

TOM: I guess she's the type that people call home girls.

AMANDA: There's no such type, and if there is, it's a pity! That is unless the home is hers, with a husband!

TOM: What?

AMANDA: Oh, I can see the handwriting on the wall as plain as I see the nose in front of my face! It's terrifying!

More and more you remind me of your father! He was out all hours without explanation!—Then *left! Good-bye!*

And me with the bag to hold. I saw that letter you got from the Merchant Marine. I know what you're dreaming of. I'm not standing here blindfolded.

Very well, then. Then *do* it!

But not till there's somebody to take your place.

TOM: What do you mean?

AMANDA: I mean that as soon as Laura has got somebody to take care of her, married, a home of her own, independent—why, then you'll be free to go wherever you please, on land, on sea, whichever way the wind blows you!

But until that time you've got to look out for your sister. I don't say me because I'm old and don't matter! I say for your sister because she's young and dependent.

I put her in business college—a dismal failure! Frightened her so it made her sick at the stomach.

I took her over to the Young People's League at the church. Another fiasco. She spoke to nobody, nobody spoke to her. Now all she does is fool with those pieces of glass and play those worn-out records. What kind of a life is that for a girl to lead?

TOM: What can I do about it?

AMANDA: Overcome selfishness!

Self, self, self is all that you ever think of!

(TOM *springs up and crosses to get his coat. It is ugly and bulky. He pulls on a cap with earmuffs.*)

Where is your muffler? Put your wool muffler on!

(*He snatches it angrily from the closet and tosses it around his neck and pulls both ends tight.*)

Tom! I haven't said what I had in mind to ask you.

TOM: I'm too late to—

AMANDA (*catching his arm—very importunately. Then shyly*): Down at the warehouse, aren't there some—nice young men?

TOM: No!

AMANDA: There *must* be—*some* . . .

TOM: Mother—(*Gesture.*)

AMANDA: Find out one that's clean-living—doesn't drink and—ask him out for sister!

TOM: What?

AMANDA: For *sister!* To *meet!* Get *acquainted!*

TOM (*stamping to door*): Oh, my go-osh!

AMANDA: Will you? (*He opens door. Imploringly*) Will you? (*He starts down*) Will you? *Will* you, dear?

TOM (*calling back*): YES!

(AMANDA *closes the door hesitantly and with a troubled but faintly hopeful expression.*)
(SCREEN IMAGE: GLAMOR MAGAZINE COVER.)
(*Spot* AMANDA *at phone.*)

AMANDA: Ella Cartwright? This is Amanda Wingfield!
How are you, honey?
How is that kidney condition? (*Count five.*)
*Horrors!* (*Count five.*)
You're a Christian martyr, yes, honey, that's what you are, a Christian martyr!
Well, I just now happened to notice in my little red book that your subscription to the *Companion* has just run out! I knew that you wouldn't want to miss out on the wonderful serial starting in this new issue. It's by Bessie Mae Hopper, the first thing she's written since *Honeymoon for Three.*
Wasn't that a strange and interesting story? Well, this one is even lovelier, I believe. It has a sophisticated, society background. It's all about the horsey set on Long Island!

(*Fade Out.*)

# Scene Five

LEGEND ON SCREEN: "ANNUNCIATION." *Fade with music.*

*It is early dusk of a spring evening. Supper has just been finished in the Wingfield apartment.* AMANDA *and* LAURA *in light-colored dresses are removing dishes from the table, in the upstage area, which is shadowy, their movements formalized almost as a dance or ritual, their moving forms as pale and silent as moths.*

*TOM, in white shirt and trousers, rises from the table and crosses toward the fire-escape.*

AMANDA (*as he passes her*): Son, will you do me a favor?

TOM: What?

AMANDA: Comb your hair! You look so pretty when your hair is combed! (TOM *slouches on sofa with evening paper. Enormous caption "Franco Triumphs"*) There is only one respect in which I would like you to emulate your father.

TOM: What respect is that?

AMANDA: The care he always took of his appearance. He never allowed himself to look untidy. (*He throws down the paper and crosses to fire-escape*) Where are you going?

TOM: I'm going out to smoke.

AMANDA: You smoke too much. A pack a day at fifteen cents a pack. How much would that amount to in a month? Thirty times fifteen is how much, Tom? Figure it out and you will be astounded at what you could save. Enough to give you a night-school course in accounting at Washington U! Just think what a wonderful thing that would be for you, Son!

(TOM *is unmoved by the thought.*)

TOM: I'd rather smoke. (*He steps out on landing, letting the screen door slam.*)

AMANDA (*sharply*): I know! That's the tragedy of it. . . . (*Alone, she turns to look at her husband's picture.*)

(DANCE MUSIC: "ALL THE WORLD IS WAITING FOR THE SUNRISE!")

TOM (*to the audience*): Across the alley from us was the Paradise Dance Hall. On evenings in spring the windows and doors were open and the music came outdoors. Sometimes the lights were turned out except for a large glass sphere that hung from the ceiling. It would turn slowly about and filter the dusk with delicate rainbow colors. Then the orchestra played a waltz or a tango, something that had a slow and sensuous rhythm. Couples would come outside, to the relative privacy of the alley. You could see them kissing behind ash-pits and telephone poles.

This was the compensation for lives that passed like mine, without any change or adventure.

Adventure and change were imminent in this year. They were waiting around the corner for all these kids.

Suspended in the mist over Berchtesgaden, caught in the folds of Chamberlain's umbrella—

In Spain there was Guernica!

But here there was only hot swing music and liquor, dance halls, bars, and movies, and sex that hung in the gloom like a chandelier and flooded the world with brief, deceptive rainbows. . . .

All the world was waiting for bombardments!

(AMANDA *turns from the picture and comes outside.*)

AMANDA (*sighing*): A fire-escape landing's a poor excuse for a porch. (*She spreads a newspaper on a step and sits down, gracefully and demurely as if she were settling into a swing on a Mississippi veranda*) What are you looking at?

TOM: The moon.

AMANDA: Is there a moon this evening?

TOM: It's rising over Garfinkel's Delicatessen.

AMANDA: So it is! A little silver slipper of a moon. Have you made a wish on it yet?

TOM: Um-hum.

AMANDA: What did you wish for?

TOM: That's a secret.

AMANDA: A secret, huh? Well, I won't tell mine either. I will be just as mysterious as you.

TOM: I bet I can guess what yours is.

AMANDA: Is my head so transparent?

TOM: You're not a sphinx.

AMANDA: No, I don't have secrets. I'll tell you what I wished for on the moon. Success and happiness for my precious children! I wish for that whenever there's a moon, and when there isn't a moon, I wish for it, too.

TOM: I thought perhaps you wished for a gentleman caller.

AMANDA: Why do you say that?

TOM: Don't you remember asking me to fetch one?

AMANDA: I remember suggesting that it would be nice for your sister if you brought home some nice young man from the warehouse. I think that I've made that suggestion more than once.

TOM: Yes, you have made it repeatedly.

AMANDA: Well?

TOM: We are going to have one.

AMANDA: *What?*

TOM: A gentleman caller!

(THE ANNUNCIATION IS CELEBRATED WITH MUSIC.)
(AMANDA *rises.*)
(IMAGE ON SCREEN: CALLER WITH BOUQUET.)

AMANDA: You mean you have asked some nice young man to come over?

TOM: Yep. I've asked him to dinner.

AMANDA: You really did?

TOM: I did!

AMANDA: You did, and did he—*accept?*

TOM: He did!

AMANDA: Well, well—well, well! That's—lovely!

TOM: I thought that you would be pleased.

AMANDA: It's definite, then?

TOM: Very definite.

AMANDA: Soon?

TOM: Very soon.

AMANDA: For heaven's sake, stop putting on and tell me some things, will you?

TOM: What things do you want me to tell you?

AMANDA: *Naturally* I would like to know when he's *coming!*

TOM: He's coming tomorrow.

AMANDA: *Tomorrow?*

TOM: Yep. Tomorrow.

AMANDA: But, Tom!

TOM: Yes, Mother?

AMANDA: Tomorrow gives me no time!

TOM: Time for what?

AMANDA: Preparations! Why didn't you phone me at once, as soon as you asked him, the minute that he accepted? Then, don't you see, I could have been getting ready!

TOM: You don't have to make any fuss.

AMANDA: Oh, Tom, Tom, Tom, of course I have to make a fuss! I want things nice, not sloppy! Not thrown together. I'll certainly have to do some fast thinking, won't I?

TOM: I don't see why you have to think at all.

AMANDA: You just don't know. We can't have a gentleman caller in a pig-sty! All my wedding silver has to be polished, the monogrammed table linen ought to be laundered! The windows have to be washed and fresh curtains put up. And how about clothes? We have to *wear* something, don't we?

TOM: Mother, this boy is no one to make a fuss over!

AMANDA: Do you realize he's the first young man we've introduced to your sister?

It's terrible, dreadful, disgraceful that poor little sister has never received a single gentleman caller! Tom, come inside! (*She opens the screen door.*)

TOM: What for?

AMANDA: I want to ask you some things.

TOM: If you're going to make such a fuss, I'll call it off, I'll tell him not to come!

AMANDA: You certainly won't do anything of the kind. Nothing offends people worse than broken engagements. It simply means I'll have to work like a Turk! We won't be brilliant, but we will pass inspection. Come on inside. (TOM *follows, groaning*) Sit down.

TOM: Any particular place you would like me to sit?

AMANDA: Thank heavens I've got that new sofa! I'm also making payments on a floor lamp I'll have sent out! And put the chintz covers on, they'll brighten things up! Of course I'd hoped to have these walls re-papered. . . . What is the young man's name?

TOM: His name is O'Connor.

AMANDA: That, of course, means fish—tomorrow is Friday! I'll have that salmon loaf—with Durkee's dressing! What does he do? He works at the warehouse?

TOM: Of course! How else would I—

AMANDA: Tom, he—doesn't drink?

TOM: Why do you ask me that?

AMANDA: Your father *did!*

TOM: Don't get started on that!

AMANDA: He *does* drink, then?

TOM: Not that I know of!

AMANDA: Make sure, be certain! The last thing I want for my daughter's a boy who drinks!

TOM: Aren't you being a little bit premature? Mr. O'Connor has not yet appeared on the scene!

AMANDA: But will tomorrow. To meet your sister, and what do I know about his character? Nothing! Old maids are better off than wives of drunkards!

TOM: Oh, my God!

AMANDA: Be still!

TOM (*leaning forward to whisper*): Lots of fellows meet girls whom they don't marry!

AMANDA: Oh, talk sensibly, Tom—and don't be sarcastic! (*She has gotten a hairbrush.*)

TOM: What are you doing?

AMANDA: I'm brushing that cow-lick down!
   What is this young man's position at the warehouse?

TOM (*submitting grimly to the brush and the interrogation*): This young man's position is that of a shipping clerk, Mother.

AMANDA: Sounds to me like a fairly responsible job, the sort of a job *you* would be in if you just had more *get-up*.
   What is his salary? Have you any idea?

TOM: I would judge it to be approximately eighty-five dollars a month.

AMANDA: Well—not princely, but—

TOM: Twenty more than I make.

AMANDA: Yes, how well I know! But for a family man, eighty-five dollars a month is not much more than you can just get by on. . . .

TOM: Yes, but Mr. O'Connor is not a family man.

AMANDA: He might be, mightn't he? Some time in the future?

TOM: I see. Plans and provisions.

AMANDA: You are the only young man that I know of who ignores the fact that the future becomes the present, the present the past, and the past turns into everlasting regret if you don't plan for it!

TOM: I will think that over and see what I can make of it.

AMANDA: Don't be supercilious with your mother! Tell me some more about this—what do you call him?

TOM: James D. O'Connor. The D. is for Delaney.

AMANDA: Irish on *both* sides! *Gracious!* And doesn't drink?

TOM: Shall I call him up and ask him right this minute?

AMANDA: The only way to find out about those things is to make discreet inquiries at the proper moment. When I was a girl in Blue Mountain and it was suspected that a young man drank, the girl whose attentions he had been receiving, if any girl *was*, would sometimes speak to the minister of his church, or rather her father would if her father was living, and sort of feel him out on the young man's character. That is the way such things are discreetly handled to keep a young woman from making a tragic mistake!

TOM: Then how did you happen to make a tragic mistake?

AMANDA: That innocent look of your father's had everyone fooled! He *smiled*—the world was *enchanted!*
No girl can do worse than put herself at the mercy of a handsome appearance!
I hope that Mr. O'Connor is not too good-looking.

TOM: No, he's not too good-looking. He's covered with freckles and hasn't too much of a nose.

AMANDA: He's not right-down homely, though?

TOM: Not right-down homely. Just medium homely, I'd say.

AMANDA: Character's what to look for in a man.

TOM: That's what I've always said, Mother.

AMANDA: You've never said anything of the kind and I suspect you would never give it a thought.

TOM: Don't be so suspicious of me.

AMANDA: At least I hope he's the type that's up and coming.

TOM: I think he really goes in for self-improvement.

AMANDA: What reason have you to think so?

TOM: He goes to night school.

AMANDA (*beaming*): Splendid! What does he do, I mean study?

TOM: Radio engineering and public speaking!

AMANDA: Then he has visions of being advanced in the world!
Any young man who studies public speaking is aiming to have an executive job some day!
And radio engineering? A thing for the future!
Both of these facts are very illuminating. Those are the sort of things that a mother should know concerning any young man who comes to call on her daughter. Seriously or—not.

TOM: One little warning. He doesn't know about Laura. I didn't let on that we had dark ulterior motives. I just said, why don't you come and have dinner with us? He said okay and that was the whole conversation.

AMANDA: I bet it was! You're eloquent as an oyster.
However, he'll know about Laura when he gets here. When he sees how lovely and sweet and pretty she is, he'll thank his lucky stars he was asked to dinner.

TOM: Mother, you mustn't expect too much of Laura.

AMANDA: What do you mean?

TOM: Laura seems all those things to you and me because she's ours and we love her. We don't even notice she's crippled any more.

AMANDA: Don't say crippled! You know that I never allow that word to be used!

TOM: But face facts, Mother. She is and—that's not all—

AMANDA: What do you mean "not all"?

TOM: Laura is very different from other girls.

AMANDA: I think the difference is all to her advantage.

TOM: Not quite all—in the eyes of others—strangers—she's terribly shy and lives in a world of her own and those things make her seem a little peculiar to people outside the house.

AMANDA: Don't say peculiar.

TOM: Face the facts. She is.

(THE DANCE-HALL MUSIC CHANGES TO A TANGO THAT HAS A MINOR AND SOMEWHAT OMINOUS TONE.)

AMANDA: In what way is she peculiar—may I ask?

TOM (gently): She lives in a world of her own—a world of—little glass ornaments, Mother. . . . (Gets up. AMANDA remains holding brush, looking at him, troubled) She plays old phonograph records and—that's about all— (He glances at himself in the mirror and crosses to door.)

AMANDA (sharply): Where are you going?

TOM: I'm going to the movies. (Out screen door.)

AMANDA: Not to the movies, every night to the movies! (Follows quickly to screen door) I don't believe you always go to the movies! (He is gone. AMANDA looks worriedly after him for a moment. Then vitality and optimism return and she turns from the door. Crossing to portieres) Laura! Laura! (LAURA answers from kitchenette.)

LAURA: Yes, Mother.

AMANDA: Let those dishes go and come in front! (LAURA appears with dish towel. Gaily) Laura, come here and make a wish on the moon!

(SCREEN IMAGE: MOON.)

LAURA (entering): Moon—moon?

AMANDA: A little silver slipper of a moon.
Look over your left shoulder, Laura, and make a wish!

(LAURA looks faintly puzzled as if called out of sleep. AMANDA seizes her shoulders and turns her at an angle by the door.)

Now!
Now, darling, *wish!*

LAURA: What shall I wish for, Mother?

AMANDA (*her voice trembling and her eyes suddenly filling with tears*): Happiness! Good fortune!

(*The violin rises and the stage dims out.*)

(*The Curtain Falls.*)

# Scene Six

---

IMAGE: HIGH SCHOOL HERO.

And so the following evening I brought Jim home to dinner. I had known Jim slightly in high school. In high school Jim was a hero. He had tremendous Irish good nature and vitality with the scrubbed and polished look of white chinaware. He seemed to move in a continual spotlight. He was a star in basketball, captain of the debating club, president of the senior class and the glee club and he sang the male lead in the annual light operas. He was always running or bounding, never just walking. He seemed always at the point of defeating the law of gravity. He was shooting with such velocity through his adolescence that you would logically expect him to arrive at nothing short of the White House by the time he was thirty. But Jim apparently ran into more interference after his graduation from Soldan. His speed had definitely slowed. Six years after he left high school he was holding a job that wasn't much better than mine.

(IMAGE: CLERK.)

He was the only one at the warehouse with whom I was on friendly terms. I was valuable to him as someone who could remember his former glory, who had seen him win basketball games and the silver cup in debating. He knew of my secret practice of retiring to a cabinet of the wash-room to work on poems when business was slack in the warehouse. He called me Shakespeare. And while the other boys in the warehouse regarded me with suspicious hostility, Jim took a humorous attitude toward me. Gradually his attitude affected the others, their hostility wore off and they also began to smile at me as people smile at an oddly fashioned dog who trots across their path at some distance.

I knew that Jim and Laura had known each other at Soldan, and I had heard Laura speak admiringly of his voice. I didn't know if Jim remembered her or not. In high school Laura had been as unobtrusive as Jim had been astonishing. If he did remember Laura, it was not as my sister, for when I asked him to dinner, he grinned

and said, "You know, Shakespeare, I never thought of you as having folks!"

He was about to discover that I did. . . .

(LIGHT UP STAGE.)

(LEGEND ON SCREEN: "THE ACCENT OF A COMING FOOT.")

(*Friday evening. It is about five o'clock of a late spring evening
which comes "scattering poems in the sky."*)

(*A delicate lemony light is in the Wingfield apartment.*)

(AMANDA *has worked like a Turk in preparation for the gentleman
caller. The results are astonishing. The new floor lamp with its rose-
silk shade is in place, a colored paper lantern conceals the broken
light fixture in the ceiling, new billowing white curtains are at the
windows, chintz covers are on chairs and sofa, a pair of new sofa
pillows make their initial appearance.*)

(*Open boxes and tissue paper are scattered on the floor.*)

(LAURA *stands in the middle with lifted arms while* AMANDA *crouches
before her, adjusting the hem of the new dress, devout and ritualistic.
The dress is colored and designed by memory. The arrangment of*
LAURA'S *hair is changed; it is softer and more becoming. A fragile,
unearthly prettiness has come out in* LAURA: *she is like a piece of
translucent glass touched by light, given a momentary radiance, not
actual, not lasting.*)

AMANDA (*impatiently*): Why are you trembling?

LAURA: Mother, you've made me so nervous!

AMANDA: How have I made you nervous?

LAURA: By all this fuss! You make it seem so important!

AMANDA: I don't understand you, Laura. You couldn't be satisfied
with just sitting home, and yet whenever I try to arrange something
for you, you seem to resist it.

(*She gets up.*)

Now take a look at yourself.
No, wait! Wait just a moment—I have an idea!

LAURA: What is it now?

(AMANDA *produces two powder puffs which she wraps in handker-
chiefs and stuffs in* LAURA'S *bosom.*)

LAURA: Mother, what are you doing?

AMANDA: They call them "Gay Deceivers"!

LAURA: I won't wear them!

AMANDA: You will!

LAURA: Why should I?

AMANDA: Because, to be painfully honest, your chest is flat.

LAURA: You made it seem like we were setting a trap.

AMANDA: All pretty girls are a trap, a pretty trap, and men expect them to be.

(LEGEND: "A PRETTY TRAP.")

Now look at yourself, young lady. This is the prettiest you will ever be!

I've got to fix myself now! You're going to be surprised by your mother's appearance! (*She crosses through portieres, humming gaily.*)

(LAURA *moves slowly to the long mirror and stares solemnly at herself.*)
(*A wind blows the white curtains inward in a slow, graceful motion and with a faint, sorrowful sighing.*)

AMANDA (*off stage*): It isn't dark enough yet. (*She turns slowly before the mirror with a troubled look.*)

(LEGEND ON SCREEN: "THIS IS MY SISTER: CELEBRATE HER WITH STRINGS!" MUSIC.)

AMANDA (*laughing, off*): I'm going to show you something. I'm going to make a spectacular appearance!

LAURA: What is it, Mother?

AMANDA: Possess your soul in patience—you will see!

Something I've resurrected from that old trunk! Styles haven't changed so terribly much after all. . . .

(*She parts the portieres.*)

Now just look at your mother!

*(She wears a girlish frock of yellowed voile with a blue silk sash. She carries a bunch of jonquils—the legend of her youth is nearly revived. Feverishly.)*

This is the dress in which I led the cotillion. Won the cakewalk twice at Sunset Hill, wore one spring to the Governor's ball in Jackson!

See how I sashayed around the ballroom, Laura?

*(She raises her skirt and does a mincing step around the room.)*

I wore it on Sundays for my gentlemen callers! I had it on the day I met your father—

I had malaria fever all that spring. The change of climate from East Tennessee to the Delta—weakened resistance—I had a little temperature all the time—not enough to be serious—just enough to make me restless and giddy!—Invitations poured in—parties all over the Delta!—"Stay in bed," said Mother, "you have fever!"—but I just wouldn't.—I took quinine but kept on going, going!—Evenings, dances!—Afternoons, long, long rides! Picnics—lovely!—So lovely, that country in May.—All lacy with dogwood, literally flooded with jonquils!—That was the spring I had the craze for jonquils. Jonquils became an absolute obsession. Mother said, "Honey, there's no more room for jonquils." And still I kept on bringing in more jonquils. Whenever, wherever I saw them, I'd say, "Stop! Stop! I see jonquils!" I made the young men help me gather the jonquils! It was a joke, Amanda and her jonquils! Finally there were no more vases to hold them, every available space was filled with jonquils. No vases to hold them? All right, I'll hold them myself! And then I—*(She stops in front of the picture. MUSIC)* met your father!

Malaria fever and jonquils and then—this—boy. . . .

*(She switches on the rose-colored lamp.)*

I hope they get here before it starts to rain.

*(She crosses upstage and places the jonquils in bowl on table.)*

I gave your brother a little extra change so he and Mr. O'Connor could take the service car home.

LAURA *(with altered look)*: What did you say his name was?

AMANDA: O'Connor.

LAURA: What is his first name?

AMANDA: I don't remember. Oh, yes, I do. It was—Jim!

(LAURA *sways slightly and catches hold of a chair*.)
(LEGEND ON SCREEN: "NOT JIM!")

LAURA (*faintly*): Not—Jim!

AMANDA: Yes, that was it, it was Jim! I've never known a Jim that wasn't nice!

(MUSIC: OMINOUS.)

LAURA: Are you sure his name is Jim O'Connor?

AMANDA: Yes. Why?

LAURA: Is he the one that Tom used to know in high school?

AMANDA: He didnt say so. I think he just got to know him at the warehouse.

LAURA: There was a Jim O'Connor we both knew in high school— (*Then, with effort*) If that is the one that Tom is bringing to din-ner—you'll have to excuse me, I won't come to the table.

AMANDA: What sort of nonsense is this?

LAURA: You asked me once if I'd ever liked a boy. Don't you re-member I showed you this boy's picture?

AMANDA: You mean the boy you showed me in the year book?

LAURA: Yes, that boy.

AMANDA: Laura, Laura, were you in love with that boy?

LAURA: I don't know, Mother. All I know is I couldn't sit at the table if it was him!

AMANDA: It won't be him! It isn't the least bit likely. But whether it is or not, you will come to the table. You will not be excused.

LAURA: I'll have to be, Mother.

AMANDA: I don't intend to humor your silliness, Laura. I've had too much from you and your brother, both!
    So just sit down and compose yourself till they come. Tom has forgotten his key so you'll have to let them in, when they arrive.

LAURA (*panicky*): Oh, Mother—*you* answer the door!

AMANDA (*lightly*): I'll be in the kitchen—busy!

LAURA: Oh, Mother, please answer the door, don't make me do it!

AMANDA (*crossing into kitchenette*): I've got to fix the dressing for the salmon. Fuss, fuss—silliness!—over a gentleman caller!

(*Door swings shut.* LAURA *is left alone.*)
(LEGEND: "TERROR!")
(*She utters a low moan and turns off the lamp—sits stiffly on the edge of the sofa, knotting her fingers together.*)
(LEGEND ON SCREEN: "THE OPENING OF A DOOR!")
(TOM *and* JIM *appear on the fire-escape steps and climb to landing. Hearing their approach,* LAURA *rises with a panicky gesture. She retreats to the portieres.*)
(*The doorbell.* LAURA *catches her breath and touches her throat. Low drums.*)

AMANDA (*calling*): Laura, sweetheart! The door!

(LAURA *stares at it without moving.*)

JIM: I think we just beat the rain.

TOM: Uh-huh. (*He rings again, nervously.* JIM *whistles and fishes for a cigarette.*)

AMANDA (*very, very gaily*): Laura, that is your brother and Mr. O'Connor! Will you let them in, darling?

(LAURA *crosses toward kitchenette door.*)

LAURA (*breathlessly*): Mother—you go to the door!

(AMANDA *steps out of kitchenette and stares furiously at* LAURA. *She points imperiously at the door.*)

LAURA: Please, please!

AMANDA (*in a fierce whisper*): What is the matter with you, you silly thing?

LAURA (*desperately*): Please, you answer it, *please!*

AMANDA: I told you I wasn't going to humor you, Laura. Why have you chosen this moment to lose your mind?

LAURA: Please, please, please, you go!

AMANDA: You'll have to go to the door because I can't!

LAURA (*despairingly*): I can't either!

AMANDA: *Why?*

LAURA: I'm *sick!*

AMANDA: I'm sick, too—of your nonsense! Why can't you and your brother be normal people? Fantastic whims and behavior!

(TOM *gives a long ring.*)

Preposterous goings on! Can you give me one reason—(*Calls out lyrically*) COMING! JUST ONE SECOND!—why you should be afraid to open a door? Now you answer it, Laura!

LAURA: Oh, oh, oh . . . (*She returns through the portieres. Darts to the victrola and winds it frantically and turns it on.*)

AMANDA: Laura Wingfield, you march right to that door!

LAURA: Yes—yes, Mother!

(*A faraway, scratchy rendition of "Dardanella" softens the air and gives her strength to move through it. She slips to the door and draws it cautiously open.*)
(TOM *enters with the caller,* JIM O'CONNOR.)

TOM: Laura, this is Jim. Jim, this is my sister, Laura.

JIM (*stepping inside*): I didn't know that Shakespeare had a sister!

LAURA (*retreating stiff and trembling from the door*): How—how do you do?

JIM (*heartily extending his hand*): Okay!

(LAURA *touches it hesitantly with hers.*)

JIM: Your hand's *cold*, Laura!

LAURA: Yes, well—I've been playing the victrola. . . .

JIM: Must have been playing classical music on it! You ought to play a little hot swing music to warm you up!

LAURA: Excuse me—I haven't finished playing the victrola. . . .

(*She turns awkwardly and hurries into the front room. She pauses a second by the victrola. Then catches her breath and darts through the portieres like a frightened deer.*)

JIM (*grinning*): What was the matter?

TOM: Oh—with Laura? Laura is—terribly shy.

JIM: Shy, huh? It's unusual to meet a shy girl nowadays. I don't believe you ever mentioned you had a sister.

TOM: Well, now you know. I have one. Here is the *Post Dispatch*. You want a piece of it?

JIM: Uh-huh.

TOM: What piece? The comics?

JIM: Sports! (*Glances at it*) Ole Dizzy Dean is on his bad behavior.

TOM (*disinterest*): Yeah? (*Lights cigarette and crosses back to fire-escape door.*)

JIM: Where are *you* going?

TOM: I'm going out on the terrace.

JIM (*goes after him*): You know, Shakespeare—I'm going to sell you a bill of goods!

TOM: What goods?

JIM: A course I'm taking.

TOM: Huh?

JIM: In public speaking! You and me, we're not the warehouse type.

TOM: Thanks—that's good news.
    But what has public speaking got to do with it?

JIM: It fits you for—executive positions!

TOM: Awww.

JIM: I tell you it's done a helluva lot for me.

(IMAGE: EXECUTIVE AT DESK.)

TOM: In what respect?

JIM: In every! Ask yourself what is the difference between you an' me and men in the office down front? Brains?—No!—Ability? —No! Then what? Just one little thing—

TOM: What is that one little thing?

JIM: Primarily it amounts to—social poise! Being able to square up to people and hold your own on any social level!

AMANDA (*off stage*): Tom?

TOM: Yes, Mother?

AMANDA: Is that you and Mr. O'Connor?

TOM: Yes, Mother.

AMANDA: Well, you just make yourselves comfortable in there.

TOM: Yes, Mother.

AMANDA: Ask Mr. O'Connor if he would like to wash his hands.

JIM: Aw, no—no—thank you—I took care of that at the warehouse. Tom—

TOM: Yes?

JIM: Mr. Mendoza was speaking to me about you.

TOM: Favorably?

JIM: What do you think?

TOM: Well—

JIM: You're going to be out of a job if you don't wake up.

TOM: I am waking up—

JIM: You show no signs.

TOM: The signs are interior.

(IMAGE ON SCREEN: THE SAILING VESSEL WITH JOLLY ROGER AGAIN.)

TOM: I'm planning to change. (*He leans over the rail speaking with quiet exhilaration. The incandescent marquees and signs of the first-run movie houses light his face from across the alley. He looks like a voyager*) I'm right at the point of committing myself to a future that doesn't include the warehouse and Mr. Mendoza or even a night-school course in public speaking.

JIM: What are you gassing about?

TOM: I'm tired of the movies.

JIM: Movies!

TOM: Yes, movies! Look at them— (*A wave toward the marvels of Grand Avenue*) All of those glamorous people—having adventures —hogging it all, gobbling the whole thing up! You know what happens? People go to the *movies* instead of *moving!* Hollywood characters are supposed to have all the adventures for everybody in America, while everybody in America sits in a dark room and watches them have them! Yes, until there's a war. That's when adventure becomes available to the masses! *Everyone's* dish, not only Gable's! Then the people in the dark room come out of the dark room to have some adventures themselves—Goody, goody!—It's our turn now, to go to the South Sea Island—to make a safari—to be exotic, far-off!—But I'm not patient. I don't want to wait till then. I'm tired of the *movies* and I am *about* to *move!*

JIM (*incredulously*): Move?

TOM: Yes.

JIM: When?

TOM: Soon!

JIM: Where? Where?

(THEME THREE MUSIC SEEMS TO ANSWER THE QUESTION, WHILE TOM THINKS IT OVER. HE SEARCHES AMONG HIS POCKETS.)

TOM: I'm starting to boil inside. I know I seem dreamy, but inside— well, I'm boiling!—Whenever I pick up a shoe, I shudder a little thinking how short life is and what I am doing!—Whatever that means, I know it doesn't mean shoes—except as something to wear on a traveler's feet! (*Finds paper*) Look—

JIM: What?

TOM: I'm a member.

JIM (*reading*): The Union of Merchant Seamen.

TOM: I paid my dues this month, instead of the light bill.

JIM: You will regret it when they turn the lights off.

TOM: I won't be here.

JIM: How about your mother?

TOM: I'm like my father. The bastard son of a bastard! See how he grins? And he's been absent going on sixteen years!

JIM: You're just talking, you drip. How does your mother feel about it?

TOM: Shhh!—Here comes Mother! Mother is not acquainted with my plans!

AMANDA (*enters portieres*): Where are you all?

TOM: On the terrace, Mother.

(*They start inside. She advances to them.* TOM *is distinctly shocked at her appearance. Even* JIM *blinks a little. He is making his first contact with girlish Southern vivacity and in spite of the night-school course in public speaking is somewhat thrown off the beam by the unexpected outlay of social charm.*)
(*Certain responses are attempted by* JIM *but are swept aside by* AMANDA'S *gay laughter and chatter.* TOM *is embarrassed but after the first shock* JIM *reacts very warmly. Grins and chuckles, is altogether won over.*)
(IMAGE: AMANDA AS A GIRL.)

AMANDA (*coyly smiling, shaking her girlish ringlets*): Well, well, well, so this is Mr. O'Connor. Introductions entirely unnecessary. I've heard so much about you from my boy. I finally said to him, Tom—good gracious!—why don't you bring this paragon to supper? I'd like to meet this nice young man at the warehouse!—Instead of just hearing him sing your praises so much!

I don't know why my son is so stand-offish—that's not Southern behavior!

Let's sit down and—I think we could stand a little more air in here! Tom, leave the door open. I felt a nice fresh breeze a moment ago. Where has it gone to?

Mmm, so warm already! And not quite summer, even. We're going to burn up when summer really gets started.

However, we're having—we're having a very light supper. I think light things are better fo' this time of year. The same as light clothes are. Light clothes an' light food are what warm weather calls fo'. You know our blood gets so thick during th' winter— it takes a while fo' us to *adjust* ou'selves!—when the season changes . . .

It's come so quick this year. I wasn't prepared. All of a sudden —heavens! Already summer!—I ran to the trunk an' pulled out this light dress— Terribly old! Historical almost! But feels so good— so good an' co-ol, y' know. . . .

TOM: Mother—

AMANDA: Yes, honey?

TOM: How about—supper?

AMANDA: Honey, you go ask Sister if supper is ready! You know that Sister is in full charge of supper!

Tell her you hungry boys are waiting for it.

(*To* JIM.)

Have you met Laura?

JIM: She—

AMANDA: Let you in? Oh, good, you've met already! It's rare for a girl as sweet an' pretty as Laura to be domestic! But Laura is, thank heavens, not only pretty but also very domestic. I'm not at all. I never was a bit. I never could make a thing but angel-food cake. Well, in the South we had so many servants. Gone, gone, gone. All vestige of gracious living! Gone completely! I wasn't prepared for what the future brought me. All of my gentlemen callers were sons of planters and so of course I assumed that I would be married to one and raise my family on a large piece of land with plenty of servants. But man proposes—and woman accepts the proposal!— To vary that old, old saying a little bit—I married no planter! I married a man who worked for the telephone company!—That gallantly smiling gentleman over there! (*Points to the picture*) A telephone man who—fell in love with long-distance!—Now he travels and I don't even know where!—But what am I going on for about my—tribulations?

Tell me yours—I hope you don't have any!

Tom?

TOM (*returning*): Yes, Mother?

AMANDA: Is supper nearly ready?

TOM: It looks to me like supper is on the table.

AMANDA: Let me look— (*She rises prettily and looks through portieres*) Oh, lovely!—But where is Sister?

TOM: Laura is not feeling well and she says that she thinks she'd better not come to the table.

AMANDA: What?—Nonsense!—Laura? Oh, Laura!

LAURA (*off stage, faintly*): Yes, Mother.

AMANDA: You really must come to the table. We won't be seated until you come to the table!

Come in, Mr. O'Connor. You sit over there, and I'll—

Laura? Laura Wingfield!

You're keeping us waiting, honey! We can't say grace until you come to the table!

(*The back door is pushed weakly open and* LAURA *comes in. She is obviously quite faint, her lips trembling, her eyes wide and staring. She moves unsteadily toward the table.*)

(LEGEND: "TERROR!")

(*Outside a summer storm is coming abruptly. The white curtains billow inward at the windows and there is a sorrowful murmur and deep blue dusk.*)

(LAURA *suddenly stumbles—she catches at a chair with a faint moan.*)

TOM: Laura!

AMANDA: Laura!

(*There is a clap of thunder.*)

(LEGEND: "AH!")

(*Despairingly*)

Why, Laura, you *are* sick, darling! Tom, help your sister into the living room, dear!

Sit in the living room, Laura—rest on the sofa.

Well!

(*To the gentleman caller.*)

Standing over the hot stove made her ill!—I told her that it was just too warm this evening, but—

(TOM *comes back in.* LAURA *is on the sofa.*)

Is Laura all right now?

TOM: Yes.

AMANDA: What *is* that? Rain? A nice cool rain has come up!

(*She gives the gentleman caller a frightened look.*)

I think we may—have grace—now . . .

(TOM *looks at her stupidly.*)

Tom, honey—you say grace!

TOM: Oh . . .

"For these and all thy mercies—"

(*They bow their heads,* AMANDA *stealing a nervous glance at* JIM. *In the living room* LAURA, *stretched on the sofa, clenches her hand to her lips, to hold back a shuddering sob.*)

God's Holy Name be praised—

(*The Scene Dims Out.*)

# Scene Seven

A Souvenir.
     *Half an hour later. Dinner is just being finished in the up-stage area which is concealed by the drawn portieres.*

*As the curtain rises* LAURA *is still huddled upon the sofa, her feet drawn under her, her head resting on a pale blue pillow, her eyes wide and mysteriously watchful. The new floor lamp with its shade of rose-colored silk gives a soft, becoming light to her face, bringing out the fragile, unearthly prettiness which usually escapes attention. There is a steady murmur of rain, but it is slackening and stops soon after the scene begins; the air outside becomes pale and luminous as the moon breaks out.*

*A moment after the curtain rises, the lights in both rooms flicker and go out.*

JIM: Hey, there, Mr. Light Bulb!

(AMANDA *laughs nervously.*)
(LEGEND: "SUSPENSION OF A PUBLIC SERVICE.")

AMANDA: Where was Moses when the lights went out? Ha-ha. Do you know the answer to that one, Mr. O'Connor?

JIM: No, Ma'am, what's the answer?

AMANDA: In the dark!

(JIM *laughs appreciatively.*)

     Everybody sit still. I'll light the candles. Isn't it lucky we have them on the table? Where's a match? Which of you gentlemen can provide a match?

JIM: Here.

AMANDA: Thank you, sir.

JIM: Not at all, Ma'am!

AMANDA: I guess the fuse has burnt out. Mr. O'Connor, can you tell a burnt-out fuse? I know I can't and Tom is a total loss when it comes to mechanics.

(SOUND: GETTING UP: VOICES RECEDE A LITTLE TO KITCHENETTE.)

Oh, be careful you don't bump into something. We don't want our gentleman caller to break his neck. Now wouldn't that be a fine howdy-do?

JIM: Ha-ha!
Where is the fuse-box?

AMANDA: Right here next to the stove. Can you see anything?

JIM: Just a minute.

AMANDA: Isn't electricity a mysterious thing?
Wasn't it Benjamin Franklin who tied a key to a kite?
We live in such a mysterious universe, don't we? Some people say that science clears up all the mysteries for us. In my opinion it only creates more!
Have you found it yet?

JIM: No Ma'am. All these fuses look okay to me.

AMANDA: Tom!

TOM: Yes, Mother?

AMANDA: That light bill I gave you several days ago. The one I told you we got the notices about?

(LEGEND: "HA!")

TOM: Oh.—Yeah.

AMANDA: You didn't neglect to pay it by any chance?

TOM: Why, I—

AMANDA: Didn't! I might have know it!

JIM: Shakespeare probably wrote a poem on that light bill, Mrs. Wingfield.

AMANDA: I might have known better than to trust him with it! There's such a high price for negligence in this world!

JIM: Maybe the poem will win a ten-dollar prize.

AMANDA: We'll just have to spend the remainder of the evening in the nineteenth century, before Mr. Edison made the Mazda lamp!

JIM: Candlelight is my favorite kind of light.

AMANDA: That shows you're romantic! But that's no excuse for Tom.
Well, we got through dinner. Very considerate of them to let us get through dinner before they plunged us into everlasting darkness, wasn't it, Mr. O'Connor?

JIM: Ha-ha!

AMANDA: Tom, as a penalty for your carelessness you can help me with the dishes.

JIM: Let me give you a hand.

AMANDA: Indeed you will not!

JIM: I ought to be good for something.

AMANDA: Good for something? (*Her tone is rhapsodic.*)
*You?* Why, Mr. O'Connor, nobody, *nobody's* given me this much entertainment in years—as you have!

JIM: Aw, now, Mrs. Wingfield!

AMANDA: I'm not exaggerating, not one bit! But Sister is all by her lonesome. You go keep her company in the parlor!
I'll give you this lovely old candelabrum that used to be on the altar at the church of the Heavenly Rest. It was melted a little out of shape when the church burnt down. Lightning struck it one spring. Gypsy Jones was holding a revival at the time and he intimated that the church was destroyed because the Episcopalians gave card parties.

JIM: Ha-ha!

AMANDA: And how about you coaxing Sister to drink a little wine? I think it would be good for her! Can you carry both at once?

JIM: Sure. I'm Superman!

AMANDA: Now, Thomas, get into this apron!

(*The door of kitchenette swings closed on* AMANDA's *gay laughter; the flickering light approaches the portieres.*)

(LAURA *sits up nervously as he enters. Her speech at first is low and breathless from the almost intolerable strain of being alone with a stranger.*)

(THE LEGEND: "I DON'T SUPPOSE YOU REMEMBER ME AT ALL!")

(*In her first speeches in this scene, before* JIM's *warmth overcomes her paralyzing shyness,* LAURA's *voice is thin and breathless as though she has just run up a steep flight of stairs.*)

(JIM's *attitude is gently humorous. In playing this scene it should be stressed that while the incident is apparently unimportant, it is to* LAURA *the climax of her secret life.*)

JIM: Hello, there, Laura.

LAURA (*faintly*): Hello. (*She clears her throat.*)

JIM: How are you feeling now? Better?

LAURA: Yes. Yes, thank you.

JIM: This is for you. A little dandelion wine. (*He extends it toward her with extravagant gallantry.*)

LAURA: Thank you.

JIM: Drink it—but don't get drunk!

(*He laughs heartily.* LAURA *takes the glass uncertainly; laughs shyly.*)

Where shall I set the candles?

LAURA: Oh—oh, anywhere . . .

JIM: How about here on the floor? Any objections?

LAURA: No.

JIM: I'll spread a newspaper under to catch the drippings. I like to sit on the floor. Mind if I do?

LAURA: Oh, no.

JIM: Give me a pillow?

LAURA: What?

JIM: A pillow!

LAURA: Oh . . . (*Hands him one quickly.*)

JIM: How about you? Don't you like to sit on the floor?

LAURA: Oh—yes.

JIM: Why don't you, then?

LAURA: I—will.

JIM: Take a pillow! (LAURA *does. Sits on the other side of the candelabrum.* JIM *crosses his legs and smiles engagingly at her*) I can't hardly see you sitting way over there.

LAURA: I can—see you.

JIM: I know, but that's not fair, I'm in the limelight. (LAURA *moves her pillow closer*) Good! Now I can see you! Comfortable?

LAURA: Yes.

JIM: So am I. Comfortable as a cow! Will you have some gum?

LAURA: No, thank you.

JIM: I think that I will indulge, with your permission. (*Musingly unwraps it and holds it up*) Think of the fortune made by the guy that invented the first piece of chewing gum. Amazing, huh? The Wrigley Building is one of the sights of Chicago.—I saw it summer before last when I went up to the Century of Progress. Did you take in the Century of Progress?

LAURA: No, I didn't.

JIM: Well, it was quite a wonderful exposition. What impressed me most was the Hall of Science. Gives you an idea of what the future will be in America, even more wonderful than the present time is! (*Pause. Smiling at her*) Your brother tells me you're shy. Is that right, Laura?

LAURA: I—don't know.

JIM: I judge you to be an old-fashioned type of girl. Well, I think that's a pretty good type to be. Hope you don't think I'm being too personal—do you?

LAURA (*hastily, out of embarrassment*): I believe I *will* take a piece of gum, if you—don't mind. (*Clearing her throat*) Mr. O'Connor, have you—kept up with your singing?

JIM: Singing? Me?

LAURA: Yes. I remember what a beautiful voice you had.

JIM: When did you hear me sing?

(VOICE OFF STAGE IN THE PAUSE.)

VOICE (*off stage*):

> O blow, ye winds, heigh-ho,
> A-roving I will go!
>> I'm off to my love
>> With a boxing glove—
> Ten thousand miles away!

JIM: You say you've heard me sing?

LAURA: Oh, yes! Yes, very often . . . I—don't suppose—you remember me—at all?

JIM (*smiling doubtfully*): You know I have an idea I've seen you before. I had that idea soon as you opened the door. It seemed almost like I was about to remember your name. But the name that I started to call you—wasn't a name! And so I stopped myself before I said it.

LAURA: Wasn't it—Blue Roses?

JIM (*springs up. Grinning*): Blue Roses!—My gosh, yes—Blue Roses!
    That's what I had on my tongue when you opened the door!
    Isn't it funny what tricks your memory plays? I didn't connect you with high school somehow or other.
    But that's where it was; it was high school. I didn't even know you were Shakespeare's sister!
    Gosh, I'm sorry.

LAURA: I didn't expect you to. You—barely knew me!

JIM: But we did have a speaking acquaintance, huh?

LAURA: Yes, we—spoke to each other.

JIM: When did you recognize me?

LAURA: Oh, right away!

JIM: Soon as I came in the door?

LAURA: When I heard your name I thought it was probably you. I knew that Tom used to know you a little in high school. So when you came in the door—
    Well, then I was—sure.

JIM: Why didn't you *say* something, then?

LAURA (*breathlessly*): I didn't know what to say, I was—too surprised!

JIM: For goodness' sakes! You know, this sure is funny!

LAURA: Yes! Yes, isn't it, though . . .

JIM: Didn't we have a class in something together?

LAURA: Yes, we did.

JIM: What class was that?

LAURA: It was—singing—Chorus!

JIM: Aw!

LAURA: I sat across the aisle from you in the Aud.

JIM: Aw.

LAURA: Mondays, Wednesdays and Fridays.

JIM: Now I remember—you always came in late.

LAURA: Yes, it was so hard for me, getting upstairs. I had that brace on my leg—it clumped so loud!

JIM: I never heard any clumping.

LAURA (*wincing at the recollection*): To me it sounded like— thunder!

JIM: Well, well, well, I never even noticed.

LAURA: And everybody was seated before I came in. I had to walk in front of all those people. My seat was in the back row. I had to go clumping all the way up the aisle with everyone watching!

JIM: You shouldn't have been self-conscious.

LAURA: I know, but I was. It was always such a relief when the singing started.

JIM: Aw, yes, I've placed you now! I used to call you Blue Roses. How was it that I got started calling you that?

LAURA: I was out of school a little while with pleurosis. When I came back you asked me what was the matter. I said I had pleurosis—you thought I said Blue Roses. That's what you always called me after that!

JIM: I hope you didn't mind.

LAURA: Oh, no—I liked it. You see, I wasn't acquainted with many— people. . . .

JIM: As I remember you sort of stuck by yourself.

LAURA: I—I—never have had much luck at—making friends.

JIM: I don't see why you wouldn't.

LAURA: Well, I—started out badly.

JIM: You mean being—

LAURA: Yes, it sort of—stood between me—

JIM: You shouldn't have let it!

LAURA: I know, but it did, and—

JIM: You were shy with people!

LAURA: I tried not to be but never could—

JIM: Overcome it?

LAURA: No, I—I never could!

JIM: I guess being shy is something you have to work out of kind of gradually.

LAURA (*sorrowfully*): Yes—I guess it—

JIM: Takes time!

LAURA: Yes.

JIM: People are not so dreadful when you know them. That's what you have to remember! And everybody has problems, not just you, but practically everybody has got some problems.

You think of yourself as having the only problems, as being the only one who is disappointed. But just look around you and you will see lots of people as disappointed as you are. For instance, I hoped when I was going to high school that I would be further along at this time, six years later, than I am now— You remember that wonderful write-up I had in *The Torch?*

LAURA: Yes! (*She rises and crosses to table.*)

JIM: It said I was bound to succeed in anything I went into! (*Laura returns with the annual*) Holy Jeez! *The Torch!* (*He accepts it reverently. They smile across it with mutual wonder.* LAURA *crouches beside him and they begin to turn through it.* LAURA's *shyness is dissolving in his warmth.*)

LAURA: Here you are in *The Pirates of Penzance!*

JIM (*wistfully*): I sang the baritone lead in that operetta.

LAURA (*raptly*): So—*beautifully!*

JIM (*protesting*): Aw—

LAURA: Yes, yes—beautifully—beautifully!

JIM: You heard me?

LAURA: All three times!

JIM: No!

LAURA: Yes!

JIM: All three performances?

LAURA (*looking down*): Yes.

JIM: Why?

LAURA: I—wanted to ask you to—autograph my program.

JIM: Why didn't you ask me to?

LAURA: You were always surrounded by your own friends so much that I never had a chance to.

JIM: You should have just—

LAURA: Well, I—thought you might think I was—

JIM: Thought I might think you was—what?

LAURA: Oh—

JIM (*with reflective relish*): I was beleaguered by females in those days.

LAURA: You were terribly popular!

JIM: Yeah—

LAURA: You had such a—friendly way—

JIM: I was spoiled in high school.

LAURA: Everybody—liked you!

JIM: Including you?

LAURA: I—yes, I—I did, too— (*She gently closes the book in her lap.*)

JIM: Well, well, well!—Give me that program, Laura. (*She hands it to him. He signs it with a flourish*) There you are—better late than never!

LAURA: Oh, I—what a—surprise!

JIM: My signature isn't worth very much right now.
But some day—maybe—it will increase in value!
Being disappointed is one thing and being discouraged is something else. I am disappointed but I am not discouraged.
I'm twenty-three years old.
How old are you?

LAURA: I'll be twenty-four in June.

JIM: That's not old age!

LAURA: No, but—

JIM: You finished high school?

LAURA (*with difficulty*): I didn't go back.

JIM: You mean you dropped out?

LAURA: I made bad grades in my final examinations. (*She rises and replaces the book and the program. Her voice strained*) How is— Emily Meisenbach getting along?

JIM: Oh, that kraut-head!

LAURA: Why do you call her that?

JIM: That's what she was.

LAURA: You're not still—going with her?

JIM: I never see her.

LAURA: It said in the Personal Section that you were—engaged!

JIM: I know, but I wasn't impressed by that—propaganda!

LAURA: It wasn't—the truth?

JIM: Only in Emily's optimistic opinion!

LAURA: Oh—

(LEGEND: "WHAT HAVE YOU DONE SINCE HIGH SCHOOL?")
(JIM *lights a cigarette and leans indolently back on his elbows smiling at* LAURA *with a warmth and charm which lights her inwardly with altar candles. She remains by the table and turns in her hands a piece of glass to cover her tumult.*)

JIM (*after several reflective puffs on a cigarette*): What have you done since high school? (*She seems not to hear him*) Huh? (LAURA *looks up*) I said what have you done since high school, Laura?

LAURA: Nothing much.

JIM: You must have been doing something these six long years.

LAURA: Yes.

JIM: Well, then, such as what?

LAURA: I took a business course at business college—

JIM: How did that work out?

LAURA: Well, not very—well—I had to drop out, it gave me— indigestion—

(JIM *laughs gently*.)

JIM: What are you doing now?

LAURA: I don't do anything—much. Oh, please don't think I sit around doing nothing! My glass collection takes up a good deal of time. Glass is something you have to take good care of.

JIM: What did you say—about glass?

LAURA: Collection I said—I have one— (*She clears her throat and turns away again, acutely shy*.)

JIM (*abruptly*): You know what I judge to be the trouble with you?
    Inferiority complex! Know what that is? That's what they call it when someone low-rates himself!
    I understand it because I had it, too. Although my case was not so aggravated as yours seems to be. I had it until I took up public speaking, developed my voice, and learned that I had an aptitude for science. Before that time I never thought of myself as being out-standing in any way whatsoever!
    Now I've never made a regular study of it, but I have a friend who says I can analyze people better than doctors that make a pro-fession of it. I don't claim that to be necessarily true, but I can sure guess a person's psychology. Laura! (*Takes out his gum*) Excuse me, Laura. I always take it out when the flavor is gone. I'll use this scrap of paper to wrap it in. I know how it is to get it stuck on a shoe.
    Yep—that's what I judge to be your principal trouble. A lack of confidence in yourself as a person. You don't have the proper amount of faith in yourself. I'm basing that fact on a number of your remarks and also on certain observations I've made. For instance that clumping you thought was so awful in high school. You say that you even dreaded to walk into class. You see what you did? You dropped out of school, you gave up an education because of a clump, which as far as I know was practically non-existent! A little physical defect is what you have. Hardly noticeable even! Magni-fied thousands of times by imagination!
    You know what my strong advice to you is? Think of yourself as *superior* in some way!

LAURA: In what way would I think?

JIM: Why, man alive, Laura! Just look about you a little. What do you see? A world full of common people! All of 'em born and all of 'em going to die!

Which of them has one-tenth of your good points! Or mine! Or anyone else's, as far as that goes—Gosh!

Everybody excels in some one thing. Some in many!

(*Unconsciously glances at himself in the mirror.*)

All you've got to do is discover in *what!*
Take me, for instance.

(*He adjusts his tie at the mirror.*)

My interest happens to lie in electro-dynamics. I'm taking a course in radio engineering at night school, Laura, on top of a fairly responsible job at the warehouse. I'm taking that course and studying public speaking.

LAURA: Ohhhh.

JIM: Because I believe in the future of television!

(*Turning back to her.*)

I wish to be ready to go up right along with it. Therefore I'm planning to get in on the ground floor. In fact I've already made the right connections and all that remains is for the industry itself to get under way! Full steam—

(*His eyes are starry.*)

Knowledge—Zzzzzp! *Money—Zzzzzzp!—Power!*
That's the cycle democracy is built on!

(*His attitude is convincingly dynamic.* LAURA *stares at him, even her shyness eclipsed in her absolute wonder. He suddenly grins.*)

I guess you think I think a lot of myself!

LAURA: No—o-o-o, I—

JIM: Now how about you? Isn't there something you take more interest in than anything else?

LAURA: Well, I do—as I said—have my—glass collection—

(*A peal of girlish laughter from the kitchen.*)

JIM: I'm not right sure I know what you're talking about. What kind of glass is it?

LAURA: Little articles of it, they're ornaments mostly! Most of them are little animals made out of glass, the tiniest little animals in the world. Mother calls them a glass menagerie! Here's an example of one, if you'd like to see it! This one is one of the oldest. It's nearly thirteen.

(MUSIC: "THE GLASS MENAGERIE.")
(*He stretches out his hand.*)

Oh, be careful—if you breathe, it breaks!

JIM: I'd better not take it. I'm pretty clumsy with things.

LAURA: Go on, I trust you with him!

(*Places it in his palm.*)

There now—you're holding him gently! Hold him over the light, he loves the light! You see how the light shines through him?

JIM: It sure does shine!

LAURA: I shouldn't be partial, but he is my favorite one.

JIM: What kind of a thing is this one supposed to be?

LAURA: Haven't you noticed the single horn on his forehead?

JIM: A unicorn, huh?

LAURA: Mmm-hmmm!

JIM: Unicorns, aren't they extinct in the modern world?

LAURA: I know!

JIM: Poor little fellow, he must feel sort of lonesome.

LAURA (*smiling*): Well, if he does he doesn't complain about it. He stays on a shelf with some horses that don't have horns and all of them seem to get along nicely together.

JIM: How do you know?

LAURA (*lightly*): I haven't heard any arguments among them!

JIM (*grinning*): No arguments, huh? Well, that's a pretty good sign! Where shall I set him?

LAURA: Put him on the table. They all like a change of scenery once in a while!

JIM (*stretching*): Well, well, well, well—
  Look how big my shadow is when I stretch!

LAURA: Oh, oh, yes—it stretches across the ceiling!

JIM (*crossing to door*): I think it's stopped raining. (*Opens fire-escape door*) Where does the music come from?

LAURA: From the Paradise Dance Hall across the alley.

JIM: How about cutting the rug a little, Miss Wingfield?

LAURA: Oh, I—

JIM: Or is your program filled up? Let me have a look at it. (*Grasps imaginary card*) Why, every dance is taken! I'll just have to scratch some out. (WALTZ MUSIC: "LA GOLONDRINA") Ahhh, a waltz! (*He executes some sweeping turns by himself then holds his arms toward* LAURA.)

LAURA (*breathlessly*): I—can't dance!

JIM: There you go, that inferiority stuff!

LAURA: I've never danced in my life!

JIM: Come on, try!

LAURA: Oh, but I'd step on you!

JIM: I'm not made out of glass.

LAURA: How—how—how do we start?

JIM: Just leave it to me. You hold your arms out a little.

LAURA: Like this?

JIM: A little bit higher. Right. Now don't tighten up, that's the main thing about it—relax.

LAURA (*laughing breathlessly*): It's hard not to.

JIM: Okay.

LAURA: I'm afraid you can't budge me.

JIM: What do you bet I can't (*He swings her into motion.*)

LAURA: Goodness, yes, you can!

JIM: Let yourself go, now, Laura, just let yourself go.

LAURA: I'm—

JIM: Come on!

LAURA: Trying!

JIM: Not so stiff— Easy does it!

LAURA: I know but I'm—

JIM: Loosen th' backbone! There now, that's a lot better.

LAURA: Am I?

JIM: Lots, lots better! (*He moves her about the room in a clumsy waltz.*)

LAURA: Oh, my!

JIM: Ha-ha!

LAURA: Oh, my goodness!

JIM: Ha-ha-ha! (*They suddenly bump into the table.* JIM *stops*) What did we hit on?

LAURA: Table.

JIM: Did something fall off it? I think—

LAURA: Yes.

JIM: I hope it wasn't the little glass horse with the horn!

LAURA: Yes.

JIM: Aw, aw, aw. Is it broken?

LAURA: Now it is just like all the other horses.

JIM: It's lost its—

LAURA: Horn!
It doesn't matter. Maybe it's a blessing in disguise.

JIM: You'll never forgive me. I bet that that was your favorite piece of glass.

LAURA: I don't have favorites much. It's no tragedy, Freckles. Glass breaks so easily. No matter how careful you are. The traffic jars the shelves and things fall off them.

JIM: Still I'm awfully sorry that I was the cause.

LAURA (*smiling*): I'll just imagine he had an operation.
The horn was removed to make him feel less—freakish!

(*They both laugh.*)

Now he will feel more at home with the other horses, the ones that don't have horns. . .

JIM: Ha-ha, that's very funny!

(*Suddenly serious.*)

I'm glad to see that you have a sense of humor.
You know—you're—well—very different!
Surprisingly different from anyone else I know!

(*His voice becomes soft and hesitant with a genuine feeling.*)

Do you mind me telling you that?

(LAURA *is abashed beyond speech.*)

I mean it in a nice way . . .

(LAURA *nods shyly, looking away.*)

You make me feel sort of—I don't know how to put it!
I'm usually pretty good at expressing things, but—
This is something that I don't know how to say!

(LAURA *touches her throat and clears it—turns the broken unicorn in her hands.*)
(*Even softer.*)

Has anyone ever told you that you were pretty?

(PAUSE: MUSIC.)
(LAURA *looks up slowly, with wonder, and shakes her head.*)

Well, you are! In a very different way from anyone else.
And all the nicer because of the difference, too.

(*His voice becomes low and husky.* LAURA *turns away, nearly faint
with the novelty of her emotions.*)

I wish that you were my sister. I'd teach you to have some confidence in yourself. The different people are not like other people,
but being different is nothing to be ashamed of. Because other people are not such wonderful people. They're one hundred times one
thousand. You're one times one! They walk all over the earth. You
just stay here. They're common as—weeds, but—you—well, you're
—*Blue Roses!*

(IMAGE ON SCREEN: BLUE ROSES.)
(MUSIC CHANGES.)

LAURA: But blue is wrong for—roses . . .

JIM: It's right for you!—You're—pretty!

LAURA: In what respect am I pretty?

JIM: In all respects—believe me! Your eyes—your hair—are pretty!
Your hands are pretty!

(*He catches hold of her hand.*)

You think I'm making this up because I'm invited to dinner and
have to be nice. Oh, I could do that! I could put on an act for you,
Laura, and say lots of things without being very sincere. But this
time I am. I'm talking to you sincerely. I happened to notice you
had this inferiority complex that keeps you from feeling comfortable with people. Somebody needs to build your confidence up
and make you proud instead of shy and turning away and—blush-
ing—
Somebody—ought to—
Ought to—*kiss* you, Laura!

(*His hand slips slowly up her arm to her shoulder.*)
(MUSIC SWELLS TUMULTUOUSLY.)

*(He suddenly turns her about and kisses her on the lips.)*
*(When he releases her,* LAURA *sinks on the sofa with a bright, dazed look.)*
*(*JIM *backs away and fishes in his pocket for a cigarette.)*
*(*LEGEND ON SCREEN: "SOUVENIR.")*

Stumble-john!

*(He lights the cigarette, avoiding her look.)*
*(There is a peal of girlish laughter from* AMANDA *in the kitchen.)*
*(*LAURA *slowly raises and opens her hand. It still contains the little broken glass animal. She looks at it with a tender, bewildered expression.)*

Stumble-john!
I shouldn't have done that— That was way off the beam. You don't smoke, do you?

*(She looks up, smiling, not hearing the question.)*
*(He sits beside her a little gingerly. She looks at him speechlessly—waiting.)*
*(He coughs decorously and moves a little farther aside as he considers the situation and senses her feelings, dimly, with perturbation.)*
*(Gently.)*

Would you—care for a—mint?

*(She doesn't seem to hear him but her look grows brighter even.)*

Peppermint—Life-Saver?
My pocket's a regular drug store—wherever I go . . .

*(He pops a mint in his mouth. Then gulps and decides to make a clean breast of it. He speaks slowly and gingerly.)*

Laura, you know, if I had a sister like you, I'd do the same thing as Tom. I'd bring out fellows and—introduce her to them. The right type of boys of a type to—appreciate her.
Only—well—he made a mistake about me.
Maybe I've got no call to be saying this. That may not have been the idea in having me over. But what if it was?
There's nothing wrong about that. The only trouble is that in my case—I'm not in a situation to—do the right thing.
I can't take down your number and say I'll phone.
I can't call up next week and—ask for a date.
I thought I had better explain the situation in case you—misunderstood it and—hurt your feelings. . . .

(*Pause.*)
(*Slowly, very slowly,* LAURA's *look changes, her eyes returning slowly from his to the ornament in her palm.*)
(AMANDA *utters another gay laugh in the kitchen.*)

LAURA (*faintly*): You—won't—call again?

JIM: No, Laura, I can't.

(*He rises from the sofa.*)

As I was just explaining, I've—got strings on me.
Laura, I've—been going steady!
I go out all of the time with a girl named Betty. She's a home-girl like you, and Catholic, and Irish, and in a great many ways we —get along fine.
I met her last summer on a moonlight boat trip up the river to Alton, on the *Majestic.*
Well—right away from the start it was love!

(LEGEND: LOVE!)
(LAURA *sways slightly forward and grips the arm of the sofa. He fails to notice, now enrapt in his own comfortable being.*)

Being in love has made a new man of me!

(*Leaning stiffly forward, clutching the arm of the sofa,* LAURA *struggles visibly with her storm. But* JIM *is oblivious, she is a long way off.*)

The power of love is really pretty tremendous!
Love is something that—changes the whole world, Laura!

(*The storm abates a little and* LAURA *leans back. He notices her again.*)

It happened that Betty's aunt took sick, she got a wire and had to go to Centralia. So Tom—when he asked me to dinner—I nat-urally just accepted the invitation, not knowing that you—that he —that I—

(*He stops awkwardly.*)

Huh—I'm a stumble-john!

(*He flops back on the sofa.*)
(*The holy candles in the altar of* LAURA'S *face have been snuffed out. There is a look of almost infinite desolation.*)
(JIM *glances at her uneasily.*)

I wish that you would—say something. (*She bites her lip which was trembling and then bravely smiles. She opens her hand again on the broken glass ornament. Then she gently takes his hand and raises it level with her own. She carefully places the unicorn in the palm of his hand, then pushes his fingers closed upon it*) What are you—doing that for? You want me to have him?—Laura? (*She nods*) What for?

LAURA: A—souvenir . . .

(*She rises unsteadily and crouches beside the victrola to wind it up.*)
(LEGEND ON SCREEN: "THINGS HAVE A WAY OF TURNING OUT SO BADLY!")
(OR IMAGE: "GENTLEMAN CALLER WAVING GOOD-BYE!—GAILY.")
(*At this moment* AMANDA *rushes brightly back in the front room. She bears a pitcher of fruit punch in an old-fashioned cut-glass pitcher and a plate of macaroons. The plate has a gold border and poppies painted on it.*)

AMANDA: Well, well, well! Isn't the air delightful after the shower? I've made you children a little liquid refreshment.

(*Turns gaily to the gentleman caller*)

Jim, do you know that song about lemonade?

> "Lemonade, lemonade
> Made in the shade and stirred with a spade—
> Good enough for any old maid!"

JIM (*uneasily*): Ha-ha! No—I never heard it.

AMANDA: Why, Laura! You look so serious!

JIM: We were having a serious conversation.

AMANDA: Good! Now you're better acquainted!

JIM (*uncertainly*): Ha-ha! Yes.

AMANDA: You modern young people are much more serious-minded than my generation. I was so gay as a girl!

JIM: You haven't changed, Mrs. Wingfield.

AMANDA: Tonight I'm rejuvenated! The gaiety of the occasion, Mr. O'Connor!

(*She tosses her head with a peal of laughter. Spills lemonade.*)

Oooo! I'm baptizing myself!

JIM: Here—let me—

AMANDA (*setting the pitcher down*): There now. I discovered we had some maraschino cherries. I dumped them in, juice and all!

JIM: You shouldn't have gone to that trouble, Mrs. Wingfield.

AMANDA: Trouble, trouble? Why, it was loads of fun!
Didn't you hear me cutting up in the kitchen? I bet your ears were burning! I told Tom how outdone with him I was for keeping you to himself so long a time! He should have brought you over much, much sooner! Well, now that you've found your way, I want you to be a very frequent caller! Not just occasional but all the time.
Oh, we're going to have a lot of gay times together! I see them coming!
Mmm, just breathe that air! So fresh, and the moon's so pretty!
I'll skip back out—I know where my place is when young folks are having a—serious conversation!

JIM: Oh, don't go out, Mrs. Wingfield. The fact of the matter is I've got to be going.

AMANDA: Going, now? You're joking! Why, it's only the shank of the evening, Mr. O'Connor!

JIM: Well, you know how it is.

AMANDA: You mean you're a young workingman and have to keep workingmen's hours. We'll let you off early tonight. But only on the condition that next time you stay later.
What's the best night for you? Isn't Saturday night the best night for you workingmen?

JIM: I have a couple of time-clocks to punch, Mrs. Wingfield. One at morning, another one at night!

AMANDA: My, but you *are* ambitious! You work at night, too?

JIM: No, Ma'am, not work but—Betty! (*He crosses deliberately to pick up his hat. The band at the Paradise Dance Hall goes into a tender waltz.*)

AMANDA: Betty? Betty? Who's—Betty!

(*There is an ominous cracking sound in the sky.*)

JIM: Oh, just a girl. The girl I go steady with! (*He smiles charmingly. The sky falls.*)

(LEGEND: "THE SKY FALLS.")

AMANDA (*a long-drawn exhalation*): Ohhhh . . . Is it a serious romance, Mr. O'Connor?

JIM: We're going to be married the second Sunday in June.

AMANDA: Ohhhh—how nice!
     Tom didn't mention that you were engaged to be married.

JIM: The cat's not out of the bag at the warehouse yet.
     You know how they are. They call you Romeo and stuff like that.

(*He stops at the oval mirror to put on his hat. He carefully shapes the brim and the crown to give a discreetly dashing effect.*)

     It's been a wonderful evening, Mrs. Wingfield. I guess this is what they mean by Southern hospitality.

AMANDA: It really wasn't anything at all.

JIM: I hope it don't seem like I'm rushing off. But I promised Betty I'd pick her up at the Wabash depot, an' by the time I get my jalopy down there her train'll be in. Some women are pretty upset if you keep 'em waiting.

AMANDA: Yes, I know— The tyranny of women!

(*Extends her hand.*)

     Good-bye, Mr. O'Connor.
     I wish you luck—and happiness—and success! All three of them, and so does Laura!—Don't you, Laura?

LAURA: Yes!

JIM (*taking her hand*): Good-bye, Laura. I'm certainly going to treasure that souvenir. And don't you forget the good advice I gave you.

(*Raises his voice to a cheery shout.*)

    So long, Shakespeare!
    Thanks again, ladies— Good night!

(*He grins and ducks jauntily out.*)
(*Still bravely grimacing,* AMANDA *closes the door on the gentleman caller. Then she turns back to the room with a puzzled expression. She and* LAURA *don't dare to face each other.* LAURA *crouches beside the victrola to wind it.*)

AMANDA (*faintly*): Things have a way of turning out so badly.
    I don't believe that I would play the victrola.
    Well, well—well—
    Our gentleman caller was engaged to be married!
    Tom!

TOM (*from back*): Yes, Mother?

AMANDA: Come in here a minute. I want to tell you something awfully funny.

TOM (*enters with macaroon and a glass of the lemonade*): Has the gentleman caller gotten away already?

AMANDA: The gentleman caller has made an early departure.
    What a wonderful joke you played on us!

TOM: How do you mean?

AMANDA: You didn't mention that he was engaged to be married.

TOM: Jim? Engaged?

AMANDA: That's what he just informed us.

TOM: I'll be jiggered! I didn't know about that.

AMANDA: That seems very peculiar.

TOM: What's peculiar about it?

AMANDA: Didn't you call him your best friend down at the warehouse?

TOM: He is, but how did I know?

AMANDA: It seems extremely peculiar that you wouldn't know your best friend was going to be married!

TOM: The warehouse is where I work, not where I know things about people!

AMANDA: You don't know things anywhere! You live in a dream; you manufacture illusions!

(*He crosses to door.*)

Where are you going?

TOM: I'm going to the movies.

AMANDA: That's right, now that you've had us make such fools of ourselves. The effort, the preparations, all the expense! The new floor lamp, the rug, the clothes for Laura! All for what? To entertain some other girl's fiancé!

Go to the movies, go! Don't think about us, a mother deserted, an unmarried sister who's crippled and has no job! Don't let anything interfere with your selfish pleasure!

Just go, go, go—to the movies!

TOM: All right, I will! The more you shout about my selfishness to me the quicker I'll go, and I won't go to the movies!

AMANDA: Go, then! Then go to the moon—you selfish dreamer!

(TOM *smashes his glass on the floor. He plunges out on the fire-escape, slamming the door.* LAURA *screams—cut by door.*)
(*Dance-hall music up.* TOM *goes to the rail and grips it desperately, lifting his face in the chill white moonlight penetrating the narrow abyss of the alley.*)
(LEGEND ON SCREEN: "AND SO GOOD-BYE . . .")
(TOM's *closing speech is timed with the interior pantomime. The interior scene is played as though viewed through soundproof glass.* AMANDA *appears to be making a comforting speech to* LAURA *who is huddled upon the sofa. Now that we cannot hear the mother's speech, her silliness is gone and she has dignity and tragic beauty.* LAURA's *dark hair hides her face until at the end of the speech she lifts it to smile at her mother.* AMANDA's *gestures are slow and graceful, almost dancelike, as she comforts the daughter. At the end of*

*her speech she glances a moment at the father's picture—then with-*
*draws through the portieres. At close of* TOM'S *speech,* LAURA *blows*
*out the candles, ending the play.*)

TOM: I didn't go to the moon, I went much further—for time is the
longest distance between two places—

Not long after that I was fired for writing a poem on the lid of a
shoe-box.

I left Saint Louis. I descended the steps of this fire-escape for
a last time and followed, from then on, in my father's footsteps, at-
tempting to find in motion what was lost in space—

I traveled around a great deal. The cities swept about me like
dead leaves, leaves that were brightly colored but torn away from
the branches.

I would have stopped, but I was pursued by something.

It always came upon me unawares, taking me altogether by surprise. Perhaps it was a familiar bit of music. Perhaps it was only a
piece of transparent glass—

Perhaps I am walking along a street at night, in some strange
city, before I have found companions. I pass the lighted window
of a shop where perfume is sold. The window is filled with pieces of
colored glass, tiny transparent bottles in delicate colors, like bits of
a shattered rainbow.

Then all at once my sister touches my shoulder. I turn around
and look into her eyes . . .

Oh, Laura, Laura, I tried to leave you behind me, but I am more
faithful than I intended to be!

I reach for a cigarette, I cross the street, I run into the movies
or a bar, I buy a drink, I speak to the nearest stranger—anything
that can blow your candles out!

(LAURA *bends over the candles.*)

—for nowadays the world is lit by lightning! Blow out your candles,
Laura—and so good-bye. . . .

(*She blows the candles out.*)

(*The Scene Dissolves.*)

# SEAN O'CASEY

# Juno
# and the Paycock

*Juno and the Paycock* was first produced by the Abbey
Theater, Dublin, in May, 1924.

# CHARACTERS

"CAPTAIN" JACK BOYLE
JUNO BOYLE, *his wife*
JOHNNY BOYLE } *their children*
MARY BOYLE
"JOXER" DALY
MRS. MAISIE MADIGAN
"NEEDLE" NUGENT, *a tailor*
MRS. TANCRED
JERRY DEVINE
CHARLIE BENTHAM, *a school teacher*
AN IRREGULAR MOBILIZER
TWO IRREGULARS
A COAL-BLOCK VENDOR
A SEWING MACHINE MAN
TWO FURNITURE REMOVAL MEN
TWO NEIGHBOURS

*Residents in the Tenement*

*Period of the play, 1922.*

# Act One

The living room of a two-room tenancy occupied by the BOYLE family in a tenement house in Dublin. Left, a door leading to another part of the house; left of door a window looking into the street; at back a dresser; farther to right at back, a window looking into the back of the house. Between the window and the dresser is a picture of the Virgin; below the picture, on a bracket, is a crimson bowl in which a floating votive light is burning. Farther to the right is a small bed partly concealed by cretonne hangings strung on a twine. To the right is the fireplace; near the fireplace is a door leading to the other room. Beside the fireplace is a box containing coal. On the mantelshelf is an alarm clock lying on its face. In a corner near the window looking into the back is a galvanized bath. A table and some chairs. On the table are breakfast things for one. A teapot is on the hob and a frying-pan stands inside the fender. There are a few books on the dresser and one on the table. Leaning against the dresser is a long-handled shovel—the kind invariably used by labourers when turning concrete or mixing mortar. JOHNNY BOYLE is sitting crouched beside the fire. MARY with her jumper off—it is lying on the back of a chair—is arranging her hair before a tiny mirror perched on the table. Beside the mirror is stretched out the morning paper, which she looks at when she isn't gazing into the mirror. She is a well-made and good-looking girl of twenty-two. Two forces are working in her mind—one, through the circumstances of her life, pulling her back; the other, through the influence of books she has read, pushing her forward. The opposing forces are apparent in her speech and her manners, both of which are degraded by her environment, and improved by her acquaintance—slight though it be—with literature. The time is early forenoon.

MARY (looking at the paper): On a little bye-road, out beyant Finglas, he was found.

(MRS. BOYLE enters by door on right; she has been shopping and carries a small parcel in her hand. She is forty-five years of age, and twenty years ago she must have been a pretty woman; but her face

369

*has now assumed that look which ultimately settles down upon the faces of the women of the working-class; a look of listless monotony and harassed anxiety, blending with an expression of mechanical resistance. Were circumstances favourable, she would probably be a handsome, active and clever woman.)*

MRS. BOYLE: Isn't he come in yet?

MARY: No, mother.

MRS. BOYLE: Oh, he'll come in when he likes; struttin' about the town like a paycock with Joxer, I suppose. I hear all about Mrs. Tancred's son is in this mornin's paper.

MARY: The full details are in it this mornin'; seven wounds he had —one entherin' the neck, with an exit wound beneath the left shoulder-blade; another in the left breast penethratin' the heart, an' . . .

JOHNNY (*springing up from the fire*): Oh, quit that readin', for God's sake! Are yous losin' all your feelin's? It'll soon be that none of yous'll read anythin' that's not about butcherin'! (*He goes quickly into the room on left.*)

MARY: He's gettin' very sensitive, all of a sudden!

MRS. BOYLE: I'll read it myself, Mary, by an' by, when I come home. Everybody's sayin' that he was a die-hard—thanks be to God that Johnny had nothin' to do with him this long time. . . . (*Opening the parcel and taking out some sausages, which she places on a plate*) Ah, then, if that father o' yours doesn't come in soon for his breakfast, he may go without any; I'll not wait much longer for him.

MARY: Can't you let him get it himself when he comes in?

MRS. BOYLE: Yes, an' let him bring in Joxer Daly along with him? Ay, that's what he'd like, an' that's what he's waitin' for—till he thinks I'm gone to work, an' then sail in with the boul' Joxer, to burn all the coal an' dhrink all the tea in the place, to show them what a good Samaritan he is! But I'll stop here till he comes in, if I have to wait till tomorrow mornin'.

VOICE OF JOHNNY INSIDE: Mother!

MRS. BOYLE: Yis?

VOICE OF JOHNNY: Bring us in a dhrink o' wather.

MRS. BOYLE: Bring in that fella a dhrink o' wather, for God's sake, Mary.

MARY: Isn't he big an' able enough to come out an' get it himself?

MRS. BOYLE: If you weren't well yourself you'd like somebody to bring you in a dhrink o' wather. (*She brings in drink and returns.*)

MRS. BOYLE: Isn't it terrible to have to be waitin' this way! You'd think he was bringin' twenty poun's a week into the house the way he's goin' on. He wore out the Health Insurance long ago, he's afther wearin' out the unemployment dole, an', now, he's thryin' to wear out me! An' constantly singin', no less, when he ought always to be on his knees offerin' up a Novena for a job!

MARY (*tying a ribbon fillet-wise around her head*): I don't like this ribbon, ma; I think I'll wear the green—it looks betther than the blue.

MRS. BOYLE: Ah, wear whatever ribbon you like, girl, only don't be botherin' me. I don't know what a girl on strike wants to be wearin' a ribbon round her head for or silk stockin's on her legs either; it's wearin' them things that make the employers think they're givin' yous too much money.

MARY: The hour is past now when we'll ask the employers' permission to wear what we like.

MRS. BOYLE: I don't know why you wanted to walk out for Jennie Claffey; up to this you never had a good word for her.

MARY: What's the use of belongin' to a Trades Union if you won't stand up for your principles? Why did they sack her? It was a clear case of victimization. We couldn't let her walk the streets, could we?

MRS. BOYLE: No, of course yous couldn't—yous wanted to keep her company. Wan victim wasn't enough. When the employers sacrifice wan victim, the Trades Unions go wan betther be sacrificin' a hundred.

MARY: It doesn't matther what you say, ma—a principle's a principle.

MRS. BOYLE: Yis; an' when I go into oul' Murphy's tomorrow, an' he gets to know that, instead o' payin' all, I'm goin' to borry more, what'll he say when I tell him a principle's a principle? What'll we do if he refuses to give us any more on tick?

MARY: He daren't refuse—if he does, can't you tell him he's paid?

MRS. BOYLE: It's lookin' as if he was paid, whether he refuses or no.

(JOHNNY *appears at the door on left. He can be plainly seen now; he is a thin delicate fellow, something younger than* MARY. *He has evidently gone through a rough time. His face is pale and drawn; there is a tremulous look of indefinite fear in his eyes. The left sleeve of his coat is empty, and he walks with a slight halt.*)

JOHNNY: I was lyin' down; I thought yous were gone. Oul' Simon Mackay is thrampin' about like a horse over me head, an' I can't sleep with him—they're like thunder-claps in me brain! The curse o'—God forgive me for goin' to curse!

MRS. BOYLE: There, now; go back an' lie down agan, an' I'll bring you in a nice cup o' tay.

JOHNNY: Tay, tay, tay! You're always thinkin' o' tay. If a man was dyin', you'd thry to make him swally a cup o' tay! (*He goes back.*)

MRS. BOYLE: I don't know what's goin' to be done with him. The bullet he got in the hip in Easter Week was bad enough, but the bomb that shatthered his arm in the fight in O'Connell Street put the finishin' touch on him. I knew he was makin' a fool of himself. God knows I went down on me bended knees to him not to go agen the Free State.

MARY: He stuck to his principles, an', no matther how you may argue, ma, a principle's a principle.

VOICE OF JOHNNY: Is Mary goin' to stay here?

MARY: No, I'm not goin' to stay here; you can't expect me to be always at your beck an' call, can you?

VOICE OF JOHNNY: I won't stop here be meself!

MRS. BOYLE: Amn't I nicely handicapped with the whole o' yous! I don't know what any o' yous ud do without your ma. (*To* JOHNNY) Your father'll be here in a minute, an' if you want anythin', he'll get it for you.

JOHNNY: I hate assin' him for anythin'. . . . He hates to be assed to stir. . . . Is the light lightin' before the picture o' the Virgin?

MRS. BOYLE: Yis, yis! The wan inside to St. Anthony isn't enough, but he must have another wan to the Virgin here!

(JERRY DEVINE *enters hastily. He is about twenty-five, well set, active and earnest. He is a type, becoming very common now in the Labour Movement, of a mind knowing enough to make the mass of his associates, who know less, a power, and too little to broaden that power for the benefit of all.* MARY *seizes her jumper and runs hastily into room left.*)

JERRY (*breathless*): Where's the Captain, Mrs. Boyle; where's the Captain?

MRS. BOYLE: You may well ass a body that: he's wherever Joxer Daly is—dhrinkin' in some snug or another.

JERRY: Father Farrell is just afther stoppin' to tell me to run up an' get him to go to the new job that's goin' on in Rathmines; his cousin is foreman o' the job, an' Father Farrell was speakin' to him about poor Johnny an' his father bein' idle so long, an' the foreman told Father Farrell to send the Captain up an' he'd give him a start—I wondher where I'd find him?

MRS. BOYLE: You'll find he's ayther in Ryan's or Foley's.

JERRY: I'll run round to Ryan's—I know it's a great house o' Joxer's. (*He rushes out.*)

MRS. BOYLE (*piteously*): There now, he'll miss that job, or I know for what! If he gets win' o' the word, he'll not come back till evenin', so that it'll be too late. There'll never be any good got out o' him so long as he goes with that shouldher-shruggin' Joxer. I killin' meself workin', an' he sthruttin' about from mornin' till night like a paycock!

(*The steps of two persons are heard coming up a flight of stairs. They are the footsteps of* CAPTAIN BOYLE *and* JOXER. CAPTAIN BOYLE *is singing in a deep, sonorous, self-honouring voice.*)

THE CAPTAIN: Sweet Spirit, hear me prayer! Hear . . . oh . . . hear . . . me prayer . . . hear, oh, hear . . . Oh, he . . . ar . . . oh, he . . . ar . . . me . . . pray . . . er!

JOXER (*outside*): Ah, that's a darlin' song, a daaarlin' song!

MRS BOYLE (*viciously*): Sweet spirit hear his prayer! Oh, then, I'll take me solemn affeydavey, it's not for a job he's prayin'!

(*She sits down on the bed so that the cretonne hangings hide her from the view of those entering.*)

(THE CAPTAIN *comes slowly in. He is a man of about sixty; stout, grey-haired and stocky. His neck is short, and his head looks like a stone ball that one sometimes sees on top of a gate-post. His cheeks, reddish-purple, are puffed out, as if he were always repressing an. almost irrepressible ejaculation. On his upper lip is a crisp, tightly cropped moustache; he carries himself with the upper part of his body slightly thrown back, and his stomach slightly thrust forward. His walk is a slow, consequential strut. His clothes are dingy, and he wears a faded seaman's cap with a glazed peak.*)

BOYLE (*to* JOXER, *who is still outside*): Come on, come on in, Joxer; she's gone out long ago, man. If there's nothing else to be got, we'll furrage out a cup o' tay, anyway. It's the only bit I get in comfort when she's away. 'Tisn't Juno should be her pet name at all, but Deirdre of the Sorras, for she's always grousin'.

(JOXER *steps cautiously into the room. He may be younger than* THE CAPTAIN *but he looks a lot older. His face is like a bundle of crinkled paper; his eyes have a cunning twinkle; he is spare and loosely built; he has a habit of constantly shrugging his shoulders with a peculiar twitching movement, meant to be ingratiating. His face is invariably ornamented with a grin.*)

JOXER: It's a terrible thing to be tied to a woman that's always grousin'. I don't know how you stick it—it ud put years on me. It's a good job she has to be so often away, for (*with a shrug*) when the cat's away, the mice can play!

BOYLE (*with a commanding and complacent gesture*): Pull over to the fire, Joxer, an' we'll have a cup o' tay in a minute.

JOXER: Ah, a cup o' tay's a darlin' thing, a daaarlin' thing—the cup that cheers but doesn't . . .

(JOXER's *rhapsody is cut short by the sight of* JUNO *coming forward and confronting the two cronies. Both are stupefied.*)

MRS. BOYLE (*with sweet irony—poking the fire, and turning her head to glare at* JOXER): Pull over to the fire, Joxer Daly, an' we'll have a cup o' tay in a minute! Are you sure, now, you wouldn't like an egg?

JOXER: I can't stop, Mrs. Boyle; I'm in a desperate hurry, a desperate hurry.

MRS. BOYLE: Pull over to the fire, Joxer Daly; people is always far more comfortabler here than they are in their own place.

(JOXER *makes hastily for the door.* BOYLE *stirs to follow him; thinks of something to relieve the situation—stops, and says suddenly*):

Joxer!

JOXER (*at door ready to bolt*): Yis?

BOYLE: You know the foreman o' that job that's goin' on down in Killesther, don't you, Joxer?

JOXER (*puzzled*): Foreman—Killesther?

BOYLE (*with a meaning look*): He's a butty o' yours, isn't he?

JOXER (*the truth dawning on him*): The foreman at Killesther—oh, yis, yis. He's an oul' butty o' mine—oh, he's a darlin' man, a daarlin' man.

BOYLE: Oh, then, it's a sure thing. It's a pity we didn't go down at breakfast first thing this mornin'—we might ha' been working now; but you didn't know it then.

JOXER (*with a shrug*): It's betther late than never.

BOYLE: It's nearly time we got a start, anyhow; I'm fed up knockin' round, doin' nothin'. He promised you—gave you the straight tip?

JOXER: Yis. "Come down on the blow o' dinner," says he, "an' I'll start you, an' any friend you like to brin' with you." Ah, says I, you're a darlin' man, a daaarlin' man.

BOYLE: Well, it couldn't come at a betther time—we're a long time waitin' for it.

JOXER: Indeed we were; but it's a long lane that has no turnin'.

BOYLE: The blow up for dinner is at one—wait till I see what time it 'tis. (*He goes over to the mantelpiece, and gingerly lifts the clock.*)

MRS. BOYLE: Min' now, how you go on fiddlin' with that clock—you know the least little thing sets it asthray.

BOYLE: The job couldn't come at a betther time; I'm feelin' in great fettle, Joxer. I'd hardly believe I ever had a pain in me legs, an' last week I was nearly crippled with them.

JOXER: That's betther and betther; ah, God never shut wan door but he opened another!

BOYLE: It's only eleven o'clock; we've lashins o' time. I'll slip on me oul' moleskins afther breakfast, an' we can saunther down at our ayse. (*Putting his hand on the shovel*) I think, Joxer, we'd betther bring our shovels?

JOXER: Yis, Captain, yis; it's betther to go fully prepared an' ready for all eventualities. You bring your long-tailed shovel, an' I'll bring me navvy. We mighten' want them, an', then agen, we might: for want of a nail the shoe was lost, for want of a shoe the horse was lost, an' for want of a horse the man was lost—aw, that's a darlin' proverb, a daarlin' . . .

(*As* JOXER *is finishing his sentence,* MRS. BOYLE *approaches the door and* JOXER *retreats hurriedly. She shuts the door with a bang.*)

BOYLE (*suggestively*): We won't be long pullin' ourselves together agen when I'm working for a few weeks.

(MRS. BOYLE *takes no notice.*)

BOYLE: The foreman on the job is an oul' butty o' Joxer's; I have an idea that I know him meself. (*Silence*) . . . There's a button off the back o' me moleskin trousers. . . . If you leave out a needle an' thread I'll sew it on meself. . . . Thanks be to God, the pains in me legs is gone, anyhow!

MRS. BOYLE (*with a burst*): Look here, Mr. Jacky Boyle, them yarns won't go down with Juno. I know you an' Joxer Daly of an oul' date, an', if you think you're able to come it over me with them fairy tales, you're in the wrong shop.

BOYLE (*coughing subduedly to relieve the tenseness of the situation*): U-u-u-ugh.

MRS. BOYLE: Butty o' Joxer's! Oh, you'll do a lot o' good as long as you continue to be a butty o' Joxer's!

BOYLE: U-u-u-ugh.

MRS. BOYLE: Shovel! Ah, then, me boyo, you'd do far more work with a knife an' fork than ever you'll do with a shovel! If there was e'er a genuine job goin' you'd be dh'other way about—not able to lift your arms with the pains in your legs! Your poor wife slavin' to keep the bit in your mouth, an' you gallivantin' about all the day like a paycock!

BOYLE: It ud be betther for a man to be dead, betther for a man to be dead.

MRS. BOYLE (*ignoring the interruption*): Everybody callin' you "Captain," an' you only wanst on the wather, in an oul' collier from here to Liverpool, when anybody, to listen or look at you, ud take you for a second Christo For Columbus!

BOYLE: Are you never goin' to give us a rest?

MRS. BOYLE: Oh, you're never tired o' lookin' for a rest.

BOYLE: D'ye want to dhrive me out o' the house?

MRS. BOYLE: It ud be easier to dhrive you out o' the house than to dhrive you into a job. Here, sit down an' take your breakfast—it may be the last you'll get, for I don't know where the next is goin' to come from.

BOYLE: If I get this job we'll be all right.

MRS. BOYLE: Did ye see Jerry Devine?

BOYLE (*testily*): No, I didn't see him.

MRS. BOYLE: No, but you seen Joxer. Well, he was here lookin' for you.

BOYLE: Well, let him look!

MRS. BOYLE: Oh, indeed, he may well look, for it ud be hard for him to see you, an' you stuck in Ryan's snug.

BOYLE: I wasn't in Ryan's snug—I don't go into Ryan's.

MRS. BOYLE: Oh, is there a mad dog there? Well, if you weren't in Ryan's you were in Foley's.

BOYLE: I'm telling you for the last three weeks I haven't tasted a dhrop of intoxicatin' liquor. I wasn't in ayther wan snug or dh'other —I could swear that on a prayer-book—I'm as innocent as the child unborn!

MRS. BOYLE: Well, if you'd been in for your breakfast you'd ha' seen him.

BOYLE (*suspiciously*): What does he want me for?

MRS. BOYLE: He'll be back any minute an' then you'll soon know.

BOYLE: I'll dhrop out an' see if I can meet him.

MRS. BOYLE: You'll sit down an' take your breakfast, an' let me go to me work, for I'm an hour late already waitin' for you.

BOYLE: You needn't ha' waited, for I'll take no breakfast—I've a little spirit left in me still!

MRS. BOYLE: Are you goin' to have your breakfast—yes or no?

BOYLE (*too proud to yield*): I'll have no breakfast—yous can keep your breakfast. (*Plaintively*) I'll knock out a bit somewhere, never fear.

MRS. BOYLE: Nobody's goin' to coax you—don't think that. (*She vigorously replaces the pan and the sausages in the press.*)

BOYLE: I've a little spirit left in me still.

(JERRY DEVINE *enters hastily.*)

JERRY: Oh, here you are at last! I've been searchin' for you everywhere. The foreman in Foley's told me you hadn't left the snug with Joxer ten minutes before I went in.

MRS. BOYLE: An' he swearin' on the holy prayer-book that he wasn't in no snug!

BOYLE (*to* JERRY): What business is it o' yours whether I was in a snug or no? What do you want to be gallopin' about afther me for? Is a man not to be allowed to leave his house for a minute without havin' a pack o' spies, pimps an' informers cantherin' at his heels?

JERRY: Oh, you're takin' a wrong view of it, Mr. Boyle; I simply was anxious to do you a good turn. I have a message for you from Father Farrell: he says that if you go to the job that's on in Rathmines, an' ask for Foreman Mangan, you'll get a start.

BOYLE: That's all right, but I don't want the motions of me body to be watched the way an asthronomer ud watch a star. If you're folleyin' Mary aself, you've no pereeogative to be folleyin' me. (*Suddenly catching his thigh*) U-ugh, I'm after gettin' a terrible twinge in me right leg!

MRS. BOYLE: Oh, it won't be very long now till it travels into your left wan. It's miraculous that whenever he scents a job in front of him, his legs begin to fail him! Then, me bucko, if you lose this chance, you may go an' furrage for yourself!

JERRY: This job'll last for some time, too, Captain, an' as soon as the foundations are in, it'll be cushy enough.

BOYLE: Won't it be a climbin' job? How d'ye expect me to be able to go up a ladder with these legs? An', if I get up aself, how am I goin' to get down agen?

MRS. BOYLE (*viciously*): Get wan o' the labourers to carry you down in a hod! You can't climb a laddher, but you can skip like a goat into a snug!

JERRY: I wouldn't let meself be let down that easy, Mr. Boyle; a little exercise, now, might do you all the good in the world.

BOYLE: It's a docthor you should have been, Devine—maybe you know more about the pains in me legs than meself that has them?

JERRY (*irritated*): Oh, I know nothin' about the pains in your legs; I've brought the message that Father Farrell gave me, an' that's all I can do.

MRS. BOYLE: Here, sit down an' take your breakfast, an' go an' get ready; an' don't be actin' as if you couldn't pull a wing out of a dead bee.

BOYLE: I want no breakfast, I tell you; it ud choke me afther all that's been said. I've a little spirit left in me still.

MRS. BOYLE: Well, let's see your spirit, then, an' go in at wanst an' put on your moleskin trousers!

BOYLE (*moving towards the door on left*): It ud be betther for a man to be dead! U-ugh! There's another twinge in me other leg! Nobody but meself knows the sufferin' I'm goin' through with the pains in these legs o' mine! (*He goes into the room on left as* MARY *comes out with her hat in her hand.*)

MRS. BOYLE: I'll have to push off now, for I'm terrible late already, but I was determined to stay an' hunt that Joxer this time. (*She goes off.*)

JERRY: Are you going out, Mary?

MARY: It looks like it when I'm putting on my hat, doesn't it?

JERRY: The bitther word agen, Mary.

MARY: You won't allow me to be friendly with you; if I thry, you deliberately misundherstand it.

JERRY: I didn't always misundherstand it; you were often delighted to have the arms of Jerry around you.

MARY: If you go on talkin' like this, Jerry Devine, you'll make me hate you!

JERRY: Well, let it be either a weddin' or a wake! Listen, Mary, I'm standin' for the Secretaryship of our Union. There's only one op-posin' me; I'm popular with all the men, an' a good speaker—all are sayin' that I'll get elected.

MARY: Well?

JERRY: The job's worth three hundred an' fifty pounds a year, Mary. You an' I could live nice an' cosily on that; it would lift you out o' this place an'. . .

MARY: I haven't time to listen to you now—I have to go. (*She is going out when* JERRY *bars the way.*)

JERRY (*appealingly*): Mary, what's come over you with me for the last few weeks? You hardly speak to me, an' then only a word with a face o' bitterness on it. Have you forgotten, Mary, all the happy evenin's that were as sweet as the scented hawthorn that sheltered the sides o' the road as we saunthered through the country?

MARY: That's all over now. When you get your new job, Jerry, you won't be long findin' a girl far betther than I am for your sweetheart.

JERRY: Never, never, Mary! No matther what happens you'll always be the same to me.

MARY: I must be off; please let me go, Jerry.

JERRY: I'll go a bit o' the way with you.

MARY: You needn't, thanks; I want to be by meself.

JERRY (*catching her arm*): You're goin' to meet another fella; you've clicked with some one else, me lady!

MARY: That's no concern o' yours, Jerry Devine; let me go!

JERRY: I saw yous comin' out o' the Cornflower Dance Class, an' you hangin' on his arm—a thin, lanky strip of a Micky Dazzler, with a walkin' stick an' gloves!

VOICE OF JOHNNY (*loudly*): What are you doin' there—pullin' about everything!

VOICE OF BOYLE (*loudly and viciously*): I'm puttin' on me moleskin trousers!

MARY: You're hurtin' me arm! Let me go, or I'll scream, an' then you'll have the oul' fella out on top of us!

JERRY: Don't be so hard on a fella, Mary, don't be so hard.

BOYLE (*appearing at the door*): What's the meanin' of all this hillabaloo?

MARY: Let me go, let me go!

BOYLE: D'ye hear me—what's all this hillabaloo about?

JERRY (*plaintively*): Will you not give us one kind word, one kind word, Mary?

BOYLE: D'ye hear me talkin' to yous? What's all this hillabaloo for?

JERRY: Let me kiss your hand, your little, tiny, white hand!

BOYLE: Your little, tiny, white hand—are you takin' leave o' your senses, man?

(MARY *breaks away and rushes out.*)

BOYLE: This is nice goin's on in front of her father!

JERRY: Ah, dhry up, for God's sake! (*He follows* MARY.)

BOYLE: Chiselurs don't care a damn now about their parents, they're bringin' their fathers' grey hairs down with sorra to the grave, an' laughin' at it, laughin' at it. Ah, I suppose it's just the same every-where—the whole worl's in a state o' chassis! (*He sits by the fire*) Breakfast! Well, they can keep their breakfast for me. Not if they went down on their bended knees would I take it—I'll show them I've a little spirit left in me still! (*He goes over to the press, takes out a plate and looks at it*) Sassige! Well, let her keep her sassige. (*He returns to the fire, takes up the teapot and gives it a gentle shake*) The tay's wet right enough. (*A pause; he rises, goes to the press, takes out the sausage, puts it on the pan, and puts both on the fire. He attends the sausage wih a fork.*)

BOYLE (*singing*):

When the robins nest agen,
And the flowers are in bloom,
When the Springtime's sunny smile seems to banish all sorrow an'
     gloom;
Then me bonny blue-ey'd lad, if me heart be true till then—
He's promised he'll come back to me,
When the robins nest agen!

(*He lifts his head at the high note, and then drops his eyes to the pan.*)

BOYLE (*singing*):

When the . . .

(*Steps are heard approaching; he whips the pan off the fire and puts it under the bed, then sits down at the fire. The door opens and a bearded man looking in says*):

You don't happen to want a sewin' machine?

BOYLE (*furiously*): No, I don't want e'er a sewin' machine! (*He returns the pan to the fire, and commences to sing again.*)

BOYLE (*singing*):

When the robins nest agen,
And the flowers they are in bloom,
He's . . .

(*A thundering knock is heard at the street door.*)

BOYLE: There's a terrible tatheraraa—that's a stranger—that's nobody belongin' to the house. (*Another loud knock.*)

JOXER (*sticking his head in at the door*): Did ye hear them tatherarahs?

BOYLE: Well, Joxer, I'm not deaf.

JOHNNY (*appearing in his shirt and trousers at the door on left; his face is anxious and his voice is tremulous*): Who's that at the door; who's that at the door? Who gave that knock—d'ye yous hear me—are yous deaf or dhrunk or what?

BOYLE (*to* JOHNNY): How the hell do I know who 'tis? Joxer, stick your head out o' the window an' see.

JOXER: An' mebbe get a bullet in the kisser? Ah, none o' them thricks for Joxer! It's betther to be a coward than a corpse!

BOYLE (*looking cautiously out of the window*): It's a fella in a thrench coat.

JOHNNY: Holy Mary, Mother o' God, I . . .

BOYLE: He's goin' away—he must ha' got tired knockin'.

(JOHNNY *returns to the room on left.*)

BOYLE: Sit down an' have a cup o' tay, Joxer.

JOXER: I'm afraid the missus ud pop in on us agen before we'd know where we are. Somethin's tellin' me to go at wanst.

BOYLE: Don't be superstitious, man; we're Dublin men, an' not boyos that's only afther comin' up from the bog o' Allen—though if she did come in, right enough, we'd be caught like rats in a thrap.

JOXER: An' you know the sort she is—she wouldn't listen to reason—an' wanse bitten twice shy.

BOYLE (*going over to the window at back*): If the worst came to the worst, you could dart out here, Joxer; it's only a dhrop of a few feet to the roof of the return room, an' the first minute she goes into dh'other room, I'll give you the bend, an' you can slip in an' away.

JOXER (*yielding to the temptation*): Ah, I won't stop very long any-how. (*Picking up a book from the table*) Whose is the buk?

BOYLE: Aw, one o' Mary's; she's always readin' lately—nothin' but thrash, too. There's one I was lookin' at dh'other day: three stories, The Doll's House, Ghosts, an' The Wild Duck—buks only fit for chiselurs!

JOXER: Didja ever rade *Elizabeth, or Th' Exile o' Sibayria* . . . ah, it's a darlin' story, a daarlin' story!

BOYLE: You eat your sassige, an' never min' *Th' Exile o' Sibayria.*

(*Both sit down;* BOYLE *fills out tea, pours gravy on* JOXER's *plate, and keeps the sausage for himself.*)

JOXER: What are you wearin' your moleskin trousers for?

BOYLE: I have to go to a job, Joxer. Just afther you'd gone, Devine kem runnin' in to tell us that Father Farrell said if I went down to the job that's goin' on in Rathmines I'd get a start.

JOXER: Be the holy, that's good news!

BOYLE: How is it good news? I wondher if you were in my condition, would you call it good news?

JOXER: I thought . . .

BOYLE: You thought! You think too sudden sometimes, Joxer. D'ye know, I'm hardly able to crawl with the pains in me legs!

JOXER: Yis, yis; I forgot the pains in your legs. I know you can do nothin' while they're at you.

BOYLE: You forgot; I don't think any of yous realize the state I'm in with the pains in me legs. What ud happen if I had to carry a bag o' cement?

JOXER: Ah, any man havin' the like of them pains id be down an' out, down an' out.

BOYLE: I wouldn't mind if he had said it to meself; but, no, oh no, he rushes in an' shouts it out in front o' Juno, an' you know what Juno is, Joxer. We all know Devine knows a little more than the rest of us, but he doesn't act as if he did; he's a good boy, sober, able to talk an' all that, but still . . .

JOXER: Oh, ay; able to argufy, but still . . .

BOYLE: If he's runnin' afther Mary, aself, he's not goin' to be runnin' afther me. Captain Boyle's able to take care of himself. Afther all, I'm not gettin' brought up on Virol. I never heard him usin' a curse; I don't believe he was ever dhrunk in his life—sure he's not like a Christian at all!

JOXER: You're afther takin' the word out o' me mouth—afther all, a Christian's natural, but he's unnatural.

BOYLE: His oul' fella was just the same—a Wicklow man.

JOXER: A Wicklow man! That explains the whole thing. I've met many a Wicklow man in me time, but I never met wan that was any good.

BOYLE: "Father Farrell," says he, "sent me down to tell you." Father Farrell! . . . D'ye know, Joxer, I never like to be beholden to any o' the clergy.

JOXER: It's dangerous, right enough.

BOYLE: If they do anything for you, they'd want you to be livin' in the Chapel. . . . I'm goin' to tell you somethin', Joxer, that I wouldn't tell to anybody else—the clergy always had too much power over the people in this unfortunate country.

JOXER: You could sing that if you had an air to it!

BOYLE (*becoming enthusiastic*): Didn't they prevent the people in '47 from seizin' the corn, an' they starvin'; didn't they down Parnell; didn't they say that hell wasn't hot enough nor eternity long enough to punish the Fenians? We don't forget, we don't forget them things, Joxer. If they've taken everything else from us, Joxer, they've left us our memory.

JOXER (*emotionally*): For mem'ry's the only friend that grief can call its own, that grief . . . can . . . call . . . its own!

BOYLE: Father Farrell's beginnin' to take a great intherest in Captain Boyle; because of what Johnny did for his country, says he to me wan day. It's a curious way to reward Johnny be makin' his poor oul' father work. But, that's what the clergy want, Joxer—work, work, work for me an' you; havin' us mulin' from mornin' till night, so that they may be in betther fettle when they come hoppin' round for their dues! Job! Well, let him give his job to wan of his hymn-singin', prayer-spoutin', craw-thumpin' Confraternity men!

(*The voice of a coal-block vendor is heard chanting in the street.*)

VOICE OF COAL VENDOR: Blocks . . . coal-blocks! Blocks . . . coal-blocks!

JOXER: God be with the young days when you were steppin' the deck of a manly ship, with the win' blowin' a hurricane through the masts, an' the only sound you'd hear was, "Port your helm!" an' the only answer, "Port it is, sir!"

BOYLE: Them was days, Joxer, them was days. Nothin' was too hot or too heavy for me then. Sailin' from the Gulf o' Mexico to the Antarctic Ocean. I seen things, I seen things, Joxer, that no mortal man should speak about that knows his Catechism. Ofen, an' ofen, when I was fixed to the wheel with a marlin-spike, an' the win's blowin' fierce an' the waves lashin' an' lashin', till you'd think every minute was goin' to be your last, an' it blowed, an' blowed—blew is the right word, Joxer, but blowed is what the sailors use. . . .

JOXER: Aw, it's a darlin' word, a daarlin' word.

BOYLE: An', as it blowed an' blowed, I ofen looked up at the sky an' assed meself the question—what is the stars, what is the stars?

VOICE OF COAL VENDOR: Any blocks, coal-blocks; blocks, coal-blocks!

JOXER: Ah, that's the question, that's the question—what is the stars?

BOYLE: An' then, I'd have another look, an' I'd ass meself—what is the moon?

JOXER: Ah, that's the question—what is the moon, what is the moon?

(*Rapid steps are heard coming towards the door.* BOYLE *makes desperate efforts to hide everything;* JOXER *rushes to the window in a frantic effort to get out;* BOYLE *begins to innocently lilt—"Oh, me darlin' Jennie, I will be thrue to thee," when the door is opened, and the black face of the* COAL VENDOR *appears.*)

THE COAL VENDOR: D'yes want any blocks?

BOYLE (*with a roar*): No, we don't want any blocks!

JOXER (*coming back with a sigh of relief*): That's afther puttin' the heart across me—I could ha' sworn it was Juno. I'd bether be goin', Captain; you couldn't tell the minute Juno'd hop in on us.

BOYLE: Let her hop in; we may as well have it out first as at last. I've made up me mind—I'm not goin' to do only what she damn well likes.

JOXER: Them sentiments does you credit, Captain; I don't like to say anything as between man an' wife, but I say as a butty, as a butty, Captain, that you've stuck it too long, an' that it's about time you showed a little spunk.

> How can a man die betther than facin' fearful odds,
> For th' ashes of his fathers an' the temples of his gods.

BOYLE: She has her rights—there's no one denyin' it, but haven't I me rights too?

JOXER: Of course you have—the sacred rights o' man!

BOYLE: Today, Joxer, there's goin' to be issued a proclamation be me, establishin' an independent Republic, an' Juno'll have to take an oath of allegiance.

JOXER: Be firm, be firm, Captain; the first few minutes'll be the worst:—if you gently touch a nettle it'll sting you for your pains; grasp it like a lad of mettle, an's as soft as silk remains!

VOICE OF JUNO OUTSIDE: Can't stop, Mrs. Madigan—I haven't a minute!

JOXER (*flying out of the window*): Holy God, here she is!

BOYLE (*packing the things away with a rush in the press*): I knew that fella ud stop till she was in on top of us! (*He sits down by the fire.*)

(JUNO *enters hastily; she is flurried and excited.*)

JUNO: Oh, you're in—you must have been only afther comin' in?

BOYLE: No, I never went out.

JUNO: It's curious, then, you never heard the knockin'. (*She puts her coat and hat on bed.*)

BOYLE: Knockin'? Of course I heard the knockin'.

JUNO: An' why didn't you open the door, then? I suppose you were so busy with Joxer that you hadn't time.

BOYLE: I haven't seen Joxer since I seen him before. Joxer! What ud bring Joxer here?

JUNO: D'ye mean to tell me that the pair of yous wasn't collogin' together here when me back was turned?

BOYLE: What ud we be collogin' together about? I have somethin' else to think of besides collogin' with Joxer. I can swear on all the holy prayer-books . . .

MRS. BOYLE: That you weren't in no snug! Go on in at wanst now, an' take aff that moleskin trousers o' yours, an' put on a collar an' tie to smarten yourself up a bit. There's a visitor comin' with Mary in a minute, an' he has great news for you.

BOYLE: A job, I suppose; let us get wan first before we start lookin' for another.

MRS. BOYLE: That's the thing that's able to put the win' up you. Well, it's no job, but news that'll give you the chance o' your life.

BOYLE: What's all the mystery about?

MRS. BOYLE: G'win an' take off the moleskin trousers when you're told!

(BOYLE *goes into room on left.* MRS. BOYLE *tidies up the room, puts the shovel under the bed, and goes to the press.*)

MRS. BOYLE: Oh, God bless us, looka the way everythin's thrun about! Oh, Joxer was here, Joxer was here!

(MARY *enters with* CHARLIE BENTHAM; *he is a young man of twenty-five, tall, good-looking, with a very high opinion of himself generally. He is dressed in a brown coat, brown knee-breeches, grey stockings, a brown sweater, with a deep blue tie; he carries gloves and a walking-stick.*)

MRS. BOYLE (*fussing round*): Come in, Mr. Bentham; sit down, Mr. Bentham, in this chair; it's more comfortabler than that, Mr. Bentham. Himself'll be here in a minute; he's just takin' off his trousers.

MARY: Mother!

BENTHAM: Please don't put yourself to any trouble, Mrs. Boyle— I'm quite all right here, thank you.

MRS. BOYLE: An' to think of you knowin' Mary, an' she knowin' the news you had for us, an' wouldn't let on; but it's all the more welcomer now, for we were on our last lap!

VOICE OF JOHNNY INSIDE: What are you kickin' up all the racket for?

BOYLE (*roughly*): I'm takin' off me moleskin trousers!

JOHNNY: Can't you do it, then, without lettin' th' whole house know you're takin' off your trousers? What d'ye want puttin' them on an' takin' them off again?

BOYLE: Will you let me alone, will you let me alone? Am I never goin' to be done thryin' to please th' whole o' yous?

MRS. BOYLE (*to* BENTHAM): You must excuse th' state o' th' place, Mr. Bentham; th' minute I turn me back that man o' mine always makes a litther o' th' place, a litther o' th' place.

BENTHAM: Don't worry, Mrs. Boyle; it's all right, I assure . . .

BOYLE (*inside*): Where's me braces; where in th' name o' God did I leave me braces. . . . Ay, did you see where I put me braces?

JOHNNY (*inside, calling out*): Ma, will you come in here an' take da away ou' o' this or he'll dhrive me mad.

MRS. BOYLE (*going towards door*): Dear, dear, dear, that man'll be lookin' for somethin' on th' day o' Judgement. (*Looking into room and calling to* BOYLE) Look at your braces, man, hangin' round your neck!

BOYLE (*inside*): Aw, Holy God!

MRS. BOYLE (*calling*): Johnny, Johnny, come out here for a minute.

JOHNNY: Oh, leave Johnny alone, an' don't be annoyin' him!

MRS. BOYLE: Come on, Johnny, till I inthroduce you to Mr. Bentham. (*To* BENTHAM) Me son, Mr. Bentham; he's afther goin' through the mill. He was only a chiselur of a Boy Scout in Easter Week, when he got hit in the hip; and his arm was blew off in the fight in O'Connell Street. (JOHNNY *comes in*) Here he is, Mr. Bentham; Mr. Bentham, Johnny. None can deny he done his bit for Irelan', if that's going to do him any good.

JOHNNY (*boastfully*): I'd do it agen, ma, I'd do it agen; for a principle's a principle.

MRS. BOYLE: Ah, you lost your best principle, me boy, when you lost your arm; them's the only sort o' principles that's any good to a workin' man.

JOHNNY: Ireland only half free'll never be at peace while she has a son left to pull a trigger.

MRS. BOYLE: To be sure, to be sure—no bread's a lot betther than half a loaf. (*Calling loudly in to* BOYLE) Will you hurry up there?

(BOYLE *enters in his best trousers, which aren't too good, and looks very uncomfortable in his collar and tie.*)

MRS. BOYLE: This is me husband; Mr. Boyle, Mr. Bentham.

BENTHAM: Ah, very glad to know you, Mr. Boyle. How are you?

BOYLE: Ah, I'm not too well at all; I suffer terrible with pains in me legs. Juno can tell you there what . . .

MRS. BOYLE: You won't have many pains in your legs when you hear what Mr. Bentham has to tell you.

BENTHAM: Juno! What an interesting name! It reminds one of Homer's glorious story of ancient gods and heroes.

BOYLE: Yis, doesn't it? You see, Juno was born an' christened in June; I met her in June; we were married in June, an' Johnny was born in June, so wan day I says to her, "You should ha' been called Juno," an' the name stuck to her ever since.

MRS. BOYLE: Here we can talk o' them things agen; let Mr. Bentham say what he has to say now.

BENTHAM: Well, Mr. Boyle, I suppose you'll remember a Mr. Ellison of Santry—he's a relative of yours, I think.

BOYLE (*viciously*): Is it that prognosticator an' procrastinator! Of course I remember him.

BENTHAM: Well, he's dead, Mr. Boyle . . .

BOYLE: Sorra many'll go into mournin' for him.

MRS. BOYLE: Wait till you hear what Mr. Bentham has to say, an' then, maybe, you'll change your opinion.

BENTHAM: A week before he died he sent for me to write his will for him. He told me that there were two only that he wished to leave his property to: his second cousin Michael Finnegan of Santry, and John Boyle, his first cousin of Dublin.

BOYLE (*excitedly*): Me, is it me, me?

BENTHAM: You, Mr. Boyle; I'll read a copy of the will that I have here with me, which has been duly filed in the Court of Probate. (*He takes a paper from his pocket and reads*):

6th *February*, 1922.

This is the last Will and Testament of William Ellison, of Santry, in the County of Dublin. I hereby order and wish my property to be sold and divided as follows:—

£20 to the St. Vincent De Paul Society.

£60 for Masses for the repose of my soul (5s. for Each Mass).

The rest of my property to be divided between my first and second cousins.

I hereby appoint Timothy Buckly, of Santry, and Hugh Brierly, of Coolock, to be my Executors.

(*Signed*) WILLIAM ELLISON.
HUGH BRIERLY.
TIMOTHY BUCKLY.
CHARLES BENTHAM, N.T.

BOYLE (*eagerly*): An' how much'll be comin' out of it, Mr. Bentham?

BENTHAM: The Executors told me that half of the property would be anything between £1500 and £2000.

MARY: A fortune, father, a fortune!

JOHNNY: We'll be able to get out o' this place now, an' go somewhere we're not known.

MRS. BOYLE: You won't have to trouble about a job for a while, Jack.

BOYLE (*fervently*): I'll never doubt the goodness o' God agen.

BENTHAM: I congratulate you, Mr. Boyle. (*They shake hands.*)

BOYLE: An' now, Mr. Bentham, you'll have to have a wet.

BENTHAM: A wet?

BOYLE: A wet—a jar—a boul!

MRS. BOYLE: Jack, you're speakin' to Mr. Bentham, an' not to Joxer.

BOYLE (*solemnly*): Juno . . . Mary . . . Johnny . . . we'll have to go into mournin' at wanst. . . . I never expected that poor Bill ud die so sudden. . . . Well, we all have to die some day . . . you,

Juno, today . . . an' me, maybe, tomorrow. . . . It's sad, but it can't be helped. . . . Requiescat in pace . . . or, usin' our oul' tongue like St. Patrick or St. Briget, Guh sayeree jeea ayera!

MARY: Oh, father, that's not Rest in Peace; that's God save Ireland.

BOYLE: U-u-ugh, it's all the same—isn't it a prayer? . . . Juno, I'm done with Joxer; he's nothin' but a prognosticator an' a . . .

JOXER (climbing angrily through the window and bounding into the room): You're done with Joxer, are you? Maybe you thought I'd stop on the roof all the night for you! Joxer out on the roof with the win' blowin' through him was nothin' to you an' your friend with the collar an' tie!

MRS. BOYLE: What in the name o' God brought you out on the roof; what were you doin' there?

JOXER (ironically): I was dhreamin' I was standin' on the bridge of a ship, an' she sailin' the Antarctic Ocean, an' it blowed, an' blowed, an' I lookin' up at the sky an' sayin', what is the stars, what is the stars?

MRS. BOYLE (opening the door and standing at it): Here, get ou' o' this, Joxer Daly; I was always thinkin' you had a slate off.

JOXER (moving to the door): I have to laugh every time I look at the deep sea sailor; an' a row on a river ud make him sea-sick!

BOYLE: Get ou' o' this before I take the law into me own hands!

JOXER (going out): Say aw rewaeawr, but not good-bye. Lookin' for work, an' prayin' to God he won't get it! (He goes.)

MRS. BOYLE: I'm tired tellin' you what Joxer was; maybe now you see yourself the kind he is.

BOYLE: He'll never blow the froth off a pint o' mine agen, that's a sure thing. Johnny . . . Mary . . . you're to keep yourselves to yourselves for the future. Juno, I'm done with Joxer. . . . I'm a new man from this out. . . . (Clasping JUNO's hand, and singing emotionally):

> Oh, me darlin' Juno, I will be thrue to thee;
> Me own, me darlin' Juno, you're all the world to me.

(The Curtain Falls.)

# Act Two

SCENE. *The same, but the furniture is more plentiful, and of a vulgar nature. A glaringly upholstered arm-chair and lounge; cheap pictures and photos everywhere. Every available spot is ornamented with huge vases filled with artificial flowers. Crossed festoons of coloured paper chains stretch from end to end of ceiling. On the table is an old attaché case. It is about six in the evening, and two days after the First Act.* BOYLE, *in his shirt sleeves, is voluptuously stretched on the sofa; he is smoking a clay pipe. He is half asleep. A lamp is lighting on the table. After a few moments' pause the voice of* JOXER *is heard singing softly outside at the door—"Me pipe I'll smoke, as I dhrive me moke—are you there, Mor . . . ee . . . ar . . . i . . teee!"*

BOYLE (*leaping up, takes a pen in his hand and busies himself with papers*): Come along, Joxer, me son, come along.

JOXER (*putting his head in*): Are you be yourself?

BOYLE: Come on, come on; that doesn't matther; I'm masther now, an' I'm goin' to remain masther.

(JOXER *comes in.*)

JOXER: How d'ye feel now, as a man o' money?

BOYLE (*solemnly*): It's a responsibility, Joxer, a great responsibility.

JOXER: I suppose 'tis now, though you wouldn't think it.

BOYLE: Joxer, han' me over that attackey case on the table there. (JOXER *hands the case*) Ever since the Will was passed I've run hundhreds o' dockyments through me han's—I tell you, you have to keep your wits about you. (*He busies himself with papers.*)

JOXER: Well, I won't disturb you; I'll dhrop in when . . .

BOYLE (*hastily*): It's all right, Joxer, this is the last one to be signed today. (*He signs a paper, puts it into the case, which he shuts with a snap, and sits back pompously in the chair*) Now, Joxer, you want to see me; I'm at your service—what can I do for you, me man?

JOXER: I've just dhropped in with the £3 : 5s. that Mrs. Madigan riz on the blankets an' table for you, and she says you're to be in no hurry payin' it back.

BOYLE: She won't be long without it; I expect the first cheque for a couple o' hundhred any day. There's the five bob for yourself—go on, take it, man; it'll not be the last you'll get from the Captain. Now an' agen we have our differ, but we're there together all the time.

JOXER: Me for you, an' you for me, like the two Musketeers.

BOYLE: Father Farrell stopped me today an' tole me how glad he was I fell in for the money.

JOXER: He'll be stoppin' you ofen enough now; I suppose it was "Mr." Boyle with him?

BOYLE: He shuk me be the han'. . . .

JOXER (*ironically*): I met with Napper Tandy, an' he shuk me be the han'!

BOYLE: You're seldom asthray, Joxer, but you're wrong shipped this time. What you're sayin' of Father Farrell is very near to blasfeemey. I don't like any one to talk disrespectful of Father Farrell.

JOXER: You're takin' me up wrong, Captain; I wouldn't let a word be said agen Father Farrell—the heart o' the rowl, that's what he is; I always said he was a darlin' man, a daarlin' man.

BOYLE: Comin' up the stairs who did I meet but that bummer, Nugent. "I seen you talkin' to Father Farrell," says he, with a grin on him. "He'll be folleyin' you," says he, "like a Guardian Angel from this out"—all the time the oul' grin on him, Joxer.

JOXER: I never seen him yet but he had that oul' grin on him!

BOYLE: "Mr. Nugent," says I, "Father Farrell is a man o' the people, an', as far as I know the History of me country, the priests was always in the van of the fight for Irelan's freedom."

JOXER (*fervently*):

> Who was it led the van, Soggart Aroon?
> Since the fight first began, Soggart Aroon?

BOYLE: "Who are you tellin'?" says he. "Didn't they let down the Fenians, an' didn't they do in Parnell? An' now . . ." "You ought to be ashamed o' yourself," says I, interruptin' him, "not to know the History o' your country." An' I left him gawkin' where he was.

JOXER: Where ignorance 's bliss 'tis folly to be wise; I wondher did he ever read the Story o' Irelan'.

BOYLE: Be J. L. Sullivan? Don't you know he didn't?

JOXER: Ah, it's a darlin' buk, a daarlin' buk!

BOYLE: You'd betther be goin', now, Joxer, his Majesty, Bentham, 'll be here any minute, now.

JOXER: Be the way things is lookin', it'll be a match between him an' Mary. She's thrun over Jerry altogether. Well, I hope it will, for he's a darlin' man.

BOYLE: I'm glad you think so—I don't. (*Irritably*) What's darlin' about him?

JOXER (*nonplussed*): I only seen him twiced; if you want to know me, come an' live with me.

BOYLE: He's too ignified for me—to hear him talk you'd think he knew as much as a Boney's Oraculum. He's given up his job as teacher, an' is goin' to become a solicitor in Dublin—he's been studyin' law. I suppose he thinks I'll set him up, but he's wrong shipped. An' th' other fella—Jerry's as bad. The two o' them ud give you a pain in your face, listenin' to them; Jerry believin' in nothin', an' Bentham believin' in everythin'. One that says all is God an' no man; an' th' other that says all is man an' no God!

JOXER: Well, I'll be off now.

BOYLE: Don't forget to dhrop down afther a while; we'll have a quiet jar, an' a song or two.

JOXER: Never fear.

BOYLE: An' tell Mrs. Madigan that I hope we'll have the pleasure of her organization at our little enthertainment.

JOXER: Righto; we'll come down together. (*He goes out.*)

(JOHNNY *comes from room on left, and sits down moodily at the fire.* BOYLE *looks at him for a few moments, and shakes his head. He fills his pipe.*)

VOICE OF JUNO AT THE DOOR: Open the door, Jack; this thing has me nearly kilt with the weight.

(BOYLE *opens the door.* JUNO *enters carrying the box of a gramophone, followed by* MARY *carrying the horn, and some parcels.* JUNO *leaves the box on the table and flops into a chair.*)

JUNO: Carryin' that from Henry Street was no joke.

BOYLE: U-u-ugh, that's a grand lookin' insthrument—how much was it?

JUNO: Pound down, an' five to be paid at two shillin's a week.

BOYLE: That's reasonable enough.

JUNO: I'm afraid we're runnin' into too much debt; first the furniture, an' now this.

BOYLE: The whole lot won't be much out of £2000.

MARY: I don't know what you wanted a gramophone for—I know Charlie hates them; he says they're destructive of real music.

BOYLE: Desthructive of music—that fella ud give you a pain in your face. All a gramophone wants is to be properly played; its thrue wondher is only felt when everythin's quiet—what a gramophone wants is dead silence!

MARY: But, father, Jerry says the same; afther all, you can only appreciate music when your ear is properly trained.

BOYLE: That's another fella ud give you a pain in your face. Properly thrained! I suppose you couldn't appreciate football unless your fut was properly thrained.

MRS. BOYLE (*to* MARY): Go on in ower that an' dress, or Charlie 'll be in on you, an' tay nor nothin' 'll be ready.

(MARY *goes into room left.*)

MRS. BOYLE (*arranging table for tea*): You didn't look at our new gramophone, Johnny?

JOHNNY: 'Tisn't gramophones I'm thinking of.

MRS. BOYLE: An' what is it you're thinkin' of, allanna?

JOHNNY: Nothin', nothin', nothin'.

MRS. BOYLE: Sure, you must be thinkin' of somethin'; it's yourself that has yourself the way y'are; sleepin' wan night in me sisther's, an' the nex' in your father's brother's—you'll get no rest goin' on that way.

JOHNNY: I can rest nowhere, nowhere, nowhere.

MRS. BOYLE: Sure, you're not thryin' to rest anywhere.

JOHNNY: Let me alone, let me alone, let me alone, for God's sake.

(*A knock at street door.*)

MRS. BOYLE (*in a flutter*): Here he is; here's Mr. Bentham!

BOYLE: Well, there's room for him; it's a pity there's not a brass band to play him in.

MRS. BOYLE: We'll han' the tay around, an' not be clusthered round the table, as if we never seen nothin'.

(*Steps are heard approaching, and* JUNO, *opening the door, allows* BENTHAM *to enter.*)

JUNO: Give your hat an' stick to Jack, there . . . sit down, Mr. Bentham . . . no, not there . . . in th' easy chair be the fire . . . there, that's bedther. Mary'll be out to you in a minute.

BOYLE (*solemnly*): I seen be the paper this mornin' that Consols was down half per cent. That's serious, min' you, an' shows the whole counthry's in a state o' chassis.

MRS. BOYLE: What's Consols, Jack?

BOYLE: Consols? Oh, Consols is—oh, there's no use tellin' women what Consols is—th' wouldn't undherstand.

BENTHAM: It's just as you were saying, Mr. Boyle . . .

(MARY *enters charmingly dressed*.)

BENTHAM: Oh, good evening, Mary; how pretty you're looking!

MARY (*archly*): Am I?

BOYLE: We were just talkin' when you kem in, Mary, I was tellin' Mr. Bentham that the whole counthry's in a state o' chassis.

MARY (*to* BENTHAM): Would you prefer the green or the blue ribbon round me hair, Charlie?

MRS. BOYLE: Mary, your father's speakin'.

BOYLE (*rapidly*): I was jus' tellin' Mr. Bentham that the whole counthry's in a state o' chassis.

MARY: I'm sure you're frettin', da, whether it is or no.

MRS. BOYLE: With all our churches an' religions, the worl's not a bit the bether.

BOYLE (*with a commanding gesture*): Tay!

(MARY *and* MRS. BOYLE *dispense the tea*.)

MRS. BOYLE: An' Irelan's takin' a leaf out o' the worl's buk; when we got the makin' of our own laws I thought we'd never stop to look behind us, but instead of that we never stopped to look before us! If the people ud folly up their religion bether there'd be a bether chance for us—what do you think, Mr. Bentham?

BENTHAM: I'm afraid I can't venture to express an opinion on that point, Mrs. Boyle; dogma has no attraction for me.

MRS. BOYLE: I forgot you didn't hold with us; what's this you said you were?

BENTHAM: A Theosophist, Mrs. Boyle.

MRS. BOYLE: An' what in the name o' God's a Theosophist?

BOYLE: A Theosophist, Juno, 's a—tell her, Mr. Bentham, tell her.

BENTHAM: It's hard to explain in a few words: Theosophy's founded on The Vedas, the religious books of the East. Its central theme is the existence of an all-pervading Spirit—the Life-Breath. Nothing really exists but this one Universal Life-Breath. And whatever even seems to exist separately from this Life-Breath, doesn't really exist at all. It is all vital force in man, in all animals, and in all vegetation. This Life-Breath is called the Prawna.

MRS. BOYLE: The Prawna! What a comical name!

BOYLE: Prawna; yis, the Prawna. (*Blowing gently through his lips*) That's the Prawna!

MRS. BOYLE: Whist, whist, Jack.

BENTHAM: The happiness of man depends upon his sympathy with this Spirit. Men who have reached a high state of excellence are called Yogi. Some men become Yogi in a short time, it may take others millions of years.

BOYLE: Yogi! I seen hundhreds of them in the streets o' San Francisco.

BENTHAM: It is said by these Yogi that if we practise certain mental exercises that we would have powers denied to others—for instance, the faculty of seeing things that happen miles and miles away.

MRS. BOYLE: I wouldn't care to meddle with that sort o' belief; it's a very curious religion, altogether.

BOYLE: What's curious about it? Isn't all religions curious? If they weren't, you wouldn't get any one to believe them. But religions is passin' away—they've had their day like everything else. Take the real Dublin people, f'rinstance: they know more about Charlie Chaplin an' Tommy Mix than they do about SS. Peter an' Paul!

MRS. BOYLE: You don't believe in ghosts, Mr. Bentham?

MARY: Don't you know he doesn't, mother?

BENTHAM: I don't know that, Mary. Scientists are beginning to think that what we call ghosts are sometimes seen by persons of a certain nature. They say that sensational actions, such as the killing of a person, demand great energy, and that that energy lingers in the place where the action occurred. People may live in the place and see nothing, when some one may come along whose personality has some peculiar connection with the energy of the place, and, in a flash, the person sees the whole affair.

JOHNNY (*rising swiftly, pale and affected*): What sort o' talk is this to be goin' on with? Is there nothin' betther to be talkin' about but the killin' o' people? My God, isn't it bad enough for these things to happen without talkin' about them! (*He hurriedly goes into the room on left.*)

BENTHAM: Oh, I'm very sorry, Mrs. Boyle; I never thought . . .

MRS. BOYLE (*apologetically*): Never mind, Mr. Bentham, he's very touchy. (*A frightened scream is heard from* JOHNNY *inside.*)

MRS. BOYLE: Mother of God? What's that?

(*He rushes out again, his face pale, his lips twitching, his limbs trembling.*)

JOHNNY: Shut the door, shut the door, quick, for God's sake! Great God, have mercy on me! Blessed Mother o' God, shelter me, shelter your son!

MRS. BOYLE (*catching him in her arms*): What's wrong with you? What ails you? Sit down, sit down, here, on the bed . . . there now . . . there now.

MARY: Johnny, Johnny, what ails you?

JOHNNY: I seen him, I seen him . . . kneelin' in front o' the statue . . . merciful Jesus, have pity on me!

MRS. BOYLE (*to* BOYLE): Get him a glass o' whisky . . . quick, man, an' don't stand gawkin'.

(BOYLE *gets the whisky.*)

JOHNNY: Sit here, sit here, mother . . . between me an' the door.

MRS. BOYLE: I'll sit beside you as long as you like, only tell me what was it came across you at all?

JOHNNY (*after taking some drink*): I seen him. . . . I seen Robbie Tancred kneelin' down before the statue . . . an' the red light shinin' on him . . . an' when I went in . . . he turned an' looked at me . . . an' I seen the woun's bleedin' in his breast. . . . Oh, why did he look at me like that . . . it wasn't my fault that he was done in . . . Mother o' God, keep him away from me!

MRS. BOYLE: There, there, child, you've imagined it all. There was nothin' there at all—it was the red light you seen, an' the talk we had put all the rest into your head. Here, dhrink more o' this—it'll do you good. . . . An', now, stretch yourself down on the bed for a little. (*To* BOYLE) Go in, Jack, an' show him it was only in his own head it was.

BOYLE (*making no move*): E-e-e-e-eh; it's all nonsense; it was only a shadda he saw.

MARY: Mother o' God, he made me heart lep!

BENTHAM: It was simply due to an overwrought imagination—we all get that way at times.

MRS. BOYLE: There, dear, lie down in the bed, an' I'll put the quilt across you . . . e-e-e-eh, that's it . . . you'll be as right as the mail in a few minutes.

JOHNNY: Mother, go into the room an' see if the light's lightin' before the statue.

MRS. BOYLE (*to* BOYLE): Jack, run in, an' see if the light's lightin' before the statue.

BOYLE (*to* MARY): Mary, slip in an' see if the light's lightin' before the statue.

(MARY *hesitates to go in.*)

BENTHAM: It's all right; Mary, I'll go. (*He goes into the room; remains for a few moments, and returns.*)

BENTHAM: Everything's just as it was—the light burning bravely before the statue.

BOYLE: Of course; I knew it was all nonsense.

(*A knock at the door.*)

BOYLE (*going to open the door*): E-e-e-e-eh. (*He opens it, and* JOXER, *followed by* MRS. MADIGAN, *enters.* MRS. MADIGAN *is a strong, dapper little woman of about forty-five; her face is almost always a widespread smile of complacency. She is a woman who, in a manner at least, can mourn with them that mourn, and rejoice with them that do rejoice. When she is feeling comfortable, she is inclined to*

*be reminiscent; when others say anything, or following a statement
made by herself, she has a habit of putting her head a little to one
side, and nodding it rapidly several times in succession, like a bird
pecking at a hard berry. Indeed, she has a good deal of the bird in
her, but the bird instinct is by no means a melodious one. She is
ignorant, vulgar and forward, but her heart is generous withal. For
instance, she would help a neighbour's sick child; she would probably kill the child, but her intentions would be to cure it; she would
be more at home helping a drayman to lift a fallen horse. She is
dressed in a rather soiled grey dress and a vivid purple blouse; in her
hair is a huge comb, ornamented with huge coloured beads. She
enters with a gliding step, beaming smile and nodding head.* BOYLE
*receives them effusively.*)

BOYLE: Come on in, Mrs. Madigan; come on in; I was afraid you
weren't comin'. . . . (*Slyly*) There's some people able to dhress,
ay, Joxer?

JOXER: Fair as the blossoms that bloom in the May, an' sweet as the
scent of the new mown hay. . . . Ah, well she may wear them.

MRS. MADIGAN (*looking at* MARY): I know some as are as sweet as
the blossoms in the May—oh, no names, no pack dhrill!

BOYLE: An', now, I'll inthroduce the pair o' yous to Mary's intended:
Mr. Bentham, this is Mrs. Madigan, an oul' back-parlour neighbour,
that, if she could help it at all, ud never see a body shuk!

BENTHAM (*rising, and tentatively shaking the hand of* MRS. MADI-
GAN): I'm sure, it's a great pleasure to know you, Mrs. Madigan.

MRS. MADIGAN: An' I'm goin' to tell you, Mr. Bentham, you're goin'
to get as nice a bit o' skirt in Mary, there, as ever you seen in your
puff. Not like some of the dhressed up dolls that's knockin' about
lookin' for men when it's a skelpin' they want. I remember as well
as I remember yestherday, the day she was born—of a Tuesday, the
25th o' June, in the year 1901, at thirty-three minutes past wan in
the day be Foley's clock, the pub at the corner o' the street. A cowld
day it was too, for the season o' the year, an' I remember sayin' to
Joxer, there, who I met comin' up th' stairs, that the new arrival in
Boyle's ud grow up a hardy chiselur if it lived, an' that she'd be
somethin' one o' these days that nobody suspected, an' so signs on it,
here she is today, goin' to be married to a young man lookin' as if
he'd be fit to commensurate in any position in life it ud please God
to call him!

BOYLE (*effusively*): Sit down, Mrs. Madigan, sit down, me oul' sport. (*To* BENTHAM) This is Joxer Daly, Past Chief Ranger of the Dear Little Shamrock Branch of the Irish National Foresters, an oul' front-top neighbour, that never despaired, even in the darkest days of Ireland's sorra.

JOXER: Nil desperandum, Captain, nil desperandum.

BOYLE: Sit down, Joxer, sit down. The two of us was often in a tight corner.

MRS. BOYLE: Ay, in Foley's snug!

JOXER: An' we kem out of it flyin', we kem out of it flyin', Captain.

BOYLE: An', now, for a dhrink—I know yous won't refuse an oul' friend.

MRS. MADIGAN (*to* JUNO): Is Johnny not well, Mrs. . . .

MRS. BOYLE (*warningly*): S-s-s-sh.

MRS. MADIGAN: Oh, the poor darlin'.

BOYLE: Well, Mrs. Madigan, is it tay or what?

MRS. MADIGAN: Well, speakin' for meself, I jus' had me tea a minute ago, an' I'm afraid to dhrink any more—I'm never the same when I dhrink too much tay. Thanks, all the same, Mr. Boyle.

BOYLE: Well, what about a bottle o' stout or a dhrop o' whisky?

MRS. MADIGAN: A bottle o' stout ud be a little too heavy for me stummock afther me tay. . . . A-a-ah, I'll thry the ball o' malt.

(BOYLE *prepares the whisky*.)

MRS. MADIGAN: There's nothin' like a ball o' malt occasional like—too much of it isn't good. (*To* BOYLE, *who is adding water*) Ah, God, Johnny, don't put too much wather on it! (*She drinks*) I suppose yous'll be lavin' this place.

BOYLE: I'm looking for a place near the sea; I'd like the place that you might say was me cradle, to be me grave as well. The sea is always callin' me.

JOXER: She is callin', callin', callin', in the win', an' on the sea.

BOYLE: Another dhrop o' whisky, Mrs. Madigan?

MRS. MADIGAN: Well, now, it ud be hard to refuse seein' the suspicious times that's in it.

BOYLE (*with a commanding gesture*): Song! . . . Juno . . . Mary . . . "Home to Our Mount'ins"!

MRS. MADIGAN (*enthusiastically*): Hear, hear!

JOXER: Oh, tha's a darlin' song, a daarlin' song!

MARY (*bashfully*): Ah, no, da; I'm not in a singin' humour.

MRS. MADIGAN: Gawn with you, child, an' you only goin' to be marrid; I remember as well as I remember yesterday,—it was on a lovely August evenin', exactly, accordin' to date, fifteen years ago, come the Tuesday folleyin' the nex' that's comin' on, when me own man (*the Lord be good to him*) an' me was sittin' shy together in a doty little nook on a counthry road, adjacent to The Stiles. "That'll scratch your lovely, little white neck," says he, ketchin' hould of a danglin' bramble branch, holdin' clusters of the loveliest flowers you ever seen, an' breakin' it off, so that his arm fell, accidental like, roun' me waist, an' as I felt it tightenin', an' tightenin', an' tightenin', I thought me buzzum was every minute goin' to burst out into a roystherin' song about

> The little green leaves that were shakin' on the threes,
> The gallivantin' butterflies, an' buzzin' o' the bees!

BOYLE: Ordher for the song!

JUNO: Come on, Mary—we'll do our best. (JUNO *and* MARY *stand up, and choosing a suitable position, sing simply* "Home to Our Mountains.")

(*They bow to company, and return to their places.*)

BOYLE (*emotionally, at the end of the song*): Lull . . . me . . . to . . . rest!

JOXER (*clapping his hands*): Bravo, bravo! Darlin' girulls, darlin' girulls!

MRS. MADIGAN: Juno, I never seen you in bether form.

BENTHAM: Very nicely rendered indeed.

MRS. MADIGAN: A noble call, a noble call!

MRS. BOYLE: What about yourself, Mrs. Madigan? (*After some coaxing*, MRS. MADIGAN *rises, and in a quavering voice sings the following verse*):

> If I were a blackbird I'd whistle and sing;
> I'd follow the ship that my thrue love was in;
> An' on the top riggin', I'd there build me nest,
> An' at night I would sleep on me Willie's white breast!

(*Becoming husky, amid applause, she sits down.*)

MRS. MADIGAN: Ah, me voice is too husky now, Juno; though I remember the time when Maisie Madigan could sing like a nightingale at matin' time. I remember as well as I remember yesterday, at a party given to celebrate the comin' of the first chiselur to Annie an' Benny Jimeson—who was the barber, yous may remember, in Henrietta Street, that, afther Easter Week, hung out a green, white an' orange pole, an', then, when the Tans started their Jazz dancin', whipped it in agen, an' stuck out a red, white an' blue wan instead, given as an excuse that a barber's pole was strictly non-political—singin' "An' You'll Remember Me," with the top notes quiverin' in a dead hush of pethrified attention, folleyed by a clappin' o' han's that shuk the tumblers on the table, an' capped be Jimeson, the barber, sayin' that it was the best rendherin' of "You'll Remember Me" he ever heard in his natural!

BOYLE (*peremptorily*): Ordher for Joxer's song!

JOXER: Ah, no, I couldn't; don't ass me, Captain.

BOYLE: Joxer's song, Joxer's song—give us wan of your shut-eyed wans. (JOXER *settles himself in his chair; takes a drink; clears his throat; solemnly closes his eyes, and begin to sing in a very querulous voice*):

She is far from the lan' where her young hero sleeps,
An' lovers around her are sighing (*He hesitates*)
An' lovers around her are sighin' . . . sighin' . . . sighin' . . .

(*A pause.*)

BOYLE (*imitating* JOXER):

And lovers around her are sighing!

What's the use of you thryin' to sing the song if you don't know it?

MARY: Thry another one, Mr. Daly—maybe you'd be more fortunate.

MRS. MADIGAN: Gawn, Joxer, thry another wan.

JOXER (*starting again*):

I have heard the mavis singin' his love song to the morn;
I have seen the dew-dhrop clingin' to the rose jus' newly born;
    but . . . but . . . (*frantically*) to the rose jus' newly born
    . . . newly born . . . born.

JOHNNY: Mother, put on the gramophone, for God's sake, an' stop Joxer's bawlin'.

BOYLE (*commandingly*): Gramophone! . . . I hate to see fellas thryin' to do what they're not able to do. (BOYLE *arranges the gramophone, and is about to start it, when voices are heard of persons descending the stairs.*)

MRS. BOYLE (*warningly*): Whisht, Jack, don't put it on, don't put it on yet; this must be poor Mrs. Tancred comin' down to go to the hospital—I forgot all about them bringin' the body to the church tonight. Open the door, Mary, an' give them a bit o' light.

(MARY *opens the door, and* MRS. TANCRED—*a very old woman, obviously shaken by the death of her son—appears, accompanied by several neighbours. The first few phrases are spoken before they appear.*)

FIRST NEIGHBOUR: It's a sad journey we're goin' on, but God's good, an' the Republicans won't be always down.

MRS. TANCRED: Ah, what good is that to me now? Whether they're up or down—it won't bring me darlin' boy from the grave.

MRS. BOYLE: Come in an' have a hot cup o' tay, Mrs. Tancred, before you go.

MRS. TANCRED: Ah, I can take nothin' now, Mrs. Boyle—I won't be long afther him.

FIRST NEIGHBOUR: Still an' all, he died a noble death, an' we'll bury him like a king.

MRS. TANCRED: An' I'll go on livin' like a pauper. Ah, what's the pains I suffered bringin' him into the world to carry him to his cradle, to the pains I'm sufferin' now, carryin' him out o' the world to bring him to his grave!

MARY: It would be better for you not to go at all, Mrs. Tancred, but to stay at home beside the fire with some o' the neighbours.

MRS. TANCRED: I seen the first of him, an' I'll see the last of him.

MRS. BOYLE: You'd want a shawl, Mrs. Tancred; it's a cowld night, an' the win's blowin' sharp.

MRS. MADIGAN (*rushing out*): I've a shawl above.

MRS. TANCRED: Me home is gone, now; he was me only child, an' to think that he was lyin' for a whole night stretched out on the side of a lonely counthry lane, with his head, his darlin' head, that I ofen kissed an' fondled, half hidden in the wather of a runnin' brook. An' I'm told he was the leadher of the ambush where me nex' door neighbour, Mrs. Mannin', lost her Free State soldier son. An' now here's the two of us oul' women, standin' one on each side of a scales o' sorra, balanced be the bodies of our two dead darlin' sons. (MRS. MADIGAN *returns, and wraps a shawl around her*) God bless you, Mrs. Madigan. . . . (*She moves slowly towards the door*) Mother o' God, Mother o' God, have pity on the pair of us! . . . O Blessed Virgin, where were you when me darlin' son was riddled with bullets, when me darlin' son was riddled with bullets! . . . Sacred Heart of the Crucified Jesus, take away our hearts o' stone . . . an' give us hearts o' flesh! . . . Take away this murdherin' hate . . . an' give us Thine own eternal love! (*They pass out of the room.*)

MRS. BOYLE (*explanatorily to* BENTHAM): That was Mrs. Tancred of the two-pair back; her son was found, e'er yesterday, lyin' out beyant Finglas riddled with bullets. A die-hard he was, be all accounts. He was a nice quiet boy, but lattherly he went to hell, with his Republic first, an' Republic last an' Republic over all. He ofen took tea with us here, in the oul' days, an' Johnny, there, an' him used to be always together.

JOHNNY: Am I always to be havin' to tell you that he was no friend o' mine? I never cared for him, an' he could never stick me. It's not because he was Commandant of the Battalion that I was Quarther-Masther of, that we were friends.

MRS. BOYLE: He's gone, now—the Lord be good to him! God help his poor oul' creature of a mother, for no matther whose friend or enemy he was, he was her poor son.

BENTHAM: The whole thing is terrible, Mrs. Boyle; but the only way to deal with a mad dog is to destroy him.

MRS. BOYLE: An' to think of me forgettin' about him bein' brought to the church tonight, an' we singin' an' all, but it was well we hadn't the gramophone goin', anyhow.

BOYLE: Even if we had aself. We've nothin' to do with these things, one way or t'other. That's the Government's business, an' let them do what we're payin' them for doin'.

MRS. BOYLE: I'd like to know how a body's not to mind these things; look at the way they're afther leavin' the people in this very house. Hasn't the whole house, nearly, been massacreed? There's young Mrs. Dougherty's husband with his leg off; Mrs. Travers that had her son blew up be a mine in Inchegeela, in Co. Cork; Mrs. Mannin' that lost wan of her sons in an ambush a few weeks ago, an' now, poor Mrs. Tancred's only child gone West with his body made a collandher of. Sure, if it's not our business, I don't know whose business it is.

BOYLE: Here, there, that's enough about them things; they don't affect us, an' we needn't give a damn. If they want a wake, well, let them have a wake. When I was a sailor, I was always resigned to meet with a watery grave; an', if they want to be soldiers, well, there's no use o' them squealin' when they meet a soldier's fate.

JOXER: Let me like a soldier fall—me breast expandin' to th' ball!

MRS. BOYLE: In wan way, she deserves all she got; for lately, she let th' die-hards make an open house of th' place; an' for th' last couple of months, either when th' sun was risin', or when th' sun was settin', you had C.I.D. men burstin' into your room, assin' you where were you born, where were you christened, where were you married, an' where would you be buried!

JOHNNY: For God's sake, let us have no more o' this talk.

MRS. MADIGAN: What about Mr. Boyle's song before we start th' gramophone?

MARY (*getting her hat, and putting it on*): Mother, Charlie and I are goin' out for a little sthroll.

MRS. BOYLE: All right, darlin'.

BENTHAM (*going out with* MARY): We won't be long away, Mrs. Boyle.

MRS. MADIGAN: Gwan, Captain, gwan.

BOYLE: E-e-e-e-eh, I'd want to have a few more jars in me, before I'd be in fettle for singin'.

JOXER: Give us that poem you writ t'other day. (*To the rest*) Aw, it's a darlin' poem, a daarlin' poem.

MRS. BOYLE: God bless us, is he startin' to write poetry!

BOYLE (*rising to his feet*): E-e-e-e-eh. (*He recites in an emotional, consequential manner the following verses*):

Shawn an' I were friends, sir, to me he was all in all.
His work was very heavy and his wages were very small.
None betther on th' beach as Docker, I'll go bail,
'Tis now I'm feelin' lonely, for today he lies in jail.
He was not what some call pious—seldom at church or prayer;
For the greatest scoundrels I know, sir, goes every Sunday there.
Fond of his pint—well, rather, but hated the Boss by creed
But never refused a copper to comfort a pal in need.

E-e-e-e-eh. (*He sits down.*)

MRS. MADIGAN: Grand, grand; you should folley that up, you should folley that up.

JOXER: It's a daarlin' poem!

BOYLE (*delightedly*): E-e-e-e-eh.

JOHNNY: Are yous goin' to put on th' gramophone tonight, or are yous not?

MRS. BOYLE: Gwan, Jack, put on a record.

MRS. MADIGAN: Gwan, Captain, gwan.

BOYLE: Well, yous'll want to keep a dead silence. (*He sets a record, starts the machine, and it begins to play "If you're Irish, come into the Parlour." As the tune is in full blare, the door is suddenly opened by a brisk, little bald-headed man, dressed circumspectly in a black suit; he glares fiercely at all in the room; he is "NEEDLE NUGENT," a tailor. He carries his hat in his hands.*)

NUGENT (*loudly, above the noise of the gramophone*): Are yous goin' to have that thing bawlin' an' the funeral of Mrs. Tancred's son passin' the house? Have none of yous any respect for the Irish people's National regard for the dead?

(BOYLE *stops the gramophone.*)

MRS. BOYLE: Maybe, Needle Nugent, it's nearly time we had a little less respect for the dead, an' a little more regard for the livin'.

MRS. MADIGAN: We don't want you, Mr. Nugent, to teach us what we learned at our mother's knee. You don't look yourself as if you were dyin' of grief; if y'ass Maisie Madigan anything, I'd call you a real thrue die-hard an' live-soft Republican, attendin' Republican funerals in the day, an' stoppin' up half the night makin' suits for the Civic Guards! (*Persons are heard running down to the street, some saying, "Here it is, here it is." NUGENT withdraws, and the rest, except JOHNNY, go to the window looking into the street, and look out. Sounds of a crowd coming nearer are heard; portion are singing*):

> To Jesus' Heart all burning
> With fervent love for men,
> My heart with fondest yearning
> Shall raise its joyful strain.
> While ages course along,
> Blest be with loudest song,
> The Sacred Heart of Jesus
> By every heart and tongue.

MRS. BOYLE: Here's the hearse, here's the hearse!

BOYLE: There's t'oul' mother walkin' behin' the coffin.

MRS. MADIGAN: You can hardly see the coffin with the wreaths.

JOXER: Oh, it's a darlin' funeral, a daarlin' funeral!

MRS. MADIGAN: We'd have a betther view from the street.

BOYLE: Yes—this place ud give you a crick in your neck. (*They leave the room, and go down. JOHNNY sits moodily by the fire.*)

(*A young man enters; he looks at* JOHNNY *for a moment.*)

THE YOUNG MAN: Quarther-Master Boyle.

JOHNNY (*with a start*): The Mobilizer!

THE YOUNG MAN: You're not at the funeral?

JOHNNY: I'm not well.

THE YOUNG MAN: I'm glad I've found you; you were stoppin' at your aunt's; I called there but you'd gone. I've to give you an ordher to attend a Battalion Staff meetin' the night afther tomorrow.

JOHNNY: Where?

THE YOUNG MAN: I don't know; you're to meet me at the Pillar at eight o'clock; then we're to go to a place I'll be told of tonight; there we'll meet a mothor that'll bring us to the meeting. They think you might be able to know somethin' about them that gave the bend where Commandant Tancred was shelterin'.

JOHNNY: I'm not goin', then. I know nothing about Tancred.

THE YOUNG MAN (*at the door*): You'd betther come for your own sake—remember your oath.

JOHNNY (*passionately*): I won't go! Haven't I done enough for Ireland! I've lost me arm, an' me hip's desthroyed so that I'll never be able to walk right agen! Good God, haven't I done enough for Ireland?

THE YOUNG MAN: Boyle, no man can do enough for Ireland! (*He goes.*)

(*Faintly in the distance the crowd is heard saying*:)

> Hail, Mary, full of grace, the Lord is with Thee;
> Blessed art Thou amongst women, and blessed, etc.

(*The Curtain Falls.*)

# Act Three

SCENE: *The same as Act Two. It is about half-past six on a November evening; a bright fire is burning in the grate;* MARY, *dressed to go out, is sitting on a chair by the fire, leaning forward, her hands under her chin, her elbows on her knees. A look of dejection, mingled with uncertain anxiety, is on her face. A lamp, turned low, is lighting on the table. The votive light under the picture of the Virgin, gleams more redly than ever.* MRS. BOYLE *is putting on her hat and coat. It is two months later.*

MRS. BOYLE: An' has Bentham never even written to you since—not one line for the past month?

MARY (*tonelessly*): Not even a line, mother.

MRS. BOYLE: That's very curious. . . . What came between the two of yous at all? To leave you so sudden, an' yous so great together. . . . To go away t' England, an' not to even leave you his address. . . . The way he was always bringin' you to dances, I thought he was mad afther you. Are you sure you said nothin' to him?

MARY: No, mother—at least nothing that could possibly explain his givin' me up.

MRS. BOYLE: You know you're a bit hasty at times, Mary, an' say things you shouldn't say.

MARY: I never said to him what I shouldn't say, I'm sure of that.

MRS. BOYLE: How are you sure of it?

MARY: Because I love him with all my heart and soul, mother. Why, I don't know; I often thought to myself that he wasn't the man poor Jerry was, but I couldn't help loving him, all the same.

MRS. BOYLE: But you shouldn't be frettin' the way you are; when a woman loses a man, she never knows what she's afther losin', to be

412

sure, but, then, she never knows what she's afther gainin', either. You're not the one girl of a month ago—you look like one pinin' away. It's long ago I had a right to bring you to the doctor, instead of waitin' till tonight.

MARY: There's no necessity, really, mother, to go to the doctor; nothing serious is wrong with me—I'm run down and disappointed, that's all.

MRS. BOYLE: I'll not wait another minute; I don't like the look of you at all. . . . I'm afraid we made a mistake in throwin' over poor Jerry. . . . He'd have been betther for you than that Bentham.

MARY: Mother, the best man for a woman is the one for whom she has the most love, and Charlie had it all.

MRS. BOYLE: Well, there's one thing to be said for him—he couldn't have been thinkin' of the money, or he wouldn't ha' left you . . . it must ha' been somethin' else.

MARY (*wearily*): I don't know . . . I don't know, mother . . . only I think . . .

MRS. BOYLE: What d'ye think?

MARY: I imagine . . . he thought . . . we weren't . . . good enough for him.

MRS. BOYLE: An' what was he himself, only a school teacher? Though I don't blame him for fightin' shy of people like that Joxer fella an' that oul' Madigan wan—nice sort o' people for your father to introduce to a man like Mr. Bentham. You might have told me all about this before now, Mary; I don't know why you like to hide everything from your mother; you knew Bentham, an' I'd ha' known nothin' about it if it hadn't bin for the Will; an' it was only today, afther long coaxin', that you let out that he'd left you.

MARY: It would have been useless to tell you—you wouldn't understand.

MRS. BOYLE (*hurt*): Maybe not. . . . Maybe I wouldn't understand. . . . Well, we'll be off now. (*She goes over to the door left, and speaks to* BOYLE *inside.*)

MRS. BOYLE: We're goin' now to the doctor's. Are you goin' to get up this evenin'?

BOYLE (*from inside*): The pains in me legs is terrible! It's me should be poppin' off to the doctor instead o' Mary, the way I feel.

MRS. BOYLE: Sorra mend you! A nice way you were in last night—carried in a frog's march, dead to the world. If that's the way you'll go on when you get the money it'll be the grave for you, an asylum for me and the Poorhouse for Johnny.

BOYLE: I thought you were goin'?

MRS. BOYLE: That's what has you as you are—you can't bear to be spoken to. Knowin' the way we are, up to our ears in debt, it's a wondher you wouldn't ha' got up to go to th' solicitor's an' see if we could ha' gettin' a little o' the money even.

BOYLE (*shouting*): I can't be goin' up there night, noon an' mornin', can I? He can't give the money till he gets it, can he? I can't get blood out of a turnip, can I?

MRS. BOYLE: It's nearly two months since we heard of the Will, an' the money seems as far off as ever. . . . I suppose you know we owe twenty poun's to oul' Murphy?

BOYLE: I've a faint recollection of you tellin' me that before.

MRS. BOYLE: Well, you'll go over to the shop yourself for the things in future—I'll face him no more.

BOYLE: I thought you said you were goin'?

MRS. BOYLE: I'm goin' now; come on, Mary.

BOYLE: Ey, Juno, ey!

MRS. BOYLE: Well, what d'ye want now?

BOYLE: Is there e'er a bottle o' stout left?

MRS. BOYLE: There's two o' them here still.

BOYLE: Show us in one o' them an' leave t'other there till I get up. An' throw us in the paper that's on the table, an' the bottle o' Sloan's Liniment that's in th' drawer.

MRS. BOYLE (*getting the liniment and the stout*): What paper is it you want—the *Messenger*?

BOYLE: *Messenger! The News o' the World!*

(MRS. BOYLE *brings in the things asked for and comes out again.*)

MRS. BOYLE (*at door*): Mind the candle, now, an' don't burn the house over our heads. I left t'other bottle o' stout on the table. (*She puts bottle of stout on table. She goes out with* MARY. *A cork is heard popping inside.*)

(*A pause; then outside the door is heard the voice of* JOXER *lilting softly:* "Me pipe I'll smoke, as I dhrive me moke . . . are you . . . there . . . More . . . aar . . . i . . . tee!" *A gentle knock is heard and, after a pause, the door opens, and* JOXER, *followed by* NUGENT, *enters.*)

JOXER: Be God, they must all be out; I was thinkin' there was somethin' up when he didn't answer the signal. We seen Juno an' Mary goin', but I didn't see him, an' it's very seldom he escapes me.

NUGENT: He's not goin' to escape me—he's not goin' to be let go to the fair altogether.

JOXER: Sure, the house couldn't hould them lately; an' he goin' about like a mastherpiece of the Free State counthry; forgettin' their friends; forgettin' God—wouldn't even lift his hat passin' a chapel! Sure they were bound to get a dhrop! An' you really think there's no money comin' to him afther all?

NUGENT: Not as much as a red rex, man; I've been a bit anxious this long time over me money, an' I went up to the solicitor's to find out all I could—ah, man, they were goin' to throw me down the stairs. They toul' me that the oul' cock himself had the stairs worn away comin' up afther it, an' they black in the face tellin' him he'd get nothin'. Some way or another that the Will is writ he won't be entitled to get as much as a make!

JOXER: Ah, I thought there was somethin' curious about the whole thing; I've bin havin' sthrange dreams for the last couple o' weeks. An' I notice that that Bentham fella doesn't be comin' here now— there must be somethin' on the mat there too. Anyhow, who, in the name o' God, ud leave anythin' to that oul' bummer? Sure it ud be unnatural. An' the way Juno an' him's been throwin' their weight about for the last few months! Ah, him that goes a borrowin' goes a sorrowin'!

NUGENT: Well, he's not goin' to throw his weight about in the suit I made for him much longer. I'm tellin' you seven poun's aren't to be found growin' on the bushes these days.

JOXER: An' there isn't hardly a neighbour in the whole street that hasn't lent him money on the strength of what he was goin' to get, but they're after backing the wrong horse. Wasn't it a mercy o' God that I'd nothin' to give him! The softy I am, you know, I'd ha' lent him me last juice! I must have had somebody's good prayers. Ah, afther all, an honest man's the noblest work o' God!

(BOYLE *coughs inside.*)

JOXER: Whisht, damn it, he must be inside in bed.

NUGENT: Inside o' bed or outside of it he's goin' to pay me for that suit, or give it back—he'll not climb up my back as easily as he thinks.

JOXER: Gwan in at wanst, man, an' get if off him, an' don't be a fool.

NUGENT (*going to the door left, opening it and looking in*): Ah, don't disturb yourself, Mr. Boyle; I hope you're not sick?

BOYLE: Th' oul' legs, Mr. Nugent, the oul' legs.

NUGENT: I just called over to see if you could let me have anything off the suit?

BOYLE: E-e-e-eh, how much is this it is?

NUGENT: It's the same as it was at the start—seven poun's.

BOYLE: I'm glad you kem, Mr. Nugent; I want a good heavy top-coat—Irish frieze, if you have it. How much would a top-coat like that be now?

NUGENT: About six poun's.

BOYLE: Six poun's—six an' seven, six an' seven is thirteen—that'll be thirteen poun's I'll owe you.

(JOXER *slips the bottle of stout that is on the table into his pocket.* NUGENT *rushes into the room, and returns with the suit on his arm; he pauses at the door.*)

NUGENT: You'll owe me no thirteen poun's. Maybe you think you're betther able to owe it than pay it!

BOYLE (*frantically*): Here, come back to hell ower that—where're you goin' with them clothes o' mine?

NUGENT: Where am I goin' with them clothes o' yours? Well, I like your damn cheek!

BOYLE: Here, what am I going to dhress meself in when I'm goin' out?

NUGENT: What do I care what you dhress yourself in? You can put yourself in a bolsther cover, if you like. (*He goes towards the other door, followed by* JOXER.)

JOXER: What'll he dhress himself in! Gentleman Jack an' his frieze coat!

(*They go out.*)

BOYLE (*inside*): Ey, Nugent, ey, Mr. Nugent, Mr. Nugent!

(*After a pause* BOYLE *enters hastily, buttoning the braces of his moleskin trousers; his coat and vest are on his arm; he throws these on a chair and hurries to the door on right.*)

BOYLE: Ey, Mr. Nugent, Mr. Nugent!

JOXER (*meeting him at the door*): What's up, what's wrong, Captain?

BOYLE: Nugent's been here an' took away me suit—the only things I had to go out in!

JOXER: Tuk your suit—for God's sake! An' what were you doin' while he was takin' them?

BOYLE: I was in bed when he stole in like a thief in the night, an' before I knew even what he was thinkin' of, he whipped them from the chair, an' was off like a redshank!

JOXER: An' what, in the name o' God, did he do that for?

BOYLE: What did he do it for? How the hell do I know what he done it for? Jealousy an' spite, I suppose.

JOXER: Did he not say what he done it for?

BOYLE: Amn't I afther tellin' you that he had them whipped up an' was gone before I could open me mouth?

JOXER: That was a very sudden thing to do; there mus' be somethin' behin' it. Did he hear anythin', I wondher?

BOYLE: Did he hear anythin'?—you talk very queer, Joxer—what could he hear?

JOXER: About you not gettin' the money, in some way or t'other?

BOYLE: An' what ud prevent me from gettin' th' money?

JOXER: That's jus' what I was thinkin'—what ud prevent you from gettin' the money—nothin', as far as I can see.

BOYLE (*looking round for bottle of stout with an exclamation*): Aw, holy God!

JOXER: What's up, Jack?

BOYLE: He must have afther lifted the bottle o' stout that Juno left on the table!

JOXER (*horrified*): Ah, no, ah, no! He wouldn't be afther doin' that, now.

BOYLE: An' who done it then? Juno left a bottle o' stout here, an' it's gone—it didn't walk, did it?

JOXER: Oh, that's shockin'; ah, man's inhumanity to man makes countless thousands mourn!

MRS. MADIGAN (*appearing at the door*): I hope I'm not disturbin' you in any discussion on your forthcomin' legacy—if I may use the word—an' that you'll let me have a barny for a minute or two with you, Mr. Boyle.

BOYLE (*uneasily*): To be sure, Mrs. Madigan—an oul' friend's always welcome.

JOXER: Come in the evenin', come in th' mornin'; come when you're assed, or come without warnin', Mrs. Madigan.

BOYLE: Sit down, Mrs. Madigan.

MRS. MADIGAN (*ominously*): Th' few words I have to say can be said standin'. Puttin' aside all formularies, I suppose you remember me lendin' you some time ago three poun's that I raised on blankets an' furniture in me uncle's?

BOYLE: I remember it well. I have it recorded in me book—three poun's five shillin's from Maisie Madigan, raised on articles pawned;

an', item: fourpence, given to make up the price of a pint, on th' principle that no bird ever flew on wan wing; all to be repaid at par, when the ship comes home.

MRS. MADIGAN: Well, ever since I shoved in the blankets I've been perishing with th' cowld, an' I've decided, if I'll be too hot in th' nex' world aself, I'm not goin' to be too cowld in this wan; an' consequently, I want me three poun's, if you please.

BOYLE: This is a very sudden demand, Mrs. Madigan, an' can't be met; but I'm willin' to give you a receipt in full, in full.

MRS. MADIGAN: Come on, out with th' money, an' don't be jack-actin'.

BOYLE: You can't get blood out of a turnip, can you?

MRS. MADIGAN (*rushing over and shaking him*): Gimme me money, y'oul' reprobate, or I'll shake the worth of it out of you!

BOYLE: Ey, houl' on, there; houl' on, there! You'll wait for your money now, me lassie!

MRS. MADIGAN (*looking around the room and seeing the gramophone*): I'll wait for it, will I? Well, I'll not wait long; if I can't get th' cash, I'll get th' worth of it. (*She catches up the gramophone.*)

BOYLE: Ey, ey, there, wher'r you goin' with that?

MRS. MADIGAN: I'm goin' to th' pawn to get me three quid five shillin's; I'll bring you th' ticket, an' then you can do what you like, me bucko.

BOYLE: You can't touch that, you can't touch that! It's not my property, an' it's not ped for yet!

MRS. MADIGAN: So much th' betther. It'll be an ayse to me conscience, for I'm takin' what doesn't belong to you. You're not goin' to be swankin' it like a paycock with Maisie Madigan's money—I'll pull some o' the gorgeous feathers out o' your tail! (*She goes off with the gramophone.*)

BOYLE: What's th' world comin' to at all? I ass you, Joxer Daly, is there any morality left anywhere?

JOXER: I wouldn't ha' believed it, only I seen it with me own two eyes. I didn't think Maisie Madigan was that sort of a woman; she has either a sup taken, or she's heard somethin'.

BOYLE: Heard somethin'—about what, if it's not any harm to ass you?

JOXER: She must ha' heard some rumour or other that you weren't goin' to get th' money.

BOYLE: Who says I'm not goin' to get th' money?

JOXER: Sure, I know—I was only sayin'.

BOYLE: Only sayin' what?

JOXER: Nothin'.

BOYLE: You were goin' to say somethin', don't be a twisther.

JOXER (*angrily*): Who's a twisther?

BOYLE: Why don't you speak your mind, then?

JOXER: You never twisted yourself—no, you wouldn't know how!

BOYLE: Did you ever know me to twist; did you ever know me to twist?

JOXER (*fiercely*): Did you ever do anythin' else! Sure, you can't believe a word that comes out o' your mouth.

BOYLE: Here, get out, ower o' this; I always knew you were a prognosticator an' a procrastinator!

JOXER (*going out as* JOHNNY *comes in*): The anchor's weighed, farewell, re . . . mem . . . ber . . . me. Jacky Boyle, Esquire, infernal rogue an' damned liar!

JOHNNY: Joxer an' you at it agen?—when are you goin' to have a little respect for yourself, an' not be always makin' a show of us all?

BOYLE: Are you goin' to lecture me now?

JOHNNY: Is mother back from the doctor yet, with Mary?

(MRS. BOYLE *enters; it is apparent from the serious look on her face that something has happened. She takes off her hat and coat without a word and puts them by. She then sits down near the fire, and there is a few moments' pause.*)

BOYLE: Well, what did the doctor say about Mary?

MRS. BOYLE (*in an earnest manner and with suppressed agitation*): Sit down here, Jack; I've something to say to you . . . about Mary.

BOYLE (*awed by her manner*): About . . . Mary?

MRS. BOYLE: Close that door there and sit down here.

BOYLE (*closing the door*): More throuble in our native land, is it? (*He sits down*) Well, what is it?

MRS. BOYLE: It's about Mary.

BOYLE: Well, what about Mary—there's nothin' wrong with her, is there?

MRS. BOYLE: I'm sorry to say there's a gradle wrong with her.

BOYLE: A gradle wrong with her! (*Peevishly*) First Johnny an' now Mary; is the whole house goin' to become an hospital! It's not consumption, is it?

MRS. BOYLE: No . . . it's not consumption . . . it's worse.

JOHNNY: Worse! Well, we'll have to get her into some place ower this, there's no one here to mind her.

MRS. BOYLE: We'll all have to mind her now. You might as well know now, Johnny, as another time. (*To* BOYLE) D'ye know what the doctor said to me about her, Jack?

BOYLE: How ud I know—I wasn't there, was I?

MRS. BOYLE: He told me to get her married at wanst.

BOYLE: Married at wanst! An' why did he say the like o' that?

MRS. BOYLE: Because Mary's goin' to have a baby in a short time.

BOYLE: Goin' to have a baby!—my God, what'll Bentham say when he hears that?

MRS. BOYLE: Are you blind, man, that you can't see that it was Bentham that has done this wrong to her?

BOYLE (*passionately*): Then he'll marry her, he'll have to marry her!

MRS. BOYLE: You know he's gone to England, an' God knows where he is now.

BOYLE: I'll folley him, I'll folley him, an' bring him back, an' make him do her justice. The scoundrel, I might ha' known what he was, with his yogees an' his prawna!

MRS. BOYLE: We'll have to keep it quiet till we see what we can do.

BOYLE: Oh, isn't this a nice thing to come on top o' me, an' the state I'm in! A pretty show I'll be to Joxer an' to that oul' wan, Madigan! Amn't I afther goin' through enough without havin' to go through this!

MRS. BOYLE: What you an' I'll have to go through'll be nothin' to what poor Mary'll have to go through; for you an' me is middlin' old, an' most of our years is spent; but Mary'll have maybe forty years to face an' handle, an' every wan of them'll be tainted with a bitther memory.

BOYLE: Where is she? Where is she till I tell her off? I'm tellin' you when I'm done with her she'll be a sorry girl!

MRS. BOYLE: I left her in me sisther's till I came to speak to you. You'll say nothin' to her, Jack; ever since she left school she's earned her livin', an' your fatherly care never throubled the poor girl.

BOYLE: Gwan, take her part agen her father! But I'll let you see whether I'll say nothin' to her or no! Her an' her readin'! That's more o' th' blasted nonsense that has the house fallin' down on top of us! What did th' likes of her, born in a tenement house, want with readin'? Her readin's afther bringin' her to a nice pass—oh, it's madnin', madnin', madnin'!

MRS. BOYLE: When she comes back say nothin' to her, Jack, or she'll leave this place.

BOYLE: Leave this place! Ay, she'll leave this place, an' quick too!

MBS. BOYLE: If Mary goes, I'll go with her.

BOYLE: Well, go with her! Well, go, th' pair o' yous! I lived before I seen yous, an' I can live when yous are gone. Isn't this a nice thing to come rollin' in on top o' me afther all your prayin' to St. Anthony an' The Little Flower. An' she's a child o' Mary, too—I wonder what'll the nuns think of her now? An' it'll be bellows'd all over th' disthrict before you could say Jack Robinson; an' whenever I'm seen they'll whisper, "That's th' father of Mary Boyle that had th' kid be th' swank she used to go with; d'ye know, d'ye know?" To be sure they'll know—more about it than I will meself!

JOHNNY: She should be dhriven out o' th' house she's brought disgrace on!

MRS. BOYLE: Hush, you, Johnny. We needn't let it be bellows'd all over the place; all we've got to do is to leave this place quietly an' go somewhere where we're not known, an' nobody'll be the wiser.

BOYLE: You're talkin' like a two-year-oul', woman. Where'll we get a place ou' o' this?—places aren't that easily got.

MRS. BOYLE: But, Jack, when we get the money . . .

BOYLE: Money—what money?

MRS. BOYLE: Why, oul' Ellison's money, of course.

BOYLE: There's no money comin' from oul' Ellison, or any one else. Since you heard of wan throuble, you might as well hear of another. There's no money comin' to us at all—the Will's a wash out!

MRS. BOYLE: What are you sayin', man—no money?

JOHNNY: How could it be a wash out?

BOYLE: The boyo that's afther doin' it to Mary done it to me as well. The thick made out the Will wrong; he said in th' Will, only first cousin an' second cousin, instead of mentionin' our names, an' now any one that thinks he's a first cousin or second cousin t'oul' Ellison can claim the money as well as me, an' they're springin' up in hundreds, an' comin' from America an' Australia, thinkin' to get their whack out of it, while all the time the lawyers is gobblin' it up, till there's not as much as ud buy a stockin' for your lovely daughter's baby!

MRS. BOYLE: I don't believe it, I don't believe it, I don't believe it!

JOHNNY: Why did you nothin' about this before?

MRS. BOYLE: You're not serious, Jack; you're not serious!

BOYLE: I'm tellin' you the scholar, Bentham, made a banjax o' th' Will; instead o' sayin', "th' rest o' me property to be divided between me first cousin, Jack Boyle, an' me second cousin, Mick Finnegan, o' Santhry," he writ down only, "me first an' second cousins," an' the world an' his wife are afther th' property now.

MRS. BOYLE: Now, I know why Bentham left poor Mary in th' lurch; I can see it all now—oh, is there not even a middlin' honest man left in th' world?

JOHNNY (to BOYLE): An' you let us run into debt, an' you borreyed money from everybody to fill yourself with beer! An' now, you tell us the whole thing's a wash out! Oh, if it's thrue, I'm done with you, for you're worse than me sisther Mary!

BOYLE: You hole your tongue, d'ye hear? I'll not take any lip from you. Go an' get Bentham if you want satisfaction for all that's afther happenin' us.

JOHNNY: I won't hole me tongue, I won't hole me tongue! I'll tell you what I think of you, father an' all as you are . . . you . . .

MRS. BOYLE: Johnny, Johnny, Johnny, for God's sake, be quiet!

JOHNNY: I'll not be quiet, I'll not be quiet; he's a nice father, isn't he? Is it any wondher Mary went asthray, when . . .

MRS. BOYLE: Johnny, Johnny, for my sake be quiet—for your mother's sake!

BOYLE: I'm goin' out now to have a few dhrinks with th' last few makes I have, an' tell that lassie o' yours not to be here when I come back; for if I lay me eyes on her, I'll lay me han's on her, an' if I lay me han's on her, I won't be accountable for me actions!

JOHNNY: Take care somebody doesn't lay his han's on you—y'oul' . . .

MRS. BOYLE: Johnny, Johnny!

BOYLE (at door, about to go out): Oh, a nice son, an' a nicer daughter, I have. (Calling loudly upstairs) Joxer, Joxer, are you there?

JOXER (from a distance): I'm here, More . . . ee . . . aar . . . i . . . tee!

BOYLE: I'm goin' down to Foley's—are you comin'?

JOXER: Come with you? With that sweet call me heart is stirred; I'm only waiting for the word, an' I'll be with you, like a bird!

(BOYLE and JOXER pass the door going out.)

JOHNNY (throwing himself on the bed): I've a nice sisther, an' a nice father, there's no bettin' on it. I wish to God a bullet or a bomb had whipped me ou' o' this long ago! Not one o' yous, not one o' yous, have any thought for me!

MRS. BOYLE (with passionate remonstrance): If you don't whisht, Johnny, you'll drive me mad. Who has kep' th' home together for the past few years—only me. An' who'll have to bear th' biggest part o' this throuble but me—but whinin' an' whingin' isn't going to do any good.

JOHNNY: You're to blame yourself for a gradle of it—givin' him his own way in everything, an' never assin' to check him, no matther what he done. Why didn't you look afther th' money? why . . .

(*There is a knock at the door;* MRS. BOYLE *opens it;* JOHNNY *rises on his elbow to look and listen; two men enter.*)

FIRST MAN: We've been sent up be th' Manager of the Hibernian Furnishing Co., Mrs. Boyle, to take back the furniture that was got a while ago

MRS. BOYLE: Yous'll touch nothin' here—how do I know who yous are?

FIRST MAN (*showing a paper*): There's the ordher, ma'am. (*Reading*) A chest o' drawers, a table, wan easy an' two ordinary chairs; wan mirror; wan chestherfield divan, an' a wardrobe an' two vases. (*To his comrade*) Come on, Bill, it's afther knockin' off time already.

JOHNNY: For God's sake, mother, run down to Foley's an' bring father back, or we'll be left without a stick.

(*The men carry out the table.*)

MRS. BOYLE: What good would it be? You heard what he said before he went out.

JOHNNY: Can't you thry? He ought to be here, an' the like of this goin' on.

(MRS. BOYLE *puts a shawl around her, as* MARY *enters.*)

MARY: What's up, mother? I met men carryin' away the table, an' everybody's talking about us not gettin' the money after all.

MRS. BOYLE: Everythin's gone wrong, Mary, everythin'. We're not gettin' a penny out o' the Will, not a penny—I'll tell you all when I come back; I'm goin' for your father. (*She runs out.*)

JOHNNY (*to* MARY, *who has sat down by the fire*): It's a wondher you're not ashamed to show your face here, afther what has happened.

(JERRY *enters slowly; there is a look of earnest hope on his face. He looks at* MARY *for a few moments.*)

JERRY (*softly*): Mary!

(MARY *does not answer.*)

JERRY: Mary, I want to speak to you for a few moments, may I?

(MARY *remains silent;* JOHNNY *goes slowly into room on left.*)

JERRY: Your mother has told me everything, Mary, and I have come to you. . . . I have come to tell you, Mary, that my love for you is greater and deeper than ever. . . .

MARY (*with a sob*): Oh, Jerry, Jerry, say no more; all that is over now; anything like that is impossible now!

JERRY: Impossible? Why do you talk like that, Mary?

MARY: After all that has happened.

JERRY: What does it matter what has happened? We are young enough to be able to forget all those things. (*He catches her hand*) Mary, Mary, I am pleading for your love. With Labour, Mary, humanity is above everything; we are the Leaders in the fight for a new life. I want to forget Bentham, I want to forget that you left me—even for a while.

MARY: Oh, Jerry, Jerry, you haven't the bitter word of scorn for me after all.

JERRY (*passionately*): Scorn! I love you, love you, Mary!

MARY (*rising, and looking him in the eyes*): Even though . . .

JERRY: Even though you threw me over for another man; even though you gave me many a bitter word!

MARY: Yes, yes, I know; but you love me, even though . . . even though . . . I'm . . . goin' . . . goin' . . . (*He looks at her questioningly, and fear gathers in his eyes*) Ah, I was thinkin' so. . . . You don't know everything!

JERRY (*poignantly*): Surely to God, Mary, you don't mean that . . . that . . . that . . .

MARY: Now you know all, Jerry; now you know all!

JERRY: My God, Mary, have you fallen as low as that?

MARY: Yes, Jerry, as you say, I have fallen as low as that.

JERRY: I didn't mean it that way, Mary . . . it came on me so sudden, that I didn't mind what I was sayin'. . . . I never expected this—your mother never told me. . . . I'm sorry . . . God knows, I'm sorry for you, Mary.

MARY: Let us say no more, Jerry; I don't blame you for thinkin' it's terrible. . . . I suppose it is. . . . Everybody'll think the same. . . . It's only as I expected—your humanity is just as narrow as the humanity of the others.

JERRY: I'm sorry, all the same. . . . I shouldn't have troubled you. . . . I wouldn't if I'd known . . . if I can do anything for you . . . Mary . . . I will. (*He turns to go, and halts at the door.*)

MARY: Do you remember, Jerry, the verses you read when you gave the lecture in the Socialist Rooms some time ago, on Humanity's Strife with Nature?

JERRY: The verses—no; I don't remember them.

MARY: I do. They're runnin' in me head now—

> An' we felt the power that fashion'd
> All the lovely things we saw,
> That created all the murmur
> Of an everlasting law,
> Was a hand of force an' beauty,
> With an eagle's tearin' claw.
>
> Then we saw our globe of beauty
> Was an ugly thing as well,
> A hymn divine whose chorus
> Was an agonizin' yell;
> Like the story of a demon,
> That an angel had to tell.
>
> Like a glowin' picture by a
> Hand unsteady, brought to ruin;
> Like her craters, if their deadness
> Could give life unto the moon;
> Like the agonizing horror
> Of a violin out of tune.

(*There is a pause, and* DEVINE *goes slowly out.*)

JOHNNY (*returning*): Is he gone?

MARY: Yes.

(*The two men re-enter.*)

FIRST MAN: We can't wait any longer for t'oul' fella—sorry, Miss, but we have to live as well as th' nex' man.

(*They carry out some things.*)

JOHNNY: Oh, isn't this terrible! . . . I suppose you told him everything . . . couldn't you have waited for a few days . . . he'd have stopped th' takin' of the things, if you'd kep' your mouth shut. Are you burnin' to tell every one of the shame you've brought on us?

MARY (*snatching up her hat and coat*): Oh, this is unbearable! (*She rushes out.*)

FIRST MAN (*re-entering*): We'll take the chest o' drawers next— it's the heaviest.

(*The votive light flickers for a moment, and goes out.*)

JOHNNY (*in a cry of fear*): Mother o' God, the light's afther goin' out!

FIRST MAN: You put the win' up me the way you bawled that time. The oil's all gone, that's all.

JOHNNY (*with an agonizing cry*): Mother o' God, there's a shot I'm afther getting'!

FIRST MAN: What's wrong with you, man? Is it a fit you're takin'?

JOHNNY: I'm afther feelin' a pain in me breast, like the tearin' by of a bullet!

FIRST MAN: He's goin' mad—it's a wondher they'd leave a chap like that here be himself.

(*Two* IRREGULARS *enter swiftly; they carry revolvers; one goes over* to JOHNNY; *the other covers the two furniture men.*)

FIRST IRREGULAR (*to the men, quietly and incisively*): Who are you —what are yous doin' here—quick!

FIRST MAN: Removin' furniture that's not paid for.

IRREGULAR: Get over to the other end of the room an' turn your faces to the wall—quick.

(*The two men turn their faces to the wall, with their hands up.*)

SECOND IRREGULAR (*to* JOHNNY): Come on, Sean Boyle, you're wanted; some of us have a word to say to you.

JOHNNY: I'm sick, I can't—what do you want with me?

SECOND IRREGULAR: Come on, come on; we've a distance to go, an' haven't much time—come on.

JOHNNY: I'm an oul' comrade—yous wouldn't shoot an oul' comrade.

SECOND IRREGULAR: Poor Tancred was an oul' comrade o' yours, but you didn't think o' that when you gave him away to the gang that sent him to his grave. But we've no time to waste; come on—here, Dermot, ketch his arm. (*To* JOHNNY) Have you your beads?

JOHNNY: Me beads! Why do you ass me that, why do you ass me that?

SECOND IRREGULAR: Go on, go on, march!

JOHNNY: Are yous goin' to do in a comrade—look at me arm, I lost it for Ireland.

SECOND IRREGULAR: Commandant Tancred lost his life for Ireland.

JOHNNY: Sacred Heart of Jesus, have mercy on me! Mother o' God, pray for me—be with me now in the agonies o' death! . . . Hail, Mary, full o' grace . . . the Lord is . . . with Thee.

(*They drag out* JOHNNY BOYLE, *and the curtain falls. When it rises again the most of the furniture is gone.* MARY *and* MRS. BOYLE, *one on each side, are sitting in a darkened room, by the fire; it is an hour later.*)

MRS. BOYLE: I'll not wait much longer . . . what did they bring him away in the mothor for? Nugent says he thinks they had guns . . . is me throubles never goin' to be over? . . . If anything ud happen to poor Johnny, I think I'd lost me mind . . . I'll go to the Police Station, surely they ought to be able to do somethin'.

(*Below is heard the sound of voices.*)

MRS. BOYLE: Whisht, is that something? Maybe, it's your father, though when I left him in Foley's he was hardly able to lift his head. Whisht!

(*A knock at the door, and the voice of* MRS. MADIGAN, *speaking very softly:*)

Mrs. Boyle, Mrs. Boyle. (MRS. BOYLE *opens the door.*)

MRS. MADIGAN: Oh, Mrs. Boyle, God an' His Blessed Mother be with you this night!

MRS. BOYLE (*calmly*): What is it, Mrs. Madigan? It's Johnny—something about Johnny.

MRS. MADIGAN: God send it's not. God send it's not Johnny!

MRS. BOYLE: Don't keep me waitin', Mrs. Madigan; I've gone through so much lately that I feel able for anything.

MRS. MADIGAN: Two polismen below wantin' you.

MRS. BOYLE: Wantin' me; an' why do they want me?

MRS. MADIGAN: Some poor fella's been found, an' they think it's, it's . . .

MRS. BOYLE: Johnny, Johnny!

MARY (*with her arms round her mother*): Oh, mother, mother, me poor, darlin' mother.

MRS. BOYLE: Hush, hush, darlin'; you'll shortly have your own throuble to bear. (*To* MRS. MADIGAN) An' why do the polis think it's Johnny, Mrs. Madigan?

MRS. MADIGAN: Because one o' the doctors knew him when he was attendin' with his poor arm.

MRS. BOYLE: Oh, it's thrue, then; it's Johnny, it's me son, me own son!

MARY: Oh, it's thrue, it's thrue what Jerry Devine says—there isn't a God, there isn't a God; if there was He wouldn't let these things happen!

MRS. BOYLE: Mary, Mary, you mustn't say them things. We'll want all the help we can get from God an' His Blessed Mother now! These things have nothin' to do with the Will o' God. Ah, what can God do agen the stupidity o' men!

MRS. MADIGAN: The polis want you to go with them to the hospital to see the poor body—they're waitin' below.

MRS. BOYLE: We'll go. Come, Mary, an' we'll never come back here agen. Let your father furrage for himself now; I've done all I could an' it was all no use—he'll be hopeless till the end of his days. I've got a little room in me sisther's where we'll stop till your throuble is over, an' then we'll work together for the sake of the baby.

MARY: My poor little child that'll have no father!

MRS. BOYLE: It'll have what's far betther—it'll have two mothers.

(*A rough voice shouting from below:*)

Are yous goin' to keep us waitin' for yous all night?

MRS. MADIGAN (*going to the door, and shouting down*): Take your hour, there, take your hour! If yous are in such a hurry, skip off, then, for nobody wants you here—if they did yous wouldn't be found. For you're the same as yous were undher the British Government—never where yous are wanted! As far as I can see, the Polis as Polis, in this city, is Null an' Void!

MRS. BOYLE: We'll go, Mary, we'll go; you to see your poor dead brother, an' me to see me poor dead son!

MARY: I dhread it, mother, I dhread it!

MRS. BOYLE: I forgot, Mary, I forgot; your poor oul' selfish mother was only thinkin' of herself. No, no, you mustn't come—it wouldn't be good for you. You go on to me sisther's an I'll face th' ordeal meself. Maybe I didn't feel sorry enough for Mrs. Tancred when her poor son was found as Johnny's been found now—because he was a Die-hard! Ah, why didn't I remember that then he wasn't a Die-hard or a Stater, but only a poor dead son! It's well I remember all that she said—an' it's my turn to say it now: What was the pain I suffered, Johnny, bringin' you into the world to carry you to your cradle to the pains I'll suffer carryin' you out o' the world to bring you to your grave! Mother o' God, Mother o' God, have pity on us all! Blessed Virgin, where were you when me darlin' son was riddled with bullets, when me darlin' son was riddled with bullets? Sacred Heart o' Jesus, take away our hearts o' stone, and give us hearts o' flesh! Take away this murdherin' hate, an' give us Thine own eternal love!

(*They all go slowly out.*)

*(There is a pause; then a sound of shuffling steps on the stairs outside. The door opens and* BOYLE *and* JOXER, *both of them very drunk, enter.)*

BOYLE: I'm able to go no farther. . . . Two polis, ey . . . what were they doin' here, I wondher? . . . Up to no good, anyhow . . . an' Juno an' that lovely daughter o' mine with them. *(Taking a sixpence from his pocket and looking at it)* Wan single, solithary tanner left out of all I borreyed. . . *(He lets it fall)* The last o' the Mohicans. . . . The blinds is down, Joxer, the blinds is down!

JOXER *(walking unsteadily across the room, and anchoring at the bed)*: Put all . . . your throubles . . . in your oul' kit bag . . . an' smile . . . smile . . . smile!

BOYLE: The counthry'll have to steady itself . . . it's goin' . . . to hell. . . . Where'r all . . . the chairs . . . gone to . . . steady itself, Joxer. . . . Chairs'll . . . have to . . . steady themselves. . . . No matther . . . what any one may . . . say . . . Irelan's sober . . . is Irelan' . . . free.

JOXER *(stretching himself on the bed)*: Chains . . . an' . . . slaveree . . . that's a darlin' motto . . . a daaarlin' . . . motto!

BOYLE: If th' worst comes . . . to th' worse . . . I can join a . . . flyin' . . . column. . . . I done . . . me bit . . . in Easther Week . . . had no business . . . to . . . be . . . there . . . but Captain Boyle's Captain Boyle!

JOXER: Breathes there a man with soul . . . so . . . de . . . ad . . . this . . . me . . . o . . . wn, me nat . . . ive l . . . an'!

BOYLE *(subsiding into a sitting posture on the floor)*: Commandant Kelly died . . . in them . . . arms . . . Joxer. . . . Tell me Volunteer Butties . . . says he . . . that . . . I died for . . . Irelan'!

JOXER: D'jever rade Willie . . . Reilly . . . an' his . . . own . . . Colleen . . . Bawn? It's a darlin' story, a daarlin' story!

BOYLE: I'm telling you . . . Joxer . . . th' whole worl's . . . in a terr . . . ible state o' . . . chassis!

*(The Curtain Falls.)*

# ANTON CHEKHOV

# The
# Cherry Orchard

## A Comedy in Four Acts

Translated by

**CONSTANCE GARNETT**

*The Cherry Orchard* was first performed at Moscow
on January 17, 1904.

# CHARACTERS

MADAME RANEVSKY (LYUBOV ANDREYEVNA) *(the owner of the Cherry Orchard)*.

ANYA *(her daughter, aged* 17*)*.

VARYA *(her adopted daughter, aged* 24*)*.

GAEV (LEONID ANDREYEVITCH) *(brother of Madame Ranevsky)*.

LOPAHIN (YERMOLAY ALEXEYEVITCH) *(a Merchant)*.

TROFIMOV (PYOTR SERGEYEVITCH) *(a Student)*.

SEMYONOV-PISHTCHIK *(a Landowner)*.

CHARLOTTA IVANOVNA *(a Governess)*.

EPIHODOV (SEMYON PANTALEYEVITCH) *(a Clerk)*.

DUNYASHA *(a Maid)*.

FIRS *(an old Valet, aged* 87*)*.

YASHA *(a young Valet)*.

A VAGRANT.

THE STATION MASTER.

A POST-OFFICE CLERK.

VISITORS, SERVANTS.

*The action takes place on the estate of*
MADAME RANEVSKY.

# Act One

A room, *which has always been called the nursery. One of the doors leads into* ANYA's *room. Dawn, sun rises during the scene. May, the cherry trees in flower, but it is cold in the garden with the frost of early morning. Windows closed.*

*Enter* DUNYASHA *with a candle and* LOPAHIN *with a book in his hand.*

LOPAHIN: The train's in, thank God. What time is it?

DUNYASHA: Nearly two o'clock (*puts out the candle*). It's daylight already.

LOPAHIN: The train's late! Two hours, at least (*yawns and stretches*). I'm a pretty one; what a fool I've been. Came here on purpose to meet them at the station and dropped asleep. . . . Dozed off as I sat in the chair. It's annoying. . . . You might have waked me.

DUNYASHA: I thought you had gone (*listens*). There, I do believe they're coming!

LOPAHIN (*listens*): No, what with the luggage and one thing and another (*a pause*). Lyubov Andreyevna has been abroad five years; I don't know what she is like now. . . . She's a splendid woman. A good-natured, kind-hearted woman. I remember when I was a lad of fifteen, my poor father—he used to keep a little shop here in the village in those days—gave me a punch in the face with his fist and made my nose bleed. We were in the yard here, I forget what we'd come about—he had had a drop. Lyubov Andreyevna—I can see her now—she was a slim young girl then—took me to wash my face, and then brought me into this very room, into the nursery. "Don't cry, little peasant," says she, "it will be well in time for your wedding day" . . . (*a pause*). Little peasant. . . . My father was a peasant, it's true, but here am I in a white waistcoat and brown shoes, like a pig in a bun shop. Yes, I'm a rich man, but for all my money, come to think, a peasant I was, and a peasant I am (*turns*

435

*over the pages of the book*). I've been reading this book and I can't make head or tail of it. I fell asleep over it (*a pause*).

DUNYASHA: The dogs have been awake all night, they feel that the mistress is coming.

LOPAHIN: Why, what's the matter with you, Dunyasha?

DUNYASHA: My hands are all of a tremble. I feel as though I should faint.

LOPAHIN: You're a spoilt soft creature, Dunyasha. And dressed like a lady too, and your hair done up. That's not the thing. One must know one's place.

(*Enter* EPIHODOV *with a nosegay; he wears a pea-jacket and highly polished creaking topboots; he drops the nosegay as he comes in.*)

EPIHODOV (*picking up the nosegay*): Here! the gardener's sent this, says you're to put it in the dining-room (*gives* DUNYASHA *the nosegay*).

LOPAHIN: And bring me some kvass.

DUNYASHA: I will (*goes out*).

EPIHODOV: It's chilly this morning, three degrees of frost, though the cherries are all in flower. I can't say much for our climate (*sighs*). I can't. Our climate is not often propitious to the occasion. Yermolay Alexeyevitch, permit me to call your attention to the fact that I purchased myself a pair of boots the day before yesterday, and they creak, I venture to assure you, so that there's no tolerating them. What ought I to grease them with?

LOPAHIN: Oh, shut up! Don't bother me.

EPIHODOV: Every day some misfortune befalls me. I don't complain, I'm used to it, and I wear a smiling face.

(DUNYASHA *comes in, hands* LOPAHIN *the kvass.*)

EPIHODOV: I am going (*stumbles against a chair, which falls over*). There! (*As though triumphant*) There you see now, excuse the expression, an accident like that among others. . . . It's positively remarkable (*goes out*).

DUNYASHA: Do you know, Yermolay Alexeyevitch, I must confess, Epihodov has made me a proposal.

LOPAHIN: Ah!

DUNYASHA: I'm sure I don't know. . . . He's a harmless fellow, but sometimes when he begins talking, there's no making anything of it. It's all very fine and expressive, only there's no understanding it. I've a sort of liking for him too. He loves me to distraction. He's an unfortunate man; every day there's something. They tease him about it—two and twenty misfortunes they call him.

LOPAHIN (*listening*): There! I do believe they're coming.

DUNYASHA: They are coming! What's the matter with me? . . . I'm cold all over.

LOPAHIN: They really are coming. Let's go and meet them. Will she know me? It's five years since I saw her.

DUNYASHA (*in a flutter*): I shall drop this very minute. . . . Ah, I shall drop.

(*There is a sound of two carriages driving up to the house.* LOPAHIN *and* DUNYASHA *go out quickly. The stage is left empty. A noise is heard in the adjoining rooms.* FIRS, *who has driven to meet* MADAME RANEVSKY, *crosses the stage hurriedly leaning on a stick. He is wearing old-fashioned livery and a high hat. He says something to himself, but not a word can be distinguished. The noise behind the scenes goes on increasing. A voice: "Come, let's go in here." Enter* LYUBOV ANDREYEVNA, ANYA, *and* CHARLOTTA IVANOVNA *with a pet dog on a chain, all in travelling dresses.* VARYA *in an out-door coat with a kerchief over her head,* GAEV, SEMYONOV-PISHTCHIK, LOPAHIN, DUNYASHA *with bag and parasol, servants with other articles. All walk across the room.*)

ANYA: Let's come in here. Do you remember what room this is, mamma?

LYUBOV (*joyfully, through her tears*): The nursery!

VARYA: How cold it is, my hands are numb. (*To* LYUBOV ANDREYEVNA) Your rooms, the white room and the lavender one, are just the same as ever, mamma.

LYUBOV: My nursery, dear delightful room. . . . I used to sleep here when I was little . . . (*cries*). And here I am, like a little child . . . (*kisses her brother and* VARYA, *and then her brother again*). Varya's just the same as ever, like a nun. And I knew Dunyasha (*kisses* DUNYASHA).

GAEV: The train was two hours late. What do you think of that? Is that the way to do things?

CHARLOTTA (*to* PISHTCHIK): My dog eats nuts, too.

PISHTCHIK (*wonderingly*): Fancy that!

(*They all go out except* ANYA *and* DUNYASHA.)

DUNYASHA: We've been expecting you so long (*takes* ANYA's *hat and coat*).

ANYA: I haven't slept for four nights on the journey. I feel dreadfully cold.

DUNYASHA: You set out in Lent, there was snow and frost, and now? My darling! (*Laughs and kisses her*) I *have* missed you, my precious, my joy. I must tell you . . . I can't put it off a minute. . . .

ANYA (*wearily*): What now?

DUNYASHA: Epihodov, the clerk, made me a proposal just after Easter.

ANYA: It's always the same thing with you . . . (*straightening her hair*). I've lost all my hairpins . . . (*she is staggering from exhaustion*).

DUNYASHA: I don't know what to think, really. He does love me, he does love me so!

ANYA (*looking towards her door, tenderly*): My own room, my windows just as though I had never gone away. I'm home! Tomorrow morning I shall up and run into the garden. . . . Oh, if I could get to sleep! I haven't slept all the journey, I was so anxious and worried.

DUNYASHA: Pyotr Sergeyevitch came the day before yesterday.

ANYA (*joyfully*): Petya!

DUNYASHA: He's asleep in the bath house, he has settled in there. I'm afraid of being in their way, says he. (*Glancing at her watch*) I was to have waked him, but Varvara Mihalovna told me not to. Don't you wake him, says she.

(*Enter* VARYA *with a bunch of keys at her waist.*)

VARYA: Dunyasha, coffee and make haste. . . . Mamma's asking for coffee.

DUNYASHA: This very minute (*goes out*).

VARYA: Well, thank God, you've come. You're home again (*petting her*). My little darling has come back! My precious beauty has come back again!

ANYA: I have had a time of it!

VARYA: I can fancy.

ANYA: We set off in Holy Week—it was so cold then, and all the way Charlotta would talk and show off her tricks. What did you want to burden me with Charlotta for?

VARYA: You couldn't have travelled all alone, darling. At seventeen!

ANYA: We got to Paris at last, it was cold there—snow. I speak French shockingly. Mamma lives on the fifth floor, I went up to her and there were a lot of French people, ladies, an old priest with a book. The place smelt of tobacco and so comfortless. I felt sorry, oh! so sorry for mamma all at once, I put my arms round her neck, and hugged her and wouldn't let her go. Mamma was as kind as she could be, and she cried. . . .

VARYA (*through her tears*): Don't speak of it, don't speak of it!

ANYA: She had sold her villa at Mentone, she had nothing left, nothing. I hadn't a farthing left either, we only just had enough to get here. And mamma doesn't understand! When we had dinner at the stations, she always ordered the most expensive things and gave the waiters a whole rouble. Charlotta's just the same. Yasha too must have the same as we do; it's simply awful. You know Yasha is mamma's valet now, we brought him here with us.

VARYA: Yes, I've seen the young rascal.

ANYA: Well, tell me—have you paid the arrears on the mortgage?

VARYA: How could we get the money?

ANYA: Oh, dear! Oh, dear!

VARYA: In August the place will be sold.

ANYA: My goodness!

LOPAHIN (*peeps in at the door and moos like a cow*): Moo! (*Disappears.*)

VARYA (*weeping*): There, that's what I could do to him (*shakes her fist*).

ANYA (*embracing* VARYA, *softly*): Varya, has he made you an offer? (VARYA *shakes her head*) Why, but he loves you. Why is it you don't come to an understanding? What are you waiting for?

VARYA: I believe that there never will be anything between us. He has a lot to do, he has no time for me . . . and takes no notice of me. Bless the man, it makes me miserable to see him. . . . Everyone's talking of our being married, everyone's congratulating me, and all the while there's really nothing in it; it's all like a dream! (*In another tone*) You have a new brooch like a bee.

ANYA (*mournfully*): Mamma bought it. (*Goes into her own room and in a light-hearted childish tone*) And you know, in Paris I went up in a balloon!

VARYA: My darling's home again! My pretty is home again!

(DUNYASHA *returns with the coffee-pot and is making the coffee.*)

VARYA (*standing at the door*): All day long, darling, as I go about looking after the house, I keep dreaming all the time. If only we could marry you to a rich man, then I should feel more at rest. Then I would go off by myself on a pilgrimage to Kiev, to Moscow . . . and so I would spend my life going from one place to another. . . . I would go on and on. . . . What bliss!

ANYA: The birds are singing in the garden. What time is it?

VARYA: It must be nearly three. It's time you were asleep, darling (*going into* ANYA's *room*). What bliss!

(YASHA *enters with a rug and a travelling bag.*)

YASHA (*crosses the stage, mincingly*): May one come in here, pray?

DUNYASHA: I shouldn't have known you, Yasha. How you have changed abroad.

YASHA: H'm! . . . And who are you?

DUNYASHA: When you went away, I was that high (*shows distance from floor*). Dunyasha, Fyodor's daughter. . . . You don't remember me!

YASHA: H'm! . . . You're a peach! (*Looks round and embraces her: she shrieks and drops a saucer.* YASHA *goes out hastily.*)

VARYA (*in the doorway, in a tone of vexation*): What now?

DUNYASHA (*through her tears*): I have broken a saucer.

VARYA: Well, that brings good luck.

ANYA (*coming out of her room*): We ought to prepare mamma: Petya is here.

VARYA: I told them not to wake him.

ANYA (*dreamily*): It's six years since father died. Then only a month later little brother Grisha was drowned in the river, such a pretty boy he was, only seven. It was more than mamma could bear, so she went away, went away without looking back (*shuddering*). . . . How well I understand her, if only she knew! (*A pause*) And Petya Trofimov was Grisha's tutor, he may remind her.

(*Enter* FIRS: *he is wearing a pea-jacket and a white waistcoat.*)

FIRS (*goes up to the coffee-pot, anxiously*): The mistress will be served here (*puts on white gloves*). Is the coffee ready? (*Sternly to* DUNYASHA) Girl! Where's the cream?

DUNYASHA: Ah, mercy on us! (*Goes out quickly.*)

FIRS (*fussing round the coffee-pot*): Ech! you good-for-nothing! (*Muttering to himself*) Come back from Paris. And the old master used to go to Paris too . . . horses all the way (*laughs*).

VARYA: What is it, Firs?

FIRS: What is your pleasure? (*Gleefully*) My lady has come home! I have lived to see her again! Now I can die (*weeps with joy*).

(*Enter* LYUBOV ANDREYEVNA, GAEV *and* SEMYONOV-PISHTCHIK; *the latter is in a short-waisted full coat of fine cloth, and full trousers.* GAEV, *as he comes in, makes a gesture with his arms and his whole body, as though he were playing billiards.*)

LYUBOV: How does it go? Let me remember. Cannon off the red!

GAEV: That's it—in off the white! Why, once, sister, we used to sleep together in this very room, and now I'm fifty-one, strange as it seems.

LOPAHIN: Yes, time flies.

GAEV: What do you say?

LOPAHIN: Time, I say, flies.

GAEV: What a smell of patchouli!

ANYA: I'm going to bed. Good-night, mamma (*kisses her mother*).

LYUBOV: My precious darling (*kisses her hands*). Are you glad to be home? I can't believe it.

ANYA: Good-night, uncle.

GAEV (*kissing her face and hands*): God bless you! How like you are to your mother! (*To his sister*) At her age you were just the same, Lyuba.

(ANYA *shakes hands with* LOPAHIN *and* PISHTCHIK, *then goes out, shutting the door after her.*)

LYUBOV: She's quite worn out.

PISHTCHIK: Aye, it's a long journey, to be sure.

VARYA (*to* LOPAHIN *and* PISHTCHIK): Well, gentlemen? It's three o'clock and time to say good-bye.

LYUBOV (*laughs*): You're just the same as ever, Varya (*draws her to her and kisses her*). I'll just drink my coffee and then we will all go and rest. (FIRS *puts a cushion under her feet*) Thanks, friend. I am so fond of coffee, I drink it day and night. Thanks, dear old man (*kisses* FIRS).

VARYA: I'll just see whether all the things have been brought in (*goes out*).

LYUBOV: Can it really be me sitting here? (*Laughs*) I want to dance about and clap my hands. (*Covers her face with her hands*) And I could drop asleep in a moment! God knows I love my country, I love it tenderly; I couldn't look out of the window in the train, I kept crying so. (*Through her tears*) But I must drink my coffee, though. Thank you, Firs, thanks, dear old man. I'm so glad to find you still alive.

FIRS: The day before yesterday.

GAEV: He's rather deaf.

LOPAHIN: I have to set off for Harkov directly, at five o'clock. . . . It is annoying! I wanted to have a look at you, and a little talk. . . . You are just as splendid as ever.

PISHTCHIK (*breathing heavily*): Handsomer, indeed. . . . Dressed in Parisian style . . . completely bowled me over.

LOPAHIN: Your brother, Leonid Andreyevitch here, is always saying that I'm a low-born knave, that I'm a money-grubber, but I don't care one straw for that. Let him talk. Only I do want you to believe in me as you used to. I do want your wonderful tender eyes to look at me as they used to in the old days. Merciful God! My father was a serf of your father and of your grandfather, but you—you—did so much for me once, that I've forgotten all that; I love you as though you were my kin . . . more than my kin.

LYUBOV: I can't sit still, I simply can't . . . (*jumps up and walks about in violent agitation*). This happiness is too much for me. . . . You may laugh at me, I know I'm silly. . . . My own bookcase (*kisses the bookcase*). My little table.

GAEV: Nurse died while you were away.

LYUBOV (*sits down and drinks coffee*): Yes, the Kingdom of Heaven be hers! You wrote me of her death.

GAEV: And Anastasy is dead. Squinting Petruchka has left me and is in service now with the police captain in the town (*takes a box of caramels out of his pocket and sucks one*).

PISHTCHIK: My daughter, Dashenka, wishes to be remembered to you.

LOPAHIN: I want to tell you something very pleasant and cheering (*glancing at his watch*). I'm going directly . . . there's no time to say much . . . well, I can say it in a couple of words. I needn't tell you your cherry orchard is to be sold to pay your debts; the 22nd of August is the date fixed for the sale; but don't you worry, dearest lady, you may sleep in peace, there is a way of saving it. . . . This is what I propose. I beg your attention! Your estate is not twenty miles from the town, the railway runs close by it, and if the cherry orchard and the land along the river bank were cut up into building plots and then let on lease for summer villas, you would make an income of at least 25,000 roubles a year out of it.

GAEV: That's all rot, if you'll excuse me.

LYUBOV: I don't quite understand you, Yermolay Alexeyevitch.

LOPAHIN: You will get a rent of at least 25 roubles a year for a three-acre plot from summer visitors, and if you say the word now, I'll bet you what you like there won't be one square foot of ground vacant by the autumn, all the plots will be taken up. I congratulate you; in fact, you are saved. It's a perfect situation with that deep river. Only, of course, it must be cleared—all the old buildings, for example, must be removed, this house too, which is really good for nothing and the old cherry orchard must be cut down.

LYUBOV: Cut down? My dear fellow, forgive me, but you don't know what you are talking about. If there is one thing interesting—remarkable indeed—in the whole province, it's just our cherry orchard.

LOPAHIN: The only thing remarkable about the orchard is that it's a very large one. There's a crop of cherries every alternate year, and then there's nothing to be done with them, no one buys them.

GAEV: This orchard is mentioned in the "Encyclopædia."

LOPAHIN (*glancing at his watch*): If we don't decide on something and don't take some steps, on the 22nd of August the cherry orchard and the whole estate too will be sold by auction. Make up your minds! There is no other way of saving it, I'll take my oath on that. No, No!

FIRS: In the old days, forty or fifty years ago, they used to dry the cherries, soak them, pickle them, make jam too, and they used . . .

GAEV: Be quiet, Firs.

FIRS: And they used to send the preserved cherries to Moscow and to Harkov by the waggon-load. That brought the money in! And the preserved cherries in those days were soft and juicy, sweet and fragrant. . . . They knew the way to do them then. . . .

LYUBOV: And where is the recipe now?

FIRS: It's forgotten. Nobody remembers it.

PISHTCHIK (*to* LYUBOV ANDREYEVNA): What's it like in Paris? Did you eat frogs there?

LYUBOV: Oh, I ate crocodiles.

PISHTCHIK: Fancy that now!

LOPAHIN: There used to be only the gentlefolks and the peasants in the country, but now there are these summer visitors. All the towns, even the small ones, are surrounded nowadays by these summer villas. And one may say for sure, that in another twenty years there'll be many more of these people and that they'll be everywhere. At present the summer visitor only drinks tea in his verandah, but maybe he'll take to working his bit of land too, and then your cherry orchard would become happy, rich and prosperous. . . .

GAEV (*indignant*): What rot!

(*Enter* VARYA *and* YASHA.)

VARYA: There are two telegrams for you, mamma (*takes out keys and opens an old-fashioned bookcase with a loud crack*). Here they are.

LYUBOV: From Paris (*tears the telegrams, without reading them*). I have done with Paris.

GAEV: Do you know, Lyuba, how old that bookcase is? Last week I pulled out the bottom drawer and there I found the date branded on it. The bookcase was made just a hundred years ago. What do you say to that? We might have celebrated its jubilee. Though it's an inanimate object, still it is a *book* case.

PISHTCHIK (*amazed*): A hundred years! Fancy that now.

GAEV: Yes. . . . It is a thing . . . (*feeling the bookcase*). Dear, honoured bookcase! Hail to thee who for more than a hundred years hast served the pure ideals of good and justice; thy silent call to fruitful labour has never flagged in those hundred years, maintaining (*in tears*) in the generations of man, courage and faith in a brighter future and fostering in us ideals of good and social consciousness (*a pause*).

LOPAHIN: Yes. . . .

LYUBOV: You are just the same as ever, Leonid.

GAEV (*a little embarrassed*): Cannon off the right into the pocket!

LOPAHIN (*looking at his watch*): Well, it's time I was off.

YASHA (*handing* LYUBOV ANDREYEVNA *medicine*): Perhaps you will take your pills now.

PISHTCHIK: You shouldn't take medicines, my dear madam . . . they do no harm and no good. Give them here . . . honoured lady (*takes the pill-box, pours the pills into the hollow of his hand, blows on them, puts them in his mouth and drinks off some kvass*). There!

LYUBOV (*in alarm*): Why, you must be out of your mind!

PISHTCHIK: I have taken all the pills.

LOPAHIN: What a glutton! (*All laugh.*)

FIRS: His honour stayed with us in Easter week, ate a gallon and a half of cucumbers . . . (*mutters*).

LYUBOV: What is he saying?

VARYA: He has taken to muttering like that for the last three years. We are used to it.

YASHA: His declining years!

(CHARLOTTA IVANOVNA, *a very thin, lanky figure in a white dress with a lorgnette in her belt, walks across the stage.*)

LOPAHIN: I beg your pardon, Charlotta Ivanovna, I have not had time to greet you (*tries to kiss her hand*).

CHARLOTTA (*pulling away her hand*): If I let you kiss my hand, you'll be wanting to kiss my elbow, and then my shoulder.

LOPAHIN: I've no luck today! (*All laugh*) Charlotta Ivanovna, show us some tricks!

LYUBOV: Charlotta, do show us some tricks!

CHARLOTTA: I don't want to. I'm sleepy (*goes out*).

LOPAHIN: In three weeks' time we shall meet again (*kisses* LYUBOV ANDREYEVNA's *hand*). Good-bye till then—I must go. (*To* GAEV) Good-bye. (*Kisses* PISHTCHIK) Good-bye. (*Gives his hand to* VARYA, *then to* FIRS *and* YASHA) I don't want to go. (*To* LYUBOV ANDRE-YEVNA) If you think over my plan for the villas and make up your mind, then let me know; I will lend you 50,000 roubles. Think of it seriously.

VARYA (*angrily*): Well, do go, for goodness sake.

LOPAHIN: I'm going, I'm going (*goes out*).

GAEV: Low-born knave! I beg pardon, though . . . Varya is going to marry him, he's Varya's fiancé.

VARYA: Don't talk nonsense, uncle.

LYUBOV: Well, Varya, I shall be delighted. He's a good man.

PISHTCHIK: He is, one must acknowledge, a most worthy man. And my Dashenka . . . says too that . . . she says . . . various things (*snores, but at once wakes up*). But all the same, honoured lady, could you oblige me . . . with a loan of 240 roubles . . . to pay the interest on my mortgage tomorrow?

VARYA (*dismayed*): No, no.

LYUBOV: I really haven't any money.

PISHTCHIK: It will turn up (*laughs*). I never lose hope. I thought everything was over, I was a ruined man, and lo and behold—the railway passed through my land and . . . they paid me for it. And something else will turn up again, if not today, then tomorrow . . . Dashenka'll win two hundred thousand . . . she's got a lottery ticket.

LYUBOV: Well, we've finished our coffee, we can go to bed.

FIRS (*brushes* GAEV, *reprovingly*): You have got on the wrong trousers again! What am I to do with you?

VARYA (*softly*): Anya's asleep. (*Softly opens the window*) Now the sun's risen, it's not a bit cold. Look, mamma, what exquisite trees! My goodness! And the air! The starlings are singing!

GAEV (*opens another window*): The orchard is all white. You've not forgotten it, Lyuba? That long avenue that runs straight, straight as an arrow, how it shines on a moonlight night. You remember? You've not forgotten?

LYUBOV (*looking out of the window into the garden*): Oh, my childhood, my innocence! It was in this nursery I used to sleep, from here I looked out into the orchard, happiness waked with me every morning and in those days the orchard was just the same, nothing has changed (*laughs with delight*). All, all white! Oh, my orchard! After the dark gloomy autumn, and the cold winter; you are young again, and full of happiness, the heavenly angels have never left you. . . . If I could cast off the burden that weighs on my heart, if I could forget the past!

GAEV: H'm! and the orchard will be sold to pay our debts; it seems strange. . . .

LYUBOV: See, our mother walking . . . all in white, down the avenue! (*Laughs with delight*) It is she!

GAEV: Where?

VARYA: Oh, don't, mamma!

LYUBOV: There is no one. It was my fancy. On the right there, by the path to the arbour, there is a white tree bending like a woman. . . .

(*Enter* TROFIMOV *wearing a shabby student's uniform and spectacles.*)

LYUBOV: What a ravishing orchard! White masses of blossoms, blue sky. . . .

TROFIMOV: Lyubov Andreyevna! (*She looks round at him*) I will just pay my respects to you and then leave you at once (*kisses her hand warmly*). I was told to wait until morning, but I hadn't the patience to wait any longer. . . .

(LYUBOV ANDREYEVNA *looks at him in perplexity.*)

VARYA (*through her tears*): This is Petya Trofimov.

TROFIMOV: Petya Trofimov, who was your Grisha's tutor. . . . Can I have changed so much?

(LYUBOV ANDREYEVNA *embraces him and weeps quietly.*)

GAEV (*in confusion*): There, there, Lyuba.

VARYA (*crying*): I told you, Petya, to wait till tomorrow.

LYUBOV: My Grisha . . . my boy . . . Grisha . . . my son!

VARYA: We can't help it, mamma, it is God's will.

TROFIMOV (*softly through his tears*): There . . . there.

LYUBOV (*weeping quietly*): My boy was lost . . . drowned. Why? Oh, why, dear Petya? (*More quietly*) Anya is asleep in there, and I'm talking loudly . . . making this noise. . . . But, Petya? Why have you grown so ugly? Why do you look so old?

TROFIMOV: A peasant-woman in the train called me a mangy-looking gentleman.

LYUBOV: You were quite a boy then, a pretty little student, and now your hair's thin—and spectacles. Are you really a student still? (*Goes towards the door.*)

TROFIMOV: I seem likely to be a perpetual student.

LYUBOV (*kisses her brother, then* VARYA): Well, go to bed. . . . You are older too, Leonid.

PISHTCHIK (*follows her*): I suppose it's time we were asleep. . . . Ugh! my gout. I'm staying the night! Lyubov Andreyevna, my dear soul, if you could . . . tomorrow morning . . . 240 roubles.

GAEV: That's always his story.

PISHTCHIK: 240 roubles . . . to pay the interest on my mortgage.

LYUBOV: My dear man, I have no money.

PISHTCHIK: I'll pay it back, my dear . . . a trifling sum.

LYUBOV: Oh, well, Leonid will give it you. . . . You give him the money, Leonid.

GAEV: Me give it him! Let him wait till he gets it!

LYUBOV: It can't be helped, give it him. He needs it. He'll pay it back.

(LYUBOV ANDREYEVNA, TROFIMOV, PISHTCHIK *and* FIRS *go out.* GAEV, VARYA *and* YASHA *remain.*)

GAEV: Sister hasn't got out of the habit of flinging away her money. (*To* YASHA) Get away, my good fellow, you smell of the hen-house.

YASHA (*with a grin*): And you, Leonid Andreyevitch, are just the same as ever.

GAEV: What's that? (*To* VARYA) What did he say?

VARYA (*to* YASHA): Your mother has come from the village; she has been sitting in the servants' room since yesterday, waiting to see you.

YASHA: Oh, bother her!

VARYA: For shame!

YASHA: What's the hurry? She might just as well have come tomorrow (*goes out*).

VARYA: Mamma's just the same as ever, she hasn't changed a bit. If she had her own way, she'd give away everything.

GAEV: Yes (*a pause*). If a great many remedies are suggested for some disease, it means that the disease is incurable. I keep thinking and racking my brains; I have many schemes, a great many, and that really means none. If we could only come in for a legacy from somebody, or marry our Anya to a very rich man, or we might go to Yaroslavl and try our luck with our old aunt, the Countess. She's very, very rich, you know.

VARYA (*weeps*): If God would help us.

GAEV: Don't blubber. Aunt's very rich, but she doesn't like us. First, sister married a lawyer instead of a nobleman. . . .

(ANYA *appears in the doorway.*)

GAEV: And then her conduct, one can't call it virtuous. She is good, and kind, and nice, and I love her, but, however one allows for extenuating circumstances, there's no denying that she's an immoral woman. One feels it in her slightest gesture.

VARYA (*in a whisper*): Anya's in the doorway.

GAEV: What do you say? (*A pause*) It's queer, there seems to be something wrong with my right eye. I don't see as well as I did. And on Thursday when I was in the district Court . . .

(*Enter* ANYA.)

VARYA: Why aren't you asleep, Anya?

ANYA: I can't get to sleep.

GAEV: My pet (*kisses* ANYA's *face and hands*). My child (*weeps*). You are not my niece, you are my angel, you are everything to me. Believe me, believe . . .

ANYA: I believe you, uncle. Everyone loves you and respects you . . . but, uncle dear, you must be silent . . . simply be silent. What were you saying just now about my mother, about your own sister? What made you say that?

GAEV: Yes, yes . . . (*puts his hand over his face*). Really, that was awful! My God, save me! And today I made a speech to the bookcase . . . so stupid! And only when I had finished, I saw how stupid it was.

VARYA: It's true, uncle, you ought to keep quiet. Don't talk, that's all.

ANYA: If you could keep from talking, it would make things easier for you, too.

GAEV: I won't speak (*kisses* ANYA's *and* VARYA's *hands*). I'll be silent. Only this is about business. On Thursday I was in the district Court; well, there was a large party of us there and we began talking of one thing and another, and this and that, and do you know, I believe that it will be possible to raise a loan on an I.O.U. to pay the arrears on the mortgage.

VARYA: If the Lord would help us!

GAEV: I'm going on Tuesday; I'll talk of it again. (*To* VARYA) Don't blubber. (*To* ANYA) Your mamma will talk to Lopahin; of course, he won't refuse her. And as soon as you're rested you shall go to Yaroslavl to the Countess, your great-aunt. So we shall all set to work in three directions at once, and the business is done. We shall pay off arrears, I'm convinced of it (*puts a caramel in his mouth*). I swear on my honour, I swear by anything you like, the estate shan't be sold (*excitedly*). By my own happiness, I swear it! Here's my hand on it, call me the basest, vilest of men, if I let it come to an auction! Upon my soul I swear it!

ANYA (*her equanimity has returned, she is quite happy*): How good you are, uncle, and how clever! (*Embraces her uncle*) I'm at peace now! Quite at peace! I'm happy!

(*Enter* FIRS.)

FIRS (*reproachfully*): Leonid Andreyevitch, have you no fear of God? When are you going to bed?

GAEV: Directly, directly. You can go, Firs. I'll . . . yes, I will undress myself. Come, children, bye-bye. We'll go into details tomorrow, but now go to bed (*kisses* ANYA *and* VARYA). I'm a man of the eighties. They run down that period, but still I can say I have had to suffer not a little for my convictions in my life. It's not for nothing that the peasant loves me. One must know the peasant! One must know how . . .

ANYA: At it again, uncle!

VARYA: Uncle dear, you'd better be quiet!

FIRS (*angrily*): Leonid Andreyevitch!

GAEV: I'm coming. I'm coming. Go to bed. Potted the shot—there's a shot for you! A beauty! (*Goes out,* FIRS *hobbling after him.*)

ANYA: My mind's at rest now. I don't want to go to Yaroslavl, I don't like my great-aunt, but still my mind's at rest. Thanks to uncle (*sits down*).

VARYA: We must go to bed. I'm going. Something unpleasant happened while you were away. In the old servants' quarters there are only the old servants, as you know—Efimyushka, Polya and Yevstigney—and Karp too. They began letting stray people in to spend the night—I said nothing. But all at once I heard they had been spreading a report that I gave them nothing but pease pudding to eat. Out of stinginess, you know. . . . And it was all Yevstigney's doing. . . . Very well, I said to myself. . . . If that's how it is, I thought, wait a bit. I sent for Yevstigney . . . (*yawns*). He comes. . . . "How's this, Yevstigney," I said, "you could be such a fool as to? . . . " (*Looking at* ANYA) Anitchka! (*a pause*). She's asleep (*puts her arm round* ANYA). Come to bed . . . come along! (*Leads her*) My darling has fallen asleep! Come . . . (*They go.*)

(*Far away beyond the orchard a shepherd plays on a pipe.* TROFIMOV *crosses the stage and, seeing* VARYA *and* ANYA, *stands still.*)

VARYA: Sh! asleep, asleep. Come, my own.

ANYA (*softly, half asleep*): I'm so tired. Still those bells. Uncle . . . dear . . . mamma and uncle. . . .

VARYA: Come, my own, come along.

(*They go into* ANYA's *room.*)

TROFIMOV (*tenderly*): My sunshine! My spring.

(*The Curtain Falls.*)

# Act Two

The open country. An old shrine, long abandoned and fallen out of the perpendicular; near it a well, large stones that have apparently once been tombstones, and an old garden seat. The road to GAEV's house is seen. On one side rise dark poplars; and there the cherry orchard begins. In the distance a row of telegraph poles and far, far away on the horizon there is faintly outlined a great town, only visible in very fine clear weather. It is near sunset. CHARLOTTA, YASHA and DUNYASHA are sitting on the seat. EPIHODOV is standing near, playing something mournful on a guitar. All sit plunged in thought. CHARLOTTA wears an old forage cap; she has taken a gun from her shoulder and is tightening the buckle on the strap.

CHARLOTTA (*musingly*): I haven't a real passport of my own, and I don't know how old I am, and I always feel that I'm a young thing. When I was a little girl, my father and mother used to travel about to fairs and give performances—very good ones. And I used to dance *salto-mortale* and all sorts of things. And when papa and mamma died, a German lady took me and had me educated. And so I grew up and became a governess. But where I came from, and who I am, I don't know. . . . Who my parents were, very likely they weren't married . . . I don't know (*takes a cucumber out of her pocket and eats*). I know nothing at all (*a pause*). One wants to talk and has no one to talk to . . . I have nobody.

EPIHODOV (*plays on the guitar and sings*): "What care I for the noisy world! What care I for friends or foes!" How agreeable it is to play on the mandolin!

DUNYASHA: That's a guitar, not a mandolin (*looks in a hand-mirror and powders herself*).

EPIHODOV: To a man mad with love, it's a mandolin. (*Sings*) "Were her heart but aglow with love's mutual flame." (YASHA *joins in.*)

CHARLOTTA: How shockingly these people sing! Foo! Like jackals!

DUNYASHA (*to* YASHA): What happiness, though, to visit foreign lands.

YASHA: Ah, yes! I rather agree with you there (*yawns, then lights a cigar*).

EPIHODOV: That's comprehensible. In foreign lands everything has long since reached full complexion.

YASHA: That's so, of course.

EPIHODOV: I'm a cultivated man, I read remarkable books of all sorts, but I can never make out the tendency I am myself precisely inclined for, whether to live or to shoot myself, speaking precisely, but nevertheless I always carry a revolver. Here it is . . . (*shows revolver*).

CHARLOTTA: I've had enough, and now I'm going (*puts on the gun*). Epihodov, you're a very clever fellow, and a very terrible one too, all the women must be wild about you. Br-r-r! (*Goes*) These clever fellows are all so stupid; there's not a creature for me to speak to. . . . Always alone, alone, nobody belonging to me . . . and who I am, and why I'm on earth, I don't know (*walks away slowly*).

EPIHODOV: Speaking precisely, not touching upon other subjects, I'm bound to admit about myself, that destiny behaves mercilessly to me, as a storm to a little boat. If, let us suppose, I am mistaken, then why did I wake up this morning, to quote an example, and look round, and there on my chest was a spider of fearful magnitude . . . like this (*shows with both hands*). And then I take up a jug of kvass, to quench my thirst, and in it there is something in the highest degree unseemly of the nature of a cockroach (*a pause*). Have you read Buckle? (*A pause*) I am desirous of troubling you, Dunyasha, with a couple of words.

DUNYASHA: Well, speak.

EPIHODOV: I should be desirous to speak with you alone (*sighs*).

DUNYASHA (*embarrassed*): Well—only bring me my mantle first. It's by the cupboard. It's rather damp here.

EPIHODOV: Certainly. I will fetch it. Now I know what I must do with my revolver (*takes guitar and goes off playing on it*).

YASHA: Two and twenty misfortunes! Between ourselves, he's a fool (*yawns*).

DUNYASHA: God grant he doesn't shoot himself! (*A pause*) I am so nervous, I'm always in a flutter. I was a little girl when I was taken into our lady's house, and now I have quite grown out of peasant ways, and my hands are white, as white as a lady's. I'm such a delicate, sensitive creature, I'm afraid of everything. I'm so frightened. And if you deceive me, Yasha, I don't know what will become of my nerves.

YASHA (*kisses her*): You're a peach! Of course a girl must never forget herself; what I dislike more than anything is a girl being flighty in her behaviour.

DUNYASHA: I'm passionately in love with you, Yasha; you are a man of culture—you can give your opinion about anything (*a pause*).

YASHA (*yawns*): Yes, that's so. My opinion is this: if a girl loves anyone, that means that she has no principles (*a pause*). It's pleasant smoking a cigar in the open air (*listens*). Someone's coming this way . . . it's the gentlefolk (DUNYASHA *embraces him impulsively*). Go home, as though you had been to the river to bathe; go by that path, or else they'll meet you and suppose I have made an appointment with you here. That I can't endure.

DUNYASHA (*coughing softly*): The cigar has made my head ache . . . (*goes off*).

(YASHA *remains sitting near the shrine. Enter* LYUBOV ANDREYEVNA, GAEV *and* LOPAHIN.)

LOPAHIN: You must make up your mind once for all—there's no time to lose. It's quite a simple question, you know. Will you consent to letting the land for building or not? One word in answer: Yes or no? Only one word!

LYUBOV: Who is smoking such horrible cigars here? (*Sits down.*)

GAEV: Now the railway line has been brought near, it's made things very convenient (*sits down*). Here we have been over and lunched in town. Cannon off the white! I should like to go home and have a game.

LYUBOV: You have plenty of time.

LOPAHIN: Only one word! (*Beseechingly*) Give me an answer!

GAEV (*yawning*): What do you say?

LYUBOV (*looks in her purse*): I had quite a lot of money here yesterday, and there's scarcely any left today. My poor Varya feeds us all on milk soup for the sake of economy; the old folks in the kitchen get nothing but pease pudding, while I waste my money in a senseless way (*drops purse, scattering gold pieces*). There, they have all fallen out! (*Annoyed.*)

YASHA: Allow me, I'll soon pick them up (*collects the coins*).

LYUBOV: Pray do, Yasha. And what did I go off to the town to lunch for? Your restaurant's a wretched place with its music and the tablecloth smelling of soap. . . . Why drink so much, Leonid? And eat so much? And talk so much? Today you talked a great deal again in the restaurant, and all so inappropriately. About the era of the 'seventies, about the decadents. And to whom? Talking to waiters about decadents!

LOPAHIN: Yes.

GAEV (*waving his hand*): I'm incorrigible; that's evident. (*Irritably to YASHA*) Why is it you keep fidgeting about in front of us!

YASHA (*laughs*): I can't help laughing when I hear your voice.

GAEV (*to his sister*): Either I or he . . .

LYUBOV: Get along! Go away, Yasha.

YASHA (*gives* LYUBOV ANDREYEVNA *her purse*): Directly (*hardly able to suppress his laughter*). This minute . . . (*goes off*).

LOPAHIN: Deriganov, the millionaire, means to buy your estate. They say he is coming to the sale himself.

LYUBOV: Where did you hear that?

LOPAHIN: That's what they say in town.

GAEV: Our aunt in Yaroslavl has promised to send help; but when, and how much she will send, we don't know.

LOPAHIN: How much will she send? A hundred thousand? Two hundred?

LYUBOV: Oh, well! . . . Ten or fifteen thousand, and we must be thankful to get that.

LOPAHIN: Forgive me, but such reckless people as you are—such queer, unbusiness-like people—I never met in my life. One tells you in plain Russian your estate is going to be sold, and you seem not to understand it.

LYUBOV: What are we to do? Tell us what to do.

LOPAHIN: I do tell you every day. Every day I say the same thing. You absolutely must let the cherry orchard and the land on building leases; and do it at once, as quick as may be—the auction's close upon us! Do understand! Once make up your mind to build villas, and you can raise as much money as you like, and then you are saved.

LYUBOV: Villas and summer visitors—forgive me saying so—it's so vulgar.

GAEV: There I perfectly agree with you.

LOPAHIN: I shall sob, or scream, or fall into a fit. I can't stand it! You drive me mad! (*To* GAEV) You're an old woman!

GAEV: What do you say?

LOPAHIN: An old woman! (*Gets up to go.*)

LYUBOV (*in dismay*): No, don't go! Do stay, my dear friend! Perhaps we shall think of something.

LOPAHIN: What is there to think of?

LYUBOV: Don't go, I entreat you! With you here it's more cheerful, anyway (*a pause*). I keep expecting something, as though the house were going to fall about our ears.

GAEV (*in profound dejection*): Potted the white! It fails—a kiss.

LYUBOV: We have been great sinners. . . .

LOPAHIN: You have no sins to repent of.

GAEV (*puts a caramel in his mouth*): They say I've eaten up my property in caramels (*laughs*).

LYUBOV: Oh, my sins! I've always thrown my money away recklessly like a lunatic. I married a man who made nothing but debts. My husband died of champagne—he drank dreadfully. To my misery I loved another man, and immediately—it was my first punishment—the blow fell upon me, here, in the river . . . my boy was drowned and I went abroad—went away for ever, never to return, not to see that river again . . . I shut my eyes, and fled, distracted, and *he* after me . . . pitilessly, brutally. I bought a villa at Mentone, for *he* fell ill there, and for three years I had no rest day or night. His illness wore me out, my soul was dried up. And last year, when my villa was sold to pay my debts, I went to Paris and there he robbed me of everything and abandoned me for another woman; and I tried to poison myself. . . . So stupid, so shameful! . . . And suddenly I felt a yearning for Russia, for my country, for my little girl . . . (*dries her tears*). Lord, Lord, be merciful! Forgive my sins! Do not chastise me more! (*Takes a telegram out of her pocket*) I got this today from Paris. He implores forgiveness, entreats me to return (*tears up the telegram*). I fancy there is music somewhere (*listens*).

GAEV: That's our famous Jewish orchestra. You remember, four violins, a flute and a double bass.

LYUBOV: That still in existence? We ought to send for them one evening, and give a dance.

LOPAHIN (*listens*): I can't hear. . . . (*Hums softly*) "For money the Germans will turn a Russian into a Frenchman." (*Laughs*) I did see such a piece at the theatre yesterday! It was funny!

LYUBOV: And most likely there was nothing funny in it. You shouldn't look at plays, you should look at yourselves a little oftener. How grey your lives are! How much nonsense you talk.

LOPAHIN: That's true. One may say honestly, we live a fool's life (*pause*). My father was a peasant, an idiot; he knew nothing and taught me nothing, only beat me when he was drunk, and always with his stick. In reality I am just such another blockhead and idiot. I've learnt nothing properly. I write a wretched hand. I write so that I feel ashamed before folks, like a pig.

LYUBOV: You ought to get married, my dear fellow.

LOPAHIN: Yes . . . that's true.

LYUBOV: You should marry our Varya, she's a good girl.

LOPAHIN: Yes.

LYUBOV: She's a good-natured girl, she's busy all day long, and what's more, she loves you. And you have liked her for ever so long.

LOPAHIN: Well? I'm not against it. . . . She's a good girl (*pause*).

GAEV: I've been offered a place in the bank: 6,000 roubles a year. Did you know?

LYUBOV: You would never do for that! You must stay as you are.

(*Enter* FIRS *with overcoat.*)

FIRS: Put it on, sir, it's damp.

GAEV (*putting it on*): You bother me, old fellow.

FIRS: You can't go on like this. You went away in the morning without leaving word (*looks him over*).

LYUBOV: You look older, Firs!

FIRS: What is your pleasure?

LOPAHIN: You look older, she said.

FIRS: I've had a long life. They were arranging my wedding before your papa was born . . . (*laughs*). I was the head footman before the emancipation came. I wouldn't consent to be set free then; I stayed on with the old master . . . (*a pause*). I remember what rejoicings they made and didn't know themselves what they were rejoicing over.

LOPAHIN: Those were fine old times. There was flogging anyway.

FIRS (*not hearing*): To be sure! The peasants knew their place, and the masters knew theirs; but now they're all at sixes and sevens, there's no making it out.

GAEV: Hold your tongue, Firs. I must go to town tomorrow. I have been promised an introduction to a general, who might let us have a loan.

LOPAHIN: You won't bring that off. And you won't pay your arrears, you may rest assured of that.

LYUBOV: That's all his nonsense. There is no such general.

(*Enter* TROFIMOV, ANYA *and* VARYA.)

GAEV: Here come our girls.

ANYA: There's mamma on the seat.

LYUBOV (*tenderly*): Come here, come along. My darlings! (*Embraces* ANYA *and* VARYA) If you only knew how I love you both. Sit beside me, there, like that. (*All sit down.*)

LOPAHIN: Our perpetual student is always with the young ladies.

TROFIMOV: That's not your business.

LOPAHIN: He'll soon be fifty, and he's still a student.

TROFIMOV: Drop your idiotic jokes.

LOPAHIN: Why are you so cross, you queer fish?

TROFIMOV: Oh, don't persist!

LOPAHIN (*laughs*): Allow me to ask you what's your idea of me?

TROFIMOV: I'll tell you my idea of you, Yermolay Alexeyevitch: you are a rich man, you'll soon be a millionaire. Well, just as in the economy of nature a wild beast is of use, who devours everything that comes in his way, so you too have your use.

(*All laugh.*)

VARYA: Better tell us something about the planets, Petya.

LYUBOV: No, let us go on with the conversation we had yesterday.

TROFIMOV: What was it about?

GAEV: About pride.

TROFIMOV: We had a long conversation yesterday, but we came to no conclusion. In pride, in your sense of it, there is something mystical. Perhaps you are right from your point of view; but if one looks at it simply, without subtlety, what sort of pride can there be, what sense is there in it, if man in his physiological formation is very imperfect, if in the immense majority of cases he is coarse, dull-witted, profoundly unhappy? One must give up glorification of self. One should work, and nothing else.

GAEV: One must die in any case.

TROFIMOV: Who knows? And what does it mean—dying? Perhaps man has a hundred senses, and only the five we know are lost at death, while the other ninety-five remain alive.

LYUBOV: How clever you are, Petya!

LOPAHIN (*ironically*): Fearfully clever!

TROFIMOV: Humanity progresses, perfecting its powers. Everything that is beyond its ken now will one day become familiar and comprehensible; only we must work, we must with all our powers aid the seeker after truth. Here among us in Russia the workers are few in number as yet. The vast majority of the intellectual people I know, seek nothing, do nothing, are not fit as yet for work of any kind. They call themselves intellectual, but they treat their servants as inferiors, behave to the peasants as though they were animals, learn little, read nothing seriously, do practically nothing, only talk about science and know very little about art. They are all serious people, they all have severe faces, they all talk of weighty matters and air their theories, and yet the vast majority of us—ninety-nine per cent.—live like savages, at the least thing fly to blows and abuse, eat piggishly, sleep in filth and stuffiness, bugs everywhere, stench and damp and moral impurity. And it's clear all our fine talk is only to divert our attention and other people's. Show me where to find the crèches there's so much talk about, and the reading-rooms? They only exist in novels: in real life there are none of them. There is nothing but filth and vulgarity and Asiatic apathy. I fear and dislike very serious faces. I'm afraid of serious conversations. We should do better to be silent.

LOPAHIN: You know, I get up at five o'clock in the morning, and I work from morning to night; and I've money, my own and other people's, always passing through my hands, and I see what people are made of all round me. One has only to begin to do anything to see how few honest, decent people there are. Sometimes when I lie awake at night, I think: "Oh! Lord, thou hast given us immense forests, boundless plains, the widest horizons, and living here we ourselves ought really to be giants."

LYUBOV: You ask for giants! They are no good except in story-books; in real life they frighten us.

(EPIHODOV *advances in the background, playing on the guitar.*)

LYUBOV (*dreamily*): There goes Epihodov.

ANYA (*dreamily*): There goes Epihodov.

GAEV: The sun has set, my friends.

TROFIMOV: Yes.

GAEV (*not loudly, but, as it were, declaiming*): O nature, divine nature, thou art bright with eternal lustre, beautiful and indifferent! Thou, whom we call mother, thou dost unite within thee life and death! Thou dost give life and dost destroy!

VARYA (*in a tone of supplication*): Uncle!

ANYA: Uncle, you are at it again!

TROFIMOV: You'd much better be cannoning off the red!

GAEV: I'll hold my tongue, I will.

(*All sit plunged in thought. Perfect stillness. The only thing audible is the muttering of* FIRS. *Suddenly there is a sound in the distance, as it were from the sky—the sound of a breaking harp-string, mournfully dying away.*)

LYUBOV: What is that?

LOPAHIN: I don't know. Somewhere far away a bucket fallen and broken in the pits. But somewhere very far away.

GAEV: It might be a bird of some sort—such as a heron.

TROFIMOV: Or an owl.

LYUBOV (*shudders*): I don't know why, but it's horrid (*a pause*).

FIRS: It was the same before the calamity—the owl hooted and the samovar hissed all the time.

GAEV: Before what calamity?

FIRS: Before the emancipation (*a pause*).

LYUBOV: Come, my friends, let us be going; evening is falling. (*To* ANYA) There are tears in your eyes. What is it, darling? (*Embraces her.*)

ANYA: Nothing, mamma; it's nothing.

TROFIMOV: There is somebody coming.

(*The wayfarer appears in a shabby white forage cap and an over-coat; he is slightly drunk.*)

WAYFARER: Allow me to inquire, can I get to the station this way?

GAEV: Yes. Go along that road.

WAYFARER: I thank you most feelingly (*coughing*). The weather is superb. (*Declaims*) My brother, my suffering brother! . . . Come out to the Volga! Whose groan do you hear? . . . (*To* VARYA) Mademoiselle, vouchsafe a hungry Russian thirty kopeks.

(VARYA *utters a shriek of alarm.*)

LOPAHIN (*angrily*): There's a right and a wrong way of doing every-thing!

LYUBOV (*hurriedly*): Here, take this (*looks in her purse*). I've no silver. No matter—here's gold for you.

WAYFARER: I thank you most feelingly! (*Goes off.*)

(*Laughter.*)

VARYA (*frightened*): I'm going home—I'm going . . . Oh, mamma, the servants have nothing to eat, and you gave him gold!

LYUBOV: There's no doing anything with me. I'm so silly! When we get home, I'll give you all I possess. Yermolay Alexeyevitch, you will lend me some more . . . !

LOPAHIN: I will.

LYUBOV: Come, friends, it's time to be going. And Varya, we have made a match of it for you. I congratulate you.

VARYA (*through her tears*): Mamma, that's not a joking matter.

LOPAHIN: "Ophelia, get thee to a nunnery!"

GAEV: My hands are trembling; it's a long while since I had a game of billiards.

LOPAHIN: "Ophelia! Nymph, in thy orisons be all my sins remem-ber'd."

LYUBOV: Come, it will soon be supper-time.

VARYA: How he frightened me! My heart's simply throbbing.

LOPAHIN: Let me remind you, ladies and gentlemen: on the 22nd of August the cherry orchard will be sold. Think about that! Think about it!

(*All go off, except* TROFIMOV *and* ANYA.)

ANYA (*laughing*): I'm grateful to the wayfarer! He frightened Varya and we are left alone.

TROFIMOV: Varya's afraid we shall fall in love with each other, and for days together she won't leave us. With her narrow brain she can't grasp that we are above love. To eliminate the petty and transitory which hinders us from being free and happy—that is the aim and meaning of our life. Forward! We go forward irresistibly towards the bright star that shines yonder in the distance. Forward! Do not lag behind, friends.

ANYA (*claps her hands*): How well you speak! (*A pause*) It is divine here today.

TROFIMOV: Yes, it's glorious weather.

ANYA: Somehow, Petya, you've made me so that I don't love the cherry orchard as I used to. I used to love it so dearly. I used to think that there was no spot on earth like our garden.

TROFIMOV: All Russia is our garden. The earth is great and beautiful —there are many beautiful places in it (*a pause*). Think only, Anya, your grandfather, and great-grandfather, and all your ancestors were slave-owners—the owners of living souls—and from every cherry in the orchard, from every leaf, from every trunk there are human creatures looking at you. Cannot you hear their voices? Oh, it is awful! Your orchard is a fearful thing, and when in the evening or at night one walks about the orchard, the old bark on the trees glimmers dimly in the dusk, and the old cherry trees seem to be dreaming of centuries gone by and tortured by fearful visions. Yes! We are at least two hundred years behind, we have really gained nothing yet, we have no definite attitude to the past, we do nothing but theorise or complain of depression or drink vodka. It is clear that to begin to live in the present we must first expiate our past, we must break with it; and we can expiate it only by suffering, by extraordinary unceasing labour. Understand that, Anya.

ANYA: The house we live in has long ceased to be our own, and I shall leave it, I give you my word.

TROFIMOV: If you have the house keys, fling them into the well and go away. Be free as the wind.

ANYA (*in ecstasy*): How beautifully you said that!

TROFIMOV: Believe me, Anya, believe me! I am not thirty yet, I am young, I am still a student, but I have gone through so much already! As soon as winter comes I am hungry, sick, careworn, poor as a beggar, and what ups and downs of fortune have I not known! And my soul was always, every minute, day and night, full of inexplicable forebodings. I have a foreboding of happiness, Anya. I see glimpses of it already.

ANYA (*pensively*): The moon is rising.

(EPIHODOV *is heard playing still the same mournful song on the guitar. The moon rises. Somewhere near the poplars* VARYA *is looking for* ANYA *and calling* "Anya! where are you?")

TROFIMOV: Yes, the moon is rising (*a pause*). Here is happiness—here it comes! It is coming nearer and nearer; already I can hear its footsteps. And if we never see it—if we may never know it—what does it matter? Others will see it after us.

VARYA'S VOICE: Anya! Where are you?

TROFIMOV: That Varya again! (*Angrily*) It's revolting!

ANYA: Well, let's go down to the river. It's lovely there.

TROFIMOV: Yes, let's go. (*They go.*)

VARYA'S VOICE: Anya! Anya!

(*The Curtain Falls.*)

# Act Three

A drawing-room divided by an arch from a larger drawing-room.
A chandlier burning. The Jewish orchestra, the same that was
mentioned in Act II, is heard playing in the ante-room. It is evening.
In the larger drawing-room they are dancing the grand chain. The
voice of SEMYONOV-PISHTCHIK: "Promenade à une paire!" Then enter
the drawing-room in couples first PISHTCHIK and CHARLOTTA IVANOVA,
then TROFIMOV and LYUBOV ANDREYEVNA, thirdly ANYA with the Post-
Office Clerk, fourthly VARYA with the Station Master, and other
guests. VARYA is quietly weeping and wiping away her tears as she
dances. In the last couple is DUNYASHA. They move across the drawing-room. PISHTCHIK shouts: Grand rond, balancez! and "Les Cav-
aliers à genou et remerciez vos dames."

    FIRS in a swallow-tail coat brings in seltzer water on a tray.
PISHTCHIK and TROFIMOV enter the drawing-room.

PISHTCHIK: I am a full-blooded man; I have already had two strokes.
Dancing's hard work for me, but as they say, if you're in the pack,
you must bark with the rest. I'm as strong, I may say, as a horse. My
parent, who would have his joke—may the Kingdom of Heaven be
his!—used to say about our origin that the ancient stock of the
Semyonov-Pishtchiks was derived from the very horse that Caligula
made a member of the senate (sits down). But I've no money, that's
where the mischief is. A hungry dog believes in nothing but meat
. . . . (snores, but at once wakes up). That's like me . . . I can
think of nothing but money.

TROFIMOV: There really is something horsy about your appearance.

PISHTCHIK: Well . . . a horse is a fine beast . . . a horse can be sold.

(There is the sound of billiards being played in an adjoining room.
VARYA appears in the arch leading to the larger drawing-room.)

TROFIMOV (teasing): Madame Lopahin! Madame Lopahin!

VARYA (angrily): Mangy-looking gentleman!

TROFIMOV: Yes, I am a mangy-looking gentleman, and I'm proud of it!

VARYA (*pondering bitterly*): Here we have hired musicians and nothing to pay them! (*Goes out.*)

TROFIMOV (*to* PISHTCHIK): If the energy you have wasted during your lifetime in trying to find the money to pay your interest, had gone to something else, you might in the end have turned the world upside down.

PISHTCHIK: Nietzsche, the philosopher, a very great and celebrated man . . . of enormous intellect . . . says in his works, that one can make forged bank-notes.

TROFIMOV: Why, have you read Nietzsche?

PISHTCHIK: What next . . . Dashenka told me. . . . And now I am in such a position, I might just as well forge bank-notes. The day after tomorrow I must pay 310 roubles—130 I have procured (*feels in his pockets, in alarm*). The money's gone! I have lost my money! (*Through his tears*) Where's the money? (*Gleefully*) Why, here it is behind the lining. . . . It has made me hot all over.

(*Enter* LYUBOV ANDREYEVNA *and* CHARLOTTA IVANOVNA.)

LYUBOV (*hums the Lezginka*): Why is Leonid so long? What can he be doing in town? (*To* DUNYASHA) Offer the musicians some tea.

TROFIMOV: The sale hasn't taken place, most likely.

LYUBOV: It's the wrong time to have the orchestra, and the wrong time to give a dance. Well, never mind (*sits down and hums softly*).

CHARLOTTA (*gives* PISHTCHIK *a pack of cards*): Here's a pack of cards. Think of any card you like.

PISHTCHIK: I've thought of one.

CHARLOTTA: Shuffle the pack now. That's right. Give it here, my dear Mr. Pishtchik. Ein, zwei, drei—now look, it's in your breast pocket.

PISHTCHIK (*taking a card out of his breast pocket*): The eight of spades! Perfectly right! (*Wonderingly*) Fancy that now!

CHARLOTTA (*holding pack of cards in her hands, to* TROFIMOV): Tell me quickly which is the top card.

TROFIMOV: Well, the queen of spades.

CHARLOTTA: It is! (*To* PISHTCHIK) Well, which card is uppermost?

PISHTCHIK: The ace of hearts.

CHARLOTTA: It is! (*Claps her hands, pack of cards disappears*) Ah! what lovely weather it is today!

(*A mysterious feminine voice which seems coming out of the floor answers her.* "Oh, yes, it's magnificent weather, madam.")

CHARLOTTA: You are my perfect ideal.

VOICE: And I greatly admire you too, madam.

STATION MASTER (*applauding*): The lady ventriloquist—bravo!

PISHTCHIK (*wonderingly*): Fancy that now! Most enchanting Charlotta Ivanovna. I'm simply in love with you.

CHARLOTTA: In love? (*Shrugging shoulders*) What do you know of love, guter Mensch, aber schlechter Musikant.

TROFIMOV (*pats* PISHTCHIK *on the shoulder*): You dear old horse. . . .

CHARLOTTA: Attention, please! Another trick! (*Takes a travelling rug from a chair*) Here's a very good rug; I want to sell it (*shaking it out*). Doesn't anyone want to buy it?

PISHTCHIK (*wonderingly*): Fancy that!

CHARLOTTA: Ein, zwei, drei! (*Quickly picks up rug she has dropped; behind the rug stands* ANYA; *she makes a curtsey, runs to her mother, embraces her and runs back into the larger drawing-room amidst general enthusiasm.*)

LYUBOV (*applauds*): Bravo! Bravo!

CHARLOTTA: Now again! Ein, zwei, drei! (*Lifts up the rug; behind the rug stands* VARYA, *bowing.*)

PISHTCHIK (*wonderingly*): Fancy that now!

CHARLOTTA: That's the end (*throws the rug at* PISHTCHIK, *makes a curtsey, runs into the larger drawing-room*).

PISHTCHIK (*hurries after her*): Mischievous creature! Fancy! (*Goes out.*)

LYUBOV: And still Leonid doesn't come. I can't understand what he's doing in the town so long! Why, everything must be over by now. The estate is sold, or the sale has not taken place. Why keep us so long in suspense?

VARYA (*trying to console her*): Uncle's bought it. I feel sure of that.

TROFIMOV (*ironically*): Oh, yes!

VARYA: Great-aunt sent him an authorisation to buy it in her name, and transfer the debt. She's doing it for Anya's sake, and I'm sure God will be merciful. Uncle will buy it.

LYUBOV: My aunt in Yaroslavl sent fifteen thousand to buy the estate in her name, she doesn't trust us—but that's not enough even to pay the arrears (*hides her face in her hands*). My fate is being sealed today, my fate . . .

TROFIMOV (*teasing* VARYA): Madame Lopahin.

VARYA (*angrily*): Perpetual student! Twice already you've been sent down from the University.

LYUBOV: Why are you angry, Varya? He's teasing you about Lopahin. Well, what of that? Marry Lopahin if you like, he's a good man, and interesting; if you don't want to, don't! Nobody compels you, darling.

VARYA: I must tell you plainly, mamma, I look at the matter seriously; he's a good man, I like him.

LYUBOV: Well, marry him. I can't see what you're waiting for.

VARYA: Mamma. I can't make him an offer myself. For the last two years, everyone's been talking to me about him. Everyone talks; but he says nothing or else makes a joke. I see what it means. He's growing rich, he's absorbed in business, he has no thoughts for me. If I had money, were it ever so little, if I had only a hundred roubles, I'd throw everything up and go far away. I would go into a nunnery.

TROFIMOV: What bliss!

VARYA (*to* TROFIMOV): A student ought to have sense! (*In a soft tone with tears*) How ugly you've grown, Petya! How old you look! (*To* LYUBOV ANDREYEVNA, *no longer crying*) But I can't do without work, mamma; I must have something to do every minute.

(*Enter* YASHA.)

YASHA (*hardly restraining his laughter*): Epihodov has broken a billiard cue! (*Goes out.*)

VARYA: What is Epihodov doing here? Who gave him leave to play billiards? I can't make these people out (*goes out*).

LYUBOV: Don't tease her, Petya. You see she has grief enough without that.

TROFIMOV: She is so very officious, meddling in what's not her business. All the summer she's given Anya and me no peace. She's afraid of a love affair between us. What's it to do with her? Besides, I have given no grounds for it. Such triviality is not in my line. We are above love!

LYUBOV: And I suppose I am beneath love. (*Very uneasily*) Why is it Leonid's not here? If only I could know whether the estate is sold or not! It seems such an incredible calamity that I really don't know what to think. I am distracted . . . I shall scream in a minute . . . I shall do something stupid. Save me, Petya, tell me something, talk to me!

TROFIMOV: What does it matter whether the estate is sold today or not? That's all done with long ago. There's no turning back, the path is overgrown. Don't worry yourself, dear Lyubov Andreyevna. You mustn't deceive yourself; for once in your life you must face the truth!

LYUBOV: What truth? You see where the truth lies, but I seem to have lost my sight, I see nothing. You settle every great problem so boldly, but tell me, my dear boy, isn't it because you're young—because you haven't yet understood one of your problems through suffering? You look forward boldly, and isn't it that you don't see and don't expect anything dreadful because life is still hidden from your young eyes? You're bolder, more honest, deeper than we are, but think, be just a little magnanimous, have pity on me. I was born

here, you know, my father and mother lived here, my grandfather
lived here, I love this house. I can't conceive of life without the
cherry orchard, and if it really must be sold, then sell me with the
orchard (*embraces* TROFIMOV, *kisses him on the forehead*). My boy
was drowned here (*weeps*). Pity me, my dear kind fellow.

TROFIMOV: You know I feel for you with all my heart.

LYUBOV: But that should have been said differently, so differently
(*takes out her handkerchief, telegram falls on the floor*). My heart
is so heavy today. It's so noisy here, my soul is quivering at every
sound, I'm shuddering all over, but I can't go away; I'm afraid to
be quiet and alone. Don't be hard on me, Petya . . . I love you as
though you were one of ourselves. I would gladly let you marry
Anya—I swear I would—only, my dear boy, you must take your
degree, you do nothing—you're simply tossed by fate from place to
place. That's so strange. It is, isn't it? And you must do something
with your beard to make it grow somehow (*laughs*). You look so
funny!

TROFIMOV (*picks up the telegram*): I've no wish to be a beauty.

LYUBOV: That's a telegram from Paris. I get one every day. One
yesterday and one today. That savage creature is ill again, he's in
trouble again. He begs forgiveness, beseeches me to go, and really
I ought to go to Paris to see him. You look shocked, Petya. What
am I to do, my dear boy, what am I to do? He is ill, he is alone
and unhappy, and who'll look after him, who'll keep him from doing
the wrong thing, who'll give him his medicine at the right time?
And why hide it or be silent? I love him, that's clear. I love him! I
love him! He's a millstone about my neck, I'm going to the bottom
with him, but I love that stone and can't live without it (*presses*
TROFIMOV's *hand*). Don't think ill of me, Petya, don't tell me anything, don't tell me . . .

TROFIMOV (*through his tears*): For God's sake forgive my frankness:
why, he robbed you!

LYUBOV: No! No! No! You mustn't speak like that (*covers her ears*).

TROFIMOV: He is a wretch! You're the only person that doesn't know
it! He's a worthless creature! A despicable wretch!

LYUBOV (*getting angry, but speaking with restraint*): You're twenty-
six or twenty-seven years old, but you're still a schoolboy.

TROFIMOV: Possibly.

LYUBOV: You should be a man at your age! You should understand what love means! And you ought to be in love yourself. You ought to fall in love! (*Angrily*) Yes, yes, and it's not purity in you, you're simply a prude, a comic fool, a freak.

TROFIMOV (*in horror*): The things she's saying!

LYUBOV: I am above love! You're not above love, but simply as our Firs here says, "You are a good-for-nothing." At your age not to have a mistress!

TROFIMOV (*in horror*): This is awful! The things she is saying! (*Goes rapidly into the larger drawing-room clutching his head*) This is awful! I can't stand it! I'm going. (*Goes off, but at once returns*) All is over between us! (*Goes off into the ante-room.*)

LYUBOV (*shouts after him*): Petya! Wait a minute! You funny creature! I was joking! Petya! (*There is a sound of somebody running quickly downstairs and suddenly falling with a crash.* ANYA *and* VARYA *scream, but there is a sound of laughter at once*).

LYUBOV: What has happened?

(ANYA *runs in.*)

ANYA (*laughing*): Petya's fallen downstairs! (*Runs out.*)

LYUBOV: What a queer fellow that Petya is!

(*The Station Master stands in the middle of the larger room and reads "The Magdalene," by Alexey Tolstoy. They listen to him, but before he has recited many lines strains of a waltz are heard from the ante-room and the reading is broken off. All dance.* TROFIMOV, ANYA, VARYA *and* LYUBOV ANDREYEVNA *come in from the ante-room.*)

LYUBOV: Come, Petya—come, pure heart! I beg your pardon. Let's have a dance! (*Dances with* PETYA.)

(ANYA *and* VARYA *dance.* FIRS *comes in, puts his stick down near the side door.* YASHA *also comes into the drawing-room and looks on at the dancing.*)

YASHA: What is it, old man?

FIRS: I don't feel well. In old days we used to have generals, barons and admirals dancing at our balls, and now we send for the post-office clerk and the station master and even they're not overanxious to come. I am getting feeble. The old master, the grandfather, used to give sealing-wax for all complaints. I have been taking sealing-wax for twenty years or more. Perhaps that's what's kept me alive.

YASHA: You bore me, old man! (*Yawns*) it's time you were done with.

FIRS: Ach, you're a good-for-nothing! (*Mutters.*)

(TROFIMOV *and* LYUBOV ANDREYEVNA *dance in larger room and then on to the stage*).

LYUBOV: *Merci.* I'll sit down a little (*sits down*). I'm tired.

(*Enter* ANYA.)

ANYA (*excitedly*): There's a man in the kitchen has been saying that the cherry orchard's been sold today.

LYUBOV: Sold to whom?

ANYA: He didn't say to whom. He's gone away.

(*She dances with* TROFIMOV, *and they go off into the larger room.*)

YASHA: There was an old man gossiping there, a stranger.

FIRS: Leonid Andreyevitch isn't here yet, he hasn't come back. He has his light overcoat on, *demi-saison*, he'll catch cold for sure. Ach! Foolish young things!

LYUBOV: I feel as though I should die. Go, Yasha, find out to whom it has been sold.

YASHA: But he went away long ago, the old chap (*laughs*).

LYUBOV (*with slight vexation*): What are you laughing at? What are you pleased at?

YASHA: Epihodov is so funny. He's a silly fellow, two and twenty misfortunes.

LYUBOV: Firs, if the estate is sold, where will you go?

FIRS: Where you bid me, there I'll go.

LYUBOV: Why do you look like that? Are you ill? You ought to be in bed.

FIRS: Yes (*ironically*). Me go to bed and who's to wait here? Who's to see to things without me? I'm the only one in all the house.

YASHA (*to* LYUBOV ANDREYEVNA): Lyubov Andreyevna, permit me to make a request of you; if you go back to Paris again, be so kind as to take me with you. It's positively impossible for me to stay here (*looking about him; in an undertone*). There's no need to say it, you see for yourself—an uncivilised country, the people have no morals, and then the dullness! The food in the kitchen's abominable, and then Firs runs after one muttering all sorts of unsuitable words. Take me with you, please do!

(*Enter* PISHTCHIK.)

PISHTCHIK: Allow me to ask you for a waltz, my dear lady. (LYUBOV ANDREYEVNA *goes with him*) Enchanting lady, I really must borrow of you just 180 roubles (*dances*), only 180 roubles. (*They pass into the larger room.*)

YASHA (*hums softly*): "Knowest thou my soul's emotion."

(*In the larger drawing-room, a figure in a gray top hat and in check trousers is gesticulating and jumping about.* Shouts of "Bravo, Charlotta Ivanovna.")

DUNYASHA (*she has stopped to powder herself*): My young lady tells me to dance. There are plenty of gentlemen, and too few ladies, but dancing makes me giddy and makes my heart beat. Firs, the post-office clerk said something to me just now that quite took my breath away.

(*Music becomes more subdued.*)

FIRS: What did he say to you?

DUNYASHA: He said I was like a flower.

YASHA (*yawns*): What ignorance! (*Goes out.*)

DUNYASHA: Like a flower. I am a girl of such delicate feelings, I am awfully fond of soft speeches.

FIRS: Your head's being turned.

(*Enter* EPIHODOV.)

EPIHODOV: You have no desire to see me, Dunyasha. I might be an insect (*sighs*). Ah! life!

DUNYASHA: What is it you want?

EPIHODOV: Undoubtedly you may be right (*sighs*). But of course, if one looks at it from that point of view, if I may so express myself, you have, excuse my plain speaking, reduced me to a complete state of mind. I know my destiny. Every day some misfortune befalls me and I have long ago grown accustomed to it, so that I look upon my fate with a smile. You gave me your word, and though I . . .

DUNYASHA: Let us have a talk later, I entreat you, but now leave me in peace, for I am lost in reverie (*plays with her fan*).

EPIHODOV: I have a misfortune every day, and if I may venture to express myself, I merely smile at it, I even laugh.

(VARYA *enters from the larger drawing-room.*)

VARYA: You still have not gone, Epihodov. What a disrespectful creature you are, really! (*To* DUNYASHA) Go along, Dunyasha! (*To* EPIHODOV) First you play billiards and break the cue, then you go wandering about the drawing-room like a visitor!

EPIHODOV: You really cannot, if I may so express myself, call me to account like this.

VARYA: I'm not calling you to account, I'm speaking to you: You do nothing but wander from place to place and don't do your work. We keep you as a counting-house clerk, but what use you are I can't say.

EPIHODOV (*offended*): Whether I work or whether I walk, whether I eat or whether I play billiards, is a matter to be judged by persons of understanding and my elders.

VARYA: You dare to tell me that! (*Firing up*) You dare! You mean to say I've no understanding. Begone from here! This minute!

EPIHODOV (*intimidated*): I beg you to express yourself with delicacy.

VARYA (*beside herself with anger*): This moment! get out! away! (*He goes towards the door, she following him*) Two and twenty misfortunes! Take yourself off! Don't let me set eyes on you!

(EPIHODOV *has gone out, behind the door his voice,* "I shall lodge a complaint against you") What! You're coming back? (*Snatches up the stick* FIRS *has put down near the door*) Come! Come! Come! I'll show you! What! you're coming? Then take that! (*She swings the stick, at the very moment that* LOPAHIN *comes in.*)

LOPAHIN: Very much obliged to you!

VARYA (*angrily and ironically*): I beg your pardon!

LOPAHIN: Not at all! I humbly thank you for your kind reception!

VARYA: No need of thanks for it. (*Moves away, then looks round and asks softly*) I haven't hurt you?

LOPAHIN: Oh, no! Not at all! There's an immense bump coming up, though!

VOICES FROM LARGER ROOM: Lopahin has come! Yermolay Alexeyevitch!

PISHTCHIK: What do I see and hear? (*Kisses* LOPAHIN) There's a whiff of cognac about you, my dear soul, and we're making merry here too!

(*Enter* LYUBOV ANDREYEVNA.)

LYUBOV: Is it you, Yermolay Alexeyevitch? Why have you been so long? Where's Leonid?

LOPAHIN: Leonid Andreyevitch arrived with me. He is coming.

LYUBOV (*in agitation*): Well! Well! Was there a sale? Speak!

LOPAHIN (*embarrassed, afraid of betraying his joy*): The sale was over at four o'clock. We missed our train—had to wait till half-past nine. (*Sighing heavily*) Ugh! I feel a little giddy.

(*Enter* GAEV. *In his right hand he has purchases, with his left hand he is wiping away his tears.*)

LYUBOV: Well, Leonid? What news? (*Impatiently, with tears*) Make haste, for God's sake!

GAEV (*makes her no answer, simply waves his hand. To* FIRS, *weeping*): Here, take them; there's anchovies, Kertch herrings. I have eaten nothing all day. What I have been through! (*Door into the billiard room is open. There is heard a knocking of balls and the voice of* YASHA *saying* "Eighty-seven." GAEV's *expression changes, he leaves off weeping*) I am fearfully tired. Firs, come and help me change my things (*goes to his own room across the larger drawing-room*).

PISHTCHIK: How about the sale? Tell us, do!

LYUBOV: Is the cherry orchard sold?

LOPAHIN: It is sold.

LYUBOV: Who has bought it?

LOPAHIN: I have bought it. (*A pause.* LYUBOV *is crushed; she would fall down if she were not standing near a chair and table.*)

(VARYA *takes keys from her waist-band, flings them on the floor in middle of drawing-room and goes out.*)

LOPAHIN: I have bought it! Wait a bit, ladies and gentlemen, pray. My head's a bit muddled, I can't speak (*laughs*). We came to the auction. Deriganov was there already. Leonid Andreyevitch only had 15,000 and Deriganov bid 30,000, besides the arrears, straight off. I saw how the land lay. I bid against him. I bid 40,000, he bid 45,000, I said 55, and so he went on, adding 5 thousands and I adding 10. Well . . . So it ended. I bid 90, and it was knocked down to me. Now the cherry orchard's mine! Mine! (*chuckles*) My God, the cherry orchard's mine! Tell me that I'm drunk, that I'm out of my mind, that it's all a dream (*stamps with his feet*). Don't laugh at me! If my father and my grandfather could rise from their graves and see all that has happened! How their Yermolay, ignorant, beaten Yermolay, who used to run about barefoot in winter, how that very Yermolay has bought the finest estate in the world! I have bought the estate where my father and grandfather were slaves, where they weren't even admitted into the kitchen. I am asleep, I am dreaming! It is all fancy, it is the work of your imagination plunged in the darkness of ignorance (*picks up keys, smiling fondly*). She threw away the keys; she means to show she's not the housewife now (*jingles the keys*). Well, no matter. (*The orchestra is heard tuning up*) Hey, musicians! Play! I want to hear you. Come, all of you, and look how Yermolay Lopahin will take the axe to the cherry orchard, how the trees will fall to the ground! We will build houses on it and our grandsons and great-grandsons will see a new life springing up there. Music! Play up!

(*Music begins to play.* LYUBOV ANDREYEVNA *has sunk into a chair and is weeping bitterly.*)

LOPAHIN (*reproachfully*): Why, why didn't you listen to me? My poor friend! Dear lady, there's no turning back now. (*With tears*) Oh, if all this could be over, oh, if our miserable disjointed life could somehow soon be changed!

PISHTCHIK (*takes him by the arm, in an undertone*): She's weeping, let us go and leave her alone. Come (*takes him by the arm and leads him into the larger drawing-room*).

LOPAHIN: What's that? Musicians, play up! All must be as I wish it. (*With irony*) Here comes the new master, the owner of the cherry orchard! (*Accidentally tips over a little table, almost upsetting the candelabra*) I can pay for everything! (*Goes out with* PISHTCHIK. *No one remains on the stage or in the larger drawing-room except* LYUBOV, *who sits huddled up, weeping bitterly. The music plays softly.* ANYA *and* TROFIMOV *come in quickly.* ANYA *goes up to her mother and falls on her knees before her.* TROFIMOV *stands at the entrance to the larger drawing-room*).

ANYA: Mamma! Mamma, you're crying, dear, kind, good mamma! My precious! I love you! I bless you! The cherry orchard is sold, it is gone, that's true, that's true! But don't weep, mamma! Life is still before you, you have still your good, pure heart! Let us go, let us go, darling, away from here! We will make a new garden, more splendid than this one; you will see it, you will understand. And joy, quiet, deep joy, will sink into your soul like the sun at evening! And you will smile, mamma! Come, darling, let us go!

(*The Curtain Falls.*)

# Act Four

SCENE: *Same as in First Act. There are neither curtains on the windows nor pictures on the walls: only a little furniture remains piled up in a corner as if for sale. There is a sense of desolation; near the outer door and in the background of the scene are packed trunks, travelling bags, etc. On the left the door is open, and from here the voices of* VARYA *and* ANYA *are audible.* LOPAHIN *is standing waiting.* YASHA *is holding a tray with glasses full of champagne. In front of the stage* EPIHODOV *is tying up a box. In the background behind the scene a hum of talk from the peasants who have come to say good-bye. The voice of* GAEV: *"Thanks, brothers, thanks!"*

YASHA: The peasants have come to say good-bye. In my opinion, Yermolay Alexeyevitch, the peasants are good-natured, but they don't know much about things.

(*The hum of talk dies away. Enter across front of stage* LYUBOV ANDREYEVNA *and* GAEV. *She is not weeping, but is pale; her face is quivering—she cannot speak.*)

GAEV: You gave them your purse, Lyuba. That won't do—that won't do!

LYUBOV: I couldn't help it! I couldn't help it!

(*Both go out.*)

LOPAHIN (*in the doorway, calls after them*): You will take a glass at parting? Please do. I didn't think to bring any from the town, and at the station I could only get one bottle. Please take a glass. (*A pause*) What? You don't care for any? (*Comes away from the door*) If I'd known, I wouldn't have bought it. Well, and I'm not going to drink it. (YASHA *carefully sets the tray down on a chair*) You have a glass, Yasha, anyway.

YASHA: Good luck to the travellers, and luck to those that stay behind! (*Drinks*) This champagne isn't the real thing, I can assure you.

LOPAHIN: It cost eight roubles the bottle (*a pause*). It's devilish cold here.

YASHA: They haven't heated the stove today—it's all the same since we're going (*laughs*).

LOPAHIN: What are you laughing for?

YASHA: For pleasure.

LOPAHIN: Though it's October, it's as still and sunny as though it were summer. It's just right for building! (*Looks at his watch; says in doorway*) Take note, ladies and gentlemen, the train goes in forty-seven minutes; so you ought to start for the station in twenty minutes. You must hurry up!

(TROFIMOV *comes in from out of doors wearing a great-coat.*)

TROFIMOV: I think it must be time to start, the horses are ready. The devil only knows what's become of my goloshes; they're lost. (*In the doorway*) Anya! My goloshes aren't here. I can't find them.

LOPAHIN: And I'm getting off to Harkov. I am going in the same train with you. I'm spending all the winter at Harkov. I've been wasting all my time gossiping with you and fretting with no work to do. I can't get on without work. I don't know what to do with my hands, they flap about so queerly, as if they didn't belong to me.

TROFIMOV: Well, we're just going away, and you will take up your profitable labours again.

LOPAHIN: Do take a glass.

TROFIMOV: No, thanks.

LOPAHIN: Then you're going to Moscow now?

TROFIMOV: Yes. I shall see them as far as the town, and tomorrow I shall go on to Moscow.

LOPAHIN: Yes, I daresay, the professors aren't giving any lectures, they're waiting for your arrival.

TROFIMOV: That's not your business.

LOPAHIN: How many years have you been at the University?

TROFIMOV: Do think of something newer than that—that's stale and flat (*hunts for goloshes*). You know we shall most likely never see each other again, so let me give you one piece of advice at parting: don't wave your arms about—get out of the habit. And another thing, building villas, reckoning up that the summer visitors will in time become independent farmers—reckoning like that, that's not the thing to do either. After all, I am fond of you: you have fine delicate fingers like an artist, you've a fine delicate soul.

LOPAHIN (*embraces him*): Good-bye, my dear fellow. Thanks for everything. Let me give you money for the journey, if you need it.

TROFIMOV: What for? I don't need it.

LOPAHIN: Why, you haven't got a halfpenny.

TROFIMOV: Yes, I have, thank you. I got some money for a translation. Here it is in my pocket, (*anxiously*) but where can my goloshes be!

VARYA (*from the next room*): Take the nasty things! (*Flings a pair of goloshes onto the stage.*)

TROFIMOV: Why are you so cross, Varya? h'm! . . . but those aren't my goloshes.

LOPAHIN: I sowed three thousand acres with poppies in the spring, and now I have cleared forty thousand profit. And when my poppies were in flower, wasn't it a picture! So here, as I say, I made forty thousand, and I'm offering you a loan because I can afford to. Why turn up your nose? I am a peasant—I speak bluntly.

TROFIMOV: Your father was a peasant, mine was a chemist—and that proves absolutely nothing whatever. (LOPAHIN *takes out his pocket-book*) Stop that—stop that. If you were to offer me two hundred thousand I wouldn't take it. I am an independent man, and everything that all of you, rich and poor alike, prize so highly and hold so dear, hasn't the slightest power over me—it's like so much fluff fluttering in the air. I can get on without you. I can pass by you. I am strong and proud. Humanity is advancing towards the highest truth, the highest happiness, which is possible on earth, and I am in the front ranks.

LOPAHIN: Will you get there?

TROFIMOV: I shall get there (*a pause*). I shall get there, or I shall show others the way to get there.

(*In the distance is heard the stroke of an axe on a tree.*)

LOPAHIN: Good-bye, my dear fellow; it's time to be off. We turn up our noses at one another, but life is passing all the while. When I am working hard without resting, then my mind is more at ease, and it seems to me as though I too know what I exist for; but how many people there are in Russia, my dear boy, who exist, one doesn't know what for. Well, it doesn't matter. That's not what keeps things spinning. They tell me Leonid Andreyevitch has taken a situation. He is going to be a clerk at the bank—6,000 roubles a year. Only, of course, he won't stick to it—he's too lazy.

ANYA (*in doorway*): Mamma begs you not to let them chop down the orchard until she's gone.

TROFIMOV: Yes, really, you might have the tact (*walks out across the front of the stage*).

LOPAHIN: I'll see to it! I'll see to it! Stupid fellows! (*Goes out after him.*)

ANYA: Has Firs been taken to the hospital?

YASHA: I told them this morning. No doubt they have taken him.

ANYA (*to* EPIHODOV, *who passes across the drawing-room*): Semyon Pantaleyevitch, inquire, please, if Firs has been taken to the hospital.

YASHA (*in a tone of offense*): I told Yegor this morning—why ask a dozen times?

EPIHODOV: Firs is advanced in years. It's my conclusive opinion no treatment would do him good; it's time he was gathered to his fathers. And I can only envy him (*puts a trunk down on a cardboard hat-box and crushes it*). There now, of course—I knew it would be so.

YASHA (*jeeringly*): Two and twenty misfortunes!

VARYA (*through the door*): Has Firs been taken to the hospital?

ANYA: Yes.

VARYA: Why wasn't the note for the doctor taken too?

ANYA: Oh, then, we must send it after them (*goes out*).

VARYA (*from the adjoining room*): Where's Yasha? Tell him his mother's come to say good-bye to him.

YASHA (*waves his hand*): They put me out of all patience!

(DUNYASHA *has all this time been busy about the luggage. Now, when* YASHA *is left alone, she goes up to him*).

DUNYASHA: You might just give me one look, Yasha. You're going away. You're leaving me (*weeps and throws herself on his neck*).

YASHA: What are you crying for? (*Drinks the champagne*) In six days I shall be in Paris again. Tomorrow we shall get into the express train and roll away in a flash. I can scarcely believe it! *Vive la France!* It doesn't suit me here—it's not the life for me; there's no doing anything. I have seen enough of the ignorance here. I have had enough of it (*drinks champagne*). What are you crying for? Behave yourself properly, and then you won't cry.

DUNYASHA (*powders her face, looking in a pocket-mirror*): Do send me a letter from Paris. You know how I loved you, Yasha—how I loved you! I am a tender creature, Yasha.

YASHA: Here they are coming! (*Busies himself about the trunks, humming softly. Enter* LYUBOV ANDREYEVNA, GAEV, ANYA *and* CHARLOTTA IVANOVNA.)

GAEV: We ought to be off. There's not much time now (*looking at* YASHA). What a smell of herrings!

LYUBOV: In ten minutes we must get into the carriage (*casts a look about the room*). Farewell, dear house, dear old home of our fathers! Winter will pass and spring will come, and then you will be no more; they will tear you down! How much those walls have seen! (*Kisses her daughter passionately*) My treasure, how bright you look! Your eyes are sparkling like diamonds! Are you glad? Very glad?

ANYA: Very glad! A new life is beginning, mamma.

GAEV: Yes, really, everything is all right now. Before the cherry orchard was sold, we were all worried and wretched, but afterwards, when once the question was settled conclusively, irrevocably, we all felt calm and even cheerful. I am a bank clerk now—I am a financier —cannon off the red. And you, Lyuba, after all, you are looking better; there's no question of that.

LYUBOV: Yes. My nerves are better, that's true. (*Her hat and coat are handed to her*) I'm sleeping well. Carry out my things, Yasha. It's time. (*To* ANYA) My darling, we shall soon see each other again. I am going to Paris. I can live there on the money your Yaroslavl auntie sent us to buy the estate with—hurrah for auntie!—but that money won't last long.

ANYA: You'll come back soon, mamma, won't you? I'll be working up for my examination in the high school, and when I have passed that, I shall set to work and be a help to you. We will read all sorts of things together, mamma, won't we? (*Kisses her mother's hands*) We will read in the autumn evenings. We'll read lots of books, and a new wonderful world will open out before us (*dreamily*). Mamma, come soon.

LYUBOV: I shall come, my precious treasure (*embraces her*).

(*Enter* LOPAHIN. CHARLOTTA *softly hums a song.*)

GAEV: Charlotta's happy; she's singing!

CHARLOTTA (*picks up a bundle like a swaddled baby*): Bye, bye, my baby. (*A baby is heard crying: "Ooah! ooah!"*) Hush, hush, my pretty boy! (*Ooah! ooah!*) Poor little thing! (*Throws the bundle back*) You must please find me a situation. I can't go on like this.

LOPAHIN: We'll find you one, Charlotta Ivanovna. Don't you worry yourself.

GAEV: Everyone's leaving us. Varya's going away. We have become of no use all at once.

CHARLOTTA: There's nowhere for me to be in the town. I must go away. (*Hums*) What care I . . .

(*Enter* PISHTCHIK.)

LOPAHIN: The freak of nature!

PISHTCHIK (*gasping*): Oh! . . . let me get my breath. . . . I'm worn out . . . my most honoured . . . Give me some water.

GAEV: Want some money, I suppose? Your humble servant! I'll go out of the way of temptation (*goes out*).

PISHTCHIK: It's a long while since I have been to see you . . . dearest lady. (*To* LOPAHIN) You are here . . . glad to see you . . . a man of immense intellect . . . take . . . here (*gives* LOPAHIN) 400 roubles. That leaves me owing 840.

LOPAHIN (*shrugging his shoulders in amazement*): It's like a dream. Where did you get it?

PISHTCHIK: Wait a bit . . . I'm hot . . . a most extraordinary occurrence! Some Englishmen came along and found in my land some sort of white clay. (*To* LYUBOV ANDREYEVNA) And 400 for you . . . most lovely . . . wonderful (*gives money*). The rest later (*sips water*). A young man in the train was telling me just now that a great philosopher advises jumping off a house-top. "Jump!" says he; "the whole gist of the problem lies in that." (*Wonderingly*) Fancy that, now! Water, please!

LOPAHIN: What Englishmen?

PISHTCHIK: I have made over to them the rights to dig the clay for twenty-four years . . . and now, excuse me . . . I can't stay . . . I must be trotting on. I'm going to Znoikovo . . . to Kardamanovo. . . . I'm in debt all round (*sips*) . . . To your very good health! . . . I'll come in on Thursday.

LYUBOV: We are just off to the town, and tomorrow I start for abroad.

PISHTCHIK: What! (*In agitation*) Why to the town? Oh, I see the furniture . . . the boxes. No matter . . . (*through his tears*) . . . no matter . . . men of enormous intellect . . . these Englishmen. . . . Never mind . . . be happy. God will succour you . . . no matter . . . everything in this world must have an end (*kisses* LYUBOV ANDREYEVNA's *hand*). If the rumour reaches you that my end has come, think of this . . . old horse, and say: "There once was such a man in the world . . . Semyonov-Pishtchik . . . the Kingdom of Heaven be his!" . . . most extraordinary weather . . . yes. (*Goes out in violent agitation, but at once returns and says in the doorway*) Dashenka wishes to be remembered to you (*goes out*).

LYUBOV: Now we can start. I leave with two cares in my heart. The first is leaving Firs ill. (*Looking at her watch*) We still have five minutes.

ANYA: Mamma, Firs has been taken to the hospital. Yasha sent him off this morning.

LYUBOV: My other anxiety is Varya. She is used to getting up early and working; and now, without work, she's like a fish out of water. She is thin and pale, and she's crying, poor dear! (*A pause*) You are well aware, Yermolay Alexeyevitch, I dreamed of marrying her to you, and everything seemed to show that you would get married (*whispers to* ANYA *and motions to* CHARLOTTA *and both go out*). She loves you—she suits you. And I don't know—I don't know why it is you seem, as it were, to avoid each other. I can't understand it!

LOPAHIN: I don't understand it myself, I confess. It's queer somehow, altogether. If there's still time, I'm ready now at once. Let's settle it straight off, and go ahead; but without you, I feel I shan't make her an offer.

LYUBOV: That's excellent. Why, a single moment's all that's necessary. I'll call her at once.

LOPAHIN: And there's champagne all ready too (*looking into the glasses*). Empty! Someone's emptied them already. (YASHA *coughs*) I call that greedy.

LYUBOV (*eagerly*): Capital! We will go out. Yasha, *allez!* I'll call her in. (*At the door*) Varya, leave all that; come here. Come along! (*Goes out with* YASHA.)

LOPAHIN (*looking at his watch*): Yes.

(*A pause. Behind the door, smothered laughter and whispering, and, at last, enter* VARYA.)

VARYA (*looking a long while over the things*): It is strange, I can't find it anywhere.

LOPAHIN: What are you looking for?

VARYA: I packed it myself, and I can't remember (*a pause*).

LOPAHIN: Where are you going now, Varvara Mihailova?

VARYA: I? To the Ragulins. I have arranged to go to them to look after the house—as a housekeeper.

LOPAHIN: That's in Yashnovo? It'll be seventy miles away (*a pause*). So this is the end of life in this house!

VARYA (*looking among the things*): Where is it? Perhaps I put it in the trunk. Yes, life in this house is over—there will be no more of it.

LOPAHIN: And I'm just off to Harkov—by this next train. I've a lot of business there. I'm leaving Epihodov here, and I've taken him on.

VARYA: Really!

LOPAHIN: This time last year we had snow already, if you remember; but now it's so fine and sunny. Though it's cold, to be sure—three degrees of frost.

VARYA: I haven't looked (*a pause*). And besides, our thermometer's broken (*a pause*).

(*Voice at the door from the yard:* Yermolay Alexeyevitch!")

LOPAHIN (*as though he had long been expecting this summons*): This minute!

(LOPAHIN *goes out quickly.* VARYA *sitting on the floor and laying her head on a bag full of clothes, sobs quietly. The door opens.* LYUBOV ANDREYEVNA *comes in cautiously.*)

LYUBOV: Well? (*A pause*) We must be going.

VARYA (*has wiped her eyes and is no longer crying*): Yes, mamma, it's time to start. I shall have time to get to the Ragulins today, if only you're not late for the train.

LYUBOV (*in the doorway*): Anya, put your things on.

(*Enter* ANYA, *then* GAEV *and* CHARLOTTA IVANOVNA. GAEV *has on a warm coat with a hood. Servants and cabmen come in.* EPIHODOV *bustles about the luggage.*)

LYUBOV: Now we can start on our travels.

ANYA (*joyfully*): On our travels!

GAEV: My friends—my dear, my precious friends! Leaving this house for ever, can I be silent? Can I refrain from giving utterance at leave-taking to those emotions which now flood all my being?

ANYA (*supplicatingly*): Uncle!

VARYA: Uncle, you mustn't!

GAEV (*dejectedly*): Cannon and into the pocket . . . I'll be quiet. . .

(*Enter* TROFIMOV *and afterwards* LOPAHIN.)

TROFIMOV: Well, ladies and gentlemen, we must start.

LOPAHIN: Epihodov, my coat!

LYUBOV: I'll stay just one minute. It seems as though I have never seen before what the walls, what the ceilings in this house were like, and now I look at them with greediness, with such tender love.

GAEV: I remember when I was six years old sitting in that window on Trinity Day watching my father going to church.

LYUBOV: Have all the things been taken?

LOPAHIN: I think all. (*Putting on overcoat, to* EPIHODOV) You, Epihodov, mind you see everything is right.

EPIHODOV (*in a husky voice*): Don't you trouble, Yermolay Alexeyevitch.

LOPAHIN: Why, what's wrong with your voice?

EPIHODOV: I've just had a drink of water, and I choked over something.

YASHA (*contemptuously*): The ignorance!

LYUBOV: We are going—and not a soul will be left here.

LOPAHIN: Not till the spring.

VARYA (*pulls a parasol out of a bundle, as though about to hit someone with it.* LOPAHIN *makes a gesture as though alarmed*): What is it? I didn't mean anything.

TROFIMOV: Ladies and gentlemen, let us get into the carriage. It's time. The train will be in directly.

VARYA: Petya, here they are, your goloshes, by that box. (*With tears*) And what dirty old things they are!

TROFIMOV (*putting on his goloshes*): Let us go, friends!

GAEV (*greatly agitated, afraid of weeping*): The train—the station! Double baulk, ah!

LYUBOV: Let us go!

LOPAHIN: Are we all here? (*Locks the side-door on left*) The things are all here. We must lock up. Let us go!

ANYA: Good-bye, home! Good-bye to the old life!

TROFIMOV: Welcome to the new life!

(TROFIMOV *goes out with* ANYA. VARYA *looks round the room and goes out slowly.* YASHA *and* CHARLOTTA IVANOVNA, *with her dog, go out.*)

LOPAHIN: Till the spring, then! Come, friends, till we meet! (*Goes out.*)

(LYUBOV ANDREYEVNA *and* GAEV *remain alone. As though they had been waiting for this, they throw themselves on each other's necks, and break into subdued smothered sobbing, afraid of being over-heard.*)

GAEV (*in despair*): Sister, my sister!

LYUBOV: Oh, my orchard!—my sweet, beautiful orchard! My life, my youth, my happiness, good-bye! good-bye!

VOICE OF ANYA (*calling gaily*): Mamma!

VOICE OF TROFIMOV (*gaily, excitedly*): Aa—oo!

LYUBOV: One last look at the walls, at the windows. My dear mother loved to walk about this room.

GAEV: Sister, sister!

VOICE OF ANYA: Mamma!

VOICE OF TROFIMOV: Aa—oo!

LYUBOV: We are coming. (*They go out.*)

(*The stage is empty. There is the sound of the doors being locked up, then of the carriages driving away. There is silence. In the stillness there is the dull stroke of an axe in a tree, clanging with a mournful lonely sound. Footsteps are heard.* FIRS *appears in the doorway on the right. He is dressed as always—in a pea-jacket and white waistcoat, with slippers on his feet. He is ill.*)

FIRS (*goes up to the doors, and tries the handles*): Locked! They have gone . . . (*sits down on sofa*). They have forgotten me. . . . Never mind . . . I'll sit here a bit. . . . I'll be bound Leonid Andreyevitch hasn't put his fur coat on and has gone off in his thin overcoat (*sighs anxiously*). I didn't see after him. . . . These young people . . . (*mutters something that can't be distinguished*). Life has slipped by as though I hadn't lived. (*Lies down*) I'll lie down a bit. . . . There's no strength in you, nothing left you—all gone! Ech! I'm good for nothing (*lies motionless*).

(*A sound is heard that seems to come from the sky, like a breaking harp-string, dying away mournfully. All is still again, and there is heard nothing but the strokes of the axe far away in the orchard.*)

(*The Curtain Falls.*)

# THORNTON WILDER

# The Skin of Our Teeth

*The Skin of Our Teeth* was first performed at the Shubert Theater, New Haven, Connecticut, October 15, 1942, and then in New York City at the Plymouth Theater, November 18, 1942.

# CHARACTERS

ANNOUNCER

SABINA

MR. FITZPATRICK

MRS. ANTROBUS

DINOSAUR

MAMMOTH

TELEGRAPH BOY

GLADYS

HENRY

MR. ANTROBUS

DOCTOR

PROFESSOR

JUDGE

HOMER

MISS E. MUSE

MISS T. MUSE

MISS M. MUSE

2 USHERS

2 DRUM MAJORETTES

FORTUNE TELLER

2 CHAIR PUSHERS

6 CONVEENERS

BROADCAST OFFICIAL

DEFEATED CANDIDATE

MR. TREMAYNE

HESTER

IVY

FRED BAILEY

ACT I. Home, Excelsior, New Jersey.
ACT II. Atlantic City Boardwalk.
ACT III. Home, Excelsior, New Jersey.

# Act One

A projection screen in the middle of the curtain. The first lantern slide: the name of the theatre, and the words: *NEWS EVENTS OF THE WORLD*. An ANNOUNCER's voice is heard.

ANNOUNCER: The management takes pleasure in bringing to you— The News Events of the World:

(*Slide of the sun appearing above the horizon.*)

Freeport, Long Island:
The sun rose this morning at 6:32 a.m. This gratifying event was first reported by Mrs. Dorothy Stetson of Freeport, Long Island, who promptly telephoned the Mayor.
The Society for Affirming the End of the World at once went into a special session and postponed the arrival of that event for TWENTY-FOUR HOURS.
All honor to Mrs. Stetson for her public spirit.

New York City:
(*Slide of the front doors of the theatre in which this play is playing; three cleaning* WOMEN *with mops and pails.*)
The X Theatre. During the daily cleaning of this theatre a number of lost objects were collected as usual by Mesdames Simpson, Pateslewski, and Moriarty.
Among these objects found today was a wedding ring, inscribed: To Eva from Adam. Genesis II:18.
The ring will be restored to the owner or owners, if their credentials are satisfactory.

Tippehatchee, Vermont:
(*Slide representing a glacier.*)
The unprecedented cold weather of this summer has produced a condition that has not yet been satisfactorily explained. There is a report that a wall of ice is moving southward across these counties. The disruption of communications by the cold wave now crossing

495

the country has rendered exact information difficult, but little cre-
dence is given to the rumor that the ice had pushed the Cathedral of
Montreal as far as St. Albans, Vermont.

For further information see your daily papers.

Excelsior, New Jersey:

(*Slide of a modest suburban home.*)

The home of Mr. George Antrobus, the inventor of the wheel. The
discovery of the wheel, following so closely on the discovery of
the lever, has centered the attention of the country on Mr. Antrobus
of this attractive suburban residence district. This is his home, a
commodious seven-room house, conveniently situated near a public
school, a Methodist church, and a firehouse; it is right handy to an
A. and P.

(*Slide of* MR. ANTROBUS *on his front steps, smiling and lifting his
straw hat. He holds a wheel.*)

Mr. Antrobus, himself. He comes of very old stock and has made
his way up from next to nothing.

It is reported that he was once a gardener, but left that situation
under circumstances that have been variously reported.

Mr. Antrobus is a veteran of foreign wars, and bears a number of
scars, front and back.

(*Slide of* MRS. ANTROBUS, *holding some roses.*)

This is Mrs. Antrobus, the charming and gracious president of the
Excelsior Mothers' Club.

Mrs. Antrobus is an excellent needlewoman; it is she who invented
the apron on which so many interesting changes have been rung
since.

(*Slide of the* FAMILY *and* SABINA.)

Here we see the Antrobuses with their two children, Henry and
Gladys, and friend. The friend in the rear is Lily Sabina, the maid.
I know we all want to congratulate this typical American family on
its enterprise. We all wish Mr. Antrobus a successful future. Now
the management takes you to the interior of this home for a brief
visit.

(*Curtain rises. Living room of a commuter's home.* SABINA—*straw-
blonde, over-rouged—is standing by the window back center, a
feather duster under her elbow.*)

SABINA: Oh, oh, oh! Six o'clock and the master not home yet.
Pray God nothing serious has happened to him crossing the Hudson
River. If anything happened to him, we would certainly be incon-
solable and have to move into a less desirable residence district.

The fact is I don't know what'll become of us. Here it is the middle of August and the coldest day of the year. It's simply freezing; the dogs are sticking to the sidewalks; can anybody explain that? No. But I'm not surprised. The whole world's at sixes and sevens, and why the house hasn't fallen down about our ears long ago is a miracle to me.

(*A fragment of the right wall leans precariously over the stage.* SABINA *looks at it nervously and it slowly rights itself.*)

Every night this same anxiety as to whether the master will get home safely: whether he'll bring home anything to eat. In the midst of life we are in the midst of death, a truer word was never said.

(*The fragment of scenery flies up into the lofts.* SABINA *is struck dumb with surprise, shrugs her shoulders and starts dusting* MR. ANTROBUS' *chair, including the under side.*)

Of course, Mr. Antrobus is a very fine man, an excellent husband and father, a pillar of the church, and has all the best interests of the community at heart. Of course, every muscle goes tight every time he passes a policeman; but what I think is that there are certain charges that ought not to be made, and I think I may add, ought not to be allowed to be made; we're all human; who isn't?

(*She dusts* MRS. ANTROBUS' *rocking chair.*)

Mrs. Antrobus is as fine a woman as you could hope to see. She lives only for her children; and if it would be any benefit to her children she'd see the rest of us stretched out dead at her feet without turning a hair,—that's the truth. If you want to know anything more about Mrs. Antrobus, just go and look at a tigress, and look hard.

As to the children—

Well, Henry Antrobus is a real, clean-cut American boy. He'll graduate from High School one of these days, if they make the alphabet any easier.—Henry, when he has a stone in his hand, has a perfect aim, he can hit anything from a bird to an older brother— Oh! I didn't mean to say that!—but it certainly was an unfortunate accident, and it was very hard getting the police out of the house. Mr. and Mrs. Antrobus' daughter is named Gladys. She'll make some good man a good wife some day, if he'll just come down off the movie screen and ask her.

So here we are!

We've managed to survive for some time now, catch as catch can, the fat and the lean, and if the dinosaurs don't trample us to death, and if the grasshoppers don't eat up our garden, we'll all live to see better days, knock on wood.

Each new child that's born to the Antrobuses seems to them to be sufficient reason for the whole universe's being set in motion; and each new child that dies seems to them to have been spared a whole world of sorrow, and what the end of it will be is still very much an open question.

We've rattled along, hot and cold, for some time now—

(*A portion of the wall above the door, right, flies up into the air and disappears.*)

—and my advice to you is not to inquire into why or whither, but just enjoy your ice cream while it's on your plate,—that's my philosophy.

Don't forget that a few years ago we came through the depression by the skin of our teeth! One more tight squeeze like that and where will we be?

(*This is a cue line.* SABINA *looks angrily at the kitchen door and repeats:*)

. . . we came through the depression by the skin of our teeth; one more tight squeeze like that and where will we be?

(*Flustered, she looks through the opening in the right wall; then goes to the window and reopens the Act.*)

Oh, oh, oh! Six o'clock and the master not home yet. Pray God nothing has happened to him crossing the Hudson. Here it is the middle of August and the coldest day of the year. It's simply freezing; the dogs are sticking. One more tight squeeze like that and where will we be?

VOICE (*off stage*): Make up something! Invent something!

SABINA: Well . . . uh . . . this certainly is a fine American home . . . and—uh . . . everybody's very happy . . . and—uh . . .
(*Suddenly flings pretense to the winds and coming downstage says with indignation:*)
I can't invent any words for this play, and I'm glad I can't. I hate this play and every word in it.

As for me, I don't understand a single word of it, anyway,—all about the troubles the human race has gone through, there's a subject for you.

Besides the author hasn't made up his silly mind as to whether we're all living back in caves or in New Jersey today, and that's the way it is all the way through.

Oh—why can't we have plays like we used to have—*Peg o' My Heart*, and *Smilin' Thru*, and *The Bat*, good entertainment with a message you can take home with you?

I took this hateful job because I had to. For two years I've sat up in my room living on a sandwich and a cup of tea a day, waiting for better times in the theatre. And look at me now: I—I who've played *Rain* and the *Barretts of Wimpole Street* and *First Lady*—God in Heaven!

MR. FITZPATRICK (*the* STAGE MANAGER *puts his head out from the hole in the scenery*): Miss Somerset!! Miss Somerset!

SABINA: Oh! Anyway!—nothing matters! It'll all be the same in a hundred years.
(*Loudly.*)
We came through the depression by the skin of our teeth,—that's true!—one more tight squeeze like that and where will we be?

(*Enter* MRS. ANTROBUS, *a mother.*)

MRS. ANTROBUS: Sabina, you've let the fire go out.

SABINA (*in a lather*): One-thing-and-another; don't-know-whether-my-wits-are-upside-or-down;    might-as-well-be-dead-as-alive-in-a-house-all-sixes-and-sevens. . . .

MRS. ANTROBUS: You've let the fire go out. Here it is the coldest day of the year right in the middle of August, and you've let the fire go out.

SABINA: Mrs. Antrobus, I'd like to give my two weeks' notice, Mrs. Antrobus. A girl like I can get a situation in a home where they're rich enough to have a fire in every room, Mrs. Antrobus, and a girl don't have to carry the responsibility of the whole house on her two shoulders. And a home without children, Mrs. Antrobus, because children are a thing only a parent can stand, and a truer word was never said; and a home, Mrs. Antrobus, where the master of the house don't pinch decent, self-respecting girls when he meets them in a dark corridor. I mention no names and make no charges. So you have my notice, Mrs. Antrobus. I hope that's perfectly clear.

MRS. ANTROBUS: You've let the fire go out!—Have you milked the mammoth?

SABINA: I don't understand a word of this play.—Yes, I've milked the mammoth.

MRS. ANTROBUS: Until Mr. Antrobus comes home we have no food and we have no fire. You'd better go over to the neighbors and borrow some fire.

SABINA: Mrs. Antrobus! I can't! I'd die on the way, you know I would. It's worse than January. The dogs are sticking to the sidewalks. I'd die.

MRS. ANTROBUS: Very well, I'll go.

SABINA (*even more distraught, coming forward and sinking on her knees*): You'd never come back alive; we'd all perish; if you weren't here, we'd just perish. How do we know Mr. Antrobus'll be back? We don't know. If you go out, I'll just kill myself.

MRS. ANTROBUS: Get up, Sabina.

SABINA: Every night it's the same thing. Will he come back safe, or won't he? Will we starve to death, or freeze to death, or boil to death or will we be killed by burglars? I don't know why we go on living. I don't know why we go on living at all. It's easier being dead.

(*She flings her arms on the table and buries her head in them. In each of the succeeding speeches she flings her head up—and sometimes her hands—then quickly buries her head again.*)

MRS. ANTROBUS: The same thing! Always throwing up the sponge, Sabina. Always announcing your own death. But give you a new hat—or a plate of ice cream—or a ticket to the movies, and you want to live forever.

SABINA: You don't care whether we live or die; all you care about is those children. If it would be any benefit to them you'd be glad to see us all stretched out dead.

MRS. ANTROBUS: Well, maybe I would.

SABINA: And what do they care about? Themselves—that's all they care about.
(*Shrilly.*)
They make fun of you behind your back. Don't tell me: they're ashamed of you. Half the time, they pretend they're someone else's children. Little thanks you get from them.

MRS. ANTROBUS: I'm not asking for any thanks.

SABINA: And Mr. Antrobus—you don't understand *him*. All that work he does—trying to discover the alphabet and the multiplication table. Whenever he tries to learn anything you fight against it.

MRS. ANTROBUS: Oh, Sabina, I know you.

When Mr. Antrobus raped you home from your Sabine hills, he did it to insult me.

He did it for your pretty face, and to insult me.

You were the new wife, weren't you?

For a year or two you lay on your bed all day and polished the nails on your hands and feet.

You made puff-balls of the combings of your hair and you blew them up to the ceiling.

And I washed your underclothes and I made you chicken broths. I bore children and between my very groans I stirred the cream that you'd put on your face.

But I knew you wouldn't last.

You didn't last.

SABINA: But it was I who encouraged Mr. Antrobus to make the alphabet. I'm sorry to say it, Mrs. Antrobus, but you're not a beautiful woman, and you can never know what a man could do if he tried. It's girls like I who inspire the multiplication table.

I'm sorry to say it, but you're not a beautiful woman, Mrs. Antrobus, and that's the God's truth.

MRS. ANTROBUS: And you didn't last—you sank to the kitchen. And what do you do there? *You let the fire go out!*

No wonder to you it seems easier being dead.

Reading and writing and counting on your fingers is all very well in their way,—but I keep the home going.

MRS. ANTROBUS: —There's that dinosaur on the front lawn again. —Shoo! Go away. Go away.

(*The baby* DINOSAUR *puts his head in the window.*)

DINOSAUR: It's cold.

MRS. ANTROBUS: You go around to the back of the house where you belong.

DINOSAUR: It's cold.

(*The* DINOSAUR *disappears.* MRS. ANTROBUS *goes calmly out.*
SABINA *slowly raises her head and speaks to the audience. The central portion of the center wall rises, pauses, and disappears into the loft.*)

SABINA: Now that you audience are listening to this, too, I understand it a little better.

I wish eleven o'clock were here; I don't want to be dragged through this whole play again.

(*The* TELEGRAPH BOY *is seen entering along the back wall of the stage from the right. She catches sight of him and calls:*)

Mrs. Antrobus! Mrs. Antrobus! Help! There's a strange man coming to the house. He's coming up the walk, help!

(*Enter* MRS. ANTROBUS *in alarm, but efficient.*)

MRS. ANTROBUS: Help me quick!

(*They barricade the door by piling the furniture against it.*)

Who is it? What do you want?

TELEGRAPH BOY: A telegram for Mrs. Antrobus from Mr. Antrobus in the city.

SABINA: Are you sure, are you sure? Maybe it's just a trap!

MRS. ANTROBUS: I know his voice, Sabina. We can open the door.

(*Enter the* TELEGRAPH BOY, *12 years old, in uniform. The* DINOSAUR *and* MAMMOTH *slip by him into the room and settle down front right.*)

I'm sorry we kept you waiting. We have to be careful, you know.

(*To the* ANIMALS.)

Hm! . . . Will you be quiet?

(*They nod.*)

Have you had your supper?

(*They nod.*)

Are you *ready* to come in?

(*They nod.*)

Young man, have you any fire with you? Then light the grate, will you?

(*He nods, produces something like a briquet; and kneels by the imagined fireplace, footlights center. Pause.*)

What are people saying about this cold weather?

(*He makes a doubtful shrug with his shoulders.*)

Sabina, take this stick and go and light the stove.

SABINA: Like I told you, Mrs. Antrobus; two weeks. That's the law. I hope that's perfectly clear.

(*Exit.*)

MRS. ANTROBUS: What about this cold weather?

TELEGRAPH BOY (*lowered eyes*): Of course, I don't know anything . . . but they say there's a wall of ice moving down from the North, that's what they say. We can't get Boston by telegraph, and they're burning pianos in Hartford.
. . . It moves everything in front of it, churches and post offices and city halls.
I live in Brooklyn myself.

MRS. ANTROBUS: What are people doing about it?

TELEGRAPH BOY: Well . . . uh . . . Talking, mostly.
Or just what you'd do a day in February.
There are some that are trying to go South and the roads are crowded; but you can't take old people and children very far in a cold like this.

MRS. ANTROBUS: —What's this telegram you have for me?

TELEGRAPH BOY (*fingertips to his forehead*): If you wait just a minute; I've got to remember it.
(*The* ANIMALS *have left their corner and are nosing him. Presently they take places on either side of him, leaning against his hips, like heraldic beasts.*)
This telegram was flashed from Murray Hill to University Heights! And then by puffs of smoke from University Heights to Staten Island.
And then by lantern from Staten Island to Plainfield, New Jersey. What hath God wrought!
(*He clears his throat.*)
"To Mrs. Antrobus, Excelsior, New Jersey:
My dear wife, will be an hour late. Busy day at the office. Don't worry the children about the cold just keep them warm burn everything except Shakespeare."
(*Pause.*)

MRS. ANTROBUS: Men! —He knows I'd burn ten Shakespeares to prevent a child of mine from having one cold in the head. What does it say next?

(*Enter* SABINA.)

TELEGRAPH BOY: "Have made great discoveries today have separated em from en."

SABINA: I know what that is, that's the alphabet, yes it is. Mr. Antrobus is just the cleverest man. Why, when the alphabet's finished, we'll be able to tell the future and everything.

TELEGRAPH BOY: Then listen to this: "Ten tens make a hundred semicolon consequences far-reaching."
(*Watches for effect.*)

MRS. ANTROBUS: The earth's turning to ice, and all he can do is to make up new numbers.

TELEGRAPH BOY: Well, Mrs. Antrobus, like the head man at our office said: a few more discoveries like that and we'll be worth freezing.

MRS. ANTROBUS: What does he say next?

TELEGRAPH BOY: I . . . I can't do this last part very well.
(*He clears his throat and sings.*)
"Happy w'dding ann'vers'ry to you, Happy ann'vers'ry to you—"

(*The* ANIMALS *begin to howl soulfully;* SABINA *screams with pleasure.*)

MRS. ANTROBUS: Dolly! Frederick! Be quiet.

TELEGRAPH BOY (*above the din*): "Happy w'dding ann'vers'ry, dear Eva; happy w'dding ann'vers'ry to you."

MRS. ANTROBUS: Is that in the telegram? Are they singing telegrams now?
(*He nods.*)
The earth's getting so silly no wonder the sun turns cold.

SABINA: Mrs. Antrobus, I want to take back the notice I gave you. Mrs. Antrobus, I don't want to leave a house that gets such interesting telegrams and I'm sorry for anything I said. I really am.

MRS. ANTROBUS: Young man, I'd like to give you something for all this trouble; Mr. Antrobus isn't home yet and I have no money and no food in the house—

TELEGRAPH BOY: Mrs. Antrobus . . . I don't like to . . . appear to . . . ask for anything, but . . .

MRS. ANTROBUS: What is it you'd like?

TELEGRAPH BOY: Do you happen to have an old needle you could spare? My wife just sits home all day thinking about needles.

SABINA (shrilly): We only got two in the house. Mrs. Antrobus, you know we only got two in the house.

MRS. ANTROBUS (after a look at SABINA taking a needle from her collar): Why yes, I can spare this.

TELEGRAPH BOY (lowered eyes): Thank you, Mrs. Antrobus. Mrs. Antrobus, can I ask you something else? I have two sons of my own; if the cold gets worse, what should I do?

SABINA: I think we'll all perish, that's what I think. Cold like this in August is just the end of the whole world.

(Silence.)

MRS. ANTROBUS: I don't know. After all, what does one do about anything? Just keep as warm as you can. And don't let your wife and children see that you're worried.

TELEGRAPH BOY: Yes . . . Thank you, Mrs. Antrobus. Well, I'd better be going.—Oh, I forgot! There's one more sentence in the telegram. "Three cheers have invented the wheel."

MRS. ANTROBUS: A wheel? What's a wheel?

TELEGRAPH BOY: I don't know. That's what it said. The sign for it is like this. Well, goodbye.

(The WOMEN see him to the door, with goodbyes and injunctions to keep warm.)

SABINA (apron to her eyes, wailing): Mrs. Antrobus, it looks to me like all the nice men in the world are already married; I don't know why that is.
(Exit.)

MRS. ANTROBUS (thoughtful; to the ANIMALS): Do you ever remember hearing tell of any cold like this in August?
(The ANIMALS shake their heads.)
From your grandmothers or anyone?
(They shake their heads.)
Have you any suggestions?
(They shake their heads.

*She pulls her shawl around, goes to the front door and opening it an inch calls:)*

HENRY. GLADYS. CHILDREN. Come right in and get warm. No, no, when mama says a thing she means it.

Henry! HENRY. Put down that stone. You know what happened last time.

*(Shriek.)*

HENRY! Put down that stone!

Gladys! Put down your dress!! Try and be a lady.

*(The* CHILDREN *bound in and dash to the fire. They take off their winter things and leave them in heaps on the floor.)*

GLADYS: Mama, I'm hungry. Mama, why is it so cold?

HENRY *(at the same time)*: Mama, why doesn't it snow? Mama, when's supper ready? Maybe, it'll snow and we can make snowballs.

GLADYS: Mama, it's so cold that in one more minute I just couldn't of stood it.

MRS. ANTROBUS: Settle down, both of you, I want to talk to you. *(She draws up a hassock and sits front center over the orchestra pit before the imaginary fire. The* CHILDREN *stretch out on the floor, leaning against her lap. Tableau by Raphael. The* ANIMALS *edge up and complete the triangle.)*

It's just a cold spell of some kind. Now listen to what I'm saying: When your father comes home I want you to be extra quiet. He's had a hard day at the office and I don't know but what he may have one of his moods.

I just got a telegram from him very happy and excited, and you know what that means. Your father's temper's uneven; I guess you know that.

*(Shriek.)*

Henry! Henry!

Why—why can't you remember to keep your hair down over your forehead? You must keep that scar covered up. Don't you know that when your father sees it he loses all control over himself? He goes crazy. He wants to die.

*(After a moment's despair she collects herself decisively, wets the hem of her apron in her mouth and starts polishing his forehead vigorously.)*

Lift your head up. Stop squirming. Blessed me, sometimes I think that it's going away—and then there it is: just as red as ever.

HENRY: Mama, today at school two teachers forgot and called me by my old name. They forgot, Mama. You'd better write another letter to the principal, so that he'll tell them I've changed my name. Right out in class they called me: Cain.

MRS. ANTROBUS (*putting her hand on his mouth, too late; hoarsely*): Don't say it.
(*Polishing feverishly.*)
If you're good they'll forget it. Henry, you didn't hit anyone . . . today, did you?

HENRY: Oh . . . no-o-o!

MRS. ANTROBUS (*still working, not looking at Gladys*): And, Gladys, I want you to be especially nice to your father tonight. You know what he calls you when you're good—his little angel, his little star. Keep your dress down like a little lady. And keep your voice nice and low. Gladys Antrobus!! What's that red stuff you have on your face?
(*Slaps her.*)
You're a filthy detestable child!
(*Rises in real, though temporary, repudiation and despair.*)
Get away from me, both of you! I wish I'd never seen sight or sound of you. Let the cold come! I can't stand it. I don't want to go on.

(*She walks away.*)

GLADYS (*weeping*): All the girls at school do, Mama.

MRS. ANTROBUS (*shrieking*): I'm through with you, that's all!—Sabina! Sabina!—Don't you know your father'd go crazy if he saw that paint on your face? Don't you know your father thinks you're perfect? Don't you know he couldn't live if he didn't think you were perfect?—Sabina!

(*Enter* SABINA.)

SABINA: Yes, Mrs. Antrobus!

MRS. ANTROBUS: Take this girl out into the kitchen and wash her face with the scrubbing brush.

MR. ANTROBUS (*outside, roaring*): "I've been working on the railroad, all the livelong day . . . etc."

(*The* ANIMALS *start running around in circles, bellowing.* SABINA *rushes to the window.*)

MRS. ANTROBUS: Sabina, what's that noise outside?

SABINA: Oh, it's a drunken tramp. It's a giant, Mrs. Antrobus. We'll all be killed in our beds, I know it!

MRS. ANTROBUS: Help me quick. Quick. Everybody.
(*Again they stack all the furniture against the door. Mr. Antrobus pounds and bellows.*)
Who is it? What do you want?—Sabina, have you any boiling water ready?—Who is it?

MR. ANTROBUS: Broken-down camel of a pig's snout, open this door.

MRS. ANTROBUS: God be praised! It's your father.—Just a minute, George!—Sabina, clear the door, quick. Gladys, come here while I clean your nasty face!

MR. ANTROBUS: She-bitch of a goat's gizzard, I'll break every bone in your body. Let me in or I'll tear the whole house down.

MRS. ANTROBUS: Just a minute, George, something's the matter with the lock.

MR. ANTROBUS: Open the door or I'll tear your livers out. I'll smash your brains on the ceiling, and Devil takes the hindmost.

MRS. ANTROBUS: Now, you can open the door, Sabina. I'm ready.

(*The door is flung open. Silence.* MR. ANTROBUS—*face of a Keystone Comedy Cop—stands there in fur cap and blanket. His arms are full of parcels, including a large stone wheel with a center in it. One hand carries a railroad man's lantern. Suddenly he bursts into joyous roar.*)

MR. ANTROBUS: Well, how's the whole crooked family?
(*Relief. Laughter. Tears. Jumping up and down.* ANIMALS *cavorting.* ANTROBUS *throws the parcels on the ground. Hurls his cap and blanket after them. Heroic embraces. Melee of* HUMANS *and* ANIMALS, SABINA *included.*)
I'll be scalded and tarred if a man can't get a little welcome when he comes home. Well, Maggie, you old gunny-sack, how's the broken down old weather hen?—Sabina, old fishbait, old skunkpot.— And the children,—how've the little smellers been?

GLADYS: Papa, Papa, Papa, Papa, Papa.

MR. ANTROBUS: How've they been, Maggie?

MRS. ANTROBUS: Well, I must say, they've been as good as gold. I haven't had to raise my voice once. I don't know what's the matter with them.

ANTROBUS (*kneeling before* GLADYS): Papa's little weasel, eh?—Sabina, there's some food for you.—Papa's little gopher?

GLADYS (*her arm around his neck*): Papa, you're always teasing me.

ANTROBUS: And Henry? Nothing rash today, I hope. Nothing rash?

HENRY: No, Papa.

ANTROBUS (*roaring*): Well that's good, that's good—I'll bet Sabina let the fire go out.

SABINA: Mr. Antrobus, I've given my notice. I'm leaving two weeks from today. I'm sorry, but I'm leaving.

ANTROBUS (*roar*): Well, if you leave now you'll freeze to death, so go and cook the dinner.

SABINA: Two weeks, that's the law.
(*Exit.*)

ANTROBUS: Did you get my telegram?

MRS. ANTROBUS: Yes.—What's a wheel?

(*He indicates the wheel with a glance.* HENRY *is rolling it around the floor. Rapid, hoarse interchange:* MRS. ANTROBUS: *What does this cold weather mean? It's below freezing.* ANTROBUS: *Not before the children!* MRS. ANTROBUS: *Shouldn't we do something about it?— start off, move?* ANTROBUS: *Not before the children!!!* He gives HENRY *a sharp slap.*)

HENRY: Papa, you hit me!

ANTROBUS: Well, remember it. That's to make you remember today. Today. The day the alphabet's finished; and the day that we *saw* the hundred—the hundred, the hundred, the hundred, the hundred, the hundred—there's no end to 'em.
I've had a day at the office!

Take a look at that wheel, Maggie—when I've got that to rights: you'll see a sight.

There's a reward there for all the walking you've done.

MRS. ANTROBUS: How do you mean?

ANTROBUS (*on the hassock looking into the fire; with awe*): Maggie, we've reached the top of the wave. There's not much more to be done. We're there!

MRS. ANTROBUS (*cutting across his mood sharply*): And the ice?

ANTROBUS: The ice!

HENRY (*playing with the wheel*): Papa, you could put a chair on this.

ANTROBUS (*broodingly*): Ye-e-s, any booby can fool with it now,— but I thought of it first.

MRS. ANTROBUS: Children, go out in the kitchen. I want to talk to your father alone.

(*The* CHILDREN *go out.*

ANTROBUS *has moved to his chair up left. He takes the goldfish bowl on his lap; pulls the canary cage down to the level of his face. Both the* ANIMALS *put their paws up on the arm of his chair.* MRS. ANTROBUS *faces him across the room, like a judge.*)

MRS. ANTROBUS: Well?

ANTROBUS (*shortly*): It's cold.—How things been, eh? Keck, keck, keck.—And you, Millicent?

MRS. ANTROBUS: I know it's cold.

ANTROBUS (*to the canary*): No spilling of sunflower seed, eh? No singing after lights-out, y'know what I mean?

MRS. ANTROBUS: You can try and prevent us freezing to death, can't you? You can do something? We can start moving. Or we can go on the animals' backs?

ANTROBUS: The best thing about animals is that they don't talk much.

MAMMOTH: It's cold.

ANTROBUS: Eh, eh, eh! Watch that!—

—By midnight we'd turn to ice. The roads are full of people now who can scarcely lift a foot from the ground. The grass out in front is like iron,—which reminds me, I have another needle for you.—The people up north—where are they?

Frozen . . . crushed. . . .

MRS. ANTROBUS: Is that what's going to happen to us?—Will you answer me?

ANTROBUS: I don't know. I don't know anything. Some say that the ice is going slower. Some say that it's stopped. The sun's growing cold. What can I do about that? Nothing we can do but burn everything in the house, and the fenceposts and the barn. Keep the fire going. When we have no more fire, we die.

MRS. ANTROBUS: Well, why didn't you say so in the first place?

(MRS. ANTROBUS *is about to march off when she catches sight of two* REFUGEES, *men, who have appeared against the back wall of the theatre and who are soon joined by others.*)

REFUGEES: Mr. Antrobus! Mr. Antrobus! Mr. An-nn-tro-bus!

MRS. ANTROBUS: Who's that? Who's that calling you?

ANTROBUS (*clearing his throat guiltily*): H'm—let me see.

(*Two* REFUGEES *come up to the window.*)

REFUGEE: Could we warm our hands for a moment, Mr. Antrobus. It's very cold, Mr. Antrobus.

ANOTHER REFUGEE: Mr. Antrobus, I wonder if you have a piece of bread or something that you could spare.

(*Silence. They wait humbly.* MRS. ANTROBUS *stands rooted to the spot. Suddenly a knock at the door, then another hand knocking in short rapid blows.*)

MRS. ANTROBUS: Who are these people? Why, they're all over the front yard. What have they come *here* for?

(*Enter* SABINA.)

SABINA: Mrs. Antrobus! There are some tramps knocking at the back door.

MRS. ANTROBUS: George, tell these people to go away. Tell them to move right along. I'll go and send them away from the back door. Sabina, come with me.

(*She goes out energetically.*)

ANTROBUS: Sabina! Stay here! I have something to say to you.
(*He goes to the door and opens it a crack and talks through it.*)
Ladies and gentlemen! I'll have to ask you to wait a few minutes longer. It'll be all right . . . while you're waiting you might each one pull up a stake of the fence. We'll need them all for the fireplace. There'll be coffee and sandwiches in a moment.

(SABINA *looks out door over his shoulder and suddenly extends her arm pointing, with a scream.*)

SABINA: Mr. Antrobus, what's that??—that big white thing? Mr. Antrobus, it's ICE. It's ICE!!

ANTROBUS: Sabina, I want you to go in the kitchen and make a lot of coffee. Make a whole pail full.

SABINA: Pail full!!

ANTROBUS (*with gesture*): And sandwiches . . . piles of them . . . like this.

SABINA: Mr. An . . . !!
(*Suddenly she drops the play, and says in her own person as* MISS SOMERSET, *with surprise.*)
Oh, *I* see what this part of the play means now! This means refugees.
(*She starts to cross to the proscenium.*)
Oh, I don't like it. I don't like it.

(*She leans against the proscenium and bursts into tears.*)

ANTROBUS: Miss Somerset!
(*Voice of the* STAGE MANAGER.)
Miss Somerset!

SABINA (*energetically, to the audience*): Ladies and gentlemen! Don't take this play serious. The world's not coming to an end. You know it's not. People exaggerate! Most people really have enough to eat and a roof over their heads. Nobody actually starves

—you can always eat grass or something. That ice-business—why, it was a long, long time ago. Besides they were only savages. Savages don't love their families—not like we do.

ANTROBUS *and* STAGE MANAGER: Miss Somerset!!

(*There is renewed knocking at the door.*)

SABINA: All right. I'll say the lines, but I won't think about the play.

(*Enter* MRS. ANTROBUS.)

SABINA (*parting thrust at the audience*): And I advise *you* not to think about the play, either.

(*Exit* SABINA.)

MRS. ANTROBUS: George, these tramps say that you asked them to come to the house. What does this mean?

(*Knocking at the door.*)

ANTROBUS: Just . . . uh . . . There are a few friends, Maggie, I met on the road. Real nice, real useful people. . . .

MRS. ANTROBUS (*back to the door*): Now, don't you ask them in! George Antrobus, not another soul comes in here over my dead body.

ANTROBUS: Maggie, there's a doctor there. Never hurts to have a good doctor in the house. We've lost a peck of children, one way and another. You can never tell when a child's throat will get stopped up. What you and I have seen—!!!

(*He puts his fingers on his throat, and imitates diphtheria.*)

MRS. ANTROBUS: Well, just one person then, the Doctor. The others can go right along the road.

ANTROBUS: Maggie, there's an old man, particular friend of mine—

MRS. ANTROBUS: I won't listen to you—

ANTROBUS: It was he that really started off the A.B.C.'s.

MRS. ANTROBUS: I don't care if he perishes. We can do without reading or writing. We can't do without food.

ANTROBUS: Then let the ice come!! Drink your coffee!! I don't want any coffee if I can't drink it with some good people.

MRS. ANTROBUS: Stop shouting. Who else is there trying to push us off the cliff?

ANTROBUS: Well, there's the man . . . who makes all the laws. Judge Moses!

MRS. ANTROBUS: Judges can't help us now.

ANTROBUS: And if the ice melts? . . . and if we pull through? Have you and I been able to bring up Henry? What have we done?

MRS. ANTROBUS: Who are those old women?

ANTROBUS (*coughs*): Up in town there are nine sisters. There are three or four of them here. They're sort of music teachers . . . and one of them recites and one of them—

MRS. ANTROBUS: That's the end. A singing troupe! Well, take your choice, live or die. Starve your own children before your face.

ANTROBUS (*gently*): These people don't take much. They're used to starving.
They'll sleep on the floor.
Besides, Maggie, listen: no, listen:
Who've we got in the house, but Sabina? Sabina's always afraid the worst will happen. Whose spirits can she keep up? Maggie, these people never give up. They think they'll live and work forever.

MRS. ANTROBUS (*walks slowly to the middle of the room*): All right, let them in. Let them in. You're master here.
(*Softly.*)
—But these animals must go. Enough's enough. They'll soon be big enough to push the walls down, anyway. Take them away.

ANTROBUS (*sadly*): All right. The dinosaur and mammoth—! Come on, baby, come on Frederick. Come for a walk. That's a good little fellow.

DINOSAUR: It's cold.

ANTROBUS: Yes, nice cold fresh air. Bracing.

(*He holds the door open and the* ANIMALS *go out. He beckons to his friends. The* REFUGEES *are typical elderly out-of-works from the streets of New York today.* JUDGE MOSES *wears a skull cap.* HOMER *is a blind beggar with a guitar. The seedy crowd shuffles in and waits humbly and expectantly.* ANTROBUS *introduces them to his wife who bows to each with a stately bend of her head.*)

Make yourself at home, Maggie, this is the doctor . . . m . . . Coffee'll be here in a minute. . . . Professor, this is my wife. . . . And: . . . Judge . . . Maggie, you know the Judge.

(*An old blind man with a guitar.*)

Maggie, you know. . . you know Homer?—Come right in, Judge.— Miss Muse—are some of your sisters here? Come right in. . . . Miss E. Muse; Miss T. Muse, Miss M. Muse.

MRS. ANTROBUS: Pleased to meet you.
Just . . . make yourself comfortable. Supper'll be ready in a minute.

(*She goes out, abruptly.*)

ANTROBUS: Make yourself at home, friends. I'll be right back.

(*He goes out.*
*The* REFUGEES *stare about them in awe. Presently several voices start whispering "Homer! Homer!" All take it up.* HOMER *strikes a chord or two on his guitar, then starts to speak:*)

HOMER:   Μῆνιν ἄειδε, θεὰ, Πηληϊάδεω Ἀχιλῆος,
         οὐλομένην, ἣ μυρί' Ἀχαιοῖς ἄλγε' ἔθηκε
         πολλὰς δ' ἰφθίμους ψυχὰς—

(HOMER'S *face shows he is lost in thought and memory and the words die away on his lips. The* REFUGEES *likewise nod in dreamy recollection. Soon the whisper "Moses, Moses!" goes around. An aged Jew parts his beard and recites dramatically:*)

MOSES:

בְּרֵאשִׁית בָּרָא אֱלֹהִים אֵת הַשָּׁמַיִם וְאֵת הָאָרֶץ: וְהָאָרֶץ הָיְתָה תֹהוּ
וָבֹהוּ וְחֹשֶׁךְ עַל־פְּנֵי תְהוֹם וְרוּחַ אֱלֹהִים מְרַחֶפֶת עַל־פְּנֵי הַמָּיִם:

(*The same dying away of the words takes place, and on the part of the* REFUGEES *the same retreat into recollection. Some of them murmer, "Yes, yes."*

*The mood is broken by the abrupt entrance of* MR. *and* MRS. AN-
TROBUS *and* SABINA *bearing platters of sandwiches and a pail of coffee.*
SABINA *stops and stares at the guests.)*

MR. ANTROBUS: Sabina, pass the sandwiches.

SABINA: I thought I was working in a respectable house that had
respectable guests. I'm giving my notice, Mr. Antrobus: two weeks,
that's the law.

MR. ANTROBUS: Sabina! Pass the sandwiches.

SABINA: Two weeks, that's the law.

MR. ANTROBUS: There's the law. That's Moses.

SABINA (*stares*): The Ten Commandments—FAUGH!!—(*To Audience*) That's the worst line I've ever had to say on any stage.

ANTROBUS: I think the best thing to do is just not to stand on ceremony, but pass the sandwiches around from left to right.—Judge,
help yourself to one of these.

MRS. ANTROBUS: The roads are crowded, I hear?

THE GUESTS (*all talking at once*): Oh, ma'am, you can't imagine.
. . . You can hardly put one foot before you . . . people are
trampling one another.

(*Sudden silence.*)

MRS. ANTROBUS: Well, you know what I think it is,—I think it's sun-
spots!

THE GUESTS (*discreet hubbub*): Oh, you're right, Mrs. Antrobus
. . . that's what it is. . . . That's what I was saying the other day.

(*Sudden silence.*)

ANTROBUS: Well, I don't believe the whole world's going to turn
to ice.
(*All eyes are fixed on him, waiting:*)
I can't believe it. Judge! Have we worked for nothing? Professor!
Have we just failed in the whole thing?

MRS. ANTROBUS: It is certainly very strange—well fortunately on
both sides of the family we come of very hearty stock.—Doctor, I

want you to meet my children. They're eating their supper now. And of course I want them to meet you.

MISS M. MUSE: How many children have you, Mrs. Antrobus?

MRS. ANTROBUS: I have two,—a boy and a girl.

THE JUDGE (MOSES, *softly*): I understood you had two sons, Mrs. Antrobus.

(MRS. ANTROBUS *in blind suffering; she walks toward the footlights.*)

MRS. ANTROBUS (*in a low voice*): Abel, Abel, my son, my son, Abel, my son, Abel, Abel, my son.

(*The* REFUGEES *move with few steps toward her as though in comfort murmuring words in Greek, Hebrew, German, et cetera. A piercing shriek from the kitchen,—*SABINA'S *voice. All heads turn.*)

ANTROBUS: What's that?

(SABINA *enters, bursting with indignation, pulling on her gloves.*)

SABINA: Mr. Antrobus—that son of yours, that boy Henry Antrobus —I don't stay in this house another moment!—He's not fit to live among respectable folks and that's a fact.

MRS. ANTROBUS: Don't say another word, Sabina. I'll be right back.

(*Without waiting for an answer she goes past her into the kitchen.*)

SABINA: Mr. Antrobus, Henry has thrown a stone again and if he hasn't killed the boy that lives next door, I'm very much mistaken. He finished his supper and went out to play; and I heard such a fight; and then I saw it. I saw it with my own eyes. And it looked to me like stark murder.

(MRS. ANTROBUS *appears at the kitchen door, shielding* HENRY *who follows her. When she steps aside, we see on* HENRY'S *forehead a large ochre and scarlet scar in the shape of a C.* MR. ANTROBUS *starts toward him. A pause.* HENRY *is heard saying under his breath:*)

HENRY: He was going to take the wheel away from me. He started to throw a stone at me first.

MRS. ANTROBUS: George, it was just a boyish impulse. Remember how young he is.

(*Louder, in an urgent wail.*)
George, he's only four thousand years old.

SABINA: And everything was going along so nicely!

(*Silence.* ANTROBUS *goes back to the fireplace.*)

ANTROBUS: Put out the fire! Put out all the fires.
(*Violently.*)
No wonder the sun grows cold.

(*He starts stamping on the fireplace.*)

MRS. ANTROBUS: Doctor! Judge! Help me!—George, have you lost your mind?

ANTROBUS: There is no mind. We'll not try to live.
(*To the guests.*)
Give it up. Give up trying.

(MRS. ANTROBUS *seizes him.*)

SABINA: Mr. Antrobus! I'm downright ashamed of you.

MRS. ANTROBUS: George, have some more coffee.—Gladys! Where's Gladys gone?

(GLADYS *steps in, frightened.*)

GLADYS: Here I am, mama.

MRS. ANTROBUS: Go upstairs and bring your father's slippers. How could you forget a thing like that, when you know how tired he is?
(ANTROBUS *sits in his chair. He covers his face with his hands.* MRS. ANTROBUS *turns to the* REFUGEES:)
Can't some of you sing? It's your business in life to sing, isn't it? Sabina!
(*Several of the women clear their throats tentatively, and with frightened faces gather around* HOMER's *guitar. He establishes a few chords. Almost inaudibly they start singing, led by* SABINA: "*Jingle Bells.*" MRS. ANTROBUS *continues to* ANTROBUS *in a low voice, while taking off his shoes:*)
George, remember all the other times. When the volcanoes came right up in the front yard.
And the time the grasshoppers ate every single leaf and blade of grass, and all the grain and spinach you'd grown with your own hands. And the summer there were earthquakes every night.

ANTROBUS: Henry! Henry!
(*Puts his hand on his forehead.*)
Myself! All of us, we're covered with blood.

MRS. ANTROBUS: Then remember all the times you were pleased with him and when you were proud of yourself.—Henry! Henry! Come here and recite to your father the multiplication table that you do so nicely.

(HENRY *kneels on one knee beside his father and starts whispering the multiplication table.*)

HENRY (*finally*): Two times six is twelve; three times six is eighteen —I don't think I know the sixes.

(*Enter* GLADYS *with the slippers.* MRS. ANTROBUS *makes stern gestures to her: Go in there and do your best. The* GUESTS *are now singing* "Tenting Tonight.")

GLADYS (*putting slippers on his feet*): Papa . . . papa . . . I was very good in school today. Miss Conover said right out in class that if all the girls had as good manners as Gladys Antrobus, that the world would be a very different place to live in.

MRS. ANTROBUS: You recited a piece at assembly, didn't you? Recite it to your father.

GLADYS: Papa, do you want to hear what I recited in class?
(*Fierce directorial glance from her mother.*)
"THE STAR" by Henry Wadsworth LONGFELLOW.

MRS. ANTROBUS: Wait!!! The fire's going out. There isn't enough wood! Henry, go upstairs and bring down the chairs and start breaking up the beds.

(*Exit* HENRY. *The singers return to* "Jingle Bells," *still very softly.*)

GLADYS: Look, Papa, here's my report card. Lookit. Conduct A! Look, Papa. Papa, do you want to hear the Star, by Henry Wadsworth Longfellow? Papa, you're not mad at me, are you?—I know it'll get warmer. Soon it'll be just like spring, and we can go to a picnic at the Hibernian Picnic Grounds like you always like to do, don't you remember? Papa, just look at me once.

(*Enter* HENRY *with some chairs.*)

ANTROBUS: You recited in assembly, did you?
(*She nods eagerly.*)
You didn't forget it?

GLADYS: No!!! I was perfect.

(*Pause. Then* ANTROBUS *rises, goes to the front door and opens it. The* REFUGEES *draw back timidly; the song stops; he peers out of the door, then closes it.*)

ANTROBUS (*with decision, suddenly*): Build up the fire. It's cold. Build up the fire. We'll do what we can. Sabina, get some more wood. Come around the fire, everybody. At least the young ones may pull through. Henry, have you eaten something?

HENRY: Yes, papa.

ANTROBUS: Gladys, have you had some supper?

GLADYS: I ate in the kitchen, papa.

ANTROBUS: If you do come through this—what'll you be able to do? What do you know? Henry, did you take a good look at that wheel?

HENRY: Yes, papa.

ANTROBUS (*sitting down in his chair*): Six times two are—

HENRY: —twelve; six times three are eighteen; six times four are— Papa, it's hot and cold. It makes my head all funny. It makes me sleepy.

ANTROBUS (*gives him a cuff*): Wake up. I don't care if your head is sleepy. Six times four are twenty-four. Six times five are—

HENRY: Thirty. Papa!

ANTROBUS: Maggie, put something into Gladys' head on the chance she can use it.

MRS. ANTROBUS: What do you mean, George?

ANTROBUS: Six times six are thirty-six.
Teach her the beginning of the Bible.

GLADYS: But, Mama, it's so cold and close.

(HENRY *has all but drowsed off. His father slaps him sharply and the lesson goes on.*)

MRS. ANTROBUS: "In the beginning God created the heavens and the earth; and the earth was waste and void; and the darkness was upon the face of the deep—"

(*The singing starts up again louder.* SABINA *has returned with wood.*)

SABINA (*after placing wood on the fireplace comes down to the footlights and addresses the audience*): Will you please start handing up your chairs? We'll need everything for this fire. Save the human race.—Ushers, will you pass the chairs up here? Thank you.

HENRY: Six times nine are fifty-four; six times ten are sixty.

(*In the back of the auditorium the sound of chairs being ripped up can be heard.* USHERS *rush down the aisles with chairs and hand them over.*)

GLADYS: "And God called the light Day and the darkness he called Night."

SABINA: Pass up your chairs, everybody. Save the human race.

(*The Curtain Falls.*)

# Act Two

*Toward the end of the intermission, though with the houselights still up, lantern slide projections begin to appear on the curtain. Timetables for trains leaving Pennsylvania Station for Atlantic City. Advertisements of Atlantic City hotels, drugstores, churches, rug merchants; fortune tellers, Bingo parlors.*
*When the house-lights go down, the voice of an* ANNOUNCER *is heard.*

ANNOUNCER: The Management now brings you the News Events of the World. Atlantic City, New Jersey:
*(Projection of a chrome postcard of the waterfront, trimmed in mica with the legend: FUN AT THE BEACH.)*
This great convention city is playing host this week to the anniversary convocation of that great fraternal order,—the Ancient and Honorable Order of Mammals, Subdivision Humans. This great fraternal, militant and burial society is celebrating on the Boardwalk, ladies and gentlemen, its six hundred thousandth Annual Convention. It has just elected its president for the ensuing term,—
*(Projection of* MR. *and* MRS. ANTROBUS *posed as they will be shown a few moments later.)*
Mr. George Antrobus of Excelsior, New Jersey. We show you President Antrobus and his gracious and charming wife, every inch a mammal. Mr. Antrobus has had a long and chequered career. Credit has been paid to him for many useful enterprises including the introduction of the lever, of the wheel and the brewing of beer. Credit has been also extended to President Antrobus's gracious and charming wife for many practical suggestions, including the hem, the gore, and the gusset; and the novelty of the year,—frying in oil. Before we show you Mr. Antrobus accepting the nomination, we have an important announcement to make. As many of you know, this great celebration of the Order of the Mammals has received delegations from the other rival Orders,—or shall we say: esteemed concurrent Orders: the WINGS, the FINS, the SHELLS, and so on. These Orders are holding their conventions also, in various parts of the world, and have sent representatives to our own, two of a kind.

Later in the day we will show you President Antrobus broadcasting his words of greeting and congratulation to the collected assemblies of the whole natural world.

Ladies and Gentlemen! We give you President Antrobus!

(*The screen becomes a Transparency.* MR. ANTROBUS *stands beside a pedestal;* MRS. ANTROBUS *is seated wearing a corsage of orchids.* ANTROBUS *wears an untidy Prince Albert; spats; from a red rosette in his buttonhole hangs a fine long purple ribbon of honor. He wears a gay lodge hat,—something between a fez and a legionnaire's cap.*)

ANTROBUS: Fellow-mammals, fellow-vertebrates, fellow-humans, I thank you. Little did my dear parents think,—when they told me to stand on my own two feet,—that I'd arrive at this place.

My friends, we have come a long way.

During this week of happy celebration it is perhaps not fitting that we dwell on some of the difficult times we have been through. The dinosaur is extinct—

(*Applause.*)

—the ice has retreated; and the common cold is being pursued by every means within our power.

(MRS. ANTROBUS *sneezes, laughs prettily, and murmurs: "I beg your pardon."*)

In our memorial service yesterday we did honor to all our friends and relatives who are no longer with us, by reason of cold, earth-quakes, plagues and . . . and . . .

(*Coughs.*)

differences of opinion.

As our Bishop so ably said . . . uh . . . so ably said. . . .

MRS. ANTROBUS (*closed lips*): Gone, but not forgotten.

ANTROBUS: "They are gone, but not forgotten."

I think I can say, I think I can prophesy with complete . . . uh . . . with complete. . . .

MRS. ANTROBUS: Confidence.

ANTROBUS: Thank you, my dear,—With complete lack of confi-dence, that a new day of security is about to dawn.

The watchword of the closing year was: Work. I give you the watchword for the future: Enjoy Yourselves.

MRS. ANTROBUS: George, sit down!

ANTROBUS: Before I close, however, I wish to answer one of those unjust and malicious accusations that were brought against me during this last electoral campaign.

Ladies and gentlemen, the charge was made that at various points in my career I leaned toward joining some of the rival orders,—that's a lie.

As I told reporters of the *Atlantic City Herald*, I do not deny that a few months before my birth I hesitated between . . . uh . . . between pinfeathers and gill-breathing,—and so did many of us here,—but for the last million years I have been viviparous, hairy and diaphragmatic.

(*Applause, Cries of "Good old Antrobus," "The Prince chap!" "Georgie," etc.*)

ANNOUNCER: Thank you. Thank you very much, Mr. Antrobus. Now I know that our visitors will wish to hear a word from that gracious and charming mammal, Mrs. Antrobus, wife and mother, —Mrs. Antrobus!

(MRS. ANTROBUS *rises, lays her program on her chair, bows and says:*)

MRS. ANTROBUS: Dear friends, I don't really think I should say anything. After all, it was my husband who was elected and not I. Perhaps, as president of the Women's Auxiliary Bed and Board Society,—I had some notes here, oh, yes, here they are:—I should give a short report from some of our committees that have been meeting in this beautiful city.

Perhaps it may interest you to know that it has at last been decided that the tomato is edible. Can you all hear me? The tomato *is* edible. A delegate from across the sea reports that the thread woven by the silkworm gives a cloth . . . I have a sample of it here . . . can you see it? smooth, elastic. I should say that it's rather attractive,— though personally I prefer less shiny surfaces. Should the windows of a sleeping apartment be open or shut? I know all mothers will follow our debates on this matter with close interest. I am sorry to say that the most expert authorities have not yet decided. It does seem to me that the night air would be bound to be unhealthy for our children, but there are many distinguished authorities on both sides. Well, I could go on talking forever,—as Shakespeare says: a woman's work is seldom done; but I think I'd better join my husband in saying thank you, and sit down. Thank you.

(*She sits down.*)

ANNOUNCER: Oh, Mrs. Antrobus!

MRS. ANTROBUS: Yes?

ANNOUNCER: We understand that you are about to celebrate a wedding anniversary. I know our listeners would like to extend their felicitations and hear a few words from you on that subject.

MRS. ANTROBUS: I have been asked by this kind gentleman . . . yes, my friends, this Spring Mr. Antrobus and I will be celebrating our five thousandth wedding anniversary.
I don't know if I speak for my husband, but I can say that, as for me, I regret every moment of it.
(*Laughter of confusion.*)
I beg your pardon. What I *mean* to say is that I do not regret one moment of it. I hope none of you catch my cold. We have two children. We've always had two children, though it hasn't always been the same two. But as I say, we have two fine children, and we're very grateful for that. Yes, Mr. Antrobus and I have been married five thousand years. Each wedding anniversary reminds me of the times when there were no weddings. We had to crusade for marriage. Perhaps there are some women within the sound of my voice who remember that crusade and those struggles; we fought for it, didn't we? We chained ourselves to lampposts and we made disturbances in the Senate,—anyway, at last we women got the ring. A few men helped us, but I must say that most men blocked our way at every step: they said we were unfeminine.
I only bring up these unpleasant memories, because I see some signs of backsliding from that great victory.
Oh, my fellow mammals, keep hold of that.
My husband says that the watchword for the year is Enjoy Yourselves. I think that's very open to misunderstanding. My watchword for the year is: Save the Family. It's held together for over five thousand years: Save it! Thank you.

ANNOUNCER: Thank you, Mrs. Antrobus.
(*The transparency disappears.*)
We had hoped to show you the Beauty Contest that took place here today.
President Antrobus, an experienced judge of pretty girls, gave the title of Miss Atlantic City 1942, to Miss Lily-Sabina Fairweather, charming hostess of our Boardwalk Bingo Parlor.
Unfortunately, however, our time is up, and I must take you to

some views of the Convention City and conveeners,—enjoying themselves.

(*A burst of music; the curtain rises.*
*The Boardwalk. The audience is sitting in the ocean. A handrail of scarlet cord stretches across the front of the stage. A ramp—also with scarlet hand rail—descends to the right corner of the orchestra pit where a great scarlet beach umbrella or a cabana stands. Front and right stage left are benches facing the sea; attached to each bench is a street-lamp.*
*The only scenery is two cardboard cut-outs six feet high, representing shops at the back of the stage. Reading from left to right they are: SALT WATER TAFFY; FORTUNE TELLER; then the blank space; BINGO PARLOR; TURKISH BATH. They have practical doors, that of the Fortune Teller's being hung with bright gypsy curtains.*
*By the left proscenium and rising from the orchestra pit is the weather signal; it is like the mast of a ship with cross bars. From time to time black discs are hung on it to indicate the storm and hurricane warnings. Three roller chairs, pushed by melancholy* NEGROES *file by empty. Throughout the act they traverse the stage in both directions.*
*From time to time,* CONVEENERS, *dressed like* MR. ANTROBUS, *cross the stage. Some walk sedately by; others engage in inane horseplay. The old gypsy* FORTUNE TELLER *is seated at the door of her shop, smoking a corncob pipe.*
*From the Bingo Parlor comes the voice of the* CALLER.)

BINGO CALLER: A-Nine; A-Nine. C-Twenty-six; C-Twenty-six. A-Four; A-Four. B-Twelve.

CHORUS (*back-stage*): Bingo!!!

(*The front of the Bingo Parlor shudders, rises a few feet in the air and returns to the ground trembling.*)

FORTUNE TELLER (*mechanically, to the unconscious back of a passerby, pointing with her pipe*): Bright's disease! Your partner's deceiving you in that Kansas City deal. You'll have six grandchildren. Avoid high places.
(*She rises and shouts after another:*)
Cirrhosis of the liver!

(SABINA *appears at the door of the Bingo Parlor. She hugs about her a blue raincoat that almost conceals her red bathing suit. She tries to catch the* FORTUNE TELLER'S *attention.*)

SABINA: Ssssst! Esmeralda! Ssssst!

FORTUNE TELLER: Keck!

SABINA: Has President Antrobus come along yet?

FORTUNE TELLER: No, no, no. Get back there. Hide yourself.

SABINA: I'm afraid I'll miss him. Oh, Esmeralda, if I fail in this, I'll die; I know I'll die. President Antrobus!!! And I'll be his wife! If it's the last thing I'll do, I'll be Mrs. George Antrobus.—Esmeralda, tell me my future.

FORTUNE TELLER: Keck!

SABINA: All right, I'll tell *you* my future.
(*Laughing dreamily and tracing it out with one finger on the palm of her hand.*)
I've won the Beauty Contest in Atlantic City,—well, I'll win the Beauty Contest of the whole world. I'll take President Antrobus away from that wife of his. Then I'll take every man away from his wife. I'll turn the whole earth upside down.

FORTUNE TELLER: Keck!

SABINA: When all those husbands just think about me they'll get dizzy. They'll faint in the streets. They'll have to lean against lamp-posts.—Esmeralda, who was Helen of Troy?

FORTUNE TELLER (*furiously*): Shut your foolish mouth. When Mr. Antrobus comes along you can see what you can do. Until then, —go away.

(SABINA *laughs. As she returns to the door of her Bingo Parlor a group of* CONVEENERS *rush over and smother her with attentions:* "Oh, Miss Lily, you know me. You've known me for years.")

SABINA: Go away, boys, go away. I'm after bigger fry than you are. —Why, Mr. Simpson!! How *dare* you!! I expect that even you nobodies must have girls to amuse you; but where you find them and what you do with them, is of absolutely no interest to me.

(*Exit. The* CONVEENERS *squeal with pleasure and stumble in after her. The* FORTUNE TELLER *rises, puts her pipe down on the stool, unfurls her voluminous skirts, gives a sharp wrench to her bodice and strolls towards the audience, swinging her hips like a young woman.*)

FORTUNE TELLER: I tell the future. Keck. Nothing easier. Everybody's future is in their face. Nothing easier.

But who can tell your past,—eh? Nobody!

Your youth,—where did it go? It slipped away while you weren't looking. While you were asleep. While you were drunk? Puh! You're like our friends, Mr. and Mrs. Antrobus; you lie awake nights trying to know your past. What did it mean? What was it trying to say to you?

Think! Think! Split your heads. I can't tell the past and neither can you. If anybody tries to tell you the past, take my word for it, they're charlatans! Charlatans! But I can tell the future.

(*She suddenly barks at a passing chair-pusher.*)

Apoplexy!

(*She returns to the audience.*)

Nobody listens.—Keck! I see a face among you now—I won't embarrass him by pointing him out, but, listen, it may be you: Next year the watchsprings inside you will crumple up. Death by regret, —Type Y. It's in the corners of your mouth. You'll decide that you should have lived for pleasure, but that you missed it. Death by regret,—Type Y. . . . Avoid mirrors. You'll try to be angry,—but no!—no anger.

(*Far forward, confidentially.*)

And now what's the immediate future of our friends, the Antrobuses? Oh, you've seen it as well as I have, keck,—that dizziness of the head; that Great Man dizziness? The inventor of beer and gunpowder. The sudden fits of temper and then the long stretches of inertia? "I'm a sultan; let my slave-girls fan me."

You know as well as I what's coming. Rain. Rain. Rain in floods. The deluge. But first you'll see shameful things—shameful things. Some of you will be saying: "Let him drown. He's not worth saving. Give the whole thing up." I can see it in your faces. But you're wrong. Keep your doubts and despairs to yourselves.

Again there'll be the narrow escape. The survival of a handful. From destruction,—total destruction.

(*She points sweeping with her hand to the stage.*)

Even of the animals, a few will be saved: two of a kind, male and female, two of a kind.

(*The heads of* CONVEENERS *appear about the stage and in the orchestra pit, jeering at her.*)

CONVEENERS: Charlatan! Madam Kill-joy! Mrs. Jeremiah! Charlatan!

FORTUNE TELLER: And *you!* Mark my words before it's too late. Where'll *you* be?

CONVEENERS: The croaking raven. Old dust and ashes. Rags, bottles, sacks.

FORTUNE TELLER: Yes, stick out your tongues. You can't stick your tongues out far enough to lick the death-sweat from your foreheads. It's too late to work now—bail out the flood with your soup spoons. You've had your chance and you've lost.

CONVEENERS: Enjoy yourselves!!!

(*They disappear. The* FORTUNE TELLER *looks off left and puts her finger on her lip.*)

FORTUNE TELLER: They're coming—the Antrobuses. Keck. Your hope. Your despair. Your selves.

(*Enter from the left,* MR. *and* MRS. ANTROBUS *and* GLADYS.)

MRS. ANTROBUS: Gladys Antrobus, stick your stummick in.

GLADYS: But it's easier this way.

MRS. ANTROBUS: Well, it's too bad the new president has such a clumsy daughter, that's all I can say. Try and be a lady.

FORTUNE TELLER: Aijah! That's been said a hundred billion times.

MRS. ANTROBUS: Goodness! Where's Henry? He was here just a minute ago. Henry!

(*Sudden violent stir. A roller-chair appears from the left. About it are dancing in great excitement* HENRY *and a* NEGRO CHAIR-PUSHER.)

HENRY (*slingshot in hand*): I'll put your eye out. I'll make you yell, like you never yelled before.

NEGRO (*at the same time*): Now, I warns you. I warns you. If you make me mad, you'll get hurt.

ANTROBUS: Henry! What is this? Put down that slingshot.

MRS. ANTROBUS (*at the same time*): Henry! HENRY! Behave yourself.

FORTUNE TELLER: That's right, young man. There are too many people in the world as it is. Everybody's in the way, except one's self.

HENRY: All I wanted to do was—have some fun.

NEGRO: Nobody can't touch my chair, nobody, without I allow 'em to. You get clean away from me and you get away fast.

(*He pushes his chair off, muttering.*)

ANTROBUS: What were you doing, Henry?

HENRY: Everybody's always getting mad. Everybody's always trying to push you around. I'll make him sorry for this; I'll make him sorry.

ANTROBUS: Give me that slingshot.

HENRY: I won't. I'm sorry I came to this place. I wish I weren't here. I wish I weren't anywhere.

MRS. ANTROBUS: Now, Henry, don't get so excited about nothing. I declare I don't know what we're going to do with you. Put your slingshot in your pocket, and don't try to take hold of things that don't belong to you.

ANTROBUS: After this you can stay home. I wash my hands of you.

MRS. ANTROBUS: Come now, let's forget all about it. Everybody take a good breath of that sea air and calm down.
(*A passing* CONVEENER *bows to* ANTROBUS *who nods to him.*)
Who was that you spoke to, George?

ANTROBUS: Nobody, Maggie. Just the candidate who ran against me in the election.

MRS. ANTROBUS: The man who ran against you in the election!!
(*She turns and waves her umbrella after the disappearing* CON-VEENER.)
My husband didn't speak to you and he never will speak to you.

ANTROBUS: Now, Maggie.

MRS. ANTROBUS: After those lies you told about him in your speeches! Lies, that's what they were.

GLADYS AND HENRY: Mama, everybody's looking at you. Everybody's laughing at you.

MRS. ANTROBUS: If you must know, my husband's a SAINT, a downright SAINT, and you're not fit to speak to him on the street.

ANTROBUS: Now, Maggie, now, Maggie, that's enough of that.

MRS. ANTROBUS: George Antrobus, you're a perfect worm. If you won't stand up for yourself, I will.

GLADYS: Mama, you just act awful in public.

MRS. ANTROBUS (*laughing*): Well, I must say I enjoyed it. I feel better. Wish his wife had been there to hear it. Children, what do you want to do?

GLADYS: Papa, can we ride in one of those chairs? Mama, I want to ride in one of those chairs.

MRS. ANTROBUS: No, sir. If you're tired you just sit where you are. We have no money to spend on foolishness.

ANTROBUS: I guess we have money enough for a thing like that. It's one of the things you do at Atlantic City.

MRS. ANTROBUS: Oh, we have? I tell you it's a miracle my children have shoes to stand up in. I didn't think I'd ever live to see them pushed around in chairs.

ANTROBUS: We're on a vacation, aren't we? We have a right to some treats, I guess. Maggie, some day you're going to drive me crazy.

MRS. ANTROBUS: All right, go. I'll just sit here and laugh at you. And you can give me my dollar right in my hand. Mark my words, a rainy day is coming. There's a rainy day ahead of us. I feel it in my bones. Go on, throw your money around. I can starve. I've starved before. I know how.

(*A* CONVEENER *puts his head through Turkish Bath window, and says with raised eyebrows:*)

CONVEENER: Hello, George. How are ya? I see where you brought the WHOLE family along.

MRS. ANTROBUS: And what do you mean by that?

(CONVEENER *withdraws head and closes window.*)

ANTROBUS: Maggie, I tell you there's a limit to what I can stand. God's Heaven, haven't I worked *enough*? Don't I get *any* vacation? Can't I even give my children so much as a ride in a roller-chair?

MRS. ANTROBUS (*putting out her hand for raindrops*): Anyway, it's going to rain very soon and you have your broadcast to make.

ANTROBUS: Now, Maggie, I warn you. A man can stand a family only just so long. I'm warning you.

(*Enter* SABINA *from the Bingo-Parlor. She wears a flounced red silk bathing suit, 1905. Red stockings, shoes, parasol. She bows demurely to* ANTROBUS *and starts down the ramp.* ANTROBUS *and the* CHILDREN *stare at her.* ANTROBUS *bows gallantly.*)

MRS. ANTROBUS: Why, George Antrobus, how can you say such a thing! You have the best family in the world.

ANTROBUS: Good morning, Miss Fairweather.

(SABINA *finally disappears behind the beach umbrella or in a cabana in the orchestra pit.*)

MRS. ANTROBUS: Who on earth was that you spoke to, George?

ANTROBUS (*complacent; mock-modest*): Hm . . . m . . . just a . . . solambaka keray.

MRS. ANTROBUS: What? I can't understand you.

GLADYS: Mama, wasn't she beautiful?

HENRY: Papa, introduce her to me.

MRS. ANTROBUS: Children, will you be quiet while I ask your father a simple question?—Who did you say it was, George?

ANTROBUS: Why-uh . . . a friend of mine. Very nice refined girl.

MRS. ANTROBUS: I'm waiting.

ANTROBUS: Maggie, that's the girl I gave the prize to in the beauty contest,—that's Miss Atlantic City 1942.

MRS. ANTROBUS: Hm! She looked like Sabina to me.

HENRY (*at the railing*): Mama, the life-guard knows her, too. Mama, he knows her well.

ANTROBUS: Henry, come here.—She's a very nice girl in every way and the sole support of her aged mother.

MRS. ANTROBUS: So was Sabina, so was Sabina; and it took a wall of ice to open your eyes about Sabina.—Henry, come over and sit down on this bench.

ANTROBUS: She's a very different matter from Sabina. Miss Fairweather is a college graduate, Phi Beta Kappa.

MRS. ANTROBUS: Henry, you sit here by mama. Gladys—

ANTROBUS (*sitting*): Reduced circumstances have required her taking a position as hostess in a Bingo Parlor; but there isn't a girl with higher principles in the country.

MRS. ANTROBUS: Well, let's not talk about it.—Henry, I haven't seen a whale yet.

ANTROBUS: She speaks seven languages and has more culture in her little finger than you've acquired in a lifetime.

MRS. ANTROBUS (*assumed amiability*): All right, all right, George. I'm glad to know there are such superior girls in the Bingo Parlors. —Henry, what's that?
(*Pointing at the storm signal, which has one black disk.*)

HENRY: What is it, Papa?

ANTROBUS: What? Oh, that's the storm signal. One of those black disks means bad weather; two means storm; three means hurricane; and four means the end of the world.

(*As they watch it a second black disk rolls into place.*)

MRS. ANTROBUS: Goodness! I'm going this very minute to buy you all some raincoats.

GLADYS (*putting her cheek against her father's shoulder*): Mama, don't go yet. I like sitting this way. And the ocean coming in and coming in. Papa, don't you like it?

MRS. ANTROBUS: Well, there's only one thing I lack to make me a perfectly happy woman: I'd like to see a whale.

HENRY: Mama, we saw two. Right out there. They're delegates to the convention. I'll find you one.

GLADYS: Papa, ask me something. Ask me a question.

ANTROBUS: Well . . . how big's the ocean?

GLADYS: Papa, you're teasing me. It's—three-hundred and sixty million square-miles—and—it—covers—three-fourths—of—the—earth's—surface—and—its—deepest-place—is—five—and—a—half—miles—deep—and—its—average—depth—is—twelve-thousand—feet. No, Papa, ask me something hard, real hard.

MRS. ANTROBUS (rising): Now I'm going off to buy those raincoats. I think that bad weather's going to get worse and worse. I hope it doesn't come before your broadcast. I should think we have about an hour or so.

HENRY: I hope it comes and zzzzzz everything before it. I hope it—

MRS. ANTROBUS: Henry!—George, I think . . . maybe, it's one of those storms that are just as bad on land as on the sea. When you're just as safe and safer in a good stout boat.

HENRY: There's a boat out at the end of the pier.

MRS. ANTROBUS: Well, keep your eye on it. George, you shut your eyes and get a good rest before the broadcast.

ANTROBUS: Thundering Judas, do I have to be told when to open and shut my eyes? Go and buy your raincoats.

MRS. ANTROBUS: Now, children, you have ten minutes to walk around. Ten minutes. And, Henry: control yourself. Gladys, stick by your brother and don't get lost.

(They run off.)

MRS. ANTROBUS: Will you be all right, George?

(CONVEENERS suddenly stick their heads out of the Bingo Parlor and Salt Water Taffy store, and voices rise from the orchestra pit.)

CONVEENERS: George, Geo-r-r-rge! George! Leave the old hen-coop at home, George. Do-mes-ticated Georgie!

MRS. ANTROBUS (shaking her umbrella): Low common oafs! That's what they are. Guess a man has a right to bring his wife to a convention, if he wants to.

*(She starts off.)*
What's the matter with a family, I'd like to know. What else have they got to offer?

*(Exit.* ANTROBUS *has closed his eyes. The* FORTUNE TELLER *comes out of her shop and goes over to the left proscenium. She leans against it watching* SABINA *quizzically.)*

FORTUNE TELLER: Heh! Here she comes!

SABINA *(loud whisper)*: What's he doing?

FORTUNE TELLER: Oh, he's ready for you. Bite your lips, dear, take a long breath and come on up.

SABINA: I'm nervous. My whole future depends on this. I'm nervous.

FORTUNE TELLER: Don't be a fool. What more could you want? He's forty-five. His head's a little dizzy. He's just been elected president. He's never known any other woman than his wife. Whenever he looks at her he realizes that she knows every foolish thing he's ever done.

SABINA *(still whispering)*: I don't know why it is, but every time I start one of these I'm nervous.

*(The* FORTUNE TELLER *stands in the center of the stage watching the following:)*

FORTUNE TELLER: You make me tired.

SABINA: First tell me my fortune.
*(The* FORTUNE TELLER *laughs drily and makes the gesture of brushing away a nonsensical question.* SABINA *coughs and says:)*
Oh, Mr. Antrobus,—dare I speak to you for a moment?

ANTROBUS: What?—Oh, certainly, certainly, Miss Fairweather.

SABINA: Mr. Antrobus . . . I've been so unhappy. I've wanted . . . I've wanted to make sure that you don't think that I'm the kind of girl who goes out for beauty contests.

FORTUNE TELLER: That's the way!

ANTROBUS: Oh, I understand. I understand perfectly.

FORTUNE TELLER: Give it a little more. Lean on it.

SABINA: I knew you would. My mother said to me this morning: Lily, she said, that fine Mr. Antrobus gave you the prize because he saw at once that you weren't the kind of girl who'd go in for a thing like that. But, honestly, Mr. Antrobus, in this world, honestly, a good girl doesn't know where to turn.

FORTUNE TELLER: Now you've gone too far.

ANTROBUS: My dear Miss Fairweather!

SABINA: You wouldn't know how hard it is. With that lovely wife and daughter you have. Oh, I think Mrs. Antrobus is the finest woman I ever saw. I wish I were like her.

ANTROBUS: There, there. There's . . . uh . . . room for all kinds of people in the world, Miss Fairweather.

SABINA: How wonderful of you to say that. How generous!—Mr. Antrobus, have you a moment free? . . . I'm afraid I may be a little conspicuous here . . . could you come down, for just a moment, to my beach cabana . . . ?

ANTROBUS: Why-uh . . . yes, certainly . . . for a moment . . . just for a moment.

SABINA: There's a deck chair there. Because: you know you *do* look tired. Just this morning my mother said to me: Lily, she said, I hope Mr. Antrobus is getting a good rest. His fine strong face has deep deep lines in it. Now isn't it true, Mr. Antrobus: you work too hard?

FORTUNE TELLER: Bingo!

(*She goes into her shop.*)

SABINA: Now you will just stretch out. No, I shan't say a word, not a word. I shall just sit there,—privileged. That's what I am.

ANTROBUS (*taking her hand*): Miss Fairweather . . . you'll . . . spoil me.

SABINA: Just a moment. I have something I wish to say to the audience.—Ladies and gentlemen. I'm not going to play this particular scene tonight. It's just a short scene and we're going to skip it. But I'll tell you what takes place and then we can continue the play from there on. Now in this scene—

ANTROBUS (*between his teeth*): But, Miss Somerset!

SABINA: I'm sorry. I'm sorry. But I have to skip it. In this scene, I talk to Mr. Antrobus, and at the end of it he decides to leave his wife, get a divorce at Reno and marry me. That's all.

ANTROBUS: Fitz!—Fitz!

SABINA: So that now I've told you we can jump to the end of it,—where you say:

(*Enter in fury* MR. FITZPATRICK, *the stage manager.*)

MR. FITZPATRICK: Miss Somerset, we insist on your playing this scene.

SABINA: I'm sorry, Mr. Fitzpatrick, but I can't and I won't. I've told the audience all they need to know and now we can go on.

(*Other* ACTORS *begin to appear on the stage, listening.*)

MR. FITZPATRICK: And *why* can't you play it?

SABINA: Because there are some lines in that scene that would hurt some people's feelings and I don't think the theatre is a place where people's feelings ought to be hurt.

MR. FITZPATRICK: Miss Somerset, you can pack up your things and go home. I shall call the understudy and I shall report you to Equity.

SABINA: I sent the understudy up to the corner for a cup of coffee and if Equity tries to penalize me I'll drag the case right up to the Supreme Court. Now listen, everybody, there's no need to get excited.

MR. FITZPATRICK *and* ANTROBUS: Why can't you play it . . . What's the matter with the scene?

SABINA: Well, if you must know, I have a personal guest in the audience tonight. Her life hasn't been exactly a happy one. I wouldn't have my friend hear some of these lines for the whole world. I don't suppose it occurred to the author that some other women might have gone through the experience of losing their husbands like this. Wild horses wouldn't drag from me the details of my friend's life, but . . . well, they'd been married twenty years, and before he got rich, why, she'd done the washing and everything.

MR. FITZPATRICK: Miss Somerset, your friend will forgive you. We must play this scene.

SABINA: Nothing, nothing will make me say some of those lines . . . about "a man outgrows a wife every seven years" and . . . and that one about "the Mohammedans being the only people who looked the subject square in the face." Nothing.

MR. FITZPATRICK: Miss Somerset! Go to your dressing room. I'll *read* your lines.

SABINA: Now everybody's nerves are on edge.

MR. ANTROBUS: Skip the scene.

(MR. FITZPATRICK *and the other* ACTORS *go off.*)

SABINA: Thank you. I knew you'd understand. We'll do just what I said. So Mr. Antrobus is going to divorce his wife and marry me. Mr. Antrobus, you say: "It won't be easy to lay all this before my wife."

(*The* ACTORS *withdraw.* ANTROBUS *walks about, his hand to his fore-head muttering:*)

ANTROBUS: Wait a minute. I can't get back into it as easily as all that. "My wife is a very obstinate woman." Hm . . . then you say . . . hm . . . Miss Fairweather, I mean Lily, it won't be easy to lay all this before my wife. It'll hurt her feelings a little.

SABINA: Listen, George: *other* people haven't got feelings. Not in the same way that we have,—we who are presidents like you and prize-winners like me. Listen, other people haven't got feelings; they just imagine they have. Within two weeks they go back to playing bridge and going to the movies.
Listen, dear: everybody in the world except a few people like you and me are just people of straw. Most people have no insides at all. Now that you're president you'll see that. Listen, darling, there's a kind of secret society at the top of the world,—like you and me,— that know this. The world was made for us. What's life anyway? Except for two things, pleasure and power, what is life? Boredom! Foolishness. You know it is. Except for those two things, life's nau-se-at-ing. So,—come here!
(*She moves close. They kiss.*)
So.
Now when your wife comes, it's really very simple; just tell her.

ANTROBUS: Lily, Lily: you're a wonderful woman.

SABINA: Of course I am.

*(They enter the cabana and it hides them from view. Distant roll of thunder. A third black disk appears on the weather signal. Distant thunder is heard.* MRS. ANTROBUS *appears carrying parcels. She looks about, seats herself on the bench left, and fans herself with her handkerchief. Enter* GLADYS *right, followed by two* CONVEENERS. *She is wearing red stockings.)*

MRS. ANTROBUS: Gladys!

GLADYS: Mama, here I am.

MRS. ANTROBUS: Gladys Antrobus!!! Where did you get those dreadful things?

GLADYS: Wha-a-t? Papa liked the color.

MRS. ANTROBUS: You go back to the hotel this minute!

GLADYS: I won't. I won't. Papa liked the color.

MRS. ANTROBUS: All right. All right. You stay here. I've a good mind to let your father see you that way. You stay right here.

GLADYS: I . . . I don't want to stay if . . . if you don't think he'd like it.

MRS. ANTROBUS: Oh . . . it's all one to me. I don't care what happens. I don't care if the biggest storm in the whole world comes. Let it come.
*(She folds her hands.)*
Where's your brother?

GLADYS *(in a small voice)*: He'll be here.

MRS. ANTROBUS: Will he? Well, let him get into trouble. I don't care. I don't know where your father is, I'm sure.

*(Laughter from the cabana.)*

GLADYS *(leaning over the rail)*: I think he's . . . Mama, he's talking to the lady in the red dress.

MRS. ANTROBUS: Is that so?
*(Pause.)*
We'll wait till he's through. Sit down here beside me and stop fidgeting . . . what are you crying about?

(*Distant thunder. She covers* GLADYS's *stockings with a raincoat.*)

GLADYS: You don't like my stockings.

(*Two* CONVEENERS *rush in with a microphone on a standard and various paraphernalia. The* FORTUNE TELLER *appears at the door of her shop. Other characters gradually gather.*)

BROADCAST OFFICIAL: Mrs. Antrobus! Thank God we've found you at last. Where's Mr. Antrobus? We've been hunting everywhere for him. It's about time for the broadcast to the conventions of the world.

MRS. ANTROBUS (*calm*): I expect he'll be here in a minute.

BROADCAST OFFICIAL: Mrs. Antrobus, if he doesn't show up in time, I hope you will consent to broadcast in his place. It's the most important broadcast of the year.

(SABINA *enters from cabana followed by* ANTROBUS.)

MRS. ANTROBUS: No, I shan't. I haven't one single thing to say.

BROADCAST OFFICIAL: Then won't you help us find him, Mrs. Antrobus? A storm's coming up. A hurricane. A deluge!

SECOND CONVEENER (*who has sighted* ANTROBUS *over the rail*): Joe! Joe! Here he is.

BROADCAST OFFICIAL: In the name of God, Mr. Antrobus, you're on the air in five minutes. Will you kindly please come and test the instrument? That's all we ask. If you just please begin the alphabet slowly.

(ANTROBUS, *with set face, comes ponderously up the ramp. He stops at the point where his waist is level with the stage and speaks authoritatively to the* OFFICIALS.)

ANTROBUS: I'll be ready when the time comes. Until then, move away. Go away. I have something I wish to say to my wife.

BROADCASTING OFFICIAL (*whimpering*): Mr. Antrobus! This is the most important broadcast of the year.

(*The* OFFICIALS *withdraw to the edge of the stage.* SABINA *glides up the ramp behind* ANTROBUS.)

SABINA (*whispering*): Don't let her argue. Remember arguments have nothing to do with it.

ANTROBUS: Maggie, I'm moving out of the hotel. In fact, I'm moving out of everything. For good. I'm going to marry Miss Fairweather. I shall provide generously for you and the children. In a few years you'll be able to see that it's all for the best. That's all I have to say.

BROADCAST OFFICIAL: Mr. Antrobus! I hope you'll be ready. This is the most important broadcast of the year.

BINGO ANNOUNCER: A—nine; A—nine. D—forty-two; D—forty-two. C—thirty; C—thirty. B—seventeen; B—seventeen. C—forty; C—forty.

GLADYS: What did Papa say, Mama? I didn't hear what papa said.

CHORUS: Bingo!!

BROADCAST OFFICIAL: Mr. Antrobus. All we want to do is test your voice with the alphabet.

ANTROBUS: Go away. Clear out.

MRS. ANTROBUS (*composedly with lowered eyes*): George, I can't talk to you until you wipe those silly red marks off your face.

ANTROBUS: I think there's nothing to talk about. I've said what I have to say.

SABINA: Splendid!!

ANTROBUS: You're a fine woman, Maggie, but . . . but a man has his own life to lead in the world.

MRS. ANTROBUS: Well, after living with you for five thousand years I guess I have a right to a word or two, haven't I?

ANTROBUS (*to* SABINA): What can I answer to that?

SABINA: Tell her that conversation would only hurt her feelings. It's-kinder-in-the-long-run-to-do-it-short-and-quick.

ANTROBUS: I want to spare your feelings in every way I can, Maggie.

BROADCAST OFFICIAL: Mr. Antrobus, the hurricane signal's gone up. We could begin right now.

MRS. ANTROBUS (*calmly, almost dreamily*): I didn't marry you because you were perfect. I didn't even marry you because I loved you. I married you because you gave me a promise.
(*She takes off her ring and looks at it.*)
That promise made up for your faults. And the promise I gave you made up for mine. Two imperfect people got married and it was the promise that made the marriage.

ANTROBUS: Maggie, . . . I was only nineteen.

MRS. ANTROBUS (*she puts her ring back on her finger*): And when our children were growing up, it wasn't a house that protected them; and it wasn't our love that protected them—it was that promise.
And when that promise is broken—this can happen!

(*With a sweep of the hand she removes the raincoat from* GLADYS' *stockings.*)

ANTROBUS (*stretches out his arm, apoplectic*): Gladys!! Have you gone crazy? Has everyone gone crazy?
(*Turning on* SABINA.)
You did this. You gave them to her.

SABINA: I never said a word to her.

ANTROBUS (*to* GLADYS): You go back to the hotel and take those horrible things off.

GLADYS (*pert*): Before I go, I've got something to tell you,—it's about Henry.

MRS. ANTROBUS (*claps her hands peremptorily*): Stop your noise,—I'm taking her back to the hotel, George. Before I go I have a letter . . . I have a message to throw into the ocean.
(*Fumbling in her handbag.*)
Where is the plagued thing? Here it is.
(*She flings something—invisible to us—far over the heads of the audience to the back of the auditorium.*)
It's a bottle. And in the bottle's a letter. And in the letter is written all the things that a woman knows.
It's never been told to any man and it's never been told to any woman, and if it finds its destination, a new time will come. We're not what books and plays say we are. We're not what advertisements say we are. We're not in the movies and we're not on the radio.

We're not what you're all told and what you think we are: We're ourselves. And if any man can find one of us he'll learn why the whole universe was set in motion. And if any man harm any one of us, his soul—the only soul he's got—had better be at the bottom of that ocean,—and that's the only way to put it. Gladys, come here. We're going back to the hotel.

(*She drags* GLADYS *firmly off by the hand, but* GLADYS *breaks away and comes down to speak to her father.*)

SABINA: Such goings-on. Don't give it a minute's thought.

GLADYS: Anyway, I think you ought to know that Henry hit a man with a stone. He hit one of those colored men that push the chairs and the man's very sick. Henry ran away and hid and some policemen are looking for him very hard. And I don't care a bit if you don't want to have anything to do with mama and me, because I'll never like you again and I hope nobody ever likes you again,—so there!

(*She runs off.* ANTROBUS *starts after her.*)

ANTROBUS: I . . . I have to go and see what I can do about this.

SABINA: You stay right here. Don't you go now while you're excited. Gracious sakes, all these things will be forgotten in a hundred years. Come, now, you're on the air. Just say anything,—it doesn't matter what. Just a lot of birds and fishes and things.

BROADCAST OFFICIAL: Thank you, Miss Fairweather. Thank you very much. Ready, Mr. Antrobus.

ANTROBUS (*touching the microphone*): What is it, what is it? Who am I talking to?

BROADCAST OFFICIAL: Why, Mr. Antrobus! To our order and to all the other orders.

ANTROBUS (*raising his head*): What are all those birds doing?

BROADCAST OFFICIAL: Those are just a few of the birds. Those are the delegates to our convention,—two of a kind.

ANTROBUS (*pointing into the audience*): Look at the water. Look at them all. Those fishes jumping. The children should see this!— There's Maggie's whales!! Here are your whales, Maggie!!

BROADCAST OFFICIAL: I hope you're ready, Mr. Antrobus.

ANTROBUS: And look on the beach! You didn't tell me these would be here!

SABINA: Yes, George. Those are the animals.

BROADCAST OFFICIAL (*busy with the apparatus*): Yes, Mr. Antrobus, those are the vertebrates. We hope the lion will have a word to say when you're through. Step right up, Mr. Antrobus, we're ready. We'll just have time before the storm.
(*Pause. In a hoarse whisper:*)
They're wait-ing.

(*It has grown dark. Soon after he speaks a high whistling noise begins. Strange veering lights start whirling about the stage. The other characters disappear from the stage.*)

ANTROBUS: Friends. Cousins. Four score and ten billion years ago our forefather brought forth upon this planet the spark of life,—

(*He is drowned out by thunder. When the thunder stops the FOR-TUNE TELLER is seen standing beside him.*)

FORTUNE TELLER: Antrobus, there's not a minute to be lost. Don't you see the four disks on the weather signal? Take your family into that boat at the end of the pier.

ANTROBUS: My family? I have no family. Maggie! Maggie! They won't come.

FORTUNE TELLER: They'll come.—Antrobus! Take these animals into that boat with you. All of them,—two of each kind.

SABINA: George, what's the matter with you? This is just a storm like any other storm.

ANTROBUS: Maggie!

SABINA: Stay with me, we'll go . . .
(*Losing conviction.*)
This is just another thunderstorm,—isn't it? Isn't it?

ANTROBUS: Maggie!!!

(MRS. ANTROBUS *appears beside him with* GLADYS.)

MRS. ANTROBUS (*matter-of-fact*): Here I am and here's Gladys.

ANTROBUS: Where've you been? Where have you been? Quick, we're going into that boat out there.

MRS. ANTROBUS: I know we are. But I haven't found Henry.

(*She wanders off into the darkness calling "Henry!"*)

SABINA (*low urgent babbling, only occasionally raising her voice*): I don't believe it. I don't believe it's anything at all. I've seen hundreds of storms like this.

FORTUNE TELLER: There's no time to lose. Go. Push the animals along before you. Start a new world. Begin again.

SABINA: Esmeralda! George! Tell me,—is it really serious?

ANTROBUS (*suddenly very busy*): Elephants first. Gently, gently.— Look where you're going.

GLADYS (*leaning over the ramp and striking an animal on the back*): Stop it or you'll be left behind!

ANTROBUS: Is the Kangaroo there? *There* you are! Take those turtles in your pouch, will you?
(*To some other animals, pointing to his shoulder.*)
Here! You jump up here. You'll be trampled on.

GLADYS (*to her father, pointing below*): Papa, look,—the snakes!

MRS. ANTROBUS: I can't find Henry. Hen-ry!

ANTROBUS: Go along. Go along. Climb on their backs.—Wolves! Jackals,—whatever you are,—tend to your own business!

GLADYS (*pointing, tenderly*): Papa,—look.

SABINA: Mr. Antrobus—take me with you. Don't leave me here. I'll work. I'll help. I'll do anything.

(THREE CONVEENERS *cross the stage, marching with a banner.*)

CONVEENERS: George! What are you scared of?—George! Fellas, it looks like rain.—"Maggie, where's my umbrella?"—George, setting up for Barnum and Bailey?

ANTROBUS (*again catching his wife's hand*): Come on now, Maggie, —the pier's going to break any minute.

MRS. ANTROBUS: I'm not going a step without Henry. Henry!

GLADYS (*on the ramp*): Mama! Papa! Hurry. The pier's cracking, Mama. It's going to break.

MRS. ANTROBUS: Henry! Cain! CAIN!

(HENRY *dashes into the stage and joins his mother.*)

HENRY: Here I am, Mama.

MRS. ANTROBUS: Thank God!—now come quick.

HENRY: I didn't think you wanted me.

MRS. ANTROBUS: Quick!

(*She pushes him down before her into the aisle.*)

SABINA (*all the* ANTROBUSES *are now in the theatre aisle.* SABINA *stands at the top of the ramp*): Mrs. Antrobus, take me. Don't you remember me? I'll work. I'll help. Don't leave me here!

MRS. ANTROBUS (*impatiently, but as though it were of no importance*): Yes, yes. There's a lot of work to be done. Only hurry.

FORTUNE TELLER (*now dominating the stage. To* SABINA *with a grim smile*): Yes, go—back to the kitchen with you.

SABINA (*half-down the ramp. To* FORTUNE TELLER): I don't know why my life's always being interrupted—just when everything's going fine!!

(*She dashes up the aisle.*
*Now the* CONVEENERS *emerge doing a serpentine dance on the stage.*
*They jeer at the* FORTUNE TELLER.)

CONVEENERS: Get a canoe—there's not a minute to be lost! Tell me my future, Mrs. Croaker.

FORTUNE TELLER: Paddle in the water, boys—enjoy yourselves.

VOICE FROM THE BINGO PARLOR: A-nine; A-nine. C-Twenty-four. C-Twenty-four.

CONVEENERS: Rags, bottles, and sacks.

FORTUNE TELLER: Go back and climb on your roofs. Put rags in the cracks under your doors.—Nothing will keep out the flood. You've had your chance. You've had your day. You've failed. You've lost.

VOICE FROM THE BINGO PARLOR: B-fifteen. B-fifteen.

FORTUNE TELLER (*shading her eyes and looking out to sea*): They're safe. George Antrobus! Think it over! A new world to make,— think it over!

*(The Curtain Falls.)*

# Act Three

Just before the curtain rises, two sounds are heard from the stage: a cracked bugle call.

*The curtain rises on almost total darkness. Almost all the flats composing the walls of* MR. ANTROBUS'S *house, as of Act I, are up, but they lean helter-skelter against one another, leaving irregular gaps. Among the flats missing are two in the back wall, leaving the frames of the windows and door crazily out of line. Off stage, back right, some red Roman fire is burning. The bugle call is repeated. Enter* SABINA *through the tilted door. She is dressed as a Napoleonic camp follower, "la fille du regiment," in begrimed reds and blues.*

SABINA: Mrs. Antrobus! Gladys! Where are you?
The war's over. The war's over. You can come out. The peace treaty's been signed.
Where are they?—Hmpf! Are they dead, too? Mrs. Annnntrobus! Glaaaadus! Mr. Antrobus'll be here this afternoon. I just saw him downtown. Huuuurry and put things in order. He says that now that the war's over we'll all have to settle down and be perfect.

(*Enter* MR. FITZPATRICK, *the stage manager, followed by the whole company, who stand waiting at the edges of the stage.* MR. FITZ-PATRICK *tries to interrupt* SABINA.)

MR. FITZPATRICK: Miss Somerset, we have to stop a moment.

SABINA: They may be hiding out in the back—

MR. FITZPATRICK: Miss Somerset! We have to stop a moment.

SABINA: What's the matter?

MR. FITZPATRICK: There's an explanation we have to make to the audience.—Lights, please.
(*To the actor who plays* MR. ANTROBUS.)
Will you explain the matter to the audience?

*(The lights go up. We now see that a balcony or elevated runway has been erected at the back of the stage, back of the wall of the Antrobus house. From its extreme right and left ends ladder-like steps descend to the floor of the stage.)*

ANTROBUS: Ladies and gentlemen, an unfortunate accident has taken place back stage. Perhaps I should say *another* unfortunate accident.

SABINA: I'm sorry. I'm sorry.

ANTROBUS: The management feels, in fact, we all feel that you are due an apology. And now we have to ask your indulgence for the most serious mishap of all. Seven of our actors have . . . have been taken ill. Apparently, it was something they ate. I'm not exactly clear what happened.
*(All the ACTORS start to talk at once. ANTROBUS raises his hand.)*
Now, now—not all at once. Fitz, do you know what it was?

MR. FITZPATRICK: Why, it's perfectly clear. These seven actors had dinner together, and they ate something that disagreed with them.

SABINA: Disagreed with them!!! They have ptomaine poisoning. They're in Bellevue Hospital this very minute in agony. They're having their stomachs pumped out this very minute, in perfect agony.

ANTROBUS: Fortunately, we've just heard they'll all recover.

SABINA: It'll be a miracle if they do, a downright miracle. It was the lemon meringue pie.

ACTORS: It was the fish . . . it was the canned tomatoes . . . it was the fish.

SABINA: It was the lemon meringue pie. I saw it with my own eyes; it had blue mould all over the bottom of it.

ANTROBUS: Whatever it was, they're in no condition to take part in this performance. Naturally, we haven't enough understudies to fill all those roles; but we do have a number of splendid volunteers who have kindly consented to help us out. These friends have watched our rehearsals, and they assure me that they know the lines and the business very well. Let me introduce them to you—my dresser, Mr. Tremayne,—himself a distinguished Shakespearean actor for many years; our wardrobe mistress, Hester; Miss Somerset's maid, Ivy; and Fred Bailey, captain of the ushers in this theatre.

(*These persons bow modestly*. IVY *and* HESTER *are colored girls*.)
Now this scene takes place near the end of the act. And I'm sorry to
say we'll need a short rehearsal, just a short run-through. And as
some of it takes place in the auditorium, we'll have to keep the curtain up. Those of you who wish can go out in the lobby and smoke
some more. The rest of you can listen to us, or . . . or just talk
quietly among yourselves, as you choose. Thank you. Now will you
take it over, Mr. Fitzpatrick?

MR. FITZPATRICK: Thank you.—Now for those of you who are listening perhaps I should explain that at the end of this act, the men have
come back from the War and the family's settled down in the house.
And the author wants to show the hours of the night passing by over
their heads, and the planets crossing the sky . . . uh . . . over
their heads. And he says—this is hard to explain—that each of the
hours of the night is a philosopher, or a great thinker. Eleven o'clock,
for instance, is Aristotle. And nine o'clock is Spinoza. Like that. I
don't suppose it means anything. It's just a kind of poetic effect.

SABINA: Not mean anything! Why, it certainly does. Twelve o'clock
goes by saying those wonderful things. I think it means that when
people are asleep they have all those lovely thoughts, much better
than when they're awake.

IVY: Excuse me, I think it means,—excuse me, Mr. Fitzpatrick—

SABINA: What were you going to say, Ivy?

IVY: Mr. Fitzpatrick, you let my father come to a rehearsal; and
my father's a Baptist minister, and he said that the author meant that
—just like the hours and stars go by over our heads at night, in the
same way the ideas and thoughts of the great men are in the air
around us all the time and they're working on us, even when we
don't know it.

MR. FITZPATRICK: Well, well, maybe that's it. Thank you, Ivy. Anyway,—the hours of the night are philosophers. My friends, are you
ready? Ivy, can you be eleven o'clock? "This good estate of the
mind possessing its object in energy we call divine." Aristotle.

IVY: Yes, sir. I know that and I know twelve o'clock and I know
nine o'clock.

MR. FITZPATRICK: Twelve o'clock? Mr. Tremayne, the Bible.

TREMAYNE: Yes.

MR. FITZPATRICK: Ten o'clock? Hester,—Plato?
(*She nods eagerly.*)
Nine o'clock, Spinoza,—Fred?

BAILEY: Yes, *sir.*

(FRED BAILEY *picks up a great gilded cardboard numeral IX and starts up the steps to the platform.* MR. FITZPATRICK *strikes his forehead.*)

MR. FITZPATRICK: The planets!! We forgot all about the planets.

SABINA: O my God! The planets! Are they sick too?

(ACTORS *nod.*)

MR. FITZPATRICK: Ladies and gentlemen, the planets are singers. Of course, we can't replace them, so you'll have to imagine them singing in this scene. Saturn sings from the orchestra pit down here. The Moon is way up there. And Mars with a red lantern in his hand, stands in the aisle over there—Tz-tz-tz. It's too bad; it all makes a very fine effect. However! Ready—nine o'clock: Spinoza.

BAILEY (*walking slowly across the balcony, left to right*): "After experience had taught me that the common occurrences of daily life are vain and futile—"

FITZPATRICK: Louder, Fred. "And I saw that all the objects of my desire and fear—"

BAILEY: "And I saw that all the objects of my desire and fear were in themselves nothing good nor bad save insofar as the mind was affected by them—"

FITZPATRICK: Do you know the rest? All right. Ten o'clock. Hester. Plato.

HESTER: "Then tell me, O Critias, how will a man choose the ruler that shall rule over him? Will he not—"

FITZPATRICK: Thank you. Skip to the end, Hester.

HESTER: " . . . can be multiplied a thousand fold in its effects among the citizens."

FITZPATRICK: Thank you.—Aristotle, Ivy?

IVY: "This good estate of the mind possessing its object in energy we call divine. This we mortals have occasionally and it is this energy which is pleasantest and best. But God has it always. It is wonderful in us; but in Him how much more wonderful."

FITZPATRICK: Midnight. Midnight, Mr. Tremayne. That's right,— you've done it before.—All right, everybody. You know what you have to do.—Lower the curtain. House lights up. Act Three of THE SKIN OF OUR TEETH.
(*As the curtain descends he is heard saying:*)
You volunteers, just wear what you have on. Don't try to put on the costumes today.

(*House lights go down. The Act begins again. The Bugle call. Curtain rises. Enter* SABINA.)

SABINA: Mrs. Antrobus! Gladys! Where are you?
The war's over.—You've heard all this—
(*She gabbles the main points.*)
Where—are—they? Are—they—dead, too, et cetera.
I—just—saw—Mr.—Antrobus—down town, et cetera.
(*Slowing up:*)
He says that now that the war's over we'll all have to settle down and be perfect. They may be hiding out in the back somewhere. Mrs. An-tro-bus.

(*She wanders off. It has grown lighter.*
*A trapdoor is cautiously raised and* MRS. ANTROBUS *emerges waist-high and listens. She is disheveled and worn; she wears a tattered dress and a shawl half covers her head. She talks down through the trapdoor.*)

MRS. ANTROBUS: It's getting light. There's still something burning over there—Newark, or Jersey City. What? Yes, I could swear I heard someone moving about up here. But I can't see anybody. I say: I can't see anybody.

(*She starts to move about the stage.* GLADYS' *head appears at the trapdoor. She is holding a* BABY.)

GLADYS: Oh, Mama. Be careful.

MRS. ANTROBUS: Now, Gladys, you stay out of sight.

GLADYS: Well, let me stay here just a minute. I want the baby to get some of this fresh air.

MRS. ANTROBUS: All right, but keep your eyes open. I'll see what I can find. I'll have a good hot plate of soup for you before you can say Jack Robinson. Gladys Antrobus! Do you know what I think I see? There's old Mr. Hawkins sweeping the sidewalk in front of his A. and P. store. Sweeping it with a broom. Why, he must have gone crazy, like the others! I see some other people moving about, too.

GLADYS: Mama, come back, come back.

(MRS. ANTROBUS *returns to the trapdoor and listens.*)

MRS. ANTROBUS: Gladys, there's something in the air. Everybody's movement's sort of different. I see some women walking right out in the middle of the street.

SABINA'S VOICE: Mrs. An-tro-bus!

MRS. ANTROBUS AND GLADYS: What's that?!!

SABINA'S VOICE: Glaaaadys! Mrs. An-tro-bus!

(*Enter* SABINA.)

MRS. ANTROBUS: Gladys, that's Sabina's voice as sure as I live.—Sabina! Sabina!—Are you *alive?!!*

SABINA: Of course, I'm alive. How've you girls been?—*Don't* try and kiss me. I never want to kiss another human being as long as I live. Sh-sh, there's nothing to get emotional about. Pull yourself together, the war's over. Take a deep breath,—the war's over.

MRS. ANTROBUS: The war's over!! I don't believe you. I don't believe you. I can't believe you.

GLADYS: Mama!

SABINA: Who's that?

MRS. ANTROBUS: That's Gladys and her baby. I don't believe you. Gladys, Sabina says the war's over. Oh, Sabina.

SABINA (*leaning over the* BABY): Goodness! Are there any babies left in the world! Can it *see?* And can it cry and everything?

GLADYS: Yes, he can. He notices everything very well.

SABINA: Where on earth did you get it? Oh, I won't ask.—Lord, I've lived all these seven years around camp and I've forgotten how to behave.—Now we've got to think about the men coming home.— Mrs. Antrobus, go and wash your face, I'm ashamed of you. Put your best clothes on. Mr. Antrobus'll be here this afternoon. I just saw him downtown.

MRS. ANTROBUS AND GLADYS: He's alive!! He'll be here!! Sabina, you're not joking?

MRS. ANTROBUS: And Henry?

SABINA (*dryly*): Yes, Henry's alive, too, that's what they say. Now don't stop to talk. Get yourselves fixed up. Gladys, you look terrible. Have you any decent clothes?

(SABINA *has pushed them toward the trapdoor.*)

MRS. ANTROBUS (*half down*): Yes, I've something to wear just for this very day. But, Sabina,—who won the war?

SABINA: Don't stop now,—just wash your face.
(*A whistle sounds in the distance.*)
Oh, my God, what's that silly little noise?

MRS. ANTROBUS: Why, it sounds like . . . it sounds like what used to be the noon whistle at the shoe-polish factory.
(*Exit.*)

SABINA: That's what it is. Seems to me like peacetime's coming along pretty fast—shoe polish!

GLADYS (*half down*): Sabina, how soon after peacetime begins does the milkman start coming to the door?

SABINA: As soon as he catches a cow. Give him time to catch a cow, dear.
(*Exit* GLADYS. SABINA *walks about a moment, thinking.*)
Shoe polish! My, I'd forgotten what peacetime was like.
(*She shakes her head, then sits down by the trapdoor and starts talking down the hole.*)
Mrs. Antrobus, guess what I saw Mr. Antrobus doing this morning at dawn. He was tacking up a piece of paper on the door of the Town Hall. You'll die when you hear: it was a recipe for grass soup, for a grass soup that doesn't give you the diarrhea. Mr. Antrobus is

still thinking up new things.—He told me to give you his love. He's got all sorts of ideas for peacetime, he says. No more laziness and idiocy, he says. And oh, yes! Where are his books? What? Well, pass them up. The first thing he wants to see are his books. He says if you've burnt those books, or if the rats have eaten them, he says it isn't worthwhile starting over again. Everybody's going to be beautiful, he says, and diligent, and very intelligent.
(*A hand reaches up with two volumes.*)
What language is that? Pu-u-gh,—mold! And he's got such plans for you, Mrs. Antrobus. You're going to study history and algebra—and so are Gladys and I—and philosophy. You should hear him talk.
(*Taking two more volumes.*)
Well, these are in English, anyway.—To hear him talk, seems like he expects you to be a combination, Mrs. Antrobus, of a saint and a college professor, and a dancehall hostess, if you know what I mean.
(*Two more volumes.*)
Ugh. German!
(*She is lying on the floor; one elbow bent, her cheek on her hand, meditatively.*)
Yes, peace will be here before we know it. In a week or two we'll be asking the Perkinses in for a quiet evening of bridge. We'll turn on the radio and hear how to be big successes with a new toothpaste. We'll trot down to the movies and see how girls with wax faces live—all *that* will begin again. Oh, Mrs. Antrobus, God forgive me but I enjoyed the war. Everybody's at their best in wartime. I'm sorry it's over. And, oh, I forgot! Mr. Antrobus sent you another message—can you hear me?—
(*Enter* HENRY, *blackened and sullen. He is wearing torn overalls, but has one gaudy admiral's epaulette hanging by a thread from his right shoulder, and there are vestiges of gold and scarlet braid running down his left trouser leg. He stands listening.*)
Listen! Henry's never to put foot in this house again, he says. He'll kill Henry on sight, if he sees him.
You don't know about Henry??? Well, where have you been? What? Well, Henry rose right to the top. Top of *what?* Listen, I'm telling you. Henry rose from corporal to captain, to major, to general.—I don't know how to say it, but the enemy is *Henry;* Henry *is* the enemy. Everybody knows that.

HENRY: He'll kill me, will he?

SABINA: Who are *you?* I'm not afraid of you. The war's over.

HENRY: I'll kill him so fast. I've spent seven years trying to find him; the others I killed were just substitutes.

SABINA: Goodness! It's Henry!—
(*He makes an angry gesture.*)
Oh, I'm not afraid of you. The war's over, Henry Antrobus, and you're not any more important than any other unemployed. You go away and hide yourself, until we calm your father down.

HENRY: The first thing to do is burn up those old books; it's the ideas he gets out of those old books that . . . that makes the whole world so you can't live in it.

(*He reels forward and starts kicking the books about, but suddenly falls down in a sitting position.*)

SABINA: You leave those books alone!! Mr. Antrobus is looking forward to them a-special.—Gracious sakes, Henry, you're so tired you can't stand up. Your mother and sister'll be here in a minute and we'll think what to do about you.

HENRY: What did they ever care about me?

SABINA: There's that old whine again. All you people think you're not loved enough, nobody loves you. Well, you start being lovable and we'll love you.

HENRY (*outraged*): I don't want anybody to love me.

SABINA: Then stop talking about it all the time.

HENRY: I *never* talk about it. The last thing I want is anybody to pay any attention to me.

SABINA: I can hear it behind every word you say.

HENRY: I want everybody to hate me.

SABINA: Yes, you've decided that's second best, but it's still the same thing.—Mrs. Antrobus! Henry's here. He's so tired he can't stand up.

(MRS. ANTROBUS *and* GLADYS, *with her* BABY, *emerge. They are dressed as in Act I.* MRS. ANTROBUS *carries some objects in her apron, and* GLADYS *has a blanket over her shoulder.*)

MRS. ANTROBUS AND GLADYS: Henry! Henry! Henry!

HENRY (*glaring at them*): Have you anything to eat?

MRS. ANTROBUS: Yes, I have, Henry. I've been saving it for this very day,—two good baked potatoes. No! Henry! one of them's for your father. Henry!! Give me that other potato back this minute.

(SABINA *sidles up behind him and snatches the other potato away.*)

SABINA: He's so dog-tired he doesn't know what he's doing.

MRS. ANTROBUS: Now you just rest there, Henry, until I can get your room ready. Eat that potato good and slow, so you can get all the nourishment out of it.

HENRY: You all might as well know right now that I haven't come back here to live.

MRS. ANTROBUS: Sh. . . . I'll put this coat over you. Your room's hardly damaged at all. Your football trophies are a little tarnished, but Sabina and I will polish them up tomorrow.

HENRY: Did you hear me? I don't live here. I don't belong to anybody.

MRS. ANTROBUS: Why, how can you say a thing like that! You certainly do belong right here. Where else would you want to go? Your forehead's feverish, Henry, seems to me. You'd better give me that gun, Henry. You won't need that any more.

GLADYS (*whispering*): Look, he's fallen asleep already, with his potato half-chewed.

SABINA: Puh! The terror of the world.

MRS. ANTROBUS: Sabina, you mind your own business, and start putting the room to rights.

(HENRY *has turned his face to the back of the sofa.* MRS. ANTROBUS *gingerly puts the revolver in her apron pocket, then helps* SABINA. SABINA *has found a rope hanging from the ceiling. Grunting, she hangs all her weight on it, and as she pulls the walls begin to move into their right places.* MRS. ANTROBUS *brings the overturned tables, chairs and hassock into the positions of Act I.*)

SABINA: That's all we do—always beginning again! Over and over again. Always beginning again.
(*She pulls on the rope and a part of the wall moves into place. She stops. Meditatively:*)

How do we know that it'll be any better than before? Why do we go on pretending? Some day the whole earth's going to have to turn cold anyway, and until that time all these other things'll be happening again: it will be more wars and more walls of ice and floods and earthquakes.

MRS. ANTROBUS: Sabina!! Stop arguing and go on with your work.

SABINA: All right. I'll go on just out of *habit*, but I won't believe in it.

MRS. ANTROBUS (*aroused*): Now, Sabina. I've let you talk long enough. I don't want to hear any more of it. Do I have to explain to you what everybody knows,—everybody who keeps a home going? Do I have to say to you what nobody should ever *have* to say, because they can read it in each other's eyes?
Now listen to me:
(MRS. ANTROBUS *takes hold of the rope.*)
I could live for seventy years in a cellar and make soup out of grass and bark, without ever doubting that this world has a work to do and will do it.
Do you hear me?

SABINA (*frightened*): Yes, Mrs. Antrobus.

MRS. ANTROBUS: Sabina, do you see this house,—216 Cedar Street,—do you see it?

SABINA: Yes, Mrs. Antrobus.

MRS. ANTROBUS: Well, just to have known this house is to have seen the idea of what we can do someday if we keep our wits about us. Too many people have suffered and died for my children for us to start reneging now. So we'll start putting this house to rights. Now, Sabina, go and see what you can do in the kitchen.

SABINA: Kitchen! Why is it that however far I go away, I always find myself back in the kitchen?
(*Exit.*)

MRS. ANTROBUS (*still thinking over her last speech, relaxes and says with a reminiscent smile*): Goodness gracious, wouldn't you know that my father was a parson? It was just like I heard his own voice speaking and he's been dead five thousand years. There! I've gone and almost waked Henry up.

HENRY (*talking in his sleep, indistinctly*): Fellows . . . what have they done for us? . . . Blocked our way at every step. Kept everything in their own hands. And you've stood it. When are you going to wake up?

MRS. ANTROBUS: Sh, Henry. Go to sleep. Go to sleep. Go to sleep.— Well, that looks better. Now let's go and help Sabina.

GLADYS: Mama, I'm going out into the backyard and hold the baby right up in the air. And show him that we don't have to be afraid any more.

(*Exit* GLADYS *to the kitchen.*
MRS. ANTROBUS *glances at* HENRY, *exits into kitchen.* HENRY *thrashes about in his sleep. Enter* ANTROBUS, *his arms full of bundles, chewing the end of a carrot. He has a slight limp. Over the suit of Act I he is wearing an overcoat too long for him, its skirts trailing on the ground. He lets his bundles fall and stands looking about. Presently his attention is fixed on* HENRY, *whose words grow clearer.*)

HENRY: All right! What have you got to lose? What have they done for us? That's right—nothing. Tear everything down. I don't care what you smash. We'll begin again and we'll show 'em.

(ANTROBUS *takes out his revolver and holds it pointing downwards. With his back towards the audience he moves toward the footlights.* HENRY'S *voice grows louder and he wakes with a start. They stare at one another. Then* HENRY *sits up quickly. Throughout the following scene* HENRY *is played, not as a misunderstood or misguided young man, but as a representation of strong unreconciled evil.*) All right! Do something.

(*Pause.*)

Don't think I'm afraid of you, either. All right, do what you were going to do. Do it.

(*Furiously.*)

Shoot me, I tell you. You don't have to think I'm any relation of yours. I haven't got any father or any mother, or brothers or sisters. And I don't want any. And what's more I haven't got anybody over me; and I never will have. I'm alone, and that's all I want to be: alone. So you can shoot me.

ANTROBUS: You're the last person I wanted to see. The sight of you dries up all my plans and hopes. I wish I were back at war still, because it's easier to fight you than to live with you. War's a pleasure— do you hear me?—War's a pleasure compared to what faces us now: trying to build up a peacetime with you in the middle of it.

(ANTROBUS *walks up to the window.*)

HENRY: I'm not going to be a part of any peacetime of yours. I'm going a long way from here and make my own world that's fit for a man to live in. Where a man can be free, and have a chance, and do what he wants to do in his own way.

ANTROBUS (*his attention arrested; thoughtfully. He throws the gun out of the window and turns with hope*): . . . Henry, let's try again.

HENRY: Try what? Living *here?*—Speaking polite downtown to all the old men like you? Standing like a sheep at the street corner until the red light turns to green? Being a good boy and a good sheep, like all the stinking ideas you get out of your books? Oh, no. I'll make a world, and I'll show you.

ANTROBUS (*hard*): How can you make a world for people to live in, unless you've first put order in yourself? Mark my words: I shall continue fighting you until my last breath as long as you mix up your idea of liberty with your idea of hogging everything for yourself. I shall have no pity on you. I shall pursue you to the far corners of the earth. You and I want the same thing; but until you think of it as something that everyone has a right to, you are my deadly enemy and I will destroy you.—I hear your mother's voice in the kitchen. Have you seen her?

HENRY: I have no mother. Get it into your head. I don't belong here. I have nothing to do here. I have no home.

ANTROBUS: Then why did you come here? With the whole world to choose from, why did you come to this one place: 216 Cedar Street, Excelsior, New Jersey. . . . Well?

HENRY: What if I did? What if I wanted to look at it once more, to see if—

ANTROBUS: Oh, you're related, all right—When your mother comes in you must behave yourself. Do you hear me?

HENRY (*wildly*): What is this?—*must behave* yourself. Don't you say *must* to me.

ANTROBUS: Quiet!

(*Enter* MRS. ANTROBUS *and* SABINA.)

HENRY: Nobody can say *must* to me. All my life everybody's been crossing me,—everybody, everything, all of you. I'm going to be free, even if I have to kill half the world for it. Right now, too. Let me get my hands on his throat. I'll show him.

(*He advances toward* ANTROBUS. *Suddenly,* SABINA *jumps between them and calls out in her own person:*)

SABINA: Stop! Stop! Don't play this scene. You know what happened last night. Stop the play.
(*The men fall back, panting.* HENRY *covers his face with his hands.*)
Last night you almost strangled him. You became a regular savage. Stop it!

HENRY: It's true. I'm sorry. I don't know what comes over me. I have nothing against him personally. I respect him very much . . . I . . . I admire him. But something comes over me. It's like I become fifteen years old again. I . . . I . . . listen: my own father used to whip me and lock me up every Saturday night. I never had enough to eat. He never let me have enough money to buy decent clothes. I was ashamed to go downtown. I never could go to the dances. My father and my uncle put rules in the way of everything I wanted to do. They tried to prevent my living at all.—I'm sorry. I'm sorry.

MRS. ANTROBUS (*quickly*): No, go on. Finish what you were saying. Say it all.

HENRY: In this scene it's as though I were back in High School again. It's like I had some big emptiness inside me,—the emptiness of being hated and blocked at every turn. And the emptiness fills up with the one thought that you have to strike and fight and kill. Listen, it's as though you have to kill somebody else so as not to end up killing yourself.

SABINA: That's not true. I knew your father and your uncle and your mother. You imagined all that. Why, they did everything they could for you. How can you say things like that? They didn't lock you up.

HENRY: They did. They did. They wished I hadn't been born.

SABINA: That's not true.

ANTROBUS (*in his own person, with self-condemnation, but cold and proud*): Wait a minute. I have something to say, too. It's not wholly his fault that he wants to strangle me in this scene. It's my fault, too. He wouldn't feel that way unless there were something in me that reminded him of all that. He talks about an emptiness. Well, there's an emptiness in me, too. Yes,—work, work, work,—that's all I do. I've ceased to *live*. No wonder he feels that anger coming over him.

MRS. ANTROBUS: There! At least you've said it.

SABINA: We're all just as wicked as we can be, and that's the God's truth.

MRS. ANTROBUS (*nods a moment, then comes forward; quietly*): Come. Come and put your head under some cold water.

SABINA (*in a whisper*): I'll go with him. I've known him a long while. You have to go on with the play. Come with me.

(HENRY *starts out with* SABINA, *but turns at the exit and says to* ANTROBUS:)

HENRY: Thanks. Thanks for what you said. I'll be all right tomorrow. I won't lose control in that place. I promise.

(*Exeunt* HENRY *and* SABINA.
ANTROBUS *starts toward the front door, fastens it.*
MRS. ANTROBUS *goes up stage and places the chair close to table.*)

MRS. ANTROBUS: George, do I see you limping?

ANTROBUS: Yes, a little. My old wound from the other war started smarting again. I can manage.

MRS. ANTROBUS (*looking out of the window*): Some lights are coming on,—the first in seven years. People are walking up and down looking at them. Over in Hawkins' open lot they've built a bonfire to celebrate the peace. They're dancing around it like scarecrows.

ANTROBUS: A bonfire! As though they hadn't seen enough things burning.—Maggie,—the dog died?

MRS. ANTROBUS: Oh, yes. Long ago. There are no dogs left in Excelsior.—You're back again! All these years. I gave up counting on letters. The few that arrived were anywhere from six months to a year late.

ANTROBUS: Yes, the ocean's full of letters, along with the other things.

MRS. ANTROBUS: George, sit down, you're tired.

ANTROBUS: No, you sit down. I'm tired but I'm restless.
(*Suddenly, as she comes forward:*)
Maggie! I've lost it. I've lost it.

MRS. ANTROBUS: What, George? What have you lost?

ANTROBUS: The most important thing of all: The desire to begin again, to start building.

MRS. ANTROBUS (*sitting in the chair right of the table*): Well, it will come back.

ANTROBUS (*at the window*): I've lost it. This minute I feel like all those people dancing around the bonfire—just relief. Just the desire to settle down; to slip into the old grooves and keep the neighbors from walking over my lawn.—Hm. But during the war,—in the middle of all that blood and dirt and hot and cold—every day and night, I'd have moments, Maggie, when I *saw* the things that we could do when it was over. When you're at war you think about a better life; when you're at peace you think about a more comfortable one. I've lost it. I feel sick and tired.

MRS. ANTROBUS: Listen! The baby's crying.
I hear Gladys talking. Probably she's quieting Henry again. George, while Gladys and I were living here—like moles, like rats, and when we were at our wits' end to save the baby's life—the only thought we clung to was that you were going to bring something good out of this suffering. In the night, in the dark, we'd whisper about it, starving and sick.—Oh, George, you'll have to get it back again. Think! What else kept us alive all these years? Even now, it's not comfort we want. We can suffer whatever's necessary; only give us back that promise.

(*Enter* SABINA *with a lighted lamp. She is dressed as in Act I.*)

SABINA: Mrs. Antrobus . . .

MRS. ANTROBUS: Yes, Sabina?

SABINA: Will you need me?

MRS. ANTROBUS: No, Sabina, you can go to bed.

SABINA: Mrs. Antrobus, if it's all right with you, I'd like to go to the bonfire and celebrate seeing the war's over. And, Mrs. Antrobus, they've opened the Gem Movie Theatre and they're giving away a hand-painted soup tureen to every lady, and I thought one of us ought to go.

ANTROBUS: Well, Sabina, I haven't any money. I haven't seen any money for quite a while.

SABINA: Oh, you don't need money. They're taking anything you can give them. And I have some . . . some . . . Mrs. Antrobus, promise you won't tell anyone. It's a little against the law. But I'll give you some, too.

ANTROBUS: What is it?

SABINA: I'll give you some, too. Yesterday I picked up a lot of . . . of beef-cubes!

(MRS. ANTROBUS *turns and says calmly:*)

MRS. ANTROBUS: But, Sabina, you know you ought to give that in to the Center downtown. They know who needs them most.

SABINA (*outburst*): Mrs. Antrobus, I didn't make this war. I didn't ask for it. And, in my opinion, after anybody's gone through what we've gone through, they have a right to grab what they can find. You're a very nice man, Mr. Antrobus, but you'd have got on better in the world if you'd realized that dog-eat-dog was the rule in the beginning and always will be. And most of all now.
(*In tears.*)
Oh, the world's an awful place, and you know it is. I used to think something could be done about it; but I know better now. I hate it. I hate it.
(*She comes forward slowly and brings six cubes from the bag.*)
All right. All right. You can have them.

ANTROBUS: Thank you, Sabina.

SABINA: Can I have . . . can I have one to go to the movies?
(ANTROBUS *in silence gives her one.*)
Thank you.

ANTROBUS: Good night, Sabina.

SABINA: Mr. Antrobus, don't mind what I say. I'm just an ordinary girl, you know what I mean, I'm just an ordinary girl. But you're a bright man, you're a very bright man, and of course you invented the alphabet and the wheel, and, my God, a lot of things . . . and if you've got any other plans, my God, don't let me upset them. Only every now and then I've got to go to the movies. I mean my nerves can't stand it. But if you have any ideas about improving the crazy old world, I'm really with you. I really am. Because it's . . . it's . . . Good night.

*(She goes out.* ANTROBUS *starts laughing softly with exhilaration.)*

ANTROBUS: Now I remember what three things always went together when I was able to see things most clearly: three things. Three things:
*(He points to where* SABINA *has gone out.)*
The voice of the people in their confusion and their need. And the thought of you and the children and this house. . . And . . . Maggie! I didn't dare ask you: my books! They haven't been lost, have they?

MRS. ANTROBUS: No. There are some of them right here. Kind of tattered.

ANTROBUS: Yes.—Remember, Maggie, we almost lost them once before? And when we finally did collect a few torn copies out of old cellars they ran in everyone's head like a fever. They as good as rebuilt the world.
*(Pauses, book in hand, and looks up.)*
Oh, I've never forgotten for long at a time that living is struggle. I know that every good and excellent thing in the world stands moment by moment on the razor-edge of danger and must be fought for—whether it's a field, or a home, or a country. All I ask is the chance to build new worlds and God has always given us that. And has given us *(opening the book)* voices to guide us; and the memory of our mistakes to warn us. Maggie, you and I will remember in peacetime all the resolves that were so clear to us in the days of war. We've come a long ways. We've learned. We're learning. And the steps of our journey are marked for us here.
*(He stands by the table turning the leaves of a book.)*
Sometimes out there in the war,—standing all night on a hill—I'd try and remember some of the words in these books. Parts of them and phrases would come back to me. And after a while I used to give names to the hours of the night.

(*He sits, hunting for a passage in the book.*)
Nine o'clock I used to call Spinoza. Where is it: "After experience had taught me—"

(*The back wall has disappeared, revealing the platform.* FRED BAILEY *carrying his numeral has started from left to right.* MRS. ANTROBUS *sits by the table sewing.*)

BAILEY: "After experience had taught me that the common occurrences of daily life are vain and futile; and I saw that all the objects of my desire and fear were in themselves nothing good nor bad save insofar as the mind was affected by them; I at length determined to search out whether there was something truly good and communicable to man."

(*Almost without break* HESTER, *carrying a large Roman numeral ten, starts crossing the platform.* GLADYS *appears at the kitchen door and moves towards her mother's chair.*)

HESTER: "Then tell me, O Critias, how will a man choose the ruler that shall rule over him? Will he not choose a man who has first established order in himself, knowing that any decision that has its spring from anger or pride or vanity can be multiplied a thousand fold in its effects upon the citizens?"

(HESTER *disappears and* IVY, *as eleven o'clock starts speaking.*)

IVY: "This good estate of the mind possessing its object in energy we call divine. This we mortals have occasionally and it is this energy which is pleasantest and best. But God has it always. It is wonderful in us; but in Him how much more wonderful."

(*As* MR. TREMAYNE *starts to speak,* HENRY *appears at the edge of the scene, brooding and unreconciled, but present.*)

TREMAYNE: "In the beginning, God created the Heavens and the earth; And the Earth was waste and void; And the darkness was upon the face of the deep. And the Lord said let there be light and there was light."

(*Sudden black-out and silence, except for the last strokes of the midnight bell. Then just as suddenly the lights go up, and* SABINA *is standing at the window, as at the opening of the play.*)

SABINA: Oh, oh, oh. Six o'clock and the master not home yet. Pray God nothing serious has happened to him crossing the Hudson

River. But I wouldn't be surprised. The whole world's at sixes and sevens, and why the house hasn't fallen down about our ears long ago is a miracle to me.

(*She comes down to the footlights.*)

This is where you came in. We have to go on for ages and ages yet. You go home.

The end of this play isn't written yet.

Mr. and Mrs. Antrobus! Their heads are full of plans and they're as confident as the first day they began,—and they told me to tell you: good night.

# BIOGRAPHIES AND BIBLIOGRAPHIES

# BIOGRAPHIES

## ANTON CHEKHOV (1860–1904)

Anton Chekhov was born in the old Black Sea port of Taganrog on January 17, 1860. His unhappy boyhood was spent helping his large poverty-stricken family. After graduating from high school at Taganrog, he entered the University of Moscow as a medical student; at the same time, in order to support himself, he wrote a large number of short stories and sketches of Russian life. In 1884 he received his degree as doctor of medicine, although by then his writing had taken on a professional character. With the publication of his first collection of short stories in 1887, his talent was immediately recognized.

Chekhov's interest in the drama was aroused at an early age, and he started writing and producing plays, none of which was a success, for at least ten years before the Moscow Art Theater was formed. In fact, when he died, he was better known as the author of several hundred short stories and sketches than as a playwright. His first minor success was *Ivanov*, produced at Korsh's Theater in Moscow in November, 1887.

Seriously ill of tuberculosis, Chekhov retired in 1890 to the Crimea, where he spent his last years. However he made frequent trips to Moscow to superintend the production at the Moscow Art Theater of his four important plays, written during this period. *The Cherry Orchard*, his last play, was produced in 1904, and at its performance Chekhov was feted as one of Russia's greatest dramatists—primarily because of his skill in recreating the atmosphere of the Russia of his day. Only a few weeks after the opening of *The Cherry Orchard*, Chekhov died in a little Russian village in the Black Forest, where he had gone in a futile attempt to recover his lost health.

The principal works of Anton Chekhov:

*Plays*

    IVANOV (1887)
    THE SWAN SONG (1889)
    THE PROPOSAL (1889)

THE WOOD SPIRIT (1889)
THE BEAR (1890)
THE SEA GULL (1896)
UNCLE VANYA (1897)
THE TRAGEDIAN IN SPITE OF HIMSELF (1899)
THE THREE SISTERS (1901)
THE CHERRY ORCHARD (1904)

*Novels and Short Story Collections*

HUMOROUS FOLK (1887)
TWILIGHT, AND OTHER STORIES (1887)
MOROSE FOLK (1890)
VARIEGATED TALES (1894)
OLD WIVES OF RUSSIA (1894)
THE DUEL (1895)
THE CHESTNUT TREE (1895)
WARD NUMBER SIX (1897)

## LILLIAN HELLMAN (1905–     )

Born in New Orleans, of Southern parents, Lillian Hellman was taken at an early age to live in New York City. She was educated at New York University and at Columbia. Her first play, *Dear Queen*, written in 1931 in collaboration with Louis Kronenberger, was never produced, and it was not until the production of *The Children's Hour* in 1934 that she began her rise to fame. This play had a run of 691 performances on Broadway before touring the country. Her next play, *Days To Come*, a drama about strike-breaking during the depression, was a complete failure. Since that time, however, her plays have been box office successes, and she is now considered one of America's leading dramatists. *Watch On The Rhine* (1941) won the New York Drama Critics Circle Award as the best play of the year. Miss Hellman divides her time among New York City, "Hardscrabble Farm," her country place near Pleasantville, N. Y., and Hollywood, where she does scenarios for MGM.

A list of Lillian Hellman's important works:

*Plays*

DEAR QUEEN (1931)
THE CHILDREN'S HOUR (1934)
DAYS TO COME (1936)

THE LITTLE FOXES (1939)
WATCH ON THE RHINE (1941)
THE SEARCHING WIND (1944)
ANOTHER PART OF THE FORREST (1946)
MONTSERRAT (1949)

*Scenarios*

THE DARK ANGEL (1935)
DEAD END (1937)
THE NORTH STAR (1944)


## HENRIK IBSEN (1828–1906)

Seven years after Henrik Ibsen's birth on March 20, 1828, in Skein, a small Norwegian coastal town, his family lost their money and their social prestige. On the wretched farm to which his family moved, Ibsen found all outlets for his literary and artistic talents closed. In 1850 he went to Christiania to enter the university as a medical student, but the fairly successful reception of his *Catalina*, published that year, made him decide in favor of a theatrical career.

Ibsen was appointed dramatist of the Norwegian Theater at Bergen in 1851 and later became its manager. After six years of hard work there, he became the "artistic director" of the Norwegian Theater of Christiania, a post he held until the theater failed in 1862. Granted a yearly pension of $450 by the King of Norway, he took up residence in Berlin and in Rome, and at these capitals he wrote his most famous plays during the next quarter century. With the production of *Brand* in 1866 and *Peer Gynt* the following year, Ibsen's success was assured, and when he finally returned to Norway in July 1891, to spend the remainder of his life there, he had become world famous.

Ibsen is an historic figure in dramatic literature, for he was the first to create the modern problem play, set in contemporary, realistic surroundings. From *Pillars of Society* (1877) to *Hedda Gabler* (1890) Ibsen dealt with many of the social problems then facing a complacent world. With his attack on the conventional treatment of women in *A Doll's House* (1879) he became world renowned, and this play, a milestone in dramatic history, marks the beginning of the modern theater.

Ibsen's principal plays are listed below:

CATALINA (1850)
NORMA (1851)
LOVE'S COMEDY (1862)

BRAND (1866)
PEER GYNT (1867)
THE LEAGUE OF YOUTH (1869)
EMPEROR AND GALILEAN (1873)
PILLARS OF SOCIETY (1877)
A DOLL'S HOUSE (1879)
GHOSTS (1881)
AN ENEMY OF THE PEOPLE (1882)
THE WILD DUCK (1884)
ROSMERSHOLM (1886)
LADY FROM THE SEA (1888)
HEDDA GABLER (1890)
THE MASTER BUILDER (1892)
LITTLE EYOLF (1894)
JOHN GABRIEL BORKMAN (1896)
WHEN WE DEAD AWAKEN (1899)


## EUGENE O'NEILL (1888–    )

Eugene O'Neill, the son of the distinguished actor James O'Neill, was born in New York City—his birthplace incidentally was on Broadway. During his early years he accompanied his family on their theatrical tours. After attending various boarding schools, he studied at Princeton for one year (1906). He worked for a time at a mail-order house, then set off, in 1909, for Honduras in search of gold, and the following year signed up on a freighter destined for Buenos Aires. Returning to the United States after a voyage to Africa as a mule-tender, he took up newspaper reporting on the New London *Telegraph*. In December of 1912 his health broke down and he was ordered to a sanatorium for the treatment of tuberculosis. His life as an ordinary seaman, his associations with stevedores and outcasts, and his rough-and-tumble existence as a vagabond made a deep impression on his personality; and the experiences of these adventuresome years are reflected later in many of his plays.

O'Neill's decision, arrived at during the winter and spring of 1913, to write verse and plays marked a turning point in his life. His need for help on technical matters led him to attend Professor Baker's famous class in play-writing at Harvard. Here he received encouragement, but he soon became bored with the routine as well as with his classmates and left. After spending the winter of 1915–1916 in Greenwich Village, O'Neill became associated with the Provincetown Players, who produced many of his early plays. By

1920 he was through experimenting with one-act plays, which he felt were too limited in scope, and had produced his first full length play, *Beyond the Horizon*. This play won him his first Pulitzer prize and definitely established him as a successful dramatist. *Anna Christie* (1922) and *Strange Interlude* (1928) were also awarded Pulitzer prizes, and in 1936 O'Neill received the Nobel Prize for Literature.

A chronological list of Eugene O'Neill's principal plays:

THIRST (1914)
BOUND EAST FOR CARDIFF (1916)
BEFORE BREAKFAST (1916)
THE LONG VOYAGE HOME (1917)
'ILE (1918)
THE MOON OF THE CARIBBEES (1918)
THE DREAMY KID (1920)
BEYOND THE HORIZON (1920)
THE EMPEROR JONES (1921)
DIFF'RENT (1921)
THE STRAW (1921)
GOLD (1921)
THE HAIRY APE (1922)
ANNA CHRISTIE (1922)
THE FIRST MAN (1922)
ALL GOD'S CHILLUN GOT WINGS (1924)
WELDED (1924)
DESIRE UNDER THE ELMS (1925)
THE GREAT GOD BROWN (1926)
THE FOUNTAIN (1926)
MARCO MILLIONS (1927)
LAZARUS LAUGHED (1927)
STRANGE INTERLUDE (1928)
DYNAMO (1929)
MOURNING BECOMES ELECTRA (1931)
AH, WILDERNESS! (1933)
DAYS WITHOUT END (1934)
THE ICEMAN COMETH (1946)

## SEAN O'CASEY (1884–    )

Sean O'Casey, born in Dublin, received very little formal schooling not only because of his family's poverty but also because of a serious eye disease. Teaching himself to read and write, however, he soon developed a keen interest in literature. At the early age of fourteen he held a job in an iron-mongery, where he toiled ten hours a day for four shillings a week. While working as a laborer, he became interested in the Irish Nationalist Movement, and as an organizer of the Irish Citizen Army, he took part in the Easter Rebellion of 1916. First known as a writer on labor and political questions, it was not until 1923 that he emerged as a dramatist when, after three of his plays had been rejected, the Abbey Theater finally accepted and produced *The Shadow of A Gunman*. *Juno and the Paycock*, his most famous play, was produced by the Abbey players in 1924.

Chronological list of O'Casey's principal works:

*Plays*

THE SHADOW OF A GUNMAN (1923)
CATHLEEN LISTENS IN (1923)
JUNO AND THE PAYCOCK (1924)
NANNIE'S NIGHT OUT (1924)
THE PLOUGH AND THE STARS (1926)
THE SILVER TASSIE (1929)
WITHIN THE GATES (1934)
WINDFALLS (stories, poems and plays) (1934)
THE STAR TURNS RED (1940)
PURPLE DUST (1941)
RED ROSES FOR ME (1943)
OAK LEAVES AND LAVENDER (1947)

*Autobiography*

I KNOCK AT THE DOOR (1939)
SWIFT GLANCES BACK AT THINGS THAT MADE ME (1939)
PICTURES IN THE HALLWAY (1942)
DRUMS UNDER THE WINDOWS (1946)
INISHFALLEN FARE THEE WELL (1949)

*Criticism*

THE FLYING WASP (1937)


# JOHN MILLINGTON SYNGE (1871–1909)

John Millington Synge was born near Dublin in 1871 and died there on March 24, 1909. In his short career only four or five years were artistically productive. After graduating from Trinity College, Dublin, he spent some time in traveling through France, Germany and Italy. In 1897 at the suggestion of William Butler Yeats, Ireland's greatest modern poet, Synge went to Aran, a group of islands at the entrance of Galway Bay in Ireland. There he lived a simple life, learning the language and habits of the peasants and discovering his own potentialities.

Synge's entry into the theatrical world of Dublin was by no means triumphant. Even his excellent *Riders to the Sea* failed to attract audiences at first, while *The Shadow of the Glen*, his first play to be performed, met with open hostility: a satire on the Irish peasantry, it enfuriated the zealously patriotic Nationalists. This enmity to Synge's work culminated two years later in 1907 in a demonstration against *The Playboy of the Western World* by the Sinn Féin, the extreme Nationalists. The leaders of the Irish National Theater, however, stood by Synge, and he, along with Yeats and Lady Gregory, played a part of great importance in the Abbey Theater.

A list of J. M. Synge's principal works and their date of first production:

THE SHADOW OF THE GLEN (1903)
RIDERS TO THE SEA (1904)
THE WELL OF THE SAINTS (1905)
THE PLAYBOY OF THE WESTERN WORLD (1907)
THE TINKER'S WEDDING (1909)
DEIRDRE OF THE SORROWS (1910)

## THORNTON WILDER (1897– )

Thornton Niven Wilder, three times Pulitzer prize winner and an outstanding figure in contemporary American letters, was born in Madison, Wisconsin, on April 17, 1897. After living with his family in China for several years, he attended Oberlin College and in 1917 entered Yale as a junior. Returning to Yale after serving a year in the Coast Artillery Corps in World War I, Wilder attracted attention as a promising young playwright, and several of his one-act plays written there were later published. After graduating in 1920, he spent a year abroad, and then returned to teach at the Lawrenceville School and later to spend six years as a member of the English staff at the University of Chicago. With the publication in 1928 of his second novel, *The Bridge of San Luis Rey*, a Pulitzer prize winner, Wilder achieved merited recognition here and abroad. His success as a playwright, however, was not achieved until *Our*

*Town* was produced on Broadway in 1938. This experimental drama, staged without scenery, won him another Pulitzer prize, as did his controversial *The Skin of Our Teeth* in 1942. After serving as an officer in the Air Intelligence Combat Force, Wilder resumed his writing at the end of the war. His first novel in over a decade, *The Ides of March*, appeared in 1948.

A chronological list of Wilder's important works:

*Novels*

> THE CABALA (1926)
> THE BRIDGE OF SAN LUIS REY (1927)
> THE WOMAN OF ANDROS (1930)
> HEAVEN'S MY DESTINATION (1934)
> THE IDES OF MARCH (1948)

*Collections of Short Plays*

> THE ANGEL THAT TROUBLED THE WATERS (1928)
> THE LONG CHRISTMAS DINNER (1931)
> THE HAPPY JOURNEY (1934)
> OUR CENTURY (1947)

*Plays*

> OUR TOWN (1938)
> THE MERCHANT OF YONKERS (1938)
> THE SKIN OF OUR TEETH (1942)

## TENNESSEE WILLIAMS (1914–    )

Born Thomas Lanier, Williams took the penname Tennessee because he came from pioneer Tennessee ancestry. A few years after his family moved to St. Louis from Mississippi, Williams entered the University of Missouri, but because he spent so much time on his own writing instead of on his studies, his father insisted that he go to work in the shoe business. After two years of working all day and staying up most of the night to write, Williams collapsed under the strain. Upon his recovery he entered the University of Iowa, where he worked his way by waiting on table. Traveling all over the country on a roving writing career after graduation, he held every conceivable sort of job from bell-hop to usher to warehouse handy man to reciter of verses at a Greenwich Village night club.

By 1939 Williams' one-act plays were gradually becoming known in theatrical circles. His first full length play, *The Battle of Angels*, produced in 1940, enfuriated a Boston audience, was banned by Boston's Watch and Ward Society, and collapsed in failure. 1943 found him writing script for MGM in Holloywood. Finally in 1945, with the enthusiastic reception accorded *The Glass Menagerie* Williams won acclaim overnight as a successful playwright. This play received the New York Drama Critics Circle Award for 1945 and had a remarkable run of 563 performances on Broadway. In 1948 *A Streetcar Named Desire* had an equally brilliant reception, and Tennessee Williams' reputation was assured.

The works of Tennessee Williams:

THE BATTLE OF ANGELS (1940)

THE GLASS MENAGERIE (1945)

TWENTY-SEVEN WAGONS FULL OF COTTON, and other one-act plays (1946)

A STREETCAR NAMED DESIRE (1947)

YOU TOUCHED ME! In collaboration with Donald Windham (1947)

AMERICAN BLUES (five short plays) (1948)

ONE ARM, AND OTHER STORIES (1948)

SUMMER AND SMOKE (1948)

*Newsweek* 4:27, November 3, 1924. 15:33, January 29, 1940.
27:100, May 13, 1946. 28:71, December 30, 1946.
*Nineteenth Century* 139:172–5, April, 1946.
*Saturday Review of Literature* 20:6, July 29, 1939. 25:5, March
21, 1942.
*Theatre Arts* 24:162, March, 1940.
*Time* 35:36, January 29, 1940.
47:102, May 13, 1946.


O'NEILL, EUGENE

Clark, B. H., *Eugene O'Neill: The Man and His Plays*, New York,
1933.
Dickinson, T. H., *Dramatists of the New American Theater*, New
York, 1925.
Eaton, W. P., *The Theater Guild*, New York, 1929. *The Drama
in English*, New York, 1930.
Flexner, E., *American Playwrights: 1918–1938*, New York, 1938.
Geddes, V., *The Melodramadness of Eugene O'Neill*, Brookfield,
Conn., 1934.
Goldberg, I., *The Drama of Transition*, Cincinnati, 1922.
Gorelik, M., *New Theaters for Old*, New York, 1940.
Krutch, J. W., *The American Drama Since 1918*, New York,
1939.
Mantle, Burns, *American Playwrights of Today*, New York, 1929.
Moses, M. J., *The American Dramatist*, Boston, 1925.
Nathan, G. J., *The Intimate Notebooks of George Jean Nathan*,
New York, 1932. *The Entertainment of a Nation*, New York,
1942.
O'Hara, F. H., *Today in American Drama*, Chicago, 1939.
Quinn, A. H., *A History of American Drama from the Civil War
to the Present Day*, Vol. 2, New York, 1927.
Shipley, J. T., *The Art of Eugene O'Neill*, Seattle, 1928.
Skinner, R. D., *Eugene O'Neill, a Poet's Quest*, New York, 1935.
Whipple, T. K., *Spokesman*, New York, 1928.
Winther, S. K., *Eugene O'Neill*, New York, 1934.
Woollcott, Alexander, *Shouts and Murmurs*, New York, 1922.
*Enchanted Aisles*, New York, 1924.


SYNGE, JOHN M.

Bickley, F., *J. M. Synge and the Irish Dramatic Movement*, Boston and New York, 1912.

Bourgeois, M., *John Millington Synge and the Irish Theater*, London, 1913.

Corkery, D., *Synge and Anglo-Irish Literature*, London and New York, 1931.

Gregory, I. A., *Our Irish Theater*, New York and London, 1913.

Howe, P. P., *J. M. Synge, a Critical Study*, London, 1912.

Masefield, J., *John M. Synge, a Few Personal Recollections*, Letchworth, 1915.

Morris, L. R., *The Celtic Dawn*, New York, 1917.

Strong, L. A. G., *John Millington Synge*, London, 1941.

Tennyson, Charles, "Irish Plays and Playwrights," *Quarterly Review*, July, 1911. "The Rise of the Irish Theater," *Contemporary Review*, August, 1911.

Yeats, W. B., *Synge and the Ireland of His Time*, Churchtown, Dundrum, 1911. *The Cutting of the Agate*, London, 1912.

## WILDER, THORNTON

Brown, J. M., *Broadway in Review*, New York, 1940. *Current Biography*, New York, 1943.

Kunitz, S. J., and Haycraft, H., *Twentieth Century Authors*, New York, 1942.

Mantle, B., *Contemporary American Playwrights*, New York, 1938.

*Who's Who in America*, Chicago, 1942–3.

*Who's Who in the Theatre*, London, 1939.

*Articles*

*Atlantic* 171:121, March, 1943.

*New York Times Magazine*, pp. 20–1, November 1, 1942.

*Theatre Arts* 27:9–11, January, 1943. 30:704–5, December, 1946.

*Saturday Review of Literature* 25:3–4, December 19, 1942. 31:11, February 21, 1948.

## WILLIAMS, TENNESSEE

*Christian Science Monitor*, p. 21, September 21, 1945.

*Current Biography*, New York, 1946.

*Harper* 197:63–71, July, 1948.

*New York Times Magazine*, pp. 28–9, March 4, 1945. p. 19, December 7, 1947.

*Theatre Arts* 30:85, February, 1946.

*Time* 45:88, April 23, 1945.